Terrien de Lacouperie

Western Origin of the Early Chinese Civilisation from 2,300 B. C. to 200 A. D.

Or, chapters on the elements derived from the old civilisations of west Asia in the formation of the ancient Chinese culture

Terrien de Lacouperie

Western Origin of the Early Chinese Civilisation from 2,300 B. C. to 200 A. D.
Or, chapters on the elements derived from the old civilisations of west Asia in the formation of the ancient Chinese culture

ISBN/EAN: 9783744796118

Printed in Europe, USA, Canada, Australia, Japan

Cover: Foto ©ninafisch / pixelio.de

More available books at **www.hansebooks.com**

WESTERN ORIGIN

OF THE

EARLY CHINESE CIVILISATION

FROM 2,300 B.C. TO 200 A.D.

R, CHAPTERS ON THE ELEMENTS DERIVED FROM THE OLD
CIVILISATIONS OF WEST ASIA IN THE FORMATION
OF THE ANCIENT CHINESE CULTURE.

BY

TERRIEN DE LACOUPERIE

LONDON:
ASHER & Co., 13, BEDFORD STREET, COVENT GARDEN,
1894.

TABLE OF CONTENTS.

Chapters.				Pages
			Introduction	ix-xiii.
1.	§§	1	A Resume and a Survey	1
II.	,,	3	General Conditions of the Problem	3
III.	,,	5	Traces in China of a Western Origin and its date	4
IV.	,,	13	(Preliminary List of) Elements of Culture received by the Civilisers of China from Babylonia and Elam ...	9, 378
	,,	13	Sciences and Arts..	9, 334
	,,	19	Writing and Literature	14, 346
	,,	25	Institutions and Religions	19, 348
	,,	27	Historical Traditions and Legends ...	21, 349
V.	,,	32	Special Proofs of an Elamite Origin	25, 348
VI.	,,	34	Items of Assyro-Babylonian and other Civilisations entered into Ancient China through later Channels 29, 85,3	50, 357
	,,	36	Ancient Dynasties of Western Origin ...	30, 350
	,,	37	Eastern Jade Traffic	31, 351
	,,	42	Ancient Route of the Eastern Sea-trade ...	36, 353
	,,	46	Ancient Routes by Land, South and South-west	38, 353
	,,	52	Trade of Shuh-Szetchuen, and the routes 46,	196, 354
	,,	81	A Resumé of the two periods, 2000-770 B.C.	69, 354
VII.	,,		Items of Babylonian, Persian, Indian, Egyptian and Greek civilisations entered into China from 770 B.C. to 220 A.D.	85
	,,	97	Retrospects	85, 357
			Fourth Period, 770-481 B.C.	
	,,	102	The Ages of Wonderism	88, 358
	,,	109	Erythræan Sea-traders and Chinese Wonderism	96, 359
	,,	130	Influences from the South-west and beginnings of Taoism...	117, 361
	,,	147	Tartar Influences in the North-west, Barbarous Customs	131, 861
	,,	155	Internal Reactions, Confucianism ...	138, 363
			Fifth Period, 480-221, B.C.	
	,,	163	Formation of Neo-Taoism or Taoszeism	145

TABLE OF CONTENTS.

	§§ 174	West Influences by the North-east	... 155
	,, 181	Innovations concerning Fire ...	... 159, 364
	,, 184	Same continued	... 164
	,, 187	Other Innovations	... 169
	,, 191	Innovations of Hindu Origin ...	... 171, 365
	,, 197	Northern Influence... ...	... 176, 365
	,, 198	Western Influence by Southern channels	... 178, 366
	,, 191	Hormuz Navy in South-east China	... 178
	,, 207	The Great Semi-Chinese State of T'su	... 190, 367
	,, 212	The Non-Chinese State of Shuh	... 196

Sixth Period, 221 B.C. to 220 A.D.

	,, 219	The Empire	... 203, 367
	,, 227	Introduction of Buddhism ...	... 210, 267
	,, 234	Private Intercourse with the West	... 213, 368
	,, 239	Official ,, ,, ,,	... 218
	,, 246	,, ,, ,, ,,	... 229, 269
	,, 249	,, ,, with South-east and South	232, 269
	,, 259	Changes and competition in the Sea-trade	... 239, 370
	,, 269	Official Intercourse with the South-west	... 249, 370
	,, 280	Foreign and Chinese Trading Navies	... 259, 370
VIII.	Excursus	... 264
	,, 284	The Si Wang Muhs and Muh Wang's Expedition to Turkestan in c. 986 B.C.	264, 370
	,, 297	On some old Geographical Knowledge of the West	... 275, 371
	,, 299	On the Gnomon and Sundial ...	... 277
	,, 302	On the Clepsydra	... 279
	,, 305	Origin of the South-pointing Chariots and Marine Compass...	... 283
	,, 309	Foreign Historical Sources of Ancient Chinese Astronomy ...	... 286
IX.	Meeting Objections	... 291
	,, 312	Southern Origin	... 291
	,, 313	Self-growth and Development ...	... 291
	,, 315	Monosyllabic Theory ...	... 293
	,, 316	Astrognosie	... 294, 371
	,, 321	On Bak as a Name of the Earliest Civilised Chinese	... 302
	,, 330	Alleged difficulty of the Journey from West to East Asia ...	. . 308
	,, 338	Silence of Western Antiquity ...	... 314
X.	Essay of Historical and Geographical Reconstruction from Traditions and Legends of the Migrations of the Civilised Bak Sings from West Asia to China 2332-2285-2283 B.C.	316
	,, 240	Sources of Information ...	... 316
	,, 343	From their original seat to the Jade Mines...	317, 372
	,, 351	From the Jade Mines to South-west Kansuh	... 325
	354	From South-west Kansuh to South Shansi...	328

XI.		ADDITIONS AND EMENDATIONS TO THE PRECEDING CHAPTERS, §§ 367-379...	... 338
XII.		CHRONOLOGICAL SKETCH OF THE PRE-CHINESE AND IMPORTED CIVILISATIONS OF CHINA IN ANTIQUITY ...	... 378
I.	§§ 380	Native Civilisation of the Pre-Chinese	... 373
II.	„ 383	Imported Civilisation by the Chinese Bak Sings	... 376
		Of their own	... 876
	„ 386	Acquired in South-west Asia	... 378
III.	„ 390	Chronological List of Western Relations with China and their Importations from 2283 B.C. to 220 A.D	... 381
	„ 390	From Hwang-ti to the Hia dynasty, c. 2280-1954 B.C.	... 381
	„ 391	From the Hia to the Shang, c. 1954-1086 B.C.	... 381
	„ 392	During the Shang-Yn dynasty, c. 1086-1111 B.C.	... 382
	„ 393	During the West Tchou dynasty, 1110-770 B.C.	... 383
	„ 394	During the East Tchou dynasty, 770-481 B.C.	... 385
	„ 395	During the Contending States, 481-221 B C.	... 386
	„ 396	Chinese Empire, 221 B.C. to 220 A.D.	... 389
	„ 397	Concluding Remarks	... 395
	„ 400	Comparative Chronology	... 396
ALPHABETICAL INDEX ...			... 398
LIST OF IMPORTANT ERRATA			

INTRODUCTION.

The just claims of the civilisation of the Chinese, the largest family of mankind, to a high antiquity uninterrupted to the present day, which makes it the young contemporary of the old civilisations, now disappeared, of the Egyptians, Babylonians, Elamites, Assyrians, Egœans, and Pseudo-Hittites, alone invest it with an unusual interest for the student of history, notwithstanding its remoteness from our western activity. While scanty remains and scattered survivals are all that have been preserved of the former glory of all these civilisations, long swept away, the case is altogether different with that of China, which is still alive, with its immense advantage, for general history of an uninterrupted continuity since its beginning.

That civilisation has long appeared unaccountable, and its similarities and dissemblances as compared with our own have caused it to be taken as evidence of most conflicting theories otherwise unsupported. But the science of history has now shown, in all known instances, that centres of civilisation never arose elsewhere than amid a conflict of races, when sparks, coming from a more enlightened quarter, have brought in an initiating and leading spirit, under the form of one or several men, or of immigrating tribes, incited by trade, religion, or in search of safety. The same science has shown moreover that man has always travelled more extensively than was formerly supposed, that "there is no such thing as the history of one country," and that intelligent nations always borrow fresh elements of civilisation whenever they have the opportunity of doing so. And it has come to be the object of the present work to show that China has been no exception to the rules here formulated, but is on the contrary an important instance of the general fact gradually disclosed by the process of historical research, that in all investigated cases, culture is the result of an introduction from abroad, and not of a spontaneous development.

It was the trade by which were imported into Chaldea lapis-lazuli, rubies, turquoises, silver, tin, asbestos, and nephrite jade, dark and white, from Khorasan, Badakshan, and Eastern Turkestan, which led western civilisation to China after 2,300 B.C. And it is also trade, alone at first, with religion afterwards, which has caused communications, although irregular and occasional, to take place uninterruptedly between the West and East of Asia, *as shown for the first time in the present work*, since 2,800 B.C. by land, and after 700 B.C. also by sea. Thus it has happened that notwithstanding its geographical distance, which always required time to traverse, China has never remained without knowledge of the progress of Western civilisation, and of this knowledge has taken advantage.

Intelligent, but lacking originality and creative power, deeply imbued with reverence for the ancients, and specially for those who had introduced civilisation in their land, blindly conservative and respecting precedents and routine, somnolent still in their worship of olden times, the Chinese in their living past, have preserved to this day in their literature and civilisation many remains and survivals from the ancient civilisations with which they happened to have had some relations. Of course no absolute proof of this fact would rest on single traits of agreement; but it is the mass of the coincidences and similarities, their appearance by groups, and the homogeneity of these groups, the historical and material circumstances agreeing, that enforce conviction due allowance being made for the idiosyncrasy and adaptive process of the borrowers. In all the cases where verification is possible we have found that innovations and changes in Western Asia have made their mark in China some time afterwards. The reverse circumstance did not happen, and the influence of one side on the other remained unreciprocated, because China in antiquity had very little to give to West Asia, with the exception of her silk, long undesired because of the Indian article, and of some of her fruits which were duly carried by the ancient trade to Persia. Staple goods were not worth the difficulties of the journeys, and for many ages trade made by pedlars could consist but of rarities and curios.

INTRODUCTION   xi.

Let us remark here that the Chinese authorities themselves claimed an origin from the north-west for a large part of their civilisation, and did not hesitate in olden times to recognise an exotic source where such was the case; and that it is only the modern native writers, authors of large compilations and mirrors of history, more patriotic than trustworthy, the only ones with whose works convenience made the ancient sinologists acquainted, who have systematically attributed every progress and innovation to their sages of antiquity, without having regard to statements to the contrary.

The problem has long attracted the attention of scholars, who have attempted with the inadequate lights of their time to find the solution it required. The oldest explanation offered has been necessarily the missionary solution of a migration from the plains of Sennaar (Jesuits, J. Edkins, 1871), McClatchie (1856). There was the suggestion of a late Egyptian colony by Deguignes in 1758, which survived in the Egyptian parentage put forward by Goodwin, the Egyptologist, 1869. Under the pressure of the progress made in the deciphering of cuneiforms appeared the suggestion of a Scythic origin in common with Babylonia, held by Pauthier, De Rosny, Fr. Lenormant (1868). The field was enlarged in subsequent suggestions, including Egypt in the scheme, favoured by Hyde Clarke (1878) and W. St. Chad Boscawen (1879). G. Schlegel in 1875 claimed in an elaborate work a native antiquity of 19,000 years for Chinese astronomy of the stone age; while in 1890, E. Faber, in a special paper asked only 4000 years for a similarly independent origin. James Legge in 1865, John Chalmers in the following year in a little book, Wells Williams, and in 1877, Freiherr von Richthofen, have on the other hand given as their decided opinion a western origin undiscernible or by way of East Turkestan. Other scholars and sinologists, overwhelmed by the intricacy of the historical literature of China—interwoven as it is by numerous generations of native commentators and thinkers, who have each improved upon the work of their predecessors —find themselves unable to throw over the yoke, and not seeing through this fictitious atmosphere, stand apart, and incline towards a blind and dangerous scepticism which goes so far as to doubt of everything, the historical existence of Confucius included.

The most recent investigator, C. J. Ball, 1890-1893, a collaborateur of *The Babylonian and Oriental Record*, in several papers, published in the *Proceedings* of the Society of Biblical Archæology, starting without acknowledgement from my own disclosures, has concluded in favour of a close relationship of the Akkadian and Chinese language, a derivation (established by me in 1888) of the Chinese characters from those of Babylonia between Gudea and Khammurabi, and a migration of civilised Akkadians to China at that time.

In 1880, after twelve years' labour (ten of them spent in testing the inefficient solutions hitherto proposed), and the help of the discoveries in Assyriology, I was enabled to launch a first and approximate sketch of my views concerning the origin in the twenty-third century of the civilisers arrived in China from South-west Asia, which fact is the first of the instances of intercourse between the West and China exemplified in the present work. This was *the first time that this solution was proposed*, and nobody had ever even suggested it before me. Approved by a few, misunderstood by many, maligned by others, unknown to most, I have continued my researches with the growing conviction that I was at last on the right path, and that the Chinese, fated as they are to have a great influence on the material future of mankind, were not apart of the concert of civilised nations in antiquity. Strong in the early approbation of such eminent scholars as the late W. S. W. Vaux and François Lenormant (1880), Sir Henry Rawlinson (1884), my friends, Prof. R. K. Douglas (1879) and the lamented Colonel H. Yule, I could hear the regretted Georg von der Gabelentz tell me at Vienna in 1887, that it would not be surprising if fifty years elapsed before that Routine, the overwhelming Ruler of Sinology, could climb down under the glaring light of my discoveries. Since then however some more confirmatory evidence has come down from several sides, and I may be permitted to say that my views have now received the approbation of no less than four scores of scholars of eminence, including some of the leading Sinologists, Assyriologists, and Orientalists of the day. Moreover my works have been laureated on two occasions by the Académie des Inscriptions et Belles-Lettres. However, vested interests, prejudices, indifference to new views, and unacquaintance with the evidence put forward—not so much probably as the clumsy way in which my disclosures have appeared piecemeal before the world, spread as they have been during the last fourteen years in some one hundred and fifty different publications (books, pamphlets, and original articles)—have not permitted as yet many other scholars to judge of the question with a fair knowledge of the case. This work, I hope, will help them to do so.

I candidly confess that when the present book was begun (writing and printing in 1889), I did not know what its conclusions would be. My object was simply (1) a resumé of a certain number of previous articles, monographs, and even books in which I had studied separate points of Chinese archæology, whose western origin from the Chaldea-Elamite civilisation had come out clearly to me and to many of my readers ; and (2) a continuance of the enquiry into such other sources as had subsequently contributed to the formation of Chinese culture. But during the five years of continuous research which have elapsed since then, I have found gradually that a few of the western elements enumerated in the first lists (pp. 9-27) had been pushed up too early on insufficient grounds, while a large number of others had been overlooked. These faults have been successively corrected by cross references as the work advanced towards its completion and specially in the chapter of Additions and Emendations (pp. 338-372). Pages 2-258 are reprinted from *The Babylonian and Oriental Record*, 1889-1894. The two most important disclosures in the interval have been the ascertained journey of Muh-wang in 986 B.C., and the arrival of Erythræan sea-traders on the coasts of China as early as the VII. cent.

One side only, limited to ancient times, of the history of Civilisation in China, is studied in the present work. The complete history forms a much larger one, on which I am now engaged.

This volume has been written and produced under unusual difficulties of a material nature, and requires every possible indulgence from the reader, who is invited *to read first the pp.* 373-397 *before proceeding with any other part.*

TERRIEN DE LACOUPERIE.

Doct. of Philosophy and of Letters (Lovan.); Laureate of the Institut de France (Académie des Inscriptions, 1889-1893) ; M. c. Philological Society ; M. hon. Royal Asiatic Society; M. C. Académie de Stanislas. Nancy; M. hon. Société Orientale, Louvain ; M. C. Peking Oriental Society; M. C. Académie des Sciences, Marseilles ; M. C. Société d'Archéologie, Bordeaux; M. Société de Linguistique, Paris ; Prof. of Indo-Chinese Philology (formerly of University College, London) ; Director of "The Babylonian and Oriental Record," &c.

FULHAM, *June, 1894.*

WESTERN ORIGIN
OF THE
EARLY CHINESE CIVILISATION.

Chapters on the elements derived from the Old Civilisations of West Asia in the formation of the Ancient Chinese Culture.

Chap. I.—A Resume and a Survey.

In beginning the following chapters I propose first to summarise, Ch. III., IV., and V., in order to grasp them with greater facility, the whole series of evidences (including probably a few immature cases which will be confirmed or replaced by better ones in the course of our enquiry), on which rests chiefly at present *my own discovery*, made since 1879-80, that the early civilisation and writing of the Chinese were simply derivations from those of Elam and Chaldæa, about and after the time of Gudea and Dungi,[1] derivations carried eastward later on to the Flowery land, namely in the XXIII. century before our era. Searching the solution of the Chinese problem has been a labour of love and duty[2] and the work of years. For long my researches were unavailing. As explained elsewhere,[3] I had worked on a wrong path. I was prejudiced by the speculative views of several eminent scholars, who, misguided by the false notion of an antiquity very remote for the civilisation of China, had suggested as plausible a common descent of that civilisation with those of Western Asia, and especially with that of Chaldæa from an imaginary centre of activity in Upper Asia. As a result of my investigations I was compelled to give up all these views in succession. The comparatively late beginnings of the Chinese civilisation showed themselves to be the outcome of an importation, not a distinct growth from common seeds, but simply a loan, a derivation, an extension eastward from a much older form of culture in the west. I was led slowly by overwhelming evidences, direct and circumstantial from the Chinese and W. Asiatic sides, to the unexpected disclosures alluded to, and which, however astonishing they may appear to those who have not followed the gradual advance of my researches, are now proved to be an assured progress of our knowledge and solid discoveries of historical facts.[4]

The inferences drawn from my investigations in the true path, as put forth in my pamphlet of 1880 on the *Early history of the Chinese civilisation*, have been to my great satisfaction, slowly but surely confirmed in their main lines, rectified and made precise in their details. The proofs I have collected, or which have been brought in the mean time to my workshop as confirmative evidence by the advancement of knowledge and the works of several enquirers, are rather scattered in an inconveniently large number of books, papers, and periodicals, and often hidden from view in the notes of some tractates. Though frequently alluded to and not yet completed in the series of monographs which I devote to them, they have not been arranged together with sufficient clearness. The provisory resumé of Ch. III., IV., and V. is intended to make up this deficiency and to show that, marshalled together, they constitute under every respect, notwithstanding its insufficiency, the most irresistible array of facts ever put forth in support of a historical discovery. But this first resumé will have to be taken as a starting ground, open to revision, as the exact date of introduction of several items of civilisation, inscribed therein, cannot be determined but by the forthcoming survey of the relations of West Asia with China in antiquity. The expected results of this survey will be twofold, viz.: a sifting of the provisory lists which deprived of a few entries cannot fail to be increased by numerous additions; and disclosures of many subsequent importations. At the end of our task, after having answered to objections past and future, we shall have to gather from these researches any conclusions that may be suggested by facts disclosed in the course of our enquiries.

NOTES.—

1) The exact date of Dungi and Gudea is not yet ascertained, and Assyriologists' opinions vary between the 25th and 28th century. One of the most learned antiquarians of China, Hwang P'u-Mi, of the third century, mentions an old legendary tradition, attributing to the Empire of Shennung-Sargon an extension of 900,000 *li* from west to east, and telling how Hwang-ti made boats and carriages to traverse this mighty territory. This looks like a forgotten souvenir of the great distance of Sargon—Shennung's domains in the west, and of the journeys of Hwang-ti and his followers to the other end in the east.

2) In connection with the building up of the philosophy of history. Cfr. my explanations pp. vii—viii. Introduction of *Les langues de la Chine avant les Chinois*, (Paris, 1888).
3) *Babylonia and China*, p. 1 (*B. & O. R.*, I, 113).
4) The number and certitude of proofs increase with the advance of knowledge and progress of research. In *Babylonia and China* (1887) I had enumerated some sixty items of Chaldæan and Elamite civilisation among the early Chinese; in the present paper more than one hundred items are indicated.

II. GENERAL CONDITIONS OF THE PROBLEM.

The general conditions of the problem which I claim to have solved are rather simple. Four distinct civilisations appear in ancient history. The oldest hitherto known is that of EGYPT, for which a length of 5500 years before Christ is required as a minimum by the Egyptologists of the present day. Next to it is the CHALDÆAN culture of unknown antiquity, though not yet enabled by the most recent research to claim on documental evidence more than 4500 years before our era. A connection of the two, either by common descent, or by development into the latter of a rude and incomplete derivation from the former, is an open question now under investigation. The peculiar civilisation of the HITTITES is the most recently discovered; its origin is still unknown, its writing undeciphered, and its age unascertained. It is undoubtedly ancient, though not as old as the two others, and may be either an independent offshoot from the same seeds which would have lingered in those quarters, or the regional development of partial loans and influences from the two older foci of culture. Its geographical proximity favours equally the two views[5].

On the other side of the Asiatic continent, at a much later date than in Egypt and in Chaldæa, we find the fourth civilisation of antiquity, that of CHINA. It appears, since its beginnings, in a curious state of relative completeness, among mongoloid races renowned for their character ultra-conservative and non-progressive. Discarding all the greatness of political power and universal knowledge, attributed to their early leaders by Chinese traditions and comments of later growth, and sifting all fabulous accounts, we find as a residue a few undisputable evidences showing a small number of families arriving in the N. W. of present China, and in possession of a comparatively advanced civilization which explains the enthusiasm of after ages for these men, and has left a deep impression surviving to the present day in the mental habits of the whole people[6]. The existence of these feelings and beliefs would have been difficult and even impossible, should traces or traditions of savage beginnings, slow development of civilization, pictorial rudiments of writing, and successive progresses of knowledge by self-growth, have ever existed among the Chinese, but nothing of the kind exists in their early souvenirs.

Therefore, at a first glance at the problem, the probabilities are in favour of an importation from S. W. Asia or Egypt, the only parts of the world endowed with civilization at that ancient time.

NOTES. 5) The best résumé on this civilisation is that of Prof. A. H. Sayce: *The Hittites. The story of a forgotten Empire.* (By-paths of Bible knowledge XII. London, 1888.) Also Dr. W. Wright, *The Empire of the Hittites.* London, 2nd edit. 1886); Perrot and Chipiez, *Histoire de l'Art dans l'Antiquité,* vol. IV. Paris, 1887.— On these questions of origin cfr. some views in my paper: *The Kushites, who were they?* (Bab. & Or. R. 1, 25. 31.)
6) We allude here, among other features, to the Ancestral worship, so prominent in all times in China, and still now the very basis of all their cult.

III. TRACES IN CHINA OF A WESTERN ORIGIN AND ITS DATE.

Everything in Chinese antiquity and traditions points to a western origin. No Sinologist who has studied the subject has been able to ascertain any other origin for the Chinese than one from the West[7].

It is through the N.W. of China proper that they have gradually invaded the country, and that their present greatness began from very small beginnings some forty centuries ago[8]. This alone would be sufficient, but there are a few traditions pointing to the same fact further west.

Nakhunte (modern: Nai Hwang ti). the first leader of the Bak tribes who reached China, had led his people into Chinese Turkestan, and then along the Kashgar or Tarym river, reaching after a time eastward of the Kuenlun, "the Flowery land," a name which its great fertility had long merited to the lands of future China[9]. Such is the lesson we learn from a comparison of the Chinese traditions about the wanderings of Nakhunte and the identification of the geographical features and names mentioned therein.

The Bak tribes though under the general command of one chief, were divided into several branches which did not reach China at the same time, as shewn by the contemporaneity of several chiefs, and their relations with the tribes of Northern Tibet among whom matriarchate was the rule[10].

Nakhunte (Nai Hwangti) having reached N. W. China did not go further than westward of the southern bent of the Yellow river, and dies to be buried, says the traditional legend, at Ning on the borders of the present Kansuh and Shensi.[11]

During their advance towards the east, some of the Bak tribes must have separated from the whole body, and travelled northwards near the upper course of the Yenisséi, where inscriptions apparently in the writing of the time have been found [12]; but we must expect some more exact copies than those we hitherto possess.

Sieh, the official scribe and officer of the *Divine* Shun, at the beginning of the *Shu King*, was a descendant from the tribes of the West, and an ancestor of the Shang dynasty.[13]

It is the opinion of some native scholars, that their writing was invented elsewhere, not in China, but in the west.[14] On the other hand it has been attempted to show that the symbol for *west* occupies a prominent place in the writing.[15] Whatever may be the value of this proof which I am not ready to support, the western origin of the Chinese writing rests now on a sounder basis than any of these views.

There are however in the ancient Chinese traditions several allusions which point in so precise a manner to the cuneiform writing, that we must mention them here. Shen-nung=Sargon was reputed to have used signs like tongues of fire to record facts, at a time when the ancestors of the Chinese were not yet acquainted with the art of writing, and Dunkit (modern Tsang hieh) whose name has the same meaning as that of the Chaldean Dungi of which it was a rendering and under whom the Bak tribes were taught to write, made marks on clay like claws of birds and animals. The primitive writing was also compared to drops of rain finely drawn out and freezing as they fall.[16] It is difficult to mistake in all this, most distinct descriptions of the cuneiform writing of south-western Asia. We shall speak again of the peculiarity of the old Chinese writing further on, but then on documental evidence.

Routine has been for so long the rule in Chinese studies, in imitation of the Chinese habits, that anything done in despite of this time-honoured and most convenient method is by many looked upon with suspicion, as unworthy of attention, uncalled for and revolutionary. The contempt for independent investigations, shown by the generality of those, who residing for a time among the Chinese, have acquired there a large dose of their routine and some tincture of Chinese knowledge and language has produced this most hindering effect. For instance, however difficult to believe it may appear to the non-initiated, it is a fact that modern books are written by *soi-disant* authorities on Chinese matters, where Chinese chronology is given as genuine and trustworthy, though its fictitiousness for ancient times has been exploded since the last century by European scholars. It was proved to have been calculated backwards upon false astronomical data, imaginary periods and fictive epochs.[17] The application of the well-known cycle of sixty to computation of historic events was only made in 104 B.C. by Szema Tsien, the author of *She-ki*. As a matter of fact the ancient Chinese had no more chronology than any other of the ancient nations. Dates and times were computed by the lengths of reigns, or the number of years elapsed of such a reign, or between such and such an event of great notoriety.[18] Unhappily there are some discrepancies between the amounts of the respective lengths of reigns, previously to 846 B.C., a date on which the various authorities agree. These discrepancies amount to three centuries or there about, making the calculations of the dates of Yao vary from the XXIst to the XXIVth century and those of Nai Hwang ti from the XXIVth to the XXVIIth century B.C. The chronology generally received among the Chinese placing Hwangti in 2697 B.C. is a work of the XIth century A.D. based upon the false basis we have spoken of.

Therefore other sources must be referred to for ascertaining the general outlines of the chronology in ancient times. These we find in computations and statements made by ancient writers and in a few astronomical data, which, however vague, are not without importance. The times of Hwangti and his successors, Yao and Shun among others, were followed by the dynasties of Hia, Shang, and Tchôu, during which last Confucius flourished (B.C. 551-479). Various statements of Yü Hung (circa B.C. 1100) Wang-sun Mwan (B.C. 606) and Mengtze (B.C. 372-289) permit to refer the period of Yao and Shun to circa 2100 B.C. The different astronomical data in the first chapter of the *Shu-king*[19] and in the calendar of the Hia dynasty are applicable to the same epoch.[20]

Now Hwang-p'u Mi, a celebrated scholar[21] of the third century (A.D. 215-282) called the "book debauchee" from his ardour in study, who had specially examined the historical traditions independently of any astronomical speculations, has come to the conclusion that Nai Hwangti's date was a year which corresponds to our 2332 B.C. This figure, which cannot be far from the truth, is one of the links of my identification of the Chinese Nakhunte of Elamite=Nai Hwangti with the Kudur Nakhunte of Elamite history. On the other hand, in removing an obvious interpolation in the mythical list of kings preserved in ancient China, the date of Shen-nung, Chinese form of Sargon, agrees with the 3800 B.C. indicated for this ruler in the cuneiform documents[22].

{It appears from all the comparative evidence and the break in the traditions and social connection that it is in the XXIIIrd century B.C. that the Bak tribes, future civilisers of China, branched off from the vicinity of Elam and Babylonia, and migrated eastwards.}

NOTES. 7) For a sketch of this important fact of history, cfr. my work *The Languages of China before the Chinese* (London, 1887), §§ 13—19 and 187—201; édition française, pp. 7--10, 109-126, and 146—148.
8) Among the most important let us quote:—Dr. Wells Williams, *The Middle Kingdom*, vol. II, p. 144; Prof. James Legge (Introduction *Chinese Classics*, vol. III, p, 189); Dr. J. Edkins, *China's place in Philology* (London, 1871); Dr. J. Chalmers, *The origin of the Chinese* (London, 1868); Prof. R. K. Douglas, *The Language and Literature of China* (London, 1875); *China* in the Encyclopædia Britannica; *China* (London, 1882); Baron F. von Richtofen, the well-known geographer of China, in the first volume of his great work, *China, Ergebnisse eigener Reisen und darauf gegründeter Studien*, pp. 48, 317, 319, 422-425, and 428, who has been able to trace back the Chinese westward as far as the Tarym basin, Chinese Turkestan.
9) *The Chinese Mythical Kings and the Babylonian Canon* (The Academy, Oct. 6, 1883). This is developed in a special monograph, still in MS.
10) *The Tree of Life and the Calendar Plant*, p. 6 (*B. & O. R.* II, p. 153). Also developed in a monograph, still in MS.
11) *The Languages of China before the Chinese*, § 13, n.
12) Ibid., n. 1, Prof. J. R. Aspelin, of Helsinfors, is now engaged in a regular study of these and other inscriptions of Siberia, as he has kindly informed me.
13) Cfr. *Shu-King* II, i, 17—19; *Shih King* IV, iii, od. 3 and 4; *K'ang hi tze tien*, s. v. 37 + 6, f. 17.
14) J. Chalmers, *The Origin*, p. 23, quoting the *Shwoh wen*.
15) Deka, *The Origin of the Chinese*, pp. 152-154, of *Notes and Queries on China and Japan*, vol. I, (Hong-Kong, 1867); Hié, *Analysis of Chinese Characters* (*The Chinese Recorder*, 1871, pp. 90-93, and 119-123).
16) All the texts are referred to in *The Old Babylonian Characters and their Chinese Derivates*, pp, 12-13 and 26 (*B. & O. R.* II, pp. 34-35 and 97).
17) Cfr. P. Souciet, *Observations Mathematiques, Astronomiques, &c.*; Paris' 1729-1732; vol. I, p. 6, vol. II, pp. 2, 9.
18) Cfr. J. Legge, *Chinese Classics*, vol. V, p. 101.—T. de L. *Traditions of Babylonia in Ancient Chinese Documents*, s. f.
19) Dr. G. Schlegel, in his important work, *Uranographie chinoise* (La Haye, 1876, 929 pp.), and *Réponse aux critiques* (La Haye, 1880, 23 pp.) where he claims an antiquity of 16,108 years B.C. for the astronomy he describes (a part of which may, I think, have been carried to

China from the West) has started from the famous statement of Yao to his four astronomers reported (perhaps inexactly) in the first chapter of the *Shu-king*). Now the learned Professor has understood this statement as implying some peculiarities which may require the length of time he has calculated, but which are not of absolute necessity for the intelligence of the text. Other scholars have understood it differently, and are satisfied that about 2000 B.C. the statement of Yao was not far from truth. Cfr. the following note.

20) Cfr. *Discussion of Astronomical Records in ancient Chinese Books*, by Prof. S. M. Russell (Journal, Peking Oriental Society, Peking 1888, vol. II, pp. 187-200); *Notes on an ancient Chinese Calendar*, pp. 1-7, by E. C. Knobel, Hon. Sec. Royal Astronomical Society, London, 1882; *Early Chinese Texts, The Calendar of the Heu Dynasty*, by Prof. R. K. Douglas, pp. 1-60; Orientalia Antiqua, edit. T. de L., London, 1882, vol. I); *Chart of the principal Stars chiefly Zodiacal*, &c., by Prof. C. Pritchard, of Oxford (Sacred Books of the East, vol. III. p. 27); *Astronomy of the Ancient Chinese*, pp. 90-102 by Dr. J. Chalmers, (Legge's *Chinese Classics*, vol. III.)—Also, T. de L., Introduction to *Historical Catalogue of Chinese Money* (London, 1889).

21) W. F. Mayers, *Chinese reader's Manual*, I. 215.

22) *Traditions of Babylonia in ancient Chinese documents*, s. f.

IV. ELEMENTS OF CULTURE RECEIVED BY THE CIVILISERS OF CHINA FROM BABYLONIA AND ELAM.

The remains and loans of Chaldean culture, which we can still now discover in the early Chinese civilization, are so numerous and bear on so many points, that we cannot without difficulty summarize them with clearness; their number increases with the progress of research, and not a few will remain behind. For the sake of convenience we shall enumerate them in their relation to: *a*) Sciences and arts; *b*) Writing and Literature; *e*) Institutions, Government, and Religion; *d*) Historical traditions and Legends; reserving for a special chapter those which show that the source of all these loans was in Elam=Susiana.

a) Sciences and Arts.

The ancient Chinese, through their civilisers, had learned from Chaldea[23]:
  the solar year,
  its duodenary division, with the system of an intercalary month,
  its sub-division into twenty-four parts,
  and into periods of five days;
  also the division of the day into double hours,
  and a certain use of a period of seven days.[25]
They preserved from their early teachers
  the same fourfold division of the year into seasons;[26]
  and they had not entirely forgotten the symbolism of the names of the twelve months.[27]

Nor had they forgotten

the allusions in the names of the planets[28]
and their symbolical colours[29]
the special colours affected to the points of space;
the superstitions relative to the lucky and unlucky days;[30]
the Babylonian words for lucky and unlucky[31] and other superstitions;[32]
the hidden properties and harmonics of numbers;[33]
a ruling idea in the repetition of events after every period of 12 years;[34]
the practice of divination,[35]
and the use of eight wands of fate like those in the hand of Marduk;[36]
the conception of *Yin* and *Yang*, principles derived or diverged from the Babylonian *Anu* and *Anat*;[37]
the sacredness and mysterious value of personal names: &c.[38]

It is also to them that must be traced back

their ancient knowledge of 24 stellar points[39] afterwards increased to 28 at the beginning of the Tchou dynasty;[40]
many names of stars such as those of the Pleiades and Polar star;
the Babylonian standard measures and weights such as the heavy mina,[41]
the twelve scales of music;[42]
the gnomon[43]; the clepsydra, &c.:
their cycle of ten, the names of which are obvious corruptions of the ten Akkadian numerals;[44]
the cycle of twelve, of which the full names, preserved from antiquity in the *Erh-ya* and the *She-ki*, stand in the same plight with reference to the names of the twelve Babylonian months;[45]
the notion of a cycle of twelve years;[46]
the knowledge of the astronomical period of nineteen years, that which was supposed to have been discovered by the Greek Meton in B.C. 432, but which existed in China long before that time, and in Chaldea much earlier still;[47]
the use of periods of 432 and 72 in their calculations,[48]
and that of 60 as a cycle and a divisible unit;[49]
the decimal notation and local value of the figures;[50]
the use of some astronomical instruments, such as one for observing the meridian passage of stars, so as to fix the time of the four seasons of the year;[51]
the conception of the sky as a convex vault;[52]
many terms from the Babylonian vocabulary of civilisation, Akkadian and Semitic,

such as those for the great year,[53]
and for the intercalary month,[54] &c;
the motion that the full length of human life ought to be 120 years;[55]
the shifted cardinal points; &c.

The latter was the occasion of
the most remarkable of the confirmatory evidences of the genuineness of my disclosures: it came from the decipherment of cuneiform inscriptions in February 1883. Three years previously, in May 1880, I had been able to state from my investigation of the Chinese documents, that the early Chinese names of the four cardinal points and the symbols to write them, were much like those of Chaldea, with the difference that they displayed a shifting of the quarter of the circle.[56] My statement, based chiefly on Chinese evidence, was splendidly confirmed at the later time at the date quoted above by the decipherment of a Babylonian tablet,[56] since then confirmed by several others, where it was shown that the Akkadian orientation was leaning to the West, their north being the north-west and so forth.[58]

In arts the ancient Chinese owed to their early civilisers:

the art of making fire by gyration[59] (fire-drill) in contradistinction to fire by friction-along so well-known in the East[60];

the arts of clay-brick building in substitution for stone;[61]

of making canals,

of embanking rivers, and of works of irrigation

and agricultural pursuits, to which they applied themselves as soon as settled in their new country, with a determination of purpose which displays an experience and knowledge of long standing;[63]

the culture of the wheat which was indigenous only in the N. and N. E. of the Persian Gulf and which they carried away with them[63];

the use of metals and the arts of casting them[64];

the erection of lofty terraces for astronomical purposes, and of large square altars;[65]

the extensive use of personal seals;[66]

the use of war chariots

and of harnessing horses abreast;[67]

the use of special emblems on their ruler's dress;[68]

the making of coracles or skin-boats[69] and many others.

NOTES. 23) Cfr. for the statements about Chaldea: A. H. Sayce, *Babylonian Literature*, pp. 54-55; *The Astronomy and Astrology of the Babylonians*,

pass. (Trans. Soc. Bibl. Archæol., vol. III, 1874).
24) On the 24 *tsieh ki* cfr. Wells Williams, *Syllabic Dictionary*, p. 974; on the 12 *tchen* (J. Doolittle. *Vocabulary and Handbook*, t. II, p. 669; J. Fergusson, *Chinese researches*, p. 165.
25) F. Porter Smith, *A Chinese Sabbath* (Notes and Queries on China and Japan, vol IV, p. 15) : C. D., *A Chinese Sabbath*, ibid. p. 38) ; A. Wylie, *On the knowledge of a weekly Sabbath in China* (The Chinese Recorder and Missionary Journal, vol. IV, Foochow, 1871, pp. 1-9 and 40-45) cfr. especially p. 44 *b*.
26) This had been already guessed by Fortia d'Urban, *Histoire Ant. de la Chine*, vol. II, p. 85; Fergusson, *Chinese Chronology*, p. 170; cfr. p. 136.
27) Cfr. Sayce, *The Astronomy*, p. 162, and R. K. Douglas. *Babylonian and Chinese literature*, p. 8; *China*, p. 232.
28) Cfr. Sayce, *Astron.* and *Astrol.*, pp p, 167-175.---R. K. Douglas, *Bab. and Chin. Lit.*, p. 7; *China*, p. 3.
29) Cfr. J. Chalmers, *Orig. Chin.*, p. 25.
30) Sayce, *op cit.*: N. B. Dennys. *The folk-lore of China*, (Hong-kong. 1876) pp. 27-32.
31) *Early hist. Chin. civil.*, p. 25; *Old. Book Chin.*, p. 262.
32) R. K. Douglas, *op. cit.*
33) F. W. Mayers: *Chinese Reader's Manual*, p. XI.
34) Tchoou-li. XXVI. 23, trad. Biot, vol. II, p. 115.---Sayce. *Astronom.* and *Astrol.*, p.151.
35) *Shu-king*, Ta Yu mo, II, (2) 18.
36) *Early history of the Chinese civilisation*, pp. 29-30; *Beginnings of writing around Tibet*, § 28.
37) Cfr. François Lenormant, *Les origines de l'histoire*, vol. I, p, 494.
38) A. H. Sayce, *Lectures on the religion of the ancient Babylonians*. pp. 304-305.
39) On these points in Babylonia. cfr. A. H. Sayce, *Astron. and Astrol.*, p. 176.
40) J. B. Biot, *Etudes sur l'astronomie Indienne et Chinoise* (Paris, 1862 p. 247.---I think most probable that the systematisation of the 24 stellar points of antiquity into the 28 *siu* was the work of the founders of the Tchou dynasty in imitation of what they had learned from the astronomy of Kwarism, where, according to Albiruni's statement, great progress had been made in that science since 1304 B.C., and among others the harmonization of the solar and lunar cycles.
41) *Babylonian and old Chinese measures* (The Academy, Oct. 10, 1885). 243-244.
42) This has been pointed out repeatedly by several writers on the subject
43) *Tchôu-li*, k. 9, ff. 16, 17, 22; k. 20, f. 40; k. 33, f. 60; k. 42, f. 19; k. 43, f. 20.
44) *The affinity of the ten stems of the Chinese cycle with the Akkad an numerals* (The Academy, Sept. 1, 1883 .
45) *Babylonian cycles, numbers, and names in ancient China* (still in MS.) For instance cfr. Chinese *Shept* = *Shebat* Babyl.
      „   *Tamot* = *Tamus*   „
      „   *Tib-tu* = *Tebit*   „
      „   *Tih-fan-noh* = *Si-ra-nu* ,.   &c.   Several of the other names are Akkadian.

46) The great year of the Chinese.—A. H. Sayce, *Astron. and Astrol.*, p. 151.
47) J. Legge, *Chinese Classics*, vol. I, introd., p. 42.—A. H. Sayce, *Astron. and Astrol.*, p. 216.
48) Cfr. Fergusson, *Chin. Chron. Cycl.*, pp. 82-86; cfr. also pp. 103, 105, and 136.
49) All this is demonstrated in the monograph above quoted.
50) Cfr. *The old numerals, the counting rods, and the Swan pan in China*, p. 312 (The Numismatic Chronicle, 1883, vol. III, pp. 297-340).— Dr. J. Edkins, who does not seem to have known the latter paper of mine, wrote *Local value in Chinese arithmetical notation* (Journal of the Peking Oriental Society, 1886, vol. I, pp. 160-169), where he claims a Babylonian origin for an old Chinese notation supposed to be from left to right; but I have shown in the above paper with the help of the ancient coins (*ibid.*, p. 315) that this notation was from right to left; besides, the writer did not know that at the time of the transmission of writing to the civilisers of China, the characters were arranged from top to bottom.
51) *Shu-king* II, i. 3.—J. Edkins, *Science and Art in China to the Ming dynasty* (Journ. Peking Or. Soc., 1888, vol. II, p. 142).
52) François Lenormant, *Chaldean Magic*, p. 152.—Alex. Wylie.
53) Cfr. Old Chinese *sut* (modern *suy*) and the Assyro-Babylonian *sattu*.
54) The Akkadian words or their cognates which are found in the Chinese vocabulary may be arranged in three series: 1) those received at the beginning with the civilisation in which they were current terms; 2) those which were the common inheritance of the two languages from the remote and original stock Turano-Scythian to which both of them belonged, and from which they have separately and greatly diverged. On this divergence cfr. for the Akkadian: T. de L., *Akkadian and Sumerian in comparative Philology* (B. & O. R., 1, 1-7); and for the Chinese: *The Languages of China before the Chinese*, sec. 20-26.
55) *Tso-tchuen*. Hi kung, 32nd year.
56) *Journal of the Society of Arts*, 1880, vol. XXVIII, p. 733.—T. de L., *Early history of the Chinese civilisation* (London, 1880), p. 29.
57) By M. Theo. G. Pinches, in the *Proceedings of the Society of Biblical Archaeology*, Feb. 5, 1883, p. 74.
58) Since then I have written a monograph on the subject with the addition of new evidence from the Chinese sources. *The shifted cardinal points from Elam to early China*, of which the first part has appeared in the B. & O. R. II, pp. 25-32.
59) W. St. Chad Boscawen, *The pre-historic civilisation of Babylonia* (Journal Anthropological Institute, 1879, vol. VIII, pp. 21-36.
60) Oscar Peschel, *Races of Man*, p. 140; Ch. Letourneau, *La Sociologie*, p. 538.—For instance the *gtsub* in Tibet (Jaeschke, *Tibetan English Dictionary*, p. 433) not quoted in these works.
61) A peculiar fact is that the Chinese and their kindreds of Tibet are the only ones in the East who build houses in bricks, and that everywhere; so much so that their quarter in a foreign town is always recognisable by that feature.
62) *Wheat carried from Mesopotamia to Early China*, p. 1 (B. & O. R., II. 134).—cfr. R. K. Douglas, *China*, p, 5.

62) *Wheat carried, &c.*, ibid. pp. 184-191; and the letter of Prof. Alph. de Candolle, *The wheat indigenous in Mesopotamia*, ibid. p. 266.

63) The sole traces of the stone period of civilisation belong to the uncivilised populations of the country when the Chinese came successively in contact with them. There is no souvenir of such a state among the Chinese traditions. Metals are mentioned since their beginning, and the casting of vases with maps and figures is spoken of under the great Yü, with all the appearances of truth. Cfr. J. Legge, *Chinese Classics*, vol. III, p. 121, vol. V, p. 293. M. Aspelin has pointed out a probable influence of Assyro-Babylonia on the bronze art of Siberia. Cfr. J. J. A. Worsae, *Des âges de pierre et de bronze dans l'ancien et le nouveau monde*, p. 406 (Mémoires de la Société des antiquaires du Nord, 1880. ---Cfr. also: Virchow, *Trans-Kaukarische und Babylonisch-Assyrische Alterthümer aus Antimon, Kupfer und Bronze* (Zeitschrift fur Ethnologie, 1887, IV, 334-337).

65) J. Edkins, *China's place*, pp. 3-5.

66) This feature is too well known to require any demonstration.

67) J. Edkins, *China's place*: "at present in N. China horses are not harnessed abreast. The farther we go back, the nearer are the resemblances (with Western Asia)," p. 7.

68) *Shu-King* yih and tsih II, 4. 4.-This item will be specially noticed in a future paper.

69) Cfr. the Chinese authorities in G. Schlegel's *Uranographie Chinoise*, p. 347.---On the *Kufas* cfr. Herodotus, I, 194, Ker Porter, Layard, Chesney, in G. Rawlinson's *Herodotus*, vol. I, p. 318 ; W. F. Ainsworth, *The Euphrates expedition*, vol. II, p. 196.

b) Writing and Literature.

As the best sign of civilisation and the great vehicle of knowledge, Writing deserves more attention than any of the items we have hitherto enumerated.

The *Bak* tribes future civilisers of China, on the border lands of Susana, at the times of Dungi King of Ur, (as shewn by their own traditions)[70] and of Gudea Priest King of Sirpulla-Lagash, learned the art of writing as spread from Babylonia,[71] and afterwards they carried away with them eastwards this knowledge, with many other elements of the Chaldean culture.[72]

When on clay as was most always the case, this writing was made of cuneiform strokes (like claws of birds, say the Chinese) the shape of which was owed to the implement used to impress them : when engraved on stone, the big apex of the strokes was not yet developed, as it came to be later on, in more complete imitation of the clay writing.[73]

The *Bak-s*, instead of baked clay[74] tablets and cylinders, were compelled by their natural surroundings and by the unsteadiness of their settlements to make use of slips of bamboo bark, on which they cut incuse the signs of the writing with a graving-knife[75]; and though this material obliged them to write in more roundish shapes, they preserved as much as possible the system of making strokes thick at one end and thin at the other. This peculiarity, which is a most salient feature of the specimens of the oldest Chinese writing or *Ku-wen* preserved to this day, and also called *Ko-tu*[76].

The forms of the Babylonian characters, not drawn in obedience to strict rules as it became the case later on in Assyria, were far removed from a pictorial stage[77]. Some of them, however, still preserved traces of hieroglyphical antecedents generally facing the reader in contradistinction to the Egyptian and Hittite hieroglyphs, which were generally drawn in profile[78]. This feature was preserved in their derivates, and the Chinese, far from forgetting this small pictorial side of their written characters, have enlarged upon it, notably in 820 B.C.[79], and have never been able to improve and advance their writing out of the limbo of ideographism and imperfect phonetism, in which it was lingering when they learnt it.

They have preserved as well the other various characteristics of the Chaldeo-Elamite antecedent of their writing at the times of Dungi and Gudea,[80] such as the disposition of the characters in vertical columns and then from right to left, their meanings and not a few of their phonetic and polyphonic values, their imperfect systen of acrology and phonetism, their limited use of determinative ideograms which they increased afterwards, and several other important peculiarities.[81]

A few hundred form the basis of this writing in the Chinese derivate as in its Babylonian antecedent. About three hundred[82] archaic forms are now known from the Babylonian side, out of which two hundred are pretty well ascertained in their respective meaning.

There are also a few peculiarities which must be noticed as not unimportant. The early Chinese writing has no simple symbol for river, but it possessed peculiarly shaped signs for a bo̱a̱t, for wi̱ṉḏ (an inflated sail); all characteristics of the Babylonian script. In the oldest texts the character *shan* 'mo̱u̱ṉṯa̱i̱ṉ' is used for country as in the cuneiform texts.

The identifications with the primitive Chinese, their derivates, bear already on nearly every one of these 200.[83]

The identifications hitherto published are much more important than their numbers would suggest, because they do not bear on such symbols as those which in the case of writing derived from hieroglyphics may be drawn in a similar fashion, as for instance the water, the sun, the crescent of the moon,[84] &c., they bear on the contrary on signs which are most arbitrary in their form, and could not be twice drawn in the same way. There is no doubt that the early Chinese characters,[85] branched off as they were from the ancient Babylonian writing, and carefully preserved in the same traditional surroundings since forty centuries, however fragmentary and altered this tradition may be in the present day, contain a large number of valuable data which will prove useful to the Assyriologist-paleographs, when they appreciate their source of information. Some proofs have already been given in support of this statement.[86]

With respect to Literature, we have the following entry to make.

A critical examination of the text, and a partial restoration of some parts of the *Yu-king* has led me to the conclusion, that the basis of that remarkable and most unintelligible among sacred books, consisted of old fragments of early times in China, mostly of a lexical character;[87] the primitive meaning of them became lost, and they were afterwards adapted, through the changes in the writing and graphical interpretations, to other purposes.[88] Many of these changes and substitutions of characters are well known. The original lists are so much like the so-called syllabaries of Chaldea, and in some cases the identity is so close, that it is impossible not to believe that their authors were acquainted either themselves or by tradition with these syllabaries, and that the question arises whether some of these were not actually carried in China by the leaders of the Bak tribes civilisers of the country.[89]

The similarity under that respect was not confined to phonetic lists like those of the Yh-king; in China as in Chaldea they were acquainted with the system of vocabularies[90] arranged by classes of objects.[91]

NOTES. 70) Cf. *supra*, part II.
71) *Chips of Babylonian and Chinese palæography*, III.
72) Cfr. notably *The old Babylonian characters and their Chinese derivates*, London 1888: (B. & O, R., pp. 73-99); *Chips of Babylonian and Chinese palæography*, (B. & O. R., pp. 257-263, to be continued).— Prof. A. H. Sayce, *Babyloni·n and Chinese chm acters* (Nature, June 7, 1888 and B. O. R. II, 218-220), accepting for Assyriology my discovery. Prof. R. K. Douglas had accepted it for Sinology long before. Cfr. his papers at note *supra*.
73) Cfr. the facsimile of the stone and clay inscriptions in L. de Sarzec, *Découvertes en Chaldee*, part I. and II.
74) The clay tablets and cylinders were baked afterwards, in Assyria only.
75) *Old Bab. char. and Chin. deriv*., pp. 20 and 25.
76) Now *K'oh töu*, transcribed with two symbols meaning ideographically "tadpoles," because of the analogy of shape of the latter with that of the strokes. This is a play on the name which, formerly transcribed "grain-measures," was so altered in the second century B.C. by King Ngan-

Kwoh. The name was probably the original one of the writing. A further resemblance has been sought for by later commentators between the waving of the tadpole's tail and the appearance of the strokes of characters eaten up and worn out on ancient inscriptions, such as the Inscription of Yü, which is, however, a forgery made about a few centuries from the Christian era. The *Ku-wen* characters are those of high antiquity, with which has been written the oldest of the canonical books; other characters of the same style and period which were used in other works are called *Ku-wen-ki-tze* in contradistinction to the former. All the *Ku-wen* and *Ki-tze* characters known to-day have been preserved from the monuments and traditional copies of the original works by the Chinese palæographers of whom the works, collections of inscriptions, comparative dictionaries and others, are almost in every case done with a precision and care worthy of European science. The mere list would be a long one; a few only of the most valuable may be quoted here: such as the *Luh shu t'ung* of Min Tsi-kih, 10 bks. 1661 (which must not be mistaken for an inferior production of nearly the same title by Yang Hüen, of the Yuen dynasty); *Luh shu fun luy* by Fu Lwan-siang, 12 bks in 1751; *Tchuen tze wei* by Tung Wei-fu in 1691; *Ku-wen Ki-tze* by Tchu Mou-wei in 1612; and others quoted in my paper on *The old Babylonian characters*, &c., sec. 8. The work of the palæographers has been much easier and more certain in their identifications by the preservation of a large number of ancient inscriptions, which permitted the verification of the calligraphical exactitude of the Archaïc characters transmitted through manuscript tradition. On the other hand the text of the canonical books have been engraved in several instances, notably under the Han, T'ang, Sung and actual dynasties, and in several styles of writing, the original Ku-wen text among others in the beginning (cfr. P'ang Yung-mei's *Shih king k'ao wen ti yao*), In A.D. 175 Tsai-yung, on the command of Ling-ti of the Eastern Han dynasty, engraved on stone tablets, eight feet high, on the two sides the five classics: *I'h King, She King, Shu King, Li Ki* and *Tchun tsiu*, in three styles of writing (cfr. *Hòu Han Shu*, biogr. of Tsai-yung; *Tai ping yü lan*, Bk.589, f. 2). During the years 240-249, Ti Wang fang of the Wei dynasty had them repaired. In 518 the remaining tablets, 46 in number, were employed in the building of a Buddhist temple; but they were rescued by special order of the Emperor, and 35 tablets found unbroken were placed in the *Kwoh tze tang* or University. These tablets contained the texts of the *Shu King* and of the *Tchun tsiu*. At the time of the author of the *Si tcheng Ki* (a work quoted in the *Tai ping yü lan* of 983 A.D. Bk. 589, f. 7), eighteen tablets only were still in existence. About the year 1050, under the Sung dynasty, Sü-wang was enabled to take squeezes of the inscriptions and engrave 818 characters which Sun Sing-yen has published in fac-simile in his work *Wei san ti shih king y tze k'ao*. On this matter cfr. also the *La suh* of Hung Kwoh published in 1188. We know that the text *Ku-wen* of the Yh-King was once in Pauthier's library. The text *tchuen* of the *Yh-King, Shu King, She King, Tchun Tsiu, Tchöu-li* and *y-li* exists in the Bibliothèque Nationale Fonds Chinois, No. 183, Paris.

77) *Old Bab. char. and Chin. der.*, sec. 11.
78) *The oldest Book of the Chinese*, sec. 111; *Early history of the Chinese civilization*, p. 22.

79) On this remarkable revival of ideographism, cfr. *Early history*, pp. 15-17; *The oldest Book of the Chinese*, sec. 24.
80) The great advance I have made in my disclosures, besides the multiplication of proofs, bear on the derivation of the written characters by the pre-Chinese Bak tribes, and on the historical certainty of the fact. They are not so much the result of my own efforts as the outcome of the progress of knowledge. In my first publication, when I felt a solid ground under my feet, *Early history of the Chinese civilisation* (1880), I could only claim a community of origin and a probable derivation from the Akkado-Chaldæan (pp. 22 and 32). In *The oldest Book of the Chinese*, sec. 110 (2nd part, April, 1883), I was still claiming for the writing of the Pre-Chinese Bak tribes a derivation from the pre-cuneiform characters, and I endeavoured from an examination of the early Chinese characters to discover some particularities of this antecedent or pre-cuneiform writing (ibid., sec. 111). But in Nov. of the same year I could point out that the derivation had taken place from the archaic cuneiform and not from the pre-cuneiform characters (*Traditions of Babylonia*, p. 3). Since then the matter has received confirmatory evidences, direct and circumstantial, from all sides and is now definitively settled.
81) *Old Babyl. Char.*, part III.
82) Cfr. A. Amiaud et L. Méchineau; *Tableau comparé des écritures Babylonienne et Assyrienne archaiques et modernes*, avec classement des 327 signes d'après leur forme archaïque. Paris, 1887.
83) On these 200, fifty and odds have already been published; the others will follow as soon as leisure and health permit.---*The old Bab. char. and their Chinese dev.*, part IV; *Chips of Bab. and Chin. palæog.*, pass.; *The Tree of life and the Calendar plant of Babylonia and China*, n. 38, p. 10; *Wheat carried from Mesopotamia to early China*, p. 5; *Early hist. of the Chin. civil.*, p. 23 and plate, &c.
84) This argument, however, is not very good, as simple objects of nature are often represented differently. Cfr. the remarks and plates in Adolphe d'Assier, *Essai de Grammaire Générale* (Paris, 1872).
85) I have explained how and by what means these ancient characters have been preserved, in *Les langues de la Chine avant les Chinois* (Paris, 1888), pp. 176-177; some bibliographical references are given in *The old. Bab. char.* &c., pp. 4-5. See also note 76 *supra*.
86) Cfr. *The oldest Book of the Chinese*, sec. 115.
87) T. de L., *Early history*, pp. 23-26: *The Yh King* (The Athenæum, 21 Jan. 9 and 30 Sept., 1882; *The oldest Book of the Chinese and its Authors*, in *Journal of the Royal Asiatic Society*, 1882, vol. XIV, pp. 237-289 and 484.—Rob, K. Douglas, *The progress of Chinese linguistic discorery* in *The Times* April 20, 1880, reprinted in Trübner's *Oriental Literary Record*, vol. I, pp. 125-127; *Chinese and Babylonian Literature*, in *Quarterly Review* of July 1882; two letters in *The Academy* July 12, 1882, pp. 121-122, and Oct. 7, same year: *China* (London, 8vo, 1882), pp. 358-359, 2nd edit. 1887, pp. 391-392. - Clement F. R. Allen, *The Chinese book of the Odes*, in J. R. A. S., 1884, vol. XVI, p. 460.---Stanley Lane Poole, *Sacred books of the Chinese*, in *Saturday Review*, 30 June, 1883.---Ch. de Harlez, *Le texte originaire de Yih King, sa nature et son interprétation*, in *Journal Asiatique* de 1887, reprint pp. 6-7.

88) Dr. De Harlez, studying the ancient text as it became after all these changes, has recognized in it an attempt at grouping under each word an enumeration of the ideas proper to the Chinese philosophy. Cfr. his remarkable paper, *Le texte originaire du Yh-King*, o.c.
89) Cfr., for instance, the comparison made § 115 of my paper *The Oldest Book of the Chinese*, l.c.
90) Cfr. § 117, *ibid*.
91) I must mention here the suggestion (Ferguson, *Chinese Reserches* p. 74) that the *Shan hai King* the Classic of the Mountains and Seas, contains a translation of the ancient work of Berosus, though it is devoid of any foundation and must have come from some one who had never read the book itself. As I have paid some attention to this work, which I have seen no where faithfully described, I may as well state that it is composed of six different works successively incorporated and forming now 18 books. The first five, *Wu tsiang*, are the older part in which short interpolations only have been made ; it is a geographical description of the hills and mountains of the country known under the Shang Tynasty. The *Hai wai* and *Hai nei* forming the 6-9 and 10-13 books respectively are two separate works describing maps of Romantic geography written under the Tchou Tynasty and added as a continuation of the former work by the editor *Liu-h:ang* in B.C. 80-9. *Liu-siu* who died in 57 A.D. arranged another edition of the work with the addition of the *Ta huang* Bks. 14-17, and of the *Hai nei* Bk. 18, two compositions of similar character as the two preceeding, but still more romantic, if possible. Finally Kwoh-poh the celebrated commentator of the IIIrd. century, inserted the *Shui King* a small composition of the Ts'in dynasty on the rivers, in the XIIIth. book. Such is the work which has reached the present time ; it contains a mass of rubbish mixed up with important data. Excepting the first five books, the work was originally illustrated with pictures of many fabulous beings, men and animals. In the VIth. century new pictures were added because the old ones had been lost. The late A. Bazin has inexactly noticed the work in the *Journal Asiatique* of 1840, t. VIII. M. Emile Burnouf has translated a portion of it in *Congrès provincial des Orientalistes* Levallois, 1875, p. 131. Prof. Leon de Rosny has begun a complete translation in *Mémoires de la Société des Etudes Japonaises*, vol. IV. pp. 81-114 (1885).

c) *Institutions and Religion.*

The early Chinese were indebted to the Bak-s their civilisers for the following items of culture from S. W. Asia, which may conveniently be enumerated under this heading :

the institution of an imperial system of government[92];

the concept of four regions or four seas, which is meaningless in China[93];

and a title of chief of the four mountains, which seems to be a sort of adviser to the early Chinese ruler and disappears soon afterwards ;[64] it was certainly a yet recent reminiscence of the famous title of the

King of the four regions, which was borne by the Chaldean sovereign and suzerain[95];

the title of pastor for their twelve leaders[96];

the appellatives of Middle kingdom for their country

and of Black-headed people for themselves, both names as in Assyro-Babylonian[97];

the custom of prefixing the divine symbol character to the names of rulers and princes, a custom which was short-lived after their arrival in China[98];

the institution of public astronomers[99];

and many minor customs, such as the right hand side as the place of honour,[100] &c.

Several entries in the two preceding sections might as well have been included in this list.

The Ancient religion of the Chinese exhibits various traces of importation from S. W. Asia by their civilisers. The singular dualism of supreme divinities which differentiates so entirely this religion from those of the other Mongoloïd races of high Asia is most worthy of attention. Besides the worship of *T'ien* the Sky-Heaven so general among these races, we find in China the cult of a supreme and personal god *Shang-ti* specially reserved to the rulers themselves. I have not yet published the monograph I have written on the subject to demonstrate this fact[101], and explain how the worship of the supreme god for the time being[102], when the Bak tribes migrated from the North of Elam developed among them into the cult of Shang-ti. There are besides, some other features pointing distinctly to a Chaldeo-Elamite origin. In the second chapter of the *Shu-King* (II. 1, III) it is said that Yao venerated the six *tsung*; these celestial spirits bear names which correspond word for word with the six minor gods of Susiana[103]. In the Annals of the Bamboo Books, Nai Hwang-ti (I. 3) is said to have taken advice from three beings whose names turn out to be those of Chaldean deities. Those points are demonstrated in the monograph spoken of.

NOTES. 92) J. Edkins, *China's place in philology*, p. 6.
93) Obviously transferred from other horizons.
94) The title is mentioned in the Shu-King and only during the reigns of Yao and Shun. (*Yao tien* 11, 12; *Shun tien*, 7, 15, 17, 23). It is alluded to by the King Tcheng of the Tchôu dynasty as one of the appointments of officers made by Yao and Shun after having studied antiquity. (*Tchôu Kwan* 8).
95) Cfr. The Assyro-Babylonian *shar Kibratim arbaim* (W. A. I., I. 3.

11, 12 ; 4, 14, 15 ; 5, 19, 21) a survival of the old tetrapole of Nimrod, (Francois Lenormant, *Essai de commentaire des fragments cosmogoniques de Berose*, Paris, 1871, pp. 27 and 323) and a usual title from the days of Naramsin, according to documental evidence (Fritz Hommel, *Die Semitischen Volker und Sprachen* (Leipzig, 1883) p. 485), and most probably older.

96) Same references as note 94. We shall have to refer to it as a souvenir of Suziana

97) *The shifted cardinal points ; from Elam to early China*, p. 1 (*B. & O. R.* II, p. 25).

90) *An*, originally an eight-pointed star in Chaldæa.—*Ti* originally derived from the same eight pointed stars in China: for instance Ti Lai, Ti Ming, &c. of the mythical canon, Ti yao, Ti Shun, in Chinese history.

99) *Shu King, Yao tien.*

100) Now it is the left hand side. Cfr. Chalmers, *Origin of the Chinese*, p. 28.

101) My task on this point has been lately lightened by the remarkable tractates of Prof. Ch. de Harlez, *Les Croyances religieuses des premiers Chinois*, 60 pp. (Académie de Belgique, 1888, vol. XLI), and *La Religion en Chine*, à propos du dernier livre de M. A. Réville, Gand, 1889, 33 pp., where this distinguished Sinologist, analysing all the ancient texts on the subject, has come independently to the same view of a complete distinction in the beginning between *Shang-ti* and *T'en*, and an importation of the cult of *Shang-ti*. Cfr. *Les Croyances*, pp. 36-37, *L a Religion*, pp. 20, 21. That which gives to these papers a much greater authority than any other recent work on the subject, is that the author being himself an eminent Sinologist has been able to collect together the original passages of the Chinese sacred books which refer to the matter, and to draw from their respective weights and comparison his own conclusions.

102) It has been remarked by Prof. A. H. Sayce that in the Chaldean civilisation of which that of Susiana was an offshoot, it was customary for a new dynasty to impose over all the other cults that of their own god which they used to worship before in their native place or region.

103) Their names were found on ancient documents at the time of the renovation of literature under the Han dynasty.

d) Historical Traditions and Legends.

In Historical Traditions and Legends, the evidences are most peculiar and striking.

They could be ascertained only since a few years, because the historical data which they represent were not known before, and because some of them, though corresponding to certain facts already known, and being somewhat isolate in the east, had not as yet attracted the attention of any scholar.

The most immediate testimony, which the Chinese Bak tribes brought eastwards of their origin was their own name of Bak, which they not only kept for themselves but which they gave to several of their first capitals.[104] Bak was an ethnic of Western Asia which appears there in not a few geographical names as we shall have occasion to show further on.[105]

The peculiar names of Middle Kingdom for their country and Black heads for their own people, were doubtless souvenirs of the same appelatives which as we know were used in Assyro-Babylonia[106] with the same acceptations or nearly so.[107]

Many proper names of S. W. Asia might be adduced here in Geography and Personal surnames. For instance, in Geography:

Su-mit for Sumir; *E-ket* for Akkad; *Din-tih* for Dintir *ki* or Babylon; *Tam-tum* for Tamdin, north of Persian Gulf; *Let-sam* for Larsam; *Sohsha* for Susa; *An-teng* for Anzan; *Sat-ki* for Susik; *U-luk* for Urnk; the *Tök-luh* river for Diglat, the Tigris,[108] &c. &c.

And among surnames, such as:

Mat-t-ki for Marduk; *Hot-Bak-Ket*[109] for Urba-u otherwise Urbagash; *Dun-kih* for Dungi;[110] *Limku* for Rimaku; *Shen-nung* for Sargon[111]; *Nak-khun-te* for Nakhunte,[112] and so forth.[113] The difference between the Chinese and the original forms of all these names being in most cases that which result from the much limited orthoepy of the Chinese.

These two lists of names might be greatly lengthened, should we quote those of the royal canon of Babylonia which appears in the ancient Chinese documents as referring to a time anterior to the existence of the Chinese as a nation.

The list of mythical kings we refer to is doubtless an early version of the Babylonian canon which existed in China from remote antiquity[114], though I am not prepared to deny the probability of the view that the rulers of the Bak tribes did carry it with them in their migration to China. Distinct allusions to names of the list and to peculiar events of the traditions concerning them are found in the Classics; the principal names are often referred to, such as those of the great Hao- Fuh hi, Shen-nung, &c.[115]. But the traditions or, better, the legends which are joined to the list have been swollen by much extraneous matter and marvellous details; there has been combined with them some legendary souvenirs referring to the Bak tribes previously to their being civilised[116]; and the original text has been so much altered in the course of centuries by ignorant copyists through the various changes of writing, that it must be carefully sifted and critically edited. The comparison could not have been made of the Chinese document with the Babylonian lists, and their identity, though different in treatment, could not have been recognized until recent years. It is only since the discoveries of the cuneiform lists of kings[117], that the Babylonian and Chinese fragments may have been studied together. Though only 27 complete names remain on the fragments of the list of Babylonian kings covered by the traditions preserved in China, the identity of the names is most remarkable[118]. Notwithstanding the subsequent rearrangement of the Chinese fragments by later mythographs in the Flowery land, it is obvious that the original data when communicated to the early Chinese, and as I have said, somewhat mixed towards the end with their own beginnings, had not been yet systematized, as they appear in the Assyro-Babylonian tablets of late date recently discovered which we alluded to.

As they stand, the Chinese fragments are divided into ten *Ki* i.e. periods or dynasties. *Ki* appears on the Assyro-Babylonian documents with the same meaning; their number *ten* reminds us of that of the antediluvian period; but the fragmentary state of the cuneiform lists does not permit us to ascertain if they were or not divided also into ten *Ki*.

The enumeration of the ten *Ki* is preceded by the mythical reigns of 13 Heavenly Kings and 11 Terrestrial Kings, each having ruled 18,000 years, or 5 *sari* of 3600 years. The total makes 432,000 years, which is precisely the number of years attributed to the antediluvian kings by the Babylonians[119]. It is still more remarkable that the unequal division of 432,000 years into 234,000 for the Heavenly Kings and 198,000 for the Terrestrial Kings (or 65 and 55 *sari*) should correspond to the zodiacal basis which has been shown to underlie these speculations[120]. And besides, the first of the Terrestrial Kings is reported to have began to rule with the zodiacal sign of the bull, in the same way as the first antediluvian reign.[121]

The first of the ten *Ki* is the reign of nine human kings, followed by five other dynasties or *Ki* of which no names of rulers have been preserved[122]; then come the seventh *Ki* of *Sumit* (for Sumir) with 22 rulers; the eighth *Ki* of *Dntih* (for Dintir *Ki*) with 9 rulers[123]; the ninth *Ki* of *Tamtun* (for Tamdin) with 24 rulers[124]. The tenth *Ki* begins with Na-khunte the Nai Hnangti of the Chinese. The names of the seventh, eighth, and ninth *Ki* are given, and their comparison with the cuneiform lists shows the most remarkable identities[125]. The last name of the Chinese list is that of *Dumung*, which is said to have been killed by Nakhunte: it is the Duma-an of the cuneiform list.

Some special traditions are most remarkable as obvious remnants of what the Bak tribes future civilisers of China, were taught previously to their migration. For instance among those already published, we find legendary souvenirs.

of a great Cataclysm which seems to refer to the flood ;[126]

of Sargon and the peculiarities of his life, under the altered form of Shen-nung ;[127]

of Dungi, as Dunkit (modern Tsanghieh) teaching the art of writing to the Bak tribes ;[128]

of Nakhunte, as Nai Hwangti, with peculiarities which point to the history of Kudur Nakhunte and his conquest of Babylonia in 2283 B.C.[129]

of successive apparitions of beings half-fish, half-men at the beginning of civilisation and in connection with the introduction of writing ;[130]

of the symbolic tree of life and its calenduric features ;[131]

of a neighbouring people, subdued by Nakhunte and having a year of ten months (an ancient Semitic feature) ;[132]

of the life of ancient men lasting 120 (or two sosses).[133]

NOTES. 104) *The Lang. of China before the Chinese*, sect. 201.
105) Cfr. below chapt. V, and note 136.—The unjustified translation of *Bak sanh*, modern *Peh sing* by *Hundred families* has long hindered all investigations on the subject. According to K'ang-hi's great encyclopædia there are in China 4657 *sing*, or surnames, out of which says Prof. R. K. Douglas (*China*, 2nd edit., p. 251) 1619 are double ones. Cfr. also addition 203 to *Les langues de la Chine avant les Chinois*, p. 160.
106) *The shifting of the card. points*, init. (B. & O. R, II, 26).
107) Cfr. *ibid*, note 2, p. 31.
108) All these names are quoted in the papers referred to, note 113.
109) This is the old form of the name which has been abraded into the modern great Hao-Fu-hi. Cfr. my demonstration in *Trad. of Babylonia in early Chinese documents*, l. c.
110) In the Chinese transcription *carrer of wood*, in the Babylonian *the man of the reed tablet*. Cfr. *Early history of the Chinese civilisation*, pp. 27-28; *The old Bab. char. and their Chinese deriv.*, note 47 (B. & C. R. II, 97).
111) The corruption of Shen-nung for Sargon is equivalent to that of Shinaar for Singar, &c. Cfr. *The wheat carried*, &c., note 11.
112) On this name, cfr. below, chapt. V, note 137.
113) For all these names cfr. *The Chinese mythical Kings and the Babylonian Canon*, l. c.; *Trad. of Bab.*, &c. l, c.: *The Wheat carried from Mesop. to early China*, l. c.; W. St. C. Boscawen, *Shen-nung und Sargon*, B. & O. R. II, 208-209).
114) I have prepared for publication a comparative list derived from the following authorities: *San Huang* ; *Sun Kia*; *Wai-Ki* ; *Lo-Pi*; *Kang Kien tcheng she-ti* ; and K'ang-hi's great encyclopædia. My first

communications on the subject appeared in *The Academy* of Oct. 6 and Nov. 17, 1883. Mr. Pinches will supply the cuneiform text.
115) Cfr. R. K. Douglas, *Further progress in Chinese studies* (The Times, Aug. 4, 1884).— Louis Rioult de Neuville, *Les origines de la civilisation Chinoise*. pp. 240-249 of Revue des questions historiques, Juillet, 1884.
116) Such, for instance, by an obvious interpolation of the names of four savage chiefs at the end of the eighth *Ki* of *Dintih* or Babylon.
117) By the late George Smith, and by Mr. T. G. Pinches.
118) As recognized by Prof. R. K. Douglas, *Further progress*, l. c.
119) According to Berosus, Abydenus, and Syncellus. Cfr. Fr. Lenormant, *Les origines de l'histoire*, I, 232 sq.
120) By François Lenormant, ibid. I, 269 sq.—Cfr. also: Robert Brown, jun., *The early Bab. Kings and the Ecliptic* (The Academy, May, 1884, pp. 386-387.—And also W. Drummond, *Origin of the Bab. Empire*, p. 9; Th. Fergusson, *Chinese chronology*, p. 84.
121) Cfr. Fr. Lenormant, *Biblical Genealogies* (Contemporary Review, April, 1880); Fergusson, O. C., p. 183.
122) They are said to have reckoned respectively 5, 59, 3, 6, and 4 rulers.
123) Four rulers are here interpolated, cfr. note 116.
124) Two names of Bak chiefs are placed besides at the beginning.
125) Cfr. my reserves however in *The Chinese mythical kings and the Bab. Canon*, s. f.
126) Cfr. *The shifted Card. points; from Elam to early China*, pp. 29-30 (B. O. R. II. .
127) Cfr. *The Chinese mythical kings and the Babylonian Canon*, p. 5 (The Academy, Oct. 6, 1883; *Wheat carried from Mesopotamia to early China*, pp. 1-2 (B. O. R. II, pp. 184-185). And the confirmation from the side of Assyriology, by Mr. W. St. Chad Boscawen, *Shennung and Sargon*, B. & O. R. II, pp. 208-209.
128) *Early history of the Chinese civilisation*, p. 27; *The Old Babylonian characters and their Chinese derivates*, pp. 13 and 25 (B. O. R. II 85-97); *Traditions of Babylonia in early Chinese documents*, p. 5 (The Academy, Nov. 17, 1883).
129) *The Chinese mythical kings*, p. 6 (l. c.); *Early history*, p. 27.— Cfr. the date of the Chinese ? Nai Hwangti in 2332 B.C. suprà.
130) *The fabulous fishmen of early Bab. in ancient Chinese legends*, pp. 1-6 (B. & O. R. II, pp. 221-226).
131) *The Tree of life and the Calendar plant of Babylonia and China*, pp. 1-11 (B. & O. R. II, 149-159).
132) *The Chinese mythical Kings*, p. 6.
133) Ibid., p. 6.

V. SPECIAL PROOFS OF AN ELAMITE ORIGIN.

Since the beginning of my publications on this subject, I have repeatedly pointed out that the elements of the Chaldean culture they possessed, had been acquired, by the leaders of the Bak tribes who civilized China, west of the Hindu-Kush, south-east of the Caspian Sea, and in the vicinity of Elam=Susiana. The reasons for my statement were and are still the following :

1. It is in this region that the ethnic *Bak*, name of the tribes which went to N. W. China, was in existence and was best preserved, e. g. B a k h d i (Bactra), B a k h t a n, B a k t h y a r i, B a g d a d, B a g i s- t a n (Bag or Bak+stan,) i.e., land of Bak,[134] B a k m e s n a g i, i.e., country of the Baks[135].

2. It was there also, that K u t t h i or the like, another appellative of the Bak tribes, met with cognate names[136].

3. The name of the ruler of the Bak tribes when they arrived in the N.W. of China proper was, *Nakhunte*, modern N a i H w a n g t i,[137] which was evidently taken in imitation of the kings of Susiana, whose generic appellative, at least for many, was *Nakhunte*[138], in honour of their "chief of the gods."

4. The six *tsung* of the early Chinese were a souvenir of the six minor gods ofSusiana[139], as shown by their names.

5. In the govermental arrangements of the early Chinese they had twelve pastors, and the country divided under their rule.[140]

6. In ancient Chinese *nam* is the South, and with the common equiva- lence n=l, it sounds like an old souvenir of *Elam* as a southern country.

7. In the Chinese synchretic legend of Shennung, which is now proved to be an alteration of that of Sargon of Chaldea,[141] and in that of Nakhunte, several geographical names point to the same country of Susiana-Elam.[142]

8. It was in 2295 B.C.. that Kudur Nakhunta, King of Susa, con- conquered Babylonia, and that the former order of things in Elam was disturbed therefrom ; now this date corresponds with the requirements of the skeleton of chronology in China, and the immigration of the Bak tribes in the XXIIIrd century B.C. therein.

9. In comparing some affinities of terms borrowed by the civilisers of China, I have pointed out that the loan could not have taken place from Chaldea, but from a cognate and intermediary country.[143]

All these reasons, as may be seen, were based chiefly on Chinese sources and excepting the indirect evidence I had drawn from an examination of the inscriptions of Susiana, it was not known when the Chaldean culture had been introduced there. A double confirmation of the correctness of my views, or better of the Chinese statements, has come from the cunei- form inscriptions. The celebrated Gudea, in one of his inscriptions (statue B) states that he conquered the town of Anzan (Elam.[145]) Now as Gudea was older by two or three reigns than one of his successors who was contemporary with Dungi, and that Dungi, the Dunki (mod. Tsang hieh) of the Chinese tradition, taught the Bak tribes the art of writing, this disclosure and indirect confirmation is most important. On the other hand, a mention of the Bak tribes has been found in the inscriptions of Elam.[146]

To resume: it is difficult to ask more evident confirmations from the cuneiform inscriptions than these statements, as the Bak tribes, being barbarians, occupying apparently a conterminous region, could not be looked upon as very important.

NOTES. 134) *The oldest Book of the Chinese*, § 112; *Wheat carried from Mesopotamia to early China*, n. 2; *Les langues de la Chine avant les Chinois*, pp. 120-121 and 159.
135) In the Susian Inscriptions. Cfr. Addit. 201 to *Les langues de la Chine avant les Chinois*, p. 159.
136) *The oldest Book*, ibid., *Les langues de la Chine*, § 202.
137) The full name may be yu Nai Huang Ti, old *Ku-Nak-Khun-te*, but yu may be a prefix, and *Nakhun* appears written in one single group in the Ku-wen style of writing. Cfr. *Fu-luan-siang, Luh shu fun luy*, s. v.; and *Tung Wei-fu, Tchuen-tze wei*, s. v.
138) *Early history of the Chinese civilisation*, p. 27.
139) Cfr. *suprà* IV, c, n. 103.
140) *Early history*, p. 29.
141) Compare Shen-nung=Sargon to Shennaar=Shingar.
142) T, de L.,- *The Chinese mythical List of Kings and the Babylonian canon* (The Academy, Oct. 6, 1883); *Traditions of Bab. in early Chinese documents* (ibid. Nov. 17. 1883; *Wheat carried from Mesopotamia to early China*, p. 2 (B. & O. R. II, p. 185).---W. St. Chad Boscawen, *Shen-nung and Sargon* (B. & O. R. II, pp. 208-209).
143) *The affinity of the ten stems of the Chinese cycle with the Akkadian numerals* (The Academy, Sept. 1, 1883): *Trad. of Bab. in early Chinese documents* (ibid., Nov. 17, 1883).
144) *Chips of Bab. and Ch. palæog.*, p. 6 (B. & O. R. II, p. 262.
145) Arthur Amiaud, *Sirpourla, d'après les inscriptions de la collection de Sarzec*, p. 13 (Revue Archéologique (1880).—T. de L., *Les langues de la Chine avant les Chinois*, 159-160.
146) By Mr. W. St. Chad Boscawen (B. & O. R., II, p.189, n. 2). Cfr. also my note and the reference to a passage of the Nimrod epos, in *Les langues de la Chine, addit.*, p. 159.

VI. Items of Assyro-Babylonian, Egyptian and other Civilization entered into Ancient China through later channels.

"The leaders of the Bak tribes do not seem to have kept up any communications on their rear with the west after their arrival in the N.W. of China proper.[147] It was only in later times, that further items of western civilisation have entered into the country. The matter is enshrouded in difficulties, because hardly anything has been preserved of the history of the conterminous states, encircling the Chinese on the east, south, and west, and through which any intercourse or communication with the outside world had to pass before reaching the royal domain, where it could be noticed by the stylus of the official recorders." On the other hand, the wretched state of the old literature of ancient China, and the preservation of many features of antiquity in compilations as late as the ages before and after the Christian era, especially after the renaissance of literature, whose authors had access to documents and traditions now lost to us, does not permit us to ascertain the respective antiquity of the entrance of not a few items of western culture. And it is not at all improbable that some minor items of the fourfold list given in this paper, may have been introduced in the country through one or the other of the later channels described in the present chapter. Every case however must be judged on its own merits, and in the absence of direct testimony, the authority of circumstantial evidence, in the west as in he east, must be resorted to. For instances, the mythical list of Kings, and the twelve names of the Babylonian months, bear intrinsic and circumstantial evidences that they most probably belong to the early strata of imported knowledge by the leaders of the Baks, although they were afterwards mixed up and combined with other data of later introduction.

The late and successive introduction we refer to, may have taken place, and to a certain extent did take place, through the trade-routes by land and by sea, west, south, and east, of which we shall speak further on, and through the arrival and conquest of the Shang and of the Tchóu peoples, whose leaders founded important dynasties of the same names.

NOTES. 147) It is most probable that some displacement of populations, perhaps hostile, stood in the way.

a) Ancient Dynasties of Western Origin.

The *Shang* whose name might suggest that they were formerly traders, while their traditions indicate a western origin near the Kuen-lun range and probably a kinship with the Jungs,[148] do not seem to have imported any progress of importance. Sich the official scribe of Shun, was reckoned as their ancestor and this implies a certain amount of culture among them.[149] The tabooing of proper names is said to have begun under their rule. The *Tchóu* who drove them away, and succeeded them in the sway of China, (XIth century B.C.) with some greatness and brilliancy for several centuries, were also intruders from the west. They were most probably red-haired Kirghizes, with some mixture of Aryan blood. Several of the explanations added to the olden texts of the *Yh king* by their leader Wen-wang were certainly suggested by the homophony of Aryan words,[150] and to their influence is due without doubt the entrance into the Chinese vocabulary of a certain number of Aryan words more or less crippled and altered. "They were acquainted with some notions derived from the Aryan focus of culture in Kwarism, probably through the route of the Jade traffic[151] which they introduced into their new country.[152] Such for instance the 28 lunar mansions instead of the 24 stellar points of older times.[153] But nothing from Assyro-Babylonia seems to have been imported by them, some important rites and regulations were established by the founders of their dynasty, who seem to have been gifted with extraordinary capability, in that respect, and have systematized in a durable manner not a few ideas and institutions which, before their time, were loose in the country. During these two dynasties, it is the Jade traffic which may have been the Channel through which Western ideas and notions have reached China. "

NOTES. 148) On the Jungs and their language, cfr. *The languages of China before the Chinese*, sec. 2, 150, 151.
149) *Ibid.*, sec. 210.
150) On the baseless theory of a supposed affinity between the Chinese and the Aryan languages, cfr. *The lang. of China before the Chinese*, sec. 208. n. 2, and the additions p. 161 of the French edition.
151) On the trade route of Jade, see further on.
152) The invention of the *boussole* or compass has been attributed to one of them, Tchou kung, uncle of Tching-Wang, first king of the dynasty, and a justly celebrated man. Dr. J. Legge, (*Chinese Classics*, vol. III, pp. 535-7), has exposed the baselessness of this story, when Tchou kung was said to have presented south-pointing chariots to some envoys of the *Suh-shin* of the North or of the *Yueh-shang* of the South. (Cfr. below in the present chapter, and note 209.
153) On the astronomy of Kwarism, an Aryan focus of civilization, east of the Caspian sea, from 1304 B.C., cfr. Albiruni, *Chronology of Ancient nations*, pass., trad. Sachau, London, 1879.

b) *The Jade Eastern traffic.*

" Jade so-called, *i.e.*, nephrite, which was not found by the Chinese in China, notwithstanding some unfounded statements to the contrary,[154] was in all times known and highly prized by the Chinese, who looked upon it as symbolizing power and authority.[155] It is not at all unlikely that the Bak tribes had been made acquainted with the Nephrit by the trade which used to bring the articles of Jade to the West. Perhaps the route of this trade was an incitement for their shaping their way eastward. Anyhow, should they have been still ignorant of that precious stone, they had occasion to hear about it when on their route to China."

With the exception of unimportant beds, in the Caucasus, and in the rivers of the Yablono and Saiansk mountains, East and S. W. of Lake Baïkal,[156] which were not known in olden times, the true jade or nephrite exists only in what is known as Chinese Turkestan. Mount Mirdjai reputed to be a mass of jade, and famous in the geographical romances of ancient China,[157] mount Sertash, both at 74 miles from Yarkand, and the rivers Ulgunkash and Karakash near Ilchi,[158] were the principal if not the sole source from where nephite jade was exported in the west and in the east.[159] This jade traffic was, according to all probabilities, of a second- and third-hand kind, which could not provide a regular channel for the introduction of S.W. Asiatic civilisation into the East. Its importance, however secondary, under that respect, must not be overlooked. There is no positive evidence that the Bak tribes in their old country were engaged in such a traffic, but the following fact is rather suggestive that they were. The excavations at Uru=Mugheir, the old town of Dungi, whose name has been referred to in connection with the early conquest of Anzan by Gudea, and their teaching of the art of writing to the Bak tribes, have revealed the use or trade of nephrite-jade.[161] As this jade could not come from any other region than that of Turkestan through the country of the Bak tribes, the connection, borne out as it is by the circumstantial evidences of the case, shows the Bak tribes to have been already at that time long previously to their migration to China, intermediary already between S.W. Asia and the East. The extension of Nephrite-Jade traffic further west, to Nimrud, Hissarlik, the Helvetian palafittes, the megalithic monuments and other places of the same period, does not belong to our field of enquiry.[162]

Once in China, the Chinese Bak tribes received nephrite-jade from their rear. The legendary accounts on the subject are not all inventions, and there is doubtless some truth underlying the magnified and fabled reports. In the ninth year of Shun, Si Wang Mu sent envoys with presents consisting of white jade rings, or archers thimbles in jade, a tube of white jade, and topographical maps.[163] Si-Wang-Mu, whatever unknown personage the name may have described originally, became the impersonation of the queen rulers, whose princedoms lay on the North of Thibet along Kuenlun, and who have had occasionally some intercourse direct and indirect with the Chinese states.[164] A Si-Wang-Mu was reported to have presented Huang-ti with topographical maps.[165] And it is near a Si Wang Mu that the great Yü is reported to have studied.[166] A Si-Wang-Mu appears again in connection with a journey which King Muh, fifth ruler of the Tchöu dynasty[167] made in the West of China, along the Kuenlun range, where he was presented by her with some jade objects,[168] and some skilful workmen and where he examined their calendar and books ! This journey[169] which I am inclined to look upon as more important than is commonly believed,[170] has been made the theme of all sorts of fables, extravaganzas and marvels, among which the historical truth and its particulars are probably lost irretrievably to history. Muh Wang's expedition is reported in the seventeenth year of his reign. On the following year the Si Wang Mu came to the Chinese court with presents and was lodged in the Tchao palace. In all that concerns Si Wang Mu and the mysterious travels of Muh Wang of Tchöu it must be remarked that jade-stones play great part,[171] and therefore the whole is so narrowly connected with the route of jade traffic that we had to mention t here, inasmuch as, there are in the traditions on the subject, some references to a transmission, however slight and shadowy it may have been, of Western knowledge, to China.[172] But there are some other proof of jade traffic from Turkestan. Some of them are found in the *Yu Kung* or *Tribute of Yu*,[173] a work of the Shang dynasty, where it is recorded that the W. provinces of Yung-tchôu and Tsiang-tchöu, corresponding to Shensi and Kansuh and to N. Szetchuen respectively, produced to the Chinese court, jade stones of several forms.[174] This jade, since it is not found in China proper,[175] could only reach these provinces through the trade from Turkestan.

Tchou Sin, the last ruler of the Yn Dynasty (circa 1120 B.C.) received as present from the *Tan-tchi* country, probably through the Tchóu people who made him some presents from the West in several instances, a pillow in Jade shaped like a tiger.[176] This was undoubtedly procured by the same traffic.

Kuan-tze, an important writer of the seventh century B.C., states that Jade comes to China from the Yü-she mountains, in the far West, where the sun sets.[177]

All the information we possess here on the Jade traffic shows it to be a second-hand one; and however ancient it may have been, the amount of knowledge which has reached the Chinese through this channel cannot have been of importance, and must have consisted only of partial, incomplete notions, sometimes transmogrified on the way.

Now let us enquire about the other trade routes through which have been imported some elements of foreign civilizations.

NOTES. 154) There are two principal sorts of jade, the **nephrite** and the **Jadeite** which differ one from another by their chemical composition.
155) We allude to the references made to the provinces of Shansi and Yunnan as producing jade.
Abel de Remusat in stating that jade was found at Tai T'ung (Northern Shansi), a statement repeated from him nearly everywhere and sometimes in a faulty manner, was mistaken by the late and loose meaning of the symbol *yü*, which has often been used for gems in general, and equally applied to Jasper. Now Jaspor and not jade figures amongst the products at *Tai t'ung* in the descriptions of the province, in Grosier. *Description de la Chine*, Wells Williams, *The middle kingdom*, and other trustworthy works.---As to the reference to Western Yunnan, it is simply a geographical error which has arisen from the fact that the Jadeite from Mogung in Upper Burma arrived in China through that province.
However Ralph Pumpelly, *Geological Researches in China, Mongolia,*

and *Japan*, p. 118 (Smithsonian contributions to Knowledge, 1886) has indicated some *blue* Jade? at Tungsan, distr. of Wu-ting. N. C. Yunnan, *green* and *blue* Jade? at Mount Mo-fu near Li-king, and *black* jade? at Manmtoz (Mungman tu sze?=) near Yung-bchang.

156) The symbol *yü*-jade has that meaning. It was formerly *ok* and its pristine form was derived from the ancient Babylonian *uk* having the same meaning Cfr. *The Tree of Life and the Calendar plant*, note 38.—Prof. Max Müller (Febr. 3, 1880) has some interesting remarks which explain (that connection of meaning apparently unknown to him) and show how important and powerful among uncivilised was a man possessing a jade-chisel which could cut iron nails and any other thing with facility. Cfr. his work *Biographies of words* (London, 1888), p. 222.

157) The Amoor in the far North rolls down jade pebbles from the Yablono Mountains of the Trans-Baikal district of Siberia (Nevil Story Maskelyne). T. W. Atkinson, *Oriental and Western Siberia* (London, 1811) has found some in the river beds among the Saiansk Mountains, S.W. of Lake Baikal, and therefore west of the preceding.

158) The *Yü shan* of the *Shan Hai King*, Bk. II, fol. 29.

159) Cfr. S. Blondel, *Le Jade, Etude sur la pierre appelée yu par les chinois*, sect. II. (Paris, 1875).- G. Schlegel, *Uranographie chinoise*, p. 787.—*Notes and queries on China and Japan*, 1868, vol. II. pp, 173, 174 and 187; vol. IV. 1870, p. 33.—An exhaustive treatise on Jade is that of Fischer: *Nephrite und Jadeit*, Stuttgard, 1875.—Cfr. also for the geography Capt. Trotter in Forsyth's *Account of the mission to Yarkand and Kashgar*, 1873-74, p. 154.

160) Of course we leave aside the jades of New Zealand and America.

161) I have proposed to recognize in the *Uk-nu* stone of the East, of the cuneiform inscriptions the Jade of Tarkestan. (Cfr. *The Tree of Life*, note 49). Four articles of nephrite-jade have been found in the ruins of Ur, and one at Nimrud, as described by Dr. O. Schoetensack in the *Zeitschrift für Ethnologie*. Berlin, 1887, pp. 125-126. At Nimrud it is a cylinder, at Ur, celts. Unless it be for a special use because of their toughness, the nephrite axes in this civilised country could only be there for trading purposes. The British Museum possesses a cylinder of ancient work from Babylon in Jade.

162) The precious nephrite worked in the forms wrongly known as celts neatly polished, with edges sharp and intact, is found along the route from Khotan in Turkestan, its starting point, to the Jaxartes, to the Oxus, then south of the Caspian sea, in Babylonia and Assyria, along the Northern Asia Minor shores, bordering upon ancient Troy, then passes to the Peloponnesus, where it directs its course to Crete, and, not touching Egypt, passes from Greece to Italy, whence it is distributed among the Helvetian lakes, the Megalithic monuments of Armorica &c., &c. Cfr. Valentine in Prof. Howard Osgood, *Prehistoric Commerce and Israel*, pp. 168-169 (The Baptist Quarterly Review, 1885, vol. VII. pp. 163-184).—Prof. Nevil Story-Maskelyne, pp. 211-214 in Max Muller's Biographies of Words.—Alex. Bertrand, *La Gaule avant les Gaulois* (Paris, 1884) pp. 130-131.—G. de Mortillet, *Le Prehistorique*. pp. 537-539.

163) *Tchuh Shu K'i nien* Shun, IX year.—*Shang shu ta tchuen*—

Ta Tai Li; *Sau tchao ki*; *Kung-tze tchi yen*; *Li töu wei y; Tsih sien luh*; *Fung suh tung*; all ancient works quoted in the *Kin ting ku kin t'u shu tsih tcheng*.

164) Si Wang Mu has absorbed the little that was known of other names of female rulers. The *Shan hai King* Bk. II. speaks also of a *Yng Mu*, cfr. note 91 of the present paper. On *Si Wang Mu*, cfr. *The Tree of Life and the Calendar Plant of Babylonia and China*, part IV. Ancient Missionaries wanted to identify Si Wang Mu with the Queen of Saba; this fancy has been refuted by G. Pauthier, *Chine*, p. 94.

165) *Tsih sien luh*, l.c.

166) According to Siün-tze, a writer of the IIIrd century B.C.—— *Shan Haï King* (gloss) Bk. II., fol. 19.

167) B.C. 1001-947 according to the usual chronology; B.C. 962-907 in the Annals of the Bamboo Books.

168) Jade is a most important factor in all that concerns Si-Wang-Mu, and Muh-Wang's journey.

169) The journey which began as a punitive expedition against the *Ki-uen Jung* tribes of Naga race on the North-east of Tibet. cfr. *The Lang. of China before the Chinese*, (sect. 150, 151) who five years before had presented some *asbestos* cloth &c. (*Lih taï ki she*: G. Pauthier, *Chine*, p. 96).—As to the details of the travels, cfr. *Ki tchung Tchöu shu*; Lieh-tze 400 B.C.; *Muh Tien-tze tchuen*, 350 B.C.; Siün tze, 300 B.C.; Shi tze, 280 B.C.; *Poh wuh tchi* by Tchang Hua, 250 A.D.; *Shih y Ki* by Wang Kia, 400 A.D., Bk. III.; *Shuh y ki* by Jen Fang, 500 A.D.; *Hou Han Shu*; *Tai ping yü lan*, 983 A.D., Bk. 85, fol. 2-3; and many more recent compilations.

170) Cfr. for instance, *The Tree of Life*, sect. IV., and notes.

171) Though not so important as would imply the legend of the ancient Iranian King Djamshid having married a daughter of *Mahang* King of *Matchin*. Cfr. Lassen, *Indische Alterthumskunde*, I. 619-622.) And the contentions of Abdal-lah Beidawy, in his general history that Mu-Wang went to Persia. Cfr. Pauthier, *China*, p. 94, as well as that of M. Paléologue, *L'art Chinois* (Paris, 1888), p. 102, who, in order to explain the Assyro-Babylonian affinities which were glaring to his eyes, wants Muh Wang in his one year journey to have gone to Media, Susiana, Chaldea.

172) It is very curious to mention here that the first enactments in which ring-weight-money *hwan* are spoken of, i.e. in 947 B.C. should have been issued under his reign, and may be the result of what he learned in his journey. The system was Egyptian and was especially in use for trade with the Asiatics, at the time of the military supremacy of Egypt, but it was not used in Assyro-Babylonia. Cfr. Fr. Lenormant, *Histoire ancienne de l'Orient*, vol. III. p. 58; and E. Babelon, *ibid*, vol. V. p, 114.

173) In the *Shu-King*. It is a description of all the engineering works made by the Chinese (and their allies under their supervision) in China to regulate the rivers and their floods. It contains also a description the products of the same geographical division of the country as known under the Shang dynasty.

174) *Shu King*, part III. Bk. I., 69 and 81.
175) Cfr. what is said above on the subject.
176) It was discovered during some excavations made in 159 A.D.. Cfr. *Shih y ki*; G. Schlegel,*Uranographie Chinoise*, p. 789; a real mine of information and where several archæological finds of jade implements are noticed.
177) Kuan tze ; G. Schlegel, *ibid*. p. 787. *K'ang-hi tze tien*, 114+4, fol. 49 verso.

c) *Ancient trade-route of the Eastern sea trade.*

On the East and South-east is the sea. The Chinese, advancing from the West, did reach the sea-shore, and this near the Shantung peninsula, five centuries only after having tntered China, *i. e.* in the XXIIIrd century B.C. They were not themselves fully established near the sea for many centuries afterwards, and the borders were in possession of non-Chinese states semi-civilized, and even less than that. On two geographical points some exceptions are important to notice, north and south of the said peninsula, as the channels through which an Egyptian influence brought in by the sea trade was introduced into China.

✓ An important emporium and sea-port, non-Chinese, *Tsi-moh*, and the surrounding country of Shantung, has played a prominent part in the development of current metallic money.[178] The first enactments on currency,[179] those concerning the weights which have proved to be based upon the mina of Carchemish,[180] in 680 B.C., are all connected with that region of Shantung reached by foreign trade.

Lang-nga,[182] an important town in that same region, was founded before the VIth century B.C.:[183] its name is singularly suggestive of an importation by the sea-traders of Asianesia and the West, Lauka (Lanka pura of Ceylon, Lanka-Balus (Nicobar), Lang-nga-sin of the north of Java, marking their route.[184]

It is there that Ts'in She Hwang-ti, the founder of the Chinese empire 221 B.C., resided for some time previously to that date. It was in these surroundings, permeated as they were by foreign ideas, that he prepared some of the important innovations, that made his name famous, and which seem to have been suggested by reports of Western ideas, institutions and events ; such, for instance, as the division of his dominion into 36 *kiun-s*, which remind us of the 36 nomes of Egypt,[185] and perhaps also the Burning of the books (213 B.C.)[186]. It is in the same vicinity that sculptures have been discovered, which, though of rather late date (147 A.D.), bear the impugnable testimony of an influence of Egyptian art, which the Chinese are unable to explain,[187] and which is mixed up with Chinese data. The mixed influences from Western Asia and Egypt through the sea-trade is so much the more remarkable that this sea-trade cannot have been important in ancient times, and grew up only in the centuries which preceded the Christian Era. Anything from the West could not reach China except in a hand to hand manner, having to change several times on the way. At the time of the Christian era, hardly anything had as yet been heard in China of the outside world by the eastern[188] coasts, and even at the time of the East Han Dynasty (A.D. 25 - 220) it is positively stated in the dynastic annals, and this by hearsay, that the seafarers did not go further than some vaguely indicated countries which cannot possibly be further than the Malacca peninsula, if so far.[189] And so late as the beginning of the fifth century, A.D., Fa-hien, the Buddhist, coming back to China from Ceylon, was compelled to make the journey in two different boats, from Ceylon to Java, and from Java to China.

NOTES. 177) *Kuan-tze*; G. Schlegel, *ibid.*, p. 787.—*K'ang-hi tze tien*, 114+4, fol. 49*v*.
178) Lat. 34° 15' in the modern Lai tchou fu, cfr. G. Playfair, *The Cities and Towns of China* (Hong-Kong, 1879) No. 663.
179) Cfr. T. de L., *Historical Catalogue of Chinese Money*, Vol. 1, pp. 4, 131-132, 213, 319, &c. Metallic money was not established in Western China before 337 B.C.
180) Cfr. *Historical Catalogue*, p. 1.
181) *Babylonian and Old Chinese Measures*. (The Academy, Oct. 10, 1885.) ——The regulations were made by Kwan Tze, a famous minister of Huan, Duke of Tsi. N. W. Shantung) at proximity of this sea-trade influence.
182) Referred to the present department of Tchu tchong (Lat. 36° Leng. 119°58) in Tsing tchou, Shantung.
183) It was conquered in 468 B.C. by the sea-border state of Yueh and became its capital until 379 B.C.
184) *The lang. of China before the Chinese*, sec. 214.—Col. H. Yule, *Notes on the oldest records of the sea-route to China from Western Asia* (Proc. R. Geogr. Soc., Nov. 1882); Alfred Maury, *Des anciens rapports de l'Asie occidentale avec l'Inde transgangetique et la Chine* (Bullet Soc. Geogr., Paris, 1846).
185) As pointed out by Thomas Fergusson, *Chinese Researches*, I. p. 59.—According to ancient authors the number of the names was reported to be 36, though as a fact, the number varied. Cfr. G. Maspero, *Histoire Ancienne*, 4e edit. p. 19.
186) It has been suggested (Fergusson, Chinese Researches, I. 41-59), that the idea of suppressing all ancient history and literature has been impressed on the mind of the founder of the Chinese Empire by reports of similar measure for the same object in the West. Berosus (Cory's *Ancient fragments*, p. 36), who lived in 340-270 B.C., states that Nabonassar collected all the mementos of the Kings prior to himself, and destroyed them, that the enumeration of the Chaldean Kings

might commence with him. It is just what did *Ts'in* She-Hwang-ti as remarked by W. F. Mayers (*Journ. North China Branch, R. A. S.*, December, 1867, p. 162).—Moses of Khorene has told the same tale of the fabled Ninus, (*II st. Armen*, ch. 13, p. 40), and so did Albiruni of the Kwarismians or Chorasmians (*Chronology of Ancient Nations*, tr. Sachau, p. 58), and also of the Persians by Alexander-the-Great or his lieutenants (*ibid*, p. 157).

187) Dr. S. W. Bushell of Peking has shown me the squeezes taken on the monument, which he exhibited at the Berlin Oriental Congress. Cfr. his notice on *Inscriptions from the Tombs of the Wu family* from the Tzü-yun shan=Purple-cloud hills, 28 li south of the city of Chia-hsiang hsien in the province of Shantung; pp. 79-80 of Ost-asiat, sect., Berlin Orient. Congr., 1881). Chia-hsiang hsien or Kia-siang hien, is in Tsi ming tchöu, by Lat. 35°32' and Long. 116°30'.—Prof. Robert K. Douglas, *Ancient sculptures in China*, and nine plates, (J. R. A. S., 1886, vol. XVIII.) has reproduced several characteristical parts of these sculptures, from the *Kiu Shih Soh* collection (1806), with their Egyptian models. They are most remarkable.

188) Should this trade have been active or regular, the Chinese would have learned earlier than they did anything about the Peng-lai islands said to be live by Lieh-tze (IVth cent . B c.) and only three at the time of She-Hwang-ti, under whose reign they were still mythical. Is *Peng-lai* = *Polo*. 'island' in Malay?

189) Namely the Naked (men) kingdom and the Black-teeth men kingdom. *Hön Han shu*, Bk. 115; tr. A. Wylie, *History of the Eastern Barbarians*, p. 81 (*Revue de l' Extreme Orient*. t. I., 1882). It was only in the sixth century that the Chinese acquired some knowledge of Java, Sumatra, &c. Cfr. W. P. Groeneveldt, *Notes on the Malay Archipelago and Malacca* (Batavia, 4to, 1872 ; also, Prof. Leon de Rosny, *Les peuples orientaux connus des anciens chinois*, 2nd edit. Paris, 1886.

d) Ancient Trade Routes by Land, South and South-West.

The oldest information we possess of any intercourse with the South and West in ancient times goes back to the beginning of the Tchou dynasty, i.e. XIth century B.C. In the *Tchöu Shu*, a work saved from the wreck of literature, and a production of that dynasty,[190] which is probably more trustworthy[191]than was formerly supposed, the arrival of some trading parties, magnified as ambassadors, is reported.[192] One of them comes from *Shou Mi* or *Tchou Mi*, a place which has been identified with Ta-yao, in the prefecture of Tsu-hiung west-centre of Yunnan.[193] This party brought to the court of Tcheng Wang, the second king of the dynasty, as a tribute, say the Chinese account, a monkey from a country where it is called *Kudang*, which is the Dravidian name for this animal; The explanations show that country to be N. E. India. No other information has been preserved about this curious and interesting event.

which gives us in the East a Dravidian word contemporaneous with those of the same languages learned by the trade of Solomon with Ophir (Kings I. 11, 22).

NOTES. 190) A large part of the following is abstracted from my paper *On three embassies from Indo-China to the Middle Kingdom* 3000 *years ago*, read before the Royal Asiatic Society on June 16, 1884, and still unpublished.
191) Prof. S. M. Russel, *Discussion of Astronomical Records in Ancient Chinese books*, l. c. p. 196, has been able to verify an eclipse of the moon in the year 1136, which is mentioned in that work on the 35th year of Wen Wang.
192) *Yh Tchou shu*, sect. 59, fol. 8.—It is also mentioned in the *Shan hai King* (edit. 1783), sect. X., fol. 2-3, sect. XVI., f. 5, and sect. XVIII., fol. 31 and in the *Shwoh-wen* (edit. 1598), sect. VIII., fol. 24.
193) It became in the IVth century B.C., part of the famous state of TSEN (331 B.C.—100 A.D. which monopolized the trade with the south, and whose name through the sea traders furnished the west with the name of CHINA. Cfr. my notices in Col. H. Yule, *Glossary of Anglo-Indian words* (London, 1886) p. 157 ; *Beginnings of writing*, sect. 80 ; B. & O. R., I., *The Sinim of Isaiah not the Chinese*, sect. 3 and below.

* *

In a much later work[194] we find that another party came to the court of the same king, Tcheng of the Tchöu dynasty, from a country called *Nélé*, or *Néré*,[195] which I have proposed to identify with the old country of Norai, on the west side of the Irawadi, between Manipuri, and Momien of S. W. Yunnan. No mention is made of anything they brought, a fact most remarkable, as their country became afterwards the Shan state of Mogaung, famous for its mines of amber and jadeite, which from th re are exported to China, since a few centuries before the Christian era. All ancient allusions to Jade referred to the north-west, and it is only in later times that we find the first allusion in literature to this jade of south-west.[196] The mines were probably not worked as yet, at the time of the two mercantile expeditions spoken of, and it is not improbable that the great prices which they saw put upon the jade stones at the Chinese Court has awakened their attention to the value of similar kinds of stones found in the country of the Noras, one of them.[197]

The references by various authors indicate an old trade route from the district of the mines, i.e. Mogaung, by Waimmo and Kakhyo, passing through Momien[198] where jade work has long been going on,[199] Yong tchang a famous mart for western products, Ta-li fu and Ta-yao to Szetchuen by Tung-tchuen and Tchao-tung, the Kin-sha Kiang and the Min river, a route of which we shall have to speak further on again, or by Ning-yuen, Tsing-Ki and Ya-tchou to Tcheng-tu, the capital of the province.[200]

The identification of the Nërë country with that of Norai=Mogaung is further supported by statements of the Chinese record on the geographical and curious features of the country which cannot leave any doubt on the matter. And about some astronomical knowledge possessed by the traders, knowledge for which the Nora people have long remained famous. This knowledge, however, being the same as that of the Chinese themselves with reference to the calendar was no gain for them, but seems to be an indice of an earlier influence of Chinese civilisation in the Nora country, though the Szetchuen traders of whom we shall speak further on.

The ascertaining of the comparatively late working of the jadeite mines of Mogaung is an important feature for the date of ancient trade of this stone, as jadeite in the east is found nowhere else than there, and is foreign to the geognostic structure of the Chinese Turkestan, where nephrite comes from. As jadeite has been found in the lacustrian dwellings of Switzerland and also in not a few places of remote times, perhaps 1500 more or less B.C. of the neolithic period, it has been rather prematurely assumed that, as in the case of the nephrite-jade, the jadeite implements had been brought from the Mogaung mines. If such had been the case, it would tend to demonstrate the existence of trade with Indo-China at that remote period.[202] But the whole is moonshine. Attention has been called to the fact that the jadeite implements of Europe belong to several varieties which are located in their respective areas, and therefore must have been brought from short distances, where their origin will be traced one day or other.[203] The difficulty has been settled from another side; chemical analysis has shown that the composition of the jadeite implements found in Europe is not the same as that of the jadeite of Upper Burma[204]. Therefore all speculations and inferences drawn in relation to an ancient trade of jade stones between that part of the world and the west are put to naught by these conclusions[205].

NOTES. 194) In the *Shih-i ki* by Wang Kia (IVth cent. A.D.), with many other souvenirs and legends of olden times saved from oblivion.
195) It is this country in which the late Pauthier wanted to recognize the name of the Nile! and therefore Egypt. Stan. Julian proposed afterwards an identification with the Indian town of *Nala*, but this town

was founded by Asoka, thus eight centuries after the event reported in the text, and its name is differently transcribed in Chinese.
196) In the *Süh Han shu* by Sié Tch'eng (250 A.D.) it is stated that the Ngai-Lao (West of Yunnan) brought forth some *Kuang-tchu* and amber (*hu-pek*) during the Han dynasty. In the *Po wu tchi* by Tchang Hwa (A.D. 232-300.) Amber is said to come from Yung-tchang, the great mart of W. Yunnan. Cfr. *Tai ping yü lan*, Bk. 88, fol. 1.— The Green jade called *pik* (cfr. W. Williams, Syll. dict. p. 691) was known to the Romantist geographers of the IVth century, Lieh-tze and Tchwang-tze, but only in the case of the latter with reference to the country of Shuh, then part of Szetchuen, and this in a fabled way. It was only under Suan-ti (73-49 B.C.) of the Han dynasty that *pih* stones were heard of more positively as found in, or better arriving through, Yh tchou i.e. parts of Yunnan and Szetchuen (*Han shu.*) The word was then applied to Jadeite which is still now one of its acceptations. The product is mentioned in the *San-tu-fu* of Tso-sze (IIIrd cent. A.D.), in the *Wei-lioh* (250 A.D.) The *Kwang-ya* dictionary (227-240 A.D.) states that two sorts of *pik*, one *p'iao* i.e. azure, the other *luk*, i.e. green, come through Yueh-sui which corresponds to a part of the modern prefecture of Tsu-hiung, West center of Yunnan. The *Tai Kang ti ki* (circa 300 A.D.) states that the *pik* stones come through Tsing ling hien (later Tayao in the same prefecture of Yunnan; cfr. G. Playfair, *Cities and towns of China*, 1167, 6893), which curiously enough as an identication of trade route is that same country of Shou Mi from where traders had come to the Chinese court of Tcheng Wang as reported in the text. (Cfr. *Tai ping yü lan*, Bk. 89, fol. 2.) The proper word for 'jadeite' is now *fei-ts'ui* ,W. W. o.c. 140 ; Geerts, *Les produits de la nature Japonaise et Chinoise*, II, 465),and that for ' Jasper ' is the above word *pih-(yüh)*.
197) *Tchuh shu ki nien*, Tchöu y wang, year II.
198) The country was visited by Capt. Hannay, Dr. Griffith and Dr. Bayfields in the years 1835-1837.—Cfr. C. H. Yule, *A Mission to Ava*, 1858. On the mines and work, cfr. also some informations in Dr. John Anderson, *A Report on the Expedition to Western Yunnan via Bhamo* (Calcutta, 1871), pp. 63, 65, 6 , 67, 327, 328 ; *Mandalay to Momien*, London, 1876), pp. 201-202.
199) Anderson, *Report*, pp. 67, 328 ; *Mandalay to Momien*, p. 201 The author says that the trade in his time had greatly diminished in importance. Capt. W. Gill in 1877, and A. R. Colquhoun in 1879, who passed through the town do not mention the jade industry. E. Reclus, *Asie Orientale*, p. 748. states that jade is sent through Mandalay to Canton. The Mohammedan rebellion has for long and in some cases disturbed for ever the old state of things.
200) The latter route to Burma is probably older than the other. Marco-Polo followed it as shown by Col. H. Yule, *Geographical Introduction* to Capt. W. Gill's journey, 2nd edit., p. 93, and *Travels of Marco-Polo*, 2nd edit. vol. II, p. 57.
201) " Ils observent le soleil et la lune pour connaitre la direction ou la position des royaumes étrangers ; ils comptent les alternatives de froid et de chaud pur connaître les années et les mois. En examinant les

époques des premières lunes dans ce royaume on trouva que leur calendier était d'accord avec celui de la Chine." (Transl. Stan. Julien. *Simple exposé d'un fait honorable*, p. 204.)—" For the Noras (the aboriginal population of the region) were a comparatively civilised people, and the few who remain are still regarded in Mogaung, Khamti and Upper Assam as a learned class, and are generally employed among the Buddhist priesthood and others as astronomers and writers." (Ney Elias, *Introd. sketch of the history of the Shans*, p. 39).

202) Fischer, *Neuen Jahrbücher für Mineralogie*, 1881, p. 131 ; Dr. Howard Osgood, *Prehistoric Commerce and Israel*, p. 169.

203) G. de Mortillet, *Le Prehistorique*, (Paris, 1883), p. 539.

204) Damour, *Compte Rendus de l'Academie des sciences*; Th. Morel, *Les differentes especes de Jades et leur classement au point de vue min. eralogique* ; Catalogue du Musée Guimet, 1883, I., 309-315.

205) No inference can be made on the same matter from the use of Jade in India, as the introduction of Jade into the country dates only from the early Mogul Emperors of Delhi. Cfr. N. Maskelyne in Max Muller's *Biographies of words*, p. 218.

* * *

The most renowned party of foreigners who reached the Chinese court in ancient times from the south, were those who came from *Yueh-Shang*, — a name which in its ideographical rendering means trail of the outside borders. It has been identified with the southern part of Tungking.[206] The unsophisticated legend[207] says that in the sixth year of the regency of Tchôu Kung, uncle to the young King Tcheng of Tchôu, they presented three elephants and a white pheasant.[208] Nothing is said of any other presents nor of their bringing any book or calendar with them, as was the case with some other parties ; they are chiefly known from the spurious statement that the Duke of Tchōu presented them with five south pointing chariots to facilitate their return to their remote country. But this account has been shown to be baseless.[209]

Like the travelling parties from Shóu-Mi and from Nêrê, the mission from Yueh-shang was of no importance for the increase of Chinese civilisation. None of them had anything to teach, while they had everything to learn: their respective countries were still uncivilised, and so far as we can judge[210] they only knew what chance had permitted them to get from Chinese culture. A fabling inference which has been developed into a regular tradition, and though unknown to the oldest statements about the journey of the Yueh-shang people has been eagerly adaptated by the doers of Annamite history, attributes to the latter trading party magnified as ambassadors, the knowledge of a writing proper to their own country.[211] This spurious story must have been concocted in putting together, the inference drawn from the statement that interpreters were employed by the travellers, and the genuine existence in Annam of a phonetic writing of unknown date which was suppressed in 186 A.D.[212] This writing may have been introduced from India, or have consisted in a syllabic derivation and simplification of the Chinese characters introduced by the trade of Shuh, but in either case it must have been several centuries later than the journey referred to.[214]

All these three trading parties had been attracted to the Chinese court by the rising fortune of the House of Tchōu just beginning its rule over the Chinese dominion, and the expectations which its wealth gave to foreign commerce.

NOTES. 206) The *Hoang viet dia du chi* of Annam (1829), states that the old country of Yueh-shang is now covered by the provinces of Nghê-an, Thuan-hoa and Quang-nam, cfr. I , 9, 11., 31.
207) In the *Tung kien kang muh* of Tchu-hi (trad. de Mailla, vol. I. p. 316-318) and in the *An nan tchi lioh* by Li-tsih of the Ming period (passage transl. in William Mesny's *Tung k ng*, pp. 10-13, Hong Kong, 1884), the story is told at great length, being swollen with extraneous matters, which show how the Chinese compilers succeed to expand the terseness of the original reports.
208) These envoys are represented among others on one of the ten sculptured stones of Hiao t'ang shan inShan tung which date of the second century u c. They are given in facsimile in the *Kin shih soh* (quoted note 187 above), but do not exhibit the same Egyptian influence as those of the Tzü yun shan, which were probably a survival of some of the Egyptian data carried there by the sea trade several centuries earlier.

M. Paleologue has reproduced a few of them in his recent work *L'art chinois*, pp. 133, 135, 137, 145, and 309.
209) Cfr. *supra* note 152. The matter is full of interest as it concerns at the same time the invention of the mariner's compass. The late W. F. Mayers, in an interesting note on *The Mariner's Compass in China* (Notes and Queries on China and Japan, Hong-Kong, 1870, vol. IV. pp. 9-10) has shown that such a knowledge in China canbe reported only to the time of Ma-Kiun, a famous mechanician who flourished at the court of Ming-ti (A.D. 227-240) of the Weidynasty. The lamented scholar thought that "several reasons exist for believing that Ma-Kiun may have derived his knowledge of the properties of the magnet from Indian sources, as he probably did of the water-wheel and other inventions which are laid claim to in his behalf." These Indian sources would then be Buddhist missionaries whose propaganda was very active under that Northern dynasty. However the mariner's compass was not known on board Indian ships as late as the Vth century. In 413 A.D. Fahien travelling from Ceylon to Java on a large merchant ship carrying about 200 men, wrote: "it is impossible to know east or west except by observing the sun, moon, or stars, and so progress. It is dark, rainy weather the only plan is to steer by the wind without guide." (*Foh kwoh-ki*, ch. XL. tr. Beal). And afterwards on board another ship of same size, from Java to China, the weather being also bad, they were in the same uncertainty as to their proper route. Dr. J. Edkins, on the other hand thinks (*On Chinese names for boats and boat-gear*, J. N. C. B. R. A. S. 1877. XI. 123-142) that magnetic iron was known in North China at the time of Kwei Kutze in the IVth century, B.C., who speaks of the south pointing chariots, and probably also known to Confucius, as the load-stone district was not far distant from the capital of the state of Lu, where the great philosopher was. Both learned writers have overlooked a most interesting statement of Liu-hiang, (80-9 B.C.) in his work *Hung fau wen hing teh'nan*, which I resume here. The Duke Hien of Tsin (822-811 B.C.) tried unsuccessfully to make south pointing chariots. Later on the Duke Huan of Tsi (N. W. Shantung, 684-642 B.C.) found out the mistake and was successful in making some, in which himself and his minister Kuan-tze (note *supra* 177) drove. The statement is very suggestive of a slow progress, perhaps under foreign influence which reached there by the sea-trade (cfr. sect. e. of the present chapter) and at proximity of the region where load-stone was found.
210) For instance the calendar of the Nërë.
211) Truong Vinh Ky, *Cours d' histoire annamite*, vol. I.. p. 11 and 27. Curiously enough the statement is not found in the highly embellished *Tungking* by William Mesny, pp. 10-13, (Hong-Kong, 1884). On the falsification and making up of the Annals of Annam, cfr. *The languages before the Chinese*, sec. 89-91, and add. p. 152, of the French edition.
212) And superseded by the Chinese characters. Cfr. my *Beginnings of writing around Tibet*, sec. 44.
213) Several such writings have been made in South-western Asia, such as the Lolo, the Shuikia, and a third one, the name whereof is not known to me, but a specimen exists in a bilingual manuscrit No. 24898, Musée d' Ethnographie du Trocadéro, Paris : Musso and ?—On the

Lolo writing, cfr. below sec. c. of the present chapter. On the Shui-Kia characters, cfr my notice *A new writing from S. W. China*. in The Academy, 19 Febr., 1887, and *Langues de la Chine*, p. 150.
214) By a singular perversion of fables, a story has been made in the VIth century of our era, of Ambassadors from Yueh-shang sent to the Emperor Yao with a written calendar. Cfr. my remarks on the subject in *The Land of Sinim, not China*, pp. 184-185 of B. & O.R.,I.: and below Chapt. VII. answer to objections.

c) The Trade of Shuh=Szetchuen.

We must come to several centuries later than the beginning of the Tchöu dynasty to find the most important trade routes through the South and South West and West, which have really exercised a great influence on the development of China. Curiously enough this trade was carried on by non-Chinese and outside the limited Chinese dominion of the time.

The traders of Shuh, i.e., Sze-tchuen, belonged to those well gifted populations of an initiative spirit, who did not shrink from being on friendly terms with the civilized Bak tribes soon after their arrival in North West China, and to avail themselves of the benefit which an acquaintance with their scientific notions and arts could procure. Some legendary accounts relate that Tchang-y, a son of Nai Hwang-ti went forward to settle in that direction,[215] and that several people of the Po'ng tribe brought books to Shao-Hao[216] a successor of Hwang-ti, who had remained in the West and did not rule in China. Arriving at more modern times, it is probable that the Shuh people had made use of their knowledge and entered into some intercourse with the outside world. The history of the country had been written by Yang-hiung (B.C. 53 - A.D. 18), the celebrated philologist[217] who was himself a native of Shuh, but his work is apparently lost and now known only through a few quotations in other works[218], which we shall refer to further on. The traders of Shuh remained for long confined to the North of the Szetchuen province, and there are reasons to believe that they did participate to the Jade traffic by the W. route which we have described. (VI, b). Their country was included in the Liang-tchöu, of the Yu-kung, which had to pay a tribute of jade: or at least from where or through which Jade articles did come, at the time of the Hia and Shang dynasties as recorded in the *Yü Kung*.[219] Much later, in 860, B.C. some of them presented Jade articles to the King Y of Tchöu,[220] and the sort of Jade indicates that it was Nephrite of Turkestan. It is apparently to this trade extended from hand to hand westwards, that western

Asia and afterwards Europe was indebted for the introduction of Chinese fruits such as the peach, the abricot, the jujube, and some others. The carrying westwards and eastwards of the famous mastiff-dogs of Tibet was also due to the same trade, at least for a part of the route, as we shall see directly.

The Peach is certainly originary from China[221], where it is cultivated since high antiquity, and where it so became a symbol of marriage and of longevity[222]. In the Brief Calendar of the Hia dynasty, which was compiled not long after the twentieth century B.C.[223], it is noted that on the sixth month the "peaches are boiled for preserves"[224]. The wild peach tree is also spoken of therein as putting forth blossoms on the first month, and forests or groves of peach trees[225] are mentioned in ancient literature[226], such as the T"ao-lin, or peach-forest in Shensi W., the oldest one known, and afterwards others in Honan[227], in Kiang-si[228], &c. Now the peach in antiquity was not known in the west[229], nor was it known to the Sanskrit-speaking people migrating into India. It must have been imported from China between the time of these migrations, and the relations of the Persians with the Greeks. It was first spoken of by Theophrastus (332 B.C.), who mentions it as a Persian fruit, and it did not reach Italy until the Christian era. It is therefore probable that this importation did take place before the fourth century[230] from China, through the route of the Shuh traders and their intermediaries.

Abricot (prunus armeniacus) is also indigenous in China[231], and may have been brought to the west by the same channel. The hing[232] is mentioned along with the t'ao=peach in the Brief Calendar of the Hia dynasty[233], but it was not so much appreciated as the latter fruit, and the references to it in ancient literature are not so numerous[234]. In the west it was not known at the time of Theophrastus, but it must have been brought before the first century as Pliny mentions it, unless it should have been already there unknown of the Greek writer. The jujube, tsao, was carried to the west, or at least to Persia, at a much earlier period than the peach and the abricot, though after the Aryan migration to India[235]. It is a native of the north of China[236], and it is mentioned in the Hia calendar already referred to.[237] The list will probably be increased by further researches on the subject.

The celebrated mastiff dogs of Tibet have been carried in antiquity in Babylonia as well as in China. Marco-Polo spoke of them as "big as donkeys."[238] François Lenormant has reproduced a slab from Babylonia where such a dog is represented with a precision which makes the identification certain.[239] In China their presentation to the King of Tchōu by some people of the West, after the overthrow of the Shang-yu dynasty has given a name to a book of the Shu-king.[240] Modern travellers have repeatedly spoken of these famous dogs.[241] The case is interesting in our enquiry as instancing communications at least occasional between a medial country, Babyloniaon the West and China on the east. In the case of China it may have been due, like the arrival of the trading parties of Shön-Mi, Nêrê and Yueh-shang, to the rising fame of the conquest of China, then very small, by the Tchōu with the help of their neighbours, the non-Chinese tribes of the West and South West.[242] Although the name of the Shuh traders do not appear, and that the party who presented the mastiffs is not given, as they are described only as travellers from the West, it is quite clear that coming from Tibet, they must have passed through the country of the Shuh traders ; therefore their journey cannot but be connected with this western trade, should they not be themselves simply a trading party from Shuh.

NOTES. 215) He dwelt near the *Joh* water. *Tchuh shuh ki nien*, I, Hwang-ti, year 77.—On relations with the Chinese in 1970 B.C.? cfr. *The lang. of Chin. before the Chin.*, sec. 113.
216) R. K. Douglas, *Chinese and Babylonian literature*, l. c. ; note 87 *suprà*.—This legend is one of those which have been combined into the fabulous account told in the *Tso-tchuen*, Tchao kung, year XVII, 3 ; edit. Legge. *Chinese classics*, vol. V, p. 667.—Tradition speaks of the P'ongs as the first rebels subdued by Hwang-ti, and afterwards friends with the Chinese, They belonged to the same family as the Mungs (Môu-Taï race). cfr. *Tai Ping yü lan*, Bk. 915, ff. 1-9; and my *Lang. Chin. before Chinese*, chap. IX.
217) I have analysed his " Comparative dictionary of dialects " in the last-quoted work, chap. VII.
218) *Shuh wang pen-tsi* in *Tai ping yü lan*, Bk. 166, ff. 3 and 10 v.
219) *Shu-king*, part III, Bk. I, 69. Cfr. text *suprà* and note 174.
220) *Tchuh shu k'i wien*. Tchōu Y wang, year II. The expression used is *Kiāng yuk* the finest sort of jade, that which is mentioned in the legend of Muh Wang and Si Wang Mu, cfr. *The Tree of Life*, pp. 5, 10, n. 35.
221) As shown by Prof. A. de Candolle from various evidences; cfr. his *Géographie Botanique raisonnée*, 1855, p. 881, and his recent smaller work *Origin of cultivated plants*, 1884. pp. 221, 229.
222) Cfr. W. F. Mayers. *Chinese R. M.*, sub. voc. *T"ao*, p. 213.
223) Cfr. E. C. Knobel, *Notes on an ancient Chinese calendar*, 1882. Above note 20.
224) *Tchu t'ao y wei tòu shih*; in the *Ta Y-li, Hia siao tcheng*, VIth month. The same calendar as edited and translated by Prof. R. K. Douglas, *The calendar of the Hia dynasty*, p. 44 (Orientalia Antiqua, I, 1882) says only *Tchu t'ao* ' Boiled are the peaches'; the other words *y wei tou*

shih, litterally ' to make dishes of fruits ' are not there.
225) Called *t'o t'ao* or *y-t'ao*, the first character having the two readings. Prof. Douglas, *l.c.* p. 26, translates mountain peach tree.
226) Spoken in the *Shu-king*, Part, V, Wu tcheng 2. It was situated about the hill of Kw'a fu in the S.C. of the present department of T'ung-tchou. Cfr. J. Legge, *Chinese classics*, vol. III, p. 309, note. The same statement is found in the *Shan hai King*. In the *Tai ping yü lan* encyclopedia of 983, in Bk. 967 ff. 1-8, there is no less than 73 references to the peach from ancient literature.
227) G. Playfair, *The Cities and Towns of China*, No. 4400.
228) *Tai ping yü lan*, Bk. 967, fol. 3.
229) The present statement and the followings are derived from Dr. A. de Candolle, *Géographie botanique* and *Origin of cultivated plants*, l.c.
230) We have spoken below of the introduction of the China peach into India at a later date.
231) De Candolle, *origin*, pp. 215-218.
232) Not *sing* as by misprint in Bretschneider, *on the study and value of Chinese botanical works*, p. 10.
233) *Hia siao tcheng*, I, 21, and IV, 54; R. R. Douglas, *o.c.* pp. 26, 37.
234) *Tai ping yü lan*, Bk. 968, ff. 1-3. Among the quotations given there, one of the Vth. cent. refers to apricot trees in Khotan, and another supposed to be earlier, speaks of an island where apricots grow, in the sea south of Shantung.
235) A de Candolle. *Origin*, pp. 194-196.
236) A de Candolle. *ibid.* p. 196.
237) *Hia siao tcheng*. VIIIth month 93 ; R. R. Douglas, *o.c.* p. 48.
238) H. Yule, *Marco-Polo*. 2nd edit., vol. II, p. 41.
239) In his work : *La langue Primitive de la chaldée*, pl., p. 383, from a terra cotta fragment found at Babylon. At the time of the Akhæ-menides, similar dogs were brought up in four villages of Babylonia, according to Herodotus, who calls them Indian, I, 192. Ktêsias has described them, 5 and fragm. VI. Cfr. *Ancient India as described by Ktêsias the Knidian*, by J. W. McCrindle, (1882), pp. 9 and 36. Also W. Houghton, *Mammalia of the Assyrian inscriptions*, Tr. S.B.A., 1877, vol. V.
240) *Liü ngao*. Part, V, BkV. in J. Legge, *Chinese classics*, vol. III, p. 345.
241) Such as G. Bogle in 1774, Manning in 1812, (Mar-khani, Tibet, pp, 88, 224) ; T. T. Cooper, P. Drand, (H. Yule, *Marco Polo*. l.c.) Capt. W. Gill, *The River of Golden Sand*, (1880), vol. I, p. 382 ; vol. II, pp. 151, 247.
242) These tribes are enumerated in the *Shu-king*, Part, V, Bk. II The Tchou were represented in China with red hair. On their foreign. origin, cfr. *Les langues de la Chine*, addit. p. 160.
243) *Si Liü*. The latter word (3837 of Basile) is not the proper name of a tribe, and means simply in that case, stranger, traveller, as in Mencius. Cfr. W. Williams. S.D. p. 559 ; J. Eitel, *Ch. C.D.*, p. 390 ; *sub. voc.*

* *

The traders of Shuh in their mercantile expeditions followed three routes going to the west, to the south-west and the south.

There was a route to Tibet and the west or south-west which, apparently starting from Tcheng-tu, passed through Darchiendo (Chinese *Ta-tsen-lu*), as in the present day,[244] and then bifurcated to the N. W. and to the S. W. The North route thither must have bent its direction to the N. W. and following South of the Kuenlun range crossed to the country of the Jade, the Khotan region. This is a mere inference from the data we have just enumerated. We have no other evidence to add in its favour nor as to the date when it ceased to be used, after the presentation to the Chinese court of Jade articles from Turkestan in 860 B.C. which we have described. The S. W. route starting from Darchiendo westwards passing through Litang, Batang, Kiangka, and then in a S. W. direction probably through Rœma, Sadiya,[245] and the course of the Brahmaputra, reached on the Ganges the important mart of Pataliputra (or Patna) which became the capital city of the celebrated Asoka (263--224 B.C.) This is the road spoken of afterwards by Tchang-Kien 123 B.C.,[246] and by the unknown author of the Periplus[247] two hundred years later.

Tchang-kien was sent in 135 B.C. by Han Wu Ti on the track of the Yueh-ti, former neighbours in the N. W. of China, who had migrated westwards in 165 B. C.,[248] in order to secure their alliance against the common foes the Hiung-nus; he arrived in the Ta-Hia country,[249] or Bactria in 125 B.C., after being a prisoner among the latter for over ten years, and there he saw, some cloth from Shuh, otherwise silk-cloth from modern central Szetchuen, and some bamboo staves from Kiung,[250] a western part of the same modern province; both articles, he was told were brought in Ken-tu, *i.e.* Hindu=India,[251] by their own traders when going to that country which lay several thousand *li* to the south-east. The acute Chinaman was unaware of the existing intercourse between Shuh and India, but he estimated rightly that with reference to the Middle kingdom, India was situate in the South-west, and therefore that some communication could be established in that direction as we shall see further on. It is to be remarked that Tchang-kieng does not allude at all to any trade of any sort through Tibet and Badakshan, which existed no more in his time, as otherwise he would undoubtedly have mentioned it, and his views would not have been solely directed to the establishment of an intercourse between Bactria and China through India, as we shall see further on. The scanty trade which as we have seen, the Shuh traders did carry in olden times by the North had long died out from the difficulties of the way, and the opening of new markets in India through the South western routes. It was after the return of the Chinese minister and his reports on the wealth of the countries West of the Tsungling mountains, that trade by the North began only to be regularly carried.

The anonymous writer of the Periplus, A.D. 80-89, has a remarkable passage on this trade.[252] "Beyond this region (*Khrusé*, i.e. Indo-China), immediately under the North, where the sea terminates outwards, there lies somewhere in T h i n a a very great city,--not on the coast, but in the interior of the country, called T h i n a, from which silk, whether in the raw state or spun into thread and woven into cloth is brought by land through Bactria to B a r u g a z a (Bharōch), or by the Ganges river to L i m u r i k é [253] (*Dimyriké*, the Tamul country, Malabar)." The author speaks of '*erion sērikon* and of *nēma sērikon* ; and in another passage he mentions furs *dérmata sērika* as exported from Barbarikon, a mart on the middle and only navigable branch of the Indus,[254] where they must have been brought from the same country as the other articles, i.e. from the S e r i c a. Pliny, somewhat earlier, mentions[255] the S è r e s sending their most excellent iron along with vestments and furs.[256] Ptolemy, is his turn, a century later, says[257] that there was not only a road from the country of the Seres and of the Sinæ to Bactriane by the Stone Tower, (i.e. by Kashgar and Pamir), but also a road to India which came through Palimbothra (i. e. Patna). The latter route is therefore that which was followed by the merchants from Shuh for their trade with India, and until the reopening of the North route, was during several centuries the way of communications between the West and the non-Chinese Szetchuen, and by rebound the Middle Kingdom. I am not in a position to say that this West-south route, or another South route whereof we shall speak further on, was opened shortly after the time of the mercantile expedition to the court of Tching Wang.[258] It is probable, but we shall not see any influence coming through them before the sixth century ;[259] as to historical facts we do not find any before the fourth century.

At that time the wealth of Szetchuen had accrued considerably in consequence of its foreign trade and made it a desirable acquisition for its powerful neighbours, in the North the state of T a n, modern sound *Ts'in*, in Shensi, future conqueror of the whole Chinese dominion, and on the East the non-Chinese state of *Tsu*, probably old T s e r u, which was not yet half-sinicised in Hukwang.

The history of the kings of S h u h by Yang-hiung[260], which I have already alluded to, gives the names of several rulers who had establishep their power in the capital[261]. After the lapse of three periods called *Ts'an tsung*, *Tcheh kuan* and *Yü y*, a certain K a i m i n g was ruling in the latter part of the fourth century[262]. His successors were P c h y u n g Y ü-w e i, and T'a-y ü. The latter, who had come from India[263], assumed the title of king, and was ruling circa 255 b.c.[264], but l e was induced to resign. according to probabilities, under the increased pressure of the kings of Ts'in, then all powerful. The latter had begun long before to show their strong hand in these regions. Prince Hwny, who did not assume the Royal dignity before 324 b.c., had conquered in 328 b.c. the region called P a t c h u n g, corresponding to the modern prefecture of Tchung King in E. Szetchuen. Five years afterwards, as king of Ts'in, he sends his prime minister, Tchang-y, to attack the Shuh[265]. Kai-ming, who was then on the throne, tried vainly to resist. and being vanquished, withdrew to Wu-yang, the modern Kia-ting fu, where he was made a prisoner soon afterwards. It was only later on[266], namely. about 218 b.c.. and in order to facilitate their communications, that Ts'in She Huang-ti, the founder of the Chinese Empire. constructed the famous five-feet causeway through the Tsing ling range. which hitherto had been a natural barrier, preventing any serious extension towards the South[267]. Previously to the establishment of this route the supremacy of the kings of Ts'in, which was only temporary, in those regions was nothing more than a sort of protectorate, the government remained in the hands of the native chiefs, who preserved their hereditary rights[268], and were entitled to receive royal princesses in marriage[269].

But it gave to the Ts'ins the right of passage for their traders and for their troops; and it permitted them to thwart the projects of the non-Chinese[270] great State of Tsu, the kings whereof had been attracted like themselves towards Ssetchuen and the south-west, and began their movements in that direction sometime earlier. They had gradually absorbed several minor states which lay on their western borders. About 330 b.c. the king Wei of Tsu[271] sent Tchwang-Kiao with troops up the (Yang-tse) Kiang to settle the boundaries of the several tribes from Pa and Kien tchung[272] westward, and attach them to his kingdom. The gallant general proceeded further on and reached the lake of Yunnan which was then called the T s e n marsh[273]; he overawed the inhabitants of the country by his military strength, and attached them also to the kingdom of Tsu. But the army of Ts'in cut his communications in the rear. seizing, as we have said above, the districts of Pa and Kien-tchung, which he had submitted. and prevented his return to his native country. " The highway being thus rendered impassable, Tchwang-kiao remained with his followers and established himself as king of Tsen, assuming the garb of the barbarians and adopting their customs, he was accepted as their chief *74.*"

NOTES. 244) Routes die hard in mountainous and unexplored lands, and the route here indicated is still said to be the only one permitted by the orography of the country. Therefore it was probably that which was followed in antiquity. Cfr. note 326 *infr.*
245) The route is indicated by the geographical conditions of the country, and that which has been severally attempted by European travellers who could not go through because of the war-like and savage dispositions of the native tribes.
246) Szema Tsien, *She ki*, Bk. 123, fol. 6 ; Pan ku, *Tsien Han Shu*, Bk. 61, Biography of *Tchang kien.*
247) Peripl. Mar. Erythr., 64. J. W. McCrindle, *The Commerce and Navigation of the Erythrean Sea* (Bombay, 1879), pp. 12-13 and 148.
248) Cfr. my paper *The Yueh-ti and the Early Buddhist Missionaries in China,* p. 5.
249) This is an important datum for the connexion of ancient geography and ethnology in the cuneiform documents and the Chinese annals. The *Tahia* of the Chinese are the Da ai of N. Persia mentioned by Herodotus 1, 125 : the Deaye of Ezra, IV, 9 : the Da hae whom Sennakhérib vanquished in 697, he seized their capital Ukku, and their King Maniya fled before him. Cfr. E. Norris, *Assyrian dictionary*, 1, 212 ; Prof. E. Schrader in F. von Richtofen, *China*, 441 n.; G. de Vasconcellos-Abreu, *De l' origine probable des Toukhares*, pp. 176-179 (Le Muséon, 1883, t. II.)—The Tahia or Da ai must be carefully distinguished from the Tokha ri and from the Yueh-ti as shown by the latter scholar. Richtofen *l.c.*, and A. Cunningham *Coins of the Indo-scythians* (Numismatic Chronicle, 1888, vol. VIII) have not avoided these confusions of ancient orientalists. Sennaherib had subdued the Tuk ha ri in his preceeding campaign, which directed more to the North.
250) Ki u n g was properly the name of a hill, producing bamboos with long joints and solid hearts, fit for making staves. A. Wylie.
251) The primitive text of Tchang-kien gave that spelling accordingly with the name as he heard it pronounced in the N. of Persia. It was corrected afterwards into S h e n-t u under the influence of Buddhist priests from India. Cfr. the gloss in Szema Tsien's *Sheki*, l.c.
252) The connection of the Greek report with that of the Chinese minister, not general, of HAN Wu-ti, has been shown by Col. H. Yule in his most valuable *Essay introductory to Capt. Gill's journey ' The River of Golden Sand'* (1880), p. 32.
253) Peripl. *Mar. Erythr*, 64 ; McCrindle, *o.c.* pp. 147-148.
254) *Ibid.* 39 ; McCrindle, *o.c.* p. 109, note. Some *nēma sērika* was also brought to Barbarikon as sta ted in the same passage.
255) Plin. *Hist. nat.* xxxiv. 41. Dr. J. Edkins has recently published in the *Journal of the Peking Oriental Society*, 1885, vol. I, pp. 1-16, a paper on *Allusions to China in Pliny'snatural history.*
256) In the *Mahábhárata*, II, 50, quoted by Lassen, among the presents

sent to Yudhishṭhira by the S a k a, T u s h â r a, and K a ṅ k a skins
are enumerated.
257) Ptolem. I, 17, circā A.D. 150.—McCrindle, *Ancient India* as described by Ptolemy, (Bombay, 1885), p. 30.—Col. II. Yule, *Cathay and the w y thither*, vol. I, introd. pp. 146-153 has collected from Ptolemy and annotated all that concerns this subject.
258) Which we have reported above.
259) Cfr. below, sect. ****** of the present chapter.
260) *Shuh Wang pen ki*. I quote it from some extracts in the *Tai ping yŭ lan* (A.D. 983), Bk. 166, ff. 3, 10. As the matter has never been treated, as far as we know, in any European work, I am compelled to speak at a greater length than I would do otherwise.
261) The modern *Tcheng-tu* as called since 221 B.C. and then pronounced T h a n h-t u. It was previously *Kwei-tcheng* or the T o r t o i s e c i t y according to the *Lung Shuh sin* in the *Shwoh ling* collection, Bk. II, f. 9.
262) The same name appears in the *Shan hai king*, Bk. XI, ff. 2-4, but so much fabled, that historical truth has disappeared under the bewildering garb.
263) The text says that he was originary from the *Tien t'o* mountains. The name (1798-1716 of Basile) is one of the many Chinese equivalents for S h i n d u or India.
264) A short notice of him is given in Mayer's Chinese R.M., I, 685, where it is said that he was styled W a u g T i. He resigned his throne and retired in the W u mountains of the West, in consequence of fabulous circumstances reported in his legend, but more probably for the reason put forth in the text above.
265) *Shuh Wang pen ki*, l.c. Bk. 166, f. 10 v. The date of this event is pretty well ascertained from a concatenation of circumstances. Prince Hwuy made himself king in the year 324 ; and the officer he sent against Shuh was Tchang-y who was in his service between the years 330-323 ; therefore it must be in 324-323 that the campaign took place Tchang-y on whose life cfr. W. F. Mayers, *Chinese R.M.*, I, 17.
266) Szema Tsien, *She ki*, Bk. 116, fol. 2.— Panku, *Tsien Han shu*, Bk. 95 : transl. A. Wylie, *History of the South Western Barbarians*, p. 4 in Journal of the Anthropological Institute, August 1879.
267) The entire route is a work of tremendous engineering, says Baron von Richtofen, in Col. H. Yule, *Marco-Polo*, vol. II, p. 26. It extended from the river Hwai opposite the district city of Pao-ki, to within a few miles of the Han river, near the prefectural city of Hantchung, (A. Wylie). It is curious that local tradition should attribute the authorship of this great work to wrong men. In Shensi, it is Liu pang the founder of the First Han dynasty in : 06 B.C. ; in Szetchuen it is the great man of the country, Liu-pi the founder of the Third Han dynasty at Tcheng-tu in 226 A.D. It is possible that Liu pang had it repaired but he did not establish it, as the statement of Szema Tsien is quite precise, and it existed previously ten years or more.
268) For instance in 255 B.C. King Tch'ao siang made a treaty with some chiefs of the Pa region, modern Tchung king, which was engraved on stone. Cfr. *Hou Han Shu*, Bk. 116, *Pan Tun* ; transl. A. Wylie, *History of the Southern and South Western Barbarians*, p. 222, in Revue de l'Extreme Orient, 1882, t. I.
269) *Hou Han Shu*, Bk. 116, *Pa Nan* ; A. Wylie, *ibid*. p. 220.

270) On this state and its non-Chinese linguistic characteristics, cfr. *The Languages of China before the Chinese*, sect. 31-33, 96-98; and in the French edition, addition p. 148.
271) Szema Tsien, *She Ki*, Bk. 116, f. 2.—King Wei ruled from 339 to 328 B.C.
272) Corresponding to W. Hunan, E. Szetshuen and N. Kueitchou provinces.
273) This name which is now decayed into *Tien* is still the litterary appellative of the province of Yunnan.
274) Szema Tsien, *She ki*, l.c. ; in Wylie's translation *J.A.I.*, l.c. p. 4.

e) *The trade of Shuh=Szetchuen.*

III.

After 320 B.C., the subjects of the Than, modern *Ts'in*, rulers had therefore a footing in the Shuh country, and could have a hand in the foreign commerce which was carried there; but we do not know how far they availed themselves of their opportunities. They certainly did so to a certain extent, and were enabled to get some geographical information on the regions of the south, and especially the region of the modern Burma. Some documents have existed about a route or routes from Ta Thanh, modern *Ta Ts'in*, as it was called at the time of its dominion[275], and Indo-China, compiled apparently at the beginning of the Han dynasty; but they have been misunderstood by a Chinese compiler of about 350 A.D. who has applied them to another purpose, and they have reached us in such a garbled and mixed up condition that it would be an invidious and dangerous task to draw any inference of positive geography out of them. It is one of the most curious cases of misgivings in the system of mosaic literary work known as Chinese composition[276].

As we have just said, a clear indication of this trade route is the geographical knowledge which was gained through it. In the Xth book of the *Shan hai King*[277], an interpolated passage of circà 210 B.C. mentions the *Kwei-lin* region[278] and afterwards the *Peh-lu* country, the *Li-ni* country, the *Tiao-ti* country, and the *Peh-ku* country, all southwards of the Yu river, which is a southern affluent of the Canton river[279]. Now all these names are, descriptive of peculiar customs; *Li-ni*=Parted-years, *Tiaoti*=tattoed foreheads, or ethnic names, *Peh-lu*=Pray and Plow, *Peh-ku*=Pgho and Pegu, all formerly of the country which is now Burma[280]. A later work mentions tin as one of the products of the country of Peh-lu, sold to foreigners[281]; and this Peh-lu is apparently the same as that we have just quoted from the Canon of the Hills and Rivers or *Shan Hai King*.

Therefore at the time of the preponderance of the *Than* or Ts'in, i. e., after 320 until 209 B.C., and probably earlier, a trade-route had existed towards the south-west, passing through the principalities of Szetchuen and Yunnan, notably through Yung-tchang in the W. of latter province, and hence by one of the two rivers, the Salwen or the Irawaddy, arriving to the emporia on the coast of Pegu[282]. We know from several testimonies, concurring to the same statement, that the coast of Pegu, was for centuries a seat of commercial activity. An ancient Hindu colony, Hinduic, not Buddhist, of merchants from Orissa under the lead of Taphussa and Bhallika had been founded in the Vth century B.C., in Ukkalamandala[283], which comprised the region S. and S.W. of the extreme Pegu yoma range[284]. The foundation of the Shwe Dagōn pagoda of Rangoon is attributed to them.

According to the *Mahá Rájáweng* or Royal history of Burma, with all reserve due to its trustworthiness, the upper part of the country had been colonised from India even before that time. Abhirájá, ruler of Kapilavastu[285], abandoned his country and crossing the mountains eastward, founded about 800 years before the time of Gautama, a new kingdom with the capital at Tagoung, on the left bank of the Irawaddy, in about 23° 30' N. lat. While Gautama Buddha was alive, i. e. *circá* 515–135 B.C., a second band of Kshatriyas from Gangetic India arrived led by Daza Rájá, and settled east of the Irawaddy[286]. The thirty-second successor of Abhirájá, named Bhiennaká, and the last king of his dynasty, who lived about the commencement of the religious Buddhist era, was driven away by invaders from his capital, the old Pagan, which they destroyed, near Tagoung, and compelled to take refuge at Malei, on the right bank of the Irawaddy, and nearly opposite the present remains of Lower Tsampenago[287]. These invaders had come from a country to the east called Gandalarit[288], in the land of Tsin or Sin, which corresponds with Yunnan.[289] Should the last name be contemporary of the event, and the "about the commencement of the religious era" indicate as it seems probable a somewhat later date,[290] namely the third century before the Christian era, if not later, we might have in this record a link with the genuine history of Yunnan which we have recorded. The Kingdom of Tsen had been established in 330 B.C., and it is very probable that the rulers of that state, enterprising as we know they were, have attempted if not succeeded to establish their sway towards the south-west of their dominion, and therefore have advanced eventually as far as the Old Pagan. This place, in some accounts was also called Tzinduè,

²⁹¹ and it seems that this name was known to the traders of S.W. China in the second century before our era.²⁹²

Anyhow, in the third century B.C., the region of modern Burma must have been largely occupied with Hindu colonists ; it was deemed of sufficient importance to be numbered among the nine realms where Buddhist missions ought to be sent ; and after the great council held about 241 B.C. in the monastery of Açokârâma at Patna, Sona and Uttara were dispatched to Suvanna bhumi,²⁹³ and according to probabilities, they landed at Golanagara,²⁹⁴ north of Thatun.

We have now carried our historical investigation about the possibilities of intercourse between Shu h and the South and South-west, as late as the third century before our era. This period ought to be later than is required for the immediate purpose of the present work. The events of the two centuries which follow, are however so important in historical results and in clearer and more precise information on the matter, that we are compelled to examine them, before proceeding to our survey of the importation of western notions and ideas which have reached the Middle Kingdom through the S.W. channels.

NOTES. 275) In the *Shan hai king*, we find *Ta Thanh*, i.e. Ta Ts'in, Ta Tsu, &c.

276) I refer to the description of *Ta T'san* in the *Wei lioh* by Yü-huan of the IVth century, a large part whereof refers distinctly to the old Ta Than (*Ta T'sin*) of N. W. China, and to Thatun near Martaban, and dates from the short period of the *Than*=Ts'in supremacy ; it was mixed up with data of later date concerning Dakshina or South India and the Ta Ts'in of further West. Tchang Kien knew nothing of Ta Ts'in. The description I discuss contains whole statements from the *Shan hai king*, (cf. II, 20, XIII, 1 and XVI, 4 of this work with sect. 77 of the description) which have crept into all the notices subsequently compiled, from the *Hòu Han Shu* downwards. The symbol *T'sin*, which as I have shown in another paper (*B & O.R.*, I, 46), was formerly *Than* and in that capacity had been used to transcribe the names of Ta Than, later *Ta Ts'in*, of N.W. China, and of Thatun, later Sadun near Martaban, was gradually decayed to *Tsin* and in the latter value, was employed in the fourth century, with the same other sign to great, for the notation of the name of Dakshina or S. India. Cfr. the Chinese version of the *Samanta-prabhâsa-sûtra*, early work like the Lalitavistara, by Tchu Fâhn or Dharmaraksha, *P'u-yao k'ng*, in 308 A.D., III, 7, fol. 5.—Another transcription for the same name was employed (Eitel, *Sanskrit-Chinese dictionary*, sub. voc.) afterwards, by Fang-yen and others but in that concerns the earliest reports the evil was done, and a case of error existed henceforth for future compilers. Much confusion has been brought about in Chinese documents by resemblances of names, and the use of well-known appel-

latives for names newly-heard of, because of a temporary and approximate similarity in sound, fancied by the transcriber according to his time and his own dialectal peculiarities. In the descriptions of *Ta T'sin* which the Chinese compilers have wrongly looked upon as that of one and unique country, there are several cases of such confusions and the result has been an inextricable entanglement. Dr. F. Hirth in his learned work *China and the Roman Orient*, Researches into their Ancient and and Mediæval relations as represented in old Chinese records, Shanghai, 1885, has published all these texts with translations and comments; but he has not recognized the extracts therein from the *Shan hai king*; he has premised that Ta T'sin applied to the Roman Orient only, and was shifting in the records according to the geographical knowledge of the time ; with a considerable amount of learning and ingenuity which deserved better subject and success, he has attempted the impossible task of making many names fit countries and towns of Anterior Asia.—I find in my own notes that the name *Ta T'sin* refers to five different countries ; *Ansih* to two ; *Tiao-tchi* to three ; *Li-kien* to three; and so forth. With reference to the old south trade-route and the documents about it which have been merged with later data concerning the Roman Orient or Ta T'sin in the *Wei lioh*, I remark the following names : T s i h-s h i h (*Shan hai king*, II, 20, XI, 3 : Legge, *Shu king*, pp. 127, 134 ; M. Guelny, *Description de la Chine occidentale*, Muséon, 1885, IV, 618-9) ; *Hien* and *Tu* in S. Szetchuen (cfr. Matouanlin, *Ethnographie*, transl. D'Hervey, I, 37, 56, 21, 175) : *Ki-fu*, not *Sze-fu*,K o-f u, in Yueh sui S. Szetchuen (Matouanlin, l.c. 147) ; *Sze-tao* in W. Kueitchou; *Tsie-lan*, E. of Tsun-y. Kueitchou (Matouanlin, l.c. 124); *A-man* = Ho-man of W. Yunnan (Matouanlin, l.c. 195); *Tiao-tchi* = T i a o-t i of Upper Burma; *Li-kien* = R a k h a i n g, modern Arakan (A. P. Phayre, *History of Burma*, p. 41); *Sze-lo* = S a d a, S. of Rakhaing. (Col. H. Yule, *Oldest Records of the sea route to China*, p. 5; Proc. R. G. S., Nov, 1882); *Sze-pin* = S a b o n a of Ptolemy = Suvarna (Lassen, in McCrindle's *Ptolemy*, p. 199); *Ta Than* later Ta Tsin, = T h a t u n, a local form (Phayre, o.c. p. 24) of Saddhamma (Dr. Em. Forchammer, *Notes* I, *The Shwe Dagon Pagoda*, pp. 3, 17) ; *Ansih*, at proximity of Tun-sun = Tennasserim (*Liong shu*, Bk. 54) = A n d h r a on the East coast of India ; *Anku* = A n g h a of the same region ; *Yü-lo* = U d r a, modern Orissa : *Lu-fen* = T a p- r o b a n e or Ceylon and its flying bridge of 230 li across the sea, = the Bridge of Rama ; and some others.—On *The Chinese name of the Roman empire*, cfr. my note in *The Academy*, 1 Oct., 1881 ; and Prof. Henri Cordier, in *Mélanges Graux*, 1884, pp. 719-721. *De l'origine des noms que les ch nois ont donnés a l' Empire Romain.*

277) *Shan hai king*, Bk. X. fol. 1 r. On this curious work cfr. note 91, *supra*.

278) The entry of this name which existed as a geographical appellative after 214 b.c. until the year 204 b.c when it was conquered by the king of Nan-yueh, who was recognised as such and as a vassal of the Han dynasty in 196 b.c. The years 214-204 b.c. or little afterwards are therefore the period of the composition of the notice.

279) A. R. Colquhoun, *Across Chrysê*, vol. 1.

280) All names and customs found still among the Karengs. Cfr. Major Spearman, *The British Burma Gazetteer*, vol. I. pp. 162-173 ; also Col. A. R. McMahon, *The Karens of the Golden Chersonese* (1876), p. 43 sq. And my *Lang. before Chin.*, sect. 145-149.
281) The *Fu-nan tu lu* by Kang-tai, quoted in the *Tai ping yü lan* (983) Bk. 789, fol. 3 r.
282) This route was again used in the second and third century of our era, as described in F. Hirth, *China and the Roman Orient*, p. 179. In the *Hou Han Shu* Bk. 116, (transl. Wylie, Rev. Extr. Orient, p. 234; also F. Hirth, o.c., pp. 36, 179) a state of *Than* or *Tan*, probably not distant from Yung-tchang, is recorded as having relations with the Chinese court in A.D. 97, and presenting to the Emperor in 120 A.D. some musicians and jugglers, whose feats are described, from Thatun (written *Ta Than*) a country in the S.W. with which the Shan or Tan had intercourse. M. Talboys Wheeler, the historian of India, has told me that the natives of South Burma are still most clever in the same tricks as those described by the Chinese annalist. On Thatun, cfr. note 276.
283) Utkalas was the classical name of the inhabitants of Orissa, E. India.
284) Cfr. Em. Forchhammer, *Notes on the Early history and geography of British Burma*, I. (Rangoon, 1883), pp. 6, 11, 12, 14 and 16. The author mentions, p. 6, that names occur in the geography of British Burma which are originally not Pali but Sanskrit, and suggestive more of ethnical and historical relations with Hinduic India than with Buddhism. Col. H. Yule has long before made the same remark. Cfr. his *Sources and authorities* in Dr. Smith's Atlas; and his *Notes on the oldest records of the sea route to China* (Proc. R.G.S. 1882) p. 11. Both scholars have remarked the transfer which has taken place of many Indian names to Indo-China.
285) Or Kapilanagara, the birth-place of Buddha Gautama, identified by Gen. Alex. Cunningham with Nagar on the Upper Maunrama or Cuni tributary of the Gogra. Cfr. his *Ancient geography of India*, p. 414 sq.—Abhiraja is said to have fled before the invasion of his country by the king of Kauthala or Oudh. (Dr. J. Anderson, *Mandalay to Momien*, pp. 26-27.) The *Mahâ Râjâweng* says, the king of P e n g-z i-l a-r i e t (Major Spearman, *British Burma Gazetteer*, I, p. 236.)
286) On the ruins of Tagoung, cfr. Sir A. P. Phayre, *History of Burma*, 1883, pp. 14-15, and Dr. J. Anderson, *Report on the Expedition to Western Yunnan*, 1871, p. 206. Little of them is apparent at first sight, but explorations and excavations there would disclose certainly some most important data. Dr. Em. Forchhammer, archæologist of the government of Burma, has just made an exploration of the magnificent ruins of New Pagan, and discovered some wonderful antiquities. Cfr. Col. Yule *Remains of Pagan*, and Dr. Forchhammer's letter in *Trübner's Record*, 1889, IIIrd s. No. 1, pp. 3-4 ; also Yule's *Mission to Av '*, 1858, p. 33 ; Howard Malcom, *Travels in the Burman Empire*, June 27, 1836. Though P a g a n is reported to have been built a long while after T a g o u n g, namely in the seventh century of our era, (*Burma Gazetteer*, p. 249) we may expect from Dr. Forchhammer's explorations some important disclosures on the inflation of the

Mahá Rájáweng in respect to the date of foundation of the first town.
287) Cfr. *Burma Gazetteer.* I, p. 286 ; Phayre, *o.c.* p. 8 ; Ney Elias, *Introductory sketch of the history of the Shans,* p. 12.
288) G a n d a l a r i t is one of the many instances of transfer of the classical localities of Indian Buddhism to Indo-China, which is current in Burma. For the Buddhist horizon in the latter country, Yunnan represents G a n d h â r a, the country about Peshawar, and is still so styled in state documents of Burma (*Gandalarit*), Cfr. Col. H. Yule, *Marco Polo* 2 ed., II, p. 59, and *An endeavour to elucidate Rashiduddin's geographical notices of India,* J.R.A.S. *n.s.,* vol. IX, p. 356. Cfr. also note 281 *suprá.*
289) Same authorities as note 287 all quoting the *Mahá Rájáweng.*
290) Bhiennaká was the 32nd ruler after Abhirâjâ who lived 300 years before Gaudama, let us say about 775 B.C. Now 33 reigns at an average of 15 years each make a total of 495 years, leaving 280 B.C. as a possible date for the recorded expedition from T s e n.
291) T h i n d u ë with the Burmese *th* is nearly *Tzinduë* which we have quoted in the text in order to avoid any misconception, cfr. Ney Elias, *o.c.* p. 11.
292) Cfr. below, end of section IV.
293) T. W. Rhys Davids, *Buddhism,* p. 227.
294) Em. Forchhammer, Notes I: *The first Buddhist Mission to Suvannabhumi,* pp. 1-6, and 10.

e) IV.

At the fall of the T h a n =(Ts'in) dynasty, 209 B.C. and the disorders which ensued, the allegiance to the Chinese government ceased to be recognised in the W. and S. W. of modern China proper ; these countries were released and the ancient roads through S h u h were reopened," and "by this traffic the communities became wealthy and prosperous.[295] ...The four regions of P a and S h u h had free communication with the Barbarians on the south and west, and by the interchange of commodities, were able mutually to supply their respective wants."[296]

The H a n dynasty which had succeeded that of Than=Ts'in was too much engaged in repelling the attacks of the Hiung-nus in the North to take any interest in the S.W., and they had left everything there go adrift. It was only after 130 B.C., under the powerful rule of Wu-ti, that some efforts were made in that direction ; the *Kiun* of *Kien-wei* was established or supposed to be so on the country connecting modern Hunan, Szetchuen and Kweitchou with its centre near the modern Kia-ting fu, and the regions of K i u n g and T s o h W. of Szetchuen[297] recognized the Chinese supremacy, the meagre resources of the Empire not permitting to do anything further.[298] At that time it was learned by the Chinese that a country named S h i n-t u h was situated about 2000 *li* to the West of K i u n g.[299] When Tchang Kien returned in 123 B.C. from his mission to the Yueh-ti, he urged his government to establish communications with Bactria through India. The North route was stopped by the Hiung-nus, and it was not possible to pass through the Kiang[300] i.e. the Tibetan tribes, who were inimical : so that he recommended to go straight through from Shuh.[301] Delighted with this suggestion, the Emperor Wu-ti gave orders that exploring parties should be sent out from Shuh and Kien-wei, by the four roads starting from there, with instructions to find their way through the S.W. barbarians, and endeavour to discover India.[302] These roads passed through the territories of M a n g.[303] J e n, S é and P'o of K i u n g, and each advanced one or two thousand *li*: [304]which is certainly a gross exaggeration of the Chinese record. At that time the M a n g and J e n,[305] both unsettled tribes, were located near the N.W. borders of Szetchuen, in what is now Mntchou.[306] The Chinese envoys who went North of these routes were stopped by the T i tribes in modern prefecture of Lung-ngan in N.N.W. Szetchuen, and by the T s o h tribes, S.W. of Ya-tchou in the N.W. of the same modern province. The southern routes passed through the Se, within the modern prefecture of Sutchou in C. Szetchuen,[307] and though the P'o of K i u n g, corresponding to the territory of Yueh-hi or Yueh-sui, W. of the same prefecture. The exploring parties through the latter routes were stopped on the W. of the state of T s e n by the K u e n-m i n g and S u i tribes, in the modern prefectures of Tali and Likiang of W. and N. W. Yunnan. The K u e n m i n g s were savages and they murdered the envoys. So that all the attempts had failed.[309]

Some knowledge however had been gained. Several of the envoys had heard of a country about 1000 *li* to the West, named *Tsen yueh*, litt. B e y o n d T s e n,[310] where the inhabitants rode on elephants, and where the Shuh traders who carried a clandestine commerce with them, occasionally went.[311]

These statements which we take from the *She Ki* of Szema Tsien, 163-85 B.C., like all that we have reported on the subject, is interesting and important. We must understand that the travelling merchants of S h u h had remained apart and refused to reveal the secret of their route S.W. towards India, which they could not reach however without some private arrangement with the tribes who had stopped the Chinese envoys; and this explains how it happened that the exploring parties sent by the Chinese Emperor did not, in their expeditions, hear anything about the country of S h i n-t u h which they had vaguely heard of before, as lying about 2000 *li* W. of the Kiung territory. The latter rumor which had come to the Chinese previously to their attempts referred to the trade route of Shuh to Patna through the S.E. corner of Tibet. The region Beyond-Tsen of which they heard in their southern exploration, was northern Burma, as I have shown elsewhere,[312] and specially the region of old Pagan named also Tzindnë,[313] but they did mistake it for India, because of the common habit of elephant driving which had been heard of by Tchang-Kien in Bactria as a peculiarity of India. Therefore they endeavoured to pass through the state of Tsen, central Yunnan, which as we have seen, had been conquered and established by a general from Tsu two centuries previously.[314]

On reaching the Kingdom of Tsen after having for four years vainly attempted to pass through the territory of the Kuen-mings who had closed the highways, the Chinese envoys were received by the King Tang Kiang who detained them on the ground that they were searching out the roads, and prevented them to pass. "Is the Han a greater Kingdom than ours ?" said he haughtily to the astonished Chinaman. Other envoys sent with the same purpose to the ruler of Ye-lang, a country extending along the South of Kien-wei had a similar reception. No passage was possible; and to use the words of the Chinese annalist: "each of these princes considering himself sovereign in his own domain, was unconscious of the magnitude of the Han empire.[315] Nothing therefore could be done for the time being.

About twelve years afterwards, the HAN Emperor, relieved of some of his harassments in the North, was enabled to act more vigorously in the South West and the South.

In 111 B.C. he put an end to the state of Nan-yueh which established in 200 by Tch'ao T'o, a refractory general of the Ts'in dynasty had extended along the South from Fuhkien to Tungking, and he occupied a part of it, i.e. Kuangtung and the eastward, which were divided for administrative purposes into nine regions.[316] Then the various populations of whom we have quoted the names, and some others, all in the West and South-west, were admitted as vassals and Chinese officers were appointed as official overseers among them.[317] The territories received special names in the Imperial dominion, and in the absence of Chinese residents among them, special officers were appointed, with residences generally on the borders to superintend their intercourse with the Empire. The treatment of the rulers of Ye-lang and of Tsen was, however, different. The former received the Chinese investiture of ruler in his own Kingdom without much resistance; but the latter objected more strongly, and he yielded only when he saw himself at the eve of being attacked. In 109 B.C. he received the royal seal from the Han Emperor, and in the words of the Chinese annalist,[318] "his people was still entrusted to his rule."

By these arrangements which with a few alterations and interruptions lasted until the third century, access and egress were secured in that direction for foreign trade with the Middle Kingdom. But the state of Tsen (now read Tien), then feudal, preserved by its geographical position its command over the trade routes towards the South, while the S.W. route to India through the S.E. corner of Tibet was also available to its people.[319]

The Tsen Kingdom for all that, deserves some attention. Its influence is still visible in the name of China itself which is derived from it, and thus far has won an everlasting fame. *T'sen* was the indigenous name of the region around the lakes of Yunnan fu and Tch'eng Kiang, of the town between them, and of the principal lake itself,[320] and its meaning in the native languages was simply the* waters, as the said lakes are the largest expanses of water in the country.[321] For the Han dynasty this feudal state was included into the great circumscription called Y h-tchou *Kiun* whose administrative centre was at the ancient capital city of Shuh, the modern Tch'eng-tu. Its king was under the immediate protectorate of the Han officer residing in the latter city. The Tsen Kingdom extended East and West of the lake region, but not at first as far in the West as the lake of Tali which was in the hands of the Kuen-mings, but in 109 B.C. this region itself was added to the domain of the king of Tsen in compensation of some territory on the east which was withdrawn from his authority. In the South its frontiers are not known, and we are not in position to state how far they advanced in the direction of the modern Shan states. The tradition quoted *suprà* from the *Mahâ Râjaweng* of Burma refers most probably to an expedition made by the King of Tsen against Old Pagan on the Irrawaddy.[322] And we may recognize perhaps a survival of the same name in that of the Shan state Tsen pho as called by the Laocians, not very far distant from the present Chinese frontier in a N.E. direction from Mandalay.[323] Referring to the Kingdom of Tsen in Yunnan, it was widely known under its name by its relations with foreign trade, and it was so for over five centuries. Established in 330 B.C., it lasted through some changes of fortune, in a state of submission to the Han dynasties or rebellion against them, until 224 A.D. Tchuko-liang, a general of the Minor Han dynasty[324].

conquered the country and put an end to the old state of things, in redistributing the land to several native chiefs under the suzerainty of the Chinese.[325] The T s e n country could be reached[326] by the trade—

a : from India; though the old route up the Brahmaputra to Sudiya, Rœma crossing the Lu-tze and Lan-tsan Kiangs,[327] and thence descending the Kin-Sha-Kiang ;

b ; from Burma and the coast : by the Salwen river and perhaps the Kiu-lung unto Tchieng-hung=Tcheli, and hence westward through Sze-mao (S. Yunnan).

c ; from Tungking; by Kattigara, the *Portus Sinarum* of Ptolemy,[328] and as a fact the nearest to and the real port of the T s e n country modern Kesho or Hanoi,[329] upwards the Red River unto Man hao, and hence straight north by land.

Let us remark that the foregoing sketch, simple as it is, gives us the solution of a long vexed question, that of the origin of the name of China which has been a puzzle for the inhabitants of the Middle kingdom as well as for many European investigators. All sorts of speculations have been made on the subject,[330] but it has been ascertained finally in recent years[331] that the first knowledge and the spread of the name *China*, did begin only in the first century of our era[332] through the southern sea trade, and not through the North and South at the same time. The arrogant and not unimportant state, then named T s e n had long been in existence at the time, and for centuries occupied a commanding position over the trade routes to the Middle Kingdom from Indo-China S.W. and S.E. Its name was spread far and wide under several cognate forms *Thin*, *Sin*, &c., and preserved for ever its predominance in the mouths of foreigners[333] as an appellative for the greatest empire of the East.[334]

The general survey we have just achieved in the present section of the historic evidence concerning the trade routes as means of communication from, through and beyond Szetchuen in antiquity, to the West, South West and South may be briefly resumed. We have thus been able to find indications of the six following routes :

1) From Szetchuen, to the Jade country in the Khotan region, from 1500 B.C. or earlier down to the ninth or eighth century B.C.

2) From Szetchuen to Patna in India, after that time and with intermissions.

3) Through Szetchuen from Shensi to Pegu, temporary, end of third century B.C.

4) Through Yunnan, from Szetchuen to India, third century B.C. and afterwards.
5) Through Yunnan, from Szetchuen to Burma, third century B.C. and afterwards.
6) Through Yunnan, from Szetchuen to Tongking, second century B.C. and afterwards.

The words however are bigger than the things and no illusion must be entertained with reference to these routes. None can be understood as having ever been regularly followed by caravanes going to and fro, and therefore as the means of steady interchange and intercourse between their extremes and along their courses. A thorough passage from one and to the other of any of these routes cannot have taken place except in isolate cases unknown to history in the ancient times. Trade was done in a second or third hand fashion, the goods passing from one to another, and being either blackmailed or increased in price along the way. In these conditions which are vouchsafed by the personal interests of the intermediaries, and the general laws of offer and demand in trade, it was only in the long run that something from one end of the route could be heard of at the other end, mangled and altered through the successive interpreters. The strictness of these observations applies of course more forcibly to the older than to the later times.

Let us now enumerate which items of western civilization did reach, and those which may have reached the Middle Kingdom through these secondary and imperfect channels. Material objects and goods may travel by them, but notions and ideas could not do so without the greatest difficulty; and besides the supply depended upon the state of knowledge in the countries which were reached by these routes.

NOTES 295) Szema Tsien, *She Ki*, Bk. 116, fol. 2 v.; Wylie's translation p. 5.—Cfr. also on this traffic, the Bk. 129 on trade in the *She Ki*, fol. 7.
296) *She Ki*, Bk. 116, fol. 3v, ibid ; Wylie, p. 7. The traders of Shuh were carrying their commerce also with the east ; for instance in 135 B.C. it was ascertained that they used to trade with the south east by the Si-kiang or Canton River, the *Tsangko* of the time. Cfr. ibid. fol. 3, and Wylie p. 5.
297) The name has been met with reference to the bamboo staves carried from there to India by the S.W., as learned by Tchang K.ien in Bactria Cfr. *suprā*.
298) *She Ki*, Bk. 116, fol. 3; *Li tai Ti Wang nien pias*, Tsien Han, fol. 6 v.—These arrangements lasted only a short time, as a few years afterwards, the *Tsoh* stopped the Chinese envoys.
299) *She Ki*, Bk. 116, fol. 4 v.

300) This must refer to a road through the Tsih shih (cfr. note 276) and the South of the Kokonor.
301) Tchang Kien's biography, in Pan Ku's *Tsien Han Shu*, Bk. 61. transl. A. Wylie, p. 48, *J.A.I.* August, 1880.
302) *She Ki*, Bk. 116. fol. 4 v.: Bk. 123, fol. 6 v.
303) It is the country misread *Long* in Matouanlin's *Ethnographie* II. p. 166.
304) *She Ki*, *T"a wan lieh tchuen*, 123, fol. 6 v.
305) In 111 b.c., until 67 b.c. the Han organised these two named tribes into a *Kiun* which received the name of *Wen shan*. The Jen moved eastwards later on, and in the sixth century they used to intercept the passages of the *San Hia* i.e. the three Yang-tze-Kiang gorges. Their descendants the Jen Kia Man are now at Shihtien and Yien-ho in the prefecture of Se-nan, in N.E. Kueitchou.
306) *She Ki*, *Si Nan y tchuen*, 116, fol. 1 v.
307) Cfr. G. Playfair, *The cities and towns of China*, N. 7635, and the other names *sub. roc*.
308) These savage tribes were probably kindreds of the K u m o n g s Mishmi tribes of the present day, who are still preventing free communications between Assam and China. The Kuen-ming seem to have been tribes of the same stock as the Hiung-nu, who had moved from N.E. Tibet southwards about the third century b.c., along the great exit of northern tribes to the South, which has been frequented in the same way from olden times to the present day.
309) *She Ki*, *Ta-wan lieh tchuen*, 123, fol. 7.
310) Or still more literally "the Beyond of Tsen."
311) *She Ki*, ibid. fol. 7.
312) In two articles of *The Academy*, May 2, and Sept. 5. 1885: *Thu-yât not India*, and *India from China*, which I confirm here. After the publication of my first article I saw that Baron von Richtofen, *China*, I, 427, had come to the same conclusion as myself. Prof. S. Beal, *Some remarks on the narrative of Fâ-hien*, J.R.A.S. XIX, 1887, p. 192 has suggested that this name might be Champa, but this is impossible because the Champa began only after 806 A.D.
313) Cfr. sect. *e*) III of the present chapter, and note 291 *suprà*.
314) Cfr. sect. *e*) ** and note 274 of the present chapter.
315) Szema Tsien, *She Ki* Bk. 116, f. 4 v.
316) *She Ki*, *Nan yueh tchuen*, Bk. 113, ff. 1-9.
317) *She Ki*, *Si nan y tchuen*, Bk. 116, f. 4.
318) *She Ki*, ibid. fol. 5 v.
319) For instance in the *Periplus*, 63 and 65, transl. McCrindle, p. 146-148, we see that the T h i n æ obtained from the Sesatai, *malabathrum* which was exported to India; conveyed down the Ganges to Gangê near its mouth; and also conveyed from the interior of India to Mouziris and Nelkunda, on the W. coast, for export.
320) It was transcribed by the Chinese with the symbol of their writing which is still used for the literary name of the Yunnan province, and in that acceptation is now read *Tien*. But the symbol with the reading *T"ien* has the meaning f u l l, a b u n d a n t and it is very probable that the significant sound has attracted the meaningless name in the subsequent corruption of the language. The *k"ang hi tze tien*

sub. voc., 85+11 gives some ancient authorities to show that the symbol was also read t c h e n, in the name of a district T c h e n-y a n g. On the other hand the Chinese dialect which has preserved the most archaic phonesis, with exceptions, the Sino-Annamite, corresponding generally to 200 B.C., as shown in my historical scheme of the Chinese family of languages *(The lang. of Chin.*, sec. 205) has still the reading *t c h a n* for this symbol. It is composed of the determinative 85 water and the phonetic, 674 of Callery's *Systema phoneticum* which has kept the reading *tchen* The same phonetic as shown by a rapid examination in Dr. Chalmer's *Concise Kang-hi's dictionary*, enters into the composition of 54 derivates as follow : 15 *tchen*, 17 *tchen* and *tien*, and 22 *tien*. Such are the reasons which show that the Chinese symbol now read *Tien* for Yunnan, must have been used at first for the same purpose with the reading *t c h e n* or *t s e n*. The latter was probably the original sound which has diverged into *tien* and *tchen*. Cfr. following note 321—M. G. Devoria, *La Frontière Sino-Annamite*, 1886, p. 119, gives *X an=S h a n* as the Annamite name of *T i e n*.
321) This native word for water was connected with the following which have the same meaning: Tchung Miao *d j e n*, Singpho n c t s i n, Kakhyen i n t z i n, Munnipuri *i s h i n g*, &c., cfr. *Beginnings of writing around Tibet*, sec. 80.—The name T c h e n has survived largely in the geographical onomasticon of the province of Yunnan and its central part, and is variously transcribed in "Chinese ; such as Tchen-tiung, Tchen-K'ang, Tchen-nan, Tchen-yuen, Tch'eng-Kiang, Tch'eng-Kung &c.
322) Cfr. end of last section *e*. III and notes 287-291.
323) The *Mung Siuen-wi*, i.e. the state of S i u e n-wi, the T h e i n-n i of the Burmese and the M u p a n g of the Chinese. M. Ney Elias has given a brief sketch of the history of that state from the *Zabu-Oke-Saung*, a Burmese work. Cfr. his *Introductory sketch of the history of the Shans*, 1876, pp. 47-51.—And perhaps also the name of K i a n g T s e n. Cfr. Holt S. Hallett, *Report on the Railway Connexion of Burmah and China*, p. 117.
324) Also called *Shuh Han* dynasty (221-263 A.D.) as called from its capital at Tcheng-tu in Szetchuen. Its dominion was one of the three kingdoms into which the Empire of the Eastern Han dynasty was divided after its fall.
325) *Shuh tchi* ; *Tai ping yü lan*, 791, I. 5 ; cfr. also *Ethnographie de Matouanlin*, transl. D'Hervey de St. Denys, vol. II, pp. 153, 186.
326) All the modern researches as to the possibility of trade routes to China, from India and Indo-China have been carefully studied by M. M. Archibald R. Colquhoun and Holt S. Hallett, cfr. A.R.C., *Across Chrysé*, vol. II, pp. 219-240 ; H.S.H. and A.R.C., *Report on the Railway connexion of Burmah and China*, 1887.
327) Kiu-lung is the name in the Shan states of the river which is called L a n-t s a n K i a n g in the North, and M e k o n g in the South.
328) *Ptolem*, Lib. I, cap. 11, § 1 ; Lib. VII, cap. 3, § 3 ; J. W. Mc Crindle, *Ancient India as described by Ptolemy*, Bombay, 1875, pp. 9 and 245.
329) The modern name *Kesho* is most likely a corruption of the ancient appellative of the country which the Chinese transcribed K a o-t i cor-

rupted into Kiao-tchi, with two symbols which are still read in Sino-Annamite K a o-t j c. The use of the sign *Kiao* has led to fabulous accounts as to a supposed antiquity of the people, 2000 B.C., which antiquity is not true. Cfr. my remarks *The languages of China before the Chinese*, sect. 89 and 90, and the addition p. 152 in the french edition.—Dr. F. Hirth, in his paper *Zur Geschichte des Antiken Orient handels*, G. f. E. z. B., Berlin, 1889, which refers chiefly to the trade after the Christian era, has pointed out in the *Tai-ping-hunn-yü-tch'*, K. 171, f. 6, a Chinese transcription *Kao-teh* which makes K a o-d n k in the archaic sounds of the Sino-Annamite dialect, and therefore would be a nearer approach to the *Kattigara* of the ancients.

330) The most plausible suggestion was that which derived the name of China from that of a great state of N.W. China which from small beginnings about 909 B.C., reached the supreme power and having absorbed all the other states of the Chinese agglomeration, became the Chinese Empire in 221 B.C. The name was represented by a symbol which is read T s i n since the fourth century of our era in the N.W. As the same name was read *T' a n* previously to that late time, there is an end, on purely philological grounds, to the suggestion, as I have shown in *The Sinim of Isaiah, not the Chinese*, III, in *B. O. R.* I, pp. 46 - 47. The ground being untenable for historical reasons as well (cfr. following note), another suggestion was made that the name may have originated with the frequent use of *jen* for m a n in Chinese ; but this is another philological impossibility as the word is a recent corruption of an ancient *r a n* or *l a n* (*The land of Sinim not China*, III, uncorrected, *ibid.* pp. 186-188), and is opened to the same geographical objections as the previous one. The latest suggestion was made by Baron von Richtofen: it is only objectionable on philological ground, but the objection is altogether fatal to the proposal. The learned geographer thought, that the commercial relations with the Middle Kingdom having taken place through Tung-King, the prototype of the name of China which was revealed by this commerce in the first century of our era ought to be found there, and he suggested the name of Jih-nan as the antecedent wanted. The name indicated by this modern Chinese reading was really that of the southern most province of Annam as divided after the Chinese conquest in 111 B.C., and corresponds roughly to the modern province of Nghê-An. But at that time it was read N i t n a m, and it is still read *Nhatnam* in Sino-Annamite. This simple fact puts an end for ever to the suggestion.

331 The identification of K e s h o-H a n o i with the old Kattigara has been established in a masterly way by Baron v. Richtofen and Col. H. Yule. cfr. B. v. R.'s papers in the Trans. of the Berlin. Geogr. Soc. for 1876, and *China*, vol. I, 1877, pp. 504–510; Col. H. Y., *Notes on the oldest Records of the Sea-route to China from Western Asia* 1882, pp. 9–11 (Extr. Pr. R.G.S.), and *A Glossary of Anglo-Indian colloquial words and phrases*, sub. voc.

332) The name of *Thin i* appears for the first time in the *Periplus Maris Erythræi*, 65, 66, dating about 80–9 of our era. Cfr. J. W. McCrindle, *The Commerce and Navigation of the Erythræan Sea*, Bombay 1879, pp. 147-149.

f) *A Résumé of the Chapter.*
§ 1.

The present section, as a conclusion to our long survey of the unsatisfactory, though various and successive, routes which permitted the introduction of western notions of civilisation in ancient China, subsequent to the great importations by the BAKs in their migration to the East, and have proved to be altogether ill-fitted if not impossible for anything strictly Assyro-Babylonian, must necessarily be little else than a rapid sketch and a short résumé.

The history of China in ancient times may be divided into six periods which we shall refer to for the convenience and clearness of our researches as follows:

1st period. From the settlement of the civilised Bak tribes arrived from the N. W. *circà* 2250 B.C. to the Hia dynasty *circà* 2000 B.C. Though interspersed with native populations, the Chinese do not extend beyond the basin of the Yellow River, nor do they reach the sea.

2nd period. From *circa* 2000 B.C. During the Hia and Shang-Yn dynasties to *circa* 1100 B.C.! Friendship with the native populations, and in some moments united strength, secure to the Chinese the predominance they are entitled to by their superior civilisation. A slight knowledge is gained of the whole country as far South as the Yangtze Kiang. The settlements are strengthened, some advance is made eastwards and the sea is reached about 1777 B.C. But there is no great extension of power through intercinal difficulties, and the seat of the central government is shifted from place to place eleven times during the Hia and eight times during the Shang-yn dynasties. During the latter dynasty, the various principalities of the dominion, withdrew no less than six times from their allegiance to the Royal authority.[335]

3rd period. From *circà* 1100 B.C. to 770 B.C.; the W. Tchou dynasty. An energetic and powerful race from the N.W. conquers the country and ensures respect everywhere. Its dominion is firmly established West and East from Sheni to Tchihli and W. Shantung, and southwards at mid-way between the Hwang-ho and the Yang-tze Kiang.

4th period. From 770 to 481 B.C.; the E. Tchou dynasty so called because in 770 they were compelled by native tribes to remove their capital westwards. The various states forming the Chinese dominion are growing gradually independent and the central power is declining. The border states grow in importance.

5th period. From 481 to 221 B.C. The contending states. The declining authority of the E. Tchou is a mere shadow, and is put to an end by the W. state of *Than*—Ts'in. The period is one of struggle for the supremacy between the various states; they are successively conquered by the state of Than which succeeds in 223 B.C. to overthrow its last and most powerful competitor, the half-Sinised and southern state of Ts'u.

6th period. From 221 B.C. to 25 A.D. Establishment of the Chinese Empire by Ts'in She Hwang-ti over two-thirds of the modern China proper. This short lived dynasty disappears in 209 B.C. and the Former Han dynasty begins in 206 B.C. The Han succeed after a century of struggle to uphold the integrity of the Empire and rule gloriously; they are followed in 25 A.D. by the After Han dynasty which ruled until 220 A.D.

Let us resume our enquiry in the progress of the ancient Chinese and their outside relations, with reference to these six periods.

NOTE 335) Under Yung-ki, 1649 or 1487 B.C.; Ho-tan-kia, 1534 or 1381; Yang-kia, 1408-1319; Siao-sin, 1373 or 1287; Tan-kia, 1258 or 1204; Ti yh. 1191 or 1111 B.C. The two dates are those of the chronology now usual in China, and of the Annals of the Bamboo Books. Under Yang-kia, the princes had not come to court for nine generations. Cfr. Szema Tsien, *Shĕ Ki*, K. III, ff. 6, 7, 7 *r*, 8*r* and 9.

§ 2.

The object of chapters III, IV and V of the present summary has been to resume the various items of civilisation during the first period in sciences, arts, writing, literature, institutions, religion, historical legends and traditions, forming with a few exceptions, the important culture of Babylonian and Elamite Origin, and which they had acquired in S.W. Asia, through their relations with the country of Elam. This civilisation, nearly complete as it was, could not have reached China otherwise than it did, i.e. through the immigration of civilised tribes and in a wholesale manner, as no successive imports, like those which took place afterwards, of shreds of western knowledge, could have produced such an homogeneous ensemble of obvious borrowings[336] from the most important civilisation of S.W. Asia. The demonstration, which is conclusive, refers chiefly to the first of the six periods we have just enumerated.

The first part of the present chapter in its five divisions and seven subdivisions (VI, a, b, c, d, i, ii, iii, e, i, ii, iii, iv), has been occupied with a survey of the various channels through which notions of civilisation from foreign countries may have reached the Middle Kingdom in times subsequent to the establishment of the civilised *Bak* tribes in the Flowery Land. We have been compelled by the difficulties of the case to go more deeply into historical details than in the former parts, because we had no longer any special papers previously published to refer to on the subject. Though eliciting not a few historical facts little known and of interest, and having to call attention to circumstances hitherto neglected or not yet extracted from their Chinese limbos, we have not been able to discover any regular channel or constant intercourse for the ingress of western knowledge in the principal state of the Far-East. The results of our enquiry so far have been most important for the purpose we are pursuing, since none of the various channels we have studied have proved to have permitted the introduction of anything better than mangled bits and bungled notions of civilisations from Central Asia (Khorasmia), India, Egypt, Oman, &c. Without entering fully into the details of acquisitions and progresses made by the civilisation of the Middle Kingdom during its third and successive periods, and therefore without benefiting of all that they will teach us, we have found historical evidences of six occasional and unsatisfactory inlets for foreign knowledge to have been brought in.

NOTE 336) In my fourfold list of these, I have omitted references to the artistic influence of Babylon and Elam on the early Chinese art. A few words only can be said here on the subject. On the most ancient bronze sacrificial vases still preserved, this influence is clear. The chief figure is the head of a horned monster, made as repulsive as possible and subsequently distorted in an ornamental manner so as to be past recognition. It was called *t'ao-t'iet*, or the "glutton," and it is now explained as intended to be admonitory against inordinate feasting at the annual sacrifices. Cfr. P. P. Thoms. *Ancient vases of the Shang dynasty*, London, 1851, p. 7. The *t'ao-t'iet* occurs on 23 out of the 42 vases reproduced in this work from the *Poh-ku-tu*, and on 9 out of the 20 vases reproduced in Pauthier's *China*, pl. 38-43 from the *Si-tsing-ku-kien*. As a fact the original object of the hideous figure was to frighten away a devouring demon. In the *T'chun-tstu* of Lu shi (250 B.C.) it is said that on the ancient vases the *t'ao-t'iet* had a head and no body, to intimate that in devouring persons, before even they can be swallowed, destruction comes upon it. Cfr. *K'ang-hi tze tien*, 184—9, f. 85. The design of the monster was traditionally preserved from that frequently represented in Chaldæa to scare away the demon of the south-west wind which was greatly apprehended there, because, coming from the deserts of Arabia, its burning breath dried up and devoured everything; the head was that of a skeleton but half decayed, and adorned with horns, *and the eyes still remaining*. The general idea was "to represent the demons under such hideous forms that it was sufficient for them to be shown their own image, to cause them to flee away alarmed." Cfr. François Lenormant, *Chaldæan Magic*, pp. 50, 52. The Chaldæan name of this demon is unknown as yet, so we cannot carry the comparison further than the resemblance of design and object. Cfr. for the figure: Lenormant, *Hist. Anc. de l' Orient*, t. v, p. 213; Perrot-Chipiez, *Histoire de l'Art*, t. II, p. 496. Other creatures on a very small scale are also represented on ancient Chinese vases, somewhat like fancy birds which become gradually entirely distorted. Their peculiarity is that they go generally by pairs fronting one another, a feature originally peculiar to the Assyro-Babylonian art, according to Von Sybel and to Perrot-Chipiez, *O.C.* II, pp. 747-748. Another of the chief ornaments on the Chinese vases is that of buds, leaf-shaped, in rows, which appear on Chaldæan ornaments (cfr. Layard, *Monuments* I, pl. 6, 9, Perrot-chipiez, *O. C.* II, pp. 702, 771-2) of bronze dishes and embroideries. It is a conventional design of the cone-fruit which is represented on the monuments in the hands of genii and others, and which has certainly a symbolical meaning. F. Lenormant, *Origines de l'histoire*, 1, 84, has pointed out a prescription of Ea to Marduk (*Cun. Inscr. W. A.* IV. 16, 2 and 29, 1) where the cedar-fruit is specially mentioned. cfr. T. de L , *The Tree of life and the Calendar plant of Babylonia and China*, n. 5, and *B. & O. R.* 11, 156. On the other hand Dr. E, Bonavia, *The cone-fruit of the Assyrian monuments*, *B.* & O. R. II, 138, 170, and 173, has shown reason to believe that in some cases at least, the represented cone-fruit was a citron. And quite recently, Dr. E. B. Tylor, *The fertilisation of the date-palm in ancient Assyria*, Academy 8 June 89, p. 396 has suggested the cone-fruit to have been the inflorescence of the male date-palm, a suggestion which seems to me to be confirmed in some other cases, such as on the alabaster bas-relief of the Louvre, figured in Perrot-Chipiez, *O. C.*, II, p. 64. A classification must consequently be made of the monuments. Returning to the early Cainese art, the chief ornament is a sort of scroll, *grecque* or *méandre*, which is employed everywhere in all sorts of varieties, and seems congenial to the taste of the Chinese. They call it *yun-lei-wen*, i e., cloud-thunder ornament, and explain it as derived from an ancient form of the symbol for cloud, as it appears duplicated in the composition of some ancient forms of the character for 'thunder.' Cfr. Min-Tsi-kih, *Lu shu t'ung*, II. 9, and Tung-Wei-fu, *T'chuen-tze-wei*, s. v. Though we may refuse to accept this explanation, there is no reason to discountenance the originality of this scroll in China, inasmuch as it is so very simple a pattern that it has occurred in several instances independently elsewhere. Curiously enough, it is almost unknown in Assyro-Babylonian Art, but it occurred frequently in ancient Egypt, Judea, Hissarlik, Greece, and in a curved form on the early bronzes of Denmark.—A peculiar form of hair-dress, represented by a small black stone object in the British Museum, *Nimroud*

Gallery, H, which has attracted the attention of Perrot, *O. C.*, II, 595n, which is exactly similar to that of important men in ancient China. Cf. with Pauthier's *Chine*, pl. 22, 36 and 51.

§ 3.

During the Second period there was no other channel than that of the eastern traffic of nephrite-jade originally from the Khotan region, this region which was to be Aryanised[3][7] from Khorasmia and Bactria through the passes of the Badakshan country,[338] about the end of that period, was yet uncivilised and could not be a source of knowledge to borrow from ; moreover, its nephrite jade did not apparently reach the Middle kingdom otherwise than after passing through several hands. And should the trade of that precious gem have been carried without intermediary, the information and notions available to be carried to the East were only those of Irano-Indian source, as the Indo-Aryans were then in occupation of the lands on the West side of the Badakshan passes and the Tsung-ling range. The Assyro-Babylonians had not reached them, and the influence of their civilisation on the latter has been nil or nearly so; even in India in later historical times, Babylonian influence has been at a minimum ; an interesting peculiarity which however is easily explained by the geographical conditions of the respective countries.[339] Any Assyro-Babylonian notion, to make its way eastward, had to pass through the Irano-Indians' mouths and minds, who were too highly spirited a race to have acted the part of middlemen and faithful transmitters of foreign ideas without stamping them anew.

The foreign relations of the Middle Kingdom, unimportant politically as the latter was at that time, were limited to native and border barbarian tribes,[340] with only two apparent exceptions, during the reign of Tai Mou of the Shang dynasty about B.C. 1466, and under the reign of Wu-ting, about B.C. 1269. In the tenth year of his reign, Tai Mou of Shang is said to have been visited by envoys of distant states, seventy-six in number according to one authority, and only sixteen according to another. No information whatever has been handed down, by tradition or documents concerning these foreign comers. They may have been trading parties magnified as is usually the case, into ambassadors from some remote countries or simply representatives of foreign tribes beyond the pale of Chinese influence. The same remarks apply to the six foreign envoys who came to the court of Wu-ting. Now one must not forget that the Chinese dominion, then within narrow limits, was surrounded on all sides by a great many communities of indigenous and independent tribes ; in the N.W. on the borders of Tibet, the Kiang tribes, some of whom submitted afterwards, numbered more than 120 ; and within modern China proper, the number of non-Chinese tribes was over 400. On the other hand the records of the Hia and Shang dynasties are often ', and not much more than mere lists of rulers and inter-reigns; they were preserved indifferently in the states of Ki and Sung which had charge of them, and we know from the words of Confucius himself, that in his time they were already in a very dilapidated condition.[341] It is not at all impossible that at the above dates some notions from the West should have reached the Chinese through some trading parties, by the Jade traffic route ; perhaps some calendaric and astronomical knowledge, inasmuch as Wu-hien prime-minister to Tai Mou, the king who received foreign envoys, is reputed to be the author of the first catalogue of stars.[342] This, however, is a mere hypothesis which no side lights support in the present state of our knowledge. No progress of importance, nor any new acquisition of civilisation seems to have been made by the Chinese at that time besides this catalogue, should it be so considered.[343] With the sole inlet we have mentioned, the reverse would be surprising, with reference to knowledge of foreign origin, and as regards the internal progress, the shaky condition of governmental affairs was not favorable to promote any advance. Astronomical studies were pursued, and the ancestral worship was extended to that of departed great men at the expense of the state.[343] The proper names of the living ruler were also tabooed for the time being ;[344] the two latter features, which tradition has preserved in use, are rather suggestive of a lower standard of mind among the rulers at the time of their introduction than was formerly the case.

337) The region of Khotan has been looked upon by several scholars as one of the oldest centres of metallurgic trade, (cfr. D'Eckstein, *De quelques légendes Brahmaniques qui se rapportent au berceau de l'espèce humaine*, in Journ. Asiat., Oct. Dec. 1855.—Fr. Lenormant, *Essai de commentaire des fragments cosmogoniques de Berose*, p. 315 ; *Origines de l'histoire*, vol. II, pp. 151-154). But the evidence collected in support of this view is very slight, and in my opinion cannot bear such a mighty construction. Legends of after time were fostered there because of its geographical position quite central. Abel Remusat has derived his *Histoire de la ville de Khotan tirée des Annales de la Chine*, Paris, 1820, from Chinese sources, and J. Klaproth, has followed a Turkish geographer in his *Histoire de la ville de Khotan*, in Mém. Rel. à l'Asie, vol. II. pp. 281-301 ; and these two works are the sole authorities on the subject referred to by D'Eckstein and Lenormant. The fertile imagination of D'Eckstein has gone too f.r in his inferences from the simple fact that Kuvera, the god of wealth of Brahmanic pantheon, corresponding to the Avestic Khshathra-Vairya (on which cfr. C. de Harlez, *Avesta*, II edit. p. xciii) and also called a Vis Ravana or Vaisrava, moreover Ruler of the North, and described as a magnificent deity residing in the splendid city Alakâ (cfr. Edw. Moor, *The Hindu Pantheon*, N. Ed., Madras, 1864, pp. 180, 183, 192), otherwise

Khotan—Kustana. He was supposed to be a local deity of pre-Aryan origin, and was worshipped by the first king spoken of, in the Legends, whose date, according to Buddhist sources, was 234 years after the Buddha's Nirvana, or about 233 B.C. The same sources either collected from Hiuen Tsang's report or from Tibetan documents, make this king contemporary and victorious of a son of Açoka who had been sent there. (Cfr. *Si-yu-ki*, *Buddhist Records of the Western World*, transl. S. Beal, vol. II, pp. 309 sq.; Woodville Rockhill, *The early history of Li'-yul* (Khoten) in his *Life of the Buddha*, *from Tibetan sources*, pp. 230 sq). It is usual with Buddhist sources to reckon the beginning of anything with or about the time of the Buddha, but in the present occasion as it begins with a failure of a son of Açoka, the information may be trusted to a certain extent, since it does not record a success in the extension of Buddhism. And it is no proof as to the Aryanisation of the country which seems to have taken place about the XIIth century.—Baron F. von Richtofen (*China* 1877, I, p. 48a) previously to our disclosures, has put forth the view that the Khotan region was the original seat of the civilised ancestors of the Chinese, but this temporary hypothesis has fallen short of what we have shown to have been the case. The civilisation which these ancestors were acquainted with was the Babylonian-Elamite which never reached in the time of its greatest extension beyond the Zagros and Paropamisus ranges.

338) The direct route from Tokharestan to the Tarym basin, passing through Badakshan, was an important trade route from early times. Cfr. E. Bretschneider, *Mediæval Researches*, vol II, p. 65.

339) Cfr. *infrà* Ch. VII.

340) Herewith the necessary résumé of these foreign relations. In these seven following statements except when otherwise stated I follow the words and dates of the *Tchuh shu ki nien* (a work of 400 B.C.)—'I) In his 8th year. i.e. 1845 B.C., Tchu the VIth ruler of the Hia dynasty, went on a punitive expedition towards the eastern sea, as far as *San-show* (central Shantung) and caught a fox with nine tails. As an instance of the magnifying and embellishing system of late Chinese compilers, here is the same event as reported in the *T"ung Kien Kang Muh* drawn by the too celebrated Tchu-hi (a.d. 1130-1260), transl. De Mailla, vol. I, p. 152 : " Pendant tout son règne, Ti Chou jonit d'une tranquillité si grande que les peuples voisins se faisaient gloire de se soumettre à ses lois. Les insulaires même de la mer orientale, qui n'avaient pas paru depuis le grand Yu, vinrent lui offrir leurs hommages et se reconnaître dépendants de l' Empire." As many lies as words.—,II). In his 21st year i.e. 1710 B.C., the same ruler conferred Chinese dignities on *the chiefs of* six tribes of Y barbarians) of the East.—(III). Fah the XVIth of Hia, in his 1st year, i.e. 1596) B.C. ; various tribes of the same barbarians came and made their submission.—(IV). Kwei, the XVIIth and last of Hia, 6th year, i.e. 1584 B.C. ; some Jung barbarian *tribes of West China* submit.---(V). T'ang, the first of the Shang dynasty, i.e. 1575 B.C., at his accession is visited by all the feudal princes, *or chiefs of families and native tribes*, to the number of 1800 with eight interpreters. At the beginning of the Tchou dynasty, which was much more powerful, their number was only 800, so that we may premise that the former figure has been magnified with the tenfold inflation so frequently met in Chinese literature, and therefore must be reduced to 180. The *T'ung*

Kien Kang Muh, says : " sa réputation de sagesse s'etendit si loin que les quarante royaumes que l' on connaissait alors avaient pour lui la plus grande vénération."—(VI). In the 19th year of the same king, i.e., 1557 B.C., the Ti-Kiang people (in Kansuh) made their submission. (VII). In the 10th year of Tai Mou, the IXth of Shang, i.e. 1466 B.C., 76 states from distant regions (*Yuen fang*) sent messengers with interpreters to his court, in admiration of his virtue. The statement is no part of the text, and is the object of a gloss. Other sources are at variance with it. The *Kang Kien y tchi luh*, a compilation of A.D. 1711 gives their number as 67 (Medhurst's *Ancient China*, p. 354. The *T'ung Kien Kang Muh* mentions 76 feudal princes of the empire and besides envoys of sixteen foreign countries (De Mailla, I, p. 192).— (VIII). In the 28th year of the same king, (i.e. 1450 B.C.) 'some West-Jung tribes (W. Shensi made their submission, and he sent Wang Mong as his envoy with presents to these hordes. In his 61st year, i.e. 1414 B.C., nine Y i.e. eastern tribes made their submission.— (IX) under Wu-ting, the XXII of SHANG-YN, in his 6th year, envoys from six states, using interpreters came to court; since that time feathers of wild birds were much used on court dresses. The first of these two statements only I find in De Mailla, t. I, p. 221, while the two are made in the *Kang Kien y tchi luh*, l.c. p. 358, and none in the *Tchuh shu ki nien.*---G. Pauthier, *Chine*, pp. 67-8, and M. Paleologue, *Art Chinois*, p. 100, in his trail, have attributed by far too much importance to this fact. Pauthier was led to do so by a misapprehension. The mythological and unhistorical character of the legend reported by Greek writers concerning a conquest of central Asia by Sesostris, had not yet been proved in his time (1839), and the French scholar thought that this arrival of foreigners in China was a result of the supposed Egyptian conquest.

341) *Lun-yu*, II, 23, cfr. below ch. VII, §1.

342) On Wu hien, cfr. *Shu King*, V, xvi, 7 ; *She Ki*, III, f. 6.—And Mayer's *Chinese R.M.*, No. 861.—*T'cheou-li*, R. XXIV, fol. 19 gloss; transl. Biot, vol. II, p. 77.

343) In the *Li Ki*, XX, 9 we hear of Kaosin-Tiknh (who was chief of the Baks before Yao) as able to define all "the zodiacal stars and exhibit their times to the people." The *T'chuh shu Ki nien*, Part I, iii, states that Kao-Yang Tchuen-hinh, predecessor of Ti-kuh. "in his 13th year invented calendaric calculations and delineations of the heavenly bodies.

CHAP. VI. ƒ) *A Résumé.* § 4.

During the third period i.e. the Tchou dynasty (*circà* 1100-770 B.C.), the situation is quite different. An important focus of astronomical and astrological lore had been established by a branch of the Aryan races in Khorasmia about 1304 B.C., and it is only what could be expected to find that the Tchou a people of Kirghize origin[346], who had settled for centuries on the N.W. borders of China, were acquainted with some shreds of knowledge from that source. The success of the Tchou may have been an incitement to the Jade traffic; some more notions from the same quarters, in a more or less dilapidated condition, have reached the Middle Kingdom at a subsequent date, through the route of Khotan then Arya-nised---and the Badakshan passes. For instance, Muh Wang[347] (circ. 1000 B.C.) who made an expedition westwards[348], was presented with nephrite-jade (of Khotan), and asbestos-cloth[349] (of Badakshan); the possibilities of intercourse, however, were partially stopped by the rising in the IXth century, of the then semi-Chinese and uncivilised state of Than,---later Ts'in on the N.W. of China, that same state which we had so often occasion to mention in the preceding sections of the present chapter. The Jade-traffic was carried on nevertheless, with increased difficulties and through Tibet, by the merchants of Shuh or Sze-tchuen, but not for a long time. Their attention was soon attracted towards the south-west by a greater facility in the communications and trade. Although no regular intercourse was established with the South, some parties of traders from Yunnan West and South, enticed no doubt by the reports of intermediary tribes about the power and wealth of the rising dynasty, came to the Chinese court with a monkey of India[350] and probably some goods of the same country, which fact seems to show that intercourse between the Malabar coast and Burmah had already begun. These trading parties were the real openers of the communications which we shall have to mention during the following period.

The sea trade through the Arabian sea and the Bay of Bengal, which later on, was extended to the Chinese seas, and imported a few western notions to the native states of the East in Shantung, through which they passed to the Chinese, seems to have begun about that period.[351] The first enactments concerning currency were issued about 1032 B.C. by a prime minister named T'ai Kung of Ts'i, an eastern barbarian less fettered to tradition than a native Chinaman, while some rules mentioning the ring-weight money were established about 947 B.C. ;[352] it seems difficult not to connect this remarkable progress with the influence of foreign trade which began about this time.

Under the guidance of the founders of the Tchou dynasty, a thorough organisation and systematization took place. Some advance and certain changes were made under the combined influence of newly-imported notions and internal progress, difficult to distinguish as to their respective importance.[353] The use of the sexagenary cycle and that of the Jupiter cycle of twelve, both of ancient date,[354] was improved ; so were those of the clepsydra, the stile of which was divided into 100 *kï* for a day, and of the sun-dial, the gnomon of which was pierced at the top. The latter permitted circà 1100 B.C., some observations to be made at Loh-yang with such accuracy that they have been verified by Laplace and Biot in the present century,[355] and found exact, without any possibility of being the result of any retrospective calculations. The knowledge of the 28 *siu* or stellar mansions and their use for prognostication, was also an acquisition made at the beginning of the period,[356] grafted upon former notions of astronomy ; their close similarity with the 27 or 28 *Nakshatras* of India, and the 28 *manazils* of the Arabs is not genealogical in one direction or the other, but simply one of common descent from an older system,[357] now known to have been systematized in Khorasmia,[358] for astrological purposes, and made to begin with the Pleiades, features which have survived long in China. The beginning of the day was fixed at midnight, while under the Shang dynasty it was at noon, and under the first dynasty at sunrise, as in Chaldæa[359]. The beginning of the year was also altered; the Baks had brought with them the Chaldæan habit of commencing the year at the vernal equinox; under the Shang, the last month, and under the Tchou, the second month of winter were made the first month [360]; but the irregular system of intercalary months seem to have somehow brought them into confusion. In arts they became also acquainted with the process of tempering iron[361].

In religion we see them adding Earth to Heaven in the denomination of the Supreme deity[362], and, among other customs we remark the sacrifice of a dog which is run over by the king in his chariot when he goes out of the kingdom[363]. Both features may be due to the Indo-Aryan influence which had undoubtedly reached the mass of the Tchou people, notwithstanding the alliance and sinicisation of their leaders reported in their legendary history.

We have also to mention the development of the use of proper names a practice due apparently to a similar influence. The notion of the five elements, which appears at the beginning of the dynasty was, however, an old idea which must be traced back to a different source[364].

344) Here are two facts from the *Tchuh chu Ki nien*, in support of my statement concerning the extension of ancestral worship to departed great men: Yuh-ting the Vth of Shang, in his 8th year i. e. B.C. 1521, appointed sacrifices to Pao-hang, temple name of *Y-yn* chief minister to the founder of the dynasty. A notice of this eminent man is given by Mayers, *Chinese R. M.*, No. 233. Later on, Wu-ting, the XXIInd ruler of Shang, in his 12th year, i.e. 1262 B.C. offered a sacrifice of thanksgiving to *Shang-Kiah Wei*, a former minister of Sieh, the Xth king of Shang.—Under the Tchou dynasty the royal temple of ancestors was seven - shrined (*Shu King* IV vi, 10;—*Tchung yung*, sec. 4), and there is no intimation in any writings of high antiquity that the practice was different under the Hia and Shang dynasties. But in the second century, J. C. Wen Yuen-shung put forth the view that under the Shang dynasty, the shrines were only five; cfr. J. Legge, *Chinese Classics*, vol. III, p. 218 notes.

345) The custom of tabooing proper names has arisen among not a few communities in a low stage of mental development from the difficulty for the undeveloped mind to s·parate, the subjective meaning from the objective value of a name, or in other words, the thing from its term. Appearing among the Chinese at that time, we take it as an influence of the pre-Chinese population yet in occupation of the greater part of the country. Its name is *pi-hway*, which in the archaic phonetism of the Sino-Annamite dialect is still pronounced *ti-bt*, and bears a resemblance to *tapi* of Tahiti, a similar custom. Cfr. the notes 2, 3, and 4 § 8 of my paper on *The Djurtchen of Manchuria*, J. R, A. S. 1889, vol. XXI. Prof. R. K. Douglas in his useful Chinese *Manual*, just published, has a specialsection, pp. 372--376 on the tabu-ed characters of the present dynasty of China, and a few others.

346) We must remark about that name which was afterwards explained by mythological legends)Girard de Rialle, *Mémoire sur l'Asie Centrale*

p. 88) that it appears in the history of the Tchou; the grandfather and really historical ancestor of Wu Wang was *ki-lik* (for Ki-rik, Kirk, &c., which cfr. to Kirgh-iz.).

347) We have already mentioned this expedition; above ch. VI, sect. *b.*, and notes 167-171. In the *Kwoh-yu*, Part 1, and in the Annals of the after-Han dynasty, it is reported that Muh Wang made a punitive expedition in the West against the *Junq Tek* barbarians and smashed their five chieftains. He seized four white deers and four white wolves, and afterwards pursued the Teks to the great source or *Tai-yuen*, perhaps in that case the sources of the Huang-ho. Cfr. *Tai ping yü lan*, K. 792, fol. 2 v.—E. Reclus, *Asie Orientale*, p. 146, records that the Mongols sacrifice every year seven white spotless animals at the sources of the Huang-ho.

348) P. Gaubil was of opinion that some new notions of astronomy from the West had reached China at the time of king *Muh*. Cfr. his *Histoire de l' Astronomie Chinese*, p. 381.

349) As recorded by Lieh-tze, 400 b.c. Cfr. *Tai ping yü lan*, K. 820, f. 8, also *suprà* VI, *b* and notes 168-169. On the *asbestos* of Badakshan, cfr. Aboulféda, *Geographie*, p. 474. Badakshan is the mountainous region including the upper part of the valley of the Oxus, on the N. of the Hindu-kush. Cfr. note *suprà*, and the following chapter.

350) Cfr. *suprà*, ch. VI, *d*, I.

351) This sea-trade was carried on from remote times along the shores of the Erythrœan sea, (i.e. Red sea, Arabian sea, and Persian gulf) by the Kushites, a Caucasian race (une race blanche, says G. Maspers, *Histoire ancienne*, ed. IV, p. 105) brown skinned, (*ibid.* p. 196) which in course of time lost of their unity by intermingling with populations negroïd or lower in type were they settled. They have left their name in many places as land marks of their settlements between Ethiopia and Gedrosia, but this name has been subsequently altered by folketymology in the various localities. (Cfr. my paper *The Kushites, who were they?* §6 and for a completion of these land marks, J. S. Stuart Glennie, *The traditions of the Archaïan white races*, §5.) They had reached S. Egypt and repelled the negroes to the South at the time of the VIth dynasty, but their seats were in South Arabia where they had several emporia, which multiplied in course of time were the points of departure and arrival of their trading ships, with Egypt, Babylonia India, &c. On the history of this trade and its extension eastwards, cfr. a special section in ch. VII.

352) Cfr. *suprà*, note 172.

353) Dr. Stern, *Göttinger Gelehrte Anzeigen* 1840, p. 2026, in his criticism of Ideler's had pointed out already eight astronomical analogies in the knowledge possessed in Chaldea and China.

354) The supposition of the Rev. Dr. J. Chalmers that those notions were introduced into India from China, has no basis, since India did possess them only in the Christian era, as we shall have the occasion to see further on.

355) On the sun-dial, gnomon and clepsydra, cfr. a special section in the next chapter.

356) Cfr. G. Schlegel, *Uranographie Chinoise*, p. 391.
357) Long discussions have taken place on the subject, cf. Ed. Biot.: *Journal des savants*, 1837-40 ; *Etudes sur l' astronomie Indienne et chinoise*, 1862, pp. 249-388.—Prof. A. Weber : *Die red'schen Nachrichten von den Naxatra* (Mondstationen), I, II, Berlin, 1860-62.— Prof. W. Whitney : *On the riews of Biot and Weber respecting the relations of the Hindu and Chinese systems of Asterims*, pp. 1-94 of J. Am. Oriental Society, 1866, vol. VIII, and pp. 382-398.
358) Cfr. Albiruni, *Chronology of the ancient nations*, pp. 342 and 227.
359) Already pointed out by Dr. Stern, *l.c.*—It was so in the calendar fixed by Tchwen-hiuh, second successor of Hwang-ti, but we do not know how it was under the last named and former ruler.
360) Under the Ts'in it was the 1st month of winter. For the Chinese changes, cfr. J. Legge, *Chinese classics*, t. II, p. 162, t. III, pp. 41, 154, 215.
361) Under Muh-wang at the time of his expedition beyond the western borders. It was not an Indo-Iranian notion at that time ; cfr. Wilh. Geiger, *La civilisation des Aryas*, p. 635, in *Muséon*, 1884, vol. III, pp. 430-438, 627-652.
362) They said *T'ien T'i*, Heaven and Earth. Cfr. *Shu-king*, V, I, 1, 3. Cfr. the Indo-Aryan *Dyárápritʰivyau*, from *dyu* the sky, and prithivâ the broad earth, when invoked together. And also the hymn to the Earth in the Rig-Veda, I, 22, 15. Cfr. Max Müller, *India, what can it teach us?* p. 158. And also A. Pictet, *Les Aryas primitifs*, t. I, pp. 666-7.
363) *Le Tchéou-li*, XXXVII, 1 ; t. II, pp. 364-5. The sacrifice seems to have originated to propitiate the two monstrous dogs, guardians of the road from which there is no return, a belief, we hear of among the early Indo-Aryans. Cfr. A. Barth, *Religions of India*, pp. 22-3. On a mythological notion of the same kind in Assyro Babylonia, M. W. St. Chad Boscawen kindly communicates to me the following note: " The double headed dog often represented on the boundary stones was the emblem of the god Tutu or Merodach as the god of the morning and evening dawns, "the begetter and restorer of the gods, like the Indian Yama or dog-headed god of death and the dawn."
364) In the counsels of the great Yu forming the third chapter of the *Shu-king*, water, fire, metal, wood, earth and grain or the six stores, are specially enumerated together, §§. 7, 8, as requiring regulations for the welfare of government and people. In the *Ts'o tchuen*, Wen Kung, year VII, 10, where the statement is quoted, they are also called the six *fu* or stores (of nature). It has been stated by the Rev. Dr. J. Chalmers that this six fold list must have come from the Avesta (*Origin of the Chinese*, p. 26) where according to his statement, the six *Amesha Çpentas* rule over a somewhat similar arrangement. And pursuing his remarks the same writer, dropping one of the six, finds a closer agreement with the five elements of the Chinese. These hasty comparisons and derivations cannot, however, stand criticism, notwithstanding the Rev. Dr. J. Edkins, *The fire elements in Persia*, in China Review, 1888, vol. XVII, pp. 49 sq., who has upheld the same views, and some more such as an identification of the six Amesha Çpentas with the six *tsung* of Shun whom we have found

simply, as proved by their names to have been a survival of the six great gods of Susiana. The two writers of China, above quoted, falling into the fault usual to Chinese authors, have neglected the strict conditions of accuracy and chronology required in historical research. Now the notion of the five elements, *Wu heng* as usually translated from the Chinese by Europeans, is mentioned in the *Shu king*, III, ii, 3 under the reign of K'i the successor and a son of the great Yu. Later on at the accession of the T c h o u dynasty, Wu Wang the first ruler was presented by Ki-tze, a follower of the former dynasty, with the *Hung fan* or great Plan, a combination of numerical categories in which were embodied the doctrine of the times of the great Yu. (*Shu-king*, V. iv). The five *heng* enumerated therein are the following : w a t e r, fi r e, w o o d, m e t a l, and e a r t h. Therefore the theory of the six *fu* and of the five *heng* is reputed, apparently with some reason, to be as old as 2000 B.C, in China, a date much earlier than anything Avestic and Persian and which would reversedly suggest a derivation from China to Persia, should any close identity exist ; such, however, is not the case. Herodotus I, 131, says that the only deities whose worship had come down to the Persians from ancient times were :— the vault of heaven to which they offered sacrifices without images, temples or altars on the loftiest mountains ; the s u n and m o o n, the e a r t h, fi r e, w a t e r, and the w i n d s. At the time of the Greek historian the Persians were still a new nation, and he duly remarks how eager they were to embrace foreign notions of civilisation. Modern research confirms these comments ; the Persians have added successively to their native Aryan notions, ideas and beliefs, others from the Magi, from Khorasmia, from Elam, from Assyro-Babylonia, from Asia-Minor and even from Egypt. Such, for instance, in the latter case is the remarkable threefold head-dress of Cyrus on the monuments, which cf. in G. Rawlinson's *Herodotus*, vol. I, p. 256; Perrot-Chipiez, *Histoire de l' Art*, vol. I, p. 723.; M. Marcel Dieulafoy, *L' art antique de la Perse*, 1884, vol. I, has pointed out the Græco-Lycian influence ruling the Persian architecture which originated after the overthrow of Crœsus about 554 and the conquests of Cyrus ; although the workmen were Persian, the architects were originary from Asia-Minor. Media had been organised towards 700 B.C. and transformed into the Persian kingdom in the VIth century. Zoroastrism had begun long before at an unknown date and was flourishing among the Hyrcanians and Caspians S.E. and S. of the Caspian sea with its chief seat at Ragha, and not at Bactra as stated in a tradition of the middle ages. It triumphed in Persia only after the accession of the Sassanides, i.e. 226 A.D. Cfr. C. de Harlez, *Le calendrier Persan et le pays originaire du Zoroastrisme*, 1881 ; and *introduction à l'étude de l' Avesta et de la religion Mazdéenne*, 1881,) The Magi, the inheritors of Zoroaster formed a part of the Persian nation, but their doctrines and the numerical categories referred to above had not yet at the time of the compilation of the A v e s t a i.e. probably between 700 and 200 B.C., reached their final development. (Cf. Fr. Spiegel, *Eranische alterthumskunde*, vol. III, p, 787; also Ph. Keiper, *Les noms propres Perso-Avestiques*, Muséon, 1885, vol. IV, pp. 211-229, 338-358, C. de Harlez, *Observation* sur l' age de l'Avesta, ibid. pp. 230-1 ; and *Origines du Zoroastrisme*, Paris, 1879;

J. Darmesteter, *Haurvatât et Ameretāt* ; Paris, 1877 ; *Ormazd et Ahriman : leur origines et ler histoire*, Paris, 1877. The six Amesha Çpentas are creations of the Mazdeism, and at first were only personifications of moral notions, such as is yet the case with four of them in the Gâthâs, (cf. C. de Harlez, *Introduction*, p. 90), which forms the oldest part of the Avesta, and whose special date of composition later by several centuries than that of the Rigveda, is fixed at the utmost by some between 1500-1200-900 B.C. (cf. L. H. Mills, *The Zend Avestā*. part III, 1887, Introd. p. 37.) Even in later times, when the Amesha Çpentas and the Yazatas were attributed a more precise control on parts of nature, no regular categories of the five elements, as in China, is apparent. Cfr. C. de Harlez, *Avesta*, Introd. pp. 88-111, where their attributes are described at length. Therefore there is no relationship between them and the six and five Chinese categories, and the similarity claimed by Dr. J. Chalmers and the Rev. J. Edkins rests only on misconceptions and misinformation. It is more likely a fact that the six *fu* and five *heng* were part of the Elamo-Babylonian categories and notions received by the early civilisers of China. We must wait for further light on the subject, when more inscriptions of ancient Susiana are discovered and deciphered. Such ideas may have been an amalgamation of Chaldean and Elamite views, and be the same that afterwards made their influence felt in Mazdeism. We may expect also some further information from the decipherment of the cuneiform inscriptions relating to numerical categories.

CHAP. VII.—ITEMS OF BABYLONIAN, PERSIAN, INDIAN, EGYPTIAN AND GREEK CIVILISATIONS ENTERED INTO ANCIENT CHINA FROM 770 B.C. TO A.D. 220.

I.

97. In the previous chapter[365] we have successively examined the various channels through which influences of the civilised Western world may have entered and in reality did enter, into Ancient China, viz.: section *a*) Ancient dynasties of Western origin; *b*) the Jade eastern traffic; *c*) Ancient trade route of the eastern sea-trade; *d*) Ancient trade routes inland, South and South-west, and *e*) the trade of Shuh (Sze-tchuen).

The second part of the same chapter (called section *f*) was occupied with a rapid survey of the general advance in foreign knowledge which was made in China, during the three first periods of its history, namely, 1) from c. 2272, Arrival of the Bak families, who were most probably a blue-eyed ruddy faced and not black haired race,[366] from the West, to the H$_{IA}$ dynasty; 2) from the time of the great Yü to the end of the S$_{HANG}$-Y$_N$ dynasty, and 3) from the beginning of the T$_{CHOU}$ dynasty to their removal to Loh-yang in 770 B.C.

98. There are several additions which further researches[367] enable me to make. The Bak families when they established their settlements in N.W. China, knew g o l d, s i l v e r, c o p p e r, and t i n (or antimony), whose symbols are all traceable to their antecedents in the mother writing of Western Asia.[368] They had great difficulty in finding s i l v e r in their new country, and the discovery of the o b s t i n a t e m e t a l (silver= *Y n*- made of *ken*, o b s t i n a t e and (*kin*) metal) under the Hia and Yn dynasties has remained historical. They owe their knowledge of i r o n at the time of the great Yü, to the native populations of North Szetchuen, who were well acquainted with it, and they called it accordingly the B a r b a r- i a n m e t a l, (*tiet*, iron, written at first *Y*, barbarian, and *kin*, metal), as well as by other names, *tiet* and *lou*, borrowed from the native dialects.

In the middle of the eighteenth century, the Chinese became acquainted with the art of Bronze. In 1741 B.C. a branah of the Kun-wus coming from the Kokonor, settled at *Hiu* (Honan, N.), introducing with them the western art of bronze (invented in Asia Minor about 2500 B.C.), which had been carried eastwards through the tin stations of Moshed (in Khorassan), of Kiu-tse (in Eastern Turkestan), and Kokonor. The initial proportions of tin to copper, which increased in the east, and diminished in the west, was 15 per cent.[370]

99. The introduction of the western art of tempering iron, which I thought to have taken place at the time of the expedition of Muhwang to the west, in the third period (*supra* VI. *f.* 4.), did not happen then.[371] A due consideration given to the texts on the matter has convinced me that they refer to the Assyrian art of inlaying metal, which was then brought to the knowledge of the Chinese,[372] while the other art was not learned by them before several centuries had elapsed.[373]

100. As we have not already done so, we must here notice the great literary and political event which had happened towards the end of the third period. It was due to the energy and foresight of *Siuen* the King of Tchou and of his able minister *Sze-tch'ou* in 820 B.C., during a temporary revival of the power of his throne.[374] The ancient *Ku-wen* writing, introduced from the West by the Bak families, had diverged to some extent, in the course of centuries, from its original forms and modes of composition; the language had varied, the area of the Chinese dominion was larger than in former times, aboriginal tribes had been absorbed and assimilated, regional variants of the spoken language had arisen, and in consequence, the phonetic spelling of ancient times suggesting a spoken term, uni- or poly-syllabic in one monogram only, simple or complex, which was largely resorted to in the written language, had ceased to be adequate with the requirements. Therefore Siuen Wang and Sze-tch'ou felt the necessity of obviating possible misunderstandings of the written commands and instructions from the Crown in any part of the Chinese dominion, and they made a bold attempt to do so. Although successful only in a small limit at the time, from want of continuity of power and recognized authority in their hands and those of their successors, the principle they laid down remained, and, followed in later centuries by powerful rulers,[375] has given to China her present wonderful writing which is understood everywhere, even in non-Chinese countries, notwithstanding the variety of the spoken languages, and has thus greatly contributed to the unity and greatness of the Chinese Empire. The principle followed by Siuen Wang and Sze-tch'ou in their recast of a large number of the written characters, was to make them more

ideographic, even more pictorial, and thus to make them more significant to the eyes than before, at the expense of the phonetic suggestion, if necessary. The original number of characters, beyond the wanted additions required by the progress of knowledge, had increased from various sources: 1°) variants resulting from the gradual neglect of the primary rules of spelling and composition, and the actual ignorance and carelessness of the scribes; 2°) local variants of the standard forms, entered into the vocabulary with an acquired shade of meaning; 3°) pictorial equivalents, of difficult or little known standard characters, actually created among the less cultivated part of the Chinese dominion. These various causes of divergencies continued to act after the reform of 820 B.C., and the new standard forms were not regularly obeyed, because of the weakness of the central authority; but as the principle of ideographism, by its suitableness to the environment, had become paramount, the written documents could henceforth be understood everywhere without great difficulty.[376] It is only in the sixth period, that we shall have to refer again to the transformation of the written characters.

101. The present chapter is practically the continuation of the second part of the preceding, since we shall continue now our survey of the evolution of Chinese civilisation, began therein for the three first periods. But the importance of the events which occurred after 770 B.C. downwards, the greater supply of documentary evidence, and the everlasting influence which these events have exercised on the subsequent history and present condition of the country, make it necessary to deal with them in a new chapter.

NOTES——

365) The numbers of the paragraphs which have been omitted in printing the previous parts of the present work may be easily ascertained by referring to the final table of contents.

366) A black-haired girl amongst them was looked upon as an extraordinary being at the time of Shun; the ruddy faces of the men and the whiteness of the women's complexions are severally praised in the *Shi King*; the indigo plant was denominated by them the eye-like plant. Cf. my paper on *The Black heads of Babylonia and Ancient China*: B. & O. R. vol. V., pp. 233-246.

367) Contained in my Monograph on *The Metallurgy of the Ancient Chinese*, which, prepared as a chapter of my *Introduction to the Catalogue of Chinese Coins in the British Museum*, was one of the chapters left aside for want of funds (unprovided for in the estimates).

368) In Gold and Tin, cf. B. & O. R. vol. V. pp. 38-39, in T. de L., *From Ancient Chaldæa and Elam to early China*, § 16.—Silver was white metal as in the west; Copper, *tung* is derived from the

original symbol for crucible as in the west. The Rev. C. J. Ball has found independently the derivation of the symbol for gold. Cf. his *Ideogram common to Accadian and Chinese*, P.S.B.A., Dec. 1890.

369) This date like that of 2282, for the settlement of the Bak sings under the leadership of Yu nai hwang-ti (Hu Nakhunte) on the banks of the Loh river in Shensi, in the 50th year of his rule, is calculated from the statements of the Annals of the Bamboo Books; the date of 2332 for the first year of Hwang-ti, verified by Hwang-p'u-mi (*supra*, Ch. III. §12); and that of 1904 B.C., lately verified by astronomy (G. Schlegel, F. Kühnert, *Die Schu-King Finsterniss*. Amsterdam, 1889), together permit a scheme of chronology much more satisfactory than the common scheme built in the XIth century on false astronomical data, or the chronology calculated from the Bamboo Books which has been frequently followed in the previous chapters. I have given a comparative table of the three schemes, so far as the history of money is concerned in my *Numismatic Chronology of Ancient China*, forming the Ch. I. of my *Introduction*, referred to, note 367.

370) The use of special ores of copper led to the discovery of Bronze. For the proofs and details, cf. my Monograph *On the Western discovery of bronze and its introduction in Ancient China*.—The various proportions of tin to copper according to the object required are stated in the *Tchou-li*, Kiv. 41 (ed. Biot, t. II. pp. 491-492). The Analyses of Chinese bronzes hitherto published concern bronze objects of comparatively recent make. Assyrian bronzes contained from 15 to 10 per cent tin.

371) It occurred only in the sixth century, as shown below.

372) For all details and proofs, cf. my paper on *The Metallurgy of the Ancient Chinese*.

373) A few of the items included in the lists forming the fourth chapter, which progress of research has proved to belong to importations of the fourth period will be indicated below.

374) I have called again, after several ancient writers, the attention of scholars to that great event, one of the most remarkable which could be quoted in the general history of writing, in several of my publications: *Early history of the Chinese Civilization*, 1880, p. 15, sq.; *On the history of the Archaic Chinese writing and texts*, 1882 p. 6; *Beginnings of writing around Thibet*, part I., §55; *Le non-monosyllabisme du Chinois Antique*, l'écart entre les langues écrite et parlée d'aujoud'hui, et l'histoire de la langue écrite, 1889, p. 14; and elsewhere.

375) In 227 and 212 B.C., in 165 and 379 A.D.

376) The own written characters of Sze-tch'ou are generally called *ta-tchuen*, Great tchuen, and those framed according to his principles *tchuen*, in contra-distinction to the same style reduced and simplified in 227 B.C., which was called *siao tchuen*, i.e., Small tchuen. The word *tchuen* means literally curved, and the usual term seal character is only an appropriate rendering.

II. FOURTH PERIOD, 770-481 B.C.

a) *The Ages of Wonder-ism*.

102. The IVth period begins in 770 B.C. when the capital of the

CHINESE CIVILISATION. 89

Tchou dynasty was transferred eastwards to Loh-yh (Loh-yang, Honan), after the death of the previous king through the hands of the Kiuen-jung,[377] western barbarians, side ancestors of the Burmo-Nagas tribes of the present day, and it lasts until 481 B.C., when began the internecine wars of the various states of the Chinese dominion contending for the Imperial supremacy. It is one of the most important in the history of Chinese civilisation. Importation by the east and by the south-west of numerous foreign ideas and notions which have had an everlasting influence on the evolution of the Chinese views, moral and religious, and the beginnings of Wonder-ism, Taoism Confucianism and Tao-sze-ism, took place during that period.

The various states and especially the border ones in contact with the outside word, less fettered than previously to accept anything new but through the authoritative channel of their suzerain the King of Tchou, were henceforth open to initiative of their own as well as to innovations introduced by foreigners.

103. The eastern sea-trade which we have noticed in the first part of the present chapter, section c, as one of the channels of introduction of foreign items of civilisation has exercised a most remarkable influence[378]. It was carried by sea traders from the Indian Ocean, who, opposed unsuccessfully after 680 B.C.[379] by the small Chinese state of Kiu (in S.E. Shantung) founded around the present gulf of Kiao-tchou, (on the South side of the peninsula), *Lang-ga* which they called after the old Ceylonese *Lanka*[380], S. of the gulf, and *Tsih-mieh*, afterwards *Tsih-moh*, their mart and mint-place on the North. They reckoned among them sea-farers from the Arabian sea[381], but their chiefs were Hindus. One of them named *Kut-lu*, i.e. Gôtra, as shown by the story of a cow connected with his visit, was the object of a grand and unusual reception at the Court of the prince of Lu (S. Shantung) in 631 B.C.[382]. They were friendly with the Chinese states and carried on with them extensive relations; their introduction of coinage about 675 was soon imitated by the Prince Hwan of Ts'i, and his able minister Kwan-y-wu. And in later times they established monetary unions for the issue with joint names of coins between themselves and inland Chinese cities[383]. They recognized the suzerainty of the Ts'i state in 550 B.C.

104. Astrology and sorcery[384] from Chaldæan source, (about 665 B.C.) tinged with Indian views, Elamo Persian notions, mythological imagery of Egypt, India, and Babylon,[385] ideas of transmutation and alchemy,[386] amongst other innovations; and besides coinage and measures[387] in

675 B.C. several material progresses such as the western art of tempering iron[388], known in 540 B.C., or perhaps before, importation of foreign products such as the Quince-fruit indigenous from Media, *circâ* 660 B.C[389], were successively introduced, (more or less inaccurate and altered as the case may be) by them into China during that period. The charactet of their knowledge was not refined, and belonged properly to the wonder-mongering spirit that could be expected from sea-traders of that age.

105. It is through their channel that the following data came into the Chinese literature.

—A hybrid list of names of the twelve Babylonian months[390];
—A list of ten names which may be that of the old Semitic months[391];
—A Babylonian list of twelve Zodiacal names[392];

These three items were chiefly used for astrological purposes and they do seem to have been adopted to that service by the sea traders in question previously to their introduction into China.

All these lists communicated orally to the Chinese scribes were transliterated by them as approximately as they could. They differ in their outwards aspect from the data of early date imported by the Bak families about 2282 B.C., such as the cycles of 10 and 12, and many others noticed in our chapter IV, *a*) sciences and art, which are thus disencumbered of several of the suspicious items which have crept among them.

106. We must also ascribe to the same influence;

—One peculiar superstition, such as the idea of exposing in the sun rays to the mercy of heaven, in time of draught, an emaciated person dying of thirst and hunger[393]; known in the state of Lu in[394], 639 B.C.;

—The annual practice of " giving a wife in Marriage to the river god Ho-peh " in throwing in the river a well-favoured Maiden, which well established at *Yeh*[395] (pres. Tchang-teh fu, N. Honan) in the state of Wei, was suppressed after 424 B.C., by a new governor named Si-men Pao[396];

—The fire-worship which was established sometime before 564 and 541 in the state of Sung[397] (Honan, E.) where it was connected with astrology[398];

—The remarkable dualist worship which was established in *Tcheng* (Honan, E.) in[399], 524 B.C., to *Hwei-luh*, god of light and fire, and *Hiuen-ming*, god of darkness and water[400], then known in Chinese mythology for the first time[401].

107. Several men of importance are mentioned in history as having promoted the astrological doctrines introduced and propagated by the active traders of the Lang-ya colony. Four of them are conspicuous;

namely : Sze yoh, whom we see giving astrological explanations to the duke of TSIN (Shansi S.) in 564 B.C.[402] ; Tze Tch'ang who died in 521 B.C., a younger son of duke Tch'eng (reigned 584-571 B.C.) of the state of TCHENG (Honan C.) where he occupied a high position and became finally chief Minister for 26 years before his death[403] : Tze Shen, in SUNG (Honan E.) in 545 and 522 B.C.[404]. And Tch'ang Hwang in TCHOU (Honan W., Shensi S.E.) who flourished in 550-492 B.C. ; Szema-Tsien says of him that he was acquainted with all matters concerning the gods and spirits, and that the sayings about the wonderful amongst the people of TCHOU date from his teachings[405].

108. These four men may be looked upon as the real founders of the Tao-sze-ism[406], and were the immedate predecessors of Lich-tze and Tchwang-tze whom we shall have to refer to in our survey of the next period. We must now examine where was the fountain head of the singularly mixed influence introduced by these foreigners of Lang-ya, influence which continued for several centuries and displayed later on a curious and instructive transformation. But during the sixth century, while this activity was going on in Shantung and the states in the vicinity, another influence of a higher standard had reached the Middle Kingdom by the South-west route, and introduced several innovations ; the most striking was a certain amount of Hindu thoughts which have deeply tinged the great philosophical work of the period, i.e. the *Tao teh king* of Lao-tze (604-520 B.C.). We shall have to enquire on the important subject of the beginning of Taoism in a subsequent section, and afterwards on that of Confucianism.

NOTES——

377) On the Jungs, cf. J. H. Plath, *die fremden barbarischen stämme in Alten China*, München, 1874, pp. 477-495 ; and T. de L., *The Languages of China before the Chinese*, par. 28, 150, 172.

378) The Rev. J. Edkins was, I think, the first to point out the introduction of Babylonian astrology and imagery in China about that time and the great movement of thought which ensued, through the ancient navigation in the Indian Ocean, and I am indebted to him for several suggestions. But he was mistaken in several of his premises which he had not worked out ; he knew nothing of the opening of the Shantung sea-trade about 680 B.C., nor of the Hindu colonies in Pegu about 500 B.C. He assumed without proof that a Babylonian sea trade to Indo-China had existed from remote date, which assumption is against scientific evidence. On the other hand he wants to begin astrology in China about 806 B.C., without any serious proof, which is too early by far, and he thinks that it could have reached the Chinese in the South of China, where they were not, inland through Indo-China,

which is not the case, as shown forcibly in my present work. I am not sure that the following list of Dr. Edkins papers and communications on the matter is complete : *Babylonian Origin of Chinese astronomy and astrology*, China Review, 1885, XIV, 90-95 ; *Babylonian Astronomy*, ibid., 104 ; *Astrology in Ancient China*, ibid. 345-52 ; *The introduction of Astrology in China*, ibid. 1886, XV, 126-28 ; *Chinese Mythology and Art*, The Academy, July 12, 1884 ; *Ancient navigation in the Indian Ocean*, J.R.A.S. 1886, XVIII, 1-27 ; *When did Babylonian Astrology enter China*, Pr. S.B.A., Dec. 7, 1886, 32-39; *The relations of the Persian and Chinese Calendars* : China Review, 1887, XVI, 95-93; also *The Yh king as a book of divination*, J.R.A.S. 1884, XVI, 360 sq.

379) Cf. *Tso tchuen*, 2, 1 : 4.—Hoh Tchib, *Tsih moh hien tchi*, 1763, Kiv. I, f. 3.

380) Vide *suprd* par. 44 ; and note 25 of my paper : *How in 219 B.C. Buddhism entered China*. B.&O.R. V, 105.

381) *Tsih-moh*, seems to have been called after the emporia of *Safar, Sophar, Zabar*, of the coasts in the Arabian sea. *Suppara* of the W. Coast of India, *Zabaj* of N.W. Jara, *Zabai* of Indo-China, all names surviving or locally adapted from a common original. Moreover we find a proof of that in their Babylonian astrology,

382) He was chief of the *Kiai* foreigners, near Lang-ya, on the south side. Cf. *Tso-tchuen*, 5, xxix, 1 and 5.

383) Cf. my introduction to the *Catalogue of Chinese coins in* the British Museum, ch. I and VII.

384) This sorcery appeared·I think for the first time in 662 B.C. (cf. *Tso tchuen*, 3, XXXII, 2). Astrology was not known in China, in 710, 669, nor even in 661 B.C., all dates where it should have been resorted to, if known then Cf. *Tso tchuen*, under these years. Besides divining by the tortoise shell or the millfoil, the chief means of forecasting events were onomancy and palmistry. Astrology appears rather abruptly in 655 B.C. when Yen the state diviner of Tsin quotes as childish ditties (*t'ung yao*) an astrological answer concerning a project of his Prince, given by some adept of the new doctrines. The native exegetes in taking the expression *t'ung yao* as meaning " the children have a sang which says" are certainly at· fault here, as children could not have made such a thing. Astrology took gradually its place as a mode of forecasting events. An instance occurs in 564 B.C. in the same state of Tsin (Shansi) ; it was followed by subsequent statements in 545, 540, etc., which show that the belief had become well established in the above state and in those of Tcheng (Honan C.) Sung (Honan E.), and in others. The twelve principal states of the Chinese dominion were, each, placed under the superintendance of one of twelve zodiacal signs whose names appear then for the first time as we shall see below (note 392). Amongst these states are those of Tcheng which begin in 806 B.C., and of Tsi'n (Shensi) which began in 770 B.C., while the name of the state of Yueh which did not appear before 537 B.C. was added either to that of Yen under *Tcheh-muh*, or to that of Wu, under *Sing ki*. As the latter state appears for the first times in history in 584 B.C. *amongst the states* the astrological arrangement must have been made between 584 and 564 B.C.—At the time of the Han dynasty some gaps have occured and the attribution

of several names forgotten ; they were restored by Tcheng-hiuen (A.D. 127-200) in his commentary of the *Tchou-li*, xxvi. 20 ; and also in the *T'ien-yuen lih li* of *Siu-fah* (A.D. 1682), with slight differences, Dr. J. Edkins, *Ancient Navigation in the Indian Ocean*, J.A.R.S. 1881, XVIII, 12, has quoted only the latter's list, and holds the view that the astrological attribution of the states may have taken place in 806 B.C. because the list begins by TCHENG, but this is no proof since we have not the original list, and the later writers have began it as they used to do in enumerating the 28 *siuh*; cf. also a rejoinder made on other grounds in the *China Review*.

385) As the mythological imagery became prominent only during the next period we shall postpone till then our enquiry on the question.

386) These notions came into effect at the end of the next period; they were too crude and vague before.

387) The coins were cast on the double basis of the light Babylonian *Mina* as unit of weight, and of the Babylonian empan of 27 mm. as unit of length. Cf. the chapter VI on *Weights and Measures*, in the *Introduction* of my *Catalogue of Chinese coins in the British Museum*.

388) This art was known in Shantung about 540 B.C. but not yet in the states more south; cf. my monograph *On Ancient Chinese Metallurgy*.

389) An ode of the *Shi-king* I, 5, X.) composed about 660 B.C. in WEI (Tchihli S.W.) praises the *Muh Kua* or quince fruit (not the *papaya* now so called in South China and introduced from America). The quince tree, indigenous in Media, is highly valued all over the east for its cardinal virtues, and its fruits are to this day the object of an important traffic from the Persian gulf to the Bay of Bengal. It was then introduced in the China by the sea trade of Lang-ya. Cf. for the details and proofs my monograph on *The Quince-fruit from Media to China*, 660 B.C.

390) The names of the cycle of twelve, which were part of the knowledge of the Bak sings, were those of the Babylonian Zodiac, on which cf. my letter in the Academy, Oct. 11, 1890, *The Zodiac and cycles of Babylonia and their Chinese derivations*; while the full names which appear in the *Erh-ya* and *She ki* are those of the twelve Babylonian months. The entry of ch. IV, section *a*, and note 45, must be altered and completed as above. See next note.

391) This is the list which appears, with the preceding, in the *Erh-ya*, and in the *She ki*, but with greater divergences which however are not too broad not to be explained as transliterations from oraldictation. Mr. E. Chavannes, in his interesting paper on *Le Calendrier des Yn* (Journal Asiatique, Nov.-Dec.1890) about the terms of the duodenary series, simple formula of good Omen, remarks p. 479, that the oldest instance of their use occurs in the *Kwoh-yu*, in the ninth year of Kou tsien of Yueh (496-465 B.C.) i.e. 488 B.C. (not 479 as he states erroneously.)—The duodenary list has been applied in a clumsy way to the duodenary cycle of Jupiter, and Dr. J. Chalmers in his paper *On the Astronomy of the Ancient Chinese* (append. in J. Legge, Chinese Classics, vol. III. 1865) has remarked that the term *sheht'i-koh*, ancient *Shepti* and *Koh*, which *Shepti* is said by Szema-Tsien to be Jupiter, in Sanskrit *Vrishaspati*, may be an approximate transcription of the Indian name. On the other hand, I have pointed above, ch. IV, *a*, note 45, the ob-

vious derivation of these names from a hybrid list of those of the Babylonian months, and the clear identity of SHEPTI with SHEBAT. Since they have been introduced into China in the sixth century only, and as astrological terms through the Indianised sea-traders of Lang-ya, the two statements are easiy reconcileable. The outwards resemblance of *shebat* with *vrishaspati* may have been one of the reasons which induced these astrologers to apply the full list to the cycle of Jupiter.

392) This list is that of the twelve *ts'e*, otherwise zodiacal signs which appear in Chinese literature in connection with the astrology beginning in the seventh century and not otherwise. Seven of them are mentioned in the *Tso-tchuen*, six of these seven, and four more are given in the *Erh-ya*. The *Shun ho*, i.e. the eleventh of the Chinese list, is mentioned in the *Tso tchuen* in 655 (5, VI, 9).—Compared with readings of the twelve Babylonian signs of the months, they present the following concordance:

Bab. 1. *shara*, chief	= *shou*, head,	10.	Chinese.
,, 2. *gu*,	= *ho*	11.	,,
,, 3. *mur*,	= *wi*	12.	,,
,, 4. *shu*,	= *shou*	1.	,,
,, 5. *bil*, fire	= *ho*, fire,	2.	,,
,, 6. *gi*, look	= *ki*, annals,	3.	,,
,, 7. *du*,	= *tche*	4,	,,
,, 8. *engar*, digging	= *hiuen hiao*, dark hole,	5	,,
,, 9. *gan* (KISLIVU)	= *kiang lou*	7.	,,
,, 10. (TEBITU)	= TSÜ TZE	6.	,,
,, 11. *ash*	= *ta liang*	8.	,,
,, 12. *she kin*	= *shi tchin*	9.	,,

The concordance fails only for the 8 and also for the 6 of the Chinese list: the latter's names for 1, 2, 3, 4, 10, 11, 12 are double instead of simple but the the additional symbol does not impair the value of the other symbol.

393) The first instance is mentioned in the state of *Lu*, in 639 B.C. (*Tso tchuen*). In the *Li-ki*, II, 11, iii, 29, the Duke Muh of Lu (409-377 B.C.) is said to have made a similar proposal which was reproved.

394) The practice however does not seem to have ever obtained any hold there, and is not known in any other part of the country.

395) *She-ki*, kiv. 126, ff. 14-16.—W. F. Mayers, *Chinese R. M.*, I, 172. —The god was represented as a man with four faces driving in a fairy chariot drawn by two dragons. Cf. *Shan hai king*, (text and gloss) kiv. 12, f. 3. His name has been assimilated to that of a certain *Ho-peh*, spoken of as an ally of the Chinese in that region, under the reigns of HIA Ti Mang, 1st year, and his successor Ti Sieh, 16th year, in the *Tchuh shu ki nien*; i.e. about 1813 and 1781 according to the rectified scheme of chronology. Ho-peh, i.e. Ho-pak was perhaps a local substitution of *Oh-pak*, a god of fire and whose worship we hear in 540 B.C. in the *Tso tchuen* in connection with fire worship, introduced in the state of Sung, apparently not long before, from the foreign source we are studying.

396) The exact year of the suppression is not stated; as Szema-tsien says simply that Simen-Pao, was the chief officer of *Yeh* during the

reign of the Marquess Wen of WEI who ruled from 424 to 387 B.C.
398) *Tso tchuen*, under those dates.
399) *Tso-tchuen*, 10, XVIII, 2.
400) *Hiuen-ming*, 'litt. : Dark-obscurity.—Once entered into their pantheon, this deity has been connected with a certain *Siu* or *Hi* said to have been a son of Shao Hao, and Superintendent of Water under Tchuan-hiu (2227 B.C.) by the authors of the Han dynasty. Cf. *Khang hi tze tien*, s.v. *ming*, 14+8, f. 22 v., and *Sacred Books of the East*, XXVII, *The Li ki*, vol. I, p. 296.
401) It is difficult not to be struck by the outward resemblance of these two names, as far as permitted by the Chinese orthoepy with those of Ahura-Mazda and Anro-Mainyus. Cf. *Huei-luh* which has no meaning in Chinese ; cf. also *Anro-Mainyus*, with *Hiuen ming*, anciently *hun-meng*. The Persians were ruling in Babylonia since 538 and on the eastern shores of the Persian Gulf for some time previously.
402) *Tso tchuen*, 9, IX, 1.
403) Cf. *Tso tchuen*, Ann. 565, 543, 541, 538, 532, and pass.—A short biography of this clever man is given in W. T. Mayers, *Chinese R.M.* I, 730, and more fully in T. Watters, *A guide to the Tablets in a Temple of Confucius*, Shanghai 1879, pp. 35-37. His tablet was admitted in the temple in 1857, which is rather surprising if we consider his astrological performance of 541 B.C. Szema Tsien, *She ki*, kiv. 129 has written his biography.
404) *Tso tchuen*, Ann. 545 and 522 B.C.
405) There are several references to this man in history. Szema-Tsien, *She-ki*, kiv. 28, f. 7 v. says that Tch'ang-Huang gave his services to the king Ling of TCHOU (whose reign ended in 544 B.C.) At that time the Princes used to come no more to the court of TCHOU, whose power was on the wane. Tch'ang-Hwang who was proficient in all matters concerning gods and spirits, shot arrows on a *pu-lai*'s head, otherwise a fox's head which symbolised the *pu-lai*, or non-coming of the Princes. He hoped that this ceremony would have contrived them to come, but they did not yield. Afterwards a man of TSIN seized Tch'ang-Huang and killed him. The wonder sayings of the people of TCHOU began with Tch'ang-Huang.—In the *Tso tchuen*, Ann. 492, par. 5, it is stated that he was put to death in that year by the people of TCHOU.—Tchuang-tze says : X, 2, Tch'ang-Huang was ripped open; and in XXVI, 1 : " Tch'ang-Huang died in Shu, where the people preserved his blood for three years, when it became changed like green jade."
406) Tao-sze-ism which has already been used by several continental scholars is used here as a convenient designation of the wonder-mongering school which has absorbed and transformed the philosophical Taoism of Lao-tze.

b) The Erythræan sea-traders and the Chinese Age of Wonderism.

109. The results of the researches resumed in the foregoing paragraphs (103-107), throw some interesting light on the state of things that existed during the 8th, 7th, and 6th centuries B.C. in the Arabian sea, the Persian gulf, and the intercourse between Babylonia and India. They suggest also that an important event must have taken place, which gave to the Erythræan Sea trade a greater impulse than before, and incited the mariners and merchants to go much further than previously in search of new lands for their commerce, and thus reach the Southern shores of Shantung about 675 B.C. Such an event had really happened, as we shall see (§116) below, by the introduction of the Phœnician navy in the Persian gulf, in 697-695 B.C., but its influence upon the extension of eastern sea trade had not hitherto been suspected.

110. Commercial relations by sea had existed from the earliest times between the Red Sea and the Aromata or Somali coast[407] with several emporia of South Arabia, and between the latter and the Western, Northern, and North eastern shores of the Persian gulf.[408] Modern disclosures go far to vindicate the tradition, handed down by the Chaldæan historian Berosus (c. 340-270 B.C.), that the civilizers of Babylonia had come by the Erythræan sea, and the Black-headed race, which in the old cuneiform texts was the traditional expression denoting originally their dusky skin,[409] have been discerned, from the later arrived Sumero-Akkadians and from the Semites, on the neatly defined statues and monuments of olden times.[410] Since the reign of Gudea, i.e. about 2500 B.C., if not previously, Kushite traders[411] of the S. Arabian ports were carrying on their trade from Coptos[412], the Sinaitic peninsula, the Midian coast, and the Bahrein islands to Babylonia[413]; but in the inscriptions of his statues where these names of stations are given, no reference is made to trade with any place of the Indian coast. And an alleged proof of teak wood which would have been discovered in ruins at Eridu of 4000 B.C. has turned out to be the result of a misconception.[414]

111. Commercial relations between the Kushite emporia of South Arabia, the West coast of India, and the South as far as Ceylon, were perhaps already opened[415] at the time of the XIIth dynasty of Egypt, i.e. circa 2400 B.C. This sea trade was certainly active in the seventeenth century, as shown by the Indian products brought back by the Egyptian fleet of the queen Hatshopsitu[416], and later on they seem to have established colonies on the Indian coast, which they probably denominated by names which recall to mind those of their trading places[417] westwards. The Indian Ophir seems to have been one of them.[418] Ancient India owes a great deal to the Sabæan traders,[419] and by rebound to Egypt, but the matter requires a special enquiry, and can only be alluded to in these pages.

112. At the time of Shalmanasar II., 828-825 B.C., commercial intercourse existed inland between India and the east of Assyria. On his Black Obelisk, a rhinoceros, a yak, and Indian animals, such as an elephant and apes[420] are brought as tribute by the inhabitants of *Mutsri*, which lay to the north-east of Khorsabad, in the mountainous district now inhabited by the Missouri Kurds, and was therefore on the route of communication with India. The caravan road from the east must have passed through it.[421] The name of the monkeys seems to be the same as that of the same animals brought from South Yunnan by the traders of *Shou-mi* to the Chinese court about 1097 B.C.,[422] and both represent the Dravidian name of the monkey.[423] More direct communications inland between Assyro-Babylonia and India were established afterwards, and the Aryan-Indians of the Sapta-Sindu became acquainted with the legend of the deluge[424] the armlet-weight *mana*[425], and perhaps other things.[426]

NOTES——

407) Aromata from there were used by the Egyptians as early as the IVth dynasty (Birch), i.e., following Mariette, 4235-3951 B.C.

408) Cf. on that question my paper on *An unknown King of Lagash* §13-29; *B. & O. R.* Aug. 1890, vol. IV. pp. 193-207.—Mr. T.G, Pinches has treated of several points of the subject in his *Notes upon some of the recent discoveries in the realm of Assyriology*, with special reference to the private life of the Babylonians, I. *Principally from an inscription of King Gudea, about 2500 B.C.* (Victoria Institute, Jan. 19, 1891.)

409) Cf. the first part of my paper on *The Black-heads of Babylonia and Ancient China*; *B. & O. R..* vol. V. pp. 233-287.—On the name of their leader, cf. my suggestion on *The name of Qannês in the Cuneiform texts*, (The Acad. June 9, 1888), and on his half-fish form in mythology: *The fabulous fish-men of Early Babylonia in Ancient Chinese legends*, Sept. 1888: B. & O. R., 11, 221-226.

410) The Semitic Assyro-Babylonian type is well known. Cf. amongst others: J. Menant, *Remarques sur les portraits des rois Assyro-Chaldéens*, 1882.—The Black-headed civilizers of Babylonia, were neither long nor

round headed, with the forehead straight, the jaws orthognathous, the cheek bones prominent, the nose large and straight, the hair curly, and a dusky complexion.—The Sumero-Akkadians of Northern origin were round headed, with the nose prominent, the chin and forehead receding, and probably an olive complexion.—Cf. my paper on *The Black heads*, O.C., and besides the monumental evidence, A. H. Sayce, *The races of the Old Testament*, 1891, pp. 137-140; and T. G. Pinches, *Upon the types of the early inhabitants of Mesopotamia*: Journ. Anthropol. Instit. Nov. 1891.

411) On the name of the Kushites as a general appellative for the early populations of the sea-borders of the Arabian Ocean, cf. my paper on *The Kushites, who were they?* B. & O. R., Dec. 1886, I., 25-31, and *suprà*, n. 351; also, *An unknown King of Lagash*, n. 48.—Prof. Sayce, *Lectures on the Religion of the Ancient Babylonians*, p. 434-435, and *Races of the Old Testament,*, pp. 43, 51, 143-4, objects to the application of the name at so early a date, because its antecedent *Kash*, which was only the name of a part of Ethiopia, was transformed into *Kush* by the Egyptians at a later period, and still later, extended to the region of Punt. As however he admits that the Kush, father of Nimrod, according to the old tradition, preserved in Gen. X, 6, 7, presents but a similarity of name with the first (cf. *Lectures*, p. 435-6), and as this tradition shows an early use of the name in the sense we attribute to it, early use which may have suggested the Egyptian alteration, I think that the name Kushite may remain as a convenient, and not altogether inaccurate appellative. Let us remember that the leading tribes of Africa, now so called, (cf. *The Black heads*, §4), are for the most part immigrated from South Arabia.

412) The foreign commerce reaching Coptos (mod. Kopf) was already so important in his time, that Pepi I., the second king of the sixth dynasty, had a special route made between it and the sea. Cf. G. Maspero, *Histoire Ancienne*, edit. IV., p. 81. The sixth dynasty, following Mariette, 3703-3500 b.c.

413) For these identifications, cf. *An unknown King of Lagash*, par. 17-23, and the references. Also T. G. Pinches, *Upon the types*, l.c.

414) Two logs of alleged teak wood discovered in the ruins of Ur in 1854, and hitherto unconfirmed by any other find, had been too readily assumed to date from the foundation of the town, some 4000 years b.c., and thus have given rise to considerable speculation; but this was a misconception, as the said logs were simply the supports of cylinders of Nebuchadnezzar (b.c. 605-562), after that maritime communications with India had been opened, as we shall see directly. Cf. J. E. Taylor, *Notes on the ruins of Mugeyer*, p. 264; J. R. A. S., 1855, vol. XV., and B. & O. R., vol. IV., pp. 205-207.—On *sindu* cloth, cf. below, n. 428.

415) The proof is not above suspicion. It consists of a shell of mother of pearl, such as those of Ceylon, which, inscribed with the cartouche of Usurtasen, was bought in Egypt in 1883 by Prof. Sayce. It may have been engraved long after the reign of that sovereign. Cf. *B. & O. R.*, I. 29 n. 28 and IV. 202, n. 58.—I have not seen Mr. Emile Dujon's *L'Egypte dans l'Inde* 4000 ans. av. J.C., Paris, Marpon, 1884, and I do not know if he has been able to support his theory with any substantial proof.

416) This comes out from the fact that when the Egyptian queen Hatsepsu (or Hatshopsitu) of the eighteenth dynasty made her expedition of five ships to the Land of Pun, the following things were brought back from there: all kinds of precious woods, Anti-Gummi, Blooming Ana Sycamores, *Taas*-wood, *Khesit*-wood, *Aham*-metal, Balsam, *Meslem* or collyrium red, two kinds of monkeys, and leopard skins. J. D. C. Lioblein, *Handel und Schiffart auf dem rothen Meere in alten Zeiten* (Christiania, 1886), p. 24-35, from whom I take the previous list, shows that this expedition, and the products brought back must be distinguished from other products brought by another expedition which had just arrived from Nubia and Ethiopia, and consisted of living giraffes, leopards, oxen, and ostrich eggs. And he refers to pl. 6 of Mariette's *Der-el-Bahari*, upper row for the first expedition's products, and lower row for those of Pun (including the monkeys), and blames this scholar as well as Lepsius and Maspero for having overlooked the distinction. Cf. also Dümichen, *Die Flotte einer Ægyptischen Königin in dem 17. Jahrhundert*, 1868, table II. p. 17; B. Graser, *Das Seewesen der alten Ægypter*, in Dümichen, *Resultate*, I. 1-27; G. Maspéro, *De Quelques navigations des Egyptiens sur les côtes de la mer Erythrée*: Rev. Histor. 1879, t. IX. p. 1-17. The name of these monkeys of Pun is given as *Kap* or *Gafi* or *Kafu*, which seems to be the same word as the Hebrew *Koph*, *Ape*, in I. Kings, X. 22. The latter has long been looked upon (erroneously, as we shall see directly), as no other than *Kapi*, the Sanskrit name for monkey, because it is among the products that were brought to Solomon from the Ophir lands by his Tarshish navy. (Cf. note 417). The names in the Hebrew text for ape, peacock, ivory, and sandal wood, were supposed to be derived from Sanskrit words, with the exception of the sandal wood which was recognized as Dravidian. This was looked upon as a proof that at the time of Solomon (c. 950 B.C.) Sanskrit had penetrated southwards to the mouths of the Indus. But this inference was premature. The name for peacock has certainly a Dravidian etymology (Caldwell, *Dravid. Gramm.*, 1875, p. 91), while the name of Ivory is now traced through Egyptian to an Assyrian source (cf. Schrader, in *Z. d. D. M. G.*, xxvii. 709). I am of opinion that the name for Monkey must also desert the Aryanists, as its source is most probably that of the Egyptian word previously cited, which is a very old one in the language (as old as the language itself, says M. Le Page Renouf). Cf. the Egyptian cognate words *ap* and *Keften* for cynocephale, in P. Pierret, *Vocabulaire Hiéroglyhique*, pp. 20, 618, 653 - Max Muller, *Physical Religion*, 1891. p. 25, says: "Here then the single word *Kapi* may possibly indicate the route of commerce from India to Judæa and Phenicia, and from thence to Egypt, in the seventeenth century B.C." But we have no evidence anywhere of such a route, and the ape *gafi* in question, was brought from *Punt*, or S. Arabia, and not all from the North.—The late Miss Amelia B. Edwards has given an interesting chapter on Queen Hatasu, and her expedition to the land of Pun in her last work, *Pharaohs, Fellahs, and Explorers*, 1892, pp. 261-300.

417) E.g. *Muziris* (mod. Cranganore) on the Malabar coast, and *Muza*, their own emporium in the Red Sea, or perhaps better, *Mitzir*, *Egypt*. —*Suppara*, (mod. Wasai, North of Bombay), and *Zafar*, in Yemen, *Zabara* in the Persian gulf, Sofala on the African coast, all probably

colonies from *Zafar*, the *Safar* of Gen. X. 30.—*Minnagara*, near the mouths of the Indus, was perhaps a survival of the once famous name of the Minæans, the leading power of Arabia in olden times. The latter is only a suggestion. Generally the onomastic resemblances of this kind are mere pit-falls, and individual cases cannot be insisted upon. On the other hand, the striving after meaning, which supplies to proper names local etymologies, must not blind the enquirer upon genuine cases which have become transformed by the regional vernacular.

418) I refer to the *Abiria* of Ptolemy (VII.), the *Abhíra* of the Hindu geographers, near the mouth of the Indus, which Lassen, *Indisch. Alterth.* I. 557, sq., II. 552, sq. had suggested to be the Arabian Ophir. The solution here suggested would solve many difficulties.—The Ophirs of Sumatra, &c. are names given by the Portuguese, as shown by J. Crawford, *Descriptive dictionary of the Indian islands*, s.v. OPHIR.

419) It received from them the Egyptian standard of weight. Cf. my *Introduction to....Chinese coins*, ch. VI.—But it did not receive from them the art of writing; the error spread by Tylor and others must be given up because it has no basis, as done by M. Philippe Berger, in his *Histoire de l'Ecriture dans l'Antiquité*, 1891, p. 229-233 ; cf. *Revue Critique*, 4 Avril, 1892.

420) Cf. the remarks of W. Houghton, *Mammalia on the Assyrian sculptures*, Part II, *Wild Mammalia*, Tr. S.B.A., vol. V, pp. 319-320; and those of François Lenormant, *Les noms de l'airain et du cuivre*, 1879, S.B.A., VI. pp. 408-409. Cf. below, note 413. Mr. Houghton identifies the monkey in question with the *Presbyter entellus*, the Hamman of India, or some closely allied species.

421) Cf. A. H. Sayce, *Records of the Past*, N.S., vol. I. p. 109, and vol. IV. p. 52, n. 2. The same country had been once laid waste by Tiglath-Pileser I., according to his own statements. *Ibid.* vol. I. pp. 109-110.

422) *Udumi* seems to be their name (cf. F. Lenormant, *Z. f. ægyptische Sprache*, 1875, p. 21; Schrader, *Keilinschr. Geschichtsfors.* p.273; F. Vigouroux, *La Bible et les d'couvertes mo Iernes*, 4. ed. III. p. 599). In the Chinese text *Kudang* is given (Cf. *supra*, ch. VI. section *d*, par. 46). Both correspond to the Dravidian word for monkey: cf. Tamil anc. *Kaduvan*; Malayalma *Kuranga*; Karnataka *Kodaga*; Toduva *Kodan*; Badaga, *Kurumba*, Irula, *Korangu*; Malabar *Kurangku*; &c. in W. H. Hunter, *A Comparative dictionary of the languages of India and High Asia*, 1868, p. 140.

423) This little fact would tend to show that the traffic was not then passing through the Aryan Indians, if there was not the word *bațiati* for elephant, which has been traced to the Sanskrit *vâsitâ* (by Finzi, *Ric. p. l. stud. dell' ant. Asira*, p. 291), a name for female elephant cf. Pott, *Ueber die Namen des Elephanten*, in Hoffer, *Zeitschr.* II. 36).—The yak is called *alap* n'ar *Sakeya*, i.e. river ox of the country of the Saka, following Lenormant, *ibid.* It would be the oldest mention of this people of western Turkistan, whom the Chinese called *Sak*, and not *Sze* as erroneously stated by some writers.

424) Lenormant, *Origines de l'histoire*, I. 421-429, has shown that it is the Chaldean legend of the Deluge and not the Biblical, which has been the source of the story of Man and the fish, in the *Satapatha Brâhmana*, of the VIIIth century, B.C. (*ibid.* p. 52) and later works.—The

latest translation is that of Julius Eggeling, *The Satapatha Brâhmana*, I. Kanda, 8 Adhyâya, 1 Brahmana; S.B.E. XII., 1882, pp. 216, 19.

425) The Assyro-Babylonian standard unit of weight, *mana*, is written phonetically *ma-na*, as if a foreign word, although sometimes by the first character only, in some contracts of the time of Khammurabi. The golden *manâ* of the Rig-Veda, VI¹., 78, 2, is looked upon by some scholars as a trace of Babylonian influence, but this view is strenlousld opposed by Max Müller, *India, what can it teach us* ? pp. 125-6, any *Biography of words*, p. 115, who argues that the word does not mean a weight (of gold), but an armlet (of gold). Is this not on the contrary a proof in favour of the other view, considering that such was the shape given to gold and bronze currency in Syria, North Assyria, and the East, just at the time when this influence, which would be that of trade from these regions and not from Babylonia, could have been felt among the Vedic Aryans. Cf. also the paper of Prof. Johannes Schmidt, and the remarks of Prof. A. Weber at the Eighth Oriental Congress of 1889.
426) Cf. De Harlez, *Introduction à l'etude de l'Avesta*, p. CCIII.—In the mythical geography, in the Vishnu Puranas and the *Mahabarata*; P. Jensen, *Die Kosmologie der Babylonier*, 1890, pp. 178-184.—Mr .J.F. Hewit, *Notes on the Early History of Northern India*, in J.A.R.S. vol. XX., 321-363; XXI., 188-359; 527-582; XXII., 319-481; 527-606, claimed a connexion between the Akkadians and the Ancient Indians, but he has not established his case.

* *

113. Direct Trade by sea began early in the VIIth century and the older trade by land became active between India and Babylonia. It is probable that the goods were no more transhipped to ascend the Persian Gulf. Teak wood was brought and used at Ur during the reign of Nebuchadrezzar,[427] but a sort of textile called *Sindhu*, in which it has been suggested to recognize *Sindu* the Aryan name of India,[428] appeared earlier in a list of the time of Assurbanipal (668-648 B.C.) and on a contract dated in the 30th year of Nebuchadrezzar, i.e. 576 B.C.[429] It seems however that the tablet of Assurbanipal's time was a copy of another document, and that the *Sindhu* cloth may have been known some time before; moreover its definition, cloth of the mountains, indicates an importation by land, and not by sea.[430] The Buddhist Jataka Bâveru gives evidence, as far as it goes, *circa* 500 B.C. of sea merchants from India going to Babylon and in the second occasion bringing there the first peacock for sale.[431] These maritime relations were not easy and therefore could not be frequent, because of the difficulties of navigation by the dangerous and tempestuous straits at the entrance of the Persian Gulf, [432] and along the inhospitable coasts of Gedrosia.

Therefore communications by sea between Chaldæa and India began directly after the time of Sennacherib's Maritime campaign in 695 B.C.

114. The Babylonians had never been a sea-faring people, and their navy of their various places on the banks of the Euphrates were only river boats, unfit to run on the high seas[433]. Hence was it that the trade had remained in the hands of the sea-farers of South Arabia. The Kushites of old had disappeared[434] in the Xth century and their inheritance had been taken by the Sabæans, whose capital was at Mariba, who jealously endeavoured to keep up the Monopole enjoyed by their predecessors. They may have carried it further east than the latter and have reached Arrakan and Pegu, but there is no clear evidence of the fact,[435] although they may have been incited to do so by the competition which they began to feel in the navy of Hiram, the Phœnician king, and of Solomon, from Eizion-gaber in the Red Sea.

115. Such was the state of things when the Assyrian Monarch Sennacherib II was confronted by a revolt which compelled him to reach by sea the district of Nagit of Elam, on the shores of the Persian gulf, where his former subjects the people of Bit-Yakîn had taken refuge when they fled from his dominions. For that purpose, shipwrights from Syria ('Hatti') built for him, at Nineveh on the Tigris, and at Tul-Barsip (opposite Karkemish)[436] on the Euphrates, sea-faring ships like those of their country, and he manned them with Tyrian, Sidonian and Cyprian sailors "whom he had made prisoners with his own hand[437]. He was thus enabled to embark with his army on board his own fleet, and invading thus by sea his powerless foes, destroyed their towns and removed the inhabitants[438]. Seven years later Babylon itself was partly destroyed by the same conqueror and remained waste until it was partly rebuilt in 680 by Esarhaddon. Nineveh, the great capital of Assyria, was destroyed and disappeared for ever in 606 B.C. In the following century, 539 B.C., Cyrus conquered Babylon, and the Assyro-Babylonian dominion existed no more.

116. The appearance of Phœnician sea-going ships on the Persian gulf (*Narru Marratu*), was, over the crafts hitherto used there, a great improvement, which we may easily appreciate from the figures represented on the Monuments of the period[439]. They presented most probably also a serious advance, vouchsafed by 250 years of maritime experience, on the larger ships which had been employed by Hiram and Solomon. And they were probably also better fitted, as sea-going vessels for long journeys and rough weather, than those of the Sabæans. In any case they have proved to be a wholesome competition to the long enjoyed Monopoly of the latter, which the Assyrian Monarch seems to have had the project of

superseding. The attempt at an expedition in Arabia which was made in the last years of his reign, and was successful as far as it went, was a first effort to that effect, and show plainly that such were his intentions for the future. His submission of Addumu and Hagar (Hedjar) in the district of Bahrein, was the result of that campaign[440].

117. After the naval expedition of 695, and the prisoners carried back to Bab-salimeti, the sea-going ships of Sennacherib are heard of no more; then useless otherwise they must have been engaged in commercial pursuits in concurrence to the Sabæans, perhaps on the command of the Assyrian Monarch himself. It appears evident that these new competitors brought a good change in the sea-trading routine of the South Arabians.[441] Being partly deprived of their old trade, though not crushed since Sennacherib was prevented by death from pursuing his projects, but in fear of what might happen in the future, and unable to dislodge the newcomers, they made them their partners. The result was a great impulse to the previous navigation, and a large extension to the area within which they used to move. They vied between themselves for the discovery of new markets, and of places well fitted for the stations which Greek authors tell us it was their custom to establish[442]. The remotest station established by the Sabæans when they were alone, and which was probably Lanka (Ceylon) could henceforth be looked upon, but as a resting place which enabled them to start anew further in the East[443].

118. The disclosures from the Chinese side, described in our previous section, with their positiveness, permit us to complete these informal inferences derived chiefly from the western facts known to history. They show how far these daring traders and sailors less than twenty years afterwards had carried their enterprises. As a fact they did reach as far as it was possible to go. The Shantung peninsula[444] and its rough South coast stretching eastwards was a sufficient barrier to prevent them going further for about three centuries, and the gulf of Kiao-tchou, which we have noticed, (§ 103), was the best sea-port which could be found at proximity of the civilised part of China.

119. The character ethnologically mixed of these sea-merchants and sailors, should we not be aware of it otherwise, would be disclosed by the singular medley of innovations and items of western culture they introduced. Their influence in China continued for several centuries, but the nature of the notions they introduced altered gradually in course of time, and this change corresponded to that which had occurred at the fountain

head, as we shall see during the following period. At first the notions introduced were Syrian, such as that of stamping the currency and the use of the Mina of Kar Khemish,[445]; and Assyro-Babylonian, consisting in scraps of mythology and legends which the Chinese arranged and combined afterwards[446] with the stories preserved amongst them from the traditional heir-looms of the ancient Bak families ; the most important were numerous notions of Babylonian astrology, made of former scientific data diverted from their original purposes, often corrupt and fragmentary, with a strong tinge of Indian views[447].

And finally, i.e. at the end of the sixth century when the Persian had superseded the Babylonian empire, some notions of Mazdeism appeared.[448]

This transformation in the influence of the sea-traders in Shantung, resulting from and following the great events which happened at the fountain head of their trade, is certainly a most remarkable fact which deserves the attention of historians[449], and shows its veracity and genuineness.

NOTES——

427) Cf. note 414.—No other specimen of the same wood has been found in any other excavations in Assyro-Babylonia ; but in a tomb on the same spot, a truncheon made of bamboo, was discovered by the same Mr. J. E. Taylor, o.c.
428) A. H. Sayce, *Hibbert Lectures*, 1887, p. 138.—The matter is I think open to a great deal of suspicion. *Sadin* of the Old Testament is not derived from the name of *Sindu*, India, as long supposed on insufficient grounds. Cf. chapter VIII, below, the excursus on S a d î n and S a t i n.
429) Cf. W. St. C. Boscawen, *Notes on some Babylonian texts* : B.& O.R. IV, 57-59, where it is suggested to be some unwoven silk. Was it not some tusser silk from India?
430) Cf. below, the excursus on the S i n d u cloth, in chapt. VIII.—Cf. on *Sindu*, W.A.I. V, 28 : 19, 20 and 14 : 30 c ; II, 29 : 50 g; and in Brunn.'s List, 1799, 1951, 5500; and on *Parsindu*, W.A.I. I. 21 : 69, 70.
431) Cf. T. W. Rhys Davids, *Jâtaka Baveru*. Translated from the original Pâli. No. 339, and my additional note, in B.&O.R. Dec. 1889, vol. IV, pp. 7-9.—Prof. Minayeff thinks that the verses of the Jâtaka date from the beginning of the Christian era, while the prose text is attributed to Buddhagosha. Cf. *Bullet. Acad. Imper. d. Sciences d. St. Petersburg*, t. XVII, col. 77.
432) Cf. E. Rehatsek, *Emporia, chiefly ports of Arab and Indian international commerce, before the Christian era*, p. 134 : J.B.B.R.A.S., 1881, vol. xv.

433) Cf T. G. Pinches, *The Babylonians and Assyrians as Maritime nations*: B.&O.R., I, 41-42 ; T. de L., *An unknown king of Lagash*, par. 20-25 and notes 48-52, 75 : *ibid.* IV, 198-203.
434) Cf. G. Maspero, *Histoire Ancienne*. p. 451-2.
435) Cf. *suprà*, ch. VI, f. 4, § 93.
436) For this improved spelling of the name of Carchemish, Gargamish, &c. cf. Joachim Menant, on *Karkemish*, in the Mém. Acad. Inscript. et B.L., 1890, t. xxxii, p. 201, sq.
437) " *Mala'hé Ḉurrai Ḉidunnai Yavnai Kisidtai Qatáya*;" G. Smith, *History of Sennacherib*, p. 91, l. 59-60, and p. 92-95 ; F. Lenormant, *Origines de l'histoire*, III, 11.—The ships being still empty passed from the Tigris, through the Araktu canal to the Euphrates which they floated down to Ubua where the king and his army went on board, and by the Bab-salimeti mouth of the Euphrates they entered in the Gulf. The king offered from his ship a sacrifice to Ea the god of the ocean, and threw in the sea, as offerings, little figures of ships and fishes in gold. Cf. G. Smith, *History of Babylonia*, p. 128-131.—There are some doubts about the decipherment of the word *yavnai* which Mr. Boscawen reads as one of the names of Cyprus.
438) The place of landing and embarking on the sea shore are now all embedded by the alluvions of the rivers. Sennacherib's fleet went from the Euphrates to the sea in order to ascend the *Ulai* or *Eulæus* river of Elam, which at present disembogues in the Euphrates. Cf. W. K. Loftus, *Chaldæa and Susiana*, 1857, p. 281-282, 424-426.—J.R. G.S.. 1855, p. 55.—W. F. Ainsworth, *Travels and Researches in Asia-Minor, Mesopotamia, Chaldæa and Armenia*, 1842.—F. R. Chesney, *The Expedition for the Survey of the Rivers Euphrates and Tigris*, 1835-37.—H. C. Rawlinson, J.R.G.S., vol, XXVI, p. 136.— Rud. Credner, Ergängzungsheft zu *Peterman's Mittheilungen*, No. 56. —Fr. Delitzch, *Wo lag das Paradies*? 1881.—E. Reclus, *Geographie Universelle*, vol. IX, p. 406-408.—Eberh. Schrader, *Die Namen der Meer in den Assyrischen Inschriften* : Ak. d. W. z. Berlin, 1877.— W. F. Ainsworth, *A personal narrative of the Euphrates expedition*, 2 vol. 1888 ; *The River Karun*, 1890.
439) Cf. the ancient boats of Chaldea in J. Menant, *Glyptique Orientale*, vol. I. pp. 65-99. from the gems and cylinders, and in Lenormant-Babelon, *Histoire Ancienne*, edit. IX, vol. IV, p. 231, and vol. V, p. 105 and F. Vigouroux, *La Bible et les decouvertes modernes*, edit. IV, vol. III, p. 574, from the Sargon palace of Khorsabad; with those of Syrian built as figured at Nimroud, in Layard *Monuments*, vol. I, pp. 71.—On the small size of the ships, cf. my paper on *An Unknown king of Lagash*, n. 49, where I have neglected to notice the great maritime event of 697-695 B.C.—Let us remark that in the list of maritime terms of olden times published by T. G. Pinches in his paper on *The Babylonians and Assyrians as maritime nations*, l.c., there are no words referring to the sails of the ships, and therefore that the lists did not concern sea-going vessels.—Moreover it is well known that the Babylonians had no timber, and in case of extensive buildings, the timber required was brought from the outside.
440) Cf. G. Smith, *History of Sennacherib*, p. 167. The Assyrian suzerainty was extended by Esarhaddon. Cf. E. Budge, *The history of*

Esarhaddon, p. 54-65.—Fox Talbot, *The Second inscription of Esarhaddon* : Records of the Past, III, 116-117.—G. Maspero, *Histoire Ancienne*, p. 453-4.

441) In 601 B.C. Neko II of Egypt sent Phœnician ships around Africa, from the Red sea, a feat which could be more easily accomplished there than from the other side. On the credibility of the fact, cf. E. H. Bunbury, *History of Ancient Geography*, 1883, vol. I, p. 289-291 and 296.—G. Rawlinson, *Phœnicia*, 1889, p. 175-180.

442) Ex. Agatharchid. 102.—E. Rehatsek, *O.C.*, p. 120.

443) It is not impossible that they had yet reached P₁gu from Lanka and the sea-coasting of West India. Cf. *supra* § 114, and references.

444) It is not unlikely that the Chinese navy of later years has preserved some of the peculiarities of their ships, such for instance the two sculls at the stern. Another curious particularity is that of painting two eyes on the bow of the ship. We know that it was a frequent habit in the Phœnician navy, as shown by the figures of boats in terra cotta found at Amathonte and now in the New-York Museum (cf. Perrot-Chipiez, *Histoire de l'Art*, vol. III, p. 517, fig. 352). A late term in Assyro-Chaldæan written : wood+eye+boat, and read *pan elippi* (Brunn. *L st.* 9314) shows that the habit had been extended to the Erythræan sea-navy, probably in 697-695 B.C. The boats of the traders and colonists from the Erythræan sea, at Lang-ga and Tsimoh had apparently such eyes, as we find these eyes spoken of inthe fourth century B.C., and such boats designated as dragon boats. Cf. the *Muh Tien tze tchuen*, a work attributed to Lieh-tze, if not to one of his disciples. Hnai-Nan-tze in his *Pen king hiun*, (150 B.C.) speaks of the bow of the ships as made like a fish-hawk's head, *yh shou*. Yang hiung, about the Christian era confirms the statement, and so does Kwoh P'oh (A.D. 276-324). (Cf. *T'ai ping yü lan*, kiv. 769, f. 2 ; *Khang hi tze tien*, 196+10, *yh*, f. 74). On the modern practice in China, cf. John Barrow, *Travels in China*, 1804, p. 37 ; W. Williams, *Middle Kingdom*, I, 753.—The practice existed also in Egypt. Cf. G. Maspero, *Archéologie Egyptienne*, p. 285, fig. 265 representing a sailing boat of Ramses III (c. 1200 B.C).

445) Cf. T. de L., *Weights and Measures*, forming the ch. VII, of the Introduction to my *Catalogue of Ancient Chinese coins*.

446) We shall have to deal with this aspect of the question and endeavour to show some of the visible points of junction in their combined mythology and traditions, before the final conclusion of the present work. The fusion of the two sources of legends, and the points of contact which they had, but which have been the occasion by the Chinese historians of many unsupported assimilations, is an interesting but at the same, time a very difficult question.

447) Cf. *supra*, § 105-6, and *infra*.

448) Cf. *supra*, § 107, and *infra*.

449) Not a few items ought perhaps to have been entered during this period, but as in some cases the evidence is not dated on the Chinese side, they will be noticed further on.

120. No record in any form, historical or fabulous that I know of has been preserved of the route they followed[450]. The myth of the Five fortunate islands which we find connected with their sea-trade on the coast of Shantung, is the only legend which conceals some vague indications on as many stations where they used to land, and on which it was their wont[451] to give as little indications as possble.

121. But this fable is not the only source from which we may derive information on the matter. These sea-traders have left the name of *Lanka* in several places on their route from Ceylon to Shantung, a fact which we have already mentioned[452], and it is not unlikely that the name of their emporium *Tsih-me* or *Tsi moh* has preserved under its folk etymology of the region a souvenir of another name dear to them[453]. That they were a mixed party from West Asia, S. Arabia and India, is ascertained, as we have shown from the hybrid character of the notions they introduced into China[454]. In our survey of the next period this will come still more prominently, and we shall have to record traces of their influence which perhaps belong to the present period, but are not as yet sufficiently ascertained as to their date.

122. The legend of the Five Fortunate isles, is a combination of the Hindu fable of the *Kurma avatâra*,[454b] with some other Brahmanical notions, and a memory of five places where the traders of the Indian Ocean used to put up before reaching the coasts of Shantung. The story is told by Lich-tze[455], who gives the names of the five islands as follows: 1) *Tai yü*; 2) *Yüen kiao*; 3) *Fang hu*; 4) *Yng-tchou*; and 5) *Pêng-lai*[456], east of *Puh-hai* (which is the gulf of Pehtchihli),[457] inhabited by Rishis (*sien shing*) whom an elixir of immortality, called *tze-mai*[458] (or Soma) preserved from old age and death. Through the machinations of giants from Lungpak, who were at proximity of the Fairy isles, and as a subsequent punishment were reduced to dwarfishness, two of the isles drifted northwards and sank in the sea.—The story is full of historical memories as we shall see further on.

123. The Maritime intercourse, which by the sailors' tales, had given rise to this fable, seems to have come to an end before the middle of the fourth century at least so far as the Shantung coasts are concerned; but it may have lasted some time longer with the Southern region of Tchehkiang coasts which were then in possession of the state of Yueh, who had her capital city at Lang-ya from 472 until 380 B.C., where it

withdrew southwards, because of the internecine wars then raging. This cessation is shown by the fact that after that time, Chinese rulers made repeated efforts to discover the three fairy isles remaining and their elixir of immortality. But having no navy, their maritime expeditions could never go far from the Chinese coasts[459]. Szema Tsien records that these expeditions began under the reign of King Wei of TS'I who ruled until 332 B.C. and were continued under his successor Sitten of TS'I, 332-313 B.C., and under King Tchao of YEN, 311-278 B.C.[460]. TS'IN She Hwang-ti himself yielded to the temptation[461], as we shall see in a later page, and the folly continued during the Former Han dynasty[462].

124. Although no identification has hitherto been attempted with the names mentioned in the above legend, we may venture to remark that, considering the circumstances of the case, namely that having been spoken of by the foreign traders of the Indian Ocean, with Brahmanical references otherwise unheard of in China, they ought to have preserved the memory of early settlements of Brahmanical Hindus in the Indian seas, or at least of places where the Hindu traders who told the story, used to put up in their onward journey. We have seen in a previous part that maritime expeditions from the eastern coast of India were already made circà 500 B.C. and perhaps earlier[463].

125. We may recognize in *Fang-hu* the name of *Bangka*, which is still at present applied with an epithet to several places about the South-eastern end of Sumatra, and is preserved alone in that of the Banca island, in the same region[464]. A variant was Fang-tchang, (anciently *Ban-tan*) which reminds us of Bantam for *Bantan*, a name of the Western end of Java.[465] The other of the Chinese names *Pêng-lai* is so much alike that of the country called *Poli* (Pali, Pari or Bari) which is said by all the Chinese geographers to be the Northern coast of Sumatra, and its neighbourhood to the Nicobar islands[466], that we have only to register it. *Yng-tchou*, which means literally 'island of the great sea' cannot be identified by the same process of onomastics, and a suggestion as to what place it was applied, may only result from further researches in all the circumstancial evidence of the case[467].

Notes——

450) A proof that sea-traders were going in high seas considerably south, is given by the astronomical statements coming from them, which Nearchos and Onesicritos have reported. Cf. on this interesting question, the just remarks of E. H. Bunbury, *History of Ancient Geography*, vol. I, p. 535.

Soma, 'the ancient intoxicating beverage of the Vedic Rishis. which
451) We know that such was the case with the Phœœnicians for their
journeys to the Cassiterides.
452) Cf. *suprà* VI, c, § 44.—On the coins which they issued there about
675 B.C. cf. my *Catalogue of Chinese coins*, p. lxv, 214.
453) Cf. the following series where the ancient names are in italics :
Sephar (Gen. X, 30) ; *Saphir* regia, *Sapphar* methopolis, *Sabe* regia,
Safar (near Sana) *Zafar* (Mahra), Zafar (Mirbat), all in S. Arabia;
Sofala (E. coast of Africa) ; *Suppara* (W. coast of India); *Sumatra*
(Indian Archipelago) ; *Samaradè* (E. Malacca peninsula) ; and *Tsimoh* (Shantung). The latter was written at first *Tsieh Mo* (Bas. 1026-50).
454) The mountain near the gulf of Kiao tchou is and was called *Lao shan* (Bas. 907-2275). The *Shan hai king*, last additions, kiv. 9, f.
3 r., states that near it were Black people. Does not this refer to the
swarthy complexion of the settlers and sea-traders of the Indian
Ocean?
454^b) The Kurma Avatâra as well as the Matsya Avatâra originally belonged
to Brahma. Cf. Muir, *Sanskrit texts*, IV, 923. Afterwards to
Vishnu.
455) Lieh tze, V. 3, who wrote (c. 397 B.C.) to the following effect : In
the east of Puh-hai,......were five mountains ;—As they were not fixed
by their base, they were floating up and down with the tide. The
holy men inhabiting them, annoyed, petitioned to God (*Ti*) who, in his
displeasure had left the islands float loose to the extreme west with all
their occupants. Then he ordered *Yü Kiang* (a god on which cf. §
178) to send fifteen huge turtles which raising their heads supported
the islands each three times alternately for 60000 years at every change.
The five islands then did not move away. But in the country of
Lung-peh (Lung-bak) were men of so enormous a stature that with a few
steps they could reach the five islands, and take them at one fell swoop.
They attached together six of the turtles and carried them away. Two
of the islands *Tai yü* and *Yüen Kiao* drifted towards the extreme No<u>rt</u>h
and sank in the high sea. The immortals who were thus carried away,
were more than 100000 individuals. God dissatisfied and in anger
reduced the people of Lung-peh to the size of dwarfs. Since the days
of Fuh-hi and Shen-nung these men had been some ten tchangs high
....On the islands, from the observatories one can see birds and beasts
in gold and jade, also trees of pure white coral, all growing and living;
there also is a juicy dainty (*tze-wei*, Bas. 5161-1191, anc. *tze-mai*) which
as a food prevents old age and death. (Instead of dying) the *rishis*
(who have taken it) fly and wander for a day and a night and then return (to their body).—Cf. *Shan hai king*, kiv. 12, f. 4, gloss ; *T.P.
Y.L.*, kiv. 38, f. 8.
456) *Tai yü*, Bas. 2293-10937.—*Yüen Kiao*, Bas. 1246-2358.—*Fanghu*, Bas. 3826-1764.—*Yng tchou* 5338-4968.—*Pêng-hai*, 9127-9092.
457) Eastwards because the starting was made in that direction. For
instance India, by the sea-route, was east of the Chinese coast. Cf.
Shan Hai king.
458) The Chinese expression which is difficult to translate by itself,
juicy-tasty, in its sound *tze-mai* seems to me a clear rendering of

was believed to bestow immortality.' *Rig-veda*, VIII, 48, 3: 'We drank Soma, we became immortal, we went to the light, we found the gods;' VIII, 48, 12. Cf. F. Max Müller, *India, What can it teach us?* p. 224.—Careful and hitherto unsuccessful researches have been made in the Hindu-kush and the Oxus valley after the modern representative of the divine Soma plant "which the priest knows." Cf. R. Roth, *Z.&D.M.G.* xxv, 680-692; M-Müller, *Biographies of words*, p. 222 sq.; O. Schrader, *Prehistoric Antiquities of the Aryan peoples*; p. 326.

459) In the second century, Chinese ships could not go much beyond the extreme point of the Shantung peninsula. Cf. *She ki*, iv. 28, f. 38.

460) *She ki*, kiv. 28, f. 11 v.—The King Wei of Ts'i had begun his reign in 378 B.C.—M. Edouard Chavannes, in his translation of this chapter, *Le traité sur les Sacrifices Fong et Chan de Se ma Ts'ien*, 1890, p. 25 n. has mistaken the first Siuen of Ts'i, for the second, and therefore given wrong dates.

461) *She ki*, kiv. 28, f. 12.

462) Namely in 133, 111, 109, 101, &c. B.C.

463) Cf. *suprà*, ch. VI, sect. *e*, div. 3. par. 64, 93, 114, 117.

464) Cf. J. Crawfurd, *Descriptive Dictionary of the Indian islands*, p. 31. Meaning of the name unknown.

465) Cf. J. Crawfurd, *O.C.*, p. 38.

466) Cf. W. P. Groeneveldt, *Notes on the Malay Archipelago and Malacca*, compiled from Chinese sources, Batavia, 1876, p. 80-84, for the statement that all the Chinese geographers make it to be the Northern coast of Sumatra, and its neighbourhood to the Nicobar islands. In the *Liang shu* A.D. 502-556, the kingdom of Poli is said to be 50 days broad and 20 days from North to South. So large a country cannot be the present island of *Bali* as proposed by Prof. L. de Rosny in *Les Peuples Orientaux connus des Anciens Chinois*, 1386, p. 141.—Lombok, near Bali, has been so called by Europeans, cf. J. Crawford, *Descriptive Dictionary*, p. 219.

467) Wang T'ai, of the third century, in his geographical work *Kwah ti tchi* has suggested the island called *Tan tchou* i.e. the isle of Quelpaerts, south of Corea.—There are however some variants of the name which are quoted in the *San fu hwang tu*, kiv. 4. f. 5 : *Hwan-tchou* (Bas. 6024-968) and *Hwen tchou* (Bas. 12751-4968) which suggest an imitation of a foreign name. There are also in the same work some variants for the two other islands: *Fang-hu* or *Fang-tchang* is also called *Lwan-wei* (Bas. 2875-7296); *Pêng-lai* is also called *Yun-shuh* (Bas. 11952-4099) and *Fang kiu* (Bas. 11756-17) but these names are descriptive. *Pêng-lai* is also said there to have on its east the *Yü-Y* (Bas. 12732-1808) or Barbarians of Kwangsi, suggesting thus an identification with the isle of Hainan.

126. The ascertained presence of Negrito-Pygmies in Indonesia from the Andaman to the Philippine islands, in juxtaposition to other races of men, is certainly a further point showing the truth of the story. Nowhere is the contrast more striking than between the Nicobarese and the Andamanese, living as they do in islands not very far distant in the Bay of Bengal. In the *Lung-pak* of the Chinese legend with its giant in habitants, we recognize without difficulty an approximate rendering of the old name of the Nicobar[468] islands and their tall sized occupants [169]; while the dwarfs of the story are the Negrito-Pygmies [170] of the two Great and Little Andaman islands in the north. And in the denomination of *Agathou daimonos nêsos* or Isle of good fortune, which the latter bear in Ptolemy, it is difficult not to recognize an echo of the same legend of the Fortunate islands which have reached the Chinese[471]. The part of the story which concerns the disparition of two of the fortunate islands in the North, through the machinations of the Lung-pak people, refers most probably to the behaviour of the Nicobarese[472], skilful as they are in the management of their canoes, who used to cut off many sailing ships. The two islands, Andaman and Nicobar, which form really two groups but appear as only two islands in Ancient relations [473], were thus lost as revictualling places for their ships, and the Ancient sea-traders were compelled to sail direct to *Pêng-lai*, i.e. Pali, the North of Sumatra. Hence they proceeded to the China sea through the strait of Malacca, the only one opened to them, since the Sunda strait which has been erroneously called the great portal of the Eastern Archipelago in Antiquity, between *Bangka*, or S. Sumatra, and *Bantam* or W. Java, and the Alas strait, were not yet opened, according to the Javanese records[474] recently published. Such is undoubtedly the truth or very nearly the truth which underlies the Legend of the Five fortunate islands, which was already known in China in the fourth century B.C.[475].

127. The remarkable feats of energy and bold enterprise which carried the sea-traders from the Arabian sea and the gulf of Bengal to the Shantung shores, during three centuries, disappeared without leaving

many more traces of their passage, than those we have recorded[476]. Their scanty tales concerning their route were passing to mythology in the middle of the fourth century, and no sea-faring crafts acquainted with their art of navigation seem to have remained behind them. The more convenient route through Indo-China had diverted the traffic.

128. The civilised Chinese, consistently with their inland habitat, before and after their settlement in the Flowery land, were not a maritime nation. They were well acquainted with river boating[477], but at the time we have reached in their history, the sea-shores included in their dominion had not permitted them as yet to develop a navy; and when the sea-farers of the Indian Ocean created their establishments on the Shantung coast, they deprived them of the opportunity of doing so. Thus when after the cessation of the maritime intercourse by the latter, the Chinese princes wanted themselves to send expeditions in search of the Fortunate islands, they had no sailors nor ships at their disposal to sail on the high sea. Their river boats could only crawl along the coasts[478].

129. The truth became apparent when at the end of the second century B.C., the extension of the Chinese empire towards the sea shores of Tchehkiang, and the non-submission of the native states of these parts, called the attention of the great Emperor HAN Wu-ti to the matter. The native populations of the S.E. coasts were "practised in aquatic warfare and skillful in the management of boats[479];" they had sea-going ships which the Chinese had not; perhaps had they learned something from the old sea-traders, although the state of uncivilisation of their country did not succeed to make it an attractive and lasting market for them. In order to incite maritime skilfulness and adventure, the Emperor who had placed in an artificial pond of Tchang-ngan his capital in 119 B.C., some figurations of the Fortunate islands each supported by its huge turtle[480], placed in another a sea-going ship of the model known in the S. East, about which all sorts of wonderful stories have been told[481]. This circumstance denotes the beginning of the Chinese navy. Maritime enterprise developed afterwards[482], and we hear no more of the Fortunate islands, which only ignorance and incapacity could have maintained in the common belief until that time.

NOTES——

468) Cf. *Long-pak* with *Lanka Barusae* of Ptolemy, *Lanka Bálús*, of the Arabs, *Láka ráram* of Rashid-eddin, *Necu veram* of Marco Polo, with the modern *Nicobar* of the Europeans and *Nancowry* of the natives. On these names cf. H. Yule, *Marco Polo*, vol. II, 290, and *Notes on*

the oldest Record of the sea Route to China, 1882, p. 7.
469) There are several races of them, but no Negritos. And they are somewhat like populations of Pegu and Burma.
470) On these Negrito-pygmies, known as Mincopies, the best work is that of E. H. Man, *The Aboriginal Inhabitants of the Andaman islands*, 1884.—A. de Quatrefages, *Les Pygmées*, 1887, has analysed all the data concerning them, pp. 98, 129-208.
471) Col. Yule *l.c.* has suggested that the name of Andaman unknown on the spot, may have been adopted from a transcript of the same name in Greek *Ag-daimon*.
472) We might perhaps detect in the legend, a fainted recollection of the occupation of the Nicobar islands by some settlers of the continent, who being skilful mariners as they are still at present interfered with the foreign ships, while the Negritos who have little knowledge of seafaring were not pirate rovers.
473) Cf. H. Yule, *Marco Polo*, vol. II, p. 290.
474 The straits of Malacca, which were still unknown to Ptolemy were thus passed through by these early travellers.—Prof. J. W. Judd, in *The Eruption of Krakatao* (Royal Society, 1888), p. 7, has called attention to an important statement of the Pristaka Raja, i.e. the " Book of Kings " of the Javanese, which work containing the chronicles of the Island, and kept secret during centuries in the Royal Archives, was only recently made public. It describes a tremendous eruption which occurred on the same spot in the year 338 Saka, i.e. A.D. 416, and it concludes by the following statement: '*This is the origin of the separation of Sumatra and Java.*'—The fact explains away many difficulties, in the geographical history of the region.—J. Crawfurd, *Descr. Dict.* p. 184, had noticed a favourite notion with Javanese chronologists that the islands of Sumatra, Java, Bali, Lombok and Sumbawa formed at one time a continuous land, and they Assign precise dates preposterously modern, to the separations, viz. Sumatra from Java in 1192, Bali from Java 1282, and Lumbok from Sumbawa in 1350. The dates therefore require correction.
475) We have thus been led far in advance of any disclosure of Archœological research in the Iudian Archipelago. The oldest colony from Kalinga, in Java, is spoken of in B.C. 75, but the fact is ill ascertained although extremely probable. The old Kalinga country embraced Orissa, and we have seen by the researches of E. Forchhammer, that the colonists in Pegu about 500 B.C. had come from there. (Cf. *suprâ* VI, *e*, iii, 64). Some other sources existed in Ancient Chinese literature, than the legend of the Five fortunate islands, about the route of the old sea-traders who came to Shantung. This is shown by the variant *Fang-tchang* or *Fang-hu*, two distinct names, and by the following fact. In 104 B.C. *Han* Wu-ti among other extravagances built the palace of *Kien tchang* at Tchang-ngan (cf. *San-fu hwang tu*, kiv. 4, f. 5) north of which he made a large pond called *Ta-yh* (Bas. 1797-5020) where the Fortunate islands were figured, supported each by their large turtle (*suprâ* note 455). Four names are given by Szema Tsien (*She ki*, kiv. 28, f. 44),.viz. the three named (*suprâ*, § 122), 3, 4, 5, and *Hu-liang* (Bas. 1764-4257). The latter is too much alike the name of *Ho-ling*, Chinese transcription of Kaling, the name

given to Java by its Kalinga colonists, not to suggest an acquaintance with that name in the Chinese traditions of the period, either from the colony in question or from the mother-land in India.

476) Some wonderful notions derived from the foreign sailors of Shantung have found a place in the later books of the *Shan hai king*. For instance in the sixth book concerning the Maritime south. (f. 3) we are told that every one in the Cross legged's state was one of the *Puh sze min*, or People of Immortals, who were of a black colour and lived for ever without dying. In the fifteenth book concerning the remote south, we hear again of the same people (f. 2v.) an I we are told 'that their name was O.—In the *Khang hi tze tien*, s.v. *sze*, death (78+3, f. 33 v.) other quotations refer to the same myth. One about the *yuen k'u shan*, probably a corruption of the name of the second of the Fortunate islands (*suprà* § 122), where a shrub of immortality grew, which statement is completed by a gloss of Kwoh poh. Another refers to a *Tsu tchou* (Bas. 7017-2381) an island of the sea where grows a grass of immortality (Lin mêng Kwei).—Other passages of the *Shan hai king* refer to Sheng-tu (India) in the East (cf. note 497), for the big bamboos of Indonesia (cf. note 477); kiv. xv, 2v., refers to a race of spirit-men called *Puh-t'ing-hu-yü*, in the Southern Ocean ; they had a human face, wearing as earrings two green serpents, and treading on two red serpents, obviously a notion of Indian imagery. Cf. below.

477) They were acquainted with the skin-boats, *Kufas* or coracles of Anterior Asia. Cf. *suprà*, ch. IV, *a*, 18.— For a definition under the Han dynasty. Cf. *Tung kwan Han ki* of A.D. 170. *T.P.Y.L.* kiv. 769, f. 1.—Numerous inventors of the Wood-boat are mentioned: Hwang-ti, Yao and Shun hollowed trees to make boats; and they cut others long and thin to make oars (*Hi-tze*, II, 16, App. III of *Yh king*).—Kungku and Ho-tih, Officers of Hwang-ti hollowed trees to make boats (*Shi pên*).— Kung-tchui *(Meh-tze*), Yü ko (*Lu she Tchun tsiu*), Pan-yü (*Shan-hai king* 1, 8, 5), Hwa Kwa (*Wuh li lun*), Peh yng (Shuh sih, *Fei Mêng ki*), are each mentioned in these authorities as *the* first maker of boats. Cf. *T.P.Y.L.*, kiv. 768, f. 7 and 769, f. 2 ; *Khang hi tze tien*, s.v.—These fabulous statements suggest that hollowing a tree was the process of making boats among the natives of China like in early Europe, but there is no other statements to that effect than those quoted here. In the *Shan hai king*, kiv. 9, f. 1, it is said that in the country of the Tall men (*Ta jen kwoh*) they hollowed out (*sioh* : Bas. 794) boats ; but this fabulous country was somewhere along the eastern coasts of Corea. In Northern Tibet, M. G. Bonvalot, *Across Thibet*, vol. I, 1891, has seen such boats.— In the *Shan hai king* kiv. 17, f. 1, an allusion is made to bamboos large enough to make boats, growing in the fields of the Wei hills which are not identified and belong to romantic geography. The notion of such bamboos had come to the author from the sea-traders of Indonesia, where it is a fact, that boats are made of a section of bamboo between two knots. Ctesias had already spoken of them. C. Acosta in his *Tractado de las Drogas....de las Indias Orientales*, (Burgos, 1578) f, 296 mentions those of Malabar. And Clusius had seen two large specimens brought from the Indian Archipelago in the University of Leyden. (Cf. Yule-Burnell, *Glossary of Anglo-Indian Words*, p. 41-42). But such boats have

never been made in China (because bamboos wide enough do not grow there), and the statement to the contrary in G. Schlegel, *Uranographie Chinoise* p. 347, is based upon the fanciful work of Ogilby, who has applied to China, the very words of Christ. Acosta referring to Malabar.—River boating is mentioned by the Chinese records since their beginnings. Neglecting the references to single boats, there are some interesting cases worth noticing. When Wu Wang, founding the TCHOU dominion, invaded the country then ruled by the Yn dynasty, he crossed the Ho river on forty-seven boats provided by Liu Shang. (Cf. *Tai kung luh tao* ; T.P.Y.L., kiv. 778, f. 6). And when TS'IN made its campaign against TS'U, one thousand river boats large and small, were built for that purpose. *Shuh wang pên ki* ; (T.P.Y.L., kiv. 769, f. 2).
478) The expedition of Siu fu seems to have reached unwillingly the Corean island of Quelpaert.
479) Memorial of Yen-tou to the Emperor in 134 B.C. (cf. *Tsien Han shu*, kiv. 64 ; Trsl. Wylie, p. 37). Concerning the populations of Min Yueh, i.e. Fuhkien.
480) Cf. note 455.
481) It was called a Yü tchang (Chinese name of the S.E. region) boat and was said to carry a myriad of men (*Miao k'i*).—The *San fu ku sze* says that there were several of them, battle-ships and ten storied boats, in the pond of Kwen-ming. Cf. *San fu hwang tu*, kiv. 4, f. 3-4.
482) The progresses of this navy were however very slow. During the first Han dynasty, one thousand kin, i.e. about fifteen tons, was enormous for a boat. Cf. *T.P.Y.L.*, kiv. 768, f. 7, v. In the third century, according to the statements of the *Wei tchi* (*San kwoh tchi*) Maritime intercourse was carried from the gulf of Petchili to S. Corea and Japan ; from then to the Liu kiu islands (the country of the Pygmies or *Tchu ju*) ; hence in the S.E., after a year of navigation, the ships reached as extreme limit the Lo or naked men country (Nicobar) and the *Heh-tchi* or Black teeth country (where they chew betel). Beyond the sea of *Kwei-ki*, i.e. Tchehkiang, were the *Tong-ti jen* forming more than twenty (not 2000 as wrong in Ma Tuanlin) states (the Philippine islands, &c.) From *Kwei-ki* and from *Tung-ye* (Fuh kien) one could not reach Tan tchou i.e. Quelpaert, and Y tchou, i.e. Japan?, except when carried away by the winds, and coming back was difficult; but people from there used to come to Kwei-ki for trade purposes.— The statement of the *Hou Han shu*, that Japan situated in the east of Kwei-ki and Tung-ye, was near Tchu-yai and Tan-erh (i.e. the Hai-nan island), can thus be understood, since it was by way of Japan that the ships used to sail south. The part played by Japan under this respect is interesting, as the navy in question was foreign to the country ; and Prof. Basil Hall Chamberlain, in the introduction (p. xxv) of his translation of the *Kojiki*, has remarked that even so late as the middle of our tenth century, navigation was in a very elementary stage and the art of sailing was but little practised by the Japanese. Mr. E. Bonar, *On Maritime enterprise in Japan* : Trans. As. Soc. Japan, 1887, xv 103-125, has concluded from his special researches that, until a far later period than the end of the IXth cent., rowing was all the Japanese knew about navigation. The attention paid to the ships of Funam (Cambodge and Siam) which visited the Chinese Coast in our third

century, and are noticed in the *Wu shi Wai kwoh tchuen* is interesting under that and other respects. They were wooden ships of twelve *sin* long (about 96 feet) and six feet wide ; having in front and behind the form of a head and a tail of a fish; cramp irons made them stronger, and they were large enough to carry one hundred men ; the men had oars long and short, and also poles; and they were thus fifty, or more than forty, from stem to stem on each side of the ship ; they used their oars according to the necessities of their course ; when seated they used their shorter oars ; in case of shallow waters they all used their poles, and in pushing off, they all sang together as a single man, (Cf. *T.P.Y.L.*, 769, f. 5.)

c) *Influences from the South West and the beginning of Taoism.*

130. We have seen in a previous part that *Shou-mi* traders of the west centre of Yunnan, who came to the Chinese court about 1100 B.C., had relations with India ;[483] but nothing whatever is known of the frequency and nature of these relations. From the Burmese sources,[484] we have learned that Hindu colonists under the leadership of the Indian prince, Abhirâja, coming through the inland Route, had settled at the old Tagoung on the Irawady, three centuries before the time of Gautama, therefore about 800 B.C. ; and also that a second colony, about 500 B.C. had come by the same route and settled like the first on the banks of the same river, but on the eastern side and at another place ;[485] while the first colonists by sea did not come from Orissa to Pegu previously to 500 B.C.[486] There is decidedly no evidence that any outside communications have been established there by the sea trade[487] previously to that time, and any speculation based on the existence of such an early trade, as we made once before, is unsafe and probably wrong.[488]

131. The important and well stated fact is that inland communications existed between the central North of India and Burma in the eighth century, and communications from them, directly or indirectly through the itinerant traders of Shub, became henceforth possible with central China, where was the great and Semi-Chinese state of Ts'u. There is no historical record that such latter communications took place, but we are justified in assuming that they did, by the influence produced in philosophical literature, superstitions and practices,[489] and perhaps also on some archæological remains in the South-west,[490] influence which could come but from

India direct or through them. This influence was one from Brahmanism, and beginning about 6C0 B.C. lasted until the last quarter of the third century B.C. when it was superseded by Buddhism, as we shall have occasion to show farther on. As the symptoms of archæology and superstitions appear more clearly during the next period, we must refer to that time our survey of their historical and ethnological character.[491]

132. On two distinct points, the S.W. influence came to its full effect during the fourth period, one concerning material progress, the other philosophy. The sea-traders of the Indian Ocean settled at Tsih-moh, had introduced about 675 B.C. the western system of stamping the actual currency,[492] which in China happened to consist of small bronze implements of daily use, while in the West it consisted of ingots of useless shape. Some seventy-five years later, more precise notions of the Western System of coinage than heretofore, reached China ; but then it came through from the inland south and reached the state of TS'U, where small ingots of bronze, bean shaped as the old Lydian coins, and stamped, were issued by Sun Shuh-ngao for his prince TS'U Tchwang wang, about 600 B.C. They are known in native numismatics under several soubriquets, the best appropriate being that of Metallic cauries (*Ho pei tsien*), because their shape suggested that of the once useful little shells they superseded.[403] This precised notion differing from that introduced and entertained in the east of China, cannot have reached the southernmost of the Chinese states otherwise than from the south, and most apparently from the west through the Indian route, inasmuch as it seems probable that the earliest cast copper coins of India, cut bits and bean shaped date from that time.[494]

133. A western contrivance which was introduced about the same age is that of the *Kao*[495] to draw water from a well. What it was exactly must be inferred from the description handed down by Tchwang tze of the fourth century B.C., quoting the words of Confucius and of one of his disciples about it,[496] which correspond exactly to the *shaduf* as we see it figured on a slab of Sennacherib,[497] and on Ancient Monuments of Egypt.[498]

NOTES——

483) Cf. *suprà*, ch. vi, sect. *d*, § 46, and also note 422 on the name of the monkey they brought with them.

484) The historical writings of the Burmese have been pronounced by the great authority of Lassen " to deserve on the whole the praise of credibility." (*Indische Alterthumskunde*, vol. IV, p. 369) ; a judgment fully endorsed by Sir Arthur P. Phayre, in his *History of Burma*, 1883, p. vii.

485) Cf. *suprd*, ch. VI, sect. *e*, div. 3, § 65.
486) Cf. *suprà*, ch. VI, sect. *e*, div. 3, § 64, and references there to the researches of the lamented Dr. Em. Forchhammer. We shall see later on, that it was this inland route which in the IVth century supplanted the sea-trade to Shantung.
487) Of course there is no impossibility to the fact, but we do not find any traces of it, and the statement *suprà* (ch. VI, sect. f. div. 4, § 93) that the sea-trade of the Arabian Sea and the Bay of Bengal seems to have begun during the third period (1100-770 B.C.) is far too positive. I have now found that the Ring money of China referred to there was a western notion most probably introduced by the TCHOU and established by them in 1091, (or the 1032 B.C. of the Bamboo Annals) and probably heard of again by TCHOU Muh wang during his expedition in the West of China. (Cf. *Introduction to the Catalogue of Chinese Coins*, ch. I, Ann. 1103-1032-1091). It was not due to the sea-trade neither of the South nor of the East.
488) Dr. J. Edkins, in the papers noticed *supra*, note 378, had assumed the existence of such maritime communications since an early date, and the presence of the Chinese in the South of China proper at the same time, but both these assumptions are historical errors, unsupported by any evidence of any kind.
489) It might be asked if the *Shindu* cloth or textile which is mentioned in the Assyrian inscriptions since the time of Assurnatsirpal (883-858 B.C.) does not refer to silk and to the name of India, hence to Chinese silk imported through India. We shall examine the question in a special excursus of chapter VIII.
490) Let us mention here:—1⁰, the horse-shoe shape of the tombs which spread from the south up to Corea, and which is clearly a figure of the *Yoni*. It was already practiced in the time of Confucius, but not as a general custom. (Cf. *Li ki*, T'an kung, I. (3) 26). On those of Corea, cf. W. R. Carles, *Life in Corea*. 1883.—2⁰) the *Wa kan* pillars, on which more below.
491) Below, part III, sect. B of the present chapter.
492) Cf. *suprà* § 104.
493) Cf, my paper on *The Metallic cauries of Ancient China*, 1888 ; J.R.A.S., vol. xx, p. 428-439 ;—*Catalogue of Chinese coins from the British Museum*, 1892, p. xii, liii, and Nos. 1575-8.
494) Cf. Sir Alex. Cunningham, *The Ancient Coins of India*, 1891, p. 54-60.—Edward Thomas, *Ancient Indian weights*, 1874, had remarked that in numismatic finds, these Indian coins were old and worn, while the Greek coins found with them look quite fresh. Cf. p. 55, sq.— According to V. A. Smith, *Græco-Roman influence on the civilisation of Ancient India* : J.A.S.B., 1890, vol. lviii, they were thought at first to belong to a much older period.
495) Bas. 4452.—In Khang-hi tze tien, 75+11, f. 89 : a machine to draw water from a well.—*Shwoh wen*, id.—Medhurst, *Chin. Engl. Dict.* p. 396 : An implement for drawing water by pulley.—The preceeding description is perhaps somewhat stretched. Joined with another word, *Kieh-kao* (Bas. 4236-4452) it is translated in Basile : Putei machina seu cylindrus.—In W. Williams, *Syll. Dict.* p. 325 : A well-sweep; they are much used in irrigating lands near rivers in the Northern

provinces. Also a water-wheel worked by the feet.—J. Eitel, *Chin. Dict.*, p. 268: A windlass over a well.—These various descriptions show that the original *Kao*, was different.—The water-wheel now so extensively used in China, and which is much like those of Syria, and the *North* of Persia, is said to have been invented by Ma Kiun of the fourth century, who is supposed to have heard about it from India. Cf. *suprá*, note 209. An accurate drawing of one of these wheels is given in Stanton's account of Earl Macartney's embassy, vol. II, p. 480. There are two appliances of that kind used in China, the chain pump, and the bamboo water-wheel. Cf. J. F. Chinese, *The Chinese*, 1844, vol. III, p. 80-84.—John Barrow, *Travels in China*, 1804, p. 540.

496) Cf. Tchwang tze, kiv. xii, § 11 : Tze kung coming from *Ts'u* and arriving North of the Han river where it was not known (therefore in Honan W.) describes it to a gardener : 'It is a lever made of wood, heavy behind, and light in front.' And in kiv. xiv, § 4, Confucius says : "When it is pulled, it bends down ; and when it is let go, it rises up." Cf. *Sacred Books of the East*, vol. xxxix, p. 320, 353.

497) Cf. G. Rawlinson, *Herodotus*, 1875, vol. I, p. 315.—Layard, *Nineveh and Babylon*, p. 109.

498) The Egyptian *shaduf*. An early Akkadian collection of agricultural proverbs say : 'The irrigation machine he puts together ; the bucket he hangs, and the water he will draw up.' A. H. Sayce, *Herodotus*, p. 111.—In Akkadian it was written *id-lal* 𒄑𒋗 haudbalance, in Assyrian *dulati*. Cf. W.A.I. II, 14, l. 17. Also Brunnow, *List* 6624.—Wilkinson, *Manners and Customs of the Ancient Egyptians*, I, p. 53, and II, p. 4.

* *

134. It was by the same route that Hindu thought and philosophical speculations were brought to the cognizance of the Chinese. in the VIth century, B.C. Li Lao Tan or Lao-tze, "the old one," once Keeper of the Royal Archives of the Tchou dynasty, worked undoubtedly upon Hindu ideas and suggestions[499] when he taught to his disciples, his *Tao teh King*, a work unique in character, and the most abstruse of Ancient Chinese literature. Established at first in the state of *Ts'u*, the southernmost of the Chinese states, whose geographical position was commanding all intercourse with the South-west, he had every facility to be acquainted with the above ideas; and as suggested by the late journey to India attributed to him in his legend, he may have travelled westwards, at least as far as the *Shuh* country, which was in direct communication with the land of the Brahmans, or travelled to India himself, unless he be himself a foreigner from those parts,[500] which case, if established, would solve many difficulties. He quotes himself from older works, but not in the usual Chinese way of referring to Antiquity.[501]

135. Several copies of his teachings, varying in accuracy, completed-

ness, and subsequent additions, out of which has been edited the present work about the third century B.C., seem to have circulated at first between his disciples. The text has obviously suffered in the transcriptions of one style of writing to another,[302] but on the whole, the work can be safely looked upon as authentic.[303] It has been translated a dozen of times into European languages.[304] But the literature of the work, both Chinese and European, appears to indicate[305] that a knowledge of the language and a philosophical training do not suffice to gain a correct understanding of it.

136. According to probabilities Lao Tan was of foreign extraction, and the Chinese writers of later ages have been unsuccessful in their attempts at putting a clearly Chinese complexion on the few statements which posterity has handed down about him. He was an exceedingly clever man, already grey haired when he appeared, in the state of TS'U, the great principality which was then commanding all possible intercourse with the South and South-west. Since 604 B.C. was the date of his birth (probably following his own statement), he ought to have appeared not before 540 B.C., and his designation of *Lao-tze*, the 'Old one' was derived from that. He was besides qualified of *Tchung erh* or 'Doubled eared,' and also of *Tan* or 'Flat eared,' from the circumstances that he had long ears pierced (in the fashion of the Shans and Burmese), a peculiarity which suggests that he may have come from the region in Burma where Abhirrja had established his Brahmanical settlement two centuries before[306] and where this custom obtained[307]. His alleged surname *Li* (plum) may also be argued as suggesting the southern origin of Lao Tan : he selected it himself and it was not a Chinese surname before his time[308].

137. Szema Tsien in his short biography of the great philosopher, knew nothing of his birth, and about his death says that it was not known when and where he died.[509] He states however that he was a man of TS'U, who become keeper of the Archives of TCHOU (at Loh-yang) where he was visited by Confucius in 517 B.C. ; he relates the conversation of the two great men,[510] and how, when he had resigned his post, and going away through the (Han-ku) passage (of S.W. Honan, therefore going westwards) he left with the keeper of the gate his work of a little over 5000 words in two parts on the *Tao* and *Teh*.[511] Therefore there is sufficient ground to assume that Lao Tan, the Old long eared man, was a foreigner who came and settled in China for a certain time. Considering the facilities offered to Szema Tsien and his father for collecting their information, and the interest which Szema Tsien himself dis-

plays for Taoism, it cannot be admitted if Lao Tan was a Chinese born and dead man, that they should have been unable to supply more data to their readers, on so remarkable a man.

138. The details furnished from later sources have a tinge of wonderful, but the sober statements which they contain, confirm rather than infirm the probability that Lao Tan was a foreigner of the South. The *Yü li* of Tchu Han,[512] in the IIIrd cent., said that he had a yellow complexion, beautiful eyebrows, long ears, large eyes, a wide forehead, parted teeth, a square mouth and thick lips, therefore a rather un-Chinese appearance.[513] He was reputed to have travelled extensively, as far as *Ta Tsin*, i.e. Dakshina or South India, and *Ken-tuh*, i.e. Hindu or North India. These statements, however valueless they may be so far as they relate to real facts of Lao Tan's life, show certainly the feeling that existed amongst his followers about a connection of his with India, and are interesting to notice in support of the views we have expressed.

139. His work shows that he was acquainted with Chinese notions as well as with Brahmanical speculations of ontology.[514] He started from the notion of the Right Way or *Tao* of the *Shu king*, and expatiated it as the Reason of nature and the first principle subordinating all creation. The treble aspect of the Tao, described in the fourteenth chapter, which was the object of the funny view that it might be a reference to Jahve, is most clearly a Hindu notion connected with similar views in the Rigveda and the Brahmanas.[515]

NOTES——
499) Prof. Ch. de Harlez says rightly : " La doctrine de Lao-tze resemble en bien des points à celle des brahmanes; le *Tao-te-king* concorde d'une manière frappante avec l'exposé philosophique qui commence les Lois de Manou. Il y a donc de grandes probabilités que l'auteur du Manuel Lao-ien ait cherché des inspirations dans l' Inde; mais à ce qu'il y a puisé, il a imprimé le caractère de son génie et en a fait un système à lui qui porte à bon droit exclusivement son nom." *Les Religions de la Chine, Aperçu historique et critique*, Leipzig, 1891, pp. 177-8.—Cf. also, but with caution. G. Pauthier : *Mémoire sur l' Origine et la Propagation de la doctrine du Tao*, fondée par Lao-tsou; traduit du Chinois et Accompagné d' un commentaire tiré des livres Sanskrits et du Tao-te-king de Lao-tsou, établissant la conformité de certaines opinions philosophiques de la Chine et de l'Inde,....suivi de deux Oupanichads des Védas, Paris, 1831, 8o pp.—Dr. E. J. Eitel, *Outlines of a history of Chinese philosophy*, states that Lao-tze's ideas of transmigration and annihilation show that he had some connection with India. Cf. *Travaux du IIIe Congr. Internation. Orient.*

St. Petersbourg, 1876, vol. II, p. 7.—Prof. R. K. Douglas, in *The Academy*, Apr. 25, 1885, favours also an Indian origin for his sources, and suggests that his name *Li* being that of a non-Chinese tribe may show his foreign origin. Anyhow we may remark that Li, plum, is said also to have been given to the child because he was born near such a tree, and that such a custom is not Chinese.—The XIVth chapt. of the *Tao teh king* contains the description of three ontological conceptions, *I, hi, Wei* which have given rise to a great deal of controversy. Several of the Ancient Jesuit Missionaries,—Abel de Rémusat, *Mémoire sur la vie et les ouvages de Lao-tseu*, 1823, (Mém. Academ. d. Inscript. tom. XII) p. 23,—V. v. Strauss, *Lao-Tse Táo-Té-king*, Leipzig, 1870,—P. Perny, *Grammaire Chinoise*, II, 1876. p. 311, 315,— Julius Grill, in *Ztschr. f. Alltetsam. Wissens.*, V, 1, 15.—support the extraordinary view that the three words are a transliteration of the name of Jehovah. On the other hand, G. Pauthier, *Mémoire.....du Tao*, 1831, pp. 32-37, who makes it an Indian notion,—Stan. Julien, *Le Livre de la Voie et de la Vertu*, 1842, pp. iv-viii,—J. Chalmers, *The speculations on Metaphysics, polity and Morality of Lao-tze*, 1868, —C. de Harlez, *Lao-tze*, Bruxelles, 1885, p. 10 ; *Le nom de Jehovah a-t-il été connu des Anciens Chinois*, Sc. Cathol, 1839, Avril,—H. A. Giles, *The Remains of Lao-tze, Re-translated*, 1888,—G. v. d. Gabelentz, *Life and Teachings of Tao-tze* : 1889, China Review, vol. XVII, p. 139, sq., who says that *wei* being anciently pronounced *mi*, the name of Jahveh cannot be recognized in *I-hi-mi*,—and J. Edkins, *On I hi-wei in the Tao-teh-king* : Chinese Recorder, vol. XVII, p. 306 sq., who thinks that Lao-tze may have got from India a notion of a (?) Babylonian trinity,—all refuse to accept the Jehovah theory which ought never to have taken so much time before being dismissed for ever.—The three terms *I, hi, wei*, which in olden times were *dzet, ki* and *m'*, singularly correspond to the *tad, svad* and *kama* of the *Rig Veda*, X, xi, and it is most probable that Lao-tze had been acquainted with it.

500) In the following paragraphs 136-138, I have collected the reasons that make to believe that Lao Tan was an Indian.

501) *Ku*, ancient, is the usual word used in classical literature when referring to the Ancients or Antiquity of China, in the *Shu king*, as in the writings of Confucius, Mencius and others. In the occasion referred to, Ch. XLI, Lao-tze says : *Ku kien yen yu tchi*, litt. ' therefore established words there are.' This peculiar mode of quoting another work seems to me to suggest a foreign source. See below n. 515.

502) I am thoroughly convinced that if we had the original text of the *Tao teh king* in *ta-tchuen* in full, instead of isolate characters, we could give a better and clearer edition in modern text than is at present known. I have already pointed out discrepancies of transcription in the text.

503) The authenticity of the *Tao teh king* had never been challenged until Mr. Herbert A. Giles, one of the best translators of modern Chinese, assailed it vigorously and in an unmeasured manner, *The Remains of Lao-tze retranslated* : Chin. Rev. 1886-1888. The translator wanted the work to be undoubtedly a forgery, containing much that Lao-tze said, but more that he did not. His canons of criticism are as follows ;

he considers as gibberish, rigmarole or nonsense all passages that he cannot understand, and as forgeries all those which in a non-exhaustive enquiry he has not found quoted in later authors of the following centuries. He brought on his work two crushing rejoinders of Dr. John Chalmers, *ibid.* vol. XIV, p. 323 sq. and of Prof. James Legge, *ibid.* vol. XVI, p. 196 sq., as well as another one in several articles of Dr. J. Edkins, and an interesting one of Prof. G. v. d. Gabelentz, *ibid.* vol. XIV, XVI, XVII, and others.

504) Notably by Pat. J. F. Foucquet (1723) mss. (Cf. H. Cordier, *Bibliot. Sinic.* col. 520); Stan. Julien, 1842 ; J. Chalmers, 1868 ; T. W. Watters, 1870 : Rheinhold von Planckner, 1870 ; Victor von Strauss, 1870 ; H. Balfour, 1885; H. A. Giles, 1886-1888 ; Ch. de Harlez, 1891 ; L. de Rosny, 1892 ; J. Legge, 1892. A latin translation mss. made in China, given by P. de Grammont to Mr. M. Rapper who presented it to the Royal Society in 1788, is now in the India Office. (Cf. J. Legge, *Texts of Taoism*, I, xii).

505) This is the judgment passed by Prof. G. v. d. Gabelentz, ibid. vol. XVII, at the occasion of Mr. H. A. Giles' work.

506) But whether (the account is) true or false, he is said to have first seen the light in the year 604 B.C. at the village of *Kiuh-jen*, or ' Oppressed benevolence,' in the parish of *Li* or ' Cruelty,' in the district of K'u or 'Bitterness,' in the state of Ts'u or 'Suffering.' R.K. Douglass, *Confucianism and Taoism*, 1879, p. 175.—The concatenation of the meanings is highly suggestive of a fabulous statement, inasmuch as divergences of opinion have existed on the identification of the above named localities, because they could not be found exactly. There were also differences of spelling in the names. Cf. the various comments added to the text of Szema Tsien, edit. of the T'ang dynasty (Kiv. 62, f. 1); the *Kwa ti tchi*, a geographical work of the third cent., the *Shen sien tchuen* of the fourth century, &c. In the third century, the dwelling and temple of Lao Tan were shown at Ku yang hien in Poh tchou (Ngan-hwei). Afterwards under the Tsin dynasty (IVth cent.,) they were shown as at present near Kwei-teh fu (Honan). The simple fact, which no assimilation can disguise, is that the village of *Kiuh jen*, or the *Li*, or the district of *Ku* referred to in the above statement, were and are still unknown in positive geography.

507) *Supra*, §§ 122 and 65.

508) Cf. Shway Yoe, *The Burman*, 1892, vol. I., p. 57;sq.—The custom of piercing and lengthening the ears was extensive in the South. In 111 B.C when Southern China was organised by the HAN, the island of *Hainan* formed the district of *Tan-erh* (Bas. 510-8337) i.e. of the 'ears falling on shoulders,' and part of that of *Tchu yai*, or Red Cliffs. (Cf. *She ki*, Kiv 113, f. 9.)—Let us remark however that Wen, Duke of Tsin (B.C. 696-628) was called *Tchung erh* (Bas. 11373-8337) like Lao Tan.

509) The taking a name from a tree near which one stands, is not a Chinese but a Himalayan custom.—*Li*, (Bas. 4076) the name in question is said by the *Fung su t'ung* of the IInd cent. A.D. to be the name of the descendants of *Peh Yang*, a name given also to Lao Tan, but it does not mention any one before bearing that surname. A feeble attempt was made after the Sung dynasty, in the *Peh Kia sing*, to create an

ancestry to the surname, by an assimilation with another surname, *Li* (Bas. 5936) of the Yn dynasty, otherwise unsupported. It is now a regular surname in China. It is also that of one of the *Hua Miao*, aboriginal tribes of Kwei-tchou, as stated in G. Playfair, *The Miaotze of Kweichou*, No. 8. Prof. R.K. Douglas, *The Academy*, April 25, 1885, thinks that the surname of Lao Tan was connected with the latter.
510) Reported in Tchwang tze, Kiv. XIV., par. 6; also XIII., 6.
511) *She Ki*, Kiv. 63, f. 2*v*.
512) This document is older than the biography written by Ko-hung about 350 A.D., in his *Shen sien tchuen*, and which has been translated by Stan. Julien, *Le livre de la Voie et de la Vertu*, 1852, p. xxii-xxxii.
513) The historical dates of Lao Tan are not ascertained. We have already stated that Szema Tsien knew nothing of his years of birth and death. Tchwang tze (Kiv. XIV., par. 5) states that Confucius knew nothing of the Tao, until his 51st year, when he called on Lao Tan at *P'ei* (a place which has not been identified, although it was the name of a region near Su-tchou, Kiang-su, which cannot be the same). This would be in 501 or 500 B.C., and Lao Tan should have been then 104 years old, which is most probably too much, if there is any truth in the alleged date of 604 B.C., given as that of his birth by some of his late biographers.
514) Cf. *supra*, note 469.—Also, D'Eckstein, *Journal Asiatique*, XIV., Sept., Oct., 1842.—Rev. J. Faber's article on Taoism in *China Review*, vol. XIII., deals also wiht the question.
515) Cf. *supra*, end of note 469.—The Sanskrit *t a d* and *s v a d* correspond pretty well to the Chinese *tzet* and *ki* (vi), but the third *k a m a*, Skr., and *mi*, Chin., differ more widely as to their sense, In Skr. it is L o v e, and in Chinese it is s u b t l e. Was this difference that of a special Hindu school with which Lao Tan was acquainted? Prof. Leon de Rosny, in his recent work, *Le Taoisme*, 1892, introd., has remarked that the absence of the great idea of love in Lao-tze's system was the greatest shortcoming of his philosophy.

* * *

140. Lao Tan makes in his work frequent quotations from sources which he does not indicate with precision[516]; although some of these quotations were not unknown to writers of the following century, it is not possible save in one case to trace them to their sources, and it is probable that for these writers the sources was the teachings of Lao-Tan himself who had derived them from his acquaintance with Hindu thoughts and views. In his capacity of Librarian at Loh-Yang, he had access to all the relics of the past which were treasured there, includng many remains and fragments handed down from remote ages and the first introduction of the Chaldeo-Elamite culture. But he did not share the Chinese worship for Antiquity, and his great contempt for all the ancient traditions is shown by his statement to Confucius. With regards to Cosmogony, the notion of the *Yn* and *Yang*, the female and male activity of nature, which existed

in the Archives could not satisfy him, since the concept of love had no place in his Ontology. Now another notion which he found most certainly there agreed with his views, and he gave it a standing in his work without quoting his source, which however, we know, was some document attributed to Hwang-ti, from where Lieh-tze has himself quoted it in his teachings during the following century.

141. As it is one of the most remarkable relics of foreign and remote Antiquity in Ancient Chinese literature,[517] let us quote it verbatim, with a word for word translation:

The Book of Hwang-Ti says[518]:
1. *Kuh shen puh se*
(The) deep's spirit not dies;
2. *She wei hiuen p'in*
It is called (the) dark-abyss's female.
3. *Hiuen p'in tchi men*
(The) dark-abyss female-ox's door,
4. *S h e w e i T'ien ti tchi k en*
It is called the Heaven (and) Earth's root;
5. *Mien mien joh ts'uen*
Perpetually as if preserved
6. *Yung tchi puh leh*
Its activity is not restrained.

We read it correctly as follows: "The spirit of the deep dies not;— It is called the Animal-mother of the dark-abyss.—The door of the Animal-mother of the dark-abyss.—It is called the Root of Heaven and Earth;—As if it was perpetually preserved,—Its activity is not restrained."

142. Some remarks are required on this noteworthy fragment of Cosmogony. The 'spirit of the deep' is the rendering of *Kuh shen*, i.e. the spirit of the *Kuh*, which *Kuh* materially means 'a valley' but which the sequence of the text requires to take in a wider sense such as an earthly deep or abyss. The two following words imply its eternal character which is furthermore described by the two last verses. *Hiuen p'in* of the second line has been variously rendered, viz. femelle mysterieuse (Julien), female mystery (Legge), generatrice de l'abime infini (De Harlez), Hidden mother (Chalmers), Abyss mother (Eitel);[519] the third and fifth of these renderings show that their authors have understood the cosmogonic character of the text. The word *p'in* has however a peculiar significance which is an important feature of the notions here expressed; it is ideographically an ox-female and it has become a generic term for the female of animals. Its acceptation of mother in the present case is

pointed out by the twenty-fifth chapter of the same work, where the same concept is described as the mother of the Universe.[520]

The euphemism of the third verse is clear enough not to require any comment, and as explained by the words following is that from where sprung heaven and earth ; the figure of speech is befitting to the general standpoint taken by Lao Tan.

143. It is needless to argue on the cosmogonic and un-Chinese character of this fragment; it is glaring to the eyes of any one engaged in antiquarian researches. It is not connected with any Indian views on cosmogony (where the dual element, male and female, by the incitement of love (*Kāṛma*) are always prominent) and this is rather striking, should we consider how much Lao Tan was indebted to Hindu thought under several other respects. Moreover, it does not belong either to Assyro-Babylonian cosmogonies of later date,—where also the male and female powers are the chief actors,[521]—which might have been introduced by the sea-traders of the Indian Ocean. But curiously enough it is much older than that period. It is a strikingly exact description of a Babylonian cosmogonic conception of remote Antiquity, which has no similar anywhere else, and which therefore cannot be mistaken for anything else.

144. In this old Babylonian cosmogony, "the mother that has begotten heaven and earth" is *Zikur*,[522] (the s p i r i t of the i m m a n e n t),[523] described as the *Apsû*, the primordial a b y ss or d e e p, out of which both earth and heaven were produced. She was "the great mother," and in the era of totemism, in early times, was known as "the pure heifer."[524] *Zikur*, and *Zigaruv* or *Zikura*, are also the names of *Gurṛa*, when regarded as the whole body of chaos, out of which the heaven and the earth were formed;[525] and it is possible that *Zi-kum* was originally considered also as the spirit of the earth alone,[526] and therefore as the spirit of a primordial terrestial deep,[527] or simply the s p i r i t of the h o l l o w.[528]

145. The identity is so close between this cosmogonic conception and that of the fragment inserted in his work by Lao Tan, that we have no choice in the explanation it forces upon us. In the archives of Tchou, he had found a work or a collection of fragments of olden times, concerning the teachings of Yu Nai Hwang ti, leader of the Bak families in China, and the Babylonian notions which he had received in the West. This collection was known as the Book of Hwang-ti, as stated by Lieh-tze when quoting the same fragment. It is a new confirmation, as remarkable as unexpected, of the existence of such documents in Ancient China,[529] which we have suspected all along this work, for many reasons explained therein.

146. The sixth chapter is not the only part of the *Tao teh King*, which shows that Lao Tan had come across some fragments of Babylonian lore. In his twenty-fifth chapter, he has grafted upon a description of the sort, his conception of the Tao: "There was something undefined and complete, —Before Heaven and Earth it existed.—It was still and formless!—Standing by itself and undergoing no change,—Reaching everywhere and not in danger!—It may be regarded as the Mother of the Universe.—I do not know its name,—and I give it the designation of T a o."

Let us substitute T i a w a t, the primordial chaos, of the earliest Babylonian cosmogonies, to T a o, and we could easily imagine that the above text is a direct translation from an ancient cuneiform text, instead of being a fragment inserted in Lao Tan's work.

NOTES——
516) Such for instance in the following passages: 2, 9; 7, 3; 8, 4; 12 ,6; 34, 7; 57, 7; 58, 6; 73, 5; 77, 5; 78, 5; 79, 3, and others.—Stan. Julien, *Le Livre de la Voie et de la Vertu*, p. 22, quoting the commentator T'u T'ao-kien of the XIIIth century, on the chap. VI, says: "On sait que Lao-tsen cite beaucoup de passages des livres appelés *fen tien*." But he does not give any information on the latter. Dr. J. Legge, *The Texts of Taoism*, 1892, I., 2, quotes the same Chinese writer to the following effect: Lao tze was accustomed to quote in his treatise, passages from earlier records,—as when he refers to the remarks of 'some sage,' of 'some ancient,' of the sentence-makers,' and of 'some writer on war.' In all these cases he is clearly introducing the words of earlier wise men. —The *fen tien* in question were the *san fen* and the *Wu tien* which Confucius threw over, with the exception of two of the five tien (*Wu tien*) when he selected the documents which composed the *Shu King*. Cf. below, §150.
517) It occurs in the *Tao teh King*, Kiv. 6, and in Lieh tze, I., 1*b*.— The statement was so satisfactory to Lao Tan, that he enlarged it in his Kiv. 25. But it is Lieh-tze only who refers to the original work.
518) Cf. the following translations: 1⁰ by Stan. Julien: "L'Esprit de la vallée ne meurt pas; on l'appelle la femelle mysterieuse.—La porte de la femelle mysterieuse s'appelle la racine du ciel et de la terre.—Il est éternel et semble exister (materiellement).—Si l'on en fait usage, on n'eprouve aucune fatigue."—Cf. *Le Livre de la Voie*, p 21.—2⁰ by Prof. J. Legge: "The valley spirit dies not, aye the same;—The female mystery thus do we name.—Its gate, from from which at first they issued forth,—Is called the root from which grew heaven and earth,—Long and unbroken does its power remain,—Used gently and without the touch of pain." Cf. *The texts of Taoism*, I., 51.—3⁰) By Prof. Ch. de Harlez: L'esprit de l'immensité ne meurt point.—C'est lui que l'on appelle la génératrice de l'abîme infini.—Sa porte est appellée la racine du ciel et de la terre.—Elle subsiste éternellement, et les êtres en usent sans jamais la fatiguer." Cf. *Textes Taoistes*, p. 292.—It is clear that in the first and second of these translations, the real object of the state-

ment has not been clearly understood. Mr. H.A. Giles, *The Remains of Lao-Tze Re-translated*, does not believe this chapter composed by Lao-tze; he does not attempt to translate it, and as he has no idea what it means, he declares it a self-evident forgery! It was difficult for this translator to give a greater proof of his incompetency in ancient matters.

519) In his *Chinese dictionary*, s.v. *p'in*.
520) see below, §139.
521) François Lenormant, *Origines de l'histoire*, vol. I. pp. 493-570 has reproduced numerous versions of this later cosmogony, where the notion of the animal mother has disappeared.
522) W.A.I, II. 48. 26; 50. 27.—A.H. Sayce, *Rel. Anc. Bab*. p. 375. n., remarks that *Zikum*, *Zi-garum*, *Zi-kura*, are all compounds of *Zi*, 'a spirit,' and are explained by *Zi(E)kura*, 'the spirit of the lower firmament.'
523) Cf. *Kum=Kur* with *Kuuma=Kuura*, rest, peace, in F. Lenormant, *Etudes Accadiennes*. III., 142, 17; E. Chossat, *Répertoire Sumerien*, p. 116.
524) Cf. A. H. Sayce, *Rel. Anc, Bab.* p. 375.—The complex ideogram Brunn. 4991, read *parû*, cow, and written ideographically (anshu-mul) beast + trebly-divine or starry, is perhaps a surviving embodiment of these views.—Or is it a survival of the notions introduced by the maritime civilisers and the "snow-white hornless cows" spoken of in the fabulous reports of South Arabia by Agatharcides (*De Rubro Mari*. Oxon., 1698, p. 64).
525) W.A.I. II., 48, 26, 27.—A.H. Sayce. *O.C.*, p. 262.—Cf. also F. Hommel, *Die semitischen Völker*, p. 38.
526) A. H. Sayce, *O. C.*, p. 375.
527) Perhaps it was neither terrestrial nor oceanic,—and thus be a clear vestige of the early time when the abyss was not yet looked upon as watery. The remark is important because it stamps the remote date of the notion embodied in the document.
528) Cf. also P. Jensen, *Die Kosmologie der Babylonier*, p. 5, 491.
529) In my paper *On the Oldest Book of the Chinese*, 1883, I expressed the opinion, then looked upon as rather bold, that the Bak families had been acquainted with lexicographic documents like the so-called syllabaries, and I am now more than ever of the same opinion, which is at present already supported by many facts. Cf. *suprà*, ch. IV., sect. *b*, §24.
530) Stan. Julien, *Le Livre de la Voie*, p. 91, translates: ne périclite point; J. Legge, *Taoist texts*, 1., p. 67, translates: in no danger (of being exhausted). The text says: *erh puh tai*, and not is-in-danger.
531) Julien: '*l' Univers*;' Legge: 'all things;' the text: *t'ien. hia*, beneath of heaven.
532) Cf. A. H. Sayce, *Rel. Anc. Bab.*, p. 370-374.

[CHAP. VII. PART II.—FOURTH PERIOD : 670-481 B.C.]

Sect. *d*) *Foreign influence in the North West. Barbarous customs.*

147. In the North-west the influence from the outside was the reverse of being beneficial or progressive. The region was properly at that time the west of the Chinese dominion, and it was occupied by the state of *Than*, mod. Ts'IN, whose population was greatly composed of non-Chinese tribes, the Jungs, whom it gradually subdued and absorbed. Although recognized as an independent fief of the Middle Kingdom in 770, when the seat of the latter was forcibly removed eastwards, it did not however take part in the concert of the other states previously to 645 B.C.[533] We have already remarked that by its position it stopped the way to any intercourse on that side between the other states and the foreign lands of the West,[534]and the little intercommunication which existed had to be carried out by a more southerly route.[535] The history states that from the time of Muh-wang's punitive expedition in the west, in 967 B.C.,[536]those who dwelt in the wild regions came no more to court,[537] and we have no evidence that the communications were renewed with the Ts'IN state. The statement is interesting to notice, in face of the changes which we shall record in the next paragraph, and the important movements which were taking place during that period in the East and South of the Chinese dominion.

148. The innovations introduced in Ts'IN denote barbarity and no improvement nor enlightenment. Its princes established new worships, such as that of the Regents of the points of space[538] and others. In 756, Ts'IN Wen Kung, having discovered on a hill a large stone shaped like a bird, instituted a regular worship to it, and its spirit was alleged to come from

time to time.[339] Teh Kung in his second year, i.e. in 676 B.C., offered for the first time the sacrifice *fuh*, i.e., the body of a dog torn asunder at the four gates of the town to avert the calamity of worms.[510] All these matters were of little importance. The worst innovations have yet to be noticed. In 746 the barbarous punishment of destroying the relatives of criminals was resorted to for the first time.[511] Also the practice of human sacrifices, of which the two first notable instances occurred in 678 and 621 B.C., when 66 and 177 persons followed (*tsung*) their prince to the grave,[542] have been severally mentioned in European literature.[543] This was obviously a satisfaction given to the Tartar element of the population, probably supported by a new influx of the same race. The next instance in the same country was that of the funerals of She Huang Ti, the founder of the Chinese Empire, when a large number of persons were buried with him in 210 B.C.[544]

149. The question arises to know if these human sacrifices were not simply a revival, in favourable surroundings, of an ancient practice which had become obsolete in the more civilized parts of the Chinese dominion, instead of being an innovation unheard of before. And the custom of placing puppets in the graves, which existed in the time of Confucius, and is at present still followed,[545] has been put forward as proof that such sacrifices existed amongst the most ancient Chinese.[546] The matter requires a more extensive inquiry than has hitherto been made, and the fresh evidence we shall adduce here placing the question on a different footing, disproves this premature conclusion. Although the Chinese chiefs and officials have never been over-scrupulous about the life of others, even for sacrificial purposes, let us remember, that there is no evidence whatever that they had ever practised human sacrifices previously to the events and circumstances which concern us here.[547] Notwithstanding their permanent influence on some superstitions and practices, the human sacrifices in China were only temporary, and under foreign influences of a passing character.

150. These human sacrifices belonged to two classes which must be clearly distinguished one from the other : 1° the sacrifices by self-devotion or supposed self-devotion of living persons to the departed ; and 2° the slaughter or burning of unwilling persons for sacrificial purposes.

The first class comprehends suttism, and the *siün*.

151. Self-sacrifices of the widows[548] is a widely spread practice,[549] and as they result from the natural feeling of devotion of the derelict towards her departed lord, it may have arisen anywhere without requiring any im-

pulse from the outside. It is needless therefore to trace the Chinese suttism to its source, although it does not seem to have begun before Indian influence was strongly felt in the land. Suttism has never been a regular institution in China, and until 1729, when it was discountenanced by an Imperial edict,⁵⁵⁰ it was limited to personal convenience and isolated cases, which nevertheless had become too frequent about that date, because of the honour which was paid to them.

152. The *Siän* practice was another affair.⁵⁵¹ It began in 678 B.C. in the west state of Ts'in, as we have already seen § 148, undoubtedly under Tartar influence. The great instance of 621, was the prelude to its extension in others of the Chinese states. The next occasion recorded in history is that of 589, at the burial of the Duke Wen of Sung (Honan E.) when the *Siän* practice was followed for the first time there;⁵⁵² such is the precise statement of Tso Kiu-ming. Afterwards we find an instance in 581 in Ts'in, when a servant of the defunct Duke Non was buried alive with his master.⁵⁵³ Then at Su-tchou (Kiangsu) in the state of Wu, about 500 B.C., the Prince Ho-lü (514-496 B.C.) having lost a favourite daughter, ran undescribed number of men and women were buried alive with her; but the act was reprobated by his subjects.⁵⁵⁴ There is also the would-be instance amongst private people which was disproved by Tze K'ang, a disciple of Confucius, who said that "to bury living persons in the grave of the dead (*siän*) is contrary to the rules of propriety."⁵⁵⁵ However the *siän* was a well known and rather extensively practised custom in the fourth century B.C., as shown by the words of Tchwang tze, who was writing about 379-330 B.C.⁵⁵⁶ The last instance of notoriety was that of the funeral of She Hwang Ti in 210 B.C. when it was compulsory. The practice had changed in character, and seems not to have been followed again by the Chinese. Such were the beginning and end of a barbarous influence in China,⁵⁵⁷ at a time when the whole country was, to some extent, anxious to adopt any novelty. It has left some survivals, as we shall now see.⁵⁵⁸

153. To imitate the new and peculiar custom of the *Siän* of the leading state,—such was the position of Ts'in at the death of Duke Muh, the fourth of the five *Pa*, in 621—was not within the reach of every one. We may easily assume that the required self-willing victims, by devotion, thirst of fame, or for a consideration, could be only the exception, and never the rule. Moreover, the practice was objectionable to the human feeling of the people at large, and was not sanctioned by the traditional rites. An ingenious device was resorted to. There was an old custom— a widely

spread one[559]—of placing in the tomb mock implements, which they called *ming-ki*, i.e. light objects,[560] imitations in bamboo, clay, or cloth of things which might be useful to the departed ; and also that of representing the defunct at the funerals by a straw effigy[561] (*tsao-ling*).[562] These led undoubtedly those who could not through impecuniosity, human feeling or otherwise practice the *sün* custom, to substitute for living persons, *yung*, or little wooden figures.[563] We can thus understand how it happened that Confucius could praise the first, and reprobate the second, as there was a danger of its leading to taking living men.[564] The departed is still represented at his own funeral,[565] and little human figures are placed in the coffin at the feet of the deceased in some parts of the land.[566] The substitution of puppets for human victims has taken place in several countries[567] and notably in Japan.[568]

154. The second class of human sacrifices in China presents only a few and occasional records, since the custom of slaughtering or burning unwilling persons as offerings was not congenial with them. They did do so only under another foreign influence, shown by the first instance here reported. In 641 B.C. the Duke of Sung, (the state where we have noticed so strong an influence from the foreigners of Lang-ga and Tsih-moh) made duke Wen of Tchu sacrifice the viscount of Tseng at the altar on the bank of the Suy, wishing to draw to him the Eastern barbarians (*yuh y shuh T'ung y*).[569] Now as these eastern barbarians were the foreigners in question, the case of their influence is clearly established. The name of the deity to whom the sacrifice was made is not mentioned, but we may remark that it was on the bank of a river, and this peculiarity makes it similar to the human sacrifices at Yeh which we have noticed previously,[570] and were due to the same influence. In 531, another human sacrifice is reported, by the Prince of Ts'u on mount Kang, but there is not perhaps in it any connection with the other,[571] although it was also a religious sacrifice.[572] Therefore all that we had to say here on the second class of human sacrifices might have been placed in our previous sect. *b* of this fourth period ; but the affinity of the subject required it to be dealt with here.

NOTES——

533) Its first appearance during the Tchun tsiu period was in that year. Cf. *Tso tchuen*, Hi Kung, Ann. XV.
534) *Suprà*, ch. VI. *f.* div. 4, par. 92.
535) *Suprà*, ch. VI., sect. *e*, div. 1, par. 52.
536) It was not the same as that already noticed (*suprà*, ch. VI., sect. *b*,

§ 39, and note 165), which occurred in 985 B.C.
537) *Kang kien y tchi luh.*—Medhurst, *Shoo king,* p. 385.
538) In 769 the Prince of Ts'in established a raised altar (*tchi*) for sacrifices to the White Ti, the Regent of the West quarter (with whom the early Ruler Shao Hao had been identified) as a set-off against the Shang Ti worship of the King of Tcnou. This led to the worship of the Five Tis as Regents of the five points of space. In 672, a similar altar was raised to the Tsing Ti, the Green-blue Regent (identified with Tai Hao or Fuh-hi) At the beginning of the Han dynasty four Tis of the four quarters only were worshipped as yet, and the series of five was completed by HAN Kao tsu in 201 B.C.—Cf. Szema Tsien, Kiv. XIV ; and Kiv. XXVIII., ff. 3. 5. 17.—*Tchuh shu Ki nien, s. d.*
539) It was called the Jewel of Tch'en (*Tch'en pao*) because it had been discovered on the north side of the Tch'en tsang (in Pao ki hien, pref. of Fung tsiang in Shensi.—Cf. Szema Ts'ien, *She Ki*, Kiv. 28, f. 4-4*v*.
540) *Shi Ki*. Kiv. 28, f. 5.
541) *Tchuh shu Ki nien.* Tchou Ping wang, ann. 25.—*She Ki*, Kiv. V., f. 6.
542) *She Ki*, Kiv. V,. f 7*v* and 26. - *Tso tchuen*, 6 : VII., 2.—*Shi King*, part I., Bk. XI., Ode *Hwang Niao.*
553) Notably by W.F. Mayers, *On the Stone figures at Chinese tombs and the offering of living sacrifices,* p, 13, 14 : J.N. Ch. Br. R.A.S., 1878. XII., 1-18.
544) *She Ki*, Kiv. VI., f. 28.—W.F. Mayers, *On the Stone figures,* l.c.
545) Cf. below § 153 and notes 560, 564, 568.
546) J.J.M. de Groot, *Les Fêtes Annuelles à Emoui,* p. 647. The author uses wrongly the term s u t t i s m for all human sacrifices at funerals (p. 645), while the term can refer only to the self-sacrifice of the widows. Cf. Yule-Burnell, *Glossary of Anglo-Indian terms,* p. 666-671, s. v. *S u t t e e*).—A. Reville, *La Religion Chinoise,* 1889, p. 200-212. The latter scholar, working only second hand, cannot be referred to as an authority on the matter, except for his own views, which have been under several respects the object of a damaging rejoinder by Prof. C. de Harlez in his paper on *La Religion en Chine,* 1889. noticed *suprà,* note 101. The facts and the texts side with the learned Orientalist of Louvain.
547) It has been rightly remarked that nothing in all that we know of the ancient state religion of the Chinese has ever countenanced human sacrifices. Cf W. Williams, *The Middle Kingdom,* II., 192, and De Groot. *Les Fêtes,* p. 281, 785.
548). Suttism is a Brahmanical rite; its Sanskrit name is *saha-gamana*, or keeping company. It was known by the Greek writers since 317 B.C., as an Indian practice (Diod. Sic., XIX., 33-34). *Suttee* is properly the Skr. *s a t i,* a good woman, a good wife. Cf. Yule-Burnell, *Glossary,* l.c.
519) Cf. Herbert Spencer, *Principles of Sociology,* ch. xiv., par. 104.— De Groot, *Les fêtes,* p. 557-558, and Yule's *Glossary,* p. 667.
550) Translated in *Self-Immolation in China* : Notes and Queries of China and Japan. vol. II., 1863, p. 3-4 ; partly reproduced in De Groot, *Les Fêtes,* p. 559-560.
551) *Siün* (Bas. 4 98) means 'to bury the (self-willing) living with the

dead ; but we may be sure that compulsion and force were often resorted to, as in the cases of c. 500 and 210 B.C.

552) The text says : *she yung siün*. Cf. *T'so tchuen*, 8, II, 5.

553) *Ibid.* 8, X. 5. —There is a story there, that the servant had dreamed that he carried his master on his back to heaven.

554) *Wu yueh tchun tsiu.—Yuen Kien lui han*, Kiv. 181, f. 5 ; W. F. Mayers, *On the Stone figures*, p. 15.

555) *Li Ki*, T'an Kung, 2 ; II. 15.

556) "Small men for the sake of gain have sacrificed (*siün*) their persons; scholars for the sake of fame have done so ; great officers for the sake of their families ; and sagely men for the sake of the kingdom. These several classes, with different occupations, and different reputations, have agreed in doing injury to their nature, and sacrificing their persons." Cf. *Tchwang tze*, Bk. VIII., Pt. II., sect. I., par. 4; Sacred Books of the East, XXXIX., 272-3.—The term *siün* is repeated in each case.

557) We must make an exception for the Tartar families who have ruled over part or the whole of China, and may have followed a custom congenial to them, when not softened as yet by Chinese influence. Even the present dynasty of Mandshu Tartars followed it at the beginning ; the only case was that of Shi Tsu, the first Emperor, who had thirty persons killed on the grave of his Empress. His son, Shang Tsu, or K'ang hi, put an end to the custom.—Cf. also below, note 572.

558) The present enquiry does not pretend to be exhaustive, and some more facts could be added, but they would not modify the aspect of the question as now stated.—In the *T'ang shu*, Kiv. 122, notice of the Eastern Kingdom of Women, *Tung niu kwoh*, also called *Suvarna Gotra*, "Golden family," situated in N. Tibet, it is stated that when the Sovereign is buried, several tens of persons followed the dead into the tomb. Cf. William Woodville Rockhill, *The Land of the Lamas*, 1891, p. 340.

559) Cf. François Lenormant, *Gazette des Beaux Arts*, 1863, p. 14, 153.

560) On the *Ming Ki*, cf. the rituals : *I li*, XII., 8-16 ; trad. C. de Harlez, 1890, p. 298-305.—*Li Ki* 2 ; I : iii., 3 and 44 ; *Sacred Books of the East*, XXVII., p. 148, 172. They consisted of vessels, vases, lutes, pipes, bells, according to the statement of Confucius in the latter work (par. 3 cited). It will be remarked that there is no mention made here of human figures, chariots, &c., on which see below. The imitations of musical instruments represented the real instruments which were employed at the ceremony according to the rites reported in the *Tcheu-li*, Kiv. 22, l. 39, 51; Kiv. 23, l. 2 , 29, 45, 48, 57, (tr. Biot, vol. II., p. 40, 45, 51, 54, 61, 63, 68.—The statement of the *T'so tchuen* concerning the funeral of the Duke of Sung, in 589, referred to in the text (§ 152), gives some interesting information on another custom. It says that the departed Duke was the first to whom they gave a great interment, using mortar made of ashes of burnt frogs for the vault in the grave, with more than the usual number of carriages and horses (*yh kiü ma*). Some commentators want to see there the (earthen) carriages and (straw) horses, which it became customary at a certain time to put in the grave. But there is no necessity of stretching the meaning of the text as far as that, since we know by the *Li Ki*, T'an Kung, 2, II., 4, that the ritual number of carriages (carrying the offerings to be put into the

grave) was seven for the ruler of a state, five for a great officer, and one for private individuals. The text of the Chronicle refers to that undoubtedly.—Confucius does not refer to earthen carriages in speaking of the *Ming Ki*, and therefore we may assume that in his time, the custom was not yet accepted and current. It is however mentioned in the *Li Ki*, ibid. I., 45, as an ancient practice ; and it is so much like the regular Phoenician custom, that we may venture to suppose that it was introduced to the Chinese by the foreign traders of Lang-ga and Tsih-Moh, (Cf. the figure of such earthen carriages found at Cyprus. in Perrot-Chipiez, *Histoire de l'art antique*, vol. III., fig. 145, 524, and the remarks on pp. 202, 212. 468, 582, 713).—At present figures in paper and bamboo slips, of sed n chairs and coolies. horses, and even boats are burnt at funerals for the use of the departed in the other world. Cf. J. Doolittle. *Social life of the Chinese*, ed. 1868, p. 131; De Groot, *Les fêtes à Emouy*, pp. 432, 580, 655, 673 ; *The Religious system*. vol. I.. p. 28, &c.—There was no sacrifice of horses amongst the ancient Chinese at funerals except for the Emperor, but it was the custom to send horses to take part in the funeral procession.—The horse was the first of the six sacred victims, the five others being the ox, sheep, pig, dog, and hen. According to the *Tchou-li*, ONE was sacrificed and buried at the Emperors' funerals (Kiv. xxxii., 50, 59) ; but not at any others' funerals. A yellow horse was offered by the Emperor at the Sacrifices to the Mountains and Rivers of the Empire (Kiv. xlii., 23). When in travelling, the Emperor happened to pass near a famous Mountain or River, the Great Prior in his name sacrificed a horse (Kiv. xxv., 5) Cf. also the *Li Ki*, Kiv. xii., 17·

561) In the *Tchou li*, ch., XXI., 46, the official in charge of the funerals (*Tchung jen*) notifies the approaching burial to the human figure (siang jen) placed on the *Lwan*-bird-ornamented-chariot. (Cf. trad., l.d. Biot, vol. II., p. 23) and which was a *tsao ling*.

562) According to Kia Kong yen of c. 700 A.D., a celebrated commentator of the *Tchou li*, this custom dated from remote antiquity.—Lao Tan (ch. V.) Tchwang tze, and also Hwai-nan-tze mention the grass-dogs, made of straw tied up in the shape of dogs, and used in praying for rain ; after the sacrifice, they were thrown aside and left uncared for. Cf. Stan. Julien, *Le Livre de la Voie*, p. 19 : J. Legge, *Texts of Taoism*, p. 50. On an ancient sacrifice of a dog, cf. *suprà*, § 95, note 363 and also § 148.

563) We are told that the *yung* were made with a figure, two eyes, and a spring, having thus the appearance of living persons. Cf. *Tai ping yü lan*, Kiv. 552, f. 3. (Comm. of the *Li ki*).

564) *Li Ki*, 2 : II. 1, par. 45. This opinion of Confucius was not understood before, because there was a confusion about the real purpose of the *tsao ling*, which confusion Kia Kong yen (*suprà* n. 562) has cleared off by his statement that the *tsao-ling* (single not several) was carried at funerals. Cf. the conflicting views of Legge, *Chinese Classics*, II, 9, n. 6 ; De Groot, *Les fêtes*, p. 645 . Albert Réville, *La Religion Chinoise*, p. 201, which would not have been put forth without it.

565) Cf. Julius Doolittle, *Social life of the Chinese*, ch. VI.—J.J.M d. Groot, *The Religious system of China*, vol. I., 1892, p. 173, 85.

566) Notably at Amoy. Cf. De Groot, *Les Fêtes*, p. 646 ; *The Relj-*

gious system of China, p. 24, 93.
567) Cf. Sal. Reinach, *Philologie Classique*, II. 224.
568) Our information on the subject is derived from the *Ko-ji-ki* or Records of Ancient Matters (712 A.D.) and from the *Ni-hon-gi*, or Chronicles of Japan (720 A.D.). The exact date of the introduction of the Chinese practice of the *Siün* is not known, but an important instance is quoted under the reign of Sū-jin of the ancient custom of burying retainers up to their necks in the neibourhood of their lord's grave. Under his successor Sui min (c. 200 A.D.), on the suggestion of Nomi no Sukune little clay figures were made as substitutes. Cf. Basil Hall Chamberlain, tr. of *Ko-ji-ki*, pp. 174, 200; *Ni-hon-gi* in Satow's transl., *Trans. R.A.S., Japan*, VIII., 329-330. Representations of these clay images (*tsuchi-nin-giyō*) are given in Henry von Siebold, *Notes on Japanese Archæology*, pl. xii., and in E. Satow, *Ancient sepulchral mounds in Kaudzuke*, in Trans. VII., 313 sq.; B.H. Chamberlain, *Ko-ji-ki*, p. xli.—For a verification of the ancient Japanese dates, cf. the excellent paper of W.G. Aston, *Early Japanese history*: Tr. A.S. Japan, XVI., 1888, p. 39-75.
569) *Tso tchuen*, 5 : XIX., 5.—The native exegetes have striven the meaning once more here, and we find in Legge's translation: "to awe and draw to him the wild tribes of the East." Ch. Cl. V. 277, which is not countenanced by the words of the text.
570) Cf. *suprà*. par. 106.
571) In 531, the viscount of Ts'u extinguished Ts'ai, and sacrificed the Marquis's eldest son *Yn* on mount Kang. Cf. *Tso tchuen*, 10 : xi., 9.
572) W.F. Mayers, in his paper *On the Stone figures at Chinese tombs*. p. 16, has quoted from the *Yun lnh mao tch'ao* of Tchao Yen-wei (c 1175 A.D.) an instance of human sacrifice in 1131 by the Kin or Djurtchen Tartars when besieging Tang t'n (mod. Tai ping fu); they drove their victims to the banks of the river, ripped open their bodies, and tore out their hearts to offer them in sacrifice for a change of wind.

Sect. e) *Internal reaction. Confucianism.*

147. We have seen thus far the Chinese community assailed, east south and west, by various influences, and the introduction of novelties in ideas, notions and superstitions, which it was but too ready to accept. The freedom enjoyed by the States since 770, (*suprà* § 102), the development of writing (§ 100), and the spirit of competition which arose between them and was the prelude of the period of civil wars which ensued, are largely responsible for the facility with which ideas hitherto strange to the Chinese mind were in some cases hailed with favour in some parts of the dominion. But when these Un-Chinese notions began to spread, when ministers of state were seen professing openly *wonderism*,[573] a keeper of the Royal Archives teach *Taoism*,[574] and Princes of States adopt barbarous practices,[575] a reaction of the Chinese natural character was unavoidable. It came to effect in the last part of the sixth century, and

was represented for the time in the teachings of Confucius to his friends and disciples. Full of the traditional spirit of respect to ancestors, ritualism and propriety, he sternly opposed all the novelties which from the east, south and west, and from pre-historic times, were invading the old domain of Chinese thought and tradition.

156. No new conception, no creation of his genius, can be found in the teachings of Confucius,[576] who claimed for himself to be 'a transmitter and not a maker, believing in and loving the Ancients.'[577] He was a Chinese amongst the Chinese, and professed with their short comings all that was best and most noble[578] in the traditions of his country. He upheld the traditional respect for the good deeds of the Ancestors, but as a rationalist, and in a limited sense as a positivist,[579] the subjects on which he did not speak, were—extraordinary things, feats of strength, disorder and spirits.[580] He professed however respect to the spirits, mixed with a sort of fear, and he believed in Omens.[581] He was a firm believer in Shang-ti, the Supreme God, as shown in several instances, but he often preferred to speak of Heaven.[582] He discountenanced all that he could not clearly understand, and deprecated the teachings of Lao Tan,[583] while on another occasion he declared that 'to go for strange doctrines is injurious indeed.'[584] We have seen previously that he condemned the recently introduced practice of human sacrifices.[585] With reference to Ancestral worship the Great philosopher of Lu has a firm hold on all his race, although his ethics, always were befitting more to the class than to the mass, because they do not give satisfaction to the emotional side of human nature, and they lack of a sanction drawn from a future life. Nowhere else has any man personified his race to the same extent, and as a natural consequence exercised so permanent an influence, as Confucius on the Chinese nation.

157. As a historian, Confucius has not deserved from posterity an unqualified gratitude. Numerous instances in the Spring and Autumn Annals, or *Tchun tsiu* of the state of Lu from 722 to 481 B.C.,[586] his own acknowledged work, that by which he wanted the after generations to pronounce their judgment upon him,[587] make the western student think very doubtfully of his merits and truthfulness.[588] His most recent editor and translator in English has shown repeatedly that he has willingly ignored, concealed and misrepresented the truth in hundreds of cases.[589]

158. There is no doubt that we are indebted to him for a mangled preservation of the *Shu King* which has come down to us still more dilapidated, but which otherwise might have been entirely lost, between

his time and the Fire of Literature in 213 B.C. Nothing has been found which throws any suspicion on the statement made on the matter by his kinsman and descendant Kung Ngin Kwoh,[590] who re-edited the classics, circâ 150 B.C. " He (Kung-tze) examined and arranged the grand monuments and records,[591] deciding to commence with Yao and Shun, and to come down to the times of Tchou. When there was perplexity and confusion, *he mowed them*. Expressions frothy and unallowable *he cut away*. What embraced great principles he retained and *developed*. What were more minute and yet of importance he carefully selected. Of those deserving to be handed down to after ages, and to supply permanent lessons, he made in all one hundred books, consisting of Canons, Counsels, Instructions, Announcements, Speeches and Charges.[592]" One third of these documents have been lost since Confucius' time, but they have never been intended to form a continuous Record. It was not a history of China which he compiled, but a collection of texts countenancing his views. "Any how besides later suppressions he has deliberately left aside and ignored any thing from old traditions, such as those which were preserved in the *San fen* or 'Three eminences' concerning Fuh-hi, Shen-nung and Hwang-ti, and in the *Wu Tien* or 'Five causes,' any thing concerning Shao Hao, Tchwen Hiüh and Kao-sin, keeping only extracts from those of Yao and Shun."[593] This method has deprived us of many a valuable tradition which in their capacity of state documents and mementos would have permitted to check the exuberancy or supply the insufficiency of the accounts which have been transmitted to posterity from irregular sources.

159. Besides the mowing, cutting away, and developing processes of editorship, the pruning pencil of the sage had recourse to another means to instil his views; this consisted in changing a word for another, or in the alteration of an ideogram by the addition or change of one of its component parts,[594] a process impossible except with an ideographic writing like that of the Chinese.[595]

160. With reference to the Western foreigners, founders of the Chinese civilization, let us understand the position assumed by Confucius. His almost complete silence towards them can be explained as the natural feeling of a Chinese among the Chinese, such as he was, and thus would confirm our discoveries about their foreign origin. The traditions of the SHANG Dynasty were preserved in the State of *Sung* (Cap. Shang-Kiu, Honan E.).[596] Those of the HIA dynasty were preserved in the principality of *K'i* which, established at first in Kai-fung fu (Honan), had been removed to the East, and in 646 B.C., had its centre at Yuen-ling (in

modern department of Tsing-tchou, C. Shangtung).⁵⁹⁷ Confucius complained of the insufficiency of their records of the two dynasties just named.⁵⁹⁸ He had therefore studied them. We are told that when the Tchou dynasty was founded, the traditions of Yao were preserved in Ki-tchou (i.e. Tchihli), and those of Huang-ti amongst the *Tchuh*, i.e. the priests.⁵⁹⁹ Those of Shao-Hao were in *Kiü* (S. E. Shantung), while those of Shun were in *Tchen* (S. E. Honan).⁶⁰⁰ Confucius may not have had access to all of them, although we know that he was not unacquainted with some of them,⁶⁰¹ and therefore his silence was voluntary.

161. Hwang-ti and his son Shao-Hao were foreigners, born outside of China ; their immediate successors Tchuen-hiüh, Kao-yang and Ti Kao-Sin were yet too much of strangers; Yao was more of a Chinese. but he was still too closely connected with his foreign forefathers.⁶⁰² Such was not the case with Shun, who was a descendant of native princes,⁶⁰³ and his association in the government by Yao has placed the latter on a different footing than his predecessor in the eyes of the patriotic Chinese. Hence it has happened that Yao and Shun have almost always been spoken of together. And it is a fact that the really Chinese history can hardly be said to begin before them. As to the myths and legends which Huang-ti and his Bak families had brought from the West, they were no part of the Chinese heirlooms, concerning as they did foreign folklore and traditions, or the past history of the Baks themselves. The consideration of these facts ought to justify the silence of the great philosopher of Lu, towards the myths, legends, and traditions anterior to the age of Yao and Shun, which were found in the ancient literature.

162. The objections of Confucius to all that was unclear to his mind, or unsatisfactory to the sternness of his doctrines, and to all recits tinged with fables and wonderism, has thrown uselessly a discredit on ancient fragments of early ages. These early documents, which as natural in the case, could be but mixed up with stories of extraordinary feats and events, have not received the care and attention which would have secured for several centuries, at least to some extent, their safety and transmission to after ages.

Such of these early statements as have come down to us, have been preserved by writers independent of Confucianism, and by Taoist writers who instead of shortening and softening them have on the contrary embellished and enlarged them by the addition of their own wonders and conceptions. They have not so much edited them as distinct works, than quoted from them, and inserted fragments in their own elucubrations. And so it has come to pass that for many a statement concerning remote antiquity, it is only in the Non-Confucianist authors than we can find them. These circumstances are extremely important for all researches on Chinese origins and must be taken into account by western scholars, as they explain the exaggerated views of remoteness or modernness in Antiquity entertained by some Sinologists according to their leaning on Non-Confucianist or on Confucianist documents, while the truth which is neither on one side nor the other, is between the two. The first section of our next part will concern the formation of Taoszeism.

NOTES——
573) Cf. *suprà*, § 108.
574) Cf. *suprà*, § 126.
575) Cf. *suprà*, §§ 106, 144.
576) B. 551—D. 479 B.C.
577) *Lun yü*, 7, I.
578) 'Not do to others as you would not wish done to yourself.' *Lun yü*, 12, II.
579) This side of his character is upheld by P. Laffitte, *Considerations generales sur la civilisation Chinoise*, 1861.
580) *Lun yü*, 7, XX.—Cf. also, 13, III, 4 : 'A superior man, in regard to what he does not know, shows a cautious reserve.'
581) Cf. *Tchung yung*, xvi, 1, 2, 4.—Cf. *Lun yü*, 6, XX : ' While respecting the spirits (*Kwei shin*), to keep also from them, may be called wisdom.
582) Cf. specia'lly *Tchung yung*, xix. 6 ; *Ta-hioh*, x, 5.—C. de Harlez *Le Religions de la Chine*, p. 160-162.—D'Hervey-Saint-Denys, *Mémoires sur les doctrines religeuses de Confucius et de l'école des lettrés*, p. 22 (Mém. Acad. Inscript., tom. xxxii, 1887).—And J. Legge, *Chinese Classics*, vol. I, introd., p. 99.
583) *Tchwang tze*, xiv, 6.—It seems however that Confucius derived some idea from his meeting with Lao Tan. Cf. the *Tchung yung*, xvi, 2, with the *I hi wei* of chap. xiv, of the *Tao teh king*.
584) *Lun yü*, 2, xvi.
585) *Suprà*, § 145.—On Confucius and his doctrines, between other works. Cf. J. Legge, *Chinese Classics* I, introd. p. 12-113.—E. Faber, Lehrbegriff der Confucius, 1872.—Samuel Johnson, *Oriental Religions*: *China*, Boston, 1881, p. 571-633.—R. K. Douglas, *Confucianism and Taoism*, 1879, p. 25-153.—Martin Hang, *Confucius, der Weise China's*, Berlin, 1880.—Ch. de Harlez, *Les Religions de la Chine*, Leipzig, 1891, p. 155-167.—Also, J. Legge, *Confucius' life and teachings*, 6th edit. 1887. - J. H. Plath, *Confucius und Seine schüler*, 1867.
586) It consists simply of a dry ephemiridis of facts or incidents, without a single practical observation. The sole peculiarity consists in the occasional selection of an ideogram instead of another, in order to show in a subrepstitions way the opinion of the writer on the recorded event.—Cf., for instance, T. de L., *The Oldest Book of the Chinese*, p.

22.—However difficult it may be for us to conciliate our expectations and the reality concerning this work, it cannot be doubted that it was looked upon as very important, since three writers have commented upon it and supplemented it soon after the death of the sage. These are Kung-yang, Kuh-liang, and Tso Kiu-ming, whose respective works have been included among the classics under the Sung dynasty. Their remarks on the special words used by the Master in such and such circumstances must be noticed as an answer to possible doubts on the authorship of Confucius in the case of that work.

587) As reported by Mencius, III, 2, ix, 8.
588) Cf. J. Legge, *Chinese Classics*, vol. V., p. 34.
589) Cf. J. Legge, *ibid*., p. 5, 6, 14, and especially, 40-49, introd. ; 34, 84, 210, 283, 404, 466, &c.—Arthur H. Smith, *Chinese characteristics*, 1892. p. 82.
590) And confirmed by Szema Tsien, *She ki*, kiv. 47, in general terms.
591) The *fen* and *tien*, cf. *supra* note 516 and *infra* note 593 and text.
592) Cf. *Chin. Class.*, III, intr. p. 4.
593) Kung Ngan-kwoh, in his preface, gives this information on these lost two works, which existed yet at the time of Confucius Lao Tan, Lieh tze, &c. The present work called *San fen* by Mao Tsien in 1084, is a made up composition which perhaps contains a few fragments of the old work, but is certainly not the lost book recovered as it pretends to be.—A *San fen shu*, with a Commentary by Yuen Han of the Tsin dynasty (400 A.D.), is included in the Han-Wei collection of reprints. On some archaisms which cannot be a forgery in that work, Cf. R. K. Douglas, *The Calendar of the Hia dynasty*, introd.
594) Cf. T. de L., *The oldest Book of the Chinese*, § 37, n. 2.
595) The Book of Poetry or *She King* existed before his time (cf. *Chin. Class.* V, 4), and the work of Confucius in editing it, consisted in the suppression, (and alteration in words or composition of ideograms) of that he did not find serviceable for the incalculation of propriety and righteousness. (Cf. *She Ki*, kiv. 46).
596) Cf. however the *Hi-tse* (II. 15) great appendix of the *Yh King*.—Tso tchuen, 10, XVII., ann. 525, and another passage of the same chronicle.
597) *Sung*, 2103 Bas.—*K'i*, 4098 Bas.—*Ki-tchou*, 9225 -2381Bas.—, *Tchuh*, 7024 Bas.—*Kiu*, 8959 Bas.—*Tchen*, 11783 Bas.
598) Cf. *Tso tchuen*. s, xiv., 1.
599) *Lun yu*, iii., 9.—In the *Tchung yung*, xxviii., 5, he makes a distinction between the two, and says that ceremonies of the Shang-yu dynasty were still continued in the State of Sung.
600) Cf, *Kang kien y tchi luh*.—Medhurst, *Ancient China*, p. 370.— Cf. also *Li Ki*, XVII., iii., 19, for slight variants.
601) Cf. *Tso tchuen*, 10, XVII.
602) According to the rectified chronology, the dates of the reigns of these founders were the following : Huang-Ti, 2285-2232 B.C.— Shao Hao 2276-2213.—Kao-Yang Tchuen hiuh hiuh, 2225-2147.—Kao Sin Ti Kuh, 2160-2085.—Ti Tchih, 2085-2076.—Yao, 2076-1976.—Shun, 202.-1955 B.C.
603) Shuh belonged to the Princely family of the native State of Yu, in

S.E. Shansi, which he had left, and which was conquered by the Chinese in 2018 B.C. Cf. Szema Tsien, *She Ki*, 1., 12 v. --*T.P.* 64, 5 v.; 135, 9 v.—*Mêng-tze*'s (iv., 2, ii., 1) statement that Shun was a *tung y tchi jen*, a man of the Eastern Barbarians, is thus explained satisfactorily; the barbarians here being the native tribes who had not yet acknowledged the government of Yao.

[CHAP. VII. PART III. FIFTH PERIOD : 481-224 B.C.]

Sect. A. *General Survey. Formation of Neo-Taoism and Taoszeism.*

163. During the period which embraces the evolution of Chinese civilisation, from the beginning of the internecine wars between the states contending for the final supremacy, to the foundation of the Empire, there was a great disorder everywhere. Each of the principalities was independent, and had ceased to take any care of the general welfare and of the time honoured habits and customs. Therefore we cannot be surprised that notwithstanding the political troubles, religious innovations and material progresses of foreign origin should characterise this period. The two channels, through which they were imported into China, were that of the sea-traders of the Indian Ocean in Shantung which ceased about 375 B.C., and the south-west route from India and the West. In the North-west the state of Ts'in whose fate it was to become the nucleus of the Chinese Empire at the end of the period, grew more and more civilised from its contact with the other states of the agglomeration, and the barbarous elements in its population were greatly softened away. No intercourse seems however to have been renewed with the further west, and there was no change in the stoppage in that direction which we have mentioned during the last period (§ 147) for outside relations.

164. The number of states forming the Chinese dominion was reduced to six important ones besides that of Ts'in[604], and the period is often called from this fact in Chinese history, Period of the six kingdoms. Some states once important, disappeared altogether[605], such as that of Ts'ao (?—866-487), Tch'en (?—854-479), Wu (?—656-473), Ts'ai

(1110-447), Tsin (?—858-376), Tch'eng (806-375 b.c.). Others were reduced to the rank of attached states[606], such were Lu (1110-409), Wei (1103-414) and Sung (1001-404 b.c.) Moreover a very large number of small principalities were absorbed and their territories contributed to enlarge those of their conquerors. The six states which survived were the following, Ts'i (1091-221); Yen (?—564-222); and Ts'u (?—1078-223) amongst the ancients, and three new ones : Tchao (517-457-228 cap. Han-tan ; Wei (453-406-231) cap. Ta Liang ; and Han (453-423-225 b.c.) cap. Tcheng. The independence of the states from the traditional allegance to the House of Tchou, is best shown by the respective dates when their rulers assumed the dignity of *Wang* or king [607], which belonged to the Ruler of the Central state : Ts'u in 671 ; Ts'i in 378; Wei in 370; Yen and Han in 332; Tchao and Ts'in in 325 b.c.

165. As to the Central Kingdom of Tchou, its fortune had fallen, and until its disappearance in 249, when the last King of this once glorious dynasty was reduced to the condition of a private man by the King of Ts'u, it had hardly any political standing during the period. It was however in charge of the traditional rites, and the famous *T'chou-li* or Ritual of the Tchou dynasty was then completed, probably about the year 430 b.c.[608] The Official Book of Tchou or *Tchou Kwan*, as such was its title at the time, was based upon the list of officers of the State administration organized by Tchou Kung[609] when regent of the Kingdom (1103 b.c.) and of which the first scheme forms one of the chapters of the *Shu King* (V. xx) also called *T'chou Kwan*. It grew by subsequent additions of offices and functions during the following centuries down to the latter part of the fifth century, when the descendants of Wen Wang and Wu Wang had fallen too low to be able to make any further regulations. It may be looked upon as the political will of the vanishing dynasty, in which was embodied the administration of the country as they had dreamed it, but not such as it ever was at any time[610].

As the *T'chou-li* contains many references to innovations introduced during the Tchou dynasty, the story of its composition required to be noticed here[611].

166. The condition of general disorder which prevailed during that period was unfavorable to the extension throughout the Chinese dominion of any uniform system of views. Lao Tan and Confucius were gone[612], sadder if not wiser men, without seeing the success of their doctrines, although the former was perhaps less unfortunate under that respect.

than his younger contemporary. Soon after their disparition their teachings flourished. The school of wonderism, which had grown out of the influence of the trader-colonists of the Indian Ocean settled at Lang-ga and Tsih-Moh who had taught Astrology and an overrated conception of the transforming powers of nature, amalgamated with the pure Taoism of Lao-tze, and formed henceforth what may be called the Neo-Taoism or Tao-szeism[613], while Confucianism remained in opposition to it, such as his founder had conceived it against the encroachments of Wonderism, Taoism, and Shamanism. It was indeed the rising of Confucianism which led to the fusion of these various elements.

167. This important transformation deserves all attention. Indifferent and matter-of-fact by nature, the Chinese had hitherto shown little curiosity and interest in all questions of historical origin and ontology, with their usual accompaniment of fabulous reports. They had neglected to investigate these problems, and the legends of early times imported from the West by Hwang-ti and his Bak tribes, and preserved in the Royal Archives, had received little care and attention. With the exception of the *Kuei-tsang* of the Hia and Shang dynasties[614], and of the *Yh-king* which had been edited from slips bearing the various meanings of some ideograms[615], little seems to have been done, and they remained as unused documents known only of the very few. But when arose the feeling of curiosity and taste for wonders, which the foreigners of Lang-ga and Tsih-moh had awaken among them, and were keeping up by their continuous flow of novelties, many Chinese found a national satisfaction in studying the old *fen* and *tien* records of their Archives, which Lao Tan had made use of in writing his *Tao teh king* (*supra*, note 516). The School of Wonderism, if it deserves to be so-called, was thus led to lay hold of the pure teaching of Taoism by itself too abstruse by far, as a peg for their elucubrations. From the fusion of these two movements so different and so opposed one another, and its absorption of the natural shamanism[617] disallowed by Confucianism, resulted the mixed school of philosophy, religion and superstition known as Tao-sze-ism which has survived to the present day, and has become one of the grossest assemblage of superstitions which have ever existed.

168. The Ancient traditions and texts were eagerly sought for, and all sorts of incidents, stories and marvellous accounts were brought to light by the writers of the new school, such as Lieh-tze, Tchwang-tze and others, in support of their views and theories ; the new ideas which were reaching China at that time were joined to old traditions[618], so as to

make new combinations illustrating their own conceptions, and every fragment of primitive legends in China became embellished with new circumstances. Romantic and wonderful accounts hitherto little known in the realistic Chinese literature of former ages began from that time. Tso Kiu-Ming in writing his precious chronicle parallel to the *Tchun tsiu* of Confucius, although fettered to some extent by some Confucianist prejudices, could not himself escape entirely the influence of this remarkable movement.

169. Lao Tan having taken his cosmogony, as we have seen in the previous part (§ 133-137) from some old texts where teachings of Hwang-ti were preserved the name of the first leader of the Chinese was associated to that of the old philosopher, to denominate the new school, and Hwang-Lao appears as a name to that effect under the HAN dynasty[619], but after that period, instead of Hwang, the use of which had become awkward since it was part of the imperial title, the name of Tchwang (tze) was used in its stead, and the appellation disappeared afterwards.

170. The old texts in which were embodied the traditional lessons of Hwang-ti were edited and commented; and thus enlarging upon the really important part occupied by the early leaders in the history of the civilisation of the country, all that was considered as fundamental and the principle of every thing, was by a regular extension of views[620] attributed to them. Shennung shared with Hwang-ti the suggested authorship of some ancient fragments, and the catalogue of Literature in the Annals of the Former Han dynasty gives evidence to that effect. The name of Hwang-ti appears in the titles of fourteen works, on philosophy, the *yn* and *yang* principles medecine, and spirits. Five works concerning Shennung, are on husbandry, the five elements, omens and spirits, and a work on diet bears the joint names of Shennung and Hwang-ti. Some of these works are stated to have been compiled during the Period of the six states, *i.e.* the period we are studying at present (cf. § 164), while others were older[621]. Compositions embodying alleged views and principles of Tchwan-hiuh, Yao, Shun, &c. were also written about that time.

171. The philosophical and literary activity of the Tao-szeists became very great during the fourth and third centuries B.C., in the states of WEI and TS'I, and still more so in the state of YEN (Petchili) which was less disturbed by the internecine wars. The descendants and disciples of Lao Tan who preserved less unsullied the teachings of their master had come to the state of WEI (N. Honan).[622] Lang-ga itself, which had been for a long time the most important centre of the new movement had become

involved in the wars.[623]

So numerous are the names of these philosophers which history has preserved, and whose writings are in some cases still existing, that this activity must have been very great.

172. Among the disciples of Lao Tan, gradually diverging from his teachings without however passing to Taoszeism, let us remember the names of Wen-tze,[624] Yang tchu[625] (c. 450 B.C.), Wang hü otherwise Kwei kuh tze (c. 380), Tchang-y (D. 312), Su Ts'in (D. 318), Hoh kwan tze (325-278 B C.) and others. Meh-tze[626] (c. 100) and Mêng-tze (372-289 B.C.) known of all as Mencius, deserve to be mentioned separately as having stated views of their own more divergent than the others.

173. Among the Taoszeists, we must mention On Kihien, and Hu-tze of TCHENG; the latter was the master of Lieh tze; Lieh Yu-kou or Lieh tze (c. 400 B.C.) who himself had many disciples, and from his native state of TCHENG went to that of WEI;[627] Tchwang-Tchou or Tchwang-tze of WEI in the IVth century;[628] Tsou-hien of Ts'i (c. 378-300), who created an important school. After visiting the King Hwei of WEI at Liang, and the Prince of TCHAO at Ping-yuen, he went, specially invited, to live near the King Tchao (311-273 B.C.) of YEN. who built the palace called *Kieh-shih Kung* (near the present Peking) for him and his followers.[629] Among his disciples the most famous were the following: Sun-K'ing of TCHAO, who was fifty years old when he adopted his doctrines, and who became later on the teacher of Li-sze, the famous prime minister of Ts'IN She Hwang-ti; Shun yü Kwan and Tien ping Tsieh tze of Ts'I, Hwan-yuen of Ts'U, Shen Tao and Sün k ing of TCHAO who were all famous for their profession of the Hwang-Lao doctrines.[630] In the state of YEN, Sung Wu-ki, Tcheng-pe Kiao, and Tch'ung shang, have also their names preserved in history.[631]—But the most famous of all were Lieh-tze, Tchwang-tze, and Tsou-hien, whom we shall have to mention again further on.

NOTES——

604) Since the time of Hiao Kung in 361 B.C., the Ts'IN state gave up the Rites of TCHOU to follow those of the SHANG dynasty. This was done to show its independence. In 336 B.C., the King of TCHOU transferred to the Prince of Ts'IN the privilege of issuing the imperial coinage, i.e. coins without name of the issuer. Cf. my *catalogue of Chinese coins*, introd. p. xiv.

605) The query shows that there is some uncertainty on their exact beginning, although it is claimed that they all began with the TCHOU dynasty, i.e. in 1110 B.C.

606) They were respectively extinguished in 249, 209 and 286 respectively.

607) *Wang*, R u l e r or King was the usual title of the Rulers of China since the SHANG dynasty, when it took the place of *H o u*, S o v e r e i g n which was used during the HIA dynasty. Previously to that time since Yu Nai Hwang ti, the name of the ruler was preceeded by *Ti* d i v i n e, such as Ti Yao, Ti Shun, which was used alone when adressing them or speaking of them. (Cf. *Shu king*, Part I). At the beginning of the HIA dynasty, *T'ien tze*, S o n o f H e a v e n appears for the first time instead of *Ti* (*ibid*. III, iv. 5). *Hwang*, an emphasized form of *Wang*, k i n g, and written ideographically s e l f + k i n g was used in speaking of the Royal Ancestors, during the same dynasty (*ibid*. III, iii. 4), and began to be employed for the living sovereign at the end of the YN dynasty (*ibid*. V, iv, 9, 10, 11, 15). The combination *Hwang Ti*, D i v i n e s e l f - R u l e r, appeared for the first time in 950, in speaking of the ancient *Ti* Yü (*ibid*. V, xxvii, 5, 6) and seems to have been seldom used until the foundation of the Chinese Empire in 221 B.C. when it was adopted as the designation of the Emperor. It has remained in use since then. The outcome of this note is that to speak of the early *Emperors* of China is a misnomer. In some historical works such as the Bamboo Annals, the prefixing of *Ti* was continued until the end of the HIA dynasty.—The statements on the subject in L. de Rosny, *La civilisation Japonaise*, p. 134, are not based on ancient authorities.

608) The inference is drawn from the following statements: "TCHOU K'ao Wang (440-426 B.C.) has appointed his younger brother to the south of the Ho. He is *Hwan* Kung ; *i suh Tchou kung tchi kwan shih*, ' for supplement to Tchou kung directions of officers." *She ki*, Kiv. 4, f. 27—Hwang Fu-mi, *Ti wang she ki*, says: *K'ao Tcheh* wang appointed his younger brother *Kieh* to the south of the Ho: *Suh Tchou kung tchi kwan*, litt.? continue (or supplement) Tchou kung's officers.

609) The observations made with the Gnomon about 1100 B.C. at Lohyang and mentioned (*supra*) § 94 as verified by Laplace and Biot, are reported in the Kiv. ix, 17 of the *Tchou li*. Cf. trad. Biot, vol. I. p. 201, and *introduction*, p. x.

610) The Kingdom of Tchou was an aggregate of principalities under the suzerainty of the successors of Wu Wang : and each of these principalities had their own administration imitated from that of the Central Kingdom but on a smaller scale. Now this Central Kingdom never did cover a large area, and after the Compulsory transfer of the Capital to Loh-yang, it was indeed a small affair. Even in the palmy days of the first period, the revenue and populations of the state would not have been sufficient to keep up so numerous a staff as that described in the *Tchou-li*. The figures are enormous. Here they are for five of the six Ministries : (i) 3920 ; (ii) 9609 ; (iii) 3633 ; (iv) 5080; (v) 3787 ; total 26029 persons in (59, 64, 58, 65 and 58) three hundred and four administrative sections. If as prob.ble the sixth Ministry was on the average of the others, the staff of the Government of the Central Kingdom would have included about 31235 individuals.

611) It has been preserved in its entirety, save the last of its six books, for which another one said to be of Ancient date has been supplied during the Han dynasty. The work has been assailed in several in-

stances, by the Hwang-ti, in 213 B.C. who wanted it to be destroyed,
and afterwards because of its regulations which displeased later rulers
For this history cf. Ed. Biot, *Introduction* to his translation, pp. ix-
xxx. J. Legge, introd. to his translation of the *Li ki*, p. 4-5; Alex.
Wylie, *Notes on Chinese literature*, p. 4.
612) Lao Tan had gone away long before the demise of Confucius which
happened in 479 B.C.
613) This convenient term, as a distinctive from Taoism has been happily coined by Prof. L. de Rosny, more than twenty years ago. Should
not the word Taoizcism have been already in use, I would have preferred myself that of Neo-Taoism.
614) The *Kuei-tsang* contained a certain number of the primitive legends
quoted as used in divination by HIA HOU Ki (1946-1937 B.C.) the
son and successor of the Great Yü. Unhappily the work is lost, and
is known to us but through quotations by ancient writers. On this
work. Cf. T. de L., *The Oldest Book of the Chinese*, 1892, pp. xi-
xiii, xxi, and 29. And some extracts in *Tai ping yü lan*, Kiv. 35, f.
1 : 373, 2 : 914, 3 ; 929, 1 ; &c. ; and in *Shan hai king*, edit. Pih
Yuen 1781, Kiv. 2, f. 14, 14v.; 7. 1 ; 17, 3 ; &c.
615) Cf. *supra*, ch. IV, sect. *b*, 24.
616) Besides the *Kuei-tsang* and the *Yh King*, we may refer also to the
fragments of Yü-hiung of the XIth century, and of Kuan Y-wu of
the VIIth. Other works concerning them have existed in antiquity
but they have not escaped the wrecks of literature in the course of
centuries.
617) The New-Taoism has gradually absorbed the gods of the aboriginal
populations of the country as well as all novelties from the outside.
The oldest information we possess on the native worship is given by
the *Shan-hai king*, but it has not yet been investigated. It consists
of descriptions of local gods made apparently by some writers of the
Neo-Taoist school.
618) Cf. the excellent remarks of Dr. J. Edkins on this precise point, in
his short paper on *Ancient Navigation in the Indian Ocean*, l.c. p.
23.—Cf. also by the same scholar on early Taoism: *Phases in the development of Tauism* : Trans. China Br. R.A.S., 1885, v. 4 ; *On early
Tauist Alchemy* : Shanghae Miscellany; *Steps in the growth of early
Tauism* : China Review, XV., 176-190.
619) For instance in Szema Tsien, *She Ki*, Kiv. 28, f. 21 v. : *Hwang-
Lao yen* ; and Kiv. 74, f. 4 : *Kiai hioh Hwang Lao tao teh tchi shu*,
they all studied the Tao and Teh of Hwang Lao. The author refers to
several writers of that school.—It also occurs in the *Tsien Han shu*,
Biographies, 32.—In the list of works existing in 983A.D. (*infra* note
621) appears a *Hwang Lao King*.
620) Cf. with reference to Hwang-ti, J. Edkins, *Place of Hwang-ti in
early Tauism* : China Review, 1887, p. 233-239.
621) *Tsien Han Shu*, Kiv. 30. Herewith the list of these works. Class 11,
On *Tao*: Hwang-ti and four Kings, 4 piens ; Hwang-ti's princes and
ministers, 10 p.; Miscellanies on Hwang-ti, 58 p.; (all said to have
been written at the time of the six Kingdoms).—Cl. 18, *Husbandry:*
—Shennung, 20 p,——Cl. 19. Talks :—Hwang ti's talks, 40 p.——
Cl. 31. Five elements: Hwang ti's Yn and Yang, 25 Kiv, ;
Discourses of the time of Hwang-ti on Yn and Yang, 25 Kiv.; Shen-

nung's Great mystery of the five elements, 27 Kiv.——Cl. 33. Divination : — On auspicious husbandry according to Shennung.— Cl. 35. Medicine: —*Hwang ti nei King*, 18 Kiv. ——Cl. 36. Local Medicine:—The tablets of Hwang-ti, 23 Kiv. (said to be a genuine work); Shen-nung and Hwang-ti on diet.. 7 Kiv.— Cl. 37. Domestic Medicine: A work on the principles of Hwang-ti, Yao, Shun, and Yu.——Cl. 3?.—Spirits and Genii:—Four works concerning Hwang-ti and one Shennung.— - In the list of 1690 works from which extracts are quoted in the *Tai ping yü lan* Cyclopedia of 983 A.D., ten bear the name of Hwang-ti.——In the Han Wei literature, a work called *Hwang-ti Shu* on divination is quoted. Al. Wylie in his *Notes on Chinese Literature*, p. 77, says that the oldest medical treatise extant (in China) is probably the *Hwang-ti su wen*, which, without admitting its claim to be the production of Hwang-ti, there is reason to believe it to have been written several centuries before Christ, and to contain a summary of the traditional knowledge of medicine handed down from the most remote times. The *Hwang-ti su wen* form the first half of the modern *Hwang-ti nei King*, of which the first European translation has been given abridged by Prof. Ch. de Harlez, in his *Textes Taoistes*, p. 341 sq.

622) *She Ki*, Kiv. 73.

623) Lang-ya was for the first time submitted to Ts'i in 547. then to Wu in 493, to Yueh in 472 of which it remained the capital until 380 B.C. when it was given up because of the civil wars, which made the place unsafe.

624) Wen-tze was the most remarkable. His literary remains are embodied in the later work which bears his name and has been translated in C. de Harlez, *Textes Taoistes*, p. 83-161.—Cf. also G. v. d. Gabelentz, *das taoistische Werk Wên-tsi* : Dec. 1887.

625) On Yang tchu's opinions, cf. J. Legge, *Chinese Classics*, vol. II, p. 95-108 of introduction.

626) Meh-Tih or Meh-tze, who taught Universal love. On his opinions cf. J. Legge, ibid., p. 103-125, and E. Faber, *die Grundgedanken des alten chinesischen Socialismus, oder die Lehre des Philosophen Micius* Elberfeld, 1877. Also G. v. d. Gabelentz, *Ueber den Chinesischen Philosophen Meh Tik* ; B.xl. K. Sachs. G. d. W. Jul. 1888.

627) Lieh-tze was flourishing in 367 B.C. as shown in *China Review*, May-June 1885, p. 409.—His full name was Lieh Yü-K'ou. The name Yü-k'ou was known in Ts'i in 550 B.C. Cf. *Tso tchuen*, 9, xxiii, 8.—Lieh tze quotes Tze-tch'an, a famous minister of Tcheng, who lived in 575-496 B.C.—He was himself belonging to the same principality which was destroyed in 375 B.C. by the Han state.—In the literary catalogue of 9 B.C., there is an entry of a work in 8 books under his name. Cf. *Tsien Han shu*, kiv. 30, sect. 11.—The work which exists at present under his name, also in eight chapters, was apparently written down by his disciples, and " may yet be accepted as a fair specimen of his teaching." Cf. J. Legge, *Texts of Taoism*, 1, p. 5.—His work has been abridged and translated by C. de Harlez, *Textes Taoistes*, pp. 180-339, with evidence of the existence of Lieh-tze which had been doubted by some writers, such as F. H. Balfour, *Leaves from my Chinese Books*, p. 83 sq., and others. Cf. also on Lieh-tze, E. Faber, *Der Naturalismus bei den alten Chinesen, oder die*

sämmtlichen werke des Philosophen Licius. Elberfeld, 1877.
628) Tchwang-tze was flourishing in 368 and also after 339 B.C. He
quotes Lieh-tze. His writings have been translated in full by : Frederic Henry Balfour. *The Divine Classic of Nanhua ; being the works
of Chuang tze*. Shanghai, 1881.—Herbert A. Giles, *Chuang tzŭ,
Mystic, Moralist and Social reformer*, 1889.—J. Legge, *The Texts of
Taoism*, 1891, vol. I. p. 125-392, vol. II. p. 1-232.—And partly by
C. de Harlez, *Textes Taoistes*, 1891. Cf. also Georg von der Gabelentz, *Die Sprache des Cuang-tsï*, Leipzig, 1888 ; *Der Räuber T'schik,
ein satirischer Abschnitt aus Tschuang-tsï*; April 1889.
629) A short resume of his views is given in *She-ki*, kiv. 74.
630) For the explanation of this term cf. *suprà* par. 169 and note.
631) Nearly all the information we possess about them comes from Szema Tsien, *Sh' Ki*, kiv. 28 and 74.

[CHAP. VII.—FIFTH PERIOD : 481-221 B.C.]

Sect. B) *Influences by the North-East.*

174. The two emporia of *Lang-ya* and *Tsih-moh* on the gulf of Kiao-tchou in S. Shantung, which the foreign traders of the Indian Ocean and Erythræan sea had established about 680 B.C. had various fortunes. In 547 B.C. they had acknowledged the suzerainty of the great state of Ts'ı, and in 493, had been conquered by the state of Wu. In 472 the latter state was destroyed by its southern neighbour, the kingdom of *Yueh*

which transferred the seat of its capital at Lang-ya where it remained for 92 years. In 380 the war raging between the states of Ts'ı, of Ts'u, and of Yueh compelled the latter to withdraw from its advanced position in the North.[632] *Lang-ya* was evacuated[633] and remained waste until 220 hen it was rebuilt by Ts'ıN she Hwang ti.[634] *Tsih-moh*, for several years previously had supported in his gradual encroachments Tien Ho, a grandee of the state of Ts'ı, who finally in 386 overthrew his legal Prince, and assumed for himself the supreme authority with the title of Tai Kung Ho.[635] The result of that support was felt all over the principality of Ts'ı by the establishment of the worship of the Eight Hindu Vasus, as we shall see below. In the year 370 the native governor of Tsih-moh was rewarded by the erection of his authority into a Chinese *ta fu*.[636] But the foreign sea traders came no more, as a shorter and more convenient route had been discovered for their commerce, as we shall see further on (sect. c).

175. Numismatics furnish monumental evidence of the great influence exercised by these Emporia. Their Monetary Unions with several inland places testify of the activity of their commercial relations. We have already noticed (§ 103) that the first stamped money in Chinese lands had been issued by the mint of Tsih-moh in 675-670 B.C., and we need not insist here again on this most important fact. Between 580 and 550, the same mint, in connection with guild-merchants of An-yang and of Kai-yang belonging to their next neighbour the state of Kıu, issued a currency of large knife-money similar to that issued before at Tsih-moh only. Between 547 and 495, the merchants of the latter place in connection with guild-merchants of Yng-ling capital city of Ts'ı, and of Kai-yang, issued also a currency of the same kind. Lang-ya, between the years 472 and 380, in connection with merchants of Yang yh and Lu, in Shansi C. and S. issued a currency of large plate (*pu*) coins. These various issues are illustrated[637] in my *Catalogue of Chinese coins, from the VIIth cent. B.C. to* A.D. *621, including the series in the British Museum* (1892).

176. We have already remarked, in a previous paragraph (108) of the fourth period, that the influence in East China, of the sea traders of the Indian Ocean having their emporia on the South coast of Shantung, displayed transformations which, after the lapse of time required by the geographical distance, corresponded or ought to correspond to changes at the fountain head of their trade. Three successive waves somewhat different in character can be discerned during the three centuries that this

influence existed.

During the seventh century, epoch of the first wave, the chief notions which radiated from their Shantung emporia were chiefly Sabæo-Phœnician, with few Babylonian and Hindu elements which they had adopted hitherto. This we have shown in our paragraphs 104 and 105. It resulted from the introduction of the Phœnician navy in the Erythæan sea (*supra*, 113-119), which we have described.

177. The second wave began much later in the seventh century, and consisted chiefly of *pyrolatric* notions, occasionally mixed with a sort of dualism, which we enumerate further on (§ 181-186 . But these notions, rather varied, cannot be ascribed in any definite manner, as far as I am aware, either to Mazdeism as described in the Gâthas, or to the Persian creed shown on the Behistun inscription. They may have been related to the variety of Zoroastrianism that was practised by the Akhæmenians when they conquered Elam under Tchaispaish (Teispês) some time about, probably before, 600 B.C.[638], for the Avestic character of several of these notions is clear and cannot be mistaken. Now we know that ships could go there inland, for Nearchus was able to take to Susa his fleet when arriving from India,[639] and therefore some of these peculiar and ancient Mazdæans may have taken part in the eastern sea-trade[640]. The more southern ports of Siraf and of Omana were not yet opened at that time[641].

The third wave of influence is more Hindu than anything else, as shown below, in the paragraphs 191-195. It began in the fifth century and does not seem to have been altered until that same foreign sea trade of the Gulf of Kiao-tchou came to an end.

178. On Wednesday, the 28th day of October 539[642], the Persians under Cyrus had conquered Babylon and thus put an end to the Babylonian Monarchy. In 525, the conquest of Egypt increased the facilities for international exchange of views and notions.[643] After 512 B.C. Darius anxious to know where the Indus emptied itself into the sea[644], sent a maritime expedition under the command of the Karian Greek Skylax with orders to sail down the river from a certain point in the Paktyica region on the upper course of the Indus. They followed the stream eastwards and westwards until they reached the sea ; *two years and a half* altogether of navigation led them to the head of the Red Sea[645]. The expedition therefore did not attempt to ascend the Persian Gulf. Herodotus (IV, 44) says that when this voyage was completed, Darius conquered the Indians and made use of the sea in those parts.

An Indian influence must therefore have been felt for a time afterwards among the Erythræan sea traders. At first mixed with the previous influence which obtained among them, it gradually became prevalent, but some time must necessarily have elapsed before it could be felt, and some longer time still before it produced a distinct and tangible effect as far as the most distant stations of the trade, such as those of the coast of Shantung.

179. When, less than two centuries later (i.e in 325 b.c.) Alexander sent out the expedition of Nearchus to explore the course of the Indus- all memory of the similar and previous voyage of Skylax would seem to have disappeared.[646] Maritime trade was in the hands of Hindus, and it is doubtless from them that Nearchus and Onesicritus[647] got the curious astronomical statements which they have reported, and which shows that those who made them used to travel in the Indian Ocean, and advanced far enough to the South to be well within the tropic.[648] We may there- fore conclude that the Northerners, i.e. the inhabitants of Northern In- dia and the region of the Persian Gulf had then little interest, if any, left in the Southern Sea trade.

180. With the removal of the capital of YUEH from Lang-ya, the sea- trade of the Gulf of Kiao-tchou in S. Shantung seems to have come to an end. The traders of the Indian Ocean and Erythræan Sea ceased to frequent the emporia of Tsih-moh and Lang-ya. They may have frequen- ted for a certain time afterwards the entrance of the Yang-tze Kiang at the proximity of the new capital city of YUEH, which was the modern Su-tchou, but we have no evidence in the present state of our researches. in favour or against this probability. About 375, the scanty knowledge which these sharp seafarers had imparted of their route, among endless fa- bles, had hardly anything left to substantiate it, and the whole had passed to mythology and fables. Difficulties on their route which arose from the hostility of natives against the revictualling of their ships, had most pro- bably for some time before diminished the frequency of journeys made by these bold adventurers. This is suggested by circumstances related in the fables concerning the *Fire* (afterwards *Three*) *Fortunate islands* which we have examined before.[649] The route through Indo-China saved a great deal of sea-faring, and, frequented since in the previous century, it took the place of the former and longer journey.

NOTES——

632) The capital was removed to *Wu*, whose name has survived as that

of the prefectural city of Su-tchou, in Kiang-su.
633) On these events cf. Szema Tsien, Kiv. 32, fol. 27.—*I'chuh shu ki nien*, V, 30, ann. 23.—*Wu yueh tchun tsiu*; T.P., Kiv. 160, fol. 6 v.—T. de L., *Catalogue of Chinese coins*, p. liv, lxii, lxiii.
634) He established there a population of 20 or 30 thousand families, cf. Szema Tsien, kiv. 6, fol. 14 v., 26; kiv. 28, fol. 12.
635) The *T'ien* family since the days of T'ien Tchang had been by themselves a state in the State. T'ien Tchang put to death Duke Kien in 481 and placed Ping Kung on the throne. In 386 his grandson T'ien Ho removed the reigning Duke K'ang from his capital, and placed him in the city of Hai-pin (60 *li* E. of Fu-ning hien in Tchihli, N.) where he might maintain the sacrifices to his ancestors, and where he led an inglorious life until his death in 379. Cf. Szema Tsien, kiv. 32, fol. 27.
636) Cf. Hoh tchi, *Tsi moh tchi*, 1753, kiv. i, f. 3.—*She ki*, Tien tai kung she kia.
637) Cf. pp. 215-219, 224-226; 105.
638) *Cylinder of Cyrus*, Inscript. l. 21.— Cf. Sir Henry Rawlinson, *Notes on a Clay Cylinder of Cyrus the Great*: J.R.A.S. 1380, XII, 70-97. —A. H. Sayce, *Herodotus*, 1883, p. 438, 482.
639) Arrian. *Indica*, c. 42.—Bunbury, Ancient Geography, I, 539.
640) The inland trade with Media and its connection with the Erythræan sea trade existed some time earlier as shown by the quince fruits which the sea-farers of Shantung introduced in China before 660 B.C. This date might require confirmation from another source of evidence than that of the Chinese critics in their classification of the odes, which is the only one on which it rests at present. Cf. *suprà* n. 389.
641) None of them is mentioned by Nearchus in his journey along the coasts.
642) According to the calculations of Dr. J. Oppert, communicated to the Academie des Inscriptions, Dec. 23, 1892.
643) Cf. *suprà* on Egyptian influences in Persia, N. 364.
644) Herodot. IV, 44. The report of the journey of Skylax of Karianda, was still existing at the time of Aristotle (Politic. VII, 13. 1).
645) E. H. Bunbury, *History of Ancient Geography*, I, 227.
646) Bunbury, *O.C.* I. 227.
647) Arrian, *Indica*, c. 25.—Pliny, VI., 23, § 98.
648) They found the shadows not to follow the same rules as in other countries, but either the sun was vertical at noon, or the shadow was cast *to the south*. He added that the constellations and stars, which had usually been high in the heavens, now were only just above the horizon, and those that were elsewhere constantly visible, 'ose and set again after a short interval.'—Bunbury, *Q.C.*, I., 534-5, 543, and 548-549.
649) *Supra* §122-126.

Innovations concerning Fire.

181. We have briefly in a previous paragraph (106) alluded to the new notions concerning fire, which made their appearance in the Chinese

states of the East in proximity with the foreign settlements of S. Shantung in the sixth century. As they continued to develop or at least to be more known during the present period, and as their influence and importance are considerable for history, we take here again the subject from the beginning, in order to enumerate the various points it concerns, although the evidence about them is not strictly in chronological order. It belongs however to the same period.

182. We may notice among other innovations:

—A state sacrifice every year at the vernal equinox for the renewal of fire; ⁶³⁰ all fires had to be extinguished for three days previously and food taken cold. The rule was established for the first time in Tsin (Shansi)⁶⁵¹ by the Marquess Wen (636-627 B.C.) who had taken as a wife *Ki-Wei*, one of the chief's daughters of the Non-Chinese barbarians Tsiang Kiu ju.⁶⁵²

—A new worship of a deity of Fire named *Hwei-luh*, and of a deity of Water named *Hiuen Ming*, previously mentioned § 106. We hear of it in 524 in *Tch'eng* (S. Honan) once only, as if it was but a local affair, but it seems connected with the pyrolatric views mentioned earlier, notably in 564, 541, and 533, in the state of Sung (E. Honan) which as we know was in close relation with the foreigners of Lang-ya and Tsih-Moh.⁶⁵³ —A female and male character attributed respectively to fire and water, which are distinctly stated, the fire to be the *fei* or wife of water, and the water to be the *mou* or husband of fire, in 533 and 525 B.C.⁶⁵⁴

183. The worship of the Fire Goddess *Hwei-luh* is highly interesting, because transformed by the ancestral and euhemeristic prejudices of the Chinese it has become the worship of the Spirit of the Hearth, the household Fire-god, commonly called the Kitchen-god⁶⁵⁵. It was sacrificed for the first time by Hia Fu-tchi Keeper of the Ancestral temple of the state of Lu, about 600 B.C., who burnt in his honour, and right in the teeth of sacrificial orders' a pile of fire-wood. Confucius whose opinion was asked in after times on the matter disapproved that mode of sacrificing in that occasion, 'at present, said he, that sacrifice is paid to a wife of old time ; the materials for it might be contained in a tub, and the (ritual) vase is the common wine-jar⁶⁵⁶.' A popular saying quoted in the *Lun-yü* : 'It is better to pay court to the kitchen fire than to the south-west corner⁶⁵⁷,' shows that this worship was not yet an ancient institution at the time of Confucius. As a fact it was then worshipped only in some parts of the land ; in 533 it existed in Honan E.⁶⁵⁸ and in the third century B.C., it was also flourishing in Kiang-su and in

CHINESE CIVILISATION.

Shansi[659]. It assumed gradually a more and more important position in the popular religion of the country, and was adopted by the Emperor himself under the Han dynasty (133 B.C.)[660]; at present it has become the most extensively worshipped divinity of China. The various names given to it show the successive and different aspects under which it was considered. That of *Hwei-luh*, its historical antecedent which has been already described, was shortened into the name of *Wei*[661], from that of Ki Wei, the Chinese lady of barbarian birth, wife of the Duke Wen of Tsin in 636-627 B.C., doubtless because her husband had made some innovations in the annual ceremony of the renewal of fire, as noticed § 182. Another denomination used in the IVth cent. B.C., for *Ki Wei*, was *Ki* which is the tuft or coiffure of a Chinese lady; the deity was then represented as a beautiful woman dressed in red[662]. Her worship as that of the First Cook, *Sien tch'uei*, was recognized as a regional one in Tsin, i.e. North half of Shansi, by Kao-tsu, the first Emperor of the Han dynasty in 206 B.C.[663]. The names of *Tsuan shin*, 'Spirit of the furnace,' and of *Tsao shin*, 'Spirit of the hearth' were and have remained the most common names of that divinity[664]. Its female character was generally acknowledged and remained undisputed until the second century of our era, when it passed to the stronger sex[665].

NOTES——
650) Fire was looked upon since early times among the Chinese as a great purifier, and large state fires were kindled at the beginning of each season to ward off the evil influences of the incoming period. Special wood fuel was selected for that object. The management of these fires was in the hands of a Director of Fire. The first appointment of the kind dates from the reign of Ti Kuh Kao Sin, the fourth ruler of the Bak Sings in China (2160-2085 B.C.). It was given to *Tchung-li*, who thus became *Tchuh-Yung*; but sent by his master against *Kwan*, intendant of public works (*Kung Kung*) who was disobedient, he was unsuccessful and fell into disgrace.
651) Cf. *Si King tsa ki* by Liu-hin (Han dyn.)—*Yeh tchung ki* by Luh-hwei (Tsin dyn.)—*King Tsu suy she ki* by Ts'ung-lin (6th cent.).— T.P. 31, 2-3.—De Groot, *Fêtes à Emouy*, I. 212.
652) The *Tsiang Kiu ju*, 2572-1213-1852 Bas; the first word also written 2196 or 5619 Bas.) are mentioned in the *Tso tchuen* in 637, and in the *Tchun tsiu* in 583 B.C. (*Ch. Cl.*, V., 186, 351, 353). The race they belonged to is not known although they were settled on the present frontiers of Shansi and Shantung. They have been reckoned as a tribe of the Red Tih or Teks (Legge, *Ch. Cl*, V., prol. 127; Plath. *Fremde barbarische Stämme im alten China*, 465; on the Teks, cf. T. de L., *Languages of China before the Chinese*, 167) because they were in proximity with the latter, but as they were attacked by them in 637, it

seems to me very doubtful that they should belong to the same race. They were finally dispersed in 588 by the states of TSIN and WEI, at the same time as the remnants of the Red Teks.
653) Cf. *Tso tchuen* under these various years, and 5, xxix., 1-5.
654) *Fei*, 1853 Bas.—*Mou*, 5647 Bas.—*Tso tchuen*, 10, ix, 3; xvii. 5.
655) At present, there are two objects of worship, as the Chinese aver, to be found in every family, viz. the Ancestral tablet and the kitchen god.' J. Doolittle, *Social life of the Chinese*, 1868, p. 417.
656) Cf. *Li Ki*, VIII, i, 23; Legge's translation, vol. I, p. 403-4.— The expression used is *Ngao shin* (Bas. 1834-1025) litt. spirit of the South-west corner (of the house) which commentators say is there equivalent to *Tsuan shin* (Bas. 5683-1025) 'Spirit of the hearth.' Cf. *Khang-hi tze tien*, s.v. *Ngao*.—In Ancient Chinese houses the door was always on the South-west side, as stated in the *Shi king*, II, iv. Ode 5. *Se Kan*, and the *Ngao* was inside, next to it.—At present the houses are so planned as to face southwards or at least to have their chief entrance on the south. Cf. Dr. C. A. Gordon, *Remarks on certain points relating to public health in China*, p. 9, and Dr. John Dudgeon, *Diet, dress, and dwellings of the Chinese*, p. 200 (London, 1885).
657) *Lun yü*, III, xiii. 1; ch. cl., I, 23. The famous philosopher Tchu-hi has remarked on this subject: 'The kitchen-fire was comparatively a mean place, but when the spirit of it was sacrificed to, then the rank of the two places was changed for the time, and the proverb was in vogue.'—Sign Carlo I uini, *Le Culte des génies tutelaires*, I, § 1, thinks that it refers to a preference of sacrifice 'à l'Esprit du Foyer plutôt qu' aux lares domestiques.' But this is stretching too far the meaning of the Chinese text.
658) This is shown by the name of a man from *Tcheng*, called *P'i Tsao*, i.e. attending the kitchen god, spoken of in the *Tso tchuen*, 10, ix, 3.
659) Szema Tsien, *She Ki*, kiv. 28, f. 17 v.—*Lü she T'chun tsiu*.—Gloss to *Shan hai king*, XVI, 5 r.—The name of *Hwui-luh* was that given to the deity in *Wu* as stated by Lü Pu-wei.
660) Szema Tsien, K. 28, f. 23 v.
661) *Wei*, 11832 B., 'hill-ghost'.—*Ki Wei*, 2072-11832 B.—Cf. *Yu Yang tsah tsu*, by Twan sheng shih, *d*. 863 A.D.—*T.P*. 186, 4.—*Tso tchuen*, Duke Hi, 23rd year; *Ch. Cl.* V., 186, 191, and prol. 127. —*Shan hai king*, ii. 21; vii., 2; xvi., 5.
662) *Ki*, 12683 B.—*Tchwang tze*, xix.—*Tze tien*, s.v. *ki*, 190+6, fol. 49.
663) *Sien tch'uei*, 580-5399 B. Szema Tsien, *She Ki*, kiv. 23, f. 17 v.
664) *Tsuan shin*, 5588-7025 B.—*Tsao shin*, 7352-7025 B.
665) *Tcheng hiuen* (127-200 A.D.) was I think the first who challenged the female character of the deity, and who put forward the view that the kitchen god was no other than the Director of Fires of Antiquity, the Tchuh hiung of the reign of Ti kuh Kao sin, the fourth of the first rulers.—He was followed in his views by several scholars who attempted to establish a connection between the Fire god of the hearth, and one or other of the early fire-makers, Sui-jen, Shen-nung, or Hwang-ti. And the deity in question became a god whose worship absorbed that of a god of fate *Se-ming*. How this has come to pass is still an open question which Dr. J. J. de Groot, *Les Fêtes à Emouy*, pp. 449 sq.,

579 sq. has not solved.—In some parts of China the Kitchen god is male and female. For instance at Fuhtchou the *Chau Kung*, 'Prince of the Hearth,' and *Chau Ma*, 'Mother of the Hearth are worshipped together. The ideographic spelling of *T'sao* in *T'sao shin* has given rise to a curious case of Mythography. This *T'sao* (7352 B.) in the *tchuen* style of writing just anterior but one to the present, is composed of three symbols meaning 'the Cave's red toad;' the popular belief has made it a wife of the house cricket (*Chou Ma*). Cf. Baldwin-Maclay, *Dict. Foochow dialect*, pp. 3 C, 100 ; Wells Williams, *Syllab. Dict.*, p. 954.

CHAP. VII.—FIFTH PERIOD: 481-221 B.C.
Sect. B. *Influences by the North-East.*

Innovations concerning Fire.

184. Among other innovations concerning fire introduced through the Sea trade of Shantung, let us describe:
—The peculiar notion of five sorts of fire. They are enumerated in full, for the first time by Sun-Wu[666] of T'si, who became a commander in the service of Hoh-liu, prince of Wu (514-495 B.C.), and is the author of the famous treatise on the Art of war, *Ping fah*, which has been preserved entire to the present time. Herewith his statement:

All fires classified are five in number:
the first is the *ho jen*[867] or 'fire in man';
the second is the *ho tsih* or 'fire accumulating';
the third is the *ho tche* or 'fire which travels' (the lightning);
the fourth is the *ho k'u* or 'fire in store';
the fifth is the *ho sui* or 'fire in the wooden fire-drill'.

The resemblance between this list[668] and that of the five fires in the Zend-Avesta is so close, so nearly identical, as shown in the note[869] below, that Sun-Wu must have been made acquainted with some Mazdean views in his native land which was in close relationship with the foreign tea-traders of Shantung.

185.—A remarkable superstition connected with metallurgy[672] which is recorded about 500 B.C. is perhaps another innovation due to the same source.

'Kan-tsiang, a man of *Wu* (Kiang-su) was, like Ngou-ye of YUEH[673], a master in the art of making swords. Having once presented a sword to the King Hoh-liu (514-494 B.C.),[674] he was commissioned to make two others which were called *Kan-tsiang* and *Moh-ya*[675]. Kan-tsiang had collected, to make these swords, the best ores from five mines which he mixed together with the addition of some fruitless blossoms, in order that the *Yn* and *Yang*, the breath of Heaven and Earth, should unite in the operation, but the essence of the Gold and Iron did not flow. Moh-ya[676] then said: 'A child should please to make the swords.' The King hearing this sent his son who worked at the swords for three years without success. Kan-tsiang then remarked: 'I do not understand his deportment.' Answered Moh-ya; 'for the transformation of human and spiritual things, a human being is necessary and then perfection will be obtained: at present the workmen make swords and find them not suitable, let them get a human being and their work will be perfect.' Kan-tsiang said: ' Formerly, in the foundry work of my master, the force of gold and iron was not exhausted, man and wife together did not enter the blast-furnace.' Moh-ya then added: 'the ancient masters themselves melted away their own bodies to get perfection in their work, as sacrificing a concubine would only result in sending down calamities[677].' On this Kan-tsiang and his wife cut off their hair and nails and threw them with a child[678] in the blasting furnace.'—The story goes on to state how the most complete success crowned the operation, and how the two swords were presented to the king[679].

Moh-ya, whose name is perhaps Indian, in this story has all the appearance of a foreigner who suggests the necessity of a human sacrifice in the furnace for success[680], instead of the elaborate arrangements which had been previously taken by Kan-tsiang, according to the geomantic views of the Ancient Chinese.

186.—The West Asiatic process of making fire by a concentration of the Sun rays with a concave metallic mirror was also introduced in China in the fifth century. It was not yet used in 617 nor in 506 B.C., as shown by statements of the *Tso tchuen* under these dates[681], and Confucius knew nothing of it[682]. As the *Tchou-li*, ch. 37, l. 27, mentions the implement under a foreign name[683], *ju*, it must have been introduced little after the time of the great sage, and as it is mixed up with one of these wonderful notions[684], which are connected with their influence in Shantung, the sea traders of Langga must have imported it from the West through the Indian Ocean[685]. In the second century B.C., when the *Li ki* was edited, the metal fire-implement, or *Kin-sui* as it was then called, had become a household utensil of general use, which was hung at the girdle[686]. The older system, the *sui* or fire-drill, which had been imported by the Bak families[687] remained in use, until its supplanting by the flint-process[688] (*huo-kwan*) which was well known to the Jews who went to China in the first century[689].

NOTES——
666) The subdivision of Fire was carried further in the Avesta than in the Veda. In the Veda we can distinguish three fires, sometimes called A g n i n i r m a t h y a, fire obtained by rubbing, A g n i a u s h a s y a, fire rising with the dawn, solar fire, and A g n i v a i d y u t a, the fire of lightning. In the Avesta (Yasna XVII) we meet with five fires. Cf. Max Müller, Physical Religion, 1891, p. 229.
667) On Sun Wu, commonly called Sun Tze, cf. *Szema Tsien*, Kiv. 65, fol. 1-2; Kiv. 31. fol. 13, who praises his work.—The really oldest work of this military class which has reached us entire, is that treatise on military tactics in 13 sections by Sun Wu, during the 6th cent. B.C. A. Wylie, *Notes on Chinese Literature*, p. 72.—Mayers, *Chinese R.M.*, l., 635.
668) *Ping fuh*, Kiv. 12.—*Tchou Ts'in shih yh tze*, Sun-tze, fol. 20 (edit. Hwang Hai-ngan).—*Tai ping yu lan*, Kiv. 869, f. 5 r.
669) *Ho jen*, 5381-91 Bas.—*Ho tsih*, 5381-7236 Bas.—*Ho tche*, 5381-6181 Bas.; the last symbol is sometimes written 6187, and at first 1090S Bas. with the meaning of travelling.—*Ho k'u* 5381-25-4 Bas. —*Ho Sui*, 5631-5552 Bas.: the latter symbol is sometimes written 11822 Bas.
670) The notion is entirely un-Chinese. In the *Tso t huen* in the years 598, 564, 545. 533, and 524 we hear only of a distinction between the human fire called *Ho-jen* and the fire from heaven, *ho tsai*, 5381-5393 Bas., i.e. the fire calamity.—The five fires have not received a place in the numeral categories of the *Li Ki*, and have remained a foreign and temporary notion.
671) Cf. the Avestic *Vohu-fryâna*, the good and friendly fire that dwells in the bodies of man and beasts, with the *ho-jen*, the fire in man :— the Avestic *Spênishta*, the bountiful, increasing fire, with the *ho-tsih*, the fire accumulating :—the Avestic *Vâzishta*, the most active fire, or fire of lightning, with the *ho tche*, the fire which travels, or of lightning ; —the Avestic *Berezisavanh*, the fire highly useful or that of the earth, with the *ho k'u*, the fire in store.—the Avestic *Urvâzishta*, the fire in the plants, kindled by friction, with the *Ho sui*, the fire in the wooden igniterebrator.— Cf. *Zend-Avesta*, *Yasna* xvii.—C. de Harlez,

Introduction à l'Etude de l'Aresta et de la Religion Mazdéenne, p. xcvii.—L. H. Mills, *The Zend-Aresta*, part III, p. 258; Oxford, 1887.—James Darmesteter, *Le Zend-Aresta*, vol. I, pp. 149-150; Paris, 1'92.

672) We have previously pointed out that the art of tempering iron had been introduced into China by these foreign traders about or before 540 B.C. A local legend near the gulf of K'iao-tchou attributed a special virtue for this operation to the water of a river near the settlement of their leader Kut-lu in 631. Cf. supra § 103-104.

673) His swords were famous, as shown by the following extract from *Tchwang-tze*, xv, 3 : Now he who possesses a sword made at Yueh preserves it carefully in a box and does not dare to use it, it is considered the perfection of valuable swords.

674) *Hop-liu*, 11718-11691, or 11718-2577 Bas.

675) *Kan-tsiang*, 2479-2196 Bas.—*Moh-ya*, 8975-8341, also written 11552-11393 or 11552-11470 Bas.

676) A version of the story says that Moh-ya was the wife of Kantsiang, but the narrative seems to show the contrary. And the two Chinese symbol perhaps conceal an Indian word such as *Maha*, g r e a t

677) Tchwang tze, VI, 10 makes probably an allusion to the human. sacrifice recorded here in the following passage : Here was a wellknown caster of metals, in whose crucible the molten metal bubbled and spurted up, saying: I am destined to be made into the Moh-ya sword.

678) One version says 'a girl,' another 'a boy.'

679) *Wu Yueh tchun tsiu.*—T.P. 848, 2.—Cf. also *Fung Tchou Lieh kwoh tchi*, kiv. 74.—A similar story is told about the casting of the great bell at Peking in the 4th year *Yung-loh* or 1406. An officer named Kwan-yu commissioned with the operation had failed twice in the attempt. His daughter Ko-ngai, then 16 years old, hearing from a soothsayer that the metals would not melt in the third attempt unless the blood of a virgin be mixed in the alloy, threw herself in the furnace to secure the success of her father, and the bell was happily cast. Cf. *La Piété filiale en Chine*, by Dabry de Thiersant, 1877, p. 217-219.—N. B. Dennys, *The Folklore of China*, p. 133.

680) As many superstitions of ancient times have been found to be connected with some crude notions suggested by experience, is it not possible that there should be under this a vague idea of cementation of the metal. It was an old practice with the founders to throw horns and bones in their melting furnaces.

681) In 617, at a great hunt organised by the Duke of Sung and the Earl of Tch'eng, every one is instructed to take his *sui* or fire drill. In 506, the King of Ts'u orders his men to take their *sui* or fire-drill and to light torches at the tails of the elephants which are sent forward against the army of Wu. Cf. *Tso tchuen*, 6. x, 7 ; 11, iv. 15.

682) *Lun yu*, xvii, 21, 3. He speaks only of the boring-wood implement.

683) It was called *ju*, variously written (Bas. 1800) in the *Tchou-li*, and (Bas. 7429) elsewhere, cf. T.1 .Y.L. 717, 3 r. The translation ' Miroir Mâle' proposed by G. Schlegel, *Uranographie Chinese*, p. 612, is therefore not acceptable.

684) There were two mirrors; one to receive the *Yang* or heat from the

sun, the other to receive dew or water or *Yn* from the moon for the sacrifices. Cf. *Tchou-li* kiv. 37, l. 27.—T.P.Y.L., *Kir.* 363, f. 2; kiv. 869, f. 8.

685) I am not aware of the date of the invention in the west, and 1 am not sure that it was unknown in Babylonia. Cf. the compound ideogram *sun+fire+enlarge*. (W.A.I. II, 27, 51 *a*; Brunn. 7864).— They were known to the Greeks.

686) Cf. *Li ki*, 10, 1, 2, 3.—Another name for it was *Yang-sui*, or solar fire-implement, which has been used instead of the older *fu-sui*.

687) Cf. *suprà* § 18 note 60.—The oldest forms of the symbol *sui* suggest its object, the fire-stick and drill, as it was ideographically composed of *a pointed stick + to go*. Cf. Min Tsi kih, *Luh shu tung*, kiv. VII, f. 47.—The Chinese term represents the Babylonian *sarul*, firestick (Brunn. 1652) on which cf. A. H. Sayce, *Rel. Anc. Bab.* p. 181.

688) The various processes of making fire were by 1°): *Gyration* of firestick by bow-drill or pump-drill : 2°) *Friction* of wood sticks by sawing or plowing ; 3°) *Percussion* of flint, pyrites and steel, 4°) *Concentration* of solar Rays by a concave mirror or a lense ; 5°) *Condensation*, as by the fire-syringe.—On the three first processes cf. the excellent paper of Mr. Walter Hough, *Fire-making apparatus in the U.S. National Museum*, pp. 531-587 of *The* Smithsonian report of the U.S.A. Museum, for 1883.—The fire-syringe or *bisiapi* of the Saribus-Dayaks of Borneo, and of the Kachins of Upper Burma.—The *friction* process by sawing which was and is perhaps still known to the Pre-Chinese populations of China, was described by Tchwang-tze in the IVth cent. B.C. Cf. *T.P.Y.L.*, kiv. 869, f. 2.— The fire-drill seems me to have been known to the Ancient Egyptians; in Paul Pierret, *Vocabulaire Hieroglyphique*, on 30 words for fire, six are written with the determinative *spt*, fl a m e, while twenty two are written with the determinative *ua* which is said to represent a sort of cord, like a fishing line. Cf. B.&O.R. Aug. 1892, pp. 42-43, my note *on fire making in Ancient Egypt*.

689) Cf. on the arrival of the Jews in China, H. Cordier, *Les Juifs en Chine* (L'anthropologie. Sept.-Oct., 1890, p. 547-551), and T. de L. *On the Entrance of the Jews into China during the first century of our era* : B.&O.R., June 1891, vol. V, p. 131-134.—They knew to produce fire by striking steel against flint (2 Macc. X, 3). Cf. C. F. Keil, *Manual of Biblical Archæology*, 1888, vol. II, p. 126.

Other Innovations.

187.—Lieh-tze[690] and Tchwang-tze[691] of the fourth century B.C., in their teachings, have often given vent to sailors' yarns learnt from the foreign sea-traders of the Shantung coast. For instance we may refer amongst others to :

—the myth of the storm-bird[692], which they called *p'êng*[693] ;—when this ird rouses itself and flies, its wings are like clouds all round the sky.— In the dark and vast Ocean, the Pool of Heaven,......on a whirlwind it mounts upwards,......it bears on its back the blue sky, and then it shapes

its course for the south, and proceeds to the Ocean there⁶⁹⁴."—This is clearly a storm myth in its inception, and perhaps the oldest version of the mythological statement which has become the Rukh of the Arabs, the Gryphon of Marco-Polo, the Garuda of the Hindus, the Simurgh of the Old Persians, the Bahr Yukhre of the Rabbinical legends, the Gryps of the Greeks, &c.⁶⁹⁵.
—a fabulous notion of the whale⁶⁹⁶;

188.—An innovation which dates from the same time is the habit of writing on skins which is, and always was, not Chinese. It began to be practiced in the state of sung and remained a local peculiarity⁶⁹⁷.

189.—An acquaintance with a religious imagery such as could only be known in the emporia of the Erythræan sea⁶⁹⁸. The fabulous fishmen civilisers and writing carriers of the legends of Babylonia, the philacteries of Egypt, and some figures of Hindu gods were brought to this knowledge, and were made use of by the Taoszeists dealers-in-the-marvellous, when they amplified the ancient Chinese traditions. . This acquaintance which had begun towards the end of the last period, was largely increased in the fifth and fourth centuries, and stamped henceforth many of the legends and fabulous reports which they compiled.

The creatures half-fish half-men who springing out of the water, brought successively written tablets to Hwang-ti, Yao, Shun, Yü, Tcheng T'ang, Wu Wang and Tcheng Wang, as stated in the glosses, not in the text, of the Annals of the Bamboo Books, are an echo of the first named of these Western notions⁶⁹⁹. Such is also the notion of the mythological hippo-centaurs. Lieh-tzǒ⁷⁰⁰ speaks of Fuh-hi, Nu Kwa, Shennung and Hia Hou (i.e. the Great Yü) has having bodies of serpents, human faces, heads of oxen and muzzles of tigers, although they had all the virtues of Saints. This conception hitherto unknown in Chinese literature is undoubtedly Egypto-Indian in character.

190.—Interpolations made in the five first books of the *Shan hai king*, and the thirteen subsequent books which with some later exceptions, belong to the period we are now studying; numerous descriptions are made of demi-gods and genii special to the regions described⁷⁰¹. The most common types are those with or without animal limbs, either holding serpents in their hands, or having serpents for earrings, and treading on or driven by two dragons or two serpents. Now we cannot take these deities as those actually worshipped in their respective countries indicated, but as those which the travellers were induced to venerate in order to be preserved from the spirits and evils of the land. They are in many cases almost so identical with Egyptian phylacteries[702] and Hindu figures[703] of deities, that the compilers of the Romantic geography we are speaking of, cannot but have seen pictures of these phylacteries and figures when they wrote their descriptions. Perhaps that the Shantung traders were not the sole channel through which the latter views have reached the Chinese states, and that some of them came in by the Southwest and through the Semi-Chinese state of TS'U.[704]

NOTES——

690) On Lieh-tze, cf. Note 627.—He was contemporary of Tze Yang who was prime minister in TCHENG. Cf. Tchwang-tse, xxviii, 4.

691) Tchwang-Tchou or Tchwang-tze was a native of the state of WEI also called *Liang* from its capital city (after 361 B.C.). He was born at Wêng (once near Kwei teh, E. Honan), and was flourishing under the reigns of Kings Hwei of *Liang* (370-361-334 B.C.) and Siuen of *Ts'i* (332-319 B.C.). He declined the offers of King Wei of *Ts'u* (339-338 B.C.). Cf. *Szema Ts'ien*, kiv. 64, fol. 3 v.—He is said to have lived in 368-319 B.C.—On the translations of his works, cf. *suprà*, N. 628.

692) Lieh-tze, V, 3.—Tchwang-tze, I, 1.—Lich-tze quotes it in his alleged dialogues between two imaginary individuals, in one of which called *Yn T'ang*, some wanted to recognize Tcheng T'ang, the founder of the Shang dynasty, because the latter's name was changed into *Yn* when it was transferred there under the reign of Pan-keng nearly 400 years later,—Tchwang-tze quotes from "a book called *Ts'i Hiai*, i.e. Talks of Ts'i (13239-10857 Bas.) which treated of strange and marvellous things," where all these sailors' tales seem to have been collected. Quotations from this work appear in the *Tai ping yü lan* cyclopedia of A.D. 983, as if it was yet in existence. Cf. Kiv. 825, f. 4v.

693) Bas. 12952. Cf. also W. F. Mayers, *Cainese R.M.*, p. 174.

694) Cf. the translation in J. Legge, *Texte of Taoism*, I, 164-167 ; *S. B.E.* xxxix.

695) My lamented friend Sir Henry Yule, has paid a particular attention to this myth, and to the partial support it may have received in the middle ages from the past existence of enormous birds such as the *Æpyornis* of Madagascar, the *Harpagornis* of New-Zealand, and the would be wings of the same represented by the immensely long midrib of the *rofia* palm, sent as such by traders of the Indian Ocean. Cf. *The Book of Ser Marco Polo*, ed. 2, vol. II, p. 408-414, 552 ; *A glossary of Anglo-Indian words*, p. 578-579.—Cf. also, L. C. Casartelli, *Cyêna-Simurgh-Roc, un chapitre d'évolution mythologique et philologique*, 14 pp. Paris, Picard, 1891 ; and the correspondence in the Academy, on *The Garuda and the famous giant-birds*, reproduced in the J.R.A.S., xxiii, 344-6.

696) Called *Kwun* (Bas. 12827) in Tchwang-tze who supposes that the *pêng* comes from its transformation, *l.c.*, while its real name is *K'ing* (Bas. 12828). It may have been known some time earlier if the latter symbol in the *Tso tchuen* 7, XII, i.e. in 597 B.C. had the same meaning, although employed there in a figurative sense. Cf. *T.P.Y.L.*,

kiv. 938, f. 1.
697) Cf. *I'sien Han Shu*, kiv. 30.—Let us recall here the *Diphtherai Basilikai* or Royal Archives of Persia, and the tradition that the writings of Zoroaster were preserved on cow's skins.
698) In the cosmogonic speculations of Babylonia, the first beings were chaotic creatures in which were combined the limbs of every species of animals. Cf. Berosus, in Euseb. *Chronic.* i, 4.—In Egypt the animal worship was officially established by Ka Kou, the second king of the second dynasty, following Manetho; and the figures of gods as half animals are supposed to have come later. Cf. A. H. Sayce, *Herodotus*, p. 262, 364.—G. Maspero, *Histo re Ancienne*, p. 28; *Revue des Religions*, 1880.—F. Lenormant, *Histoire Ancienne*, t. III., p. 211. —As to the Egyptian worship of animals cf. A. Wiedemann, *Le Culte des Animaux en Egypt*: Le Muséon, 1889, pp. 211-225 and 309-318, tom. viii.
699) I have reprodced the Western and the Chinese statements in my paper on *The fabulous fishmen of Early Babylonia in Ancient Chinese documents*, 6 pp.; B. & O. R., Sept. 1888. Cf. also my note on the *Centaurs and Hippocentaurs of Western and Eastern Asia*, B. & O. R., VI, 167-168.
700) *Lieh tze*, Kiv, II. Cf my paper on *The Deluge tradition and its remains in Ancient China*, note 60.
701) The purpose of the descriptions of countries, such for instance as those inscribed on the ancient vases which were supposed to have been reproduced in the *Shan hai King*, was to enable the traveller to avoid any injury. Cf. *T'so tchuen*, 7, iii., 4.
702) Cf. for instance the Egyptian phylactery of Hor on the crocodiles, in the British Museum, engraved in F. Lenormant, *H istoire Ancienne*, tom. III. p. 183.
703) Cf. Edwd. Moore, *Hindu Pantheon*, pl. 6, 16, 23, &c.
704) In 548, according to the *Tso-tchuen* 9, xxv., 9, Wei Yen Grand Marshal of Ts'u, 'set about describing the different lands, measuring the forests ; defining the meres; marking out the higher lands and the downs; distinguishing the poor and salt tracts; enumerating the boundaries of flooded districts ; &c..' Although this was done chiefly in Ts'u's interest, it may have been the ground work of a part of the *Shan hai King*.

Innovations of Hindu Origin.

191.—the worship of the *Pah Shen*[705] or Eight Demi-gods which are simply the Hindu Eight Vasus. It was established all over his state, probably if not before, by Tai Kung of Ts'ɪ who ruled in 390-384 B.C.[706] He was the founder of the *Tien* dynasty, the second one in Ts'ɪ, and owed much to the foreign element of the sea-shore population of his state, which supported him as they had done his fathers in their encroachments against the regular authority of the lineage of princes founded in the XIth century by Kiang Tai Kung whose last descendant was d eposed by him. This circumstance explains partly his adoption of the foreign worship of the *Pah Shen*, which it will be sufficient to enumerate in comparison with the Hindu *Vasus* to establish their identity and unquestionable derivation.

Eight *Vasus* (Hindu)		Eight *Shens* (Chinese)		
Dhruva,—Sky	=	Heaven (Lord of),	*Tien Tchu*	
Dhava,—Earth	=	Ea·th	,,	*T'i* ,,
Dhanu,—*Arcitenens*	=	War	,,	*Ping* ,,
Pratyusha,—Dawn	=	Light	.,	*Yang* ,,
Prabhasha,—Twilight	=	Darkness	,,	*In* ,,
Soma,—Moon	=	Moon	,,	*Yueh* .,
Anala,—Agni	=	Sun	,,	*Jeh* ,,
Anila,—Wind	=	4 Seasons	,,	*Sze she*

The respective places of worship of each of these deities which are indicated by Szema Tsien are all within the limits of the state of Ts'ı, and principally in the North of the Shantung peninsula.[707] The Hindu origin of these Demi-gods cannot be doubted.

In India they are a class of semi-divine beings impersonations of natural phenomena belonging to the Vaidic period; they are alluded to bodily[708] in the Rig Veda, and described individually in other works.[709]

NOTES——

705) *Pah Shen*, 611-6173 Bas.—These must be clearly distinguished from the *Pah Sien* or Eight worthies of Chinese legend and art.

706) Szema Tsien, *She ki*, Kiv. 28, f. 10, recording that She Hwang ti offered sacrifices to the famous mountains, great rivers, and to the *Pah shen*, says that the latter "were acknowledged since antiquity, and that it was said also that they had been introduced by Tai Kung. The state of *Ts'i* (Bas. 13239) was so called because of the navel of Heaven, *Tien ts'i* (Bas. 1798-13239). The sacrifices had been interrupted, and I do not know when they were begun again."—The pun on the sound of Ts'ı (Bas. 13239) Regulated, name of the state, with that of *Ts'i* (Bas. 8628) navel, (same character with det. flesh) because of a pool near the capital which was thus named, does not deserve criticism. As to the *Tai Kung* or Great Duke, the one referred to cannot be Kiang Tai Kung the founder of the state in 1091 B.C. (Rectified Chronology) who had no knowledge of such matters, and who is always called Kiang Tai Kung in history; while the other Tai Kung Ho, also a founder of dynasty (the second) is certainly the one referred to, although the author does not speak positively on the point.

707) As the authority of the Princes of *Ts'i* was not established there before the middle of the sixth century, the cult of the eight gods in *Ts'i*, could be but of a later date.

708) *Rig Veda*, X., 98, 1.—*Atharva Veda*, XVIII., 2, 49.—*Satapatha Brahmana*, IV, 5; 7: 2.—Trsl. Julius Eggeling, II., 411; S.B.E. XXVI.—

709) *Vishnu Purana*, trsl. Wilson, p. 120.—*Nala*, trsl. Monnier-Williams. p. 215.—*Bhagavad Gita*, p. 145.—*Mahá Bharata, Adi Parva*, xcix.. p. 295-297, trsl. Pratapa Chandra Ray.

192.—A monster god of the North, called *Yü-Kiang*,[710] i.e. Kiang of the remote corner, also called: *Kiang-liang*,[711] which was represented with the face of a man the body of a bird; as earrings it has green serpents, and it treads on two other similar animals.[712] Its description vouchsafes its Hindu origin.[713]

193.—A notion of thirty three superior beings, as in the Rig Veda,[714] and the Avesta.[715] They were in India deities of the Sky, the Earth, and the Waters, eleven for each.[716] The result was that when the Chinese compiled their information about the fabulous period, and found amongst their earliest relics, statements concerning the existence of thirteen and eleven Kings or periods of 18000 years each, according to astrologico-cosmogonic calculations once made in Babylonia and which they could not understand,[717] they were by this later notion led to add nine more *Kings*, or periods of 18000 years each, which as a computation of years, clash with all the other calculations and have no *raison d'être*. But the number of *thirty three* primitive beings was thus secured and took its place in their cosmogony.

194.—Notions of Hindu cosmogony and cosmography, such as the avatar of the tortoise, the Sumeru, and the Soma. Lieh-tze (c. 400 B.C.) seems to be the oldest Taoszeist who has combined Hindu ideas and conceptions learned from the foreigners of Shantung with legends long before in possession of the ancient Chinese. In my special paper on *The Deluge-tradition*, I have pointed out the influence of the avatar of the tortoise on the flood legend which the Chinese had preserved[718], and therefore it is needless to say here[719] anything more on the subject.

The wonderful fancies of the Hindu poetical descriptions of the imaginary Sumeru and its four rivers were applied to the scarcely less imaginary Kwen-lun of the West of China ; and the scraps of positive knowledge about it, with the few traditions preserved about the expeditions of TCHOU Muh Wang outside the W. borders in the Xth century[720], served as a peg for all sorts of wonderful accounts, due for the greatest parts to the immediate disciples of Lieh-tze.[721]

The *S o m a*, Chinese *Tse-mai*[722] is the plant and elixir of immortality, food of the *Sien* or Richis, which is spoken of in the fabulous reports of the Five islands of the Genii (*suprà* § 122-126).

195.—By his adaptation of Hindu thoughts on Cosmogony and Cosmology, Tsou-hien (c. 378-300 B.C.) whom we have already mentioned, has exercised a great influence on Taoszeism[723]. He began to teach towards the end of the reign of King Wei of Ts'i (d. 331 B.C.) And under that of his successor Siuen (332-831 B.C.) He wrote first a very large work on supreme holiness[724], and later on when established in the *Kieh shih* palace, in YEN, he composed his treatise on the chief evolution of the *Yn* and *Yang*[725]. He explained that by the influence of the Five elements[726] the world was formed, and proceeding from smaller things to greater things, he described a scheme of cosmogony similar to the *Sakwala* of the Hindus.

196.—The seventh year (i.e. 305 B.C.) of King Tchao of YEN, the protector of Tsou-hien (§ 173 *suprà*) saw the arrival of a man professing the doctrines of Tao(?), and called *She-lo*[727]. His name recallss the Sanskrit *Sila*, moral purity, usually transcribed by the same symbol[728]. He said that he was 130 years old, and that he had come from the country of *Muk-tu*[729] or *Magadha*, also known as *Shen-tu*[730] or India, which he had left five years previously. He performed numerous magical tricks, one of which is described in the traditional report of the event[731].

Nothing is said of the route which the Indian Monk had followed; it may have been through the South-west, as we shall see further on that certain circumstances suggest that relations with Burma and India became active in the fourth century. The arrival of *Sila* was certainly an important circumstance and he may have been the first of the Sramans whom we shall hear of in N.E. China at the beginning of the next period.

NOTES——
710) *Yu Kiang*: Bas. 7107-2646.—*Kiang liang*: Bas. 2646-8303.
711) *Shan Hai King*, Kiv. 8 f. 4 v; Kiv. 17, f, 20.—It is mentioned in Tchwang-tze, VI. vi., 7, and in Lieh-tze, V. 2.— *Khang-h' tze tien* s.v.
712) An old authority says also that it was figured, the body, hands and feet black, riding on two dragons. Cf. *Shan hai King*, ibid. gloss.— These two descriptions are combined in its modern figure, where it is represented with its human face and bird's body driving on two dragons. Cf. for instance the fig. 58 in Charles Gould, *Mythical Monsters*, p. 241.
713) It is not without some resemblance to Garuda, or perhaps to Kuvera.
714) Rig-Veda, I. 34, 11; 139, 11; VIII, 35, 3; IX, 92, 4.—Muir. *Sanskrit texts*, vol. IV, f. 9.—Max Muller, *India, what can it teach us*, p. 144-5.—*Satapatha Brahmana*, III, 5; 7:4: transl. Eggeling, S.B.E. xxvi, p. 411. And in many other works such as the Aitareya Brahmana, the Atharva Veda, the Mahâbhârata, the Ramayana, the Taithirya Sanhita, &c.
715) *Avesta*, Yasna I. 10, the 33 *rataras*.—Transl. Mills, S.B.E. xxxi, p. 198.—M. Haug, *Essays*, ed. West, p. 276.—
716) The thirty-three gods have been carried by Buddhists in Central Asia. The *Man-Han Si-fan tsyeh-yas*, a *Buddhist repertory in Sanscrit, Tibetan, Mandshu, Mongol and Chinese*, tr. De Harlez, gives sect. xiv, 2: *Trayastrinça*. The group of the 33 gods; Tibetan, *sum c'u*

gsum pa, id. ; Chin. Mandshu, the 33 heavens (*abka*) ; Mongol, the 33 tekin.—B.&O.R. IV, p. 168.—Cf. also J. G. Schmidt, *Forschungen in Gebiete der alteren religiosen....der Völker Mittel-Asiens*, 1824. —C. de Harlez, *La Religion Nationale des Tartares Orientaux*, 1889, p. 173.

717) Cf. *suprà*, ch. IV, sect. *d*, 30, and notes 119-121.
718) Cf. *The Deluge legend*, § 51, and note 120.—B.&O.R. iv, 108-109.
719) The sundering of the earth, mentioned in the Chinese legend is referred to in the *Yh King*, Kwa II. 1.—The five dragons of the first Ki in the Chinese mythical list of Akkadian kings, are mentioned in the same work, Kwa I.—These two references in the oldest book of the Chinese would be sufficient by themselves to show the existence of ancient documents bearing on these subjects in early China and their introduction by the Bak families of Nai Hwang-ti. But there are some more proofs. The early Babylonian cosmogony quoted in the *Tao teh king* (*suprà*, 133-137) is referred to in the same work: Kwa I. 1.—The legend of Nu-hwa repairing the rent in the heaven, was already among the documents used for divination under the second ruler of the Hia dynasty as shown by the *Kuei-tsang*.
720) Cf. *suprà*, notes 165-169, § 52, note 347.
721) *l.c.* The story of Muh, the Son of Heaven, *Muh t'ien-tze-tchuen*, is a most valuable relic of antiquity which has not received the attention it deserves. It has not the glowing of a production of the Neo-taoist school, and contains a great deal of geographical lore, *which it seems to me refers to a genuine journey to Khotan and Kashgaria*. Dr. E. J. Eitel, who has translated it (China Review, 1889, XVII., 223-240, 247-258) "is convinced that the main portion of the narrative is of a very ancient date (10th cent. B.C.)," and I agree with him in that respect. I intend to make a special study of the work.
722) Suprà, notes 455, 458.
723) His works are now lost, but they were still existing in the Imperial library of the Han dynasty in B.C. 9. Cf. *Liu hwang pieh luh*. And an analysis of his views is given by Szema Tsien, *She Ki*, kiv. 74, f. 2-3.
724) *Ta sheng tchi pien*, in more than one hundred thousand words. Cf. *She ki*, kiv. 74, f. 2.
725) Called *Yn yang tchu yun*, ' chief permutations of the Yn and Yang.'— Cf. *suprà*, § 173.
726) His views on the five elements were followed by Liu Hiang in the *Wu heng tchi*, and by Pan-ku in the *Peh hu tung y*, of the Han dynasty. He is believed to have annotated the *Tchou-li*. Cf. Mayers, *Chinese R.M.*, i, 746 ; ii, 127.
727) *She-lo*, 2230-8176 Bas.
728) Eitel, *Sanskrit Chinese dictionary*, p. 127a.
729) *Muk-ta*, mod. *Muh-sü*. 4880-8476 Bas. The old sounds are given by the Archaic dialects notably by the Sino-Annamite, the oldest of all, on which cf. B.&O.R. V, 24.
730) *Shen-tu*, 6173-4772 Bas.
731) 'One of his tricks consisted in causing a ten storied *fou-t'u* or pagoda, with images of people 5 or 6 inches long, walking and dancing round it, to grow out of the tip of his fingers. Cf. *Shih y ki*, kiv. 4, by Wang Kia of the fourth century.—Mr. Herbert J. Allen, *Simi-*

larity between Buddhism and Early Taoism : China Review, 1886-7, vol. xv, p. 97, was the first to translate this interesting statement. But the proposed identification of *Muk-tu* with Magadha is mine. As to the trick described, I would suggest that it was an image seen through, a magnifying glass which Sila was holding in his hand.

Northern Influence.

197) Towards the middle of the fourth century a new and rather curious influence became apparent in the states of TCHAO in Shansi, and of YEN in N. Tchihli[732]. We have seen that the Neo-Taoists were flourishing in the latter Kingdom[733]. North and West of these states were the teritories of *Lin-hu* and *Lou-fan* belonging to the non-Chinese *Wu-hwan* who were the west branch of the *Tung-hu*, the eastern branch of whom were the *Sien-pi* or Coreans[734]. In the same region which in the sixth century formed the N. of the state of TSIN, there was a famous breed of horses which it is reported in the *Tse-tchuen* had never been taken advantage of for the benefit of the state. In 333, Su-Ts'in[735] the famous statesman of TCHOU went to YEN to enlist it in his league of the six states against the encroachments of TS'IN, then aiming already at the Empire[736]. A result of his sojourn there was the organization of a body of 6000 horsemen, being the first cavalry which had ever existed in the Chinese states[737]. The first instance of horseriding astride had occurred nearly two centuries before, but has never been put into practice for army purposes[738]. Wu-ling, the King of the aforesaid state of TCHAO, who ruled in 325 until 298 B.C. conquered the Hu state of *Lin-hu* and *Lou-fan*, in 307 B.C. and introduced from there several new customs and habits. Horsemanship[739] and archery were henceforth extensively practised, contrily to former times, and the costume of the *Hu* people was adopted[740]. Among these innovations may be noticed that of the *hüe* large leather boots to go on horseback, which are worn to the present day[741].

NOTES——
732) Suprà, § 164.
733) Suprà, § 173
734) *Lin-hu.* 4I36-8472 Bas.—*Lou-fan,* 4466-5491 Bas.—*Wu-hwan*, 5421-32 Bas., also written 5421-4235 Bas.—*Tung-hu*, litt. Eastern Hu, 4108-8472 Bas.—*Sien-pi*, 12S13-1006 Bas.
735) Szema Tsien, *She Ki*, kiv. 43, fol. 22 v ; kiv. 69, f. 2 v.
36) Szema Tsien, kiv. 69, f. 1, says that the Su-Ts'in was a native of

Loh-yang, in the *Tung Tchou* or Eastern Tchou Kingdom. The Kingdom of TCHOU was thus called since its transfer at Loh-yang in 770 B.C. and its fallen fortunes.—The league organised by Su-Ts'in was between the YEN, TCHAO, HAN, TS'I and TS'U states, but internal strife destroyed the combination, and he was assassinated in 318 B.C. The history fills the 69th book of the *She Ki*. W. F. Mayers has given a short notice of this remarkable man in his *Manual*, I, 626.

737) Cf, *She Ki*, kiv. 34, f. 5. And below, note 739.
748) Cf. *She Ki*, kiv, 69, f. 2 v.—*I'cheng tze tung.—Khang-hi tze tien*, s.v. *K'i* (12535 Bas.).
739) Cf. my notes on *Earliest Horse-riding in Western and Eastern Asia*.
740) *Tsien Han Shu*, Kiv. 94.—*She Ki*, Kiv. 43, fol. 22 sq.
741) *Hüe*, 12067 or 121 2 Bas.—*Khang hi T'ze tien*, s.v.—*Kwang yun*, s.v.—*T.P.*, 698, 6.—The *Shih ming* of the Han period says that *hüe* is a word of the *Hu* language. Cf. the Corean wood *hey*.

CHAP. VII.—FIFTH PERIOD: 481-221 B.C.
Sect. C. *Western Influences by Southern Channels.*

a. Hormuz Navy in South-Eastern China.

198. The few double-eyed, dragon-like Merchantmen [742] of the Erythraean Sea which continued to carry an international trade notwithstanding the temporary check caused by some unknown event on their route, to be guessed only through their fabled accounts of the Five Fairy islands, did not cease entirely to frequent the eastern coast of China after 380 B.C.[743] The removal of the capital of YUEH to *Wu* (i.e. Su-tchou in Kiang-su), and the internecine wars in the vicinity of the Gulf of Kiao-tchou (S. Shantung) had ruined the foreign trade of the once great emporium of *Tsih-moh*. As we suspected, they shifted their arriving station towards the South, in the Hang-tchou bay, near which Kou-tsien, King of YUEH had began to start at Kwei-ki, a market town in 473 B.C., in the vain hope of enticing to remain there his exminister Fan-li, the greatest Chinese merchant of his age.[744] But there was for a time a marked slackening of activity.

199. In 334 B.C. the powerful state of TS'U was finally successful in its protracted struggle against its eastern neighbour of YUEH; Wu-Kiang king of the latter state was killed, and the territory from Su-tchou (in Kiang-su N.W.) on the S. borders of Ts'I, to the Tchekiang river, near Kwei-ki, was absorbed by the Ts'U kingdom. The rulers of that state

could thus get for themselves the rarities which the foreign traders used
to import. Accordingly when Hwei, Duke of Ts'in, assumed for the first
time in 324 B.C., the title of King, Siang Wang of Ts'u could send him
some valuable presents. Besides a hundred of chariots, he presented him
with a large ring of *ye-kwang*, i.e. of the stone which shines at night,
otherwise of *yakut* ruby of Badakshan[745], and a *hiaiki* rhinoceros, i.e. a
Rh. lasiotis, ear-haired, of Northern India, two varieties usually imported
by these traders.[746]

200. Their influence made itself felt also by several material innovations;
for instance the curious system of casting coins in clusters shaped like
trees, which was then obtaining in the western world.[747] Some time
before important progress, traceable to the same source, in Astronomy
and Mathematics, is shewn by the *Tchou pi swan king*, which an astronomical statement recorded therein proves to have been written within
the years 527-450 B.C.[748] It is the only ancient work we have on the
Kai-tien system of Astronomy, in which the heavens are represented as a
concave sphere.[749]

201. The conquest of YUEH in 334, did no tresult in the complete
extinction of her Royal house. Several princes fled further South along
the Coast and created centres of influence which developed into States
and Kingdoms. About the site of the present Ning-po,[750] grew a Marqui-
sate of *Mou*, which was a trading centre at the beginning of the third
century B.C.[751] The south-west of this saw the rising of the Kingdom
of *T'ung-hai*, whose centre was in the present prefecture of Tai-tchou in
Tchehkiang C., and which extended to the sea borders. South of the
preceding, with its centre at Tung-yeh, the present Fuhtchou of Fuhkien,
and its southern limit N. of the present Tsinen-tchou, rose the Kingdom
of *Min-yueh*.[752] The Month of the *Min* river was therefore a centre
of foreign trade in the first quarter of the fourth century B.C.

202. The state of TS'U was then engaged in its deadly struggle with the
TS'IN of Shensi, and by its system of encroaching everywhere possible, was
rather disquieting its weaker neighbours. It became consequently the
policy of the small states to seek alliances wherever they could. We are
made aware of two instances of such a conduct by the king of the new
state of YUEH. In 312 B.C. he sent an ambassador named Kung-se Yu
to the king of WEI, which state by its commanding position in Eastern
Honan, between the Hwang-ho and the Hwai river, had acquired a political importance. The envoy took away with him as presents 300 boats
laden with five hundred thousand arrows,[753] rhinoceroses (*sze*)[754] horns

and elephants *siang*,[755] tusks.[756] On the other side of the Shantung peninsula, in the present Tchih-li province was the state of *Yen* then ruled by spirited kings, enamoured with novelties, as we have seen in previous paragraphs,[757] and holding a high position among their co-princes of the Chinese agglomeration. In 310 B.C. perhaps at the occasion of his recent accession to his throne, the King Tchao of YEN was presented by the same southern king with a Red ship; a large vase, carved and ornamented, containing a rare sort of grease, lamps with asbestos wicks[758] and a peculiar sort of fish oil giving a great light ; and besides these objects, two beautiful dancing girls.[759] Tradition says that they had come from the east of *Fang-tchang*, one of the Fortunate islands, which may be identified with some island North of Sumatra, either Banca as already suggested,[760] or more probably Bintang at the eastern extremity of the straits of Malacca. As Asbestos wicks could not be got from elsewhere than Badakshan and the rainless plains of North India, where we know that such wicks were made,[761] we have here as well as in a fable connected with it some indications about the country which supplied these seatraders, and from the vicinity of which they used to come to the Chinese Ocean,[762] i.e. the North-west sea borders of India, and the entrance of the Persian Gulf. We shall see some other evidence to the same effect in the following paragraph.

203. S e s'a m u m, introduced after Quinces by the same eastern sea trade in the sixth century,[763] testifies, by its earliest Chinese name *Kusheng*,[764] obviously connected with the Persian *Kundjud*, Malay *widjin*, and *bendjam* in Sumatra, of its route of importation. *Ye-kwang*=Yakut of *c*. 400 B.C. has been spoken of in a previous page.[765] It was about the same time that pearls began to be imported in China, as we shall see directly and little afterwards that cubebs of Java were known in western Asia.[766]

The Chinese, contrarily to an oft repeated statement[767] were not acquainted with the p e a r l before *c*. 400 B.C. They knew the thin and nacreous fresh water mussels of the Hwai river since the days of the *Yü kung*, and probably the seed-pearls from the Mouths of the Yang-tze since the seventh century.[768] The earliest references to the p e a r l occur in writers of the fourth century Meh-ti, Lieh-tze, Tsou-hien, and others, in such prizing terms that its novelty cannot be doubted.[769] In some cases it is coupled to the *Ye-kwang*.[770] And the name of M i n g-g w e t, a transfer and folk-etymology of the western word for it, shows moreover its Western Origin,[771] most probably from the pearl fisheries of the Persian Gulf, not of Ceylon.⁷⁷² In the second century B.C. we are told that those who imported them were no other than the *Hwang-tche*,⁷⁷³ or yellow-fingered traders of the Erythræan sea, at the entrance of the Persian Gulf, and we know that there was the emporium for the pearl-trade. The Chinese became thus acquainted with the p e a r l little after the Western world.⁷⁷⁴

204. We may derive also from the statements of 316 B.C. a precious indication on a part of the Sea route followed by these merchantmen which must have ceased to pass through the straits of Malacca. The loss of two of their five stations about 400 B.C., drifted away in the North by the wickedness of some neighbours, as told in the Fable of the Fortunate Islands,⁷⁷⁵ disguised most probably some event which had led to a change of route and the adoption of a more southern course. The slackening of their Activity which activity about 375 B.C. they did not transfer bodily from their Northern Emporia in Shantung to another one in the South,⁷⁷⁶ shows an hesitation in their adoption of a new route. And this new route is first indicated by the circumstances of the present event. The route of these dealers in Asbestos we are told, led east of *Fung tchang*. Further more, the *Shen y king*⁷⁷⁷ of Tung-fang to (150-100 B.C.) says that this asbestos came from, i.e. through, *Hwo-lin*, otherwise, *Hu-liang*⁷⁷⁸ in Szema Tsien, otherwise *Ho-ling* (in later times) a name of the S.E. of Java as a Kalinga colony from Eastern India established there about that time.⁷⁷⁹ As the Sunda straits were not opened before A.D. 416, and the Bali, Lombok and Allas straits along afterwards,⁷⁸⁰ the Merchantmen in question must have passed through the Sapy straits, East of Sumbawa. This physical circumstances had a rather important influence on the articles of trade in subsequent centuries as we shall see further on, and led to the discovery of cloves and nutmegs.

205. No denomination has appeared yet in any of the occasions referred to about these West Asiatic traders who had then frequented the coasts of China for several centuries. A convenient name for them, justified by the nature of their imports, for want of a more precise knowledge, might be that of E r y t h r æ a n s which covers all their possible sea-coasts of departure, for the period preceding the fourth century, and some time afterwards. In the absence of any written record of this circumstance,—absences as much due to the fact of their emporia in China being outside the Chinese dominion for the time being, as to the wrecks of literature,—all that we have been able to say about them has come from gathering chance allusions, isolate facts and scrap statements in various

works, which hitherto had neither been put together nor studied in a comparative manner. As we advance in time, more statements have escaped the havoc of ages, and less curtailed they have been in the transmission, so that we hear at last of their name.

206. These foreign importers of Quinces, Sesamum, precious pearls, yakut gems, Asbestos, magnifying glasses, Rock crystal, Indian Rhinoceroses, already referred to, and of Jessamine, Sambac, Henna, Sugar, colouredglass, and other rarities afterwards, were called the *Hwang-tche*.[783] The name means ideographically the yellow-fingered and refers to their practice of dying the fingers tips with the *henna*. still at present followed by the Arabs, Persians and people of British India.[784] Their country was situated at 30000 *li* distance of South China.[785] As there are variants in the way of spelling it, we may be sure that it is a phonetic transfer, altered by the limitations of Chinese orthoepy and ideographic rendering of their own name. And taking these reservations into account, we recognize in this *Hwang-tche* a distant imitation of *Harmozia*, later Hormuz, the famous emporium which shifted several times its position at the entrance of the Persian Gulf.[785] This unexpected find, which throws some more light on the whole subject, concurs entirely with all the foregoing circumstances.

Notes——
742) *Suprà*, § 118, note 444.
743) *Suprà*, § 180.
744) Cf. Szema Tsien, *She Ki*, Kiv. 41, fol. 11-12. and kiv. 139, fol 3 vers.— Some circumstances of the biography of Fan-li are partly resumed in F.W. Mayers, *Chinese R.M.*, I., 127.—Fan-li had been a minister in YUEH for over 20 years, when after the successes of his native state over the kingdom of Wu, in 472 b.c., probably sick of his politics, he withdrew into private life and started a lucrative trade, probably at Kwei-ki; but he left the place and went to the Five lakes (*Kiang hu*), and from there. under an assumed name, he went to Tao, the modern Ting-t'ao of S.W. Shantung, which, placed in the centre of the Chinese dominion, was more convenient for his commercial purposes. —According to the *Wu yueh tchun tsiu* : *Tai ping yü lan*, Kiv. 935, fol. 7., it was at the instigation of Fan-li that piscieulture was started at Kwei-ki. On the Chinese piscieulture, cf. Hue, *L'Empire Chinois*, II., 433-4.—St. Julien & P. Champion, *Industries de L'Empire Chinois*, 230.—J.H. Gray. *China*, 291-2.
745) They used to import *yakut* ruby stones since the fifth century. Cf. my paper *On Yakut precious stones from Oman to N. China*, in B.& O. R., June, 1893, vol. VI., p. 271.
746) Let us remark however that, as far as I am aware, this was the first case of importation of a rhinoceros, which, as shown by its curious name, was different from those which were found in the South of the

country. The words used are *hiui-ki tchi se*, 12514-11929-41-5671, Bas., i.e. a chicken-frightening rhinoceros, or Rh. of *Hiui-ki*, if the latter are the transfer of a proper name. It became an usual article of importation by the sea-traders of Ta-tsin=Tarshish, and is described in the commentaries of the *Hou Han shu*, as a Rh. that has something hanging about him. (Cf. the quotation in F. Hirth, *China and the Roman Orient*, p. 41, 73, 79, where no identification is suggested.) Now the Rhinoceros is rather an unwieldy animal, and there is only one species of it which has anything unusual hanging about its body. It is the *Rh. lasiotis* that has hair on the ears. The traders of olden times in search of curiosities had hit upon this animal, and we see one of them figured on the black obelisk of Salmanazzar with monkeys and elephants of India. Cf. Perrot-Chipiez, *Chaldee-Assyrie*, p. 565; F. Lenormant, *Hist. Anc.* IV, 191. The hair of the animal has suggested several critics unaware of the particularity that, notwithstanding the horn, it was not the figure of a rhinoceros. François Lenormant, *Noms de l' airain*, l.c. p. 409, gives the name *susu*, rhinoceros. Cf. the Chinese *se*. The explanation contained in the present note ought to dispel any hesitation.

747) Cf. S. W. Bushell, *Roman and Chinese Coinage*: China Review, I, Sept. 1892.—Alex. Cunningham, *Coins of Ancient India from the earliest times*, 1881, p. 60.—T. de L., *Catalogue of Chinese coins*, 1892, introd. xxix.

748) Cf. J. B. Biot, *Astronomie Indienne et Chinoise*, pp. 298, 304. &c.

749) A. Wylie, *Notes on Chinese Literature*, p. 86.—On the nine trigonometric propositions in the first part of this work which shows an undoubted connection with Western Science, cf. A. Wylie, *The Science of the Chinese*, Arithmetic: in the *North China Herald*, 1852 and *The Chinese and Japanese Repository*, 1864 -5 †11-1, §0-57, 491-500, II, 69-73. Also T. de L., *On the numerals, the counting rods and theSwan pan in China* (Numismatic Chronicle 3, III, 1883) p. 33.—Herodotus (II, 109) attributes to Sesostris (? Ramsès II) the beginnings of geometry which statement can be but the result of a confusion, as Prof. Eisenlohr has discovered that mathematics were studied at the court of the Hycsos princes, as the Rhind papyri contain a work on geometry (written for Apepi I) which may be described as a treatise on applied arithmetic.

750) Cf. for instance the history of Tchu-tchung, a famous dealer in pearls established at Kwoi-ki during the reigns of Kao hou and of King-ti of the First Han dynasty, in the *Lieh sien tchuen* of Liu-hiang, b.c. 80-9 : *T P.* 803, 6.—Tsou yen (378-300 B.C.) on whom cf. *supra*, § 195, could say that Pearls grow in the southern seas. Cf. *T.P.* 803, 2 r and § 203.

751) Called *Mou hou* (cl. 163+10444—293 Bas.) territory. Cf. T.P. 171, 3.—*Mou*, 10414 Bas., means "exchange, barter."

752) Cf. Szema Tsien, *She Ki*, kiv. 114, fol. 1, and gloss.—*Tai ping yü len*, 170, 10 vers.

753) *Tchuh shu ki nien*, V, xxxiv, 3.—The mission went apparently along the sea-coast and by the Hwai river and an affluent.

754) Rhinoceroses existed in China in historical times, as shown by the following evidence. A few years before the overthrow of the SHANG-YN dynasty by the Tchou-ites, 1110 B.C., Tai Kung Wang the famous

minister of TCHOU, procured from Y-Kiü, modern King-yang fu in E. Kansuh, a rhinoceros—*sze* which he presented to Shou, the king of Shang-yn. C. *Han shi wai tchuen*, by Han Yng, 173-156 B.C.—T.P. 890, 2.— A visible amplification of a slender truth says that when the Duke of TCHOU, smote the native state of YEN, corresponding to the present *Yen-tchou* of S.W. Shantung, he drove far away, from these and other places tigers, leopards, rhinoceroses (*si*), and elephants. (Cf. *Mencius*, III, 2, ix, 6). This would have happened between the years 1107-1099 B.C. (cf. *Chin. Class.* III, introd. 144-145. and p. 493).—In his 16th year, i.e. 1025 B.C. King *Tch'ao* of TCHOU having crossed the Han river, N.W. Hupeh, met with a large rhinoceros-*sze*. King)" of the same dynasty, in his 6th year, i.e. 879 B.C., when hunting in the forest of Shay, Honan, captured a rhinoceros-*sze*, and carried it home. Cf. *Tchuh shu ki nien*, s.a.—In 818 B.C., in the Royal hunting grounds near the Western Capital i.e. Hao king, modern Si-an, S. Shensi, the King Sinen of TCHOU hunded a large rhinoceros (*sze*). (Cf. *Shi King*, II, iii, 6).—The King Tchwang of TS'U, (613-590 B.C.) while hunting at Yun-mêng, the present Teh-an fu in Hupeh E., killed a rhinoceros (*sze*). Cf. Lu she, *Tchun tsiu* : T. 1'. 890, 4 v.— In the *Er-ya* vocabulary (c. 500 B.C.) Rhinoceroses-*sze* and elephants are said to be numerous in the mountains of Liang, i.e. of N.E. Szetchuen.—The *Shan hai king* the celebrated Romantic geography of the TCHOU period, mentions Rhinoceroses-*si* and elephants in the *Min shan*, i.e. N.W. Szetchuen (kiv. V, fol. 29), and in the S.W. of Kansuh (kiv. II, fol. 6 r.), many rhinoceroses *sze* and *si* in W. Kwangsi (kiv. I, fol. 8), rhinoceroses-*sze* in the south of the Siang river, S.E. Hunan, (kiv. X, fol. 2), rhinosceroses-*si* in W. Hunan (kiv. X, fol, 2 *vers.*), and white (?) rhinoceroses-*si* in Hupeh (kiv. V, fol. 27 r.- In the *Tso tchuen*, Ili kung, xxiii, 4, i.e 637 B.C., we hear that the I rince of Ts'u could get no..... &18u. and rhinoceroses' hides in his own dominion, i.e. Hupeh. And in the same wo.... of.. k, rk, Sinen kung, II. 1, i.e. 607 B.C., a popular song says that the want w... as not of rhinoceroses, *si* and *sze*, to supply skins for buffcoats, but of courage to animate the wearers.— The so-called Tribute of Yü, chapter of th.... home *Shu King*, mentions (I, 40, 52) elephants teeth and hides (supposed to... be rhinoceroses' hides), among the products of Yang-tchou, i.e. the South of the Hwai river, and of King-tchou, i.e. Hunan.—The outcome of all t... the evidence piled up here is that rhinoceroses were not unfrequent in Ancient China, even in the Northern provinces, and that in course of time they gradually receded to the Southern parts of the country. It is not certain that the two words for rhinoceros, however promiscuously used in some instances where they are quoted together, were not applied to two different species of rhinoceros. *Si* would be a rh. with two horns of equal length, and *sze* a rh. with one horn sometimes long of three spans. With one exception one in Mencius' statement) where it may be a clerical error, the two species are rather well distinguished by their geographical habitat. the *si* species in the West, not South-west, and the *sze* species in the East and the South East.—In their original writing of Western descent, the Chinese had no distinct character for rhinoceros, and where they came across the animal they called it *si-niu*, 2255 Bas. - cl, 93, the obdurate bull, by two characters which afterwards combined together have made the symbol *si*, 5671 Bas. In the East they adopted a pictorial modification of their symbol *she*-pig, cl. 152 which subsequently altered, has become the special symbol *sze*, 591 Bas. Cf. the successive forms of the two symbols in Min Ts'i kih, *Luh shu tung*, kiv. I, 23, 26, and V. 18. It seems that the symbol *sze* was one of those which were framed for convenience, in ignorance of the principles of composing new characters of the standard writing, by some fraction of the Chinese community more illiterate than the others. Cf. on this phenomenon my historical *Catalogue of Chinese Coins*, Early period, introd. p. xxxiii ; and *The oldest Book of the Chinese*, vol. I, 1892, par. 150.

755) The Chinese character, *Siang*, e l e p h a n t is one of the most interesting of the writing. It is one of the few hieroglyphics which have been looked upon as indigenous evidence against the extraneous origin claimed by us for the early written characters of China. Of course we intend to speak of the usual character for e l e p h a n t (10352 Bas.) and not of the rude picture which appears on some Ancient vases as a special mark, and not as a character of the writing.—In their stock of written symbols of Western Origin, the ancient Chinese had no sign for e l e p h a n t as happened with the rhinoceroses afterwards. As they became acquainted with the elephant when crossing Honan little after their entrance in China proper, they framed a new symbol for it by combining together two actual symbols of their writing. In accordance with the traditional principles of the script, they took into consideration the form of the object to be represented and the sound to be expressed, in so far as permitted by the internal arrangement of the strokes composing the signs at their disposal. The native name of the great pachyderm was *sam, sham, tsam, sang, song*, &c. Consequently they selected their character *she*, p i g, as recognized by the first author of the *Shwoh Wen*, and they have written over it a contracted form of *Mien*, effort, (586 Bas. Cf, Min Ts'i kih. *Luh shu t'ung*, k. vi, f. 24. By this process the scribes contrived to figure the intended animal in a sort of clumsy way, and at the same time to suggest the sound to be read, from bottom to top S H E + M, as is most usual in *ku-wen*. A positive proof of this phonetic intention consists in the variants of spelling which exhibit *Mien*, f a c e (12033 Bas.) or *Muh*, e y e, cl. 109, instead of *Mien*, e ffo rt. These substitutes were perhaps used afterwards, in the occasions where the compound symbol was not intended for e l e p h a n t, as the shapes of these two characters, though placed also above the character *she*, did not display the same suggestiveness of an elephant's head. When in after times the old mode of orthography was forgotten and disappeared under the encroachments of the processes of ideo-phonetic formation, i.e. symbols made either of characters having each their sound and their meaning, or of an ideographic character mute joined to a phonetic character meaningless, such compounds as those made according to the old method like those referred to, were no longer in harmony with the current views of the scribes and were open to change. *She* was preserved as a silent ideograph, and the sign *tchem*, to a b s o r b (1013 Bas.) as a phonetic was substituted to the M—characters of Antiquity. The Ancient scribes have always displayed a considerable amount of ingenuity and taste in their attempts at satisfying the various conditions here described, and they have often attained better results than clumsy shapes

and approximative sounds. The phonetic system of orthography by a rude process of Acrology and syllabism was lost before the Tchou dynasty, but the scribes of after ages have been real worshippers of their written characters, and in their arrangements and combinations have made of the Chinese writing a most remarkable art. On the early orthography in Ku-wen, cf. *The oldest Book of the Chinese*, par. 28 and n., 46-52 ; *Beginnings of writing* par. 50 ; *Languages of China before the Chinese*, par. 167, n. 2, 185, n. 1 ; R. K. Douglas, *Further progress in Chinese studies*, &c.

756) *Elephants* were living as far as the north of Central China, when the Chinese dominion first extended in the land. A younger brother of the famous Shun (2004-1996 B.C. rect. chronol.) was sent away to settle in *Yü Pi* (South Honan not Hunan) cf. *Shu King*, I, iii, 12 ; Mencius, V, i, 3.—In the geographical and hydrographical survey of the Shang dynasty called the *Yü kung*, the same South of Honan and the adjacent lands were denominated *Yü-siang tchou*, (shortened into *Yü tchou*) which means province of the docile elephants. These two names are clear evidence that elephants were then living in the region. The same document, as shown in our note on *Rhinoceroses*, mentions elephants teeth as products of N. Hunan, and of the S. of Hwai river. —Elephants are spoken of in 1107, S.W. of Shantung, and about 500 B.C. in the N.E. and N.W. of Szetchuen. (Cf. preceding note).— Elephants teeth could be procured from Hupeh, in 637 B.C. (*ibid.*)— In 506 B.C. elephants were used in N. Kiangsi for war against Wu by the state of Ts'u. (Cf. *Tso-tchuen*, Tingkung, iv, 14).—Writing in A.D. 89, the author of the *Shwoh wen* described the elephant as an animal of *Nan-yueh*, i.e. Kwangtung and Kwangsi.—The name of Elephants' province, *Siang kiun* was given in 215 B.C. by Ts'in She Hwang-ti to the region including the South of Kwangtung, Kwangsi, and part af Tungking (Szema Tsien, *She Ki*, kiv. 113, fol. 1) covering perhaps the provinces of Tai nguyen, Son-tay, Hung hoa, Nghê-an and Thanh Hoa, (*Hoang Viet dia du ch*, II. 9 r. ; I, 47 ; II, 3, 31, 16), but the limits were rather undefinite and lasted only ten years.—We may consider the foregoing evidence as showing a gradual retreat of the elephant in China from the North centre to the S.S.W. borders. Liu-Sün, *Ling piao luh y*, of the 7th cent., says that in the departments of *Siun* and *Tch'ao*, in the S.E. of the present province of Kwangtung, wild elephants were still numerous, while among the Mêngs (=Muongs, Shan districts) of Southern Yunnan, the elephants were employed to carry burdens like oxen and horses in the Middle Kingdom. Cf. *T.P.* 890, 8.—

757) Cf. *supra* §§ 173, 195.

753) These could come but from Badakshan and Northern India. Cf. note 761, *On Asbestos*.

759) Cf. Wang tze nien, *Shih y ki*.—*Tai ping yü lan*, kiv, 9^0, fol. 9 vers., and 816, 8.—The King is said to have received these foreigners in his famous *tang* or Audience hall of *T'ung yun*.

760) Cf. *suprá*, § 125-126.—On *Bintang*, cf. H. Yule, *Marco Polo* (2) II, 261.

Sect. C. *Western Influences by Southern Channels.*

a. *Hormuz Navy in South-Eastern China.*

NOTES *continued*——
761) Asbestos came to the knowledge of the Chinese during the reign of *Tch'eng*, the second king of the Tcuou dynasty. Barbarians of the West, coming by the Kukunor presented him with some asbestos cloth. (Cf. *Ki tchung Tchou shu*).—The next instance in date is that of Muh Wang who was presented also with asbestos by Kiaen-Jungs inhabiting the same region, about 990 B.C. (Cf. *supra*, notes 169 and 249).—Badakshan near the source of the Oxus was the chief producer of lapislazuli and of asbestos,—the stone for wicks—according to the Arab travellers. Cf. M. Reinand - Stan. Guyard, *Géographie d' Abulféda* II, ii, 203 quoting Ibn Hankal and the *Lobáb* of Ibn-el-Athir. —Cyprus was another country producer of Asbestos in Antiquity. Cf. G. Maspero, *Histoire Ancienne*, p. 237?—Pliny was aware that the asbestos cloth was produced in the rainless deserts of India, (xix, 1, 4). —Silky amianthus occurs in flat beds or veins above the Khost valley south of the Kurram, Afghanistan) where the hill people there twist it still at present into ropes. (Cf. E. Balfour, *Cyclopoed. oj India*, 1385; I, 129).—We have just seen in our text an importation by sea of asbestos wicks in North China, 310 B.C., which had been brought by Hormuz Merchantmen. From the HAN period down to the fifth century, Asbestos cloth was reckoned among the Tats'in—or Tarshish—. imports. (Cf. *Hou Han shuh*, k. 88; *San Kwoh tchi*, *Wei lioh*, k. 30; *Tsin shu*, k. 97; *Sung shu*, k. 97; F. Hirth, *China and the Roman Orient*, pp. 41, 45, 46, 74.) Tung Fang-so of the second century B.C. said that it was coming from (*i.e.* through) the Southern Ocean. (*Shea y king*; T.P. 820, 8 *v.*; 869, 7; *Shih tchou ki*, T.P. 863, 8).—In 381-3 A.D., Hindus from Cabul presented asbestos cloth to the court of the FORMER Ts'IN at Tchang-an. (Cf. *Tsien Ts'ir luh*; *Shih luh kwoh tchun tsiu*: T.P, 820, 8; Bunju Nanjio, *Catal Budd. Tripitaka*, p. 403). It was probably from the same region that in 235 A.D. had come the men from the Si-yü who accompanied with double interpreters presented asbestos cloth to the court of WEI at Loh-yang (cf. *Wei tchi*: T.P. 820, 8).—In the 2nd cent. A.D. Asbestos was discovered in China, in the *Yü shan* or Feathers'-hill, on the common borders of Shantung and Kiangsu provinces. (Cf. Wang kia, *Shuh y ki*; T.P. 820, 9 *v*, and 12, 10). And the famous conspirator Liang-hi who died in 159 A.D., was enabled to play the joke, practised at the court of the Emperor Charles V, which was well known at the time of Pliny. (Cf. F. Hirth, *China and the Roman Orient*, p. 250-1), with an unlined garment made of Asbestos cloth from the *Yü shan*.

(cf. *San kwoh tchi, Wei tchi*; Wang Kia, *loc. cit.*) Some more asbestos cloth came from the same place to the court of the TSIN dynasty at Loh-yang in the years *Tai-k'ang* 280-9 A.D. The local population claimed to have presented some of their identical veined stone to Yao and Shun, amplified into a woven cloth by later tradition. (Cf. T.P. 820, 9 r.) On the asbestos of Shantung and its use for stoves, crucibles, and so forth, by the inhabitants there. (Cf. Alex. Williamson, *Journeys in North-China*, 1870, I, 129.) Under the YUEN dynasty asbestos was discovered in Szetchuen. (Cf. *Yuen she*; *Sheng ngan tsih* by Yang-shen, 1483-1559; G. Schlegel, *Nederl. Chin. Woortl.* iii, 1066). Consul Alexander Hosie, *Three years in Western China*, 1890, p. 160, reports having seen some asbestos cloth there.

762) Fabulous account of the Asbestos, making it the hair of a burrowing animal of volcanic (Sunda) islands, already current at the time of Tung-fang So, circ. 150-100 B.C., and confirmed by later reports (*T. P.Y.L.*, kiv. 820, 8; 868, 8; 869, 7; and 78, 8), refer most positively to East Java, where no asbestos is found any more than in any other of the Sunda islands. — The story of the Salamander passing unhurt through fire is at least as old as Aristotle, but it was not known when the fable arose that asbestos was a substance derived from the animal. (H. Yule, *Marco Polo*, I, 217). The Chinese sources permit us to say that it was current in the second cent. B.C. It was a Persian story. Bakin says the animal is found at Ghur near Herat and is *like a mouse*. Another author quoted by D'Herbelot, says it is *like a marten*. Similar animals are found in the deserts of Chinese Turkestan since antiquity between Kharo Khodjo and Khotan. They were spoken of as yellow rats, *hwang shä*, in the old *Muh T'ien tze tchuen* (China Review. 1889, xvii, 233) of the 10th cent. B.C. containing Records of the Journey of Muh Wang in Turkestan. They were described also in the *Si yä tchu kwoh tchi* of the 5th cent. (cf. T.P.Y.L. 911. 6; description of the *Shä wang kwoh*); in the *T'ang shu*, (kiv. 258 *b*, *Yä-tien*) and later works. (Cf. Stan. Julien, *Mél. d. Géogr. Asiat.*, p. 99). Dr. E. Bretschneider says that they are jumping hares or *Gerboas* (cf. *Chinese intercourse with the Countries of Asia*, Art. *Huo chou*). Their presence gave rise in the middle Ages to the location there of the old Afghan Myth, and Marco Polo has reported at length a statement denying its veracity. Cf. *Marco Polo*, ed. Yule, I, 215).—Another fabulous origin of Asbestos is that which made it the bark of trees growing on a volcanic island East of Funam, in Java. The story came to China through the trade with Funam=Phnom=Cambodia, in the third and 4th cent. A.D. (cf. T.P.Y.L., kiv. 820, 8; 868, 8 r.; 869, 5; 960, 9 r.

763) Liu Hiang, *Lieh sien tchuen*.—T.P.Y.L., 989, 5 r.
764) *Ku-sheng*, 11420-20. Bas.
765) Cf. *suprà*, par. 199.
766) Cf. *Kômakon* in Theophrastes and the Javanese *Kumu kus* as pointed out by Col. H. Yule, *Marco Polo*, II, 380.
767) Based upon the *pin-tchu* (9608-5917 Bas.) of the Hwai river in the *Yü kung*, i, 35. Now these *pin-tchu* of fresh water could not be pearl-oysters of the sea. They have been identified with the *pang* (9401 Bas.) of later times, the *Uniouidæ*, fresh water mussels; the addition of *tchu* was to indicate a selection of the best and most nacre-

ous ones.
763) Cf. *Kwan-tze*: T.P. 803, 1 v.
769) Cf. *Lieh-tze*.—*T'sou h'en*.—*Tchwang-tze*—*Tchun Kwoh tsih* —T.P. 803 ; 2, 2v., 4.
770) Cf. *Meh-ti*.—T.P. 941, 5.
771) Med. *Ming-yueh*, shining moon, (3890-cl. 74 Bas.)—Cf. Sanskr. *marakata*; Greek *maragdos*; Latin *margarita*; Persian *marwid*; &c.
772) Nearchus speaks of an island of the gulf, noted for its pearl fishery which was carried there in the same manner as in the Indian Ocean. (Arrian, *Indica*, 38, 3). Pliny is the first who spoke of the Pearl fishery at Tylos, Bahrein islands. *Hist. nat.*, vi, 28: 148) cf. E. Bunbury, *Hist. Anc. Geogr.*, I, 462, 538.—Tch'ang-teh, a Chinese traveller has described those of Shiraz. in 1258. Cf. E. Bretschneider, *Mediæval Researches*, 1, 1-5. The Arab geographers, Masudi, i, 328, Edrisi, i, 373-4, Ibn Batuta, ii, 246, have also described them. Modern descriptions have been made by Col. D. Wiison, *Pearl Fisheries in the Persian Gulf*, J.R.G.S., iii, 1834, 283-286.—Brenner, *Report on Pearl Fishing in the Bay of Bahrein*; Peterm. Geogr. Mitth. 1873 ; 37 ; E. Bretschneider, *Med. Res.*, I, 146, II, 130.—On the history of the pearl fisheries of Ceylon cf. Emersen Tennent, *Ceylon*, II. 561.
773) Tung Fang So, *Lin yh ki.—Kwang tchi*.—T.P.Y.L., 803, 9, 10 v.
774) There is no world for p e a r l in P. Pierret, *Vocabulaire Hieroglyphique*. I do not see any mentioned in Assyrian. The ancient classical authors, such as Herodotus do not speak of pearls. No mention is made of it in Perrot-Chipiez, *Histoire de l' Art Antique*, vol. I-IV.
—The pearl-fisheries of the isle of Hainan were not opened before the second century ; cf. below.
775) Cf. *supra* note 455.—Although Lieh-tze was living in 597 B.C., the legend may have been heard of by him 25 years later.
776) I have explained the political reasons which have led to this change, *supra* § 174.
777) *Tai ping yu lan*, kiv. 820, 8 v.; 869, 7.
778) These various spellings belong to the time when an official mode of writing the name in question had not yet been adopted. The same difficulty occurs with the *Muh T'ien tze tchuen* and the *Shan hai king* where geographical names are written differently of what they were afterwards.—Kalang was for long an ethnic in Java.
779) The native traditions indicate about 75 B.C. The Chinese evidence suggests some fifty years earlier.—Kwoh-Poh the famous commentator of A.D. 276-324, gives for the same region and the same story the name of *Tche-pu* (8285-7622 Bas.), variant *Tchu-pu* (10173-7622 Bas.) which is oldest appearance of the name of Java.
780) Cf. *supra*, notes 474 and 475.
781) Many gaps remain at present in reconstructing the whole fabric, but we may expect that some if not all of them will be filled up by further finds in the fragments of ancient literature.
782) In the *Tsien Han shu*; T.P.Y.L., 785, 2 v.
783) There are several spellings which show the foreign origin of the name, *Hwang* is the cl. 201 ; but the other character is *tche*, cl. 66, branch. sometimes *tche*, 4140 Bas., same meaning, sometimes *tche*,

3345 Bas., finger.—In the second century they introduced in South China the *tche-kia hwa*, the finger-nail flower, as we shall see later on.
78) Cf. Edw. Balfour, *Cyclop. of India*, II, 37.
785) *T'sien Han shu*, 1. c.—The same distance is given later on for the country of Oman, said to be near the sea of Persia, in A.D. c. 250. Cf. Kang-tai, *Funam tu suh tchuen*; T.P., 787, 4.—Tsui Pao, *Ku kin tchu*; T.P., 961, 9 *v*.
786) It was spoken of by Nearchus, 325 B.C. who stopped there, but does not mention its trade (Arrian, *Indica*, 33-35). Perhaps was it on one of the neighbouring islands. We have seen already that he and Onesicritus were acquainted with reports of Mariners travelling far to the South. Cf. *supra*, § 179, n. 648.

b. *The Great State of* Ts'u (Hukwang, &c.)

207. It was already one of the largest and most powerful states of the Chinese agglomeration when it became part of it in the 7th century, and for a certain time afterwards it was able to keep in check the Princes of Ts'in during their struggle for the Empire. Its area was very large, but much of it was not Chinese, thinly inhabited and uncivilised. The reigning house claimed to have been founded by a certain Ki-lien (meaning 'heaven in the Hiung-nu language),[787] himself alleged to be a great-grandson of Tchuen-hiuh at the fifth generation.[788] Their surname was Me, bleating, and for long their language was not Chinese, as its meaning suggests.[789] They were settled at first in the Tchung Kwoh, or Honan, and in *Wei*, or the west of Yun-yang fu of N. Hupeh, among Taic-Shan populations. A certain Yit-Hiung is mentioned as instructor of Tchou Wen Wang,[790] and it is probably to the influence of his family that the Wei native tribes responded to the call of Wu Wang to overthrow the Shang-yn dynasty and conquer the Chinese dominion.[791] In 887 B.C. their chief Hiung k'iü assumed the title of king for the first time.[792] Their centre was between Y-tchang and King-tchou of S. Hupeh, on the banks of the Yang-tze kiang. Known at first by the old name of King, famous for this region since the days of the *Yü Kung*, it became Ts'u in 659 B.C.[793] It extended its territory in every direction until its extinction by its more powerful rival the kingdom of Ts'in in 223 B.C. Ts'u *Tchwang* wang who ruled in 613-591 B.C. had indeed reached already such a high rank that he was for the time being Leader of the Princes, exercising therefore the part of Protector which the decayed prestige and authority of the kings of Tchou did not permit them to occupy anymore.

208. A few circumstances show the gradual extension of the dominion of Ts'u.[794] In 696 B.C., it extended east as far as *Yen-ling* (south border of Kiang-su).[795] In 591, complimentary envoys[796] came to the capital, near the present *Y-tchang* on the Yang-tze, from Hunan, which was soon afterwards partly conquered. In A.D. 400, the region of *T'sang-wu* (South Hunan) was subdued and the minister Wu-ki, was sent more south to establish intercourse with the Barbarians there.[797] This was an important event, as it is the first opening of relations with the South, viz. the modern Kwang-tung province. Then in 334, the Kingdom of Yueh (Tcheh kiang) was submitted,[798] and about 330 the important Tsu-ite kingdom of Tsen in Yunnan was founded.[799] Although the communications between the new state and the mother country were not always easy and required a good deal of warfare, they were seldom interrupted notwithstanding the efforts of the kings of Ts'in.[800] The new state of Tsen has played an important part in the history of the trade routes of the South-west, which we have told in a previous part of this work.[801] About 280 B.C.[802] the Tsenites had made an expedition to the South and according to the Burmese history destroyed the Old Pagan, the capital of Burma. It is the first appearance in history of the name of *Tsen* for China,[803] and therefore it deserves a special notice.

209. Notwithstanding its inland position, the Kingdom of Tsu succeeded, in course of time as we have just seen, to open outlets and inlets with the outside world, East, South, West and South-west. We know very little of its internal history, but that little is enough to show that its political importance and its wealth attracted much from the exterior. The competition of its various races made it a centre of activity which had some influence on the civilisation of China in general, at that time. Not a few foreign notions and things were half-sinicised therein and thus became more acceptable to the Chinese minds of the central North. Such for instance were the coinage of stamped lumps on the Lydian pattern in 590-600 B.C., the hand-swipe or *shaduf*, in the same century, which we have already mentioned.[804] The horse-shoe shape of the tombs and the *wei-tan* pillars, both reminding the natural worship popular in India,[805] must also be added to the preceding.

210. It was undoubtedly through the Southern advance of the Tsuites towards the South, that the Chinese became acquainted for the first time with the cinnamon tree[806] of North Kwang-si, in the fifth century, when Fan-li the famous merchant made a trade of it,[807] probably not with foreigners.[808]

Some other Southern and foreign plants came thus to be imported in Central China. Kiü-yuen, 314 B.C., in his famous poem *Li sao*[809] has enumerated several of them ; for instance the *Kün kwei*, a small sort of cinnamon which grows in Tungking .[810] he speaks also of the *hu-tcheng* or foreign rope, which has not been identified.[811]

As to philosophical advance we have only here to remind our readers that it was in Ts'u that the famous Lao-tze is reputed to have flourished at first.[812]

But it was not only in putting forward foreign things that the state of Ts'u has played an important part in the history of China civilisation. Material progress was actually made in the land. The *Kieh* or hooked spear was invented there about 690 B.C.[813] A short time before 500 the cross-bow was invented among the Ki-tze a native population, and soon attracted the attention of the Chinese.[814]

211. In 548 B.C. a rather important thing had been achieved in Ts'u. Wei-yen, Marshal of the Kingdom[815] had been commanded to make a complete survey of the lands and their products. Nothing so important had been done in the States since the days of the *Yü kung* and it was looked upon as a great achievement. It is most probable that a large part of it was embodied in the *Shan Hai king* ;[816] and we consider as more probable still that the survey imitated by the Great Yü being thus recalled to mind and imitated, it was at this occasion that was erected for the first time the (original of the) famous tablet known as the inscription of *Yü*.[817] Comparative palæography permits to assign it to about that age. The wriggling shapes of the characters increased in the hand copies of subsequent times have nothing common with the *Koh-tou* or thick and thin strokes of the early writing ;[818] they were simply the outcome of the ages on the inscribed stone.[819] It was made partly of sentences taken from the *Shu King*.[820]

NOTES——
787) Cf. Mayers, *Ch. R.M.* 309.
788) Szema Ts'ien, *She Ki*, Ts'u she kia, 40, fol. 2.— I have just seen i. a note of Dr. J. Edkins, *On the chronology of the Chu kingdom* (Chin. Rev. xvi, 305-6) that Yuen Shao (A.D. 160) tells us, in his *Fêng su tung,* that the sovereigns of Chu,—or Ts'u, counted 64 generations from the Emperor Tchuen Hiüh, to Fu-tchu, who was king when Ts'in Shi Hwang conquered his kingdom (223 B.C.). Counting 30 years a generation as usual with the Chinese, it makes 2143 B.C. This is an unexpected confirmation of my corrected scheme of chronology which acknowledges the years 2225-2147 to Tchuen-hiüh. Cf. *suprâ* note 603, and *in rà* : chronological sketch.

789) Their language belonged to the Taic-shan family. Cf. *Les Langues de la Chine, avant les Chinoise*, §§ 31-33, 96-97, and addition 31, p. 148.
790) Cf. Mayers, *Ch. R.M.* 947.—There is a work existing still at present under his name which probably contains some of his views.
791) Cf. *She King*, V. ii, 3.
792) Under the pretext that they were Man-y, i.e. Non-Chinese natives, and that they did not bear Chinese appellations, he gave to his three sons Royal titles, viz. *Keu Tan Wang, Ngo Wang*, and *Yueh tchang Wang*. Cf. *She ki*, 40, 3 v.
793) Cf. *Tchun tsiu Tso tchuen*, Hi kung ann. 1.—In the *Shi King*, it is called KING Ts'u. Cf. Chin. Class. IV, 644 ; V, 134.
794) In 821, a brother of Hiung siang settled among the *Yung-pu*, opposite Tchung king, south of the Yang-tze kiang. Cf. *She ki*, 40, 4 v.
795) Cf. *Hou Han shu*, kiv. 116 ; trad. Wylie, R.E.O., I, 208.—In 678, it had become an important state. Cf. *She ki*, 40, 6.
796) *Hou Han shu*, ibid.
797) The future *Nan-yueh*. Cf. *Hou Han shu*, ibid.—On the extension of Ts'u over 5000 li cf. Su-Ts'in, *c.* 333 B.C. in the *She ki* : T.P. 167. l v.—
798) Cf. *supra* §§ 199, 202.
799) Cf. *supra*, par. 61 and seq., note 271 &c.
800) The Tsu-ites were thus compelled in 294 B.C. to destroy the native state of *Ye-lang* which stood on the way,
801) Cf. *supra*, ch. VI, sect. *e*, div. III. par. 75.
802) Cf. *supra*, note 240.
803) I have given *supra* par. 75, 77 and notes 320, 321 the historical origin of that name, which has had nothing to do with the state of Ts'is of Shensi.
804) Cf. *suprá* §§ 132-133.—It is not uninteresting to remark here that the first allusion about the three legged crow supposed to roost in the sun occurs in the *Li sao* of Kiü-yuen, the poet of Ts'u 314 B.C. in China, and that a three legged bird in various forms was figured on coins of Pamphylia and Lycia of older times, Comte Goblet d' Alviella has reproduced some of them in his interesting work on *La Migration des Symboles*, 1891, p. 242.
805) Cf. *supra*, note 490. For figures of the *wei kan* pillars, cf. A. Colquhoun, *Across Chrysi*, II, 162, 138, 156, 161, 172.
806) The *Kwei muh*, 4212—cl. 75 Bas., or *Muh kwei*; on which see E. Bretschneider, *Botanicum Sinicum*, II, 247, 552.— *Kwei* or *Kwei hwa* 4222-8344 Bas. was used for the *Olea flagrans*. (Cf. E. B., *Bot. Sin* l.c.) and thus appears in the *Shan hai king*, I, 1, on the Tchao-yao Mount which I suspect was near Hang-tchou. The *Si hai* of the text (which has misled Prof. L. de Rosny, *Chan Hai King*, I, p. 5) is the *Si hu*, as shown by the names of the neighbouring mountains.—The *Kwei n.nh*, (like the *Kwei*) is unknown to the Great Classics. It appears in the *Shan Hai King*, II, 7, *v*, about a mountain of N. Kwangsi. It is spoken in the *Er-ya*, in *Tchwang-tze, Su Tsin, Hwai wan-tze*, &c. The Kao-sin-forest, or Cinnamon-tree forest, *Kwei-lin*, which has given its name to the site in 214 B.C., is still at present that of the capital of Kwang-si, is spoken of in a later book of the

Shan Hai King, x, 1 v.

807) Cf. *Lieh sien tchuen*, 1st cent. n.c.; T. P. 957, 5 v.—We have had already occasion to speak of that remarkable man, cf. note 744 and text.

808) The question here is particularly interesting because of the *Cinnamon* of *Exod.* xxx, 23; *Prov.* vii, 17; *Song of Sol.* iv. 14, and of the *Cassia* of *Ps.* xlv, 8, which had been erroneously supposed to have come from China, while there is no doubt that they were imported from the Malabar Coast and from Ceylon, where they grow naturally. The Kassia as a cheaper and coarser kind would be that of the continent which for long was wrongly supposed to be a distinct species, as stated by A. de Candolle, *Origin of Cultivated Plants*, p. 146. Flnckiger and Hanbury have thoroughly investigated the matter in their *Pharmacographia*, or History of the Principal Drugs of vegetable Origin, p. 467 sq.—The word *Kinnamón* is traceable to the Singhalese Kakynnama. As to *cassia* it has come through the Septuagint from the hebrew which means 'cutt off.'

809) It has been translated into French by the late Marquess D'Hervey St. Denys in 1'70.

810. Cf. E. Bretschneider, *Botanicum Sinicum*, II, 552.

811) Cf. E. B., *Bot. Sin.*, II, 420.

812) Cf. *supra*, note 505.

813) Cf. *Tso tchuen*, ann. 690.—*Chin. Class.* V, 77.—Fan-li, when minister to *Yueh*, 493-473 b.c., is attributed the invention of a catapulte throwing stones of 12 pounds at 400 paces. Cf. *Khang-hi tze tien*, s.v. *pao*, 11:+16.—Pellet-bows had been invented about 607 b.c. Cf. following note.

814) *On Bow, Composite Bow, Pellet Bow, and Cross-bow.* The B o w-a n d- A r r o w are not a weapon so primitive in its character that it may have been invented anywhere. Comparative ethnography shows to this effect that not a few nations and populations hav never been acquainted with it. (Cf. Lane Fox, *Catalog. Anthrop. Collect.*, 1877, p 41-45). Three different sorts of bows have appeared in Antiquity.1⁰ The Arcus, or plain Bow, made of a single piece in one bend : 2⁰ the Angular B ow, apparently made of two pieces, of the Egyptians and Assyrians, and probably the antecedent of the following ; 3⁰ the Composite bow, made of wood, horn, glue and sinews, of which there were two sorts, *a* the Greek bow, or Cupid's bow, forming a doub e arch, used by Parthians, Daces and generally near the Black sea ; notwithstanding the adverse opinion of Theocritus and Locrophron who dis inguished them, it seems doubtful that when unstrung the Greek bow should have differed much of the: *b* the Scythian bow, forming a C in its backward curve when unstrung. This peculiarity is noted in Herodotus, vii, 69, of Arab's bows ; and may be seen at Karrak with the bows of captives made by Sheshonk (Rawlinson, *Her.* iv. 64). The C o m p o s i t e B o w appears on monuments of Anterior Asia as early as the old carved slabs of Telloh, and it was that same bow which the civilised Bak Sings carried with them to Eastern Asia. It was that sort of bow which was pictured by the old Babylonian symbol writing used for it, still recognizable in its descendant the Chinese character *Kung*. (Cf. *The old Chinese characters and their early Chinese derivates* § 42). The Arcus or plain bow was known in pre-Chinese China

among the natives of the East, the Y. whose name was written with a symbol meaning pictorially the *Great Bow*-men. The most famous makers of Arrows were the *Y-mou* of Shantung, according to the *She pên*. Curiously enough one of the mythical inventors of the Bow, in the *Shan Hai king*, (xviii, 5 and gloss.), was named *P'an* which is the word for Bow, in Akkadian, in Malay, &c.—A *Kiñt*, (4868 Bas.) sort of thimble or ring fitted on the thumb was used to assist in drawing the bow. (Cf. *Shi King*, II, iii, Ode 5, *Kiu kung*) as in Assyro-Babylonia (cf. Perrot-Chipiez. *Hist. Art. Antiq.* II, fig. 5 of Assurbanipal) must have been brought from the west in China by the Bak Sings along with the composite bow. On the early knowledge of the implement at the time of Hwang-ti and of Shun, cf. note 163 and its add. in the present work).—Two improvements were made among the Chinese and Non-Chinese, the *t'an* or pellet-bow and the *Nu* or Cross-bow.—1°, The *t'an* (2645 Bas.) is a bow with a socket fixed on the string for holding bullets or pellets, whence its name. It was used in 607 B.C. at first as an amusement, by the Duke *Ling* of Tsin (Shansi) and was an introduction of Tung-tze, or .iu Tung, his minister. (Cf. *Tso tchuen* VII, ii, 4 ; *Han shi wai tchuen* ; *Shi shwoh* ; *T'ai ping yü lan*, kiv. 350, fol. 6 vers. ; 55, fol. 6 vers.) Pan Tchao the famous general of the first century, sent in 74 A.D., 36 men to Khotan to practise arrows and pellet-bows. (*T.P.Y.L.* 350-6). Besides China, it is now used by Afghans and others in the North-west of India, where it is called *gulel*. (Cf. Wilbraham Egerton, *An illustrated Handbook of Indian arms*, 1880. p. 130, and Lane Fox, *Catal.*, p. 52).—2° The *Nu* (2631 Bas.) ideographically the e n s l a v e d b o w, once called also *Kiü-shu* (10662-cl. 202, or 11420 cl. 202, Bas.), by the Non-Chinese, which is still preserved in the Tibetan. *gzu*. Its first appearance was made among the *Ki-tze man* (10316-cl. 39-9633 Bas.) a native tribe of West Hunan on the borders of Ts'u, in the sixth century B.C. Through Sun-Wu the military author of 500 B.C. (*supra* note 667) and subsequent writers, it became soon famous because it permitted to shoot an arrow at 600 double-paces. (Cf. *T.P.Y.L.*, 348, 1-82) ; *She ki*, 76, 2 ; 65, 2).—The crossbow does not seem to have been known in Roman Europe before the sixth century A.D. (Cf. E. B. Tyler, *Anthropology*, p. 196). The Lateran council of 1139 forbade its use as being too murderous a weapon for christians to employ against one another, and Anna Commena who described it said that " a truly diabolical affair it is."—Crossbows are still characteristic weapons of many of the wilder tribe) of Chin-India and of non-Chinese parts of China. (Cf. W. Egerton, o.c., pp. 85-87 for details, and also H. Yule, *Marco-Polo*, II, 67-68)
815) *Tso tchuen*, Siang kung, xxv, 9.
816) Cf. *supra*, note 91 and add.
817) On this tablet cf. in favour of its authenticity : Amiot, J. Hager (1802), J. Klaproth (1311), G. Panthier (1868) ; and against it : J. Legge, (1865), W. H. Medhurst (1868), Christopher T. Gardner (1864). Nothing shows it to be the clumsy forgery of a Taoist under the Han dynasty which Dr. J. Legge declares it to be. Copies and copies of copies only exist at present, and they represent clearly in my opinion a genuine inscription of *circa* 500 B.C., partly defaced and eaten up by ages.

818) On the *Koh tou*. cf. *supra* n. 76.
819) Cf. the same effect on ancient texts, in the native collections of inscriptions.
820) Cf. *Shu King*, II, iv, 8.

c. The State of Shuh (Szetchuen.)

212. We have had occasion in a previous part of the present work,[821] when enquiring about the channels of introduction of foreign civilisation, in China, to speak of the trade of Shuh[822] and of the state of the same name, the first king of whom claimed an Indian descent, and was ruling in 475 B.C.[823] He was succeeded by some other *Kai-mings*[824] or Rulers, the last of whom named *Tze-kwei Kai-ming* was on the throne in 324 B.C. when the king of Ts'in by superchery succeeded in conquering the country,[825] or at least submitting it under his protectorate.[826]

The Indian descent here referred to deserves more than a passing remark as previously done. Some more fragments of the native history of the kings of Sze-tchuen, *Shuh Wang pên ki* by Yang-hiung (53 B.C.—A.D. 18), which had escaped my attention before, are most important on these intercommunications, because they permit us to determine the date when they began, and that of the cave remains of West China.

213. According to the native history, the oldest masters of the country were the *Ts'an-tsung* or gatherers of silk-worms, the *7 cheh kwan* or Breakers of the Bushy-forests, and the *Yü yh* or Fish traders; afterwards the *Kai-mings*.[827] Then came *Peh yung*, or Baron Yung, and after him *Yü wei* and *Wei tien* who settled in the hills of the *T'sien* river and lived there as the first Anachorets (*sien*).[828] After them there was a king named *Tu-yü* coming from India.[829] A daughter of the chieftain of *Tchu-she*,[830] whose name was *Li* and who was coming from the sources of the *Kiang*, became his wife, and then he assumed the Royal dignity with the title of *Wang-Ti* or Expecting Emperor, and established his residence in *Pi yh*, or city of the tablet, (the later *Tcheng-tu*).

214. The foregoing statement about the anachorets is most interesting as the first historical information about the once inhabited hermit-caves of the Min river. The *Tsien shan* lies near the upper course of the Min,[831] in the neighbourhood of Li-fang which Capt. W. Gill visited in 1878 when travelling in N.W. Szetchuen, and where he saw a great many caves on the sides of the hills.[832] Now as to the date. The history says that these first anachorets came after *Peh yung*, one of the historical rulers. It just happens that we hear of this Baron Yung in the classics.[833] In 611 B.C., as he had led a conspiration of native MAN tribes

against the state of Ts'u, his state was destroyed,⁸³⁴ and he was compelled to flee westwards, in Shuh where he established a new state as the native history tells us.

And as to the arrival of these anachorets, the statement of the *Shuh wang pên ki* is supported by some further evidence in the historical literature. For instance the *Yü kwei king* and the *Yh tchou tchi*, description of Szetchuen, two ancient works, record that Recluses (*sien*) were established in caves of the Mount of Tsing tcheng (in the modern prefecture of Kia-ting, on the Min river) at the time of the six Kingdoms, i.e. 481 B.C.⁸³⁵ The region of Tso, near the present Tatsienlu or Darchiendo of W. Szetchuen was reputed in 97 B.C. to be since ages productive of the *shin-yoh*, the divine drug (of immortality) on Mount Shantu which was also inhabited by Recluses.⁸³⁶

215. Therefore we know, as the outcome of the previous paragraphs, that in the first half of the 6th century B.C. some hermits, or *Sien*, i.e. Richis, came and settled in N.W. Szetchuen, in the vicinity of the central route of the Shuh traders with India.⁸³⁷ This date coïncides with a visible influence of India on China, and the same century saw the arrival of Lao-tze with a certain baggage of Indian views.

216. Several of these caves, cut in the hills in a remarkable manner have been visited by European travellers. It seems that their former occupants were ignorant as yet of the art of writing : carved ornaments representing the vadjra, the trisula, the sun, and the existence therein of large water basins for ablutions purpose suggest and confirm the Hinduism or Brahmanism of these Anachorets. They continued to be inhabited thus for long and finally some of them and similar other ones were occupied by Buddhist, and by natives. They are commonly called Mantze caves because of the latter circumstance and the Non-Chinese character of their occupants.⁶³⁸

217. It is in the usual sequence of events that these anachoretes and proselytisers should not have come and settled in the country of S h u h otherwise than by a well known trade route and on the trail of traders. Their arrival in the sixth century implies the existence of the trade route through P a t n a, S a d i y a and D a r c h i e n d o some time earlier.⁸³⁹ We have been able in previous pages of the present work to adduce some evidence of the activity of the merchants of S h u h in several directions west and south-west. The import of Tibetan Mastiffs (*ngao*) by travellers, ⁸⁴⁰ about 1105 B.C., which concerns most probably the eastern portion of that route, is the oldest instance known, and concurs with the

precited circumstances. Jujube, Peach, Abricot, &c. were carried by their trade inland. (*Supra* ch. VI, sect. *a*) to the N.W. of India. Wild-silk and woollen cloth of *Shuh*, curious bamboo staves of *kiung*, precious furs of Hukwang, and special ironware of *Liang* (N. of Shuh) became gradually regular articles of trade of these merchants of Shuh to West India across the S.E. corner of Tibet.[841] We have no precise data as to its actual beginning, but it cannot be, according to probabilities much later than 650 b.c. It was through their channel that were introduced in the west and in the centre of China several innovations rather characteristic of their origin which he have previously mentioned.[842]

218. While dealing with the imports and exports which took place through this trade route between China and India during that period, we must necessarily mention the question of the South Açoka or Mauriya written characters. The North Indian writing, also called Bactro-Pali is based undoubtedly on the Semitic writing, probably, on that which was employed in Ancient Persia, and was introduced by Cyrus in North-India as tradition suggests. It was there subsequently brought to perfection by the Brahmans. The South-Açoka, so-called, although brought likewise to perfection by the same systematizers, rests on a different basis. Various attempts have been made to find this basis in South-Arabian and others characters. But they have proved to be complete failures, which further enlightenment from recent researches shows to be greater than were supposed at first.[843] Traders can ill afford to manage their business without writing, and the travelling merchants of the country of Shuh, where Chinese script was known, cannot have journeyed then into India, where on the contrary the art of writing was still unknown, without having introduced for their business transactions, some of their own written characters. This they could do easily with their most simple symbols and the syllabic sounds inherent to them, as has been the case in China when dealing with foreigners in later times. Such for instance the Tsuan or Lolo characters framed in a.d. 9, or before,[844] the Yao Shuikia and Miaotze characters in the South-west ;[845] the small characters of the Djurtchens,[846] and others. Now a classification of the Chinese characters in the *tchuen* style[847] current during that period, such as made in the *Shwoh wen* vocabulary of the first century,[848] shows that among the numerous characters, most generally cumbrous and complicated in form, there was a comparatively small number of them, about a hundred, quite simple and most convenient for use. And a close comparison of the Indian characters, *in shape and sound* with these elementary Chinese symbols shows

in 32 cases out of 34 such resemblances and similarities, that it is most difficult to believe that the Hindu Brahmans have not availed themselves of the Rude writing of these merchants, as a material already known, to make out of it, with improvements imitated from the Northern alphabet, the so-called South Açôka characters.[649]

NOTES——
821) Cf. *suprà* pp. 46, 52, 55.
822) *Shuh*, *Shuk*, 9457 Bas., now written eye (cl. 109) bundle (cl. 20) and warm (cl. 142) arranged in a single group-character, was originally written w o r m, *tsung* (cl. 142) under κien, l o o k i n g, thus making a phonetic suggestion ts-k. Cf. Min Ts'i-kih, *Luh shu tung*, ix, 10.
823) As shown by the complimentary mission he sent to Li kung, Duke of Ts'IN, at the occasion of his accession to the throne in 476 B.C.— The year 255 of p. 52 was a misprint.
824) *Kai-ming* was a title, not a proper name as mistaken *supra* p. 52. An its connection with the name of the *Kuen-mings*, cf. *infra*.
825) The superchery consisted in the offer by the king of Ts'IN to that of Ts'U, of five stone oxen about which the Ts-inites had reported the wonderful story that some gold (secretly placed there at night) found every morning under their tail, was really made by them. The king of SHUH invited to take them away if he choosed, was compelled to open a route across the Kiu-lung range, to do it. The Ts'inites afterwards availed themselves of the passage hitherto impracticable and their army conquered the country.—Cf. Yang-hiung, *Shuh wang pen ki* : T.P. 900, 2. In 1868, Alexander Wylie has travelled through the same road which he has carefully described in his *Notes on a journey from Ching-tao to Han-kow*; Proc. Rog. Geo. Soc., June 7th 1870, p. 175-9. It is known as the *Shih niu tao*, the Stone-Oxen Road.
826) As shown *supra*, p. 52.
827) This paragraph is intended to replace the lines 2-7 of page 52 which contain several misapprehensions.
828) The Chinese text there is extremely concise : *Yü-wei Wei-tien Yü Tsien shan teh sien*, but I think the statement is clear enough. Cf. T.P.Y.L., 166, 3 v.
829) Cf. *supra* note 263.
830) *Tchu she* was the name of a locality famous for its silver mines. S.W. of *Y-pin* hien in Szetchuen. (Cf. G. Playfair, *The cities and towns of China*, Nos. 1470, 8574) near Sin tchou.—The Min river was for long supposed to form the head waters of the Kiang, and is marked Ta kiang on the ancient maps of the contending states period. Cf. the *Lih tai ti li yen koh tu*.
831) Cf. *Khang hi tze tien*, s.v. Tsien, 85+9, fol. 77.—The *Tsien Han shu*, Ti li tchi, says : In the *Shuh* province, district of *Mien-se*, the *Tsien* river flows from the *Yü lei* hills.— Mien-se is at present the district of *Wen tchuen*, in *Mou tchou* of N.W. Szetchuen.
832) *The River of Golden Sand*, 1880, vol. I, p. 346-353.
833) The *Shu King*, Speech at Muh, v, ii, 3, enumerates the Yun among the native tribes, who came to the help of the TCHOU when the

conquered China. They were settled near the present Yun-yang, in N.W. Hupeh, not far from the Kia-lung range and the N.E. of Szetchuen.
834) *Tchun Tsiu, Tso tchuez.*, Wen kung, xvi, 6.
835) *Tai ping yü lan.* Kiv. 44. fol. 4 r.
836) *Hou Han shu.* Kiv. 116.—We shall hear of them under the She Hwang-ti. Cf. below.
837) Their influx must have lasted for several centuries as they settled also on the cliffs of the Kia-ling, and Wu rivers.
838) Cf. A. Wylie *O.C.* (*supra* N. 825).—W. Gill. *O.C.* (*supra* n. 832).—E. Colborne Baber, *Travels and Researches in Western China*, 1882, p. 129-141.—F.S.A. Bourne, *Report of a Journey in Southwestern China*, 1888.—E. C. Baker has studied several of these caves with his usual carefulness, and has published plans and drawings.
839) On this route cf. *supra* § 56 and notes 214-7; also § 55 and notes 238-243.
840) Cf. *supra*, note 243 on the meaning of *liu*.
841) Tchang Kien, in Ta-Hia, 128 B.C. (not 125), saw there only the bamboo staves and the *puh* of Shuh. (*Sup.* n. 249-251). The Chinese word may be singular or plural, and the vagueness of the term, instead of the easier precision if one sort of cloth only had been spoken of, suggests that he meant the two well known sorts of cloth made in the Shuh country. The woollen cloth was called *mao-yü*, litt. hairfeathers (cloth). The wild-silk could not be the object of a great demand because of the somewhat similar *tusser* (not tussah) silk of North India. As to the fine silk cloth of the East of China, it could not be exported at first by that route, and does not seem to have been so before the Han period. Silk culture was introduced from the East in the Ægean isle of Cos before the overthrow of Darius and seems to have flourished until about 222 A.D., when it ceases to be spoken of in history. (Cf. S. Reinach, *Philo. Class.* (2) I. 255, 4.—S. Sharpe, *History of Egypt*, I, 263.—Edw. Balfour, *Cyclop. Ind.*, I, 819). Their silkworms fed on cypress-turpentine-, ash-, and oak-trees (Plin. xi, 17). On the silkworms of Cos, cf. also. Aristotle, *Hist. An.* v. 19, 17; 11, 6, and Plin. xi, 26 (22). It is said that their cocoons were first wowen in the said island by Pamphile, daughter of Plates. (Cf. G. Birdwood, *Indian Arts*, 267).—Silk industry in the island has survived or has been revived to the present day, and is the object of a yearly export of £50000—in Roman times, the insufficiency of local production in quality and quantity led to the importation there of plain silk-stuffs of China which were split and rewoven. (Cf. on the latter question. F. Hirth, *China and the Roman Orient*, 256-60).— The silk-worms of Cos did not belong to the mulberry-feeding, but to the oak feeding sort; therefore to that which is still at present abundant in Szetchuen, with an important market at Pao-ning fu; (cf. *Silk-China, Imperial maritime Customs*, 1881, p. 8). It was in the vicinity of the head quarters of the Ancient trade route we are speaking of.—A sort of cloth, or textile stuff called *Sindhu* is mentioned in cuneiform inscriptions; for instance on a list of cloths of the time of Assurbanipal (B.C. 668-625). perhaps a copy of an older list, and on a tablet of 576 B.C. under Nebuchadnezzar, were four manas of *sindhu* are handed over to the workman (cf. *B.&O.R.*, iv, 57). This

suggests an unwoven stuff, not necessarily valuable. Wool and Iron were likewise weighed by Manas. (Cf. T. G. Pinches, *B.&O.R.*, i, 9 ; and *Guide Nimroud*, 119). The word is written ideographically "striped- or ribbed-cloth," and thus far cannot be muslin of *Sindhu*, or India (as suggested by Prof. A. H. Sayce, *Relig. Anc. Babyl.*, p. 138) where no such thing was made at the time. The industry began much later in Muaslipatam. Moreover there are two fatal objections; the *Sindhu* is described as a cloth of the mountains (*gurri*) showing that it came through an inland route, or more probably that it was made inland. (Cf. *Parsindu*, a town of Namri in the inscriptions of Assurnazirpal) ; the other objection is the equation $h = s$ which could not have been avoided by a land route from India, as shown by the *Hidu* on the Darius inscription of Naksh-i-Rustam, *Hoddu* in Esther, i, 1 and viii, 9.—The resemblance with *Sindu*, India, is a coincidence, as the word is not isolated in the Assyrian vocabulary, (cf. Brunnow's *List*, Nos. 1799, 1951, 4776, 5500, &c.) and is probably cognate with the Egyptian *sent sentu* (cf. Paul Pierret, *Vocab. Hierogl* 512).—As to a suggested connection with the *sindon* of the Bible, I think that the latter is decidedly Egyptian in origin. Cf. *Suten* in P. Pierret *V.H.* 564.—The forgoing reasons show an impossibility in interpreting, *Sindu* by silk, as has been suggested also. (Cf. *supra* n. 428-30).— The *sherikoth* of Isaiah, 19, 9, refers decidedly not to silk.

842) Cf. *supra* par. 209.

843) Cf. *supra*, note 419.—It is unnecessary to quote here the unsuc- cessful essays of A. Weber, I. Taylor, J. Halevy, &c.—For the Northern writing cf. T. de L.. *Did Cyrus introduce writing into In- dia?* (B. & O. R., Feb. 1887, I, 58, 4.

844) Cf. *Miao Man hoh tchi*, ii, 2.—*Yun-nan t'ung tchi* : Nan Man tchi, 31, i, 4 *v.*; 32. ii, 13.—Also, G. Deveria, *Les Lolos et les Miao- tze* : J. A, 1891.—I have myself found 450 different signs on Lolo Mss.—376 different characters were all those that a Lolo man could remember, at the invitation of Consul F. S. A. Bourne. Cf. the list in his *Report of a Journey in South-western China*: Parliamentary Papers, 1888, China s.c. 5371.

845) Cf. T. de L., *A new writing from South Western China*: The Academy, 19 Febr. 1887.—And G. Deveria, *Les Lolos*, p. 15.

846) Cf. F. Hirth, *The Chinese Oriental College*, Shanghai, 1887.—G. Deveria, *Examen de la stèle de Yen-t'ai* ; *dissertation sur les carac- teres d' écriture employés par les Tartares Jou-tchen* ; 1882.—T. de L., *The Djurtchen of Mandshuria* : *their name, language and litera- ture* : J.R.A.S. 1889.

847) Cf. *supra* n. 376 on the *tchuen* styles of writing.

848) Compiled in A.D. 89-99 on Imperial Command, by the famous Hü shen.

849) This question forms the object of a special paper of mine *On Indo- Chinese elements in the formation of the South-Açôka alphabet*.

CHAP. VII.—SIXTH PERIOD : 221 B.C.—A.D. 220.
Sect. A. *The Empire.*

219. After over a century of uninterrupted war of a most sanguinary character, the state of Ts'in[850] established at last its sway all over the Chinese dominion[851], and in 221 B.C. Wang Tcheng in the 26th year of his reign assumed the title of She Hwang-ti, intended to mean the First Universal Emperor. The policy of general conquest[852] had been initiated by Tchao Siang Wang, 300-250 B.C., and it may be asked if the fame of the extensive conquests of Alexander the Great did not give an impetus to the natural ambition of the Ts'inite princes.[853] Anyhow the unity of government with a centralised administration, and the progressive assimilation of the various parts of the country changed henceforth the conditions in which foreign influences could be felt in the Flowery Land. The personal character and turn of mind of the autocratic sovereign for the time being could but have thenceforth a peculiar importance for outside relations according to his sympathy or dislike for novelties and foreign things.

220. Two great Emperors have shone and left an imperishable mark during this period, the last that can concern the present work. Ts'in She Hwang-ti founder of the Empire on principles somewhat differing from those of respectful tradition which had hitherto obtained in Chinese surroundings, and HAN Wu-ti who first opened relations with foreign countries by all the means in his power.

It is interesting for us here to know from recorded history where from She Hwang-ti derived the un-Chinese proclivities which he displayed more specially after 237 B.C. on the counsels of his minister Li-sze, when the latter was promoted to a higher rank than he occupied previously.[854] The king of Ts'in, Wang Tchêng as he was then called, conceived an aversion against foreigners, and in the aforesaid year issued an edict in order to shut his kingdom to them. Li-sze himself a native of Ts'u and a pupil of the known Taoszeist Sun-k'ing, protested openly against it and the reasons put forward in his memorial to the throne convinced the sovereign who cancelled his order.[855]

221. Li-sze began in reminding his sovereign of the useful services which his predecessors had derived from foreigners, and of the precious things and curios which he would not get anymore from foreign parts. The list he gave of these things is peculiarly instructive. He said that His majesty obtained: Jade from the *Kwen* mountains (i.e. from Khotan, *gloss*.[856]) ; moreover that he had the jewel of Sui Ho (otherwise Pien Ho,[857] which afterwards was made into the State Seal by She Hwang-ti himself, *gloss*.) ; pendant pearls of *Ming-yueh*[858], swords of *Tai-ngo*[859], which he wore, horses of *Ts'ien-li*[860] which he rode ; banners ornamented with king fishers feathers,[861] and drums of the *K'ien, Shu* and *Ling* patterns in skin of iguana,[862] made on his command; all rare things which the Ts'in territory did not produce. Continuing his enumeration, Li-sze mentioned rings of *Ye-kwang* gem,[863] articles in ivory and rhinoceros horn, [864] nice girls from Tcheng and Wei (E. Honan), stately and good *Kiuh-ti* horses of the North,[865] and gold and silver of the South of the Kiang, which could not be got anymore ; vermilion and green paint of west Shuu which it would no more be possible to gather,[866] hair-pins in pearl from *Wan* (Honan), earrings in pendant-pearls, undyed silk cloth, and embroidered ornaments,[876] which would not be procurable as before.[868] On the eighteen articles enumerated there, it can be seen that no less than eight were introduced by the trade from foreign and distant lands ; all the others were obtainable in China proper though not in the Ts'in dominion.

222. Li-sze was then promoted to a superior rank and acquired a great influence on his Royal Master, a prince of great energy and skill whom he converted to his views.

It was with the help of his able minister that Ts'in Wang Tchêng proceeded as much by the force of his well organized armies as by political ability to complete the conquest of the six other Chinese States. One of the most clever steps to that effect was the adoption within the various parts of his actual dominion of an uniform style of writing the

Tchuen characters,[869]abbreviated and simplified in a filiform way. This was in 227 B.C., and Li-sze was himself the principal author of this new style called *Siao tchuen*.[870] Fifteen years later, the hair pencil had been considerably improved by the general Mêng-tien, and by the increase in the number of characters, so many variants had occurred that it became necessary to adopt a new style of writing which was the *Li shu*,[871] made of strokes thick and thin according to the convenience of the brush pencil for rapidity.

223. Acting on the advice and with the help of his faithful minister, the king of Ts'in assumed in 221 B.C. the Imperial authority and selected for his future denomination *She Hwang-ti*, probably in imitation (we do not suggest it without diffidence) of the name of Iskander whose fame as we know was echoed in the remotest corners of Asia,[872] and whom he seems to have imitated in several of his deeds. He divided his Empire in 36 provinces.[873] In 214 B.C., to guard his dominion from Tartar invasions, he decreed the building of a line of defensive works from Lin-tao (S.W. Kansuh) to Liao-tung in the N.E., utilising for the purpose such previous works built successively since 359 B.C. by several of the Chinese princes in the North, as well as the precipitous hills, water-courses and ravines on the borders.[874] General Mêng-tien, residing in *Shang Kiun* i.e. N.E. Shensi, was put in command there for over ten years, and built series of earth-works, which in later years, repaired and in some places built in full became the Great wall of China.[875] It grew in repute as in material importance and it became identified by a geographical dislocation in the minds of western Orientals with the long famed Wall of Gog and Magog. (*Sadd Yádiúdj wa Madjúdj*).[786]

224. In 213, three years before his death, She Hwang-ti decreed the Burning of the Books. In view of putting an end to the incessant complaints of the literati that he did not follow the ways of Antiquity, he approved of a report of his Premier Li-sze, of which the following is the most important part : "I pray that all the Records in charge of the Historiographers be burned, excepting those of Ts'in ; that, *with the exception of those officers belonging to the Board of great scholars*, all throughout the Empire who presume to keep copies of the *She King* or of the *Shu King*, or of the discourses[877] of the various schools, be required to go with them to the officers in charge of the several districts, and burn them; that all who may dare to speak together about the *She* and the *Shu* be cast away on the market place ; that those who make mention of the past, so as to blame the present, be treated likewise with their relatives ;

that officers who shall know of the violation of those rules and not inform against the offenders, be equally guilty with them ; and that whoever shall not have burnt their books within thirty days after the issuing of the ordinance, be branded and sent to labour on the great walls. The only books which should be spared are those on medecine and drugs, divination and augury, seeds and trees."

The decree was strictly put in force but not for long,[878] as it was neither renewed nor repealed by the successor of She Hwang-ti, 210 B.C. A great deal of harm was certainly done to literature, though not so much as could have been feared, considering that the edict was not officially cancelled before 23 years, i.e. in 191 B.C. Much of the Confucian literature against which it was specially directed, escaped through the retentive memory of the literati and the numerous finds of hidden copies of the forbidden books.[979] In 209 B.C. a large part of the country had ceased to recognize[830] the yoke of the Ts'ɪɴ dynasty, and therefore its literary proscriptions. The wreck of Chinese literature is due as much if not much more to the havoc of ages and to the four great bibliotecal catastrophes which occurred in the following centuries,[381] than to the Burning of the Books.

225. Like Alexander the great with the Avestic Nasks on medicine and astronomy ¿(?) She Hwang-ti had excepted from the fire, the books on medicine and astrology,[882] some 120 years after him. It can hardly be doubted that the founder of the Chinese Empire was acquainted with some circumstances concerning the Macedonian conqueror.

As we have said before She Hwang-ti had become deeply imbued with the ideas and novelties of the Neo-Taoists.[883] In several occasions we hear of his relations with them, and of their excentricities which he adopted. In 219 he sent an expedition[884] from Tsihmoh in search of the Three fortunate islands and of the drug of immortality ;[885] and in 201 B.C., dissatisfied with the failure of[886] the attempts made to that effect, he went himself along the sea-shore and partly by sea in the hope of being more successful, from Kiang-tch'êng[887] to Lang-ya (Tsihmoh) and died soon afterwards.

226. Disorders followed his death as could be expected after an imperial reign of only twelve years, and no less than eighteen different states[888] arose on the ruins of the Empire he had founded for 10000 years, but which his weak son and successor was unable to keep together. In 206, but exactly in 202 B.C. the HAN dynasty began to reign over the Empire once again united under one sway, with a glory and power which have

not been surpassed. The Chinese dominion was extended in the west so far as Transoxiana, and in the south included Tungking, while conterminous states acknowledged its suzerainty. Intercommunications were opened everywhere available, and the ancient history of China thus comes to an end.

NOTES——.
850) As Ts'IN has long been supposed to have given its name to China, let us remark that in the Annamese history where archaic names are preserved, this state and its short lived dynasty are called TAN; and as the name of China originated with the Southern trade as shown by several scholars, the supposition must be given up for ever as contrary to historical evidence, cf. *supra*, n. 330 ; and P.J.B. Truong Vinh-ky, *Histoire Annamite*, I., 16, for the sound of the name.
851) According to the figures given in the *She Ki* of Szema Tsien, kiv. xv., the Ts'inites would have butchered some 1500000 people during the struggle. Some of the figures making this total are obviously exaggerated.
852) An Imperial spirit of general conquest is attributed to Huan Kung of Ts'i in the 7th cent. cf. an extract from *Kwan-tze*, in *China Review* xviii., 196.
853) We give below reasons to believe that it was really so.
854) Li-sze was a native of Ts'u and a pupil of the famous Taoszcist Sun-k'ing disciple of Tsou-yen. (Cf. supra § 173). He went to Ts'IN before the accession of Wang Tchêng the future Ts'IN She Hwang-ti. In 237 B.C. he was successful in deciding the king to withdraw a decree of expulsion against foreigners. In his memorial he mentions several instances where foreigners had proved useful to his predecessors, notably that of *You-yu* (6171-170 Bas.) a *Jung* by birth whose advices were followed by Muh Kung and enabled him to conquer vast lands over 20 tribes of Western Jung Tartars (*She Ki*, 87, 3, and 5. 14) about 626 B.C.
855) Cf. De Mailla, *Histoire générale de la Chine*, II, 383.
856) This is a direct confirmation of the Jade traffic which has often been spoken of in the present work. Cf. p. 31 and pass.
857) On the history of this gem discovered in the 8th century B.C. Cf. Mayers, *Chinese R.M.*, I, 393, 551. It was probably a piece of Jade which had come to Ts'u through the traders of SHUU.—An alleged figure of this seal is thoroughly Persian.
858) Cf. *supra* Note 871.
859) This was a name for swords made of iron tempered in the *Lung tsiuen* or Dragon source (of Si Ping, Yu-ning fu, Honan). They are enumerated in the biography of Su Tsin, 4th cent. B.C., (*She Ki*, 69, 9) with those of WEI made at *Ming shan*, the Moh-ya swords of Meihyang, and the deadly ones of the TENG state, all permitting to cut across in two, at one blow, a bull or a horse.—On *Moh-ya* cf. *supra* par. 185 ; on Su Ts'in, note 736.
860) The horses of Ts'ien-li like those of Pu Shao, N. Shansi were a fine breed of horses. Cf. T. de L., *Earliest Horse-riding in Western and Eastern Asia* : B.&O.R., 1893, vi, 200 and *supra* par. 197.

861) *Ts'ui fêng tchi ki*, 8253-12393-41-3852 Bas.—The *ts'ui* or king fisher a southern bird said to have been first seen when some were presented to TCHOU Tcheng Wang from *the region later named* Tsang-wu. Cf. *Kih tcheng Tchou shu*, Wang Hwei : T.P. 924, 7 r.—It was known in Ts'u in the 4th century as shown by the *Li sao*.—Tchao t'o, of Nan yueh, sent a thousand of these birds to HAN Weh-ti, 179 B.C. Cf. *T.P.Y.L.*, 934, 7 *J.*

862) *Kien Shu ling t'o tchi ku*, 2535-4482-12020-13134-41-cl. 207 Bas.— The *Kien* drum was the standard drum in metal of the Shang dynasty of which the Ts'in state had adopted the rites when it repudiated those of the TCHOU. The *Shu* drum means the Wooden drum as made with trees from *Yü-tchang*, i.e. Kiang-si. The *Ling* drum sexangular was used specially for the Earth sacrifice. Cf. *Tu Tchou tcheng yoh* : T.P.Y.L. 532, 6 and 338, 3.—Skins of Aguanas were used especially for drums. The *t'o* of the Ancient Chinese was probably an alligator, whose species has now almost disappeared. Cf. Dr. A. A. Fauvel's interesting article on *Alligators in China* : Journ. China Br. R.A.S., 1879, xiii.—Two specimens of the *Alligator Sinensis* have at last been discovered and sent to the Zoological Gardens of London in September of 1890.

863) Cf. *supra* § 199. One of these rings had been sent to Ts'in in 324 B.C.

864) Cf. also *supra* § 199.

8 5) Such horses are said by the *Kih tchung Tchou shu* to have been presented to Tchou Tcheng Wang. —*Tsiun liang kinh ti*, 12525-8803-12490-12544 Bas.

866) The text of my copy of the *She Ki*, 87, 4 *rers.* has *tchou-tsing*, cl. 137- cl. 174, boat-green which is certainly a misprint for *tan-tsing*, 34- cl. 174 Bas., red-green, which has become a current term for painting in general.

867) Manufactured in eastern China.

868) The statement in the *She Ki*, 87, 4 and 4 *rers.* is interspersed with remarks which had nothing to do with the description of the articles.

869) On the previous periods of the writing, cf. *supra* § 100.

870) Cf. *She Ki*, Ts'in She Hwang pên ki, 12, 15.—Hu Shen, *Shwoh wen*, intr. fol. 3,—*Tsien Han shu*, kiv. xxx.—Under the reign of HAN Tchang-ti, A.D. 76-88, it was decided to make a dictionary of the *Tchuen* characters. The task was performed in A.D. 89-99 by Hu shen, and the result of his efforts is the famous *Shwoh-wen* dictionary, the standard work of its kind. He collected 9353 characters which in their most s ber and simple forms respecte l the old rules of Sze-tchou (*supra*, § 100 and his introduction fol. 7), and he quoted occasionally some 441 characters of olden times which had been simplified afterwards. It is therefore a mistake to suppose that the characters of the *Shwoh wen* represent the oldest Chinese characters as some Sinologists have done, such as done by Mr. L. C. Hopkins, *Ancient writing in Babylonia and in China* : Academy, May 18, 1889. Cf. my rejoinder on *The oldest Chinese characters* : ibid. June 15, 1889.

871) Its invention is attributed to a certain Tcheng Mao.—Cf. same authorities as in preceeding note. Also *Tai ping yü lan*, 749, 3-4.

872) Iskander was the form of the name among the Persians through whom it was spread eastwards. Cf. for instance my paper *Sur deux*

ères *inconnues de L'Asie Anterieure*, 330 et 251 *ar. J. C., d'après un document Chinois*, Muséon, 1891.
873) Cf. *supra* note 185.
874) Cf. *Tchuh shu ki nien*, V, xxxii, 10, and the following.
875) Cf. *Tsien Han Shu*, kiv. 94—*She Ki*, Meng tien lieh tchuen, kiv. 88, f. 1 vers. ; Ts'in She Hwang pěn ki. Kiv. 6,⁴ fol 19v.-20.—The *Ku kin tchu* of Tsui-Pao, c. 350 B.C. tells us that the great defensive works of the Ts'inites were made of earth, chiefly red in colour. Cf. T.P.Y.L. 192, 5r.—Some parts of it were built in stone and earthworks under the Han dynasty, cf. *Hou Han shu* : T.P. 334, 6 vers.— It was rebuilt under the Ming dynasty.—Cf. O.F. van Mollendorf, *Die grosse Mauer von China* ; Z. f. D.M.G., 1881, xxv.—L'Abbé Larrieu, *Rapport sur la grande Muraille de la Chine*, où il est prouvé que cette Muraille telle qu'elle est communément décrite non seulement n'existe pas, mais même n'a jamais éxisté ; *Rev. Extr. Orient*, 1885, III., 347-361.—J.S. Brazier, *Analysis of brick from the great wall of China*, J. Ch. Br. R.A.S., 1887, xxi, 252.—H.N.Stove, *The Great Wall of China*: Illustr. Naval and Milit. Magaz. 1887, p. 227.—E. T C. Werner, *The Great wall of China*: Archæolog., 1889, I, 45, 180, p. 379-389.— E. Martin. *La vérité sur la Grande Muraille* : L' Anthropologie, 1891, II, 438-444.
876) Neither Marco-Polo nor Odoric de Pordenone speak of the Great wall, but Radshideddin and Albufeda do so.—Alexander the Great was reputed to have erected ramparts of this sort (cf. Procop., *Bell. Pers.*, i, 10) in the Caspian gates, the Gate of Gates, near Derbend, where inscriptions in cufic of A.D. 465, Pahlevi and Cuneiform have been found. (Cf. E. Schuyler, in H. Yule, *Marco Polo*, II, 537 ; also i, 55, 283-235.—Eichwald, *Periplus des Kasp. M.*, i, 128.—Ker Porter, *Travels*, ii, 520.—F. Lenormant, *Origines de l' Histoire*, ii, 425.) —The cuneiform inscriptions would be Vannic of the viiith cent. as those found in Georgia. Cf. A. H. Sayce, *The Cuneiform Inscriptions of Van*, J.R.A.S., 1888, xx, 1.—Another *Sadd-i-Iskandar* or Rempart of Alexander at the S,E. Angle of the Caspian, has been described by Arm. Vambery, *Travels in C. Asia*, 54 sq.
877) Cf. She Ki, vi, 21-21v. - I follow the translation of Dr. J. Legge, *Chin. Class.*, I, 8-9, except in the following cases. I translate "discourses of the various schools " *peh kia yü*, hundred families phrases or speeches, instead of his " the books of the Hundred schools." Further on " cast away on the market place " instead of his " be put to death and their bodies exposed on the market place " ; the Chinese words are *Ki-she*, 4291-2406 Bas. which I have rendered word for word. G. Pauthier, who in his Premier *Mémoire sur l' antiquité de l' histoire et de la civilisation Chinoises*, J. A. Sept. Oct. 1867, has given a translation (rather inaccurate) of the same document, has rightly remarked that the punishment of the *Ki she* is described in the *Li ki*, Wang tchi, kiv. 3 (sect. ii, 11), and did not imply death. Cf. *Sacred Books of the East*, xxvii, 215. The culprit lost any post or situation he occupied, nobody could come to his rescue and he was compelled to live to go away from the country. Cf. also *T.P.Y.L.*, 646, 6r.
878) We have evidence that the edict was strictly put in force by the following circumstance. The year after, i.e. in 212, literati of the Capital *Hien-yang* (mod. Si ngan) having continued to vilify the acts

of his government as contrary to the teachings of Confucius, 460 of them were buried alive. (*Kang*, 11752 Bas.). Cf. *She Ki*, vi, 24.— Cf. on this supplice, note 563 *supra*.

879) In 26 B.C. by Imperial order a catalogue was prepared of all the books saved from olden times and others, and when finished reached a total of over 13000.—G. Pauthier, in his pre-cited *Memoire* has given an analysis of this catalogue, full of interest notwithstanding the numerous mistranslations, from Pan Ku, *Tsien Han shu*, kiv. 30. Cf. *supra*, note 621. The books were only those of the Imperial library.

880) Cf. below note 888.

881) On the five bibliotecal catastrophes, cf. A. Wylie, *Notes on Chinese literature*, p. iii-vii.

882) Cf. J. Darmestater, *Le Zend Avesta*, 1893, III, viii and xxviii.— Also C. de Harlez, *Introduction á l' Étude de l'Avesta*, xvi and xxxiii.—And *supra* note 186,

883) Supra §§ 220 and 173.

884) It was an expedition made on the proposal and under the command of Siü-fuh of Ts'i, with a large number of young men and girls, reported in the *She Ki*, vi, 16 *r.* and which was wrecked, according to the *Kwa ti tchi* of the third cent. on the *Tan tchou* or Quelpaert Island. The result may have been an unwilling colonisation, and some of the ships may have been carried on the southern coast of some Japanese island. Prof. L. de Rosny tells us that there is a temple in the honour of Siü-fuh at Kumano, province of Ki-i, Japan. Cf. *La civilisation Japonaise*, 1883, p. 93-4.

885) The notion of such an elixir had come from the fabled reports about the *Soma*, as we have shown *supra* § 132 and note 458.

886) Siu-fuh, saved from the wreck of his expedition, had reported himself to the Emperor, and given some wonderful excuses for his failure, in that same year.

887) Kiang-tch'öng, the modern Shang-yuen, in Kiang-ning fu, Kiangsu —The *She Ki*, 28, 12 tells us that he went himself on the sea.

888) Herewith a short list of these states :—i. *Ts'u*, 209-205 B.C.—ii. *Si Tsu*, 206-202 B.C.—iii. *Hong-shan* or *Tchang-Shao*, 206-157 B.C.— iv. *Lin Kiang*, 206-202 B.C.—v. *Kiu-Kiang*, 206-204 B.C.—vi. *Tchao* or *Tai*, 209-204 B.C.—vii. *Tchang-Shan*, 206 B.C.—viii. *Ts'i*, 209-206 B.C.—ix. *Lin-tchi*, 206-204 B.C.—x. *Ts'i peh*, 206 B.C.—xi. *Yen*, 209-201 B.C.—xii. *Liao tung*, 206 B.C.—xiii. *Wei*, 209-206 B.C.— xiv. *Si Wei*, 206-203 B.C.—xv. *Yn*, 206-264 n.c.—xvi. *Han*, 208-205 B.C.—xvii. *Ho-nan*, 208-207 B.C.—xviii. HAN 206 B.C.

Sect. B. *Introduction of Buddhism.*

227. The religion of the Light of Asia was introduced no less than three times in China, twice in an indistinct and unsuccessful manner, and a third time under Imperial protection with permanent success. In the two first instances the BuddhistShamans came on the trail of Brahmanist ascets, and it is difficult to know from the Chinese side when they began exactly. In the North-east after centuries of Indian influ-

ence through the Sea trade, we have heard of Sila, arrived from Magadha after a journey of five years in 305 B.C.[889] He is not called a Shaman and although an amplified tradition makes him exhibit Buddhist images, it is not at all probable that he belonged to the persuasion of Sakyamuni unless the early Buddhism should have differed from what it became subsequently. After him flourished also in the *Yen* country, Sung-wu-ki, Tcheng-peh-k'iao, Tchung-shang[890] and later on the Shaman T z e-k a o who was a contemporary of Ts'in She Hwang-ti. All these men had thus settled in the native land of Taoszeism. And Szema Tsien the historian himself imbued with Taoist views does not separate them from the school of Tson-hien. He tells us that "they were skilled in the Path of the Richis, divested themselves of their bodily frames, were dissolved and transformed, and relied on the worship of saints and genii." These ideas which did not belong to Tsou-yen and look like a garbled view of the mental condition of the Buddhist shamans, thus transformed into a physical notion, were most probably proper only to Tze-Kao and his disciples. He is the first Buddhist bonze known with some probability, and he was seen by She Hwang-ti, at Puh hai (gulf of Petchili, near Lai tchou) in 219 B.C.[891] He seems afterwards to have gone and settled in the Tchao hills, in the North of Honan.[892] Some years later, in 215, the same Emperor being at Kieh-shih[6 93] in Liao-si, near the present Tcheng-teh, N. Tchihli) sent a certain Lu-sheng of Yen to fetch another Shaman, named K a o-s h e.[894] Nothing more is known of these two nor of any other Shamans there afterwards. In 112 B.C. the soothsayer[895] Luan-ta persuaded HAN Wu-ti that he had travelled by sea, and seen the residences of Ngan-ki sheng, a former magician, and of the Shamans.[96] His boasting shows in any case, if nothing more that Shamans had ceased at that time to inhabit any part of the Chinese dominion, and that their former presence in 219-215 B.C., in the east and in the west, as we shall see directly, had been decidedly an unsuccessful attempt.

228. A remarkable incident occurred in 221 B.C. on the Western borders, in the town of *Lin-tao* (S.W. Kansuh, near the Tibetan frontier).[897] Twelve men of very high stature, dressed like Teks (barbarian Turks) arrived there. The event was looked upon as so important that the Emperor had their statues cast in bronze, of an enormous size, weighing some 1500 kilos each."[98] These were broken and sent to the foundry to cast coins in 189 A.D. by order of Tung Tchoh, the destroyer of Loh-yang.[899] No accurate description of these statues seems to have been preserved and we do not know what they exactly represented. It has been sug-

gested that they may have been buddhist, but there is no evidence that they were so, and the Buddhists have never clearly claimed them for their own.[900]

229. On the other hand the following story which undoubtedly concerns them shows that they were Hindus or at least that they were professing Hindu views. " She Hwang-ti was very fond of all that concerned spirits and genii, and he sought for marvels all over the empire. Now at that time there were some people of *Yuan-kiu*[901] (in N.W. Szetchuen), who floating upwards the Black River (a N.W. affluent of the *Min* River) on *li* boats (or coracles),[902] thus reached the *Yung* region or *pu* (i.e. the S.W. of Kansuh where was *Lin-tao*). She Hwang-ti had a long conversation with them about the beginning and transformations of the Universe ; they told him that the sun and moon were at certain times sunk in the water 90000 lis deep, and that there were then a day and a night of 10000 years each. They gave him some peculiar stone which during that time was used as a substitute to give light, and which being pierced or broken produced fire as large as grains of rice and illumined.[903] This was the first introduction of the pyrites in China, therfore older than we supposed.[904]

It is clear that these Brahmanists or Hindus coming from the N.W. of Szetchuen, belong to the same people that had settled as anchorets and made caves in the cliffs of the Min and other rivers in the sixth century and afterwards.[905]

230. The same wave of penetration of Brahmanic views must be looked upon as the cause of the influences evidently Hinduic which had been at work among the Hiungnus on the Northern borders of China 200 B.C. According to the Annals of the First Han dynasty their horses were arranged according to symbolical colours of the points of space, pure white on the west, white-faced greys on the east, black on the north, and bays on the south : a Hindu arrangement as far as could be.[906]

In 121 B.C., the golden statue of a god worshipped by the Hiung-nus, was taken from the *kiu-tu*,[907] i.e. *ordo* or residence of one of their princes, in the northern vicinity of Liang-tchou, (Kansuh) by the young Chinese general Ho-Kiu-ping, and brought back at Yun-yang a district of Tchang-ngan.[908] It was apparently not a statute made according to the canons of the Buddhists who have refused to acknowledge it, although the probabilities are in favour of its Buddhist character.[909]

231. On the other hand, a distinct mission of Buddhists is claimed by them to have taken place in 217 B.C., when a Shaman Li-fang [910] and

seventeen companions is reputed to have come from India to Lohyang. The story has come to us through two sources,[911], both Buddhist and somewhat amplified with marvellous details, but all the probabilities indicate that a genuine historical fact underlies the account in question. As was the case with the Shamans of Shantung and Tchihli, they disappeared altogether during the temporary collapse of the political edifice built up by the She Hwang and the disorders which preceded the rise of the HAN dynasty.

232. It is rather remarkable that for three centuries after the unsuccessful attempts we have just noticed, nothing should be known of the Buddhist infiltrations, which considering the activity of Buddhist propaganda everywhere else, must have reached China, one way or another.[912] Influences of foreign origin were possible at a time of separate states, without much of them be known to the outside; but in a centralised Empire, as was that of the Han dynasty according to the written history, any fresh influence or activity of importance, such as a Buddhist movement, could occur unknown only in the non-Chinese parts of China. These were the west of Szetchuen until 110 B.C., the *T'een* state of Yunnan until 109 B.C., the *Tung-hai* and *Min-yueh* states of Fukien until 111 B.C., and the *Nan-yueh* state of South Hunan, Kwang-tung, Kwang-si and Tungking, until 111 B.C., which were all subdued either as protectorates or as Chinese provinces, and more or less temporarily in some cases. But as far as I am aware there is no available information as yet on the matter.

233. At the beginning of the reign of HAN Ming-ti. A.D. 58, tidings of Buddhism had reached the Imperial court, and one of the brothers of the Emperor, Prince of Tsu, was deeply interested with its doctrine in view of comparing them with those of the Hwang-Lao or Taoszeist school.[913] In A.D. 63, Ming Ti made his famous dream of a flying golden figure, which the historiographer Fu-yh already acquainted with Buddhism, explained as connected with the Buddha. The outcome of the movement was the expedition of an Imperial commission to India at the end of A.D. 64[914] to get proper information. It came back in the year 67 with two shamans named *Ka-siap Ma-tang*, i.e. Kasiapa Matanga and *Gap-lan*, i.e. Gobharana[915] who settled at Loh-yang, in the *Lan-tai* or Orchid gallery, where the Sutra in 42 sections was then for the first time completed.[916] The *Peh Ma Se* or White horse monastery, west of the Capital, was built for them, and finished in A.D. 71, and they died there not long afterwards.

NOTES——

889) Cf. *supra* § 196.
890) Cf. *supra* § 173 on the school of Tsou-hien.
891) Cf. Szema Tsien. She Ki, kiv, 28, fol. 10, 11.—Herbert J. Allen, *Similarity between Buddhism and early Taoism*, China Review, 1887, xv, p. 96-99.—T. de L., *How in* 219 B.C. *Buddhism entered China* : B.&O.R., May 1891, p. 97-99 ; *The Introduction of Buddhism into China* : Acad. Oct. 3. 1891.—H. J. Allen, same subject, Acad. Sept. 12, and Nov. 14, 1891. The hypercriticism of the latter note, goes beyond the mark.
892) The last book of the *Shan hai king*, which book as we know was compiled by Liu-hin about our era from older documents, tells us that, " East of the Hwa mount and of the Tsing river, on the Tchao hills, lived men called Peh and Tze Kao", whom the gloss says were Recluses.
893) It was there that the king of Yen had built a palace for Tsou-hien about 310 B.C. cf. *supra* par. 178.
894) Cf. *She Ki*. vi, 13r.
895) On Luan-ta and other magicians, cf. below par. 237.
896) Cf. *She-Ki*, kiv. xii, 6 v. ; xxviii, 28 r.
897) The town had been founded in 239 B.C. and populated with the removed inhabitants of *T'un-liu* (in Shansi) by Tcheng Ts'in Wang, the future She Hwang-ti. Cf. Szema Tsien, *She Ki*, kiv. vi, fol. 3. And for the history of the latter town, cf. my *Catalogue of Chinese Coins, Early period*, p. lxiv.
898) Cf. *She Ki*, kiv. 6, fol. 1 —*Tsien Han shu*, Wu heng tchi.—She Hwang-ti h ving pacified the Empire, had collected at the capital, Hien-yang, all the weapons and implements of war, which were then made chiefly of bronze. The weight of each statue was of one thousand *shih* (*She Ki*), and therefore according to the weights list in my book on Chinese coins, about 1560 kilos.—In the Han annals, *l.c.* these foreigners are said to have been 5 *tchang* (i.e. 50 feet) in height, with feet six *tch'ih* or spans long.—Cf. also T. de L., *The Introduction of Buddhism into China* : The Academy, 3 Oct. 91.—Four large bells with their stands were cast at the same time with the same material.
899) *San fu hwang tu*, kiv. i, fol. 4 vers. : kiv. v, fol. 4 vers.
900) Cf. Herbert J. Allen in *The Academy*, and my rejoinder, 3 Oct. 91.—I had not yet found the story quoted in the text when I wrote this rejoinder.—The *Tsin shu* or Annals of the TSIN dynasty (265-419 A.D.) tells us that in a palace of Fêng tcheng (the present Siu-tchou of Kiang-su) was preserved drawings of Buddhist statues, made by the hand of a former Emperor, after the model of Lin-tao, which the Tek barbarians had made, but which was found not to be according to the Buddhist principles. Cf. T.P. 657, 2r.
901) *Yuan-lin*, 2118-5078 Bas.— Also called *Siä-kiü*.
902) *Li*, 9618 Bas., litt. "calabash." On the Coracles of West China, cf. No.e 69 and add.
903) Cf. Wang tze nien, *Shih y Ki* : T.P.Y.L., 869, 1-2 for the full story.
904) Cf. *supra* § 136 and note 680.—The legend concludes by a most curious statement. It tells us that in the days of Shennung (Sargon)

the Arabs (*Ta-shik*) had presented similar stones to him.
905) Cf. *supra*, par. 215 and note 838.
906) White horses in the absence of yellow were substituted for the western colour, white-faced greys for white east, black for black north, bays for red south.— C. Pau Ku, *Tsien Han shu*, Kiv. 91 ; tr. A. Wylie, J.A.I., 1873, p. 412.—H. de Charencey, *De la Symbolique des points de l'espace chez les Hindus* : Revue de Philologie, 1874. I., 174.
907) A gloss says that *hiu-tu* in the Hiung-nu language means *town*.
908) Cf. *Han tchi.—T'i kiao ki tchi*.
909) A commentator has suggested that it was perhaps *K'ai lo shen*, the God of the Roads, which was probably worshipped by this people, but the suggestion is entirely gratuitous and contrary to probabilities.
910) Sometimes called *Ts'i-li ja.g*, which could represent *Srirana*.
911) Cf. *Po sie lun* by Fa-lin, 624-640 A.D.—*Fah wan tchu lin*, by Hiuen-yun, 668 A.D.—*Kin'ting ku kin t'u shu tsih tch'eng*, sect. 18, kiv. *Shi kia*. *Kwang poh wuh tchi*, kiv. 16.—R. K. Douglas, *China*, 1887. p. 344.—S. Beal, *Four lectures on Buddhist literature in China*, p. 2 ; *Buddhism in China*, p. 48.
912) The *Wei lioh* of Yü-hwan (300 A.D.) in its article on *L é m-n i* (mod. *Lin-er*, 8660-588 Bas.), i.e. the Lumbini, birth place of the Buddha, quotes an extract from a *Fou-t'u king*, relating the birth of the great Sage, and the following circumstance. "In Middle India, moreover, there existed a saintly man named *S a l u* (mod. *Shu-liu*, 4888-2687 Bas.; i.e. a *S á l a*, writ. *Sha-lo*, 4883-8176 Bas. ; a title given to every Buddha ; cf. Eitel, *Skr. Chin. Dict.* s.v.) Formerly in A.D. 2, a disciple of that Master, *King-lu*, on the advice of (*tsung*, 2700 Bas.) the *Yueh-ti* King, sent Y-tsun-kou with a *Fou-t'u king*, or Buddhist Book (to China). Its contents agreed with that of Lao-tze of the Middle Kingdom ; it went away and came back, for the reason that Lao-tze went away from the Gate (the *Han kuh kwan*) to the Tsen-tuh (mod. *Tien tchu*) of the Si-yü (W. Asia) to teach the *Hu* (bearded barbarians) and become *Fou-t'u* (the Buddha). Cf. *Tai ping yü lan*, kiv. 797, 6r. A similar text, with additions and suppressions, has often been quoted in various later works and compilations. I am unable to follow either G. Pauthier, *Examen méthodique des faits qui concernent le Thien-tchu*, 1839. p. 14-15, or Mr. E.J. Specht, *Etudes sur l'Asie Centrale*, I., 1890, p. 34-40, in their disagreeing renderings of the text. Its importance lies in two points, viz., that the *Yueh-t* were rulers in India in 2 A.D. and that Buddhist teachings were then sent to China. *King-lu* is said to have been originally from Ts'IN.
913) For this paragraph cf. *Hou Han Ki* by Yuen Hung of A.D. 400. in T.P.Y.L., Kiv, 654, fol. 1.—*Kao seng tchuen* : ibid. 655, 2.—Sam. Beal, *Buddhist Literature in China*, p. 3.
914) Or the beginning of the following year. Hence the frequent mistaken date of 65 for the Introduction of Buddhism in China instead of A.D. 67.
915) Modern *Kia yeh mo t'ang*. In the Archaic dialecte *yeh*, 9051 Bas., I e a f, makes *j i e p*, such as in Sino-Annamese.—The full Chinese name of the second bonze which is read at present *Tchu Fah lan* has been variously rendered by European scholars, Dharmaraksha, Dharmananda, and by the Tibetans, rightly I think *Gobharana*. The first *Tchu* is the usual determinative prefix of all the names of Buddhist monks of In-

dian origin. (Cf. T. de L., *The Yueh-ti and the early Buddhist missionaries in China* : Acad. Dec. 31, 87). The second character *Fah, Fap*, 4917 Bas , L a w. is made of the cl. water and the phonetic *K'u, Kop*, 143 Call, a w a y, whence its use by the Buddhist transcribers for the sound *ku, ko, kap*, as in the syllabary of Sangharama (cf. St. Julien, *Méthode pour déchiffrer les noms Sanskrits-Chinois*, n. 274), orin the name of Kashgar by Hiuen Tsang and others. (Cf. J. Eitel, *Sanskrit-Chinese Dict.* s.v.)

916) The Chinese text says : *tch'u kien*, 764-7932 Bas., first bound or sealed up.—Therefore it was not in the White horse Monastery (which was not yet built) that this famous Sutra was completed, as misstated in Bunyu Nanjio. *Catalogue of the Tripitaka*, p. 376.

CHAP. VII.—SIXTH PERIOD : 221 B.C.—A.D. 220.
Sect. C. *Private trade and Official opening of inland intercourse with the West.*

234. Since the reign of Duke Hwei of Ts'in (399-386 B.C.) the Ts'in-ites used to go as far west as the present Kwa-tchou of Kansuh W.[917] But they did not otherwise entertain or favour any foreign relations,[918] and the foundation of the Empire by their Princes did not attract traders through the Kansuh N.W. Route. Commercial intercourse in the second century B.C. was carried through the route of Lintao, (at present Min tchou), also Wu-tu and Han tchung. Beyond Lin-tao[919] to the west, the route followed is not known, but in a fragment added to the *Shan Hai King* under the Han dynasty from older documents, two names of localities seem to refer to stations of that trade. It says that in the west, in the Region of the Flowing Sands, there is a country called Market of the valley, *Ioh she*[920]; and further in the west beyond the sands another country called *Se-yep*[921]. The latter would remind us of *So-yep*, which in later writers is described as a place where the merchants used to congregate, should it not be so far in the west.[922]

235. Among the natural products imported into China by this inland trade, were brimstone from *Tsiu-mi*,[923] and Nephrite Jade from Khotan.[924] In 133 B.C. we hear of the arrival of merchants from, i.e. through Yen-ki (? Karashar) with a large mirror of black metal, measuring four spans :[925] rubbing it with felt and powder of black tin kept it shiny.[926] It was the beginning of Greek notions and arts in China.

236. Since the conquests of Alexander, the influence of Greek civilisation was paramount in the West of Asia. The Seleucidian dominion had been broken up in the East by the rising of two separate kingdoms, in the middle of the third century.[927] Diodotus had founded the Greco-Bactrian, and Arsaces the Parthian,[928] on the west and north of the other. The Arsacidæ were so far grecised that their coins bore Greek legends,[929] and we know from Chinese history that they were the self-made intermediaries between the west and the Chinese by the inland north route.[930] We have seen that some tidings of the feats of Alexander the Great had reached the Flowery Land in the 3rd cent.[931] The Chinese were indebted to the Greeks for many things in the following century, such as industrial processes,[932] modes of issuing coins,[933] astronomical theories,[934] and notions of Alchemy.

237. Among the many novelties which appeared in China during the first period of the reign of HAN Wu-ti, the most striking was certainly the last named, i.e. Alchemy. And if we consider that cinnabar[935] and orpiment[936] were the principal ingredients used for the wanted transmutation into gold, as they were in the west long before, since the days of the Persian Ostanes and his pupil Democrites,[937] it is difficult not to believe that these new views were a foreign importation and had come from the countries where they were known. The first Alchemist in Chinese history was a certain Li-tchao kiun, (145-132 B.C.) a familiar of the Marquess of Shen-tsê (in Tchihli) under the reign of King-ti (156-141 B.C.), who had come no-body knew from where. He was 70 years of age, when his views about transmutation and a worship of the furnace[938] were adopted by the credulous HAN Wu-ti in 132 B.C.[939] These new notions joined to the older ones concerning the drug of immortality and the transformation of the five elements, produced a most unhappy movement which lasted for centuries, and, in China (as in the West), had a destructive influence on the mind of several Emperors and an injurious effect on the common sense of many. In the 9th century it cost the life of four emperors, who died poisoned by an alleged Elixir of immortality.[940]

238. The earliest introducers of alchemy arrived by the west route, viâ Lin-tao or Wu-tu, and repaired to the east region where only they could find congenial surroundings. It was a repetition of what had occurred with the early Buddhists (§227). After the death of Li-tchao kiun, a certain Kwan-shu, a man of Shantung East was appointed his successor.[941] After him appeared *Shao-ong* 119 B.C. who came from Ts'i, i.e. the West of Shantung.

In 113 B.C. came to court *Lwan-ta* from Kiao tung (E. of the Gulf of Kiao-tchou, Shantung East) who was a pupil of the same master as Shao-ong. And in the same year appeared also at court *Kung-suu-king*, of Ts'i who professed the same views.⁹⁴² Alchemy had therefore found in the cradle-land of Tao-szcism⁹⁴³ favourable circumstances where it was eagerly accepted, and this explains the alliance which took place between it and the brahmanical ideas current there, as well as the hold it soon assumed among the Tao-szeists.

NOTES——
917) *Tai ping yü lan*, kiv. 65, f. 6.
918) Par. 148 *supr.*, we have remarked that several barbarous innovations in Ts'IN, 7th cent. B.C. should have been due to Tartar influence, and in the note 854 we have been able to record that Duke Muh of Ts'IN, had a Western Jung as principal adviser previous to 626 B.C.— Cf. also *Tsien Han Shu*, kiv. 94 ; *History of the Heungnoo*, trad. Wylie ; J.A.I., Dec. 1873, p. 404.
919) In Lin-tao, the second word is the name of a river, not the word for 'route.'—Cf. supr § 228 and note 897 for the arrival of foreigners, most probably through the Sung-pan ting route from the South. In 1884-5, Potanine the Russian traveller has explored these routes, which are entered from his report in map 13 of Dutreuil de Rhins, *Asie Centrale*, 1889. From Min tchou, southwards, an available route passes through Si-ku, and Nan-ping, to Sung-pan ting. From Min-tchou, North-westwards, a route passes through Djoni and Labran to Si-ning.
920) *Hoh she*, 1740-2406 Bas. —*Shan Hai King*, 18, 1.
921) *Se-yep*, 4854-9051 Bas., or *Fan-yep*, 4837-9051 Bas.; the two characters *Se* and *Fan* being nearly similar.
922) *So yeh*, *So-yep*, 7786-9051 Bas. ; also *Sui-yeh*, 6886-9051 Bas.— Cf. *Hiuen-Thsang*, tr. Beal, i, 26. It was situated between the Ili river and Taraz. Cf. E. Bretschneider, *Notices on the Mediæval Geography*, p. 36-7.
923) Brimstone, *shih liu hwang*, stone-flowing-yellow, which as learned afterwards by the Chinese was brought from certain hills, 800 li distant from Kiü-sze (Kao tchang, Karakhodjo), called *Tsiü-mi*. (Cf. *Poh wuh tchi* : T.P., 987, 3, and *Peh she* : T.P. 796, 4-5). The exact date of its first introduction is not ascertained, but it is spoken of in the work bearing the name of Pien-Tsiao, the celebrated physician of the 6th cent. B.C. ; it is spoken of anyhow in literature, 200 B.C. —It arrived through Han-tchung, which fact indicates the route through North Tibet. (cf. Fan-tze, *Ki-jan* : T.P. 987, 4).—In the south of the *Yueh-Pan* country, north-west of the Wu-suns, there was a Fire Mountain, *Hwo shan*, from which flowed sulphur in large quantities. This country is spoken of in the Dynastic Annals of the NORTHERN WEI, and in those of the SUI, which fact suggests that it was not known before the fifth century (Cf. T.P. 795. 2 ; 796. 4, and 987, 3). Now this was the Northern country where the W. Hiung-nus had fled after their defeat by the Chinese General Tou-hien in A.D. 89. It extended far in the West, and answers to Sarmatia. In the fifth century the Huns

had conquered the European *Sarmatia* (De Guignes, *Hist. des Huns*, ii., 301). According to Strahlenberg, *Description*, p. 448, the only place where sulphur is found is in the kingdom of Casan (Kazan), and this answers to the foregoing indications. Curiously enough the modern Chinese *Yueh-pan*, restored by the archaic dialects, makes *Sol-pan*, *Sol-po*, therefore equal to Sor-ma, a sufficiently approximate rendering of Sarmatia. The fact is interesting in several respects, but it is not necessary that this first Sulphur should have come from Kasan. There are nearer places. Sulphur was at one time collected on the *Poh shan* North of Kucha (cf. Mushketoff, *Turkestan*, 1886, i., 172 ; E. Bretscsneider, *Mediœv. Res.* ii., 244). The summit of Mount Demavend, near the Caspian, is a mass of sulphur. Allusion is made to sulphur trade in the *Shan Hai King*, xi., 2 and xviii., 3.—Sulphur from Tu-kun, i.e. Tagaung in Burma, was imported into China in our 3rd cent. Cf. *Wu shi Wai kwoh tchuen* : T.P. 788, 6 and 982, 2. On the sulphur of Tagaung, cf. Balfour, *Cyclop. Ind.*, iii., 759.

924) Cf. *suprà* § 221.

925) It was placed in the Wang shen *Koh* or gallery.—Cf. De Mailla, *Histoire générale*, iii., 25.—*Tung ming ki*, T.P.Y.L., 717, 5.—The Greeks used to make very large metallic mirrors. Cf. Beckmann, *History of Inventions*, 1846, ii., 65, and the following note.

926) Hwai-nan-tze (d. 122 B.C.) tells us that the polished metallic mirrors were at first somewhat dim, and one could not see one's features in them ; but on rubbing the mirror with some white felt and yuen-tin (?) well ground, even curly hair and whiskers would be easily seen in it.—Cf. *T.P.Y.L.*, 717, 2v., and 812, 8.—*Yuen-sih*, may be g o o d t i n, or b l a c k t i n, because of the tabued *hiuen*, b l a c k in the T.P.Y.L. edition of 1807 to which I refer ; but b l a c k t i n, *hiuen sih* in Chinese is unknown to me. The thing referred to may have been an amalgam of Mercury, which as we know was indeed used by them. Cf. on on this point. Stan. Julien—P. Champion, *Industries anciennes et modernes de la Chine*, p. 63-65.—It is curious that we should find the process, obviously current in the Greek world, described in the classical writers, not with reference to metallic mirrors, but for mirrors of glass or another material. Cf. Beckmann, *Hist. Invent.*, ii., 66 ; Marquis de Jouffroy, *Dict. des Invent.*, 1860, ii., 455 . Victor Fournel, *Le Vieux neuf*, ii., 148 ; iii., 557 ; S. Reinach, *Philol. Class..* i., 90 ; ii., 149, 276 The process seems to have been known in India. Cf. *Archives des découvertes*, xv., 365 ; V. Fournel, *Vieux Neuf*, ii., 267.

927) A clear sketch of this complicated period is given by M. Ed. Drouin. in his *Notice sur la Bactriane* (Extr. de la Grande Encyclopedie), 1887. —Cf. also Percy Gardner, *The Coins of the Greek and Scythic Kings of Bactria and India*, 1886, introd.

928) Cf .T. de L., *L'Ere des Arsacides en* 248 Ar. *J.C., Lourain*, 1891.

929) Cf. Percy Gardner, *The Parthian Coinage*, 1878, (Intern. Numism. Orient., I., v).

930 *Hou Han Shu*, kiv. 88, Ta Ts'in.— *Wei lioh* ; *San Kwoh tchi.* kiv. 30): par. 24, 45.—F. Hirth, *China and the Roman Orient*, p. 42, 70, 72.

931) Supr. par. 225.

932) For instance the polishing of metallic mirrors (note 926) ; and burning lenses in Hwai-nan tze. Cf. *T.P.Y.L.*, 869. 3-4. and for the same expanded : the *Poh wuh tchi* ; cf. G. Schlegel, *Uranographie*

Chinoise, p. 142.

933) The Mints of Athens and Rome were under the superintendence of three Mint masters. In 116 B.C., HAN Wu-ti reorganized the State mint on the same system. (*Tsien Han Shu*, Shih ho tchi); Fr. Lenormant, *La Monnaie dans l'Antiquité*, iii., 50 sq.; T. de L., *Catalogue of Chinese Coins*, introd. xxix.

934) For instance the circulating movement of the earth in the heavens, in Hwai-nan-tze, ap. Cibot and Grosier, *Chine*, vol. vi.—The theory was taught by Pythagoras, 500 B.C., and by Aristarchus of Samos, c. 260 B.C. Cf. Th. H. Martin, *Etudes sur le Timée*, ii., 123.—The same view was entertained by the Egyptians, according to : F. Chabas, *Sur un texte Egyptien relatif au mouvement de la terre*. Zeits. f. Ægypt. Spr. 1864, p. 97 ; and J. Lieblein, *Les Anciens Egyptiens connaissaient-ils le mouvement de la terre?* (Congr. Prov. Orient., St. Etienne, 1880, p. 127.—We have mentioned before in note 804, the notion of a three legged bird in the Sun from Asia Minor which appears in the *Li sao*, and is spoken of also by Hwai-nan-tze. Cf. T.P.Y.L., 3, 3 ; 920, 6, 935) Cf. *She ki*, xxviii, 23.

936) Or yellow sulphuret of Arsenic.—In the writings of Hwai Nan tze d. 122 B.C. Cf. T.P.Y.L., 985, 1 v., 3 r.

937) According to Synesius, Cf. *Notices et Extraits des Manuscrits*, t. vii, p. 223. Also t. vi, p. 306.—Plin. *H.N.* xxxiii, 22 says that Caligula also, when he tried to make gold, used orpiment (like Democrites); Victor Fournel, *Le Vieux Neuf*, III, 500-502.

938) One cannot fail to remark the importance attached to the furnace by the alchemists; a further connection of Chinese alchemy with that of the west.

939) Cf. *She ki*, kiv. 28, fol. 22 r., 23.—On the worship of the furnace, cf. *supra* par. 183, note 665.—The earliest works on Alchemy in China are those of Hwai-nan-tze, d. 122 B.C. ; *Tchun tsiu yun tou tch'u*, 50 B.C. ; *Ts'an tung k'i* by Wei Peh-yang, 150 A.D. ; and that of Pao-p'oh-tze, 300 A.D.—In 1855, Dr. J. Edkins, *On Early Tauist alchemy* (Shanghae Miscellany), and in *Phases in the development of Tauism* (Trans. Ch. Br. R.A.S., V) has suggested a Chinese origin for the Alchemy of the West. W.A.P. Martin, in his *Alchemy in China*, China Review, 1879, reprinted in his *Han lin papers*, 1881 has taken again the same view. But the two scholars have over-looked the older antiquity of the West.—On the latter's history cf. the special works of Marcelin Berthelot, *Les Origines de l'Alchimie* 1885 ; *Collection des Anciens Alchimistes Grecs*, 1887-8 ; *La Chimie dans l' Antiquité et au Moyen-Age* : Rev. 2 Mondes, 15 Sept. 1 Oct. 93 ; and also *Transmission des Industries Chimiques de l' Antiquité au Moyen-age*, ibid. 1 Sept. 92, p. 39-55.

940) The researches made for long by sea and even by land to find the plant producing the drug of immortality i.e. the *tze-mai* or *soma* (cf. *supra* §§ 123, 214, 225, notes 458, 462) had proved unsuccessful. The current notion was that it was like the *ku* plant or *hydropyrum latifolium* (cf. Tung Fang so, *Shih tchou ki* : T.P.Y.L. 60, 4 r.—E. Bretschneider, *Botan. Sinic.*, ii, 88, 350). So that the Taoszeist alchemists endeavoured to compose an Elixir of immortality. Four Emperors of the *T'ang* dynasty, Hien tsung in 820, Muh tsung in 824, Wu tsung in 846 and Süen tsung in 859, died from the Elixirs of im-

mortality given to them by the Taoszeists who were then in favour at court. (Cf. De Mailla, *Hist. Gen.* vi, 430, 412, 492, 503). The avowed purpose of these alchemists was the transmutation of the body into an incorruptible substance by means of the absorption into it of special elixirs compounded principally of mercury and mica as in India, cf. A. Barth, *Religions of India*, p. 210.—Researches by sea after the fortunate islands and the drug of immortality, were still going on at the time of Sun kwang founder of *Wu*, one of the Three Kingdoms, 3rd cent. Cf. *Wu tchi*.

941) In § 173 *supra*, we have enumerated the names of the principal thaumaturgists of YEN and of Ts'ı during the fifth period. Sung Wu ki was followed during the reign of She Hwang ti by Ngan ki sheng and by Siu-fuh (cf. note 884). Under HAN Hiao Wen-ti flourished about 165 B.C. Kung-sun Tch'en, and Sin-yuen Ping of Ts'i, cf. *She ki*, kiv. 28, fol. 19-19 *v*.—On Sung-Wu ki, and Ngan-ki sheng, cf. Mayers, *Chinese R.M.*, i, 641 and 523. In 163 B.C. Sin yuen-ping is attributed (De Mailla. *Hist. Gen.*, ii, 563, and Ed. Chavannes, *Le Traité sur les Sacrifices Fong et Chan*, p. 44) a high feat which could vie with that of Joshua, as he would have effectually commanded the sun to retrograde in heaven. I am afraid a misunderstanding has crept there from the frequent confusion of the characters *hou*, p r i n c e, (217 Bas.) and *hou*, e x p e c t (293 Bas). It is the second character, not the first, which occurs in the text (cf. *She ki*, xxviii, 20 *v*.). The statement is the following : Ping, speaking to the Emperor, said: "Your servant expects the sun will be repeated in the centre (of the sky); and in only a moment, the sun stopped and was again in the centre." This is clearly a phenomenon of parhelion, which Sin yuen ping had foreseen from its preliminary phases.

942) Cf. *She ki* kiv. 28, fol. 22 *v*., 23 *v*., 25 *v*., 30, and 32.—Kiao-tung had been created into a small feudal state in 207 B.C. cf. *She ki*, xvi, 10.

943) This circumstance might suggest that Alchemy was carried to China by the sea-traders of Hormuz (*supra* § 198-206) to the South-east Coast of China and from there to the Shan-tung peninsula. But in 110 B.C. those who came from the states of Yueh (§ 201) to the Chinese court where alchemy was so much in favour, speak only of their worship of special genii, and of their divination by (alectromancy) birds which were immediately adopted. (*She ki*, xxviii, 40 *v*., 41). Their silence about transmutation is rather significant. The art was Greek, and the Greeks were then near the route of the trade to China from Western Turkestan. Cf. par. 234, 236 and 242.

* *

239. Since the last years of the Ts'IN, the Hiung-nus said to be Turkish stock,[944] outside the north borders of China, who had long been in enmity with the states, had increased in boldness and their frequent raids on the Imperial territory where they advanced as far as the south centre of Shansi and of Shensi, resulted in a state of incessant warfares. In 176 B.C. they had pushed forward to the west of their former quarters

and established their sway over a large area ; the *Yu e h-t i*⁹⁴⁵ were finally
crushed. the *Wu s u n*, who from the *Tien shan* range had advanced
South-east, as far as Kwa-tchou of Kan-suh west, had been compelled to
withdraw, and the state of *L o u l a n* (for Labran, later Shen-shen) recognized their authority as did the *H u-k i t*⁹⁴⁶ and 26 other states. The
Yueh-ti removed gradually westwards⁹⁴⁷ until in 143 B.C. they settled for
a time on the banks of the Oxus. When HAN Wu-ti came to the throne
140 B.C., being desirous of getting rid of the obnoxious Hiung-nus, he
wished to make an alliance to that effect with his former neighbours the
Yueh-ti. Tchang-kien, it is well known, was sent in official mission to
them in 13 9 B.C., but he was stopped on his way for ten years by the
Hiung-nus ; he finally escaped from their territory to that of Ta-yuan,
from where he went to Kang-kiu (Samarkand) and reached the *Yueh-ti*.
He followed them during their conquest of the Ta-hia, but could not de-
cide them to resume an offensive action in common against their former
foes. After a sojourn of one year, he started for his return journey, and
travelled along the *Nan shan*, in view of passing through the Kiang
route, i.e. that leading to *Sung pan ting* or to *Lin-tao*. But he was again
stopped by the Hiung-nus who kept him a prisoner for another year, so
that he did not reach his native country prior 126 B.C.⁹⁴⁸

240. Tchang kien having personally visited the three countries precited
reported upon them, and with additional details on five or six others⁹⁴⁹.
He spoke of the marvellous Nisæan horses, blood perspiring, fed with lucern in Ta-yuan, and of the products of Shuh (Szetchuen) which through
India were carried in the *Ta-hia* country. It was then estimated that
India could not therefore be far from the South-west of the Empire, and
that *Ta-hia* could be thus reached without difficulty.⁹⁵⁰ Unsuccessful
attempts were thus made for several years to pass through the South-
west border states,⁹⁵¹ as the Hiung-nus in the North stopped the way of
Turkestan. Some partial successes having at last cleared the region of
the Nan-shan of these indomitable foes, Tchang-kien, on his proposal in
119 B.C. was sent a second time, as Imperial envoy, with a large retinue
of official assistants, to negociate an alliance with the *Wu-suns* against
the Hiung-nus and a free intercourse with *Ta-yuan*, *Ta-hia* and other
countries.⁹⁵² He started by the *Lin-tao* route and reached the *Wu-suns*
whom he could not make accept the Chinese proposals. He came back in
116 B.C. accompanied with a mission from them to China. Whilst
amongst the Wu-suns he had dispatched his assistant Envoys to Ta-yuan
Kang kiu, the Yueh-ti and Ta-hia. Nearly all came back about a year

later, bringing some of the natives of these countries with them. "And thus, Szema Tsien tells us, the intercourse of China with the countries of the North-west commenced from this time."⁹⁵³

241. By a singular concourse of circumstances the famous Nisæan horses of classical history⁹⁵⁴ became then the cause of the Chinese power being established in Central Asia. It was reported to Han Wu-ti, that the King of Ta-yuan (Farghana) kept a large stud of marvellous horses, blood perspiring, descending from a heaven's stallion and travelling a thousand lis in a day. Their native place was $Ni\text{-}se$⁹⁵⁵ but the capital of the kingdom was *Kwei-shan* (modern Kasan)⁹⁵⁶ one of the seventy cities of the Kingdom. Their name was *p'u-shao* in which we recognize a curtailed transfer of *topicha*, "the long-necked and long-legged Turkoman horse."⁹⁵⁷ The Chinese envoys could not get any of these horses for their Emperor who having been deceived once⁹⁵⁸ finally decided to get some of them at any price. Military stations were established as far as Tun-hwang (N.W. Kansuh) in 109 B.C., to facilitate the intercourse with the North-west kingdoms independently of the fortuitous caprice of the Hiung-nus.⁹⁵⁹ A special envoy named Tchai-ling was sent with a golden horse and a thousand *kin* of gold to purchase one of the much coveted horses, but Megas the king of Ta-yuan refused, the envoy was murdered and the golden horse stolen. Hostilities were resumed by the Hiung-nus and an important expedition sent in 104 B.C. was wrecked by them. At last in 101 B.C. a large army under the command of Li Kwang-li, titled Nisæan general for the purpose, reached Ta-yuan, imposed a treaty and came back decimated with *ten Nisæan horses*, which had cost to China fifteen years of efforts and sacrifices of all sorts, including a total loss of about 300000 men.

242. A circumstance of peculiar interest, also unnoticed, in that event, is that Greeks and Chinese came there into contact for the first time.⁹⁶⁰ *Ta Yuan* was then occupied by Greeks. The evidence of this fact rests partly on words and names quoted in the Chinese record which happen to have an hellenic appearance notwithstanding their Chinese garb. Herewith a short list of these words:

Ch.					
Muh-tuk,	lucern,	for	*medikai*	in Greek⁹⁶¹	
P'u-tao,	vine,	„	*botrus*	„	
Tsai-kwa,	cucumber,	„	*sikuos*	„	
Hung-hua	safflower,	„	*knikos*	„	
Mu-ku,	name of the King,	„	*megas*	„	great

Although we may regret that their list should not be longer, their evidence is sufficiently conclusive, and finds a further confirmation in the name of the country itself. *Ta-yuan* means greater *Yuan* as shown by the contemporary existence of a *Siao Yuan* or Lesser *Yuan*, as in the case of the *Ta Yueh-ti* and *Siao Yueh-ti*. The name is therefore *Yuan* only, which, the Archaic dialects indicate, was pronounced *Yuen* or *Yuan*, surely a transfer of *Iaon*, G r e e k.⁹⁶² We must therefore translate *Ta Yuan* or *Ta Wan Kwoh*, the G r e a t e r G r e e k Country.⁹⁶³

243. The victory of a Chinese Army over Ferghana was a most important event in the political history of Central Asia.⁹⁶⁴ It gave to the Son of Heaven a leading position for two centuries among the potentates of that part of the world. Many states recognized his Imperial authority or asked for his alliance, and in 59 B.C. a Governor Generalship was established at *Wu-ley* (S.W. of present Karashar) had under its supreme jurisdiction no less than 36 states on the east, north and west of the Tsungling range.⁹⁶⁵ In 51 the outposts extended as far west as *Sha-kiu*, i.e. Yarkand. The Chinese authority on the west of the Pamir range was then strong enough to avenge the injuries done to former envoys by *Hippostratus*,⁹⁶⁶ King of Kophen (Kabulistan); the entreaties of the son of that king were disregarded, a plot was entered with the son of the king of the Greeks, *Hermæus*,⁹⁶⁷ which resulted in an attack on the country, when the king was killed, and Hermæus, receiving the investiture from China was enthroned as King of Kophen.⁹⁶⁸ In 1 B.C., by partitions and additions, the number of western states bowing to the Chinese Emperor had been increased to fifty, and the Chinese seals and ribbons of office were received by no less than 376 officials, chieftains and rulers, although several of the more distant states had ceased to do so some time before.⁹⁶⁹

244. The Chinese greatness there was short lived, and less than 75 years after the establishment of a Governor General of the *Si-yü* (West Asia), all the states beyond Sha-kiu, i.e. Yarkand, had swerved from their former allegiance.⁹⁷⁰ This was in the years 10-16 A.D. during the usurpation of Wang Mang. When the Eastern Han dynasty arose at Loh-yang in A.D. 25 the Chinese Government, again engaged against the Hiungnus, was unable to interfere, and the last faithful states gave it up in 38 and 41 A.D. Later successes over the hereditary foes permitted to resume intercourse and Imperial interference with the West. Pan-Tchao, the famous General, was the chief agent in the affair. From 73 to 98, he restored the authority and prestige of the Chinese name in these regions. The states of Eastern Turkistan were either compelled or induced to recognize their former suzerain, and friendly relations were reopened with the states

West of the Pamir. Pan-Tchao himself, in 97 A.D. went as far as HIEN-TU, i.e. ANTIOchia *Margiana*,[971] and dispatched his lieutenant Kan-yng to the unknown *Tats'in*,[972] while himself returned to *Ku-tse*, i.e. Kutcha. Kan-yng went as far as the Persian Gulf (not the Caspian Sea)[973] and returned afraid of the sea voyage to the head of the Red Sea. Pan-Tchao returned to his native land in 102 to die, and five years later the dilapidated condition of the Imperial finances caused a withdrawal of all the Chinese Representatives and forces beyond the N.W. borders (of pres. Kansuh), which resulted in the loss of nearly all the advantages gained by the great politic general. Some years afterwards a fresh advance was made, an outpost was established at *Liu-tching* (pres. Lu-ko-ts'in, 60 li S.E. of Turfan) in 123, and *Yen-Ki*, i.e. Karashar, was conquered in 126 A.D.,[974] but the former position and political influence was not recovered.

245. Several missions or embassies implying an untold number of private caravans, from the west, at that time, have been recorded in history. Among the first in 115 B.C. was: one from Parthia (An-sih) with Ostriches' eggs of Mesopotamia and jugglers of *Li-kien*=Reken;[975] and one from the Wu-suns with horses.[976] In 51 B.C. an Imperial Princess given into marriage to the *Kun-mi* or King of the Wu-suns came back in 105 B.C. bringing home the *pi-pa* or tamburah of Persia.[977] Missions from *Kang-kü* (Samarcand) and from *Pan-tu* (=Parthuva) arrived in 11 B.C.[978] Thirteen years later Buddhist books were brought by Y-tsun kou, from the Yueh-ti.[979] The Arsacidæ in A.D. 87 sent lions and *jupas* (hornless unit corns.[980] In A.D. 101 the King Bankü of Ansih (i.e. Pacorus II. the xxivth Arsacidæ) sent lions and ostriches' eggs. Until four years later several envoys from India reached China by the same route. Another mission from Parthia arrived in 106,[981] but any further communications were stopped by the revolt of the Si-yü in A.D. 107.[982] The travellers of Maes Titianus who went to *Sera Metropolis* at that time, and supplied Marinus Tyrius with the information which appears in Ptolemy, must have gone as subservient only to the Parthian envoys, if they have been there themselves at all. The details they give about the seven months journey from the Stone tower to the Sera Metropolis, as already remarked by Ptolemy himself, look like second hand information.[983] They remained probably at the Stone-Tower, expecting the return of the Parthian envoys, as we know from the Chinese side that the Arsacidæ were the self-made middlemen[984] between the West traders and the *Sera Metropolis*,[985] the Eastern city.

NOTES——

944) The Hiung-nus appeared for the first time *eo nomine* in history in 318 B.C. cf. Szema Tsi'n, *She ki*, v. 24.—They traced the ancestry of their chiefs to *Shun-wei* a descendant of the Chinese Royal family of Hia, who had removed from China a thousand years before the time of Tou-man, their Shen-yu in 209 B.C. (cf. *She ki*, fol. 9, and *Tsien Han shu*, kiv. 94)—Klaproth and Remusat have taken them to be Turks, because the *T u h-k i ū h* (ancient *Tol-kul*, *Tul-kwet*), whose words in Chinese books are really Turk, are said in the same books to have been descendants of Hiung-nus. So are said to be the *Kao-kiu* or Uigurs, the *Puloki* and the *Kun-mi* ; the Tungusic *To-pah* are said also to have the same origin as the Hiung-nus. (Cf. T.P.Y.L., 791, 12 ; 801, 1 v., 4.) Now the *Puloki* and *Kun-mi* were not Turks. Moreover in twelve words of the Hiung-nu language given in the *She-ki*, two or three only are Turk, two are Tungusic. The Hiung-nus seem to have been a political, not a racial unity.—Cf. also T. de L., *Khan, Khakan, and other Tartar titles*, 1888, note 31.

45) The *Yueh-ti* were spoken of first in the geographical work of Y-yn (Shang dynasty) cf. Pih yuen, *Shan hai king*, comm. 13, 1 r.—In 209 B.C. they were in a flourishing condition in Kansuh, N.W. (cf. *She ki*, 113, 6 r.).

946) Klaproth mistook these for the *Hu-ṭe*, identified by him with the Goths.

947) In 143 B.C. their neighbours compelled them to move again further west and it was then that they reached the Oxus. They were sinicised to some extent and carried with them not a few Chinese notions. They had a coinage of Chinese pattern, on which cf. my paper *Une monnaie Bactro-Chinoise bilingue du premier siècle ar. n.è.* (Extr. Cte-R. Acad. Inscript. 1890), pp. 7, 14. Two specimens are known apparently of different date. A small one which must have been issued chiefly among the Yueh-ti. A larger one of later date which bears apparently the name of Hermœus in Bactro-Pali, and may have been issued when this king was instated by the Chinese about 51 B.C. (Below par. 243). The previous existence of the Chinese type of coinage it represents, introduced by the *Yueh-ti*, would justify its maintenance in that circumstance, instead of the newer type of the HAN dynasty.

948) Cf. Szema Tsien. *She ki*, 123, 1-3.—*Tsien Han shu*, kiv. 61.

949) Such is the precise statement of the *She ki*, 123, 2 r.—He had passed also through Kang-kü, and reported upon the *An-sih*, (Arsacida).

950) Cf T. de L., *Tin-yüt, not India*: Acad., May 2. and *India from China* : ibid. Sept. 5, 1885.

951) On these attempts, see below, par. 269.

952) It was then that he visited the alledged sources of the Hwang-ho, the *Sing su hai* or *Oduntala*, i.e. Starry Sea, which he thought was in communication underground with the Pu-tchang Hai or Lopnor, and made the Hwang-ho a continuation of the Tarym. The most interesting information on the subject has been translated by M. Gulay in his *Description de la Chine Occidentale*, Suppl. ; Muséon, Oct., 85, p. 612-7.

953) *She Ki*, Kiv. 123, fol. 8, 9, 9v.

954) These were the large horses personally used by the Kings of Persia and the Princes, which Herodotus (i., 497; iii., 106; iv., 39) and other classical writers have described, as horses of *Nisa* in Media : Strabo, 11; Aristot., *De Hist. Anim.*, 9 ; Amm. Marcell, 23, 6 ; Eustath. ad Dionys. Per. ; Appian, 1.—On an early history of these horses, cf. W. St. Chad Boscawen, *The Horses of Namar* : B. & O. R., vi., 139-40.— The Nisæan plain famous for its horses must have been near Behistun, as Alexander passed it on his way from Opis to Ekbatana (Cf A.H. Sayce, *Herodotus.* 282.

955) This name and the consequences which ensue for the identification of the horses has hitherto been passed unnoticed by former Sinologists because they have been satisfied to read it with the corrupted sounds of the present day, *eul-she, er-she, urh-she* in Pekinese and Mandarin, and therefore did not perceive its historical interest. *Ni-se* (10484-8430 Das.) is still at present read *ni-sz* in the Shanghai, *nhi-soai* in the Sino-Annamite, and similar sounds in other archaic dialects. The present sound *er* in Chinese was *ni* in the Buddhist transcriptions as shown in Stan. Julien, *Méthode*, Nos. 266, 268-9 ; Eitel, *Sanskr. Chin. Dict.*, p. 83, &c.

956) *Kasan*, now a small place N.W. of Namaghan, was formerly the capital of Ferghana, according to the early Arabian geographers. Cf. E. Bretschneider, *Mediæv. Res.*, ii., 52.

957) *T'obich'a*. cf. *topchay* in Shaw, *Vocabulary of the Turki language*, p. 71 ; Pavet de Courteille, Mém. de Baber, pref. ;E. Bretschneider. *M.R.*, i., 140, ii., 125, 264. These horses are now called *Arghamak* in Samarcand, but there seems to be some differences in the breed, (cf Edw. Balfour, *Cyclop. of India*, ii, 109).--The Turkoman horse has been often described, and lately by Heinrich Moser, *Le Pays des Turcomans*, Rev. 2. Mond. 15 Mai, 1885, and in his large work *Durch Centralasien*, Leipzig, 1888.—La faculté de suer du sang que l'on sait aujourd'hui être due à l'éxistence de filaires longs d'environ un demi millm. pourrait être moins rare qu'en le croit; elle a été trés souvent constatée sur les chevaux hongrois. Cf. C.A. Pietrement. *Les chevaux dans les temps préhistoriques et historiques*, 1883, p. 29.

958) The Wu-suns had sent him some of their own horses which at first were received as celestial horses, but the superchery was discovered on the return of other envoys. (Cf. *Shi Ki*, 123, 28 ; *Tsien Han shu*, 41, 4).

959) Envoys were then sent to *Ansik*, i e. the Arsacidian Empire: *Yentsai*, i.e. the Aorsi, N. of Parthia : *Li-kien*, i.e. Rekem, the emporium N. of the Red Sea : *Tiao-tchi*, i.e. the Arab settlements N. of the Persian Gulf, and *Shen-tuh*, i.e. India. Cf. *Tsien Han shu*, kiv. 61, fol. 4 , Wylie, *Western Regions*, 51.—For Aorsi and Rekem, cf. F. Hirth. *China and the Roman Orient*, p. 139, 157.—Perhaps that *Likien* was *Rakkan* in Persian.

960) Strabo, xi. 11, tells us that the Greek Kings of Bactriana extended their dominion as far as the country of the Seres. Cf. Reinaud, *Relations politiques et commerciales de l'Empire Romain avec l'Asie Orientale*, p.*113. Of course we must understand countries under the dominion of the Seres fo the time being. Does this refer to the *Sias* or *Lesser Yuan* ? See below in 963.

961) The Lucern had been called *medikai* by the Greeks because it had been brought from Media at the time of the Persian wars, about

470 B.C.; in Central Asia its native names are *Rishka, Shasta, isfist,* which leave no doubt on the Greek origin of the Chinese word. Cf. A. Candolle, *Origin of Cultivated plants*, p. 102; V. Hehn, *Wanderings of Plants*, p. 306—The comparison with *botrus* and *medikai* was first made by Mr. Kingsmill of Shanghai.—Two more words from Ta-yuan are quoted, but one seems to refer to an old Persian and Sanskrit words: such as *hu-tao* for walnut tree; cf. *akhôda*; and one to Turki *pu-shao*, horse, cf. *topicha*.

962) Dr. J. Edkins, *Philological importance of Geographical terms in the She-ki*: J. Ch. Br. R.A.S., 1886, xxi, 200, says: Greek Kingdom in Ferghana, *Wan* (Javan).

963) The identification of *Yuan* with *Yaon* or Greek, gives interest to the existence of the *Siao Yuan* with their capital Yü-ling or Han-ling, consisting of 150 families, 1050 people. 200 soldiers, at 7210 li from Tchangngan; and at 2558 li N.W. was the seat of the Governor General. (Cf. *Tsien Han Shu*, 96; A. Wylie, *Western Regions*, 9). Shen-shen was at 6100 li and Khotan at 9670 li from Tchang-ngan. The *Siao Yuan* were on the route North of Tibet, between these two places. Yü-ling should be one of the buried cities, and looks like a small colony of Greeks.

964) After the Ta-yuan war, Chinese posts and military colonies had been established at *Lun-tai* or Round Tower, (at 680 lis=194 modern lis, West of *Yen-ki* or Karashar, near present Bugur according to Father Hyacinth ap. E. Bretschneider, *Mediœv. Res.*, i., 16) and at *Yü Kiü-'i*, near Turfan, where a Deputy Protector had his residence, cf, *Tsien Han shu*, 96, 1; A. Wylie, *Western Regions*, 3; and De Mailla. *Hist. Gen.*, iii., 75.

965) This measure was taken after the defection from the Hiungnus and the submission to China of a Hiungnu Prince with 50000 followers. Cf. *Li tai T'i Wang nien piao*.—*Tsien Han Shu*, Kiv. 94.—A. Wylie,, *Heung-noo*, 451.—De Guignes, *Hist. 'des Huns*, 2, 86.—De Mailla *Hist. Gen.*, iii., 140.—The office of Slaves Protector General which had replaced the former was then suppressed and a Governor General appointed instead.—*Wu-ley*, his new residence was near the present Kurla, S.W. of Karashar, on the pass of the Kuruk-tagh (figured on map 19 in E. Reclus, *Asie Orientale*, 113).

966) In Chinese Bu To Lo.
Greek hi PPosT Ratos.

967) In Chinese mod. *Yu-muh-fu* (=Yn-mn-vn for Yr-mu-vn)=*Ermaion*, the Greek name.—The Chinese word is *Yung-kiu*=Younaki, the country of the Greeks. Cf. Ed. Drouin, *Notice sur la Bactriane*, p. 16 for these two identifications. Cf. *supra* note 947.

968) Cf. *Tsien Han Shu*, Kiv. 96; Wylie, *Western Regions*, p. 17. Wen-tchung, the Chinese envoy who had installed Hermæus, having returned to China to report on his mission was replaced by the Marquis Tchao-tih who had difficulties with Hermæus and was kil'ed with his retinue of 70 persons. Han Yuan-Ti who had just ascended the throne refused to interfere because of the distance and the difficulty of the route through Badakshan. In 25 B.C. under his successor a request from Kophen received a similar answer. Cf. *Tsien Han Shu*, kiv. 96; Wylie, *Western Regions*, p. 17-18.

969) Cf. *Li Tai Ti Wang nien piao*.—And the previous note.

970) This occurred successively in the years 10, 13, and 16 A.D.
971) We have here a fresh instance of the double suggestion of sound and suitable meaning in the transfer of a foreign name. The two Chinese characters *Hien tu* (7981-11240 Bas.) mean '*Métropole of district*.'
972) Cf. *infra*, par. 263.
973) Cf. F. Hirth, *China and the Roman Orient*, p. 3, 13, 138, 164.— Also E.C. Taintor, *Advance of a Chinese General to the Caspian Sea*: Notes and Queries, 1868, p. 60-62, and A. Wylie, ibid. p. 153 for the various texts on the subject.
974) Cf. *Li tai Ti Wang nien piao*, s. a.—De Mailla, *Hist. Gén.*, iii., 417, 423.—E. Bretschneider, *Mediæv Res.*, ii., 184.
975) On Li-kien = Reken, cf. *infra* par. 263,— *She-Ki*, kiv. 123.
976) *She Ki*, 123, 8.—*Tsien Han Shu*, 41, 4.
977) Cf. *Po yuen pipa sū*. T.P.Y.L., 583, 3.—De Guignes, *Hist. de Huns*, ii., 61.—Mayers, *Chinese R.M.* 872.
978) *Li tai Ti Wang nien piao.*
979) *Supra*, note 912.
980) *Hou Han Shu*, kiv. 88.—F. Hirth, *Chin. and Rom. Or.*, 39.
981) *Si yū tchi*.—Cf. Pauthier, *Examen Méthodique*, J.A. Oct., 1839, p. 266, 282.
982) De Guignes, *Hist. des Huns*, i., 31, and previous paragraph.
983) Cf. on this point the *History of Ancient Geography*, by E Bunbury, ii, 529-531.
984) *Supra* note 930.
985) No satisfactory explanation has been given as yet of the name of *Sêres*, *Séra*, *Serica*. The name appeared in Western writers (not since Ktesias where it is an interpolation, but) since Apollodorus of Artemita (of the 1st cent. B.C. in his lost History of Parthia), Virgil and many others. t was known in North India at the time of Kanishka and in Ceylon in the 1st cent. Pausanias in the second century speaks of the great river *Ser* in that country. The same writer, Hesychius, Photius, Clemens Alexandrinus, and others say that *ser* is a worm and also a nation. Klaproth in *Journal Asiatique* of 1823, p. 243, R.G. Latham, *On the existence of a nation bearing the name of Seres* in Classical Museum, 1846, and Reinaud, *L'Empire Romain et l'Asie Orientale* : J.A. Mars 1863, p. 123, have suggested the own name of the silk, *se* Chines, *sir* Korean, *sirek* Mongolian, and *sirghe* Mandshu. We may add *dar* Tibetan, and should we trust the oldest Chinese phonetic spelling which wrote the word occasionally *siao*+L*u* (litt. small bone) the present Chinese SE would be an abraded sound of S*ə*L for S*ə*R. But the final was lost in Chinese long before our era.—The suggested etymology however ingenious cannot be accepted as it is not supported by any evidence that China has ever been so called by any of those nations through which only the name of Sêres could have been learned by the travellers of the West. Moreover it is not suitable for the name of the great river of the land, the *Hwang-ho* or Yellow river. Now let us remark that yellow is *ser* in Tibetan, *sari* in Turki, s*h*a*ra* in Mongolian, and therefore that the name of the river was thus translated. Besides the name of the Sêres was learned by the Singalese traders travelling North as well as by the travellers coming through the North-west highways. Tibetans were on the route on both

sides, and it is from their language that a name given to their eastern neighbours should have been learned. Such indeed was the case, as the same word as for yellow means East, Eastern, *shar* in Tibetan. Yellow is also a natural colour for silk. We can thus understand how the confusion arose in the explanations of travellers. Furthermore there is evidence that the North-west of China was so called by foreigners, and I do not know if the name of Sharshen since the Han dynasty is not a survival. *Suh* now Suh-tchou of Kansuh was an old name of the region which was SoL for SoR, as shown by its archaic phonetic spelling and outside evidence. On the latter cf. my paper on The *Diurtchen of Mandshuria*, part i.—The Sung-p'an-ting traders, in the present day are called *shar-ba*, among the Golok and other Tibetan tribes of N.E. Tibet. Cf. W. Woodville Rockhill, *Tibet from Chinese Sources* : J.R.A.S., Jan. 1891, p. 89 n.—It means simply inhabitant of an eastern country. Cf. Jaeschke, *Tibet. Dict.*, p. 557.

Chap. VII.—Sixth Period : 221 b.c.—a.d. 220.

Sect. C. *Private trade and Official opening of inland intercourse with the West.* (cont.)

246. It is difficult to appreciate in detail all the western things and notions that came to China through the frequent relations which occurred after the openings of 126 and 115 b.c. West Asia was then in the hands of the Greeks, of the Parthians, of the Romans and of the Buddhists. The old Persian culture had disappeared, as had before the older Assyro-Babylonian which had become mythical[986]save in one place[987] ; they were no more in current use and could not be transmitted through common intercourse of politicians, still less of soldiers or of merchants. This state of things limitates the character of the items of western culture which can have reached the Chinese Empire duringthat period. The Greek character of several of the innovations has already been pointed out[988], and some more will have undoubtedly to be added to the list by the progress of research.

247. Thanks to the great care always paid by the Chinese to botany[989] and to their numerous records on the matter, we know approximately which new plants and fruits were then introduced from the *Si Yü* to the Flowery Land. Herewith a short list of them : lucern, vine, cucumber, and safflower, with their Greek names[990], walnut tree, with its Aryan name ; *hu-tou* or common bean, *hu-sui* or parsley, *hu suan* or great garlic[991], *hu-ma* or sesamum identified with that introduced earlier by the sea trade[992], and the *an-shih lu*, or nar of the Arsacidæ, i.e. the pomegranate[993] and others. In 87 b.c., the king of *Yueh-ti*, from W. Asia where

they had removed sent four oz. of a most valuable spice called *King-tsing*[994], and produced by a tree growing in the island of *Tsü-kwot* in the Western Ocean[995].

248. Amongst the most interesting articles then introduced from the West inland was amber which came then first to the knowledge of the Chinese. HAN Wu-ti was presented by one of the western emissaries who accompanied the assistant envoys of Tchang-kien on their return[996], with a swallow made of Amber and with pieces of the same precious material[997]. It was in Kophen (Kabulistan) that according to the reports, Amber could be procured[998], and in the Chinese *hu-peh* for Amber we should see a distant imitation of the native term which has become the Persian *kehribar*[999]. In the following century Amber came through the South sea trade (*infra* §274).

We may be sure that many additions will have to be made to these preliminary lists by subsequent researches. For instance alum shale or *fan-sheh*, now an article of export, was then imported in the Middle Kingdom[1000], through *Wu-tu*[1001], a district of S.W. Kansuh established in 111 B.C. in view of commanding the route there from the West.

NOTES——

986) Cf. for instance the ignorance of Herodotus, Ctesias and others, on history and accurate notions.

987) At Babylon, chiefly in the great temple E-sag-gil.—The latest cuneiform tablet at present known was dated in the 5th year of Pacorus, *King of Persia*, i.e. 55-56 A.D., as shown in my monograph on *L' Ere des Arsacides en 248 av. J. C. selon les Inscriptions Cuneiformes*, 1891, p. 32-35.

988) *Supra*, § 235-237, notes 926, 933, 934, 937-939.—It cannot be a coincidence that at this very moment when Greek influence was penetrating into their land that the Chinese should have felt the necessity of reforming their calendar. In 104 B.C. the reform was made according to views of their own with the help of foreign notions permitting a greater accuracy than before. Szema Tsien, the *Ta she ling* or Great Astrologer, in his *She ki*, built up from relics of Antiquity a system of astrological calendar which was not put into use. Cf. on this calendar, *Le Calendrier des Yn*, by E. Chavannes; J. A., Nov. Dec. 1890, p. 463-510.—The *T'ai tch'u* calendar established in 104 was based upon an alleged relation between the measure of time and musical proportions on a scale of 81 divisions. Cf. *Tsien Han shu* : kiv. xxi.

989) For instance HAN Wu-Ti, in 138 B.C. collected in the park of *Shang-lin* near the capital Tchang-ngan, all the plants and fruits which could be gathered from all parts of the Empire, numbering 3000, (cf. *san fu hwang tu*, iv, 1 v) not all different. The poet and statesman Szema Siang-ju who was present at the opening of the park, described it in a poem, some parts of which have been preserved by Szema Tsien,

She Ki, kiv. 117, fol. 5 sq.; numerous names mentioned there, when identified, cannot fail to be highly interesting.
990) Cf. *supra*, § 242.—For all these names and identifications, cf. E. Bretschneider, *On the study and value of Chinese botanical works*, p. 15; *Botanicum Sinicum*, ii, 29, 35 3.—Also *Pên tsao kang muh*; *Han shu*; *Poh w th tchi*; *Tai ping yü lan*, 996, 3, *r.*—The *hu* there denotes the bearded populations of the west.
991) The small garlic had been introduced by the Early Chinese civilisers. Cf. *infra*.
992) This *hu ma* or sesamum which was known by that name to Hwainan-tze who died 122 B.C., was first eaten by one Lu-an-sheng in the Tchang-lo palace of Tchang-an. Cf. *San fu hwang tu*, iii, 7 *v*. and ii, 2; T.P.Y.L., 989, 5 *r.*—On the earlier introduction of Sesamum, cf. *supra* § 203; for the identification of *hu-ma* with the older *Ku-sheng* cf. the *Wu she pên tsao* : T.P., *l.c.*
993) Cf. my note on *The Pomegranate from Persia to China*, 116 B.C. in B.&O.R., vi, 239-240. The fruit was coming then from *Tu-lim*, for *Turira*, one of the two satrapies which the Arsacidæ had wrested from Eucratides (*Strabo*, XI, ii, 2).—The pomegranates of Khodjend were famous in the middle ages as shown in E. Bretschneider, *Mediæv. Res.*, i, 19-20, but the Chinese sources of the 1st cent. do not mention it amongst the products of Ferghana and suggest therefore that it was not yet cultivated there.
994) *King-tsing* (12500-7698 Bas.) or Essence of fright, also called *tchen-ling-wan* or marvellous pills for awe, *fan-sheng hiang* or returning-life spice, *kioh-se* hiang or rej cting-death spice.—The name of the island, mod. *Tsü-kuh*, 8365-7312 Bas., anc. *Tsü-kwet*, may be that of Socotra. The identification of this spice thus carried through the sea and continent would be interesting.—On a use of that drug under HAN Wu-ti, therefore in 87 B.C. his last year, cf. T.P. 981, 3.
995) *Shih tchou ki.*—T.P.Y.L., 983, 7.
996) *Supra*, § 240.
997) Wang tze nien, *Shih y ki*.—Shen-yoh, *Sung shu*,=T.P.Y.L., 808, 1-2.—The amber in pieces was mounted into a golden pillow for Li Kuan, the favorite concubine of the Emperor. *Ibid.*
998) *Tsien Han shu*, 9 i, Si yü tchuan, Art. *Ke-pin*.—In the *Si yü tchu kwoh tchi*, of A.D. 400, we hear of a fable connecting amber with burnt wasps' nets of the Sandy bank of the river of *Mu-lu* or Merv. This river is the Murgab. (Cf. T. P. Y. L. 808, 2). Does this not refer to the ants, flies and other insects often found embedded into it which show that it belongs to late tertiary age.—The amber trade from the north-sea and Baltic shores began early as shown by the beads of *Baltic amber* found at Mycenæ (cf. *Schliemann's Excavations* by Dr. C. Schuchhardt, p. 196).—Amber, according to Perrot-Chipiez has been found everywere in Italy, doubtfully in Sardinia, and not in Egypt, Assyria, Syria nor Cyprus. *(Cf. Hist. Art Ant.* i, 840; ii, 768-9: iii, º54-5; iv, 108,. Cf. also D'Arbois de Jubainville, *Les Premiers habitants de l' Europe*, 1889, p. 090-2.= O. Schrader, *Zur Bernsteinfrage* : Naturwiss. Beitr. z. Geogr. n. Kulturgesch. Dresden, 1888, p. 177, sq.—Kirwan, *Les Conifères*, ii, 25 ; V. Fonınel, *Vieux Neuf*, iii, 668.—Prof. Clifford Allbutt has lately lectured on *The trade in Amber in Ancient times* : Cambridge-Antiquarian

Society, May 17, 1893. It seems that Amber was found also in other places. Ctesias in 400 B.C. spoke of amber found near a river Hypobarus in India, which is a corrupt information, as no amber has ever been found in India (E. Bunbury, *Hist. Anc. Geogr.*, vol. i.) It refers probably to the Red Amber of the Nicobars, where its abundance has made it an object of trade since an unknown date (cf. Rashideddin (1300) and Barbossa (1510), in Yule-Burnell, *Gloss. Anglo-Indian*, p. 478. Cf. also *Hypobarus* with *Barusæ*, name of the Nicobars in Ptolemy.—A Chinese itinerary of the Ming period speaks of Amber in Oman, (cf. E. Bretschneider, *Chinese intercourse with the countries of C. and W. Asia in the 15th cent.*, Part ii, 1877), and the statement has been confirmed by the recent discoveries of large quantities of Amber in that region. Perhaps it was also alluded to in Pliny, 37, 39 when he speaks of the amber of *Carmaniæ* (Kerman, East South of the Persian Gulf, not Germaniæ). Dr. A. B. Meyer. *Wurde Bernstein von Hinterindien nach dem Westen exportirt?* Dresden, Isis, 1893, who has collected there besides the passages of Ctesias and Pliny alluded to here, some other statements from ancient Authors, thinks that they refer to the amber of Burma. But we cannot accept this suggestion, because Burmese amber was not known at that time.—Cf. besides: K. G. Jacob: *Neue Beitrage zum Studium des Kasp sch-baltischen Handels in Mittle-alter*, I. *Neue Studium; den Bernstein im Orient betreffend*: Z.D.M.G., xliii., 353-87.—W. Fischer, *Der Weg des steinzeitlichen Bernstein-Handels*: Globus, ix., 268f., 1891.—L. Wilser, *Bernstein und Bronze in den Urzeit*, 1892 Globus, lxi., 184-6.—O. Schneider, *Nochmals zur Bernsteinfrage*, 1891 : Z.D.M.G., xlv., 239-44.—P. Orsi. *Ueber prahistorischen Bernstein aus Sicilien*, 1892: Z. f. Ethnol., xxiii,, 690 f.
999) Cf. F. Hirth. *Roman Orient*, p. 245.
1000) The alum-shale, *Fan-shih* or trellis-stone, also called *yü nieh* or feather-mud, is mentioned in the *Pen-Ts'ao*, 100 B.C. as coming from the West of the Ho, and in the *Fan tze ki jan* of our era as imported through *Wu-tu*. Later on it came through S.W. Kansuh (Lung-ti).— It is only in the 5th cent. that we hear of alum found in China, at Kien-ping (mod. Wu-shan in N.E. Szetchuen) according to the *King tchou ki* by Tcheng Hung-tchi. Cf. *T.P.Y.L.* 988, 4.—Fourteen localities of alum are mentioned in Pumpelly's list. The great importation of alum is now from China. Edw. Balfour, *Cyclop. Ind.* i, 84.— The source of the imported *Fan shih* is not stated. Let us remark that the famous *Peh shan*, near Kutcha produces alum.
1001) *Wu-tu*, was 80 *li* W. of pres. Tcheng. in Kiai-tchou near the borders of Tibet, on the frontiers of Kansuh and Szetchuen. Its position was important as commanding the routes. *Supra* n. 919.

Sect. D. *Foreign Sea-trade and Official opening of the South.*

a) *South-East and South.*

249. The *Hwang-tchi* or yellow fingered sea-traders of Hormuz continued to frequent the non-Chinese coasts of South China until the conquest of the latter and their reduction in Chinese provinces, 111 B.C. As was

the case for the previous centuries, there is generally the same absence of Records, but the imported objects are historical witnesses of the Indo-Persian trade with the Non-Chinese states of the South which was then going on, and of the arrival of other competitors in the field as we shall see further on.[1002]

250. On the South-East the states of *Tung-hai* in Tchehkiang and of *Min-yueh* in Fuhkien had acknowledged the Suzerainty of the First Chinese Emperor. In 192, the first of the two, faithful to the Han dynasty saw its name changed into *Tung-ngou*, and in 138 its population removed into Anhwei. The *Min-yueh*, on the contrary was submitted to the Empire of *Nan-yueh* from 179 to 138 b.c.; it was then rebaptized *Tung-yueh*, and finally conquered in 110 b.c. by the Chinese, who however did not occupy it and left it vacant, i.e. in the hands of the natives, after having removed all the chiefs and leaders.

251. On the South was the Empire of NAN-YUEH, founded in 204 b.c. by Tchao-t'o a rebel general of She Hwang-ti.[1003] Having assumed authority over the territory corresponding to the modern provinces of Kwang-tung and Kwang-si,[1004] he proclaimed himself Martial king of Nan-yueh, a title which was acknowledged by the Chinese in 195 when Luh-kia was sent for that purpose on Mission to him,[1005] In 179 having extended his dominion over the *Min-yueh* in the East, and in the West over the Kingdom of *Ngou-Lo*,[1006] he assumed the Imperial dignity, which however was never admitted by the Chinese in their dealings with him. The *Ngou-lo* was the present Tung-king and part of Annam. Tchao-t'o died in 137 and 26 years later under his 4th successor, his empire was conquered and annexed by the Chinese who divided it into nine provinces.

On the west stood the Kingdom of Tsen in Yunnan commanding the Shan-Burmese trade route, which must be reserved for later paragraphs (272 ff.).

It was necessary to notice these general circumstances to appreciate more easily the following importations which occurred at that time before the Chinese conquest, and thus save a repetition of the facts.

252. *Sugar-of-palm* was heard of in China before the Sugar of Cane. A fabled entry in the *Shan Hai hing*, concerning the *Puh-se Min* or Immortals (i.e. the Richis who eat the Soma or drug immortality[1007]) tells us that the sweet tree is their food. It was part of the tales told by the Erythræan sea traders.[1008] Kü-yuen in the *Li-sao* (314 b.c.) speaks of the *tche-tsiang*, or sweet-of-tree, which is understood as a refer-

ence to the same sort of Sugar, then introduced in the Ts'u kingdom.

Sugar-o j-Cane, called in Chinese *Shek-mih* or Stone honey was not heard of before the beginning of the Empire. A doubtful tradition says that the Hindu Sramanas of Shantung[1009] were supplied with some *shek*-honey for their own wants. A more satisfactory statement is that Wu-tchu,[1010] king of *Min-yueh*, whose capital city was at Tung-yeh (pres. Fuhtchou of Fuhkien) sent to Kao-tsu, founder of the HAN dynasty, therefore within the years 201-195 B.C., two *huh* measures of *shek-mih* or Sugar.[1071] It was reknown to dissipate the bad effects of intoxication. The next importation took place by the central route of the West, as about 100 B.C., *shek-y*, also sugar-of-cane, was to be found at *Wu-tu*[1012] of S.W. Kansuh). In the two names, the sound *shek* is prominent and represents undoubtedly the Sanskrit name *Sarkara* of the article. India was for long the sole sugar producing country,[1013] Sugar-cane which is not indigenous in Indo-China,[1014] was only introduced there afterwards,[1015] and in China, near Canton, not before 28) A.D., from Cambodja.[1016]

253. Another trade of older standing with the same mariners was that of big pearls from the Persian Gulf.[1017] One Tchu-tchung, in 187-140 B.C. was trading in pearls at Kwei-ki.[1018] A pearl of three inches was worth 500 *kin* of gold, of four inches 700 *kin* of gold. About 156 B.C. the same merchant had several tens of pearls of three inches.[1019]

254. The rising of the *Nan-yueh* kingdom attracted the foreign trade to the region of present Canton as shown by the following instances of Indo-Persian articles.

Jasmine, Chinese *ye-si-ming*, from the Persian *yâsemin* was found in Nan-yueh by Luh-kia, the Chinese envoy to Tchao-t'o in 195 B.C. He reported that the *ye-si-ming* and the *mo-li*, both fragrant plants had been introduced by bearded foreigners (*hu jen*) of the West, and adopted there because the local grains had no taste and the flowers no fragrance.[1020] *Mo-li*, from the Tamil *Mallai* is the Jasminum S a m b a c.[1021]

255. In 179 B.C. the King of Nan-yueh sent to the Chinese Emperors, as presents[1022] : a pair of *pih*, or round rank-token, of white gem, 1000 kingfishers. ten horns (of rhinoceros), 500 purple cowries, a case of cassia grub,[1023], 40 pairs of living kingfishers, and two pairs of peacocks. The last article is interesting. It is one of the first appearances of these much vaunted birds exported by Indian trade since the days of Salomon.[1024] The length of the journey and lack of comfort at sea on the smaller ships of older times had probably prevented their successful

importation as far as China with any regularity[1025].

256. The next western products were corals and henna. *Corals*, which appeared c. 140 B.C.[102 6]or before, indicate a new source of sea-trade, if not the appearance of new sea-traders. Tchao-t'o, king of Nan-yueh (d. in 137 B.C.) sent to Han Wu-ti for the *Tsih tsao* pond of the *Shang-lin* park, inaugurated in 138 B.C., four hundred and sixty-two stalks of coral, *shan-hu*, which were arranged into a large tree, 12 spans high, having one stern and three branches. This coral was of the red sort as shown by the name given to it by Tchao-t'o[10:7], and therefore must have come from the Mediterranæan, the only sea where true red coral, *corallium rubrum*, is found[1028]. This name *jung-ho* (litt. beacon-fire tree, *shu*) reminds us of the Hind. *Manga*, while the other name, *sham hu*, transmitted from its native country is probably a corruption of a Semitic word connected with the hebrew *ramuth*. We learn therefore from these names that the coral in question was carried by the Red Sea trade to one of the emporia of the Indian coast and from there to China. The circumstance is interesting as a forerunner of the arrival of the Red Sea traders themselves, if it does not indicate it as an actual fact.

257. *Henna*, the *Lawsonia alba*, in Chinese the finger nail flower, *tchi-kia hwi* (probably from the Skr. *sakachera*), was brought by bearded foreigners (said by a later source to be from the *Tats'in Kwoh*) who planted it in *Nan-hai*[1029] (South of Kwangtung and Kwangsi), perhaps at the same time as corals or more likely some time afterwards.[1030] It is spoken only because of its fragrance, although the name is suggestive enough of its use by the foreigners, and the fact of its plantation is interesting, since it was the plant of the *Hwang-tchi* or Yellow fingers of Hormuzia.

258. In 127 B.C.[1031] some fragrant plants *shen-tsing*, also called *tsuan-mu* (from an original word connected with the Arab *sumbul*)[1032], were brought from the country of *Po-dji*[1033] (in N.W. Sumatra). This I take to be N a r d. The event suggests some remarks. The necessarily frequent stations of the mariners in the Sunda isles for revictualling on their route to Chinese lands led gradually to the establishment of regular stations, which in some cases developed into small colonies. It may be that this place was one of them which had temporarily acquired some importance.

NOTES—
10"2) Cf. below par. 256.
1003) Cf. Mayers, *Chinese R.M.*, 727, 234, 50.

1004) *T'u sui*, the first general sent in 220 by She Hwang-ti to conquer the South was killed in 218 in fighting not far from Canton. His successor *Jen Hiao* was successful and conquered in 21b the regions of *Kwei-lin*, *Nan-hai* and *Siang-kiun*, corresponding to the provinces of Kwangtung a id Kwangsi, but not beyond as sometimes stated by unaware writers. *Jen Hiao* died in 209 and advised Tchaot'o to make himself independent, which he did the same year.

1005) *She Ki*, 113, 2 r.

1006) Ibid. fol. 3. 3 r.—Tchao-t'o declared himself having extended his authority eastwards as stated, and in the west as far as the *Ngou-Lo state*. The denominations in the historical geography *Hoang viet dia du chi* of Annam, show that the two provinces of *Nan-hai* and *Siang* were extended in a somewhat curious, though intelligible manner. The *Nan-hai* extended from Kwangtung along the sea-coast over the delta of Tungking. The *Siang kiun* which comprehended the savage and unruly parts, extended, south of Kwei-lin or North Kwangsi, through the centre of the province westwards around the *Nan-hai kiun* and southwards of the delta as far as the present Nghê-an province.—The *Ngou-lo kwoh* had been founded in the middle of the third cent. among the *Lo-yueh* at Ki kien (near pres. Si-ngan in S.W. Kwangsi) by a son of a former King of Shuh (destroyed in 316) who assumed the title of An-yang wang. He figures in the Annam history as the second dynasty called *Thuc*, and the house of Tchao-t'o, as the third dynasty called *Trieu*.

1007) Cf. par. 122, notes 455-458, 475.

1008) *Shan Hai king*, xv, 2 v., Tung-hai tchi wai.—The statement is an amplification of another entry, kiv. vi, 3, Hai wai nan king, which says that this people of black colour live and never die. The Comm. says that the shrub of immortality grew on the Yuen-kiu (one of the Fairy islands).

1009) *Supra*, par. 227.

1010) *Wu-tchu* received in 201 B.C. his investiture from the HAN Emperor who died in 195 B.C.—On Wu-tchu, cf. Szema Tsien, *She-ki*, 114, 1 r.—The *huh* or *huk* was a measure of three *t'ou* or pecks.— For the event, cf. Liu Hin, *Si king tsa ki*, of our era ; T.P.Y.L., 988, 5 r.—On *Min-yueh*, supra par. 201.

1011) Szema Siang-ju, *Lo-ho*.—E. Bretschneider, *Study and Value*, p. 46.—Sugar was known to Pliny only as a medicinal drug.

1012) *Pen tsao king*.—T.P. ibid.—On *Wu tu*, supr. n. 1004.—We must also mention the *fu-tze* (cf. *bish*, in Beng. Hind.) or Aconitum introduced there at that time. Cf. *Fan tze ki jan* ; T.P. 990, 1 r. ; and note 722 *add*.

1013) Nearchos and Megasthenes have spoken of the Sugar-cane of India. History speaks of the Ikshvâkns, the sons of the Sugar-cane or of the sweet flag (skr. *ikshu*), one o whom Ikshvâku Virudhaka Ancient king of Pôtala, was reckoned as an ancestor of Sakyâmuni. Cf. Rig-Veda, x, 60.—Zimmer, *Attindische Leben*, p. 130.—J. Eitel, *Skr. Chin. dict.*, s.v.

1014) Dr. C. Thorel, naturalist of the *Voyage d' Exploration en Indo-Chine*, 1866-8, states it most possitively, vol. II, p. 428: " Nulle part nous n'avons trouvé la canne-à-suore croissant à l'état spontané en Indo-Chine."

1015) It was only in 252 A.D., that some cakes made of Sugar-cane were received from Tongking, and that Chinese geographies mention Sugar-cane, there. Cf. *Kiang piao tch'uan*: *Wu luh ti li tchi*: *Nan tchou y wuh tch*ı : *Nan jang ts'ao muh tchuang*: T.P.Y.L., 874, 4-5 r.
1016) At Ho-yuen, near Canton. Cf. *Wu she pen ts'ao*; T.P.Y.L., 988, 5 r.
1017) *Supra*, par. 203.—The pearls of Ceylon were small. Cf. below n. 1112.
1018) Where a Market had been established two centuries previously, cf. par. 198.
1019) Cf. *Lieh sien tch'uan* by Liu-Hiang, B.C. 80-9.—T.P.Y.L., 803, 6.
1020) Lah Kia. *Han Yueh heng ki*; *Nan jang ts'ao muh tchuang* : W. F. Mayers, *Henna and the Jasmine in China*: N. and Q., Hongkong, 1868, ii., 33.—Lah Kia's biography in *She Ki*, 97, 6-9.
1021) No explanation had been made yet of *Mo-li*.
1022) Cf. with the list of presents sent by the king of Min-yueh in 312 B.C. *Supra*, par. 202.
1223) The comm. explains that on cassia trees one finds some grubs *hoh-tchung* (cl. 142-4018—9589 Bas.) which feed of cassia and are not bitter; soaking them one gets some edible honey, cf. *Ku wen shih y sin vien*, v, 42.—I suspect the *ko-tchung* (10377-9589 Bas.) of the Yung-tchang trade were the same grubs.
1024) In Chinese *Fung tsiok*, (B..s 2061-11882). We may probably in *Kung* find a p onetic imita-o (of -*l'hin*, in *Sikhin*, the Skr. name of the bird.—Some western people p · ented some *Kung-tsiok*, litt. great sparrows, in Tchou Tcheng Wang's reign (*Tchou shu*).—*Kop-hen* country produces peacock, (*Han sh.u*).—The South Barbarian country of *Tsen* (Yr man fu) produces peacocks (*Suh Han Shu*)—The country of Tiao-tch'i near the Western Ocean produces peacocks and lions. (*Suh Han Shu*: Tchang P'an, *Han ki*). Cf. T.P.Y.L. 924, 4-5.—On the introduction of pe cocks from India in Babylonia, cf. the *Ja aku Bureu*, tr. T. W. Rhys Davis : B.&O.R., iv. 7-9.
1025) Peacocks are mentioned in the Eleg es of *Tsu*. c. 300 B.C. cf. T.P.Y.L., 924, 6.—*Supra*, par. 210.
1026) Coral was spoken of and described by Szema Siang-ju, in his *Shang lin ju*, cf. *Khang hi tze tien*, s.v., 96, 5, f. 12 : and T.P., 807, 5.
1027) *Sa.i ju hwang lu*, iv., 6 r. The story says that Tchao-t'o in sending t' em said that they were *Fung-ho* (i.e. beacon) trees, bright and sh.ning even at nigh .—The same text is given in Liu-hin, *Si King tsa ki* of our era. Cf. T.P.Y.L., 807-4.
1028) Coral fishery was carried on in the Red Sea in later times to the knowledge of the Chinese, as shown by the notice of the *Siu T'ang shu*, kiv. 221. Cf. F. Hirth, *China and Roman Orient*, 59, 76, 246. Dr. E. Bretschneider, *Mediæv. Res.*, i., 151, quoting the old *T'ang shu*, kiv. 258 b, thinks that it refers to the Mediterranean fisheries, but the text of the *Siu T'ang shu* does not permit this interpretation.—The *Hou Han shu*, kiv. 88, and the *Wei-lioh*, mention coral as a product of Tatsin.
1029) Cf. *supra*, par. 206.—F. Hirth, *China*, p. 268-9.— A. de Candolle, *Origin of Cultivated Plants*, p. 138.—*Henna in China*, by Cantoniensis, W.F. Mayers, H.T. Hance, E.C. Taintor, Thomas Sampson, in the N. and Q. of Hong-kong, 1867-68.
1030) *Henna* was not brought to the Chinese capital before 111 B.C., i.e.

after the conquest. Should Tchao-t'o have had any specimens of it about 140 B.C., he would certainly have sent some with the corals.
1031) Cf. *Tung ming ki* by Kwou-tze Hêng, a contemporary—T.P.Y. L.. 983, 7*c*.
1032) Cf. Edw. Balfour, *Cyclop. Ind.*, iii.. 719, 765.
1033) *Po-t'hi*, 4924-7018, or 4924-Cl. 56 Bas.—(*Pulo*) *Perjah* or *Putjah* is the indigenous name of a part of Sumatra. Cf. R. D. Verbeck, *Sumatra, sa Géologie et ses mines d'or* : Annal. Extrem. Orient., i, 186. H. Cordier, *Odoric de Pordenone*, 1891, p. 154. A.H. Keane, *Ethnolog. app.* in A.R. Wallace, *Australasia*, p. 653, gives *Pertya*. The name in question is perhaps related to that of the *Pasei* kingdom, on which cf. H. Yule, *Marco Polo*, ii., 270-7.

Chap. VII.—Sixth Period : 221 b.c.—a.d. 220.

Sect. D. *b) Changes and Competition in the Sea trade.*

259. A great change occurred about that time with the western Sea traders frequenting the Chinese seas. The progressive advance of the Chinese power over the land had gradually driven them away from the emporia of their selection. Let us remark that they always chose, for their trading stations, places on the sea-coast at proximity of the Chinese, but not within the Chinese dominion. What their object was is clear enough. They wanted to be enabled to trade easily with the Chinese centres, without loosing their own independance, and running the risks of seizure of their goods or extra mulcts and taxes. At first when the Chinese were ettled chiefly around the basin of the Hwang-ho, the

greater part of the remainder of the country being uncivilised and wild, they established their settlements on the South side of the Shantung peninsula, in the Gulf of Kiao-tchou, which they frequented during three centuries (c. 675-375 B.C.). When the civil wars and the advance o the Ts'ı-Chinese drove them away from *Lang-ya* and *Tsihmoh*, they went to *Kwei-ki*, near pres. Ning-po, and to the entrance of the Min river, near Fuhtchou. The first was given up when the Han Empire extended its sway there in 201 B.C., and the second when internecine wars (140-110 B.C.) disturbed the country. They shifted their quarters to the Annamese coast and the S.W. of Hainan, trading with the Nan-yueh, near the present Pakhoi leading to the Hêng shan market[1034].

260. The Indo-Persians of Hormuz and the Sabæans of the Arabian coast, hitherto hand-in-hand, ceased to be alone to share the spoils of the Chinese trade. New competitors had come with the Tatsin traders of the Red Sea who had began to appear[1035]. At this juncture the older traders established stations and marts at all the points of vantage. The emporium of *Kattigara* was founded on the southern borders of the Nan-yueh (in pres. Ha-tinh, S.E, of Nghê-an province[10 6]); and *Hwang-tchi* mariners acquainted with the pearl-fisheries of the Persian gulf and of Ceylon, discovered pearls on the W. coast of Hainan and created the pearl-fisheries of *Tchu-yai*, litt. the Coast of Pearls[1037], (pres. Yai tchou). The Chinese conquest of 111 B.C. made amongst others, special districts for both; the latter under the precited name, and the other under that of *Nhit-nam* or South of the Sun, probably because of its position as the southernmost point of their dominion. As in the previous circumstances of a similar character the Erythræans shifted away once more their central quarters from the Chinese possible supervision. They settled *west* of Cape Cambodia, East side of the gulf of the Siam, in *Tcham*, the *Zabaı* of Ptolemy, *Tchu-po* of the Chinese, and *Sanf* of the Arabs[1038]. It was there that the merchantmen from O m a n landed with his companions the Hindu *Kun-tien* who founded the Cambodjan kingdom[1039]. Known to the Chinese as the *Funam*, or P h n o m kingdom it absorbed the old *Tcham* and remained for several centuries the great centre of foreign trade east and west[1040]. We cannot therefore be surprised that when Alexander trading agent of Maës Titianus went to Kattigara about 100 A.D., nearly all the geographical names he met with were Hindu names[1041].

261. *Hêng shan* remained for centuries the principal market for exotic goods imported by foreign merchantmen.[1042] It was situated, east (not

west) of Nan-ning in S.W. Kwangsi, on the Yü Kiang leading by the Pearl river to Canton. The nearest sea shore for landing goods was near the present Pakhoi, and it was there that the merchantmen used to come after or not a landing at *Nhit-nam* (Kattigara). It was called *Hop-pu* or Estuary of Meeting, which became the name of the district in 111 B.C. These circumstances are interesting to remember, as they explain much of subsequent history. Canton did not begin to be an arrival port for foreign trade before 159 A.D.,[1043] and then only yet as a secondary station, the first being always *Nhitnam*.

Notes——
1034) On this important market place of old, cf. par. 261.
1035) About 140 and 136 B.C. *Supra* par. 256-7. On *Tatsin* as *Tarshish*, cf. *infra* par. 263.
· 1036) At the time of the conquest by Tchao-t'o, in 179 B.C. the region was still wild and not separately mentioned. In 111 B.C. it became *Nhit-nam*. When after 40 years severance from the Chinese dominion, 186-226 A.D., the court of Wu at Nanking reestablished Chinese authority over the country, and gave fresh administrative denominations, that province received the name of *Kotik* (*Kotak, Kuuduk*) which shows a close connection with the Hindu name. Cf. *Fung yü tchi*: T.P.Y,L., 172, 11 *v.*—*Hoang viet dia du chi* (Annamese), ii, 31 *v.*— Dr. F. Hir*h, *Zur Geschichte des Antiken Orienthandels*, Berlin, 1889, p. 19, has justly pointed out the connection of that name with that of Kattigara. The notes 329 and 331 must be amended and completed by the statements here, as Kesho-Hanoi was not the place.
1037) The *Yen tieh lun* of 86-63 B.C. mentions irregular pearls coming from there through the Kwei-lin district. Cf. *T.P.Y.L.*, 803, 4 *v.*— In A.D. 87 a pearl of three inches, and in 103. one of five inches came through the *Yü lin* district. Cf. *Ku kin tchu* by Tsui Pao of 350 A.D. Cf. *T.P.Y.L.* 803, 5.—The latter may not have come from the Hainan fisheries as the market of *Héng shun* (cf. par. 261) seems to be the place referred to.—Grosier, *Chine*, i, 201, mentions oyster-pearls on the coasts of Hainan.—The *Han shu* says that at *T'chu-yai*, the habits and customs were like those of the *Hwang-tchi*, cf. *T.P.Y.L.*, 785, 2 *v.*—Pearl fisheries stopped since as not productive existed in the xvth century on the coasts of the Kwang-tung province, prefectures of Lien-tchou and Ley-tchou. Cf. Dr. J. Macgowan, *Pearls and Pearl making* : Shanghai almanack, 1855 ; and W. F. Mayers, *Ancient Pearl Fisheries in the province of Kwang-tung* : N. and G. on China and Japan, 1867, i, 1-2.—The Chinese possess particular skill in drilling holes into the pearls, (China, Port Catalogues at Exhibition of Vienna, 1873, p. 427). They may have learned it from the Pearl traders of Hormuz who were celebrated for their ability under that respect, and to whom Ceylonese pearls were sent for that purpose.
1038) *Tchu-po*. 4046-4924 Bas., which was not Burma as unwarrantedly stated by some, was a name very little used by the Chinese, because that of Funam overshadowed it altogether. For the identification of

Zabai with the later *Sanf* and their geographical position, cf. H. Yule, *Sea-route to China*, p. 9.

1039) This interesting fact, yet unnoticed, is reported in the *Funam tu suh tchuan* of Kang-tai, 3rd cent. cf. T.P.Y.L., 787, 4.—*Kun-Tien* represents the two names *Kumé* and *Thong* of this founder in the *Chronique des Anciens Rois du Cambodge*, trad. et. comm. by E. Aymonnier, in *Cochinchine Française, Excursions et Reconnaissances*, 1880, p. 149.

1040) On the expedition of Kangtai, cf. below par. 233.

1041) Quoted in Marinus Tyrius whose work was made use of by Ptolemy. Col. H. Yule was the first to notice the fact in his *Sources and Authorities* for India in W. Smith's *Atlas of Ancient Geography*, 1874, p. 22-4; *Oldest sea-route to China*, 1882, p. 11.—Dr. Schlichter, *The African and Asiatic coasts of the Indian Ocean in Antiquity*, 1891, gives no new information on this subject, but he places Kattigara in Borneo, overlooking the old Chinese evidence on the subject.

1042) It is mentioned in these terms by the *Nan she* in 347 A.D.—The Chinese officials of Kiao-tchou and Jih-nan used to levy from 20 to 30 per cent on these goods, and the kings of Tchampa (Lam-ap) were then desirous to extend their own frontier north to that market.—M. Archibald Colquhoun has visited the place in his journey *Across Chrysé*, 1883, i. 126 sq.—It was spoken of as an important mart as late as the 12th century in the *Kwei hai yü heng tchi* by Fan shi hu.—Its present name is Hwang or Hung tchou.

1043) Cf. below § 265.

262. In 109-108 B.C., corals were brought for sale to the market of *Hêng-shan* :[1044]the *Tatsin* men presented a *hwa-ti niu* (flower-hoof-bull)[1045] and shewed how to make use of the leaves of the *Mulan*[1046](magnolia obovata, *Roxb.*) This is apparently the third recorded appearance in China seas of the traders from the Red Sea. There may have been some more in the interval, and some traces of them will perhaps be disclosed by further researches. But it is the first time that their name appears connected with the event in so early a source; as the authority, so far as their name is concerned in the preceding cases, is later in date, and therefore may have been completed from some knowledge acquired in later years.

263. Much has been written about the origin of that name of *Tatsin*, which became that by which the Roman Empire and specially the Roman Orient was known to the Chinese, but no satisfactory explanation has been given as yet. The ground is clearer now than it was in previous investigations on the matter, and much of the dimness has disappeared [1047]. Let us remark that the name cannot mean Great Ts'in, or Greater Ts'in, because there is no Lesser Ts'in, and that *Ta* great is never used by the Chinese in foreign names but for that distinctive purpose; therefore Tats'in must be taken as a whole. When the Symbol *Ts'in* represented the names of the N.W. State of the Chinese agglomeration and

of the Empire in the 3rd century B.C. it was still read *Tan, Ten*. But in the first century a wave of phonetic changes had come over the land by the supremacy of the Honan dialect for court dialect by the Han dynasty, and the older sound *Ten* had become *tjen, tsen, tsin*. At present it is *tch'in*[1048].

Now recent researches[1049] have shown that the centre of the *Tats'in* traders arriving then into China was the Red sea and that their emporium was Rekem, (later Petra)[1050] near the old sea port of Eziongaber, in the Ailatha gulf, from where Hiram and Salomon, Jehoshaphat and Ahaziah[1051] with more or less success, had started their Tarshish navy. As an emporium it began to grow as an independent state after that Tyr had been taken and more or less ruined five times successively, by Alexander and the Ptolemies (from 332 to 287 B.C.) and that some of her sea merchants had sought for other quarters for their enterprise. It continued to develop nothwithstanding the emporia built by the Ptolemies on the N.W. side of the Red Sea to attract the old Phœnician traders and their commerce, and lost its independance by the hands of the Romans only in 137 A.D.[1052]. The sea-going trade ships of Rekem-Ailana were Tarshish ships, or ships like those once going to Tarshish, and we think that the Chinese *Tats'in* represents simply *Tarshish*[1053], which they have easily mistaken for a name of country. This solution fits well enough with the conclusions arrived at on other grounds. The Tarshish ships that went to China in 140, 127, 109, 73 B.C.[1054] were not Greek, still less Roman; they belonged to the independent trade of Rekem-Ailana, plying in concurrence with the Greeks, with all the boldness and experience of their elders, the Phœnician Mariners, and their first importation in China was that of Red corals from the Mediterranean (cf.

§ 256).

264! Greco-Romans from Egypt were trading with India in the first century, but it was by mesaventure that one of them reached Ceylon about 41 A.D.[1055], and apparently as a consequence that about 47 A.D., Hippalus of Alexandria was the first Greek navigator who availed himself of the monsoon winds[1056]. About 85 A.D., they did not as yet go beyond the South of India according to the evidence of the *Periplus*[1057]. The first quarter of the second century saw the Greco-Romans, then masters of the Tarshish-Tatsin navy in relation with South Burmah[1058], and probably not as far east as Kattigara. The latter probability results from the report of Alexander trading agent of Maes Titianus, who seems to have gone no further than Burma and have heard of the further journey from Hindu Mariners. We do not know of any Chinese evidence in favour of an arrival of Greco-Romans at that time in any part of China.

265. In 166 A.D. the famous Roman mission alleged to have been sent by Marcus Aurelius Antoninus (*An-tun* in Chinese) was really the first direct arrival of Romans in the Flowery Land.[1059] It has been suggested that this was only a private expedition of traders who availed themselves of the name of their Emperor as a commendation.[1060] The circumstances of the case justify this view. The Parthian war begun in 162 had interrupted the silk trade which used to be carried inland, and commercial interest into a trade producing a profit of ten and hundredfold per cent, was a powerful inducement for merchants to make by themselves an attempt to open a direct intercourse. The object of the mission required that they should be well received, and in order to secure the good will of the Emperor and officials, according to the long-established practice of foreigners, they offered ivory, rhinoceros horns and tortoise shells all articles of Annam and neighbouring trade, which they must have procured at Kattigara, and which we should understand as choiced articles and not as staple goods. The result was a beginning and the continuation afterwards of an intercourse which recorded in general terms in the Anuals, is not mentioned again, but in exceptional cases[1061]. For instance in 226 A.D. a Roman merchant who had come to the court of Wu at Nanking, was entrusted with 20 Negrito Pygmies[1062] to bring home with him, but the scheme fell through; and in 284 an important arrival of Roman merchants which took place at Canton, offered 30000 rolls of aloes paper which paper appears to have been then manufactured in Aunam, or perhaps in Funam[1063].

NOTES——
1044) Cf. *Shuh y ki*: T.P.Y.L., 807, 4 v. The text says in *Yü-lin kiun*, where the market was.

1045) The *hwa-ti niu* is described as six feet high, swift and powerful, with a long wagging tail and four-branched horns. Sent to the capital it was employed to draw cart-loads of bronze and stone for the *Wang sien* gallery (then in construction at Tchang-'an); the prints of its hoofs on the stony-road were like flowers, whence the soubriquet given to it. Cf. the *Tung ming ki* by Kwoh-tze Heng of our era: T.P.Y.L. 900, 1 v.; 958, 6-7. This text is often corrupted in quotations as in the case translated by M. E. H. Parker. *China Review*, xix, 191.

1046) *Tung ming ki*, ibid.—The juice was used in dyeing a black colour, Cf. Kwoh-Poh, &c. in E. Bretschneider, *Botan. Sin.*, ii, 18.—It is undoubtedly that use which was shown by the merchants in question.

1047) In *The Chinese name of the Roman Empire*: Acad. Oct. 1, '81:

we had suggested that *Tatan* was for *Dadan* a name of Syria. But since *Tatsin* does not appear early enough to have been yet *Tatan*, and that it refers to the upper Red sea and not to Syria, the suggestion is untenable.

1048) Herewith the list of the reading of Ts'in in the various dialect s. Pekinese *tch'in*, Shanghai *dzing*, Ningpo *dzing*, Wentchou *zang*, Futchou *ching*, Amoy *chin*, Hakka *ts'in*, Canton *ts'un*, Korean *chin*, Japanese *shin*, Annam *ten* ; in the dictionaries of M. H. A. Giles and of Dr. S. W. Williams.

1049) By Prof. F. Hirth, in his *China and the Roman Orient*, frequently quoted in our pages.

1050) Cf. on Petra, *Mount Seir, Sinai anp Palestine*, 1884, and *The Rock-hewn Capital of Idumæa*, by Prof. Hull : Victoria Institute, May 2, 87.

1051) I, *Reg.* x, 22.—II, *Par.* ix, 21 ; xx, 36.

1052) On the history of Rekem and the facts alluded to here, cf. *Erathosthen* ap. Strabo, xvi, 4, 2, 21.—*Agatharchid.* 87.— *Diod. Sic.*, iii, 42.—*Dion. Cassius.* lxviii, 14.—*Ammian. Marcell.* xiv, 8, 13.—Also E. Bunbury, *Hist. Anc. Geogr.*, i, 647 ; ii, 59, 160, 167. 321.— G Rawlinson, *Phœnicia*, 225-7.

1053) On the meaning of Tarshish ships ; cf. Ign. Guidi, *Geographia Antica dell' Arabia* : Bull. Soc. Geogr. Ital. 1872. vii, 501 sq.—A. H. Sayce, *The Races of the Old Testament*, p. 47.—The Tats'in men were those who make Tarshish, i.e. who trade on ships like these which were going to Tarshish. The Tats'in men were looked upon as *Hai lao* or sea hunters as showed by a quotation of the *Ts'eh fu yüan kwei* (F. Hirth, *O.C.* 22).

1054) The entry of 78 B.C. here rests on a statement of the *Liang Shu*, 54, 1. that envoys with presents came to Nhitnam, from Tats'in and India during the reign of Han Suan ti, 73-49 B.C. cf. Groeneveldt, *Malacca*, 3.

1055) Cf. below § 275.

1056) Cf. *Pliny*, vi, 23 : 104—*Peripl.* 57.—E. Bunbury, *Hist. Anc, Geogr.*, ii, 351, 445, 470.

1057) E. Bunbury, *O.C.*. ii, 472-5.

1058) Cf. the statement of the jugglers sent by a Shan King in 120 A.D.

1059) The Chinese sources are most precise on this point.

1060) F. Hirth, *China and Roman Orient*, 175.

1061) W. Williams, *Middle Kingdom*, ii, 409, quoting the Annals of Canton says that in the reign of Hwan-ti, 147-168 A.D., Tien-tchu (or better Tsen-tuh), Tatsin and other nations came by sea with tribute, and from this time trade was carried on at Canton wich foreigners.

1062) Negrito-Pygmies were part of the native population of China, and were known since the days of Yao. Cf. T. de L., *The Negrito-Pygmies of Ancient China* : B.&O.R., v, 169, 203, sq.

1063) Cf. *Ling piao luh yh* ; *Nan yueh tchi* : T.P.Y.L., 982, 4.—The first work mentions the fabrication of aloes paper.

266. After the conquest of Nan-yueh the Chinese Emperor Han Wu-ti established in the Imperial park of the capital (*Yü siäh yuen* at Tchang-'an) the *Fu-ti* gardens, where a large number of trees and plants were brought from the New provinces. In the following list which has been preserved in a description of the Metropole,[1064] thirteen names are given with the number of roots in each case: *tch'ang pu*, or sweet flag, Acorus calamus;—*Shan Kiang*, or Indian shot, Canna indica;—*Kan-tsiao* or Banana tree;—*Liu-kiu tze* or Quisqualis indica;—*Kwei*, or Cinnamon Cassia;—*Mih hiang* or Agila wood;—*Tchi-Kiah hwa*, or Finger-nail flower, Henna;—*Lung-yen*, or Nephelium longan;—*Li-tchi*, or Nephelium Litchi;—*Pin-lang*, or Areca Catechu;—*Kan-lan*, or Canarium;—*Tsien-sing tze*, or Thousand years;—and the *Kan-yü*, or Sweet Orange tree.[1065] We are told that notwithstanding fresh plants sent again from Kiao-tchi, the plantations could not be kept up, and that most of them became dry and died.

Besides its botanical interest, the above list discloses old foreign importations in Nan-yueh in addition to those we have noticed. The *Tch'ang-pu*[1066] and *Kan-tsias*[1067] denote by their names that they were introduced by the traders of India; the *shan-kiang* and the *liu-kiu tze* were likewise imported from the Indian continent.[1068]

267. Soon afterwards we hear again that the *Hwang-tchi* (of Hormuzia) whose country lay at 30000 *li* from Hop-pu and Nhitnam, presented a large quantity of bright pearls[1069], some coloured glass[1070], curious stones and strange objects, such as a large round pearl, perfectly spherical[1071]. The coloured glass which appears here for the first time, was then manufactured in Kabulistan, which as we have had already occasion to notice had frequent relations with Hormuzia. Han Wu Ti was so pleased with the glass that he wanted some more and sent a special envoy by sea to purchase a quantity of the article. The name of the emporium which the envoy must have visited is not recorded, but we may assume that it was Zabaj[1072]. In A.D. 2, some *Hwang-tchis* presented living rhinoceroses[1073].

268. The name of *Hwang-tchi*, in its acceptation of yellow fingers for the West-Orientals who used to dye their fingers with Henna, was then too vague a term, as several races of yellow fingers were then trading with China by sea. It became necessary to distinguish among them and several names began then to appear.

Commercial missions from *Tzen-tu*, commonly T'ien-tchu[1074], for Sindu or India, are said to have arrived in China after 73 B.C. by the port of Nhitnam[1075] (or Kattigara) and after 89 A.D.[1076]; again in 159 A.D. by Nhitnam and Canton[1077]. It was the first arrival in the latter place[1078]. These dates are not without interest as it is in 75 B.C. that the Kalingas, the famous sea-traders of India S.E. are reputed to have established settlements in Java[1079]. And during the last portion of the 2nd century, the King of Saurashtra Mandala was sending ships with cargoes to Mahácina, Cina and Bhota[1080]. It is most interesting to find another name of ships arriving in China was that of *Oman*, a maritime state, consisting almost chiefly of ships, in the Sea of Persia, 30000 *li* distant. They frequented the ports of Funam, and they imported into China ebony wood[1081].

NOTES——
1064) *San fu hwang-tu* of c. 200 A.D., ed. 1784, kiv. iii., fol. 8.—Ten *Shan kiang*, twelve *Kan-tsiao*, ten *Liu-kiu tze*, and a hundred of each of the others, save the *Mih-hiang*, of which the number is not given. — Cf. suprà, note 989. on a former collection made by HAN WU TI.
1065) For these identifications, cf. E. Bretschneider, *Study and Value*, pass., and *Botanicum Sinicum*, vol. I.——On *Kan-tsiao* and its probable Sanskrit etymology, cf. my note *On Eastern names of the Banana*: B. & O.R., July, 1890, p. 176.
1066) Cf. *Tch'ang pu* from Tamil vassambu, Maylayal, vashambu. It is said to be not indigenous in India, but an importation from northern lands. Cf. Edward Balfour, *Cyclop. Ind.* sub verb. This etymology and the introduction of the plant about that time dispose of the rendering of *Tso tchuen*, V., xxx., 7 in J. Legge, *Chin. Class.*, v., 217, and of the assimilations of native scholars in E. Bretschneider, *Botan. Sinic.*, ii., 376.
1067) *Kan-siao*, anc. K a n t h a, from Sanskr. K a d a l a, was known by Szema Siang-ju, i.e., prior to 126 B.C., in S. Szetchuen. cf. below, par.
1068) *Han shu*: T.P.Y.L., 785, 2 r.
1069) *Ming yueh*, of the Persian gulf, cf. par. 203, 253, note 771.
1070) Coloured glass. *liu-li* for *pih-liu-li*; cf. Hind. *balur*, Arab. *ballur*, &c. T. de L., *On the Ancient history of glass and coal in China*: T'oung Pao, 1891; F. Hirth, *China*, 228-232.—It was known as a product of *Ke-pin* in the reports on that country, *Tsien Han Shu*, 96; A. Wylie, *Western Regions*, 16. And it was from there that the travelling merchants came who taught the process in China about 435 A.D.
1071) The text says that this pearl was so perfectly round, that once placed on a plain surface, it could not be still for a whole day.
1072) *Han shu*: Ti li tchi.—T.P. 80 ?. 8 v.—And *supra* 260.
1073) *Hou Han shu*, 116.—They used also to import *shui-ts'ing* or Rock Crystal. Cf. T.P.Y.L., 826, 6.
1074) *Tien-tchu* is a misreading of modern Scholars. *T'ien*, h e a v e n was *Tsen* during the Han dynasty. It is rightly given in Giles' Dictionary p.xv as the probable reading about 100 B.C. when the Chinese Princess sent as a wife to the Kun-mi of the Wusuns who introduced the *pi-pa* in China was lamenting her unhappy fate in a song which

has been preserved to the present day.

1075) *Liang shu*, 54, 1. Cf. supra note 912 on an introduction of Buddhist Books in 2 B.C.; and par. 233.

1076) *Hou Han shu*.—Pauthier, *Examen Methodique*, p. 266.—The place of arrival in this case is not mentioned. It may have been inland.

1077) An Shi-kao, a Buddhist Missionary from Parthia who had arrived in China by the North in 149 A.D., went before 170 A.D. to Canton to see other Missionaries, but he was killed there by the people. Cf. S. Beal, *Buddhist Literature*, 7; Bunyu Nanjio, *Tripitaka*, 381.

1078) *Hou Han shu*: Hüan-ti tchuan.—W. Williams, *Middl Kingdom*, ii, 409.—Subsequent arrivals are noticed in 357, 428, 477, 502, 504, 507, 508, 515, 571, 641, &c. The gap between 159 and 357 is rather remarkable.

1079) Cf. Ed. Balfour, *Cyclop. Ind.*, ii, 481.

1080) Cf. A. Weber, Ueber das *Çatrunjaya Mahatmyam*; Abh. D.M.G. 1858, i, 4, p. 43; L. Rodatsek, *Emporia*, p. 111.

1081) Modern *O-wen*, crow-ornament.—Cf. Ts'ui Pao, *Ku kin tchu*.— Kang-tai, *Funam tu suh tchuan*.—T.P.Y.L. 961, 9 v.; 787, 4.

CHAP. VII.—SIXTH PERIOD : 221 B.C.—A.D. 220.
Sect. D.   c) *South-West*.

269. The report of Tchangkien in 126 B.C. on his first mission in Turkestan gave to HAN Wu-ti a high opinion of the wealth of Bactria, Parthia, and Ferghana,[1034] and "the importance of securing their attachment to the Middle Kingdom, *whose territory would thus be expanded* 10,000 *li*, embracing people of every custom, and requiring a nine-fold staff of interpreters ; while the prestige of the Empire would be all-pervading from sea to sea."[1083] It showed moreover that the route by the Kiang, or border tribes of Tibet, being dangerous because of their enmity, and the North route cut by the Hiungnus, it would be safer to start through Szetchuen and India to reach Bactria, since goods from Shuh arrived there in that direction. The Emperor was transported with delight, and after several unsuccessful missions in four directions, acting on their reports, he sent Tchang-kien himself in 122 to open the route through the Kingdom of *Tsen* in Yunnan.[1] [84] The haughty answer and refusal of the latter's king stopped for a time Chinese enterprise towards the South West. After the conquest of the *Nan-yueh*, fresh attempts were made, and the *Tsen* kingdom acknowledged the Chinese suzerainty, but any route further in the S.W. towards India remained impassable through the Kunmings or Kunmis occupying the West of Yunnan. We have alluded to these various events in previous pages.[1085]

270. The Kun-mings who thus occupied such an important position with reference to intercommunications with the South-West, deserve a special notice. They became the chief population in the west portion of the

Tesn Kingdom of Yunnan in whose king had been compelled to come to terms with them.¹ ⁶⁶ They were immigrants from the North who had come to settle there in the first quarter of the 2nd century B.C. They had separated from the main body of the Wusuns or Kunmis people, a fair haired and blue eyed race, when the latter were driven away from their quarters near Tun-hwang (in N.W. Kansuh) by the Yueh-ti, and fled southwards,[1087] while the main body went N.W. of the Hiungnus.[1088] We shall hear again of this red haired people in a curious circumstance hitherto unintelligible (see below 278).

271. The policy of the Chinese government, which had extended its dominion in Szetchuen West and South-East since 130 B.C., was to advance towards the South-West in every available occasion[1089]. In 111 B.C. a serious progress was made towards the South and West, and four new administrative districts were created, all about the limits of present Szetchuen province, *as the commencement of a conterminous chain, intended to extend onward to Bactria*[1090]. Although precarious and temporary as shown by subsequent history, this authority was all that was possible for the time being. The successful conquest of *Nan-yueh*, in that same year permitted a farther advance. The King of *Tsen* in 110 B.C. was induced to received investiture from the Chinese Emperor, whose suzerainty the year after was recognized by the Red-haired Kun-mis. "After this envoys were again sent, but to the end they never succeeded in opening up a passage[1091]."

272. The military expedition of the TSEN kingdom towards Old Pagan on the Iwawaddy about 280 B.C., had undoubtedly facilitated commercial intercourse with the Hindu mercantile colonies of Pegu. It was through this route that had come the bearded travelling merchant, who before the foundation of the Empire[1092], arrived in S.W. Hunan carrying some valuable spices such as *ngai-nap* or mint-palm?, and *mi-sung*, a sort of Narcotic[1093]. When Sema-Siang-ju, about 130 was superintending Chinese affairs in the South-West of present Szetchuen, he became acquainted with c o c o a-n u t s, (imported by traders), and made them known to his countrymen[1094].

273. Some Indian paper seems to have been carried over to China through that route, before 12 B.C. We know from Nearchus that Hindus used some c o t t o n w e l l b e a t e n t o g e t h e r to write upon[1095]. Now the biography of Tchao Hwang-hou, Empress of HAN Hao Tcheng-Ti, says[1096] that she had some paper called *hak-tai*, (a foreign name variously written) which is described as a sort of small paper made of s p r e a d

and pounded grass-fibres. The description is therefore similar to that of Nearchus. In the absence of cotton a similar article was imitated in China with *siä* or silk refuse[1097], but this was only an intermediary stage and in 105 B.C. the Marquess Tsaï-lun started the manufacture of papers made of *Broussonetia papyrifera*, and of rags[1098].

274. HAN SUAN-TI, who reigned in 73–49 B.C., is reported to have received from India, a precious mirror, large as a coin of the 8 *tchu* type[1099], and fixed into a box made of Amber. The jewel in question had been brought by a route passing through the district of Fan-kiun (pres. Sin Fan, S.E. of Tcheng-tu). It was lost or stolen at the death of the Emperor[1100]. These minutiæ of history in the absence of general statements are interesting because of the information, otherwise unknown, which they procure on Ancient intercourse.

Many other articles will have to be added to the list of that trade with the progress of research, as it could not fail to have had some importance. Certain political events which occurred in the first century appear to have been caused by the desire of cutting this profitable route. South of the State of TSEN, some native tribes happened to settle on the tract of this commercial route, and derived advantage from the merchants in levying taxes on their goods.

275. Singhalese traders,[1101] finding probably that the overcharges made that route too expensive, and desirous to avoid them, took a more western route sometime about the Christian era. Starting from *Hippuri* (of Pliny, in Taprobane[1102]), N.E. along the Indian coast, up to *Desarênê* or Orissa, they struck across the bay to *Sada* in *Argyrê* or Arakan,[1103] then by the long famed Aeng pass, the Irawady and Shwêli rivers, eastwards across the Lu-kiang or Salwen river, they arrived on the banks of the Lan-tsan kiang or Upper Mekong river, where the barter took place.[1104] Pliny tells us that the Singhalese Rachias, who about 47 A.D., had been sent on embassy to Rome, after the journey by sea misadventure of a Roman agent of Annius Plocamus to Ceylon, said that his father used to go and trade, on the banks of a river, beyond the *Hemodii* mountains (i.e. the Himalayas, and here their spurs the Burmese Yoma) with the SERES men of high stature with red hair and blue eyes.[1105] In them we can easily recognize the Red-haired Kun-mis. Subjects of the Chinese Empire since 108 B.C., they could boast of being themselves SERES, the name by which they had known the Chinese since the time of their Northern habitat. We find thus explained the two difficulties hitherto unsolved about red-haired Chinese, and the northern name of Seres which occurred in the

South on that single occasion.[1106]

276. The Singhalese trade by the western route we have just described was undoubtedly successful, and detrimental to the former route more south, as it soon raised the envy of the *Ai-lao* tribes. In 69 A.D. some of them advanced as far as *Yao* (in pres. Tsu-hiung, Yunnan E.) head station of the west route, which they occupied, thus cutting off any outside communication with the Kun-mis otherwise than through them, and tendered their submission to the Chinese Empire. The event was hailed with the greatest satisfaction by the Chinese, and a new government called *Yung-tchang*, or Ever-prosperous, was intended to be the head-land of all South-west intercourse. It extended from the west of the present Tsu-hiung-fu to the banks of the Lan-tsang kiang, and Northwards over the present territories of Ta-li and Li-kiang between the pre-cited river and the Kin-sha kiang. Eight years later (i.e. 77 A.D.) an insurrection which arose among the Ai-lao was quelled by the Kun-mis on behalf of the Chinese government. The country was in a frequent state of quasi rebellion, and the authority of the Han dynasty was well respected there but by frequent interference of military forces.

277. The *Yung-tchang* trade was looked upon with great interest, and not a few allusions were made to it in the historical literature. Some lists of the staple articles of that trade have been preserved. In the Annals of the Eastern Han dynasty,[1109] at the opening in 69 A.D., it consisted of copper, iron, lead, tin,[1110] gold and silver,[1111] of bright pearls,[1112] amber,[1113] crystal, vitreous ware,[1114] Ko-tchung grubs,[1115] oyster-pearls, peacocks, kingfishers, rhinoceros, elephants, apes, and tapirs, all products from Shan-Burma, Malacca, Ceylon, India, Kabulistan, &c., but not as yet from the Red Sea.

Some time afterwards the *Kiu-yuen*[1116] used to arrive once a year at the Yung-tchang mart, with tin, iron, chicken tongues,[1117] parrots of red, white and other colours, according to a notice of the same date.[1118] A later document enumerates the goods which used to be carried from the country of the *Kun-lun*[1119], 81 days journey from the Si-er-ho (an affluent of the Lan-tsang Kiang near Ta-li fu), as elephants, fragrant *tsing-muh* (aristolochia), fragrant sandal wood (*tchan-tan*), fragrant red sandal, *pin-lang* (*Areca Catechu*), vitreous ware, crystal, *li-pei* or shell-cups and rhinoceros-horns[1120].

In the year 97 A.D., a *Shan* king, Yung-yu tiao entered into relations with China, and in 120, conjurors presented by him to the Emperor said that they were Tatsin men, communications existing then with *Tat-*

in by the South-west of the Shan states[1121].

278. We owe more than a passing reference to the *Clove*, in Chinese *Ki-shet*, or chicken-tongue which was for the first time spoken of at the court of Han Hwan-ti (147-167 A.D.) as a wonderful product of nature, according to Yng-shao, a scholar of some eminence for that time.[1122]. It was then a novelty. In the west at the time of the Periplus of the Erythraean Sea (c. 63-75 A.D.) it was still unknown, and Pliny (d. 79 A.D.) in his description from hear-say does not distinguish it from its congener the nutmeg. The sumptuary laws of 176-180 show that it was then well known. The Chinese heard from the Report of Kang-hai who had been sent on a scientific mission to Camboja (280-343 A.D.) that the chicken-tongue fragrant were imported from the *Ma-ngu tchou*[1123] or five islands *Ma*, i.e. the Moluccas[1124], east of Java, which is an accurate fact, as the five islets west of Gilolo are the original *Malukas* and the native country of the Clove. It is rather curious that this spice should not have been introduced in China by the Southern Coasts and should have first reached the Middle Kingdom by the Shan-Burmese Route.

279. An event of no mean importance for the introduction of western notions in China was the arrival, about 72 A.D.[1125], of seventy families of Jews who settled between Lü shan (Ya-tchou fu, Szetchuen W.) and Tcheng-tu. One of their inscriptions at Kai-feng fu tells us that they came from India[1126], i.e. through India by the trade route from Bactria to Szetchuen. Only five families, still preserving their Jewish features, have survived to the present day, but their old faith has gone[1127]. The influence of these 3 or 400 people of an energetic and insinuating race must have been much more important than it has been customary to suppose. They were doubtlessly full of their own lore and of the notions of western civilisation of the time, which they cannot help having spread around them[1128].

Notes ——
1082) I thus write for convenience the Chinese *Ta-hia*, *Ansih*, and *Toyuan*.
1083) Such are the exact terms of Tchang kien's report in Szema Tsien, *She ki*, 123, Gr. It was therefore an idea of conquest which was prominent at first in the Chinese mind.—All these details and the following are given in the biography of Tchang-kien by Szema Tsien.
1084) Cf. *Li tai Ti Wang nien piao*.
1085) On these various circumstances, cf. *supr.*, p. 60-63; but the date of 123 for the return of Tchang kien must be corrected into 126, and his own mission in 122 added to the recit.—Envoys to the South were severally sent on two occasions, 126-122 and 111 B.C.—Cf. also my

articles, *Tin-güt not India*: Acad. May 2, and *India from China*. ibid. Sept. 5, 1885.

1086) The Chinese were still in ignorance that routes through Yunnan were too meridional and did not lead to India but to Indo-China.

1087) In the *Tang shu*, their northern origin is fully stated, as well as their original friendship with the Hiungnus. Cf. T.P.Y.L., 791, 12. — This gives a contenance to the traditional claim of the Karengs of Burma, that they came originally from the North, beyond the Flowing Sands, and after a stay near the present Ya tchou, Szetchuen W., came south and settled near Taungu. Cf. MacMahon, *The Karens*, 113 ; Spearman, *British Burma Gazetteer*, i, 163 : T. de L., *Languages of China before the Chinese*, 147-8.

1088) Cf. *Tsien Han shu*, lxi, Biography of Tchang kien ; A. Wylie, *Western Regions*, 4º.—In 176 B.C. the Shen-yu of the Hiungnus said in his despatch to the Chinese Emperor that Lowlan (Labran), Wusun, and other states had submitted to him. Cf. *Tsien Han Shu*, kiv. 94; A. Wylie, *Heungnoo*, 415.

1089) It was in that year that the administrative provinces of *Kien-wei* and *Yai-lang* in the S.E., and of *Kiung* and *Tsok* on the borders West had been established.—Szema-siang ju was the statesman who acted in the circumstance, and we know that he was interes ed in western products.—On trad· of native articles by the traders of Shuh, cf. Szema Tsien, *She ki*, 116, 2-3.

1090) Cf. *Li tai Ti Wang nien piao*.--The underlined sentence comes from the *Ts'en Han shu*, kiv. lxi : A. Wylie, *Western Regions*, 51.

1091) Cf. *Tsien Han shu*, ibid.

1092) Cf. *supra* p. 56 ; note 282 must therefore be completed the present information.

1093) *Ngai-nap*, 8818-7759 Bas., unidentified, but said to come through *Pao* or *Pegu*, *Ni-sung*, 11038-11048 Bas., also unidentified and said to come from the Western Ocean. Cf. T.P.Y.L. 982, 3 r., 6-7.— In the notice of Tatsin in the *Wei-lioh*, these two spices are mentioned ; unhappily in the text reprinted in Dr. Hirth, *China and the Roman Orient*, p. 113, they appear as *mi-mi-tou-nah*, instead of *mi-sung, ngai-nah*.

1094) Cf. T. de L., *Le Coco du Roi de Yueh* (Oriental Congress of 1892) p. 903. On Szema-Siang-ju, cf. note 1089.— These articles as shown by their Chinese names did not come there by the Annam route. Cf. note 1047.

1095) Cf. Strabo, xv, 67.—·Also, Max Müller. *On the introduction of writing in India* : Hist. Anc. Sanskr. Lit., 1859, p. 515.

1096) *Tsien Han shu*, kiv. 97 (2).—Comm. of Yng-Shao, 2nd cent.— *Hak-tai*, mod. *heh-ti*, 10549 or 12719-10740 Bas., might be compared to the skr. *aktu*.

1097) Cf. Hii Shen, *Shwoh wan*, in 89-99 A.D.

1098) Cf. F. Hirth, *Die Erfindung des Papiers in China*, p. 1-14 ; T'oung Pao Archives, i, 1890.—J. Edkins, *On the Origin of paper making in China* : N, and Q., Hongkong, 1867, i, 67-8.—G. Pauthier, *Mémoires sur l' Antiquité*, ii, 395-404.

1099) The coins weighing 8 *tchu* were issued for the first time in 183 B.C. cf. my *Chinese Coins*, Early period, p. 342.

1100) Cf. *Si King tsu ki*, a Record of incidents at Teh'ang-an, by Lin-hin, of our era.—*T.P.Y.L.*, 717, 1 r. and 808, 1 r.
1101) The navy employed in that trade was probably that of the Kalingas.
1102) Identified with a port called *Kudremale*, the name of which has the same meaning, i.e. *horse-tails*, in Sanskrit.
1103) Cf. H. Yule, *Notes on the oldest Records of the Sea-route to China*, p. 4-5, and following note.
1104) It is rather remarkable that here we find again the old trade route followed by commercial missions since those of *Shou-mi* and *Nélé* (p. 38-40 and n. 196) at the time of Tcheu Tcheng Wang about 1079 B.C. and later. Eastwards of the Mekong it passed through *Ta-yao* or *Yao* district, which was occupied by the Ai-lao when they wanted to cut off the Sirghalese trade, as shown par. 276. Cf. also note 196.
1105) Cf. Pliny, vi., 22: 84, 86, 88, 89, 91.—Periplus, 60.—Reinand, *L'Empire Romain et l'Asie Orientale*, p. 325.—J. Edkins, *Allusions to China in Pliny's Natural History*, Peking, 1885, p. 10-12.—E. Rehatsek, *Emporia*, 119.
1106) Ptolemy's statements represent the Chinese as *Seres*, when reached by the long land route through Central Asia, and as *Sinae*, when reached by the sea-voyages. Cf H. Yule, *Notes*, p. 2. The circumstance of the fair-haired Kunmis, Chinese subjects, and intermediaries, explains the difficulty in Pliny's text.
1107) Cf. *Hou Han shu*, kiv. 116.—*Tang shu*.—T.P.Y.L., 786, 2.
1108) On the *Ai-lao*, cf. *Hou Han shu*, kiv. 116.—And on the legends of their origin, G. Deveria, *La Frontière Sino-Annamite*, 1886, p. 117, sq.—T. de L., *The Languages of China before the Chinese*, 1886, par. 99-102; edit. française, 1888, suppl., p. 153.
1109) The *T.P.Y.L.*, 786, 2, quotes the same list from the *Kiu tchou ki* of Ho-yen, 3rd cent.
1110) The great beds of tin ore of Malacca were probably not yet worked out, as we hear nothing about them. Kang-tai, in Cambodja, c. 240, A.D., heard of a *Peh-lu* district, South-east of *Tchu-po* or Java, producing tin, which was resold outside the country. Cf. T.P.Y.L., 786, 3r. As there is no tin-producing land S.E. of Java, and since the tin districts extend from Tavoy to Billiton, the statement shows that *Peh-lu* was heard of in Java by sea-traders travelling along the west coasts of Sumatra and eastwards to Java, properly the extreme east of Java; *Peh-lu* or *Pak-lu* could hardly be Perak, (whose tin has long been worked) because it is too far in the Malacca Straits, but it could be Junk-Ceylon or another of the Mergui islands.
1111) Extensive mines of silver exist on the East of the Irawaddy from the N.E. of Mandalay to the South of Yunnan. - Wan Tchen of the 3rd cent. in his *Nan tchou y wuh tchi*, says that the *Kin-lin* country, 2600 *li* from Funam (Cambodja) produces silver; the people there are fond of hunting, and ride on large elephants. Now *Kin-lin* was Kamlun, i.e. the *Kanran*, natives of Burma, who first settled near Prome. Cf. T.P.Y.L., 790, 9r, and 712, 5. - Spearman, *British Burma*, i., 238. —Ancient silver mines are said to have been found in the isle of Banca.
1112) *Kwang-tchu*, i.e. bright pearls, of Ceylon, different in name from the *Ming-gwet* pearls of the Persian Gulf (cf. par. 203, note 771 *supra*).

The *pang-tchu*, or oyster pearls, also from Ceylon.—Small fine pearls only were generally found there, the big ones occasionally found were bad. Cf. *Merveilles de l'Inde*, edit. Van der Lith et Devic, p. 179-180. —The *Periplus* mentions the pearl fishery, and the manufacture of stuffs ornamented with small seed pearls. Cf. Ptolemy, vii., 1. 10.— E. Bunbury, *Anc. Geogr.*, ii., 473. On the pearl-fishery of Ceylon, cf. Vincent, *Commerce and Navigation of the Ancients*, ii., 489-490. —E. Tennent, *Ceylon*, ii., 561.—H. Yule, *Marco Polo*, ii., 321, 359-361.—Cf. also on the better quality of the Pearls of the Persian Gulf, E. Reclus, *Asie Antérieure*, 861.

1113) Amber; we have already heard of it. *Supra*, § 248. note 998.
1114) On *liu-li*, or vitreous ware, *supra* note 1070.
1115) On Ko-tchung (grubs) *supra* note 1023.
1116) *Kiu-yuen*, 7272-1064 Bas. The archaic dialects in Giles' Dict. do not suggest any serious change in these sounds.
1117) Chicken-tongues, *K'i-shit*, or cloves, infra 278.
1118) *Wu shi wai kwoh tchuen* : T.P. 790, 10.
1119) Name of the Kokarit hills, Dana mountains and Poung-loung range, east of Tennasserim and Pegu. Cf. T. de L , *Formosa notes* par. 38.—The name has misled several scholars because of its similarity with the Kun-lun range of North Tibet.
1120) *Nan y tchi*.—T.P.Y.L., 789, 5 and 982, 2 r.
1121) *Hou Han shu*, 116.—T.P.Y.L., 791, 8 r.—Cf. *supra* note 282.
1122) Yng-Shao, author of the celebrated antiquarium treatise entitled *Fêng suh tung*, in his *Han-kwan-y*. Cf. T.P.Y.L., 981. 6 r.
1123) *Fu-nan tu suh tchuen* : T.P., 787, 3 r.—*Wu shi wai Kwoh tchuen*.—*Nan tchou y wuh tchi*.—According to the *Tsien yh ki tsuen*, an old western foreigner of an outer country explained that it comes from a tree of which the flowers become the chicken-tongues.—Cf. T.P., 981, 6-7.—Kang-tai had understood that they were small fruits, but the cloves are not the fruits, but the unexpanded flower-buds, and therefore the old foreigner was right.
1124) It is not impossible that the combination *Ma-ngu*, was an attempt at an imitation of *Maluka*, the name of the islands, while showing that they were five.—The proper Moluccas are the five islets on the west side of the large island of Gilolo : they constitute the native country of the clove, and are the celebrated islands which mainly prompted the European nations of the 15th century to the discovery of the new world, and of a navigation which made known to them a portion of the old one, equal to the new in extent. Cf. J. Crawfurd, *Descript. Dict. Indian islands*, p. 283.—In the 7th cent., the Moluccas are mentioned in Chinese descriptions as *Mi-li-kiä*, but it is not said that their ships were then going there as they did under the Ming dynasty. Cf. W. P. Groeneveldt. *Malay Archipelago*, p. 58, 117.
1125) The date is generally stated to be the Han period, reign of Ming-ti, 58-76 A.D.; but the year 72 was indicated by the first Jesuists who came in contact with them. It is not however well ascertained, and may have been some years earlier.
1126) Inscription of 1488. Cf. A. K. Glover. *The Tablet Inscriptions of the Chinese Jews discovered at Kai-fung fu* in 1 '5) : B.& O.R, v., 250.—In face of this positive statement it is curious to read in Grosier, *Chine*, 1819, iv. 490, resuming the reports of Missionaries : " Il paroît

par tout ce qu'on a pu tirer d'eux, que ce pays d'Occident (*Si-yü* d'où ils sont venus) est la Perse, et qu'il vinrent par le Khorassan et Samarkand ; ils conservent même encore dans leur langue plusieurs mots persans."

1127) A recent traveller, M. Armand, at Kaifung fu, where they settled since 1163 A.D. gives this information and says that on the site of their ancient temple, an inscription has been set up with the dates of construction and destruction.

1123) In my notice *On the Entrance of the Jews into China during the first century of our era* (B. & O. R. v., **131-4**), I have expressed my opinion that these Jews must have branched off from those settled in Babylon, Seleucia, and Ctesiphon, when the persecution which followed the mismanagement of their countrymen Asinai and Alinai compelled them to remove.—Cf. also H. Cordier, *Les Juifs en Chine* (L'Anthropologie, 1390, p. 547-51.

Sect. D.—*Foreign and Chinese Trading Navies.*

280. We have noticed in previous pages,[1129] that after some event which the vagueness and fabled character of the recit does not permit to ascertain, the Indo-Persian mariners had been compelled to shift their sea-route and give up passing through the Malacca Straits.[1130] The Sunda Straits being still unopened,[1131] they passed through some of the straits further east. The circumstance deserves some attention as it explains several historical problems. It permits us to understand how Ptolemy was misled in the extraordinary length he gave to the Malacca peninsula, and how it was he knew nothing of the Malacca Straits. It explains also how it happened that the Hindu colonists in Java settled at the farther east of the island instead of any nearer spot. It led to the discovery of clove and nutmeg, natives of the Moluccas and Banda Islands respectively. We know that the Indo-Persian mariners were passing through there and northwards in the second century B.C. as shown by their stories of Fire Islands and volcanic mountains, connected by them with the Asbestos legends,[1132] which mountains they were seeing near the Moluccas.[1133] They do not seem however to have discovered the clove and nutmeg at that time as the first intimation we have of these spices dates only of the first century of our era (see par. 278).

281. A descriptive work now lost was then written about the famous ships of people from the outer west, then trading in China Sea. A quotation from it in another work, also lost, of the third century, tells us that these ships were over 200 spans long, raising from 20 to 30 spans above the water; they carried 600 or 700 men, and their cargo filled 10,000 pecks.

The term *tchuen*, *shun*, Malay jung, whence the Portuguese and our *junk* was gradually applied chiefly to Chinese ships, and that of *bak* or *p'ak* was applied to the ocean going ships of foreigners who called them thus.[1135]

In a previous chapter we have had occasion to quote a Chinese description of the ships of Funam-Cambodja in the third century, on board which were transhipped Indian goods for China (note 482).

The Periple of the Erythrœan Sea enumerates five kinds of vessels engaged in the trade of the Hindus: *Madratæ*, stitched boats, like the Masula boats of Madras, and the smaller Patamar boats of Bombay; *Trappagæ* and *Kotymbæ*, long fishing boats and pilot boats at the mouths of rivers; *Sangaræ*, sea-boats or double-banked canoes, *i.e.*, the Jangars now used on the rivers of the Malabar coast like the Malay prahus; and the *Kolandiophantæ* or Bantings, ships of great size, which as well as the Sangaræ, were employed in the Chersonese trade.[1136]

282. The First HAN dynasty saw the birth of the Chinese navy; the south-east coasts, *i.e.*, those of Yueh or Tchehkiang S., and Fuhkien, were its birthplace. The skilfulness of their populations in the management of boats had long been known, and the Chinese conquest made their navy its own. We have had already occasion of speaking of their ships and of the peculiarities they derived from the Erythrœan merchantmen. In 138 B.C. the state of *Min-yueh* (*supr.* 201) had thrown over the yoke of the *Nan-yueh* Empire (*supr.* 251) and attacked in the same year their northern neighbours the *Tung-Ngou* (*supr.* 250), and in 135 B.C. the Nan-yueh itself. For these purposes they had gone into building themselves some pooped-junks (*lou-tchuen*).[1137] In 112 B.C. the king of *Tung-yueh*[1138] was able to send in his own pooped-junks 8,000 men from the present Fuhtchou to pres. Tchao-tchou (near Swatow, then Kieh-yang, in Kwang-tung East), but the unruly waves of the ocean partly disturbed his fleet, as his mariners were yet unexperienced. The year after the Chinese built some pooped-junks at Kü-tchang, near pres. Ningpo, in order to attack by sea[1139] and by land the Tung-yueh[1140] which was conquered and given up as told before.[1141] The pooped-junks built for war purposes were sea-going ships,[1142] and the Chinese Emperor was enabled to

send envoys by sea to get for him some glass from the emporium of the western traders.

288. In 41 A.D. the Chinese navy proved useful in the reconquest of Tunking (then *Kiao-tchi*) after the rebellion of Trung-trac, the Tungkinese Joan of Arc, and again in 226 A.D. when the Wu Kingdom with its capital at Nanking (then Kien-yeh), conquered Annam, independent since 186 A.D., down to *Autek*, or Kattigara.[1143] About 280 a maritime expedition, under the command of Kang-tai and of Tchu-yng, was sent to report upon the Funam (*i.e.* the country of the Phnom, or Cambodja),[1144] and other countries.[1145] The importance of this scientific mission as shown by the fragments which remain of its record cannot be overestimated for the history of those countries. Fifty years later, the WESTERN TSIN dynasty gave some impetus to the navy, and no less than ten different sorts of ships were exhibited in the ponds of the Imperial park. A large junk of 120 double-paces long was built, exceeding in its size and number of oars anything that had been made before.[1146] A boat with a south-pointing magnet[1147] was exhibited in 342 A.D. in the *ming ho tchi*, or pond of the cakling crane, at Lin-tchang (then *Yeh*, in Tchangtehfu, Honan), but this great invention remained for long a toy and nothing more; perhaps it was looked with contempt because the invention of a Tartar named Hinifei, for Shih-hu, fourth king of the small Tartar dynasty of the AFTER TCHAO, then ruling in North China (380-351 A.D.). At the beginning of the fifth century Chinese ships were not yet going as far as Java. Soon afterwards maritime enterprise developed and Chinese junks, about 450 A.D., were navigating as far as Ceylon and also as far as Hira, at the Head of the Persian Gulf.

NOTES.—

1129) Cf. *supra* par. 204, also 180, 198, and notes 474-5.

1180) In the primitive times of near coasting navigation it can be understood that they should at first have passed through the Malacca Straits; but in later times when the larger size of the ships permitted to have on board a greater supply of fresh water, and thus save many stations, a bolder course could often be taken, and land lost sight of for some time when required.

1181) The great eruption of 416 A.D., which according to the *Pristaka Raja* of Java, opened the Sunda Straits (sup. note 474) was apparently felt as far as Pegu, as the Burmese historians date the retreating of the ocean at Prome from a terrible earthquake which took place in the fifth century. Cf. E. Forchhammer, *Notes on the Early History of British Burmah*, ii. 8.

1132) *Suprà*, notes 761-2.

1133) Cf Tung Fang So, *Shen y King.—Shih tchou Ki.*—T P.Y.L. 820, 8; 868, 8; 869, 7.—*Shan Hai King.* xvi. 4, 5, and Kwoh-poh's comm.—*Wu luh ti li tchi.—Pao poh tze:* T.P., 786, 8.—*Hiuen tchung Ki.—Nan she.*—Kang tai, *Fu-nam tu süh tchuen.*—Wan Tchen, *Nan fang y wuh tchi:* T P. 787, 4 *v.*; 820, 10.—*The names of *Suh kiü* and *Ma-ngu* islands are mentioned with reference to these Fire Islands in the writers of the third century. *Ma-ngu*, i.e., the Moluccas and *Suh-kiü* which was the Fire Island. It is most probably *Sangir*, N. Celebes, which its recent eruption has made famous.—*Ho-ling*, or Java, was also referred to, as shown in note 762. ° Cf. also *Matouanlin*, tr. D'Hervey, ii. 449, 519.

1134) The *Wai yü jen ming tchuen* author unnamed, in Wan tchen, *Nan tchou y wuh tchi*, or Description of remarkable things of the South ; *T.P.Y.L.*, 769, 6.

1135) Cf. The *Bayla* of the west coast of India, unchanged since the days of Alexander. Cf. Ed. Balfour. *Cyclop. Ind.* i. 396.—Anc. Tamil *pakada*, Arab *markib*.

1136) Cf. T. Braddell, *The Ancient Trade of the Indian Archipelago*, Singapore, 1857, l.c.p. 143.—Ed. Balfour, *Cyclop. Ind.*, art. *Boats*.

1137) The *Yueh tsüeh shu* (cf. 150 A.D.) tells us that on the removal of the capital of *Yueh* to Lang-ya in 472 B.C. (*supr.* par. 174) *Mukoh*, i.e., the wood guest, brother of *Kou-tsien*, the king, commanded that 2800 soldiers should be sent there on *lou-tchuen*, or pooped junks. (T.P.Y L., 771, 2 v.) The soubriquet given to the leader and the names of the ships show that these belonged to the Erythræan navy then frequenting the coasts for commercial purposes. Cf. *lou* (137. 1944 or 4466 Bas.) and skr. *nau*, ship.—*Tchou*, was a small boat, and *tchuen* a larger one requiring five wooden boards. (Cf *Hou Wei Tong tu ki:* T. P., 770, 1.)—On 800 *tchou* sent from *Yueh* in 312 B.C. cf. par. 202.—Kung Tsung-tze made a great praise of the mariners of *Yueh* to the King of *Han*, a short time before the conquest of the latter by *T'sin* in 231 B C. Another praise was made by Yen-tsu in 134 B.C.—Cf. also n. 444, 477-482. The precited *Yueh tsüeh shu* contains a curious answer of *Tze-sü* to Hoh-lü, King of Wu, 514-495 B.C., on the arrangement at sea of a squadron comprising small and cargo boats, pooped-junks *Kiao*-junks and leader's junk. Cf. T. P. Y. L., 770, 1 *r*. On *Tze-sü*, or Wu-yun. Cf Mayers, *Chinese Readers' Manual*, 879. Also *Tso tchuen* xii, xi., 4.—The story looks like a later amplification.—Pleasure boats are mentioned for the first time at the same date. Duke *King* of Ts'i 517-489 B.C. is reputed to have made a pleasure boat called "Lotus leaf," which was manned by the "Dames du Palais." Before 484 B.C. Fu-tcha, King of Wu, had a boat called the "Green Dragon," on which he made a daily trip in an artificial pond called "The Celestial Pond," with the peerless beauty *Si-shi*. These are given as the earliest instances of the so called Flower Boats by Prof. G. Schlegel, *A Canton Flower Boat*, Intern. Arch. of Ethnogr., 1894.—Cf. *Koh tchi King yuen*, Kiv. 28, ibid. ; W. F Mayers, *Chinese Readers' Manual*, i., 139, 571. And also Jules Arènes, *La Chine familière et galante*, 1876.

1138) The Chinese interfered, and while Yen-ts'u, the general in command, was collecting boats at Kwei-ki, near pres. Ningpo, to attack Min-yueh, the latter withdrew their troops. And the Marquis Kung-wu, King of Tung-ngou (near pres. Wen-tchou of Tchehkiang, S.), was enabled to remove with 40,000 men and settle in Lü Kiang Kiun, w. of Lu-tchou in Anhwei W.—Cf. *She-ki*, 114, 2 v., and comm.

1139) Han Wu Ti in 119 B.C. had a pooped-junk of that pattern exhibited in a pond of the capital. Cf. Supr. par. 129, note 481.

1140) Or Eastern Yueh. A new title assumed by the brother, murderer of the King of Min-yueh, with Chinese approval.

1141) Cf. Szema Tsien, *She-ki*, 114, 3, 4.

1142) Cf. for a similar case in the Persian Gulf. *Supr.* 116.

1143) Cf. *Supra.* §§ 260, 261.

1144) *Phnom* is mountain in Cambodian. A high mountain near Chantabon was the landmark for mariners and slave dhows. Cf. Reinaud, *Relation des Voyages faits par les Arabes*, i. 18.—J. Crawfurd, *Journal of an Embasy to Siam*, 1880, ii. 206.—H. Yule, *Notes on the oldest records of the Sea-route to China*, 1882, p. 8.

1145) Cf. *Liang shu*, kiv. 54.—T. P. Y. L. 787, 3.—"They went to or heard from a hundred or more countries and made an account of them."—Kang-tai wrote a work on the native customs of Funam, *Funam tu suh Tchuen*; his companion wrote Historical Record of Funam, or *Funam ki*, and a description of the curious things of Funam, or *Funam yh wuh tchi*. Several works written in the third century contained many information derived from the same expedition, viz., a description of curious things of southern provinces, or *Nan tchon yh wuh tchi*, by Wan shen. Reports on foreign countries under the Wu period, or *Wu shi wai kwoh tchuen*. Only quotations from these works have been preserved.—The founder of Cambodia arrived there from India on board of an Omanite merchantman, about 50 B.C.

1146) *Tsin-shu.—Tsin Kung Ko ming.*—T. P. Y. L., 768, 3 v., 5 v., 769, 1 v.

1147) Cf. Excursus on *South-pointing Chariots and Maritime Compass* §§ 305-308.

CHAP. VIII.—EXCURSUS.

The Si Wang Mu and Muh Wang's Expedition to Turkestan in 986 B.C.

281. The name of *Si Wang Mu*, which means literally Royal Mother of the West, has been a peg for all sorts of fables and myths in the romantic school of Chinese literature. European writers have somewhat improved upon the Chinese under that respect, and some of the good Jesuits of the eighteenth century have seriously suggested that the Royal Mother of the West was no other than the Queen of Sheba! All this nonsense once discarded, it is undeniable that there is a substratum of truth concerning the personages so denominated in the course of Chinese history, and that the Si Wang Mus have played an important part in the ancient relations of China with the west.

285. A genuine queen may have been the person referred to when the name was written down for the first time, in the allusive mode of meaning and sound combination, proper to the Chinese scribes.[1148] And in the later ages, the presence of Queendoms in the north west and east parts of Tibet, which have survived in comparatively modern times,[1149] has helped to keep the popular notion that a *Si Wang-mu* had always a feminine character, and was only one immortal queen. There is however *nothing in any of the ancient texts on the subject to indicate that Si Wang-mu was a woman.*

286. According to tradition Yu-Nai Hwang-ti, leader of the Bak sings was presented by a *Si Wang-mu* with some white jade rings, archers' thimbles and topographical maps. This is probably an amplified view

of a circumstance that took take place when he was travelling eastwards through Turkestan to the Flowery Land. During Yao's reign Hou y, the famous archer, obtained from a *Si Wang-mu* some of their famous drug[1150] (against consumption). Under the reign of Shun a *Si Wang-mu* presented some rings of white jade. The great Yü also had some relations with a *Si Wang-mu*. SHANG Tai Mou sent Wang Mêng, c. 1588 B.C., with some presents to the *Si Wang-mu*, to get some of the valuable drug. In 986 B.C. Muh Wang of TCHOU started for his expedition in the west, during which he visited the *Si Wang-mu*, who in 984 came to the Chinese court.[1151]

287. The most important references to the Si Wang-mu are those which occur in the *Muh T''ien-tze tchuen*, a narrative concerning the journey we have just spoken of made in the west by Muh, the king, called Son of Heaven.[1152] This work had always been undervalued because of the wondrous amplifications of the Taoszeist writers on the subject. Stripped of a few exaggerations, the original relation has all the characters of a genuine work of very ancient date concerning the various journeys of Muh Wang, 1001-946 B.C., the fifth ruler of the TCHOU dynasty. Dr. J. Eitel who has published it in English, in 1889, tells us that he is convinced that the main portion of this narrative is of very ancient date, not long after the events it records, and I agree with him in the matter.

In the longest of these journeys, which alone lasted twelve months of travelling and four months of rest, Muh Wang went as far as Karashar, if not further west, and he paid a visit to the country of Si Wang-mu and to its sovereign.

NOTES—

1148) *Si, W e s t* is no part of the transcription of the name, and must be taken in its geographical sense. Cf. *Shan hai King*, xvi., 2 r.— On the mythological aspect of *Si Wang-mu*, cf. W. F. Mayers, *The Western King Mother:* Notes and Queries, Hong Kong, 1868, ii. p. 12-14, and his *Manual*, n. 572.—Cf. Also, *suprà* p. 82, and the references, n. 163-168, and add. 164.

1149) Cf. Note 164 and *add*.

1150) A fir balsam with asafœtida. Cf. below Note 1162.

1151) *Shuy yng t'u.—Kwa ti tu.—Bamboo Annals*. IV., ix., 26; vv., 15, 17.—*Tai ping yü lan*, 85, 2-3; 693, 5 r., 7 r.; 790, 4; 872, 12.

1152) On this title cf. *suprà*, Note 607.

288. We shall enumerate briefly the principal stations of his journey. On the 169th day of the narrative, Muh Wang bound for his west journey, crossed the Ho, or Yellow River.[1153] After 53 days travelling and several stations he stopped at the out-lying hills of the Kwen-lun (*i.e.*, the Nan-shan), in front of the river *Tchih* (Red, *i.e.*, the Hung-shui of Kansuh), where he saw the remains of a palace of Hwang-ti. On the 231st day, he started northwards and ascended the mount *Tchung*[1155] (*i,e.*, the north side of the Nan-shan), near which is a genial and pleasant place, which the kings of antiquity had called accordingly *Hiuen-pu*, or Sombre Garden[1156] (in the present Kan-tchou of Kansuh). A few days later he reached the country of the *Tch'ih-Wu* tribe, whose chief traced his descent back to the family of the Tchou dynasty. On the 244th day he crossed the *Yang* river,[1157] and the day after he arrived at the country of the *Ts'ao-nu* tribes, then marching northwards and turning round for two days towards the east, he reached the *Heh* (black) river[1158], which is called *Hung-lu* by the people of the western desert (*i.e.*, the Bulunghir river), and going northwards he followed the course of that river. On the 257th day he arrived at the mount of *Ki'un-yüh*[1159] (lit. mass of gem, near Turfan), which was guarded by the *Yung-shing* tribe. He obtained there three cart-loads of gem-slabs. Here was the place which the kings of former times called *Tch'ëh-fu*.[1160]

289. On the 261st day he marched northwards, passing through the country of another tribe (name lost) and arrived westward three days later to that of the *Ki-lü* or *I-lu* tribe near mount *T"ieh*,[1161] in Turfan. West of these, four days afterwards, he reached the country of the *Yn-han* tribe. On the 273rd he arrived near the *Hiuen tch'i*, or Sombre Lake, and near the *Loh tch'i*, or Delightful Lake, near which he planted bamboos, whence the after name of *Tchuh-lin*, or bamboo grove given to that spot. Continuing his route westwards he arrived six days later at *K'u shan*,[1162] which the people of the western desert call *Mou yuen*, *i.e.*, Luxuriant Gardens. Here it was that he tasted the *K'u* fruits. Advancing westwards he stayed overnight on the spur of the *Hwang shu*, or Yellow Rats Hills, and four days later, still more west he reached the *Si Wang-mu* people. He stayed there for six days in feasts and and receptions near the *Yao tch'i*, *i.e.*, Gemmy Lake and the *Yen* hills.[1163] On the 332nd day he settled on the banks of the *Juh* river, near which is a place where the birds shed their

feathers. On the 382nd day, after a sojourn of three months in *Kwang-yuen*, *i.e.*, the great plain, he turned eastwards on his return journey.

290. Ninety days' stay in *Kwang-yuen*, make Muh-Wang arrive there six days only after he had first reached the country of Si Wang-mu. It was therefore in the vicinity of the latter country. Several features reported in the narrative permit most probable identifications of the localities referred to in the last instances. Deducting seven days of rest on the route, Muh Wang had journeyed for 22 days from the Mass of Gems to the country of the Western Wang-mu. The remarkable heap of agate stones in question being situated between Pidjan and Turfan, is a landmark that cannot be mistaken. Muh Wang therefore should have gone further west between Karashar and Kutcha, where there is a level plain spoken of by Hiuen-Tsang[1104] which should be the *Kwang-yuen*, where he made his long sojourn. The sand rats, or yellow rats, which he met before, have been severally spoken of by travellers in Eastern Turkestan. They are frequently met with between Turfan and Khotan;[1105] and although the fact of their being spoken of in the narrative vouchsafes its genuineness and accuracy, it does not by itself indicate which spot between the two regions is referred to.

291. As to the place where the birds cast their feathers in such numbers that a hundred cars were laden with feathers alone, we do not find any such place spoken of in the scanty information we possess on this part of Eastern Turkestan, *i.e.*, between Karashar and Kutcha. One may have existed there, as in other parts of Turkestan, unless these so-called feathers should not be feathers at all, and be pampas grass which as we know is also found in central Asia;[1106] but we have not heard that any such feather-grass should have been found in the Tarym Valley. The most probable explanation is that the meaning of the text is more extensive geographically than could be supposed at first. The *Juh* river, anciently *Nuh*, and meaning literally "water defiled by mud," seems to apply to the *Khaidu-gol*, or River of Karashar, which deverses its waters in the *Bagaratch* Kul or lake from where under the name of *Khaidin-kwa*, or *Kontche-daria*, it flows into the great Tarym river.[1107] The latter disembogues or dies into the Lop-nor, just southwards of Karashar, and it is in the Lop-nor that

since remote times such a place is spoken of, where birds roost and moult.

292. The narrative is silent on what Muh Wang did or heard of during his three months near Karashar. Hunting would seem to have been his sole occupation. But having advanced so far as that into Turkestan, it would have been surprising that his expedition should not have learned or seen something from lands further in the west. This may have been the object of another recit which may have been lost, but from which scraps of information have been preserved in other works. For instance, we are told that Muh Wang received there a mirror or magnifying glass (*hwo t'si*) from the country of *Tsiñ-kiñ* (or Yarkand?)[1168] And from the narrative itself we learn that when coming back on the banks of the Black River, he instructed the people to fuse certain stones found there, so as to make with various sorts of objects for ornament.[1169] This looks much like a recently acquired knowledge of making some sort of glass and false gems.[1170] We may mention also as suggesting that Muh Wang, while in the great plain of Eastern Turkestan, had some relations with the farther west, the well-known legend that he married his daughter to the King of Persia, which Firdousi has reported. It may have had some slight foundation in the fact of an alliance of a daughter of Muh Wang with one of the princes of Khorasan. A circumstance interesting to remark is that at Herat (old Alexandria, Chinese *O-yk-shan-li*), when the notice about it was compiled during the First Han dynasty, it was reported that the elders there were acquainted with the Si Wang Mus and the Weak Waters (the emboguing waters of the Tarym river in the Lopnor lake) The interest of this lies in the fact that Herat was the arrival or departure place of the great trade route with China.[1171]

NOTES.—

1153) His advance-guard was under the command of Poh-yao throughout his march to the countries of the far west. He was a descendant of *Wu y* (5454-1808 Bas.), otherwise Ho-tsung, *i.e.*, the Venerable of the (Yellow) River, to whom Muh Wang offered two sacrifices. Cf. par. 11, 13-15, and 16 of the narrative. On Ho-tsung, or Ho Poh, cf. *suprà* note 895.

1154) On this river, cf. the authorities in Dutrueil de Rhins, *Asie Centrale*, p. 117. It is still at present called Red River, Hung shui, and flows into the Tola.

1155) Mount *Tchung*, or *Mortar* Mountain (8695 Bas.) The word is sometimes written (also 11522 or 11583 Bas.) *Bell*, whence a confusion from some writers with the mountains of the same name on the borders of Shansi. The original was probably intended to be the *Tchung*, 11378 Bas., or piled up mounts because of their height, and thus might be the *Bayan shan*, Great Mountains.

1156) Cf. *Tchang ye ki*. Tai ping yü lan, kiv. 65, 3. *Shan Hai King*, ii., 14, 15, text and commentaries.

1157) He met there the *Tchang Kung*, or Long Armed people. On the *Yang* and *Heh* rivers, cf. *Shang Hai King*, ii., 18, and for the *Ki Kung* people, vii. 1 r.

1158) The *Bulunghir* River, or Sule River, deverses its waters in the Kara nor. *Hung-lu*, the local name in 1000 B.C., suggests the Mongol *Khara*, Turk *Kara*. In Hiuen Tsang's life the same river is called *Hu-lu*. Cf. tr. Beal, i., 17, and *Life*, 18. Also Dutreuil de Rhins, *Asie Centrale*, 125. The *Heh*, i.e., Black River, is said to flow from the San-wei hills (two miles S.E. of Sha tchou in W. Kansuh), and afterwards to run east and west. Cf. *Shan Hai King*, com. ii., 16, 21, which description applies to the Bulunghir.

1159) The All-Gems' mountain has also been called *Bak-yüh* mount (i.e., *Peh-yüh*, white gems). The *Shan Hai King*, xiii., 10 r., speaks of the west lake (*Si hu*. 8472 for 5108 Bas.), with the *Peh yuh shan* on the S.W. of which run the moving sands. In the neighbourhood is a hill of very hard and bright stones white like bones, spoken of by travellers (cf. E Bretschneider, *Mediæval Researches*, ii. 189), which is undoubtedly the Hill of White Gems, or All-gems' Mountain of our text. The old geographers tell us of a hill, west of Turfan, " S'élevant en terrasses superposées, toutes formées par des galets d'agates. . . . La roche ne doit son éclat qu'aux brillantes agates " (cf. Amiot, in *Mémoires concernant les Chinois*, xiv.; E. Reclus, *L'Asie Orientale*, p. 160). It has long been known to the Chinese. Nai-Hwang-ti, going east, is said to have stopped there. Under Tchuan-hiuh, the Red Hills State, i.e., the Hwo tchou near Turfan is said to have sent him water pitchers made of agate. Later on agate brought from there passed through the country of the Yueh-ti (An-si tchou of W. Kansuh) and it is from there that the Chinese get their best agate to the present day. Some confusion have occasionally been made between the heap of agate and the *Bogdo ola*, or *Ling shan*, the Sacred Mountain near Urumtsi.

1160) *Tch'ëh-fu*, 7457-2514, Bas., translated by Dr. Eitel: Record-office.

1161) Probably the *Yen-tze shan* of later times (cf. *Shan Hai King*, ii., 28 v. The Chinese travellers speak in all this region of a kind of iron yelded by magnetic iron ore, cf. E. Bretschneider, *Mediæval Researches*, ii., 180, 183, 193. *Ki-lü*, 809-11691, or *Y-lü* 4612-11691 Bas., is perhaps an antecedent of that of Ili which has survived to the present day further west.

1162) *K'u shan*, 8874-cl. 46 Bas., litt., Bitter's Mount, cannot be understood as Mount Brinjal as translated by Dr. Eitel (probably because of *K'u-kwa*, 8874, cl. 97 Bas. litt., bitter gourd, which was wrongly supposed to be the *solanum melangena* or brinjal. For instance in Doolittle's *Vocab.*) But Dr. Bretschneider, *Botan Sinic.*, ii., 387, tells us that the *K'u kwa* is the *momordica churantia*, which, the *Pên tsao kang-muh* of 1578 says, was introduced from the south, and therefore cannot be the intended plant, which I think was one of those producing *asafœtida*, for which the region north of Karashar has been renowned since antiquity. *Asafœtida*, from the Persian *aza*, mastic, which is largely used as a condiment by Asiatics, was with fir-bark and birds' fat the principal ingredients of the famous fir-balsam employed as a successful drug against consumption ; it was therefore a life-prolonging medicine, and gave rise to the opinion amongst the Chinese of the contending states period, that Si Wang-mu, like the foreigners coming by the eastern coasts, was in possession of the drug of immortality. The balsam in question, it is alleged, was already known in the age of Yao. The word *Ku* must be taken as an imitation of the local name of the asafœtida, which local name at the time of Muh Wang was apparently of Aryan origin (cf. *Ku* with the later Chinese *a-gwei*, *a-'wei* imitating the Persian *anguzeh*, and the Sanskrit *hingu*). In the *Pên tsao King* of the first century containing information on the materia medica of olden times, the medical virtues of the pine are registered ; the pine's fingers (*i e.*, the kernels), and the grease or fat (*i e.*, the resine), if used lighten the body and prolong the years of life (T.P., 953, 6 *r.*); they were imported into China for that purpose from the N.W., according to the *Ki jan* of Fan-tze (T.P., 953, 6), therefore from the direction of Si Wang-mu's country. The marvellous character attributed to this plant and fruit of that region has been extended to others. For instance, the *Lycium* of Turkestan and Kansuh, of which the red berries once dried are imported, at first in Kansuh only, and more recently in other provinces, has received several names to that effect, viz. : *k'u k'i*, 8874-4098 Bas., or bitter k'i ; *kou k'i*, 4149-4098 Bas.; *Sien jen tchang* or Richi's staff, Si Wang-mu's staff, heavenly essence or *t'ien tsing*, none oldness or *kiuh lao*, earth bone or *ti ku* (the root). For the foregoing facts, cf. : *Pên tsao King* (150 B.C.), *Wu shi Pên tsao* (250 A.D.), *Pao p'oh-tze* (300 A.D.), *Hiao King yüan shen k'i* (our era), *Hwai-nan-tze* (150 B.C.) ap. T.P.Y.L., 984, 5 *v.*, 990, 8 *v*; E. Bretschneider, *Chinese intercourse with the countries of Asia*, art *Hwo-chou*, and *Botanicum Sinicum*, ii., 526 ; *Description de la Chine Occidentale*, trad. Gueluy, ch. iv., Kreitner, *Oestr. Mon. f. d. Orient*, 1883, p. 78-6.

1163) *Yen* hills, same character than in Yen-tze hills. *Suprà* Note 1161. Cf. *Shan hai King*, ii., 18 *v*.

1164) Cf. *Life of Hiuen Tsang*, tr. Beal, p. 37.

1165) Cf. *Suprà* note 761 on asbestos. On the sand rats of Turfan, cf. the Ming geography and Bretschneider, *Mediœval Researches*, ii., 192. On these on the route to Khotan, cf. *Shih tao An'si yü tchi*, quoted in the *Y Yuan* of A.D. 400 : T.P.L.Y., 797, 8-9, and

911, 6. *Hiuen Tsang* (tr. Beal, ii., 315) at Khotan, was told the same story that Herodotus, ii., 141, had preserved of an enemy's army disabled by rats having gnawed the weapons leather at night. The story is so similar that its importation into Khotan is clear. On the Greek story, cf. A. H. Sayce, *Herodotus*, p. 205; G. Rawlinson, *Herodotus*, vol. ii., p. 220. The same sand rats are at the bottom of the fable of the Golden Ants of Herodotus, iii. 102. Megasthenes (ap. Strab. xv., 706), Nearchus (ap. Arrian *Indic.* 15), Dio, Pliny, Mela, &c, the *pippilika* of the *Mahabharata*, i., 375, *v.* 1860; as shown by Mrs. Spiers, *Ancient India*, p. 216; Sam. Beal, *l.c.*; Bunbury, *Hist. Anc. Geog.*, i., 227, 257; G. Rawlinson, *l.c.*; Lassen, *Ind. Alter.*, i., 849.

1155) The text says that in the wilderness of the great plain there is a swamp with fresh water and hills and plains where birds shed their feathers. This might permit us to understand the Lop-nor which is right south of Karashar, therefore not so far distant after all, and where such a station for birds has been spoken of for centuries. See for instance the *Shan hai King*, ii. 21 *v.*; vii., 1; xv., 1; and in modern times the report of *Ye-lu Tchu-tsai's* journey in the thirteenth century, ap. E. Bretschneider, *Chinese Mediæval Travellers*, 113.

1166) For instance in the desert near the River Ischim grows a sort of grass which exactly resembles white plumes or feathers, and may be dried and preserved a great while. Cf. P. J. van Strahlenberg, *Description*, p. 362.

1167) Cf. E. Reclus, *L'Asie Orientale*, p. 118.

1168) *Tsiü Kiü — So-Kiü* and *Sha-Kiü*, T. P. Y. L., 717, 4 r. This *Tsiü-Kiü*, 14-5078 Bas., must not be confused with the *Tsiü-Kiü*, 4892-5078 Das., said to be an official title among the Hiung-nus, and the family name of the NORTHERN LIANG Tartar dynasty which ruled in Kansuh, A.D. 397-428. Cf. the original *Shih luh kwoh tchun tsiu*, Peh Liang luh, of Ts'uy Hung, ap. T. P. Y. L., 124, 8.

1169) *Muh Tien-tze tchuen*, § 72.

1170) Chinese are famous in the art of making false gems, but not in that of making glass. The latter process was finally introduced amongst them in A.D. 435 from Cabul. Cf. F. Hirth, *China and the Roman Orient*, p. 280; and T. de L., *On the Ancient History of Glass and Coal in China*: T'oung pao, 1891.

1171) For Muh Wang and the marriage, cf. Firdousi, *Shah Nameh*. G. Pauthier, *Relations Politiques de la Chine avec les puissances Occidentales*, 1859, p. 14. And for Alexandria, cf. *Tsien Han Shu*, Kiv. 96; tr. Wylie, *l.c.* p. 19. In later texts this simple statement has been replaced by a quotation without reference from the *Shan Hai King* (cf. *suprà* note 276) which made it unclear, and an occasion of useless speculations by several orientalists. On the trade route and Herat, cf. n. 1288. On the marriage, cf. n. 171 and *add.* 171.

293. We gather from other sources some more information about the location of the state of Si Wang-mu which confirm and concur with that derived from the narrative of Muh Wang's journey.

The second book, one of the oldest of the *Shan Hai King*[1172] tells us that in the west of the Flowing Sands is the Mount of Gems (*Yü shan*) where the Si Wang Mus reside. This mount is identified by all the commentators with the mount Mass of Gems (*K'iun yü*) of Muh Wang's journey which we have seen to be the Mount of Agate spoken of by the old travellers, near Turfan, W.

From a mythological account in a later book of the same work,[1173] we are given to understand that the Si Wang Mus had on their south the region where birds roosted (near the Lop-nor, as seen before) and that the latter place was northwards of the spurs of the Kwen-lun range, which is exact.

A further statement of the same work[1174] says that "on the margin of the Flowing Sands, after the Red River (of Kansuh, S.W.), and in front (*i.e.* south) of the Black River (of Kansuh, N.W,) are the great mountains of the Kwen-lun; at the bottom of these are the weak waters (of the Lop-nor); beyond these is the *Yen hwo shan*, or Mountain of the Blazing Fire, which throws things suddenly in the air, on the spurs of which the Si Wang Mus reside." The mountain referred to cannot be mistaken for any other than the *Aghir*, or Fire Mountain, the *Peh shan* of modern Chinese maps, visited by a Russian traveller in 1881, at 16 versts north-east of Kutcha, which sends away smoke and sulphurous gas; its fires are said not to be volcanic as supposed before, and to proceed from burning coal.[1175]

The foregoing statement of the *Shan Hai King*, which came from different sources and various dates, indicate the region between Karashar and Kutcha, on the slopes of the Tien shan as the residence of the Si Wang Mus. It is exactly that which our examination of the narrative of Muh Wang's journey has led us to recognise.

294. Confirmative evidence may be quoted from other works. Hwai-nan-tze was aware that the domain of the Si Wang Mus was beyond the brink of the Flowing Sands.[1176] In the geographical chapter of the Han dynastic Annals, the same country is said to be in the north beyond the Lop-nor.[1177] The Records of Sha tchou (W. Kansuh) of the T'ang period,[1178] and the History of the Sixteen Kingdoms by Ts'uy Hung, of A.D. 500,[1179] tell us that the hills of

Tch'u-pu, where the Si Wang Mus used to reside, were N.E. of Yang-Kwuh (whose name underlies that of Yanghi-shar, east of Kutcha, which appears on some maps).[1180] The mounts spoken of would be the Bairak tagh, on the west of Karashar, and the authority given by the author of the *Sha tchou ki* for his statement is not borrowed from literature; it rests on the local tradition among *Kiang* Tibetans and *Hu* or western people.[1181]

These identifications permit us to recognise in the *Mou yuen*, or Luxuriant Garden of Muh Wang's journey, the *Yulduz* plateau, covered with luxuriant herbage, and celebrated throughout central Asia to the present day for its beauty, which Przevalsky was the first European to visit in 1877.[1182]

295. Feminine memories would seem to linger round the country which we have been able to identify with the former residence of the Si Wang Mus. In the south-east of Kutcha, one finds the *Baba kul* or Lake of Women;[1183] it might be the result of a reaction of the Chinese fabled account, as the queen-ruled states belong to the northern territory of Tibet, west and east, but not the north side of the Tarym valley. Should we trust the Chinese description which from its inception has never varied, a queen should have been the ruler, when the first relations began with the Chinese, but it does not follow that she should have always been succeeded by other queens. As remarked at the beginning of this note, there is no evidence in any of the ancient texts that the Si Wang Mus were queens.

296. *Si Wang-mu*, as we have seen, means the *Wang-mu* of the west, and this *Wang-mu* is undoubtedly an attempt at imitating with an appropriate meaning the foreign name or title of the sovereign referred to. The word has happily not suffered much from phonetic alteration. It should have been $K a m - m u$, $K w a m - m u$, or nearly so.[1184]

This gives us a well-known royal denomination among the population of antiquity inhabiting the north-west from the skirts of the Chinese province of Kansuh, to the north of the Tarym valley and the *T'ien shan* range, population called *Wu-suns* in Chinese history.[1185] *Kun-mo* was the title of their sovereign, which has become Kam-mu, and afterwards the *Wang-mu* of the west of the Chinese. Their queens seem to have enjoyed royal prerogatives,[1186] and one of them may have ruled when the Chinese became acquainted with them for the first time. Their country corresponded to that which the Chinese sources have shown us to be that of Si Wang Mus. An interesting problem of history has thus received its solution.

NOTES.—

1172) *Shan Hai King*, ii., 18, 19. In ch. xvi. 2 *c*. it says that the mountains of Si Wang-mu are the *Itoh shan*, 1740, cl. 46, Bas. or, Hill of the Moat, and the *Hai shan*, 4993, cl. 46, Bas., or Hill of the Sea. Let us remark that unlike the other lakes of East Turkestan, that which is near Karashar, the *Bagaratch Kul* is generally called *Denghiz*, *t h e s e a* (cf. E. Reclus, *Asie Orientale*, p. 113), and therefore justifies the *Hai shan*.

1173) *Shan Hai King*, xii. 1.

1174) *Ibid.*, xvi. 4, 5.

1175) It is described in the *Wei shu* of the 5th cent., in the *Peh she* of the 6th, in the *Si yü t'u ki* of the same age, ap. T. P. Y. L., 792, 7, 8; in the *Description de la Chine Occidentale*, trad. Gueluy, ch. ii.; *Muséon*, Juin, 1885. Cf. Also J. Klaproth, *Tabl. Hist. As.*, 109: Ritter, ii. 333; Kisseloff, in Turkestan Gazette, 6 Oct., 81; Mushketoff, *Turkestan*, 1886, i. 131-133 and 172; E. Bretschneider, *Med. Res.*, ii., 190, 243-6. It produces sulphur, sal ammoniac, and alum.

1176) *Shan Hai King*, comm., ii., 19.

1177) *Han shu*, Ti li tchi; T.P., 65, 3 *v*.

1178) *Sha tchou ki* by Twan Kwoh ; T. P., 50, 5.

1179) *Shih luh Kwoh tchun tsiu*, by Ts'uy Hung; *Tai ping yü lan*, 50, 5. This is a quotation from the original work preserved in the latter cyclopædia of A.D. 983, and not from the alleged forgery under the same title of the Ming period.

1180) Unless it be *Yang shar*, new town, as in R. Shaw, *High Tartary, Yarkand, and Kashgar*, 1871, p. 175; but probably a false etymology of an older name.

1181) *Ibid.*, T.P., 50, 5. In the fables piled up on the deceptive name of Si Wang-mu, we find a connection established between her and the Tortoise Mountain (*Tai ping Kwang Ki : Kwang po wuh tchi :* W. F. Mayers, *N. and Q.* l. c) Now Kutcha was formerly called *Kuh-tse* or *Kwei-tse*, lit. Tortoise here.

1182) *Travels from Kuldja to Lobnor*, p. 42, 21 ; E. Bretschneider, *Med. Res.*, ii., 230.

1183) E. Reclus, *L'Asie Orientale*, p. 112.

1184) In an old form of the Tchou period which I take to be a phonetic suggestion, it is made of *Kam* cl. 13 below *Kan* cl. 51. Cf. Min Ts'i-Kih, *Luh shu tung*, iv., 12, 13. In the oldest *fan-tsieh* transcriptions, the initial is indicated by *yü*, rain, which was *r u* in the Han period.

1185) They were repulsed by the Hiung-nus towards the region of I-li about 143 B.C. In former times they covered a large area, and their dominion extended as far as the west borders of Kansuh. Cf. the sources in T. de L., *Khan Khakan and other Tartar titles*, 1888, par. 4 and notes 18-22.

1186) We must infer this from the fact that *Kun-mo* was the title of the king, and *Kun-ti* that of the queen, a peculiarity which may have not been remarked by the ancient Chinese.

Sect. II.—*On some Old Geographical Knowledge of the West.*

———o———

297. A certain amount of geographical knowledge of the west has been handed down from the SHANG period. Y-yn, prime minister to the founder of that dynasty (Rect. Chr., 1686 B.C.) in a fragment quoted from a geographical work bearing his name by the *Kih tchung Tchou shu* of the TCHOU dynasty, says that northwards of China were the countries of the *Yueh-ti* and of the *Ta Hia*.[1187] As a certain Lao-shing-shing had come to the court of Kieh Kwei, the last ruler of the HIA dynasty, from the country now called Karashar,[1188] situated on the route leading from the further west, the geographical information may have been obtained from him.

In 1538 B.C some men from the west having come to Tai Mou, the seventh ruler of the SHANG dynasty, the Chinese sovereign sent envoys who went as far as Karashar [1189] Some information may have been also derived from their report.

298 The *Shan Hai King*, kiv., xiii., fol. 1, in a chapter made of several fragments has preserved some interesting relics of that knowledge. " The country beyond the Flowing Sands (desert of Gobi) are those of *Ta-hia*,[1190] *Shu-sha*,[1191] *Kü-yao*,[1192] and *Yueh-ti*. The Western *Hu* (bearded people) and the Mount of White Gems are east of *Ta-hia* . . . all west of the Flowing Sands.

The narrative of Muh Wang's journey to Karashar, which we have examined, shows that this mountain of White Gems was situated in the immediate west of Turfan. Neglecting the well-known name of the *Yueh-ti*, who were settled in the north-west Kansuh, the three other names by their respective meanings, Great Summer, Raised-up Sands, Settled and Luxuriant, suggest stations in travelling to the west in Eastern Turkestan.[1193] Any attempt at seriously identifying them with modern localities would be most difficult. However the country of Great Summer could be that which near Turfan has been afterwards called *Hwo tchou*, or Fire District, because of the enormous heat resulting there in summer from the sun's rays on red hills. The Raised-up or Firm Sands indicate a region which must have been just outside the moving sands of the desert, while the Settled and Luxuriant refers undoubtedly to the Yulduz plateau, north-west of Karashar, the celebrated garden of central Asia.[1194]

NOTES—

1187) The work of Y-yn has long been lost; fragments only have survived as quotations, *eo nomine*, in several ancient work, such as the *Kih tchung Tchou shu*, and the *Lu she Tchun tsiu*. Cf. Pih Yuen *Shan Hai King*, comm. i. 4, 4, 4 *r*.; ii. 4, 15, 16; v. 35; x. 3; xi. 2; xiii. 1; xv. 1, 4; &c. Another ancient geographer of the same period was Hia Koh, who also compiled a work now lost, a few fragments only have been preserved as quotations. Cf. *Shan Hai King*, vi. 1, and *Lieh-tze*, Tang wen pien, &c.

1188) *Hwai-nan-tze*. *Shan Hai King*, comm., ii. 19 v.

1189) *Kwoh ti tu*; T. P. Y. L., 7904. *Bamboo Annals*, ix. 26.

1190) *Ta hia*, cl. 37-1780, Bas., *i.e.*, Great Summer. The symbols are the same as those used afterwards by Tchang-Kien and others as an equivalent for the name of the *Dahæ*, on whom cf. note 249.

1191) *Shu-sha*, 10333-4888 Bas., "Raised Sands." A late variant gives *Kien-sha*, 1635-4888 Bas., "Firm Sands," probably as an equation of meaning.

1192) *Kü-yao*, 2240-8013 Bas., "Settled Yao." As in the case preceding a late variant gives *Shuh-yao*, 2270-8013 Bas., "Dependent Yao." This country is most probably spoken in other books of the *Shan Hai King*, vii. 3; *Tchu yao* and xvi. 2 *r*.

1193) Curiously enough the name of *Ta hia* amongst them has misled some writer of the Ts'in and Han period, who has taken it for the *Ta hia* of Tchang Kien; and finally the list has taken place in the curious Mosaic of the *Wei lioh*, on Ta Ts'in, cf. supr. note 276. It is also this vague *Ta hia* which is mentioned in the inscription of Ts'in She Hwang-ti at Lang-ya, which M. Ed. Chavannes has translated, *Les Inscriptions des Ts'in*: J. A., 1893, p. 500. Under the Han dynasty, *Ta hia* was the name of the present Ho tchou in Lan tchou fu of south-west Kansuh.

1194) *Suprà* on *Muh Wang's* journey, § 294

Sect. III.—*On the Gnomon and Sundial.*

———o———

299. The Gnomon and Sundial, in a more or less primitive condition must have been brought into China by the western civilised Bak-sings, under the leadership of Hwang-ti, who is traditionally ascribed their invention, as without them they could not have determined their solstices and equinoxes which the first book of the *Shu-King* show them enabled to do. Moreover we see from the *Shi-King* that in the seventeenth or eighteenth century the Chinese knew how to determine by the measure of the shadow the position of a town, or more exactly how to determine the four cardinal points by the observation of the solar shadow.[1195] Therefore the early Chinese had been taught the process, ingenious and simple, which permitted the Babylonians, as it did the Egyptians, to set their monuments on a regular orientation.[1196] We do not know if the implement made use of by the Chinese was anything more than a gnomon or vertical staff set up on a measured ground, as the Book of Poetry in its terseness says only this: "he shadowed" (*ki-yng*), in the sense of measuring the shadow.[1197] Anyhow at the beginning of the Tchou dynasty, *i.e.*, *circà*, 1100 B C., observations made at their capital city with the gnomon have been verified by Laplace [1198] and by Biot, who have found them to be substantially correct within an approximation, which from the complication introduced in the case by the obliquity of the ecliptic never understood by them, cannot have been calculated backwards by the Chinese in subsequent ages.[1199]

300. In the Ritual of the Tchou dynasty some information is given on the system of the sundial; the gnomon *piao* had eight feet in height, with a dial *t'u-kwei*, *i.e.*, measuring table, of one foot five-tenths for the length of the shade at the summer solstice.[1200] *Jeh-kwei*, or simply *kwei*, as a term for a sundial complete, is a later expression of the HAN dynasty.[1201]

An improvement of great importance for the scientific accuracy of observations made with the gnomon, and consisting of a hole at the top instead of a point, was introduced under the Tchou dynasty at a time it is difficult to ascertain, but which must have been before the sixth or fifth century B.C.[1202] As the invention is commonly attributed to the Arabs, its existence in China is worth noting at that early period.

301. In the west the history of the gnomon and sundial is uneventful until comparatively late. In the eighth century B.C., Akhaz of Juda, then a vassal of Tiglath Pileser, had a sundial[1203] perhaps about 732 B.C., and through the relations existing between his country and that of his suzerain. In Isaiah xxxviii. 8, and 2 Kings xx. 9-11, the shadow is said to have been brought "ten degrees," or malûth, backwards, by which it had gone down on the dial of Akhaz. Anaximander set up the first gnomon in Sparta in B.C. 560,[1204] probably with some improvements which wrongly caused his name to be looked upon as that of the genuine inventor. Rome had no sundial before B.C. 263, and even then only an inexact one,[1205] which was not put to right until B.C. 163 by G. Marcius Philippus.[1206]

Notes.—

1195) *Shi King*, iii., ii., vi., 5. This is said to have been done by a Chinese Duke Liu, who went to live with the *Tehou* people, then uncivilised and even ignorant of making for themselves kiln-shaped huts, an art in which they were taught by Tan-fu. Cf. the same work III , i. It was most probably nothing else that the cave dwelling of Shensi (in the loess).

1196) Cf. Edward Biot, *Recherches sur les mœurs Anciennes des Chinois, d'après le Shi-King*, Journ, Asiat, Nov., Dec., 1843 ; J. Legge, *Chinese Classics*, vol. iv., pp. 162 intro. and 487-8.

1197) " Le tracé de la ville ou du monument était précédé d'observations astronomiques, faites avec un gnomon vertical pour déterminer la ligne méridienne par la bissection de l'arc de cercle compris entre les ombres solaires du matin et du soir." J. B. Biot, *Advertisement* to the Tcheou-li, p. 27 ; *Le Tcheou-li*, K. xlviii., f. 21, transl. Ed. Biot., v. ii., p. 554.

1198) P. Gaubil, *Mémoire sur les observations du gnomon faites à la Chine* in Additions à la connaissance des temps, 1809, pp. 393 sq. Laplace, *Ibid*, 1811, pp. 429 sq. *Tcheou-li*, K. ix. f. 17.

1199) J. B Biot, *Astro. Ind. Chin.*, p. 320. Teng fung hien in E. Honan, is famous by the astronomical tower and gnomon erected there by Tchou Kung. Cf. Grosier, *Chine* (3), i. 188 ; De Mailla, *Hist. Gen. Chine*, xiii. 58.

1200) *Tcheou-li*, K. ix., 16, 17, xlii. 19 ; transl. Biot. v. i., pp. 200-202 ; v. ii. pp. 522, 523.

1201) It is explained in the *Shwoh wan* of 89 A.D., and in the *Shih Ming* of 175 A.D. Cfr. *Tai ping yü lan*, K. 4, ff. 4r. 5r.

1202) It is described in a part of the *Tchou pei* which an astronomical statement recorded therein reports to a date within B.C. 572-450. Cfr. J. B. Biot, *Astron. Ind. Chin.* pp. 238, 304 &c.

1203) Cfr. the remarks of G. Wilkinson's notice in G. Rawlinson's *Herodotus*, vol. ii. p. 330, on *måláth, step degree*.
1204) *Diog. Laert*. ii. 1. We know that the Greeks have often substituted *invention* to *adoption* in their claims for things known for several centuries before in other countries.
1205) Built for Catana in Sicily, 4° S. of Rome and therefore presenting a big error which was not perceived for a century. Cf. Sal Reinach, *Phil. Class*. i. 275.
1206) On the sundials, cfr. G. Rayet, *Annals de Chimie et de Physique*, s. v., and vi., p. 52 ; Hermann, *Privat alterthümer*, pp. 122 v. 2, 142 v. 8 ; Marquardt, *Handbook*, v. 2, 271 ; S. Reinach, *Phil. Class.*, ii. 212, i. 275.

Sect. IV.—*On the Clepsydra*.

302.—We have no historical statement that the Bak Sings were acquainted with the Clepsydra, as they were with the gnomon, when they came into China. It may be said, however, that they could not without it have made any stellar observations at night with any precision, if, as probable, they were able to do.[1207] And circumstancial evidence from the west originary quarters show that if they had not then been made acquainted with it, they could not afterwards have received it in the same condition or preliminary stage of development. Herodotus (ii. 109) speaks of the Babylonian sundial, gnomon, and division of the day into twelve hours, but he does not speak of the clepsydra. It is only Sextus Empericus of the second century who has said that it was with the clepsydra that the Babylonians had made their system of duodecimal division of the day.[1208] Now we are aware that this division along with the reform of the calendar was made about or after 2500 B.C.,[1209] and this shows a respectable antiquity for the clepsydra. Some of the poles figured on Chaldean cylinders are probably gnomons, but I have not remarked any possible representation of the clepsydra on these monuments. The oldest known as yet is that which occurs in Egypt in the great Temple of Bubastis, at the time of Osor-Khon II., *circ.*, 875 B.C. It is a single object with an animal shaped top.[1210]

303. The clepsydra is alluded to in the Annals of the Bamboo Books as being neglected in 895-870 B.C.,[1211] and in the *Tchou-li* we find it was in charge of special officers.[1212] In the camps it was

hung on a pole to be seen from afar. Its mode of construction was most simple, and consisted of a single vase with a leaking spout and a cover with an opening; a graduated rod on a floating base emerging as a signal was gradually lowering as the water diminished. It could not differ much from its western antecedent, and likewise rested chiefly on the principle of leaking,[1213] while the rude time-checks used in India, Burma, and among the Malays rest on the principle of sinking, which shows their different origin, and the western source of the Chinese implement.

The names for the implement in China was $K'it$-hu, $Kich$-hu, the Raised Jar, and KAK-LU, $K'eh$-lou, the graduated leak, which names singularly enough are much like the Sanskrit $ghati$, for time piece, and the Hindi $ghari$, for clepsydra.[1214]

The Rod was graduated with one hundred degrees for the whole length of the day, i.e., daylight and night.[1215] Such a regularity in the division of time, independent of the respective seasons-length of day and night is a highly scientific conception, thoroughly Babylonian, which the Chinese could not have got from anywhere else, and which was long unknown to the Greeks and Romans.[1216]

304. In ancient India a regular division of daytime and a system of clepsydra were known, but they rest on different bases. The water-clock described in the *Vishnu Purâna*[1217] is just the reverse of the Chinese one; it is in use in other countries such as Java[1218] and Burma,[1219] where it was carried by Hindu influence, and the system is most simple: a smaller basin with a hole at the bottom is placed floating on the water in a larger basin, where it fills itself gradually and sinks in a fixed time. In the Laws of Manu and the Puranas, the day and night are divided into sixty *muhûratas* of thirty *kalas* each,[1220] which division is obviously different from the 100 $k'ehs$ of China. I do not know which were the sub-divisions of the $k'ehs$,[1221] but their relation with the duodecimal division employed in Babylonia suggests a division by thirds, which would make 25 thirds of a $k'eh$ correspond to a twelfth part of a day and night or nyctemeron. It has the appearance of a substitution made to a former duodecimal system, the original one, (?) which would have been discarded as not sufficiently minute for the purpose, though otherwise preserved.[1221] The centigrade division was the work of the Tcuou, but we do not know when it was done, nor from which quarters the notion may have come

to them, if it was not an improvement devised by themselves. It has been inferred from the fact that the *Jyotisham* or Vedic calendar and the Chinese traditions present an identity of specifications on the duration of the longest days, which duration applies to the latitude of Babylonia, that this specification originated in the latter country, and had been carried to India and hence to China. But the inference goes too far, as the units of calculation differ, and the two countries appear to have received it indipendently.[1222]

Notes—

1207) The astronomical confusion of the first chapter of the *Shu King* is not without throwing doubts on the matter.

1208) *Adv. Math.* cap. 21.

1209) Let us remember that the necessity of a change in the calendar was brought about by the accumulated errors of supputation and by precession of equinoxes. The sun at the vernal equinox was entering Taurus from 4698 to 2540, and Aries from 2540 to 382 B.C. Now the tablets translated in *The Astronomy and Astrology of the Babylonians*, by A. H. Sayce, 1874, show that Aries was the first zodiacal sign (cf. p. 237).

1210) Cf. *The Festival Hall of Osor-Khon II. in the Great Temple of Bubastis*, by Ed. Naville, 1887-89; London, 1892, pp. 6, 8, 9, &c. It was called *s h e b*. Brugsch, in *Zeits f. Æg.*, 1870, 156, gives an Egyptian word *merkhet* for h o r l o g e in P. Pierret, *Voc. Hierogl.* 226. Another system according to Professor G. Maspero, which existed also in ancient Egypt, consisted of several stone-basins emptying one another. On a similar system made of bronze basins in China, during the T'ang dynasty, cf. G. Schlegel *Uranographie Chinoise*, p. 190.

1211) *Tchuh shu Ki nien.* V. vii.

1212) *Tchou li* xxx. 29, 30. It was under the guard of a special officer, *K'it hu she*, who had to keep the water warm in winter that it should not be frozen; hang up the horary vase for certain signals of a fixed length of time; and measure the day and night at the equinoxial and solsticial times, as explained in the *Sui shu.* Cf. Stan. Julien, in J. B. Biot, *Astronomie Indienne et Chinoise*, p. 290. Cf. the picture of a clepsydra-vase of the Han dynasty in the *K'ao ku tu*, ix. 26.

1213) Cf. J. L. Ideler, *Ueber der Ursprung des Thierkreises*, p. 16. G. Schlegel, *Uranographie Chinoise*, p. 191. Cf. Also F. A. Seeley, *Time Keeping in Greece and Rome*, pp. 377-397 : Smithsonian Report, 1889. In later times in China, in order to obtain a greater accuracy the number of recipients was increased from two to five. For instance in the T'ang dynasty as shown by the figure given by Tchu-hi in the *T'si king tu* Ed. Biot, *Le T'chéou-li*, ii. 202, and G. Schlegel, *Uran. Chin.*, 190. On great clepsydras of Quinsay or

Hang-tchou, cf. Martini, in H. Yule, *Marco Polo*, 2, ii. 198; of Peking in 1272, cf. Bazin, *Chine Moderne*, p. 26; of Canton in 1317, cf. *Chinese Repository*, xx. 480.

1214) *K'ieh-hu*, 3346-1764 Bas. *Keh-lou*, 789-5189 Bas. For the Indian words, cf. Wilson, *Indian Terms*, 174, and Edw. Balfour, *Cyclop. Ind.*, i. 195.

1215) Cf. *Shwoh wen*, sub. voc., *Lu*. P. Gaubil, *Hist. Astron. Chin.*, p. 239-40.

1216) The division in hours was unknown to Homer, and was posterior to Anaximander. Pollux enumerates fifteen divisions of the day and seven of the night (*Onamasticon*, i. c. 7). After the introduction of the clepsydra by Ctesibius, the Athenians had two sorts of hours, the e q u a l or 1,24th of the day of 24 hours, and the v a r i a b l e, or 1/12th of the length of the daylight. In Rome the day and night were not divided in any regular manner; even after 159 B.C., the clocks indicated not the equinoctial hours, but the twelfths of the natural day, so that the hours were shorter in winter than in summer. Cf. S. Reinach, *Ph. Cl.*, i., 222, 223, 275, 276.

1217) Transl. H. H. Wilson, 1840, p. 531.

1218) G. Schlegel, *Uranographie Chinoise*, p. 191.

1219) Shway yve, *The Burman, his life and notions*, London, 1882, vol. ii. 294. In-Burma, it is only at the vernal and autumnal equinoxes that the hours of the day and night are equal in time. At other times they vary, as formerly in Rome. Cf. *Suprà* n. [1216] The length of a day and night is complete in sixty *nayes* (or *nari*), but this division is only used for astrological purposes.

1220) *The Laws of Manu*, i. 64, G. Buhler, p. 19. It is only slightly different from the astronomical divisions. Cfr. Ebenezer Burgess, *Translation of the Surya Siddhanta*, with notes by Whitney, i. 12.

1221) In the first year *Tai teh'u*, *i.e.*, 104 B.C., twenty divisions were added to the former of 100 of the graduated rod in the *Keh-lu*, making 120 for the night and day. Cfr. *Nyai Ti K'i* in *Tai Ping yü lan*, K. II. f. 12.

1222) Cf. Alb. Weber, *Ueber die Identität der Angaben von der Dauer des längsten Tages bei den Chaldäern, Chinisen, Indern.* Mon. d. Kön. Akad. d. Wiss, Berlin, 1862; cfr. from the same scholar, *Ueber den Veda Kalender*, namens *Jyotisham*, pp. 29, 30, 107, 108. Abhand Kön. Akad. d. Wiss, Berlin, 1862; *Die redischen Nachrichten von den Naxatra*, i. 361-363, ii. 400. J. B. Biot, *Astronom. Ind. Chin.*, pp. 292-293. And the Severe Criticisms of Prof. W. D. Whitney, *Biot and Weber on the Hindu and Chinese Asterisms*, pp. 63-64. Prof. Max Müller in 1860, J. A. S. B., xxix. 200, has claimed that the Jyotisha account of the position of the colures fixed the twelfth century B C. as the date, not the fourteenth as Colebrook had concluded. Cf. also Dr. James Burgess, *Notes on Hindu Astronomy and the History of our Knowledge of it*; J. R. A. S., Oct., 1893, pp. 717-761; before the Greek influence Indian astronomy consisted of primitive and rough methods of observations, without even a knowledge of the 19-year period. Cf. ibid. p. 752-3.

Sect. V.—*Origin of the South-pointing Chariots and Maritime Compass.*

305. The question is more complicated than would appear from the suggestion of the Nestor of Sinologists in his not inexhaustive enquiry on this subject,[1223] quoted *suprà*, note 159. (1.) The polarity of the magnet; (2) its utilisation for route indicating; (3) its application for that purpose to chariots (4) and to boats—are different and successive questions, probably solved successively in the history of progress. It seems that the first notion was very old in the west. The Egyptians were acquainted with the magnetic iron which they called *bàa-n-pe*, c e l e s t i a l i r o n,[1224] and the expression *res-mehit-ba*, s o u t h-n o r t h i r o n, if correctly read, in the inscription of the pyramid of Unas (last Pharaoh of the fifth dynasty), would show them also acquainted with the artificial isolation of the magnet for direction purposes. Plato and Aristotle were acquainted with it, and among the Arabs it was to the latter that the discovery was attributed.[1225] The same notion has also been found in the ancient literature of India.

I am not aware that any trace of a similar knowledge has been hitherto disclosed in the Babylonian civilsation, but as our acquaintance of these matters therein is still fragmentary, we may expect that it was common, as so many other things were, to Egypt and Babylonia.

The leaders of the Bak Sings, future civilisers of China, while settled yet near the Bakhtyari range, could therefore have become acquainted with it, and we might thus understand as a later amplification of a genuine fact the legend reported, not by Szema Tsien, but by other compilers, that Hwang ti made use at war of a south-pointing chariot. But the evidence in favour of this tradition is romantic and nearly nil.

306. The same incertitude does not concern Tchou Kung, the virtual founder of the Tchou dynasty, who appears to have really

been acquainted with the *polarity of the magnet*. He may have learned it in the same way as they had learned the other notions of western knowledge which we have mentioned in the present work.[1226] The fifty-sixth chapter of the *Shu King*, which ought to have contained a statement of the fact is lost, and we only know it through an amplified version of the fourth century B.C. by Kwei Kuh tze.[1227] We have seen (*supra*, note 209) that south-pointing chariots could not be made in 822-811 B.C., and that it was only in the seventh century that an experiment is reported to have been successful. The tradition indicates probably nothing more than an improvement in the make of the magnet which one could take on oneself when driving, while the suggestion of some modern Chinese that the south-pointing article was connected with the axles of the chariot is pure childishness.[1228] It is almost certain that nothing definite had been arrived at in the make of special chariots for the purpose, as they are not described in the *Tchou-li*, and subsequent writers, such as the well informed Hwai nan tze (T. P., 752, 6) speak only of the magnet. All that could be done was to have the magnetic needle fixed in the chariot, without being impaired in its movement.

807. We must come to the first century of our era to hear that a certain Tchang Heng had reconstructed one for astronomical purposes. Then we arrive to the third century at Lohyang under the reign of Ming-ti (227-240 A.D.) of the WEI dynasty, where it being said that the ancients never had any south-pointing chariots, Ma-Kiun, the mechanician, made the attempt and was at last successful in making one.[1229] The *Shu Wang Ki* of the fifth century, describing the system says that on the top of the chariot was placed a wooden figure of a *sien-jin* holding a trusty flag ; inside of the chariot was the pointing to the south (cf. T. P., 775, 1*v*.)

A century later the same success does seem to have partly rewarded the efforts of Hiai-fei in 342, and of Hu-sheng, 394 A.D., to make similar chariots for Shih-hu, fourth king (335-349 A.D.) of the AFTER TCHAO, a small Tartar dynasty of North China, and for Yao-hing, 394-415, second king of the HOU TSIN.

When the first of these chariots came into the possession of Wu Ti of the LIU SUNG dynasty (420 A.D.), it was claimed that these Jung-Tek, otherwise Tartars, who had made it had not worked well, and that often they did not indicate the true south.[1230] This damaging report was probably prompted by the wounded amour propre of the Chinese, when seeing all the great things which these Tartars had made. Shih-hu, in 342, had rebuilt the city, already magnificent, of *Yeh* (modern Lin-tchang in Tchang-teh fu of North Honan). On the *Ming-hoh tch'i*, or Pond of the Cackling Crane, a special boat with a south-pointing magnet (*Tchi nan tchou*) was built on his commands in that year, and this may be taken as the *first instance of the maritime compass*. It is mentioned in the *Tsin Kung Koh Ki* of the fourth century.[1231] I do not know when this mere toy was improved and adopted for practical navigation ; it remained undoubtedly slumbering for centuries, as the oldest mention of the maritime compass (as shown by Dr. J. Edkins, Trans. Asiat. Soc. Japan, Dec., 1880, viii. 475), dates only of 1122 A.D., on board of the ship which starting from Ning-po carried the Chinese ambassador to Corea.

308. In 1876, Mr. William Chappell,* *Nature*, June 15, has tried to show that we owe the appearance of the compass in Europe in the twelfth century to independent discovery, and not to importation from China. Herr A. Schüch, *Die Sage von Kompass in China*, 1891, Natur, Halle, 51, 606-8 ; 52, 618, 5, and *Ausland*, 1892, 4-10, has collected historical data to show that it has been received by the Arabs from Europe, and not by Europe from the Arabs. However, the Arabs who were then, long before and afterwards, frequenting the Chinese ports must have been blind and deaf if they did not hear something of this novelty. And although a positive link proven by a definitive fact is missing between the Chinese and Arab implement, the corresponding dates and the known intercourse are rather too much for an independent invention.

NOTES.—

1223) *Chin. Class.* iii. 536-7. Cf. also J. Klaproth, *Lettre sur l'invention de la Boussole*, 1834. Ed. Biot, *Note sur la direction de l'Aiguille Aimantée en Chine*. C. R. Acad Scienc 1844, t. xix.

1224) According to T. Deveria, *Le Fer et l'Aimant dans l'Ancienne Egypte*, 1870.

1225) Cf. Reinaud, Introd., *Géographie d'Aboulféda*, 1848, p. clll.

1226) Cf. Notes 149-153, 346, and the text corresponding.

1227) T.P., 775, 1 v.

1228) Cf. the negative note of Dr. J. Chalmers, *China and the Magnetic Compass:* China Review, 1891, xix. 52-54.

1229) Cf. *Fu-tze.* T. P., 752, 7.

1230) Cf. Tch'en Yoh, *Sung Shu.* Shih-hu, *Yeh tchung Ki.* T P., 752, 2, 2 v. The *Ku yü tu*, Illustrations of Ancient Jades by Tchu Tch-jun, 1341 (re-published 1603), in two books, gives, i. 2, a picture of a little figure in jade on its pivot, from a south-pointing chariot, which has been reproduced in the *San ts'ai tu huy* cyclopædia of 1609, and elsewhere, and was sixteen inches high. The right arm extended in front is supposed to have always indicated the south from a loadstone concealed inside. In the oldest southpointing chariots the indicator was a hand hanging inside of the car; the little figure outside was an improvement of the fifth century.

1231) Cf. T. P., 769, 1 v; 197, 4; 973, 3.

Sect. VI.—*Foreign Historical Sources of Ancient Chinese Astronomy.*

309. When the Bak Sings arrived in China some of the native populations had already a rough sort of astronomy. Several of them, star-gazing, had noticed in course of years the recurrence at regular times of the same celestial bodies in the starry heavens;[1232] and with reference to sowing and harvest times they had paid a peculiar attention to the position of *Ursa Major.*[1233] When he took possession of the supreme authority of the East of China the famous *Kao Yang Tchuen hiuh*, in his thirteenth year (*i.e.*, *c.* 2213 B.C.), is said to have made some calendaric calculations and delineations of heavenly bodies[1234] His successor *Ti Kuh Kao-sin* (2147-2076 B.C.), with his foreign minister, *Tchung-li*,[1235] was able to define the zodiacal stars and exhibit their times to the people.[1236] Szema Ts'ien, who has preserved[1237] a bare list of the celebrated astrologers of olden times, begins with the name of Tchung-li, and passes to *Hi* and *Ho* of the time of *Yao*, spoken of in the *Shu King.* The most famous afterwards was *Kun-gu*, who arrived with his tribe by the Kukunor route, introducing the art of bronze about 1741 B.C. Under the reign of Tai Meu, of the SHANG dynasty, who is said to have received numerous envoys from foreign parts, flourished *Wu-hien*, a foreigner, who made the first catalogue of the stars, and in *c.* 1553 B.C.

organised the state worship of the hills and rivers.[1238] During the Tchou dynasty, at the outset, under Wu Wang, lived *She yh*, who was *Ta she*, or great historiographer.[1239]

310. *Tch'ang-hung*, who has also made himself famous in astronomy, was a *ta-fu*, or great officer, in the time of Ling Wang (571-544 B.C.) Later on flourished *Tze Wei*, in the state of Sung, and Pi Tsao in the state of Tcheng, whom we have already met as a well known sacrificer to the foreign Kitchen god in 533 B.C.[1240] In the principality of T'si, *Kan Kung*, who lived in the time of the Contending States, about 350 B.C., wrote a work called *Tien wen sing tchen*, Divination by the starry signs of the sky, in eight books. In the kingdom of T'su lived *T'ang Mei*, and in that of Tchao, *Yu Kao*, after 400 B.C. In that of Wei about the same date lived *Shih Shên* who wrote the *T'ien Wen*, or Signs of the Sky, in eight books[1241] The *Tien wen sing tchen* and *Tien wen*, of Kan and Shih, are said to have become the *Sing King*, The Book of Stars, that was edited under the Han dynasty,[1242] and recast under the T'ang dynasty,[1243] when Hindus, Greeks, Romans, Persians, Mahommedans had furthermore contributed to enrich the Chinese stock of notions of astronomy.

311. The Annals of the Tsin dynasty (265-419 B.C.) section of astrology, say that the astronomical works of the *Ta she-ling*, or great astrologer, Tch'en-tch'oh and others, of Kan and Shih, and of Wu-hien, altogether three schools, had mapped out the stars, in a total of 288 kwan or constellations including 1464 stars.[1244] The list of fixed stars published by Mr. A. Wylie, the translator of Herschell, contains 2872 fixed stars, of which 1398 only were Chinese.[1245] In Dr. Gustave Schlegel's *Uranographie Chinoise*, 755 different names of stars are given.[1246]

Notes—

1232) Dr. Gustav Schlegel, in his *Uranographie Chinoise*, 1875, 929 pp., has collected a considerable mass of evidence on the subject. But he thinks that it cannot be explained but by an antiquity of 18000 years, which I think unnecessary. Cf. below, §§ 316-320.
1233) This is shown by the teaching of Shun (who was a native prince) in substitution to the teaching of Yao, which it seems had been misunderstood in the transmission, as explained in the following note.
1234) *Tchuh shu Ki nien*, I., iii. In the Literary Catalogue of the

first Han dynasty, *Tsien Han shu*, kiv. 30, section of calendar, *Lih-pu*, several works bear titles concerning that early period. *Hwang-ti wu kia lih*, Hwang-ti's five schools' calendar, in 33 kiv. The earliest astronomical statements in Chinese legends and traditions are most interesting to notice here for their intrinsic value, and also because of the numerous misgivings which are fancied about them. I.—Szema Tsien, *She Ki*, i. 4, tells us that " Hwang-ti had acquired a valuable tripod, and that he calculated the lists of the solar movements." And at xxviii. 32, he reports a legend told in 112 B.C., from which it appears that Hwang-ti utilised the astrological slips of the tripod (*i.e.*, contained in it as in ancient west) and calculated as said before; the legend says also that Hwang-ti remarked that after about twenty years the winter solstice was coming again on the first day of the month, and thus calculated the calendar for twenty times that period, or 380 years. The last part of the legend is almost certainly spurious as the 19-year cycle appeared only in 655 B.C. (see *add.* n. 47), and the seven intercalary months which it requires meanwhile were not made, otherwise than in a haphazard fashion, as shown by J. Chalmers, *Astronomy of the Ancient Chinese*. II.—Tchuan-hiüh is said in the Bamboo Annals to have made a calendar with figures (of the heavenly bodies ?). The text gives only *lik siang*, which might be translated somewhat differently, but as the *Shu King* in the canon of Yao has the same words followed of sun, moon, planets, and constellations; their meaning is allowed to be as we have translated. The Imperial Library in B.C. 7 contained a calendar of Tchuan-hiüh in twenty-one books, and a work under the same name on the Five Stars or planets in fourteen books, where probably the views commonly attributed to him had been embodied (cf. *Tsien Han shu*, kiv. 30, fol. 31). Tradition also wanted him to have first made the sky round while Hwang-ti had made it a vault (cf. Liu she *Lih tchang wan* of the Han period, T. P., ii. 8 *v.*) It was soon inferred from it that he had actually made an astronomical instrument on that principle. III.—In the first chapter of the *Shu King*, Yao instructs his astronomers that a year being complete on the 366th day, they should have to use intercalary months to make the seasons right and the year exact. There is no question here of a bissextile year, although Norman Lockyer, in his *Origin of the Year*, has shown that the year length of 365¼ days was known in ancient Egypt 2500 B.C.; but the migration of the Bak tribes took place before the Chaldean reform of calendar of about 2243 B.C.(?) It is in the same chapter of the Book of History that are given the famous instructions of Yao, to four astronomers for observing the four leading stars of the seasons, which would be roughly right, instead of being incomprehensible, had not an inversion crept between the characters for west and east as shown by the actual and unmistakable derivations of the four symbols of the cardinal points from those of the Chaldeo-Elamite script (T. de L., *The Loan of Chaldeo-Elamite Culture to Early China*, 1891, §§ 20-30; and *The Oldest Book of the Chinese*, 1892, §§ 185-8. IV.—It appears that this astronomical method did not work well, as in the following chapter of the *Shu King*, we see that Shun, as soon as he assumed the supreme authority, provided his subjects with another and more simple process—" He fixed on the *siun-ki*, or pearly revolving (the first four stars), and the *yüh heng* or gemmy balance (the three stars of the tail of Ursa Major), to be the seven controllers (of the seasons)." It is the same idea suggested by nature which caused the Greeks to call this constellation *helikè*. This use of these stars for calendaric indicators was said to have been always known; it was described at length in the fourth century B.C. by Hoh Kwan-tze; and about 190 B.C. the old Fuh sheng, after the literary persecution, had still preserved the notion that the four words of the text in question were referring to the north pole. But after 150 B.C., with Kung-'an Kwoh, another view began to prevail; the oldest explanation was not grand enough, and it was stated that these words were the description of a jewelled astronomical instrument, which in the later commentators has become an armillary sphere made of pearls with a transverse tube of jade! The astronomical fact that *Draconis* was yet pole-star at the time of Shun, just above the so-called balance, fully justifies the names he gave to these stars, and the whole thing shows, in our opinion, that this teaching of Shun was based upon native astronomical folk lore.

1235) Tchung-li, anciently Tung-li, for Tungri = *Tengri*, heaven, in Turkish languages, which fact may suggest that he was a foreigner, and probably a Turk. Among the Turko-Tartars the following star names appear to have been anciently known:— (1) the North Star, *Altin Kazuk*, or golden pole or stake, in Uigur, *temir Kazuk*, or iron pole or stake, in Djagatai. (2) In *Ursa Minor*, two stars called *Kök-bozat* and *Ak-bozat*, or White and Blue Horses. (3) Three stars in the same constellation called *Arkan-jolduz*, or Rope Stars. (4) *Jeti-karakchi* = the Seven Robbers. (5) *Sekiz-jolduz*=the eight stars on the eastern horizon of the steppes. There is the unlucky star, *zejan-jolduz*=Scorpio Star, called in central Asia and Persia *Kerwankush*, the grave-digger of caravans, because as long as the caravans observe its rising with Orion in the morning, robbers and death follow the stations. (6) The Morning Star. (7) The Seven Stars, *i.e.*, the Pleiades. (8) The Milky way, called the Bird's Path. Cf. H. Vambery, *Die Primitive Cultur des Turko-Tatarischen Volkes*, 1879, pp. 154-6. Considering that Turkish tribes formed part of the Pre-Chinese population of North China, the almost complete absence of connection between their astronomical folk-lore and that of the Pre-Chinese shows that the astronomical knowledge of the latter was small, regional, and various. On names of stars introduced from the ancient west cf. *add*. 28.

1236) *Li Ki*, xx. 19. *Sacred Books of the East*, xxviii. 208.

1237) *She Ki*, Tien Kwan shu, xxvii. 40, 41,

1208) *Supra* sect. 98, 91, note 340, and *add*, 342. *Tchuh shuh ki nien*, IV., ix. 11 Wu-hien was a man of the west. His country was called *Fuk-mok*; it was situated in the N.W. of the Lop-nor, near the

T'ien-shan, therefore in Karashar. Cf. *Shui King. Si yü tchi*, T. P. Y. L., 50, 6. His name, anciently Mukan, Mogan, is perhaps suggestive of an ultimate origin farther in the west. It reminds me of *Makan* in Takla Makan, the region east of Yarkand, and of the plain and town of *Mogan* near the Caspian (on which cf. Ed. Bretschneider, *Med. Res.*, i, 294; Barbier de Meynard, *Dictionnaire Historique de la Perse*, 548; H. Cordier, *Odoric de Pordenone*, 36.

1239) Khang hi tze tien, s. v. yh. 9 + 5, fol. 19.

1240) *Suprà*, sect. 183 and note 658.

1141) It will be remarked that these various astronomers lived in the east, and at the period of astrological influence imported in Shantung by the mariners of the Erythrœan Sea who were acquainted with the astronomical peculiarities of the southern hemisphere. The latter circumstance coupled with the double sowing and double harvest times for some plantations has introduced a good deal of confusion in the astrological folklore of China.

1242) The section of *T'ien wen* or astrology in the HAN Catalogue includes 445 sections forming 21 works, and that on calendar 18 works, forming 606 sections.

1243) A. Wylie, *Notes on Chinese Literature*, p. 98, has the following information on this work: "Old catalogues mention a Book of the Stars, with the title or *Sing King*, written during the Han, by Kan Hung and Shih Shen. An ancient work with the same title is still extant; some have thought it to be the same, but it has been concluded on critical evidence that it cannot be older than the T'ang dynasty."

1244) *Tsin shu*, Tien Wen tchi. In *She Ki*, kiv. 27, fol. 16.

1245) In Doolittle's *Vocabulary and Handbook*, 1872, vol. ii., p. 617-632.

1245) *Uranographie Chinoise*, 1875, p. 86.

CHAPTER IX.—MEETING OBJECTIONS.

I.—*Southern Origin*.

312. So far as I am aware four objections of a general character have to be met by my disclosures of an early importation of West-Asiatic culture in China.

The first objection in date was made by two reviewers of my book on *The Languages of China before the Chinese*, in 1888 (prized in 1889 by the Academic des Inscriptions). An anonymous critic wondered why I had not left the native populations of China alone (*sic*), as these miserable tribes did not deserve to be studied, and another advocated the suggestion that the Chinese people ought to have come from the south, even from the Malacca peninsula and not from the north west. Now let us remark that he mixed the two questions of population and civilisation, which are different in the case.

When the west civilised Bak families under the leadership of Hwang-ti arrived in the Flowery Land they found the country inhabited by tribes of several races, originating from the south and from the north; and the present Chinese nation has come out under the activity of these civilisers and of later conquerors from the gradual fusion of these various ethnical elements. The formation has taken 3500 years to be completed.

II.—*Self-Growth and Development*.

313. Another objection consists in the hypothesis, once cherished by theoricians, that the civilisation of the Middle Kingdom was the

result of a self-growth, slowly evolved from the limbos of savagery. This view could be put forward, but when Chinese antiquity had not yet been the object of a systematical enquiry which it entirely disproves, as the Chinese themselves attribute the establishment of most items of their civilisation to the foreign founders of their nation arrived from the west. The last attempt[1247] at finding a native origin for the Chinese written characters, in neglecting several conditions of the problem, such as a possible foreign origin, has proved to be a complete failure, as shown by the remarks and criticisms of several scholars. The author has attempted to show a hieroglyphical and therefore an independent origin for all the written characters of China. He has neglected the conditions of preservation of these characters, the political state of the country which led to the creation of new pictorial characters in some of the illiterate circuits, and the natural increase of all systems of writing belonging to the semi-ideographic semi-phonetic stage, as that imported by Hwang-ti and his people. Pictorial characters of new make would not appear as they do on coins of the fourth century B.C. if it was not so. We may refer for this to our remarks *suprà* § 100.

314. For the sake of argument let us for a moment neglect this pictorial evidence. It cannot be doubted that identical hints rather often lead to developments and results somewhat identical. The question therefore is to know wherefrom the hint has come. It may be from inner or outer nature, such for instance as the awe of spirits in the one case, and a veneration for the polestar on the other, or it may be a communication from another nation. In the latter circumstance, when the similarity turns out on things which are not what they are by necessity of nature, and might as well be altogether different, as far as this necessity is concerned, it must be a coincidence or an importation. Historical circumstances and physical possibilities must be surveyed to make sure of the importation, and in the absence of historical records, numerous similarities of the kind justifying and supporting one the other, must be established for the same object. In the long array of items of culture collected in the present work, with the shortcomings of the author and the difficulties of all pioneering investigations, it is unavoidable that within long series of finally established instances there may be some misapprehensions, premature

identifications, suggestive of further researches, which shall only disprove or confirm them individually.

NOTE—

1247) Rev. E. Faber, *Prehistoric China*: J. Ch. Br. R. A. S., xxiv., 1890, and the refutations by Dr. J. Edkins and others, *Ibid*, p. 211, sq., by Prof. G. Schlegel, *T"oung Pao*, 1891, ii. 105-110; cf. also T. de L., *The Loan of Chaldeo-Elamite culture to China*, note 35. Dr. Faber does not seem to have been acquainted with my papers on the subject.

III.—*Monosyllabic Theory*.

315. The most curious objection is undoubtedly that which was made to me by Prof. J. Legge, of Oxford, at the International Congress of Orientalists of 1892, here in London. The Nestor of Sinologists said that although he had heard of my works on the Babylonian sources of the early Chinese civilisation, he did not look at any of them because, as he learned from Prof. Sayce, the Akkadian language is polysyllabic, while that of the Chinese is monosyllabic, therefore their civilisation must be older than that of the Akkadians, instead of the reverse (*sic*).

My answer to this is twofold. Firstly, the linguistic question has nothing to do in the matter; secondly, I have never held that Akkadian was ancestor of the Chinese, since my contention is that the two languages are related by common descent from a remote stock,[1248] and not so to speak in the relation of mother to daughter.[1249]

NOTES--

1248) Cf. my remarks on this subject in *The Oldest Book of the Chinese*, 1893, i. 106-8.

1249) The latter view is nearly that of the Rev. C. J. Ball, in his papers on the *New Accadian*, 1890, to which I have demurred. In my opinion we do not know enough of the old forms of the Chinese words to make many safe comparisons, inasmuch as the monosyllabic words of a limited phonetism as that of the Chinese (where a single sound has as many as 1200 different meanings), can be compared with any monosyllables of any language as done by John Webb (1669), Daniel Webb (1787), Julius Klaproth (1811), M. Hyde Clark, *Protohistoric Comparative Philology*, 1875; M. R. P. Grey *Comparative Philology of the Old and New Worlds* in relation to Archaic speech, 1893, &c. On the other hand we are aware that many present words monosyllabic in Chinese are crippled forms of former polysyllables. Cf. T. de L., *Le Non-Monosyllabisme du Chinois Antique*, l'écart centre les langues écrite et parlée d'aujourd-'hui et l'histoire de la langue écrite, 1889 ; Raoul de la Grasserie, *Des Recherches Récentes de la Linguistique relatives aux langues de l'Extrême Orient*, principalement d'après les travaux de M. Terrien de Lacouperie, 1891 ; C. de Harlez, *Existe-t-il des langues purement Monosyllabiques?* 1893 ; in his latest paper *The Accadian Affinities of the Chinese*, 1898, Mr. C. J. Ball, has admitted the neo-monosyllabism of the Chinese. Cf. also T. de L., TIBET, *Philology* in *Encyclopædia Britannica*, 1888, xxiii, 847-8.

IV.—*Astrognosie.*

816. Some of the Pre-Chinese tribes appear to have had a taste for star-gazing, and the result, as referred to previously, has been a traditional amount of astronomical lore in connection with their customs and agricultural pursuits. The immigration of the Chinese with a stellar lore of their own, the introduction of new plants, and the successive importation of further astrological notions in the course of centuries, have made the symbolism derived from the stars in China most complicated. This symbolism looked upon as a whole forms the fourth objection which we shall now meet. It is the only theory which has been developed with any show of serious arguments.

The claim of the present work goes against that theory put forth with great erudition and ingenuity some nineteen years ago by Dr. G. Schlegel in his *Uranographie Chinoise.*[1250] The contention of the learned author was and is that 19,000 years ago astronomy was already cultivated in China, and that traces of that astronomy exist in the symbolical names given to asterisms in the literature, and can be recognised in alleged relations between them and popular customs. The peculiar and multiple attributions of symbolism to the same stars and identical attributions to different stars are better explained in our view by the variety of foreign sources, north and south, which have successively contributed to the formation and increase of the astronomy of the Chinese—joined to their own observations—than by a theoretical array of thousands of years, unsupported by a tithe of evidence from any other source, and which nothing justifies. Let us remember here that according to the astronomer, John Reeves, in his appendix to Morrison's Dictionary, I. ii. 1063 : " To our surprise we find that the Chinese know little or nothing about astronomical science." It consists chiefly of a mass of facts and notions ill-digested and ill-understood until they received the help of the Hindus and Mohammedans to put them into some sort of shape. And as to the accordance claimed by Dr. Schlegel of the names of asterisks and constellations with the natural history, ethnography, and customs of China, no one acquainted with the remarkable cleverness of the Chinese writers at combining information and finding allusions to anything in everything,[1251] unthought of before their own combinations, will attribute any value to the alleged accordance as a traditional evidence of 16 or 18,000 years standing.

317. Prof. G. Schlegel (p. 498) avers that the Chinese have reached China by the north west, between the 30th and 27th century B.C., and that a striking agreement exists between the names of western constellations and those of Chinese asterisms,[1252] whose invention which should be attributed to the Pre-Chinese races,[1253] and which would denote a state of uncivilisation, of the stone age, like among savages of the present day,[1254] would have wandered from east to west. We think it has been the reverse, and that the resemblances, like most of the imported notions enumerated in the present work, have all the appearances of a clumsy learning of western notions. As recognised by the learned author himself, peoples without writing have a short memory. Now we cannot admit, as a human possibility, that symbols fancied in the relative position of some stars could, without written records to keep up the interpretation, have had a sufficient hold on uncivilised minds to last unaltered for twelve thousand years, when the alleged symbolism had long ceased to exist as a result of the precession of equinoxes. Moreover the etymology of the Chinese characters, first written some 4500 years ago and transmitted by tradition, through which most of the supposed astronomical symbolism is examined, is most difficult to ascertain, and although we may often recognise the component parts of a symbol, we are by no means sure of their individual meaning, still less of their symbolism. The Chinese themselves vary on their interpretations, which are often biassed by the current ideas of the time of the exegete, and we have seldom the possibility of correcting them, inasmuch as we are ourselves exposed to prejudices of the same kind. Furthermore the difficulty is enhanced by the multiplicity of names,[1255] sometimes six or eight, amongst which the most suitable are unavoidably selected for a theory

in view, while another theory could select as well and with the same success suitable names among the others.

318. We cannot but find, notwithstanding the remarkable amount of ingenuity and erudition displayed by the author of the *Uranographie Chinoise*, that such a symbolism forms a basis by far too slender and utterly inadequate for the huge construction made upon it beyond five thousand years ago. Should the theory be true there would not be a gap of some twelve thousand years of dead silence, between the supposed symbolisms of 17,000 and 3000 years B.C.[1256] We are utterly convinced that adequate explanations, more in accordance with historical traditions, can be found for the remote cases alleged in the work: and as to those of later date which might resist criticism at close quarters, it is easier to understand some of them as introduced from older centres of culture where writing was known several thousand years earlier, than to suppose their preservation without writing among savages.

319. All the foregoing reasons are not however sufficient to disprove all the suggestions put forward in support of his views by so great a scholar as my friend Dr. Schlegel. Some cases may have been explained away by the progress of research since the publication of his work.[1257] Others may have resulted from misconceptions[1258] and overstretching the symbolism.[1259] But my readers will agree with me that there must be some other cause, more general in character which pervades the whole edifice. It is this cause which we have yet to describe. The learned author of the *Uranographie Chinoise* has not taken the usual means to make safe his basis before building his monument; he has not made any *text-critik* of his documents, nor has even classified them chronologically.[1260] Should he have taken this preliminary step, he could not have failed to be struck by the fact that the names from which he was able to derive his inferences of oldest antiquity are not the oldest denominations that they ought to be. For the readers of the present work there is nothing surprising in that. Let them remember the numerous items of western astrological-astronomy introduced in North China by the trading mariners of the Erythrœan Sea, who frequented the emporia of Shantung during three centuries, 675-375 B.C., and then removed gradually their stations to the south. Denominations of stars accompanied the names of months, zodiac and

cycles (distinct from those of early times) for astrological purposes, which they imported among the Chinese. And let them remember also, that about 400 B.C., if not before, through some circumstances historically unexplained, although they are facts, they changed their sea route and henceforth passed south of Sumatra-Java, therefore south of the equator, where the seasons are the reverse of those of the north, and where, also, the stars had and have just the reverse of their usual symbolism in the north. This southern symbolism which they communicated to the Chinese has naturally thrown into the *astrognosie* of the latter some disturbing notions unaccountable but by the historical circumstances of their introduction in North China, or by the stupendous hypothesis of the *Uranographie Chinoise*, which, written when the aforesaid circumstances were yet undiscovered, has thus become unnecessary. History within its limited period is sufficient to explain the whole thing.

320. Dr. G. Schlegel says in his last answer that "the disbelievers in Chinese antiquity will firstly have to prove by undeniable astronomical testimony that Elam and Chaldea have an older history than China, which is impossible, the oldest astronomical observation in the world being the eclipse of the sun in B.C. 7 May, 2165." Let us first remark that in his paper on this eclipse with Dr. Kuhnert, he gives an alternative date of B.C. 12 May, 1904, which alone fits the lengths of reigns in Chinese history. But this is a secondary point. The learned author has forgotten that according to Berosus, the astronomical observations sent by Kallisthenes from Babylon to Aristotle in B.C. 331 reached back to B.C. 2243 (Pliny N. H. vii. 57). But this is nothing compared to the evidence put forward by the well known astronomer, Prof. Norman Lockyer, in his recent work on *The Dawn of Astronomy*,[1262] about astronomical observations in the sixth and fifth milleniums B.C. Dr. Schlegel (p. 768, 770) gives the date of 2852 for Fuhi, the fabulous inventor of the Chinese writing. At the Academie des Inscriptions, on the 8th and 23th September, 1893, Prof. J. Oppert gave the translation of an inscription of Bingani-sar-iris, a Semitic King of Nippur, older than 4000 years B.C., and since then Mr. Joachim Menant, has read in the same place a paper on three Chaldean rulers older than 4000 B.C.. such as Sangani, Sarluti, Bingani Sarluti. These answers are conclusive. They are strengthened moreover by the historical circumstances of foreign sources for the

Chinese astronomy (*supra* 309). Besides the notions imported from the west by Hwang-ti and his followers, we have learned that the first catalogue of the stars was made by Wu-hien, a man from the west, who had come from or through Karashar, and that the two astronomical works by Kan Kung and Shih Shen which form the substratum of the Book of Stars, *Sing King*, were written in the north east of China, after that the trading mariners of the Erythræan Sea had there spread their astrologico-astronomical notions for three centuries.

NOTES—

2050) Cf. *supra*, § 309, and note 1284, also note 1255, and the references. About double crops, Wells Williams, *Middle Kingdom*, revised edition, 1883, ii. 5, says: "Grain is not sown broadcast, and this facilitates hoeing and weeding the fields as they require. Two crops are planted, one of which ripens after the other; maize and pulse, millet and sesamum, or sorghum and squash, are thus grown together."

1251) *Uranographie Chinoise, ou Preuves directes que l'astronomie primitive est originaire de la Chine, et qu'elle a été empruntée par les anciens peuples occidentaux à la sphère Chinoise*. La Haye, 1875, 929 pp. and atlas. *Réponse aux critiques de l'Uranographie Chinoise*, 23 pp., 1880. *China or Elam*, in T'ung Pao, Sept., 1891, p. 243-5; the latter is intended to be an answer to a criticism of mine in *From Ancient Chaldea and Elam to early China* : B. and O. R. v. 34, 84 ; the sole remark to be noticed is that the greater facility for communications between the west and the east was equal between the east and the west.

1252) The remains of ancient Chinese literature have been overhauled unceasingly during twenty centuries or more, in more or less indifferent and clever manner, most generally indifferent, and it has now become an almost Herculean task to get through the whole fabric and get rid of the inaccurate interpretations which have been piled up over them by the native commentators.

1253) *Uranographie*, 728, 738, &c., 655-712.

1254) *T'ung Pao*, iv. 493. *Uranographie*, 766.

1255) Curiously enough when it became necessary to distinguish every star by a name, some of the denominations possessed only by a central star were distributed around it. For instance with Regulus, Cassiopée, &c. ; Sirius, the Dog Star, the Bow Star of the Chaldeans has near it a Bow Star, and a Chacal Star in the Chinese uranosphere. Cf. also below *add.* 28, and on the lateness of the conception of the four Animal Quadrants of the Sky, *add.* 392.

1256) *i.e.* Between 14,671 and 2700 B.C., cf. O.C., 498.

1257) The argument derived from the astronomical statement of Yao about the most prominent stars that were to be observed for each of the four seasons comes to nought, and is explained away by the shifting of attribution between the symbols of the cardinal points which occurred during the migration of the Bak families, as shown by their obvious derivation from the older Chaldeo-Elamite symbols and the discrepancies in other legendary accounts. The compiler of the chapter of the *Shu King* which is not a contemporary document, has undoubtedly mistaken the information when expanding the brief original statement. Cf. on the subject: T. de L., *Early History*, 1880, p. 29; *The Shifted Cardinal Points, from Elam to Early China:* Jan., 1888; *The Loan of Chaldeo-Elamite Culture to Early China*, 1892, p. 9-14; *The Shifting of the Names and Symbols of the points of space from Chaldea to China*, as evidence of the South-West Asiatic Origin of Early Chinese Civilisation: London and China Telegraph, Sept. 13, 1892; *The Oldest Book of the Chinese* 1893, vol. i., p. 111-4.

1258) The star *Deneb*, alpha Cygni, was Polestar, some 17,500 years ago, and some traces of so important a fact should be found in the *Astrognosie Indestructible*, if the alleged 18,000 years of Chinese astronomy were based on evidence and not on misconceptions. But there is nothing. *Deneb* is one of eight stars forming what is called a *T'ien tsin*, or Heaven's Ford, probably because the Milky Way branches there in two lines (which continue running in parallel to the south west). Professor G. Schlegel, however, thinks (p. 208) that he has found a tradition of 16,000 years of age in the following statement of Ko-hung, an alchemist of our fourth century:—"The Heaven's River (*i.e.*, the Milky Way) coming from the north pole separates into two branches, reaching to the south pole; one branch goes by the *Nan tou* (λ Sagittarii on the east), and the other goes by the *Tung tsin* (Gemini on the west)." As I have given in brackets the relative positions of the asterisms indicated, which both are on the ecliptic, at 12 h. R.A., one from the other, the two branches in question cannot be the two lines branched off in Cygnus, as inadvertently supposed in the *Uranographie Chinoise*, and therefore *Deneb* or its region has nothing to do in the affair. Ko-hung was speaking of what he could himself see in the heavens, and we may be sure that he knew nothing of the North Pole of 16,000 years before his time. A glance at the stellar chart shows that the Milky Way has a sort of head, in the north of Cepheus, between the stars γ and β Alphirk; and this is its nearest point to the North Pole which was then nearer to the present Pole Star than of *Kokhab*, the former one (1000 B.C.). Ko-hung was certainly speaking of the central point, equidistant from Sagittarius and the Gemini, which would not have been the case with *Deneb*. Therefore we may be satisfied that there is no evidence there of any antiquity for the Chinese astronomy.

Rastaban, γ Draconis, as a Pole Star 13,000 years ago has left no record in the Chinese astronomy. This is what we expected. On the other hand *Shuban*, Chinese *Si fan*, α Draconis, the Pole Star of 3000 B.C. is well described as such. It was called in early

Chaldea, the Great God of Heavens, the *yoke* or pivot of the heavens (Sayce, *Anc. Relig. Bab.*, 291), all denominations which have been received and preserved in the Chinese nomenclature (*Uranographie Chinoise*, 506-8). β Ursæ Minoris, the Pole Star of 1000 B.C., is still called the God's Star, *Ti sing* or *Tien Ti sing*. The present Pole Star (*a* Ursæ Minoris) besides the name of *Kou-chen*, from the Arab *Kachab*, which it shares with several surrounding stars, now enjoys the polestar title of *Tien Hwang Ta Ti*, the Great God Emperor of Heavens.

1259) It is interesting to examine how the symbolism of the *Astrognosie Indestructible* (Uranographie Chinoise, 75) can be obtained. Let us see for instance *Lou*, the sixteenth *siu* (the second sih of Babylon) which is given us (p. 331-2) as the "Moissonneuse," whose symbol *lou* represents, " Une femme portant sur sa tête un faisceau d'épis." No Chinese authority is given for the interpretation. If we refer to the *Shwoh wan* (89 A.D.) the phonetic *Shwoh wan* (1833), the *Luh shu t'ung* of Min Ts'i Kih (1661), the *Tchuen tze wei* of Tung wei fu (1691), we find that the symbol in question was a self-spelling character $\overset{-K}{\underset{LU}{}}$—, composed of NIU=LIU, woman, suggesting the initial, and placed above it to suggest a final —K, one or other of the following characters: *Kiu*, mortar, *Kwan*, pierced through, *Kwai*, empty basket, *Kin*, looking crossways, or *Kwan*, accustomed. In course of time the phonetic suggestion has been forgotten, and the upper symbol has been altered: *Kiu* written with two eyes became only one, *muh*, afterwards *mu*, mother, and *mu* not, and another symbol joined to it has become *tchung*, middle. The meaning of the whole is, a secluded woman, emptiness, seclusion, fagged, or troublesome member, &c., which are rather the reverse of the alleged symbolism. And among the ideo-phonetic derivates from the same we find words for: to drag, to plunder, to hollow out, basket for carriages, sowing machine, &c., in fact nothing suggesting the harvest.

Now let us examine another case. *Mao*, the Pleiades, which shows a curious confusion, made during the Han dynasty. *Mao* (*Mul* in Chaldea) is written sun—open door; the latter sign is and has always been *Mao* (the fourth sign of the duodenary cycle); the former represents the three stars which figured in the oldest forms, as shown (save the *Shwoh wan*) by the standard works above mentioned. This *Mao* is much like another character *yu* (*liu* in compounds) a closed door, barred at the top; the only difference between the two being a bar at the top of the latter which is lacking in *Mao*. This *yu* or *liu* joined with the sign for tree, makes *liu*, the tree-liu, or willow, which is the name given to six, afterwards eight, small stars of *Hydra*. In the *Shi King*, ode on small stars, *Siao Sing*, the poet says: " Small are those starlets, and there are *Tsan* (Orion) and *Mao* (the Pleiades). So the modern commentators have it (cf. J. Legge, *Chin. Class.*, iv. 32), but the oldest interpreters did not think so. When Mao Tchang edited the *Shi King*, 129 B.C., he understood *Tsan* as referring to some stars in *Scorpio*, and the now alleged *Mao* as being *Liu*, the aforesaid star in *Hydra*. He could not understand that so conspicuous star points as Pleiades and Orion should be spoken of as small stars. The author of the *Tchun tsiu yuan ming pao* of the following century, quoted in the *K'ang hi tse tien*, s.v. *Mao*, shared the same view, and said that the stars of the Ode were the six (not seven) star *Liu* (of Hydra). It must not be forgotten that the use of determinatives had not yet reached its later fixity. In *Uran. Chin.* we are told that *Mao* was composed of s u n and *Liu*, d o o r s h u t, and therefore that it must have indicated the autumn, thousands of years before, and that the composition s u n—o p e n d o o r was an after thought and a mistake. We have seen that such was not the case and we have seen also how the misconception arose. *Mao*, the Pleiades, the stars of the Open Door announced the spring c. 2250 B C. The astronomical book of *She ki* 27, 12v.) says that between the *Mao*. Pleiades, and *Pyh*, the Hyades (where passes the ecliptic) was a (or the) route of heaven, *Ti'en Kiai*, which is an interesting confirmation of the meaning of *Mao*.

With reference to the Gates of Heaven through which passes the ecliptic, herewith another instance which shows the late and western sources of the Chinese astronomical notions; the *Nan ho* (α Procyon, β and η Canis Minor) and the *Poh ho* (Castor, Pollux, &c., Gemini), respectively the South and North River, and also called Gates of Heaven, occupy this position just south and north of the ecliptic, east of the Milky Way.

1260)   As unhappy result of this, Cf. for a typical instance, p. 368 : " Ce qui a donné lieu au fameux passage du *Chou King* que *l'y* (the 19th *Siu*) aime la pluie;" in the foot note we find a Chinese quotation to that effect from a *commentary* (by Tsai Yung, 175 A.D.) on the Great Plan, *Hung fan*, chapter of the *Shu King*, but not from the text, where as a matter of fact the word *py* does not appear at all ! The text, par. 38, says only that " some stars love the wind and some love the rain. Another instance in another way is the myth of the C o w h e r d and S p i n n i n g D a m s e l, identified with stars near the Milky Way, either with the River's Drum, *Ho K'u*, β γ Aquila, or the constellation of the O x *Niu* (parts of Capricornus and Sagittarius), and W e g a, α Lyre. Hwai nan tze (d. 122 B.C.) first gave currency to a romantic idea on the subject by declaring that the two are separated all the year round, except on the seventh night of the seventh month, when " Magpies fill up the Milky Way and enable the Spinning Damsel to cross over." (Cf. Mayers, *Ch. R. M.* 311.) In the *Uran. Chin* , p. 494, we are told that the myth must date 16,000 years ago, because at that time the two constellations were culminating together at the winter solstice ! But there is no evidence whatever that the myth existed in remote historical times. The learned author refers to some customs of the Dames du Palais in *Wei* and *Tsin*, mentioned in the *King Ts'u shui shi ki* of our sixth century, as customs of these states during the Tchou dynasty, while they are simply those of two contemporary dynasties reigning in north and south China about 400 A.D. This is shown by several other contemporary works, cf. T. P. Y. L , kiv. 31, fol. 6-11. My explanation is much more simple. When HAN Wu-ti had become Emperor in 140 B.C., attention was called by the courtiers and myth-mongers frequenting his court to the seventh day of the seventh month which was his birthday. Now that time of the year is that of the annual appearance of a shower of shooting stars in the vicinity of the two constellations in question. These shooting stars became the magpies of the myth which was built upon these circumstances. I just find in the T. P. Y. L., 875, 7, 7 v. instances of shooting stars near the Spinning Damsel in 198 and 356 A.D., in the middle of the year. In order to work out the matter more completely, cf. Ed. Biot, *Catalogue Général des Etoiles filantes, &c., depuis le VIIe siècle ar. J. C., d'après les documents Chinois*: Mem. pres. Acad. des Sc., 1848, x. 129-352, 415-422; P. Parker, *Observations made at Canton on the Shooting Stars of the 10th and 11th August, 1839:* Silliman Journal, 1840, xxxviii. 301-6.

1261) *China or Elam*, T'oung Pao, Sept, 1891, p. 246.

1262) Cf. the following articles of the same scholar in *Nature:* *On some points in Ancient Egyptian Astronomy:* January 28, Feb. 18, 1892. *On the Early Temple and Pyramid Builders:* May 18. *The Early Asterisms:* Sept. 7, 28, Dec. *The Origin of the Year*: March 29, June 2, Nov. 10, 1892, Jan. 5, 1893. Cf. Also P. Jensen, *Die Kosmologie der Babylonier*, Strasburg, 1890; Fritz Hommel, *Die Astronomie der alter Chaldäer:* Ausland, 1891-2. With the progress of research in Chaldean Astronomy grows the evidence of the Chinese indebtedness to it. Cf. *Mul, Mao*, Pleiades, *Ku, Kio Spica*, &c.; part of Draco, an enclosure, in both countries, &c. Cf. *add.* 41.

V.—*On BAK, as a Name of the Earliest Civilised Chinese.*

321. *Bak Sing* is the earliest denomination in their historical literature which the Chinese used to give to themselves, exclusively of the native populations they had subdued. The Bak Sings were the followers of Hwang-ti who came with him from the north-west, and settled at first in the south-west corner of Kansuh. Since more than ten years I have several times objected to the common rendering of Bak sings by Hundred Families,[1263] and I have said that in my opinion, an early ethnical name of the people underlies this denomination. This view has been accepted by many scholars, ignored by several, and once or twice protested against. My readers may therefore be glad to find here the various reasons, never as yet put together, on which are based my conclusions to that effect.

322. Sing, a compound symbol meaning literally, "born (sheng) from one woman (niu)," was apparently applicable originally to all those born from one wife only and to their descendants, all necessarily bearing the same surname.[1264] In the oldest etymological dictionary, the Shwoh wan of the first century, it is described as "that with which a man is born." And in the historical texts since the most remote times it is applied to the clans, or their names, belonging exclusively to the Chinese proper. Their number was very small at first, and we hear of the "eight most ancient surnames," as if this was an established fact.[1265] The descendants of Hwang-ti are said to have borne only twelve surnames,[1266] and the Emperor Shun was praised in after ages for having given government employment to all the chiefs of the Sings, less than twenty in number. Since that remote time they have multiplied to thousands, but those which are most frequently met do not reach a total of beyond four hundred and fifty.[1267]

323. BAK was a self-spelling symbol made of two superposed characters in the script of oldest times.[1268] It was composed of Pei, p r e c i o u s, or P eh, w h i t e, or Pi, n o s e, or M uk = Bak, e y e, for the initial and of KHa, hia b e l o w, or of K'ao e f f o r t, for the final consonant. The selection of these symbols traditional as it was is rather instructive. The nose among the Chinese as in the west, was looked upon as the beginning of the child,[1269] hence the use of the character denotes here that the meaning of B a k had once in itself something initial; the e y e was most important as a suggestion which we shall have to remember further on.

As a significative symbol, BAK occurs in ancient literature with three different meanings :—

(1) A hundred, as a definite number.[1270]

(2) A collective and indefinite number, all the things or beings appearing to the front of their class or kind.

(3) To the front, forward, to incite, exertion, &c.

324. In the expression Bak Sing, the first symbol cannot have had in China the meaning of one hundred as a definite number, for the conclusive reason that the number of Sings in early times was not one-fifth of that, as we have just seen. If the Sings ever numbered

a hundred before, it would be at the original seat of the race in West Asia, in the country from where Hwang-ti had originated with his followers.[1271] The use of a numeral as a people's own name is a well-known feature of some Ural-Altaic races. Let us remember here the name of the Kirghizes, from *kirk*, f o r t y, and that of the *Yüs* Usbek tribes, meaning properly the H u n d r e d.[1272]

325. Kung Yng-ta the famous commentator of the classics (A.D. 574-648) in his remarks on the first book of the *Shu King* has shown most positively that *Baksing* was a designation of the foremost families of the state, and that it was still so, under the Tchou dynasty. The Chinese families alone having sings and forming the elite of the population, the exalting meaning was befitting to the case. It included them all,[1273] whence the expression Wan Sings the 10,000 surnames occasionally used in its stead. The same reason of exclusiveness applies to the expression *Bak Kwan*, all the officers because they were necessarily all belonging to the elite or Chinese *sings*. And it does not follow from the equation Bak=*Wan* with reference to the Sings that *Bak* had a wholesale meaning. As an evidence of this, one may remark that the expression, which should be expected otherwise, of *Bak Min* for all the people does not exist at all in the *Shu King*, nor in the *Shi King*; it is *wan min* which occurs, and the use of *wan*, and even that of *tchau*, m i l l i o n, as a collective term is usual in the classics. *Bak* appears fourteen times in the *Shu*, and twice in the *Shi*, with *Sing*, and in thirty expressions in the two works.[1274] On the other hand *wan*, t e n t h o u s a n d, is met with a hundred times or more as a wholesale collective noun in the two great classics we have just named.

326. To resume, the term *Bak* occurs in the ancient literature,[1275] with reference only to choice or foremost beings or things,[1276] and it does apply generally to a complete body of beings or things, as far as that body is by itself an elite in its kind.

Let us remark before proceeding any further that BAK appears also to be a family surname, although it has not been preserved to the present day in its singleness. In the list of the mythical kings we find a *Bak Wang*, i.e., King of Bak. During the Tchou dynasty we meet such names as *Bak Li*, *Bay Fêng*.[1277] And in the *Peh Kia Sing* we find *Peh*, indifferently written with the symbol h u n d r e d or white. *Bak Sing* can be compared to such expressions as *Li min*, the *Li*, or able-bodied people,[1278] *Yao jen*, the men Yao, *Tchung Kia*, the family Tchung, the *Sung Kia*, the family Sung, the *Ts'ai Kia*, the family Ts'ai, the *Lung Kia*, the family Lung, &c. BAK was not a proper name of forgotten or foreign origin whose meaning was lost. It was a word still preserving its pristine transparent form, whose meaning was yet fully understood by the people, being helped to that effect by the ideographism of the writing. It was that and it was also an indefinite collective, meaning the foremost and the utmost.

327. It appears from the foregoing remarks that the Chinese sources alone cannot give a satisfactory explanation of the various acceptations of BAK. The Mother writing and the cradle land of the earliest civilisers of China happily have much to say in the matter, and they come to the rescue. We have had to notice in the Ku-wen spellings of BAK, that the ideogram for eye was most important. Now in the old Babylonian writing from which the earliest Chinese symbols were derived, more or less directly, the symbol for eye has the sound BAKH, and the meanings to see, foremost, before, and the like. It means also a thousand. The symbol for hundred, *me*, which looks like the crippled form of the other, means also numerous.[1279] In the Akkadian vocabulary, which is the oldest representative of the large linguistic formation to which the Chinese belongs, we find such words as *Bakh*, prince, *Baku*, strong, numerous, *Bah*, abounding, flourishing, &c.[1280] We may compare to these the Turkish *bogh*, prince, the Mongolian *bagha*, thousand, the Chinese *Bak*, *Puk*, &c.,[1281] great, &c.

The existence at the fountain head of their civilisation of a word and similar symbol having the same meanings as those preserved by the Chinese is more than suggestive in favour of our views.

328. But this is not all. The same word appears to have been used extensively as a geographical and ethnical term in that same region from which the early civilisers of China have come according to all probabilities. Bakhtyari, Bagistan (Behistun), Bagdad, Bakhdi (Baktra) are instances of the case. Moreover we hear in the Elamite inscriptions of a King of Baks,[1282] which fact shows that sister tribes of the

early civilised Chinese were still in existence in later historical times.

329. Therefore we cannot but be satisfied that the word Bak was used as an ethnical qualificative, and that in calling themselves Bak Sings or Bak families, the early Chinese were only preserving the traditional and limited used of a word, whose meaning was still clear to them. We may call them the BAKS or the BAK SINGS without hesitation, but not the *Hundred Families*.

NOTES—

1263) Cf. *The Chinese Mythical Kings:* Acad. 6th October, 1883; *The Language of China before the Chinese,* 1887, p. 116-8; Wheat carried *from Mesopotamia to early China,* 1888, p. 6; *Les Langues,* 1888, add. p. 159-160.

1264 There is no evidence available that the meaning suggested by the composition of the ideogram was yet understood at any earliest time of Chinese history.

1265) Cf. Herbert A. Giles, *On the Surnames of the Chinese:* Historic China, 1882, p. 359.

1266) *Kwoh-yu,* Sü tch'en. R. K. Douglas, *China,* 1887, p. 250-1, has given these twelve surnames.

1267) In the well known *Peh Kia Sing,* compiled under the Sung dynasty, where are found the names of 408 single and 30 double of the Sings most commonly met, more than one hundred of them claim Hwang-ti as their ancestor. In the *K'ang hi tze tien,* 1678 simple, 168 double, and 8 triple Sings are mentioned; while in the great Cyclopædia *Ku Kin t'u shu tsih tch'eng* there are as many as 4657 entered, 3038 of which are single, as stated *suprà* note 105. An interesting statement, although somewhat unclear, occurs about the Sings, in the *Tso tchuen,* Yn Kung, viii. 10, or 715 B.C.; *Chin. Class.* v. 26.

1268) Min Ts'i Kih, *Luh shu tung,* x. 1 v. Fu Lwang-siang, *Luh shu fun hay,* ii. 46 v. Tung Wei fu, *Tchuen tze wei.* In the old Tchuen style we find the expression *Bak sing* written in one complex symbol, made of *Muk-Buk,* e y e, with *shang,* l i f e, over it, suggesting distantly the reading; as there are two instances of the case, there is no mistake in the decipherment.

1269) Notably among the Egyptians. In Chinese, *pi tsin,* n o s e a n c e s t o r, means f i r s t a n c e s t o r.

1270) In some ancient texts, as for instance in the old MS. of Lao tze's work, the symbol BAK has cl. 9 as an adjunct for the meaning of 100. But such is not always the case in other texts.

1271) But there is no evidence of such a thing which must remain in the dark of the past, long before the migration eastward of the early

Chinese, and is apparently contradicted by the evidence collected below.

1272) Cf. W. Radloff, *Zeits. f. Erdk.*, 1871, p. 505. Cf. *tume*, all in Mandshu, *tumen*, 10,000 in Mongol, *tumen*, name of a leader among the Hiung-nus.

1273) *Wan Sing* occurs only five times in the *Shu* and twice in the *Shi* Kings.

1274) In some of these however the meaning h u n d r e d is clear. In the *Shu King*, *Shi King*, *Lun-yu*, *Tchun-yung*, *Ta hioh*, *Tchun tsiu*, and *Mêng-tze*, I have counted thirty-two different expressions composed with Bak; in nine of them the meaning h u n d r e d is clear, and in some cases imperative, while in the twenty-three others the word means the foremost and utmost of the kind or class referred to. Cf. J. Legge, *Chinese Classics*, vol. iv. p. 371, 429, 440, 486, 548, 949, 967; vol. i. p. 352; vol. ii. p. 246; and vol. iii. p. 49, 55, 64, 198, 341, 348, 381, 410, 432, 441, 460, 498, 515, 545; vol. iv. p. 357, 362, 492, 551, 586, 638; vol. ii. p. 31; vol. i. p. 190.

1275) With a few exceptions in late times arisen from the usual abuse of terms.

1276) Cf. for instance *Shu King*, v., x. 10, and xvi. 9.

1277) *Bak-li* of the State of Ts'in in the seventh century. *Bak fung* a disciple of Lieh-tze. But this BAK had probably no connection with the original Bak Sings.

1278) Cf. On this name my paper on *The Black Heads of Babylonia and ancient China*, 1891, par. 21. The use of *Kia* was originally reserved for family in speaking of the native population of the country in contradistinction with *Sing* chiefly used for the Chinese themselves.

1279) M. C. J. Ball, *The Accadian Affinities with Chinese*, 1893, has suggested on other ground the same confusion that is noticed here of the two symbols by the civilisers of China.

1280) Cf. Rud. Brunnow, *Classified List of Cuneiform Characters*, Nos. 9257, 9265, 9287; 10,354, 10,372, 10,374, 10,356, 7267, 7269, 7272, &c. Cf. also the Assyrian words: *bakhar*, to collect, group; *bakhar*, splendour; *bakhlat*, the own people of the king (Sarg. 46).

1281) The latter have been studied by G. Schlegel, *Sinico-Aryaca*, p. 85.

1282) As shown by Mr. W. St. Chad Boscawen. Cf. *Les Langues de la Chine avant les Chinois*, p 159. Another name of interest belonging to a portion of the early Chinese is that now read *Hia*, which the Ku-wen spellings show to have been originally read Ketchi = Ket-si = Katse. The name is known in West Asia. The best instance occurs in the famous *Stèle des Vautours*. There we see Eannada King of Sirpurra or Lagash, son of Akurgal, and grandson of Urnina, striking victoriously at his enemies who belonged to the country of *Ish-han* or *Kashtu*. These enemies deformed their skulls as the Bak Sings used to do in later times. Could they be the ancestors of the latter? Cf. B. and O. R., vi. 96, and *Tapered Heads in Anterior Asia and Early China*, ibid. p. 195. On Sirpurra, cf. W. St. Chad Boscawen, ibid. vii. 2.

VI.—*Alleged difficulty of the Journey from West to East Asia*.

330. One of the semi-objections first made against my discovery of the south-west Asiatic origin of the Chinese civilisation was the great distance, and the difficulty of the route between west and east Asia for large caravans and migratory tribes. The objection is specious, but must disappear on further consideration, geographical and historical. Some or the following facts have already been put forward by me as an answer to the objection, but as I have some new facts to quote I may as well marshall all of them together.

The chief difficulty of the route has always been the passage through the Bolor, or Pamir, or Tsung-ling mountains, impracticable except at one season of the year to reach the Chinese Turkestan. The more circuitous route by the north, *i.e.*, through Ferghana, which was not suggested by the existence there of gems or valuable products coveted by traders does not seem to have been known and used, but much later, when the growing bulk of the trade made it necessary to find a more convenient route than the older one. At first the trade route to the east was only that which was made imperative by nature and the localities of the products to get. This was the route through Badakshan, Wakhan, and Yarkand to the jade mines as we shall see further on (note 1291).

331. Two routes were known and used by the Chinese about the Christian era. They are described in the Annals of the first Han dynasty,[1283] as follows :—" From Yü-men (jade gate) and Yang barrier (north-west Kansuh) there are two roads to the western regions. That by Shen-shen, skirting the river Po, on the north of the Nan Shan (southern range) and leading west to *Sha-Kiu* (Yarkand) is the southern road. After, this road passes the Tsung-ling mountains, and leads to the country of the great Yueh-ti and of the Arsacidæ. The northern road starts from the Royal Palace of the Anterior Kiü-tze (*i.e.* from Turfan),[1284] following the course of the river Po, in the direction of the Peh Shan (northern range) as far as *Su-lih* (Kashgar).

This road passing westward across the Tsung-ling range, goes on to Ta-yuan (Ferghana, K'ang Kiu (Sogdiana), and the Yen-tsai (Alani, near the Caspian Sea)."[1285] The two roads were thus following the Yarkand daria and the Kashgar daria respectively.[1286]

332. In more remote times the route to the eastern lands was that which trade and nature had opened long before the migration of the Bak Sings. It was the trade route leading to the asbestos[1287] and ruby mines of Badakshan, to those of Lapis-lazuli (in Khorasan and) in the same region,[1288] which was so highly prized in Babylonia and Egypt, and also to those of Nephrite Jade of Khotan, also highly valued in the Euphratean valley.[1289] The unaccountable taste and partiality, traditionally displayed for jade by the Chinese since the earliest dates, suggest strongly that the early chieftains of the Bak families in Western Asia were engaged themselves in the commerce, and therefore were well acquainted with the trade route. Passing by the Khorasan, Meshed and Baktra, then through Badakshan along the upper course of the Oxus,[1290] crossing either the Chichiklik or the Kandar Pass, of the Pamirs, reaches the Kashgarian Plain,[1291] and the long renowned jade quarries[1292] of the Yarkand daria and Khotan.

333. Once over the Tsung-ling range, the country leading to China was neither so bare and wild nor the objectionable tracts of later times.[1293] And the geographical isolation in which China stands is greatly the result of geological phenomena which have occurred in historical ages, and have become obstructive only long after the Christian era.

In the western part of the Tarym valley, cities still mentioned during the First Han dynasty, in the eastern vicinity of the present Khotan, Yarkand, and Kashgar, were gradually sand buried in the following centuries. It is there that Bactro-Chinese coins older than the Christrian era, also manuscripts of the fifth century, and other antiquities have been dug out in recent years.[1294] The Annals of the pre-cited dynasty recorded that in *Yen-Ki* (Karashar) and the various kingdoms of these western regions, the land was covered with cities, villages, cultivated fields, and domestic animals.

334. Advancing in the direction of China it is the same thing. The geography of the *Heft Iklim*, or seven climates, says that instead

of a sandy desert, the route from Khotan to Kathay in fourteen days was formerly covered with towns and villages.[1295] Several cities which existed at the time of the Chinese pilgrim Sung-yung (518 A.D.) had been buried in the sand when his illustrious fellow-countryman travelled on the same route in 629 A.D.[1296] Ruins of cities have been discovered in the eastern desert near the Lopnor.[1297] The history of Mirza Haidar, called *Tarikh-i-Rashidi*, in describing the great Basin of Eastern Turkestan, says:—" Formerly there were several large cities in this plain ; the names of two have survived—*Lob* and *Kank*, but of the rest there is no trace or tradition, all is buried under the sand."[1298] According to a tradition reported by Johnson, 360 cities were buried in a single day by the sands of the Takla Makan desert (east of Yarkand). The *Liu-sha*, or drifting sands, west of *Yü men Kwan* (An-si tchou of Outer Kansuh), were known to the ancient Chinese, and are mentioned already in the *Yü Kung* of the *Shu King*, although they may not yet have assumed their importance of later times. When Muh Wang of Tchou, in 985 B.C. came back from his expedition in Turkestan, he went further east than when starting, and was compelled to cross the sandy desert, where he happened to be famishing with thirst.[1299] These circumstances are interesting because of some orological details which vouchsafe the genuineness of this recit,[1300] and because of the last peculiarity we have mentioned. We must remark also that the traditional accounts speaks only of a sandy desert, not of shifting sands.[1301]

335. The foregoing notes make it therefore certain that the Eastern Turkestan was different in antiquity of what it is at present, and that numerous states have arisen and disappeared there in the course of ages. The long-famed Flowery Land was more easily approachable by this route than in later centuries. The difficulties of the journey were therefore not in the way when the Chinese Bak Sings chose to migrate to China. There are several instances of such migrations. If I am not mistaken the KUN-WU, about 1900 B.C., and the TCHOU, about 1325 B.C., are instances of the case, but they are, perhaps, too much undistinguishable in the dim history to be accepted as convincing evidence.

336. Let us take some more recent cases of migrations from west to east. An important instance already put forward was that of the

Kalmuck Torguths, who emigrated in 1772 from Russia into China.[1302] But as they had been banished from the Chinese dominion not very long before, and as they came back to their ancient possessions on the invitation of the Emperor, their case is not near enough to that of the Bak Sings of antiquity.

337. Another instance quite satisfactory under that respect is that of the Turks Salar. They are still at present one of eight nations of the Turkomans, east of Meshed, on the road to Bokhara.[1303] During the Ming dynasty a part of them, driven from their country by internal discord, migrated to the Tibetan borders of China. In 1370 three or four of them arrived from Samarkand to the banks of the Yellow River, and founded the present Salar head-village of Katze-Kun (about eighty miles of Kimbun-Lusar); they were rapidly followed by others of their countrymen, and now the villages they occupy are 75 or 100 in number, with a population estimated at 8000 families at the lowest.[1304]

NOTES.—

1283) *Tsien Han Shu*, kiv. 96, 1. In another page we find the following statement: The southern road passing Shen-shen tends southerly to *Wu-yh-shan-li*, which is its terminus. *Ibid.*, Wu-yh-shan-li=O-yk-san-ri=Alexandria=Herat of the present day. Its position is given as follows in the same work : " Wu-yh-shan-li joins *Ke-p'in* (Kabulistan) on the east—it joins Bactria on the north—*Ke-p'in* joins it on the south-west—and Ansik (Parthia) joins it on the east." It was therefore between Bactria, Kabulistan and Parthia. Cf. A. Wylie *Western Regions*, pp. 2, 15, 19, 20.

1284) *Peh She*. T. P., 794, 5v. Also E. Bretschneider, *Med. Res.*, ii. 189.

1285) The *Yem-tsai* under the Second Han Dynasty were called *A-lan-na*; under the After Wei, *i.e.*, after 386 A.D., the country was called *Suh teh*, and also *Uan-na-sha*. Cf. *Tung-tien*: T. P., 793, 10, and 797, 7 v., also Klaproth, *Tableaux Historiques de l'Asie*; F. Hirth, *China and the Roman Orient*, p. 139. Dr. Hirth proposes the equation Yem-tsai=An-tsai=Aorsi of Strabo.

1286) With the increased intercourse during the Han dynasty, we hear of more routes. A branch of the south route was passing through the *Hien-tu-shan*, or Hindu Kush, to Kabulistan ; its difficulties are graphically described in the notice on Ke p'in in the *Tsien Han Shu*. Cf. A. Wylie, *Western Regions*, p. 18, and also on the northern route, p. 33.

1287) On asbestos, *suprà*, p. 31 and note 761.

1288) Deposits of lapis-lazuli are few. Arab geographers and mineralogists mention mines of lazulite at Hastan, Batahá-ristan hill, north-east Persia. Cf. Teifashi, in Cl. Mullet, *Essai sur la Minéralogie Arabe*, pp. 152, 198; J. A. Fev-Mar., 1868. Abulféda, *Géographie*, tr. Reinaud, p. 474; Edrisi, *Géographie*, tr. Jaubert, 478. On those of Badakshan, Kuram valley; cf. J. Wood, *A Journey to the source of the Upper Oxus*, 1872, p. 169-172, and H. Yule, Marco Polo, i. 170. On lapis-lazuli in Assyrio-Babylonia, cf. Perrot-Chipiez, *Art Antique*, ii. 906.

1289) Microscopic structure has shown that the Nephrite objects found in Assyro-Babylonia have come from the Turkestan mines, cf. below add. 162.

1290) On Rock inscriptions in cuneiforms said to have been seen in Wakhan, E. of Badakshan, cf. B. and O. R., vi. 968; cylinders with cuneiform inscriptions have years ago been found in the same region. Cf. Proc. R. G. S.

1291) On the occasional necessity for some travellers to reach first Kashgar; cf. H. Yule, *Marco Polo*, i. 191. Since the time of Wood, 1888, and especially since 1868, not a few British, French, Russian, and even Greek scholars, explorers and hunters, have crossed the Pamirs, partly or entirely in various directions. Among them we may mention: Hayward 1868, Potagos 1871, Gordon, Trotter, Biddulph 1874, Kostenko 1876, Severtsoff 1877, Oshanin 1878, Mushketoff 1879, Regel 1881, Ney Elias, 1885, Grombchewsky, Bogdanovitch 1888-91, Bonvalot, Capus, Pepin, 1888, Littledale 1888-90, Cumberland 1890, Younghusband 1890-1, Bower 1891, Dunmore 1892, Taylor and others. Passing by the mines of Baddakshan and the valley of the Panj to Kala Panjah (capital of Wakhan), then by the valley of the Wakan-su, Sarhad, Bozai Gumbaz, the Tchakmak Kul, the valley of the Aksu river and the Neza tash Pass the natural route leads to Tash-Kurgan, which is probably the famous Stone Tower of Ptolemy. From Tash Kurgan two sides could be taken *according to the seasons;* one passing at a short distance of the Tagh Dumbash valley, then turning east across the Kandar pass into the Tung valley, and from there passing into that of the Yarkand daria, and leading not far from the jade mines; the other by the Chichiklik and Torut passes, Chihil Gumbaz, and the Kashkasu pass, leading to Kashgar, and therefore necessitating occasionally an extra journey to reach the mines. This route from Bakakshan to Yarkand-Kashgar is recognised by experienced travellers as the most practicable and appears to have been always followed unto modern times. Horses and pack animals can be used but no carts. I am indebted to Mr. Ney Elias himself for some important information included in the present note. Cf. also F. D. Forsyth, *Report of a Mission to Yarkand*, Calcutta, 1875, pp. 222-277; H. Bower, *Report of a Journey in Chinese Turkestan*, in 1889-90, Calcutta, 1891; and Henri Lansdell, *Chinese Central Asia*, 1890, ii. 11-19.

1292) The jade mines of Khotan have been specially studied by H. Cayley 1871, H. v. Schlagintweit 1873, F. Stoliczka 1874, and more recently, 1889-91, by Grombchewsky and Bogdanovitch who have visited the rocky banks of the Reskem daria (Yarkand daria), chiefly formed of white jadeite (like that of Upper Burma), within which exists a huge dyke of dark nephrite, from which was taken the tombstone of Tamerlan now at Samerkand. On a curious tradition about this white and dark jade seen by Hwang-ti in his migration to the east, cf. below, § 348.

1293) It is important to remark that in the relation of Muh Wang's journey to Turkestan, in 986 B.C., two places are mentioned by names said to have been given to them by the kings of older times. Cf. *suprà* § 288.

1294) Percy Gardner. *Coins from Kashgar*, 1879; *suprà* note 947; and my *Catalogue of Chinese Coins*, 1892, p. 893-4. The Bower MS., of about 470 A.D., which proves to be the older Sanskrit MS. in existence has been discovered near Kuchar, Kucha, Kutche. Cf. *Proc. As. Soc. Bengal*, Nov., 1890; Dr. Hoernle, *Journ. As. Soc. Bengal*, 1893, lxii. 9-18; *The Academy*, Aug. 12, 1893, p. 136. Cf. also Capt. F. Bower, *Report of a Journey in Chinese Turkestan*, in 1889-90: Gov. Printing Office, Calcutta, 1891.

1295) E. Quatremère, *Notices et Extraits des Manuscrits*, vol. xiv. 476, 477. It was the southern route followed by Fa-hian on his way to India; by Hiuen Ts'ang on his way back; and by Shah Rukhs's ambassadors on their return from China in 1421. Cf. H. Yule, *Marco Polo*, vol. i. p. 198.

1296) S. Beal, *Si yü Ki*, vol. i., intr. 85-6; vol. ii. p. 324-5.

1297) Dutreuil de Rhins, *Asie Centrale*, 1890, p. 148. We may expect some fresh information on these regions from the recent journey of M. St. George Littledale, and from the exploration of the Nan Shan range between the Lop-nor and the Kuku-nor by the expedition of Capt. Roboroffsky and Lieut. Kozloff, this year, 1894.

1298) Cf. H. Yule, *Marco Polo*, 2, vol. i. p. 201. On the buried cities cf. Johnson, J. R. G. S., 1870, xxxix.; Douglas Forsyth, *On the Buried Cities of the Shifting Sands of the Great Desert of Gobi*; ibid., 1878, xlvii.; Bellew, *Kashmir and Kashgar*, p. 370-1.

1299) " The Son of Heaven then marched forthwith in an easterly direction, and, by a turn to the south, crossed the sandy plain. On the 424th day (of this journey) the Son of Heaven was famishing with thirst in the sandy plains, when some went to search for drinking water. But before it was brought, one of the commanders of the seven detachments (of his body guard) called Kao Pen-jung, cut the throat of his left-hand carriage horse, gathered the pure blood, and gave it to the Son of Heaven to drink. The Son of Heaven found it delicious." *Muh T'ien-tze chuen*, tr. Eitel, §62.

1300) The *Muh Tien-tze chuen* records the following : " On the 412th day (forty days after he began to return), the Son of Heaven reached the river *Hien*. Thence he marched forthwith eastwards (stopping merely) to (let the people) drink, and proceeded again. He then turned forthwith towards the south-east. On the 422nd day he reached the mountains of *Kwa-lu*, which form a triple ring like a walled city. This is the region guarded by the Yah and Hu tribes." ibid. §§ 60-61. According to the stations mentioned in the recit, the region they reached was that of Khamil or Hami. Modern geographers have remarked that Barkul is surrounded on the side of Khamil by three mountain ridges. Cf. E. Reclus, *Asie Orientale*, p. 161.

1301) On the east of Khamil is the desert called *Han-hai* in Chinese, d r y s e a, and not d r i e d s e a, as wanted by Richtofen, *China*, i. 24, in support of his theory of the existence there in historical times of a vast lake, for which there is no evidence whatever in the Chinese traditions and records. *Han-hai* is the Chinese transcript, not translation, of a foreign name which appeared for the first time in 119 B.C. Cf. E. Bretschneider, *Mediaeval Researches*, i. 15, 57, and ii 191.

1302) Cf. on the migration of the Torguths : *Description de la Chine Occidentale*, trad. M. Gueluy : Muséon, Avril, 1886, vol. v., p. 238-246. *Mémoires concernant les Chinois*, i., 408. H. H. Howorth, *History of the Mongols*, i. 575, 579.

1303) Girard de Rialle, *Asie Centrale* 2, p. 105. Abu Zeid, in the ninth century said that between the Sogdiana and China, the journey takes two months. Cf. Reinaud, *Relation des Arabes*, p. 114.

1304) Cf. Woodville Rockhill, *The Land of the Lamas*, and his letter 1st March, 1892, in J. R. A. S., July 1892, p. 592.

VII.—*Silence of Western Antiquity.*

338. It has been remarked that the existence of a mighty and highly civilised empire in eastern Asia in antiquity is not consistent with the complete silence of the ancients. The first part of the remark is answered by the fact that no such great empire was in existence. The Chinese formed for long only a small and comparatively poor State, or agglomeration of States, struggling to establish their sway over the native populations of the country of their adoption. They were too far away to be entangled in any of the wars and political movements which occurred in Western Asia. Travelling merchants were only those who could know something about them, and we are aware that traders' records were not mentioned in history.[1305] On the other hand we do not know what undiscovered or undeciphered texts may not have in store about relations hitherto unsuspected on that side with the east. The geographical horizon of the ancient civilisation of the west has already been considerably enlarged by the progress of research.

339. As to China herself, the Middle Kingdom, long surrounded by semi-barbarous states, could not but through them have any relations with the outside world. As soon as powerful and rich enough we see it moving and attracting foreigners. My readers will be surprised in perusing the chronological list at the end of the present work of the number of communications with the west which have taken place. There are no less than a score of instances previous to 1000 B.C., three of which are journeys made westward, but not far, by Chinese. In 986 Muh Wang of Tchou made his famous journey in Turkestan, and the seventh century saw the first arrival of sea traders of the Indian ocean. Afterwards relations became more frequent, and have not been interrupted ever since. And when the Chinese Empire had been barely established for a century, we hear of an Emperor entertaining for several years the project of conquering Baktria, and the intervening lands by the route through India.[1306]

NOTES—

1305) The same thing occurs in the large Chinese historical works, and it is only in special books on separate subjects that we find here and there special references made to these small facts so interesting to know for the history of civilisation.
1306) Cf. *suprà* sections 269, 271.

CHAPTER X.

ESSAY OF HISTORICAL AND GEOGRAPHICAL RECONSTRUCTION FROM TRADITIONS AND LEGENDS OF THE MIGRATION OF CIVILISED CHINESE BAK SINGS FROM WEST ASIA TO CHINA ABOUT 2332-2285-2282 B.C.

---

340. The following chapter is an attempt at restoring pages of history, hitherto unwritten, from fragments of information scattered in historical works, traditions, and legends, put together chronologically and geographically with the help of extraneous sources, chiefly western, of that period of antiquity. No comprehensive history of these ages has been preserved in China from olden times. But a peculiarity of the Chinese mind comes happily to the aid of the enquirer. In their reverence for any sort of precedent, the Chinese writers, either philosophers or politicians, moralists, poets or historians, who were generally well informed of their ancient literature and traditions, have always been fond of making allusions to circumstances and events of antiquity. These allusions form by themselves an additional source of information which we could not neglect.

341. Szema Tsien, the great astrologer historian, appears from his own statement not to have been able to get at the meaning of the broken traditions concerning the early period; his silence about the government of Shao-Hao, contemporary of Hwang-ti and of Tchwan Hiuh, which forms so conspicuous a feature of the gradual advance of the Bak Sings in China, and his inaccurate geographical statements, show his difficulties about these beginnings. It was said against the

complaints of inefficiency of his work which were made soon afterwards, that he had not access to many ancient books which saved from the persecution of literature had found their way in other collections than the Imperial Library, such as that of Tch Hien, king of Hoh-Kien. Anyhow, in 60 A.D., Pien-piao, Chief Recorder of State, was commissioned to supply the deficiencies of the *She Ki*, and his first move was to get access to these valuable treasures, but he died soon afterwards, and the matter remained in suspense until Pan-Ku who, after 76 A.D., compiled to the same effect a *Tsai-Ki*, or Complete Record, which unhappily has long been lost.

342. A later compiler and genuine investigator, Hwang-p'u Mi, has worked out the same materials with criticism and care. Unhappily again his valuable researches, which we have had occasion to praise before, are only available to us in fragments, through the quotations made of them in later works, such as in the great Cyclopædia of extracts, the *Tai ping yü lan*, of 988 A.D., in 1000 kiv. As to the great historical works of the Sung dynasty, commencing with the *Ki ku luh* of Sema Kwang, the *Tung kien wai ki* of Liu Shu, and the *Tung kien kang muh*, edited by Tchu Hi, they are not reliable authorities for the period preceding the fourth century B.C. The least use made of them the better for those who wish to have a view as accurate as possible of the early times. The sole aim of these patriotic authors was the magnifying of the past; their ignorance of ancient geography, and their lack of historical criticism has led them most often to a blind acceptation of all favourable traditions and legends, and rejection of the unfavourable; they have not been able to distinguish the old and original ones and those which have accrued in course of time from foreign sources, or from undue inferences developed out of simpler statements of antiquity.

I.—*From their original seat to the Jade Mines.*

343. In the second half of the third millenium B.C., the region east of the Zagros and north of the Bakhtyari hills, in the vicinity of Elam, was occupied by various populations, Ugro-Altaic of an early type, Semites, and Allophylians. Among them some were Semitic warlike nomads, whence their designation of TSAB MANDAS, which has this meaning.[1307] Others were not wanderers, and were addicted on the

contrary to agricultural pursuits and also to trade. Some of the latter were known as the BAKS, *i.e.*, the numerous, flourishing, and foremost.[1308] Their principal articles of commerce were salt from the great steppe of Khorasan, lapis-lazuli and tin from Meshed,[1309] rubies, turquoises, silver, asbestos, also lapis from Badakshan, and jade, dark and white, from Eastern Turkestan. The civilisation of Babylonia had penetrated among them from early times, principally through Elam.[1310]

The Baks, at least the Bak Sings, those of the Baks who became the civilisers of China, if they belonged to the yellow races, which seems more than doubtful, had none of their exaggerated characteristics. We know that they had blue eyes, not turned up, and no black hair; moreover they used to taper their heads.[1311] Their language was connected with those of the Sumero-Akkadians, and of the Turano-Scythian stock of languages at large.[1312]

844. The Baks had submitted for some 300 years to the rule of the successors of Sargon, Shennung in Chinese,[1313] perhaps since the days of Dungi (Dumkih-Tsang-kieh), under whose reign they had learnt the art of writing like footprints of birds (*i.e.*, in the cuneiform style), when about 2382 B.C., Kung-Sun, son of the Chief of Sho-ten (? the King of Shushan, Elam), and then ten or fifteen years old, became Prince of the *Hien-yuen*, or Kom-the-long-robed, a part of the BAK tribes.[1314] The authority of the successors of Shennung (Sargon) was on the wane, and under the reign of the seventieth of these kings, named DUMANG (? *Uru* DU MAN *sun* of the cuneiform lists),[1315] the regional princes fighting each other became cruelly oppressive to the Bak Sings, and levied heavy duties on their salt. The Shennung King being powerless to re-establish order, the *Hien-yuen* chief then compelled them to submit (to him), with the exception of the *Tchivus*[1316] (? the Tsabs), who continued to be most outrageous, but dared not come forward and attack. Kung-sun thus established his authority at defiance with that of the former suzerain. The Dan-tik (=Dintirki, Babylon,) king projected then to invade and oppress the rebel princes who rallied around the Hien-yuen chief. The latter consolidated his power, and then called to arms and to help several tribes bearing names of animals[1317] (a habit common in anterior Asia), and fought against the said king in the plains of *Fan-tsiuen*, Reverting Source (? a tidal river), three different battles. The result was that afterwards he could do what he had wanted.[1318] *Lih muh* (anc. Lehmuh; ? Bab.

Lukmuh), *Tang sien, Ta hung,*[1319] *Shen nung hwang tchih* (a Shennungite controller), *Fung Kii, Ta Tchen, Ta shan ki* (great mountain reverer), *Kwei-yü Kiii* (demons classifier), *Fung hu, Kung Kia* (great buff coats), and others formed his officers and army. He distributed them over the four regions as superintendents.[1320]

245. The Tchivus (Tsabs), however, proved obdurate; they were eighty-one brothers, all descendants of Shennung (Sargon), had a year of ten months, and were skilful at using war weapons. In accord with the other princes the Hien-yuen leader sent Lih-muh and the Shennung-ite Imperial Officer, to their chief, but he refused to obey the imperial commands. The struggle was long and severe as fighting took place on fifty-two different occasions. They pursued him as far as the plain of Tchub-lu (anc. Tiuk-lu,? Tiklat, the Tigris); and finally Yng lung was dispatched to put the chief of the Tchi-vus to death,[1321] near the hills of Hungli, in the region of *Tsuh-bi* (Zab river).[1322] After this all the princes honoured the Hien-yuen prince, who became *Tien-tze*, Son of Heaven; he succeeded the Shennung-ite *in authority*, and became Hu NAKHUNTE, or Yu-Nai Hwang-ti.[1323] All those who beneath heaven were not obedient he pursued and punished, the pacific he let go. Then he opened the mountains with routes leading to not yet pacified lands, and he settled, on the last as far as the sea, &c. The *She Ki* of Szema Ts'ien, from where we extract the statement, goes on with the names of the places that where supposed to have formed the limits of the empire of Hwang-ti within China proper.

346. Although the whole story is one of glorification, one cannot fail to notice the subdued tone with which some parts of it are told. The presence near the Hien-yuen prince of an officer representing the suzerain king, successor of Shennung, shows that some arrangement had been made with the latter after the war, which therefore could not have been concluded by a victory so complete as some interpreters wanted it to have been. Furthermore, nothing is said of the reasons, probably overwhelming, that afterwards compelled the leader of the Baks to open the mountains with routes to yet not pacified lands, and settle in China. The historian in his patriotism could not clearly understand that Hwang-ti and his followers had not always inhabited the Middle Kingdom,[1324] although as far as the latter country is concerned, the first fifty years of his reign were a blank.

347. The recit calls for some more remarks. It is astonishing to see how closely the account preserved by the Chinese coincides with the circumstances and events, geographical and personal, of the history of anterior Asia for the time indicated by the tradition. Several equations of names in brackets and some of the notes may have permitted to grasp a part of the facts, as we understand them. A further consideration discloses some more coincidences and suggest strongly that through the dim of ages, oral tradition and legendary exaggerations of later times, the recit really refers to a genuine period of primitive history of the Bak Sings in Anterior Asia. A similar concatenation of circumstances and proper names on the two sides form indeed a strong body of evidence. We know from the Babylonian sources that Chaldean suzerainty over the border lands of the East was at that time at a low ebb. A powerful king then arose in Elam; his name was *Kudur Nakhunte* (*i.e.*, Servant of *Nakhunte*, the Elamite Chief God), and he made a successful campaign against Chaldea, then held by the successors of Sargon, either by regular descent or more probably in chronology only. This was before 2285 B.C., while Sargon as stated by the Cylinder of Nabonidus had reigned about 3800 B.C. The lapse of time between the two dates (1465 years) answers admirably to the seventy reigns spoken of by the Chinese tradition. In 2285 Kudur Nakhunte returned in Elam, carrying away to Susa, as one knows, a much venerated statue of the goddess Nana and other spoil. A part of the land remained in his power, but the kingdom he had established there was captured not many years later by Khammurabi, who first united all Babylonia under his sway. These circumstances, which belong to written history, suggest forcibly the event which the Chinese account has left untold. The coinciding dates have been written on the two sides thousands years ago, and no interference or correction of a European hand has been required to make them concur.[1325]

348. In 2285 Kudur Nakhunte, King of Elam, comes back victorious to his capital, after an expedition which, however successful, must have taken a certain lapse of time. In 2282, Hu Nak Kunte, chief of the Baks, in the fiftieth year of his reign, arrives on the banks of the Loh river in South Shensi, and offers a sacrifice. The Chinese account shows that the chief of the Baks, inflated by the successes over the Tsabs, in which he appears as the leading spirit, had assumed the

Imperial authority, and therefore thrown over any suzerainty. The return to Susa of Kudur Nakhunte, whose name he had imitated, must have frightened him, as the victorious Elamite would not have permitted the existence on his borders of a rival sovereign. Hu Nak Kunte, Yu Nai Hwang-ti, must therefore have migrated then with some of his followers, either on their own accord for fear of reprisals, or perhaps only after having been threatened with war in case they would not withdraw. Anyhow no actual fight seems to have happened, but the migration took place nevertheless. Hu Nak Kunte was accompanied with a certain number, apparently some twelve or fifteen, of the BAK tribes. Amongst them were some *Ketsa* (whose name crippled in course of time is now read *Sha* and *Hia*), belonging probably to the Kassi or to the Kashtu once inhabiting the same region as the BAKS in Anterior Asia.[1326]

849. The route which they followed in their migration was not for them a matter of choice. It could be but in a north-east direction, as this quarter was the only one where they could make good their escape, and where they could go in search of desirable lands to establish new settlements. It was that which some of them knew best from their former experience of traders. Therefore the highest probabilities are that they followed the trade route leading to the mines of Khorasan, Badakshan, and Eastern Turkestan (sect. 332). The probability becomes almost a certainty with the additional evidence derived from the written symbols of the cardinal points which they had learned like the other characters of the writing from the Chaldeo-Elamites. The signs for south-west or front, and the north-east or back, of the diagonal orientation of the Sumero-Akkadian became forcibly for the tribes migrating to the north-east, those for Back and Front, and have remained so to the present day.[1327]

850. Meshed and Baktra further east are thus indicated as the two first principal stations of the emigrants; from the latter place the Upper Oxus leading by Badakshan and Wakhan over the Pamir to the Chichiklik or the Kandar pass form the natural route between Khorasan and Eastern Turkestan, through which the Tarym valley and the celebrated jade mines are reached (see note 1291). Let us remark here that cuneiform inscriptions have been seen in Bactria and apparently also in the Wakhan country, while cuneiform cylinders have been discovered near the Pamir.[1328] Their respective dates are still

unknown, and we ignore if they are older, contemporary, or later than the migration of the Baks, but their existence confirms most positively that the route in question has been followed since remote antiquity.[1329]

NOTES—

1307) Cf. A. H. Sayce, *Records of the Past*, n.s., iii., xiv.

1308) See our sections 321-9.

1309) The existence, hitherto unknown, of tin beds and ancient mines near Meshed, discovered only a few years ago, is a most important fact for the history of bronze. They have been discovered at Utshan-mion-abot, 20 farsangs, and at Raboji, Askaband, 6 farsangs, distance from Meshed, by P. Ogorodnikow. Cf. Baer, *Archiv. f. Anthrop.*, ix., 265.

1310) The inscriptions discovered at Seripul, near the old Lulubi, are amongst the oldest hitherto deciphered, and older than those of Gudea. Sargon long before had conquered Elam. Cf. B. & O. R., v. 272, *Cuneiform Inscriptions near the Pamir*, vi., 168, and W. St. Chad Boscawen, *The Elamite origin of Chinese Civilisation*, vii, 17.

1311) Cf. T. de L., *The Black Heads of Babylonia and ancient China*, 1892; *Tapered Heads in Anterior Asia and Early China*. B. O. R., vi., 193-6, and 264; and on modern times, cf. *Les Déformations Crâniennes en Chine*, by Dr. Ernest Martin: Revue d'Ethnographie, 1883, p. 504-6. Dr. A. B. Meyer, in 1881, has published an important monograph, *Ueber Künstlich deformirte Schädel von Borneo und Mindanao, nebst Bemerkungen ueber die verbreitung der sitte der Künstlichen Schädel-deformirung*, Dresden, dealing with the question in general.

1312) Cf. *Add.* 54, and note 1249.

1313) The identification of the legend of Sargon with that of Shennung is at present a fact for all those who have taken the trouble of studying the question. Cf. the references, *suprà* note 127, and also T. de L., *The Loan of Chaldeo-Elamite Culture to Early China*, 1892, par. 34-44; W. St. Chad Boscawen, *The Elamite Origin of Chinese Civilisation*, 1893; B. & O. R., vii., 17. Tchwang-tze of the fourth century B.C., says that O-ho-Kam (Orkham?) had received the same lessons as Shennung. Cf. T.P., 78, 6 v. There was a tradition that the Hien-yuen chief lived three hundred years, which we understand as meaning that the chieftainship lasted that lapse of time. But the Chinese compilers could understand only that Hwang-ti, the Hien-yuen chief, was referred to, and an explanation was difficult. The *Ta Tai Li*, or Ritual of the Elder Tai, of the first century B.C., attributed to Confucius the following : " Hwang-ti reigned 100 years, his people mourned for him 100 years, and venerated him another 100 years, hence 300 years " (T.P, 79, 4), which is more convenient than genuine and conclusive Seven names of rulers are given before Hwang-ti as having ruled 306 years. Cf. also *Kia-yu*, v. 22 v. On the other hand let us remember the 300 winters of the *Zend Avesta* (edit. J. Darmesteter, ii., 21).

1314) The denomination of *Hien-yuen*, or Kom-the-long-robed, was perhaps assumed only at the beginning of Kung-sun's reign. The *Tchuh shu ki nien* says that he invented then the cap with pendents and the robes to match.

1315) Eight names of Shennung-ites, including *Dumang*, appear on the Chinese list of mythical kings in the same order as in cuneiform lists of Sumero-Akkadian and Kassite names of kings, which were first deciphered by T. G. Pinches in 1882, and published again by A. H. Sayce in 1883 and 1888. Unhappily the fragmentary condition of the cuneiform tablets, where no headings remain, does not permit us to know where these kings ruled, nor how the names are arranged in the lists.

1316) *Tchi-yu*, anc. *Tchi-vu*, which may be translated s t u p i d-and-e x t r a o r d i n a r y, has thus all the appearance of a transcription of a foreign word. If the assimilation, I suggest, could be proved, many difficulties would disappear as the name would be simply an appellative as its repetition shows. *Tchi-vu*=*Tsa-bu*.

1317) Cf. the wolves, tigers, dragons, dogs, eagles, flies, wasps, horses, &c. of Anterior Asia, in Rawlinson, vol. i., 698, 700, iii., 546 of his *Herodotus*. On the names of animals amongst the Sings, cf. H. A. Giles, *Historic China*, p. 363.

1318) The statement here is interesting because it shows that the Shennung-ite king was not thoroughly vanquished and destroyed. The various readings of the tradition are the following: Szema Ts'ien: " and after he obtained his will," Ta Tai Li, " after that he carried on his will; Hwang P'u Mi: he subdued him." The battle of Fan-tsiuen is referred to in the *Tso-tchuen*, v., xxv.

1319) *Ta hung* was a title of officer, not a personal name. Hwang-ti himself was at a time called *Ti Hung She*, the Emperor Hung (*Ti wang She Ki*: T. P., 79, 2). He is thus mentioned in 609 B.C. in the *Tso tchuan*, Wang Kung, xviii. 9. Kwei-yü Kiu who appears to have come to China with Hwang-ti, and whose funeral mound was said to be near present Fung-tsiang, in south-west Shensi, was titled *Ta Hung*, hence the name of *Hung Mung* for his tomb (*She Ki* xxviii. 18 *v*. and 83). One officer of Yao had the same title (*K'ang-hi tze tien*, s.v. *hung*, 196+6). It means the G r e a t W i l d S w a n.

1320) These various names will probably yield interesting disclosures when properly studied. The Great Mountain Reverer and the Demons' Classifier speak for themselves. The most interesting is perhaps the *Shen-nung hwang tchih*, Shennung's imperial straightener, who seems to have been a sort of controller representing the authority of the Shennung-ite King. His mission to the Chief

Tchi-vu, and the qualified victory of the Hien-yuen Prince before explain the position which he occupied.

1821) Szema Ts'ien, *She Ki*, i. 3, in his precise account does not mention the previous organisation nor these details. He says simply : Tchi-yu made disorder and did not acknowledge the imperial command ; thereupon Hwang-ti collected his army and the princes, fought against Tchi-yu in the plain of Tchoh-lu ; he pursued, seized, and killed Tchi-yu." Szema Ts'ien, *ibid*., speaks of *Fung-hou Lih-muh, Tang tien*, and *Ta Hung*, who were raised to be superintendents of the people, when Hwang-ti was settled in his (new) dominion. *Fung-hou*, Prince of the Wind, seems to correspond to *Fung-hu*, Appointed dew-lapped, *Fung-Kü*, Appointed Noble, is mentioned also in the *She Ki*, but in the Kiv. 28, fol. 44, with *Fong-hou*.

1322) *Yh Tchou shu :* T. P., 162, 6 *v*. *Kwei-tsang*. *Ti Wang She Ki*. *Shan Hai King*, xvii. 8 *v*.

1323) *Yu Nai*, Hu Nak, is said by the *Tchu shu ki nien* to be where he resided when king. The *Ku She K'ao* says it was his name as chief, *Yu Nai she*; so says the *Ti Wang She Ki*. Cf. T. P., 79, 1 *v*., 2*r*.

1824) And it is not at all unlikely that in reproducing the terms of the tradition of oldest times concerning the migration, the Chinese historian did not grasp their meaning to their original and full extent.

1825) The date of 2285 has been given by Nabonidus. That of 2282 for the first event of the reign of Hwang-ti in China, has been given by Hwang-p'u mi, one of the greatest archeologists China has ever produced, in the third century.

1326) On *Kutche-Ketsa = Sha=Hia*. Cf. *The Languages of China before the Chinese*, § 202. J. Oppert, *La Langue Cissienne ou Kassite, non Cosséenne :* Zeits. f. Assyr. 1888, iii. 421-3. *The Tapered Heads in Anterior Asia and Early China :* B. O. R., Mar., 1893, vi. § 7. I have pointed out that the people vanquished by Eannada, of the country of Ish-ban or Kashtu (Brunn. List, 9100), with tapered heads may have been the ancestors of the civilisers of China.

1227) Cf. *From Ancient Chaldea and Elam to Early China* : sections 25-29. B. and O. R., Febr., 1891.

1328) Cf. *Cuneiform Inscriptions near the Pamir :* B. and O. R., vi., 168. When the *Yü King* was compiled intercourse existed with the country of *Kiñ-su*, later Fei-kan or Wakhan. Cf. *add*. 1187.

1329) The Puh-Tchou shan, anciently Put-dzok shan, cf. Badsakshan, famous in the Chinese legend of the deluge, was placed in the north-west (*Shan Hai King*, ii. 13). According to the geographers of the Han period, this mountain was in the north-west of the Kwen-lun, and near the country of Khotan (*ibid*. comm.) which is not far from the truth. Modern Badakshan.

II.—*From the Jade Mines to South West Kansuh.*

351. Once arrived to the jade mines, Hwang-ti is said[1330] to have taken there some beautiful pebbles[1331] of jade from *Mit*, where white jade is abundant and where its effluvium produces dark jade (a curious statement which reminds us of the white and black jade found there by modern travellers.)[1332] He carried them away with him to the south of Mount *Tchung*[1333] (where he settled afterwards, as we shall see below).

Continuing their journey, the emigrants must have followed the Yarkand daria, as we find them arriving next to the country of *Hwa sü* (west of Yen-tchou or Karashar, and north-west of Hoh tchou, the meeting place of ancient travellers, modern Kurla), which was most probably near the present Kutcha.[1334] They came after to the country of the *Yao Min* further east, where they sojourned some time, for the tradition has preserved the memory of a station of Hwang-ti there.[1335]

352. At a short distance eastward they reached the residence of the Kam-mu (Wang Mu, a western sovereign), from whom Hwang-ti received some rings of agate or white jade and some (?) maps of the country.[1336] We have seen in previous pages that the country in question was on the west of Karashar.

Following the southern course of the Tarym, afterwards the Bulunghir, and the north slopes of the Altyntagh range, they arrived near the Nan-Shan, and there we are told,[1337] east of the Drifting Sands and west of the (head water of the) Black River, or Bulunghir, where the countries of the *Tchou Yun*, Morning Clouds, and of the *Se-Tche*, R e a r i n g S w i n e s, where Hwang-ti married *Lei-tsu*,[1338] who became the mother of Tchang-y, were situated. The region in question would be right south-west of An-si fu in Kansuh. Further east they stopped at the Red River. A legend has been based on the circumstance that Hwang-ti ascended a hill of the Kuenlun range, north of the upper course of that river to look about the route.[1339] Near this Red River, according to the description of its course in ancient books, was the *Hung shui* (same meaning) of the present day, which rises from the mountains, south of Suhtchou of Kansuh west, and flows north.[1340] The chief of the Bak families went on a hill near its upper course, and obtained some information on the route from an old man there.[1341] Their march was impeded further on by some warlike tribes, the *Ku* of White Tek race, and the *Kin-pei*, who attacked them from the south and killed some of them.

353. Being thus prevented from seeking a route right south-east to the coveted pastures of the Flowery Land, the Hwang-tites followed east the north slopes of the *Tchung-shan*, *i.e.*, the Nan Shan range,[1342] where are at present Kantchou and Liangtchou. It was there that Hwang-ti could take his revenge against the *Ku* and *Kin-pei*, and destroy them, near the Yao hills.[1343] From the region of the present Liangtchou, it seems that the immigrants followed the natural route by Lantchou and Ti-tao, as they finally arrived to Kung-shan, later Kung-tchang-fu, of the south-west of Kansuh, where they established their central quarters. The site was well chosen, being partly surrounded by high hills, and thus well protected from unforeseen attacks. It was there that Hwang-ti founded his Chinese kingdom, known in legendary history by the name of *Hien-yuen-Kwoh*;[1344] and it is there also that unto the present day, Chinese have venerated some tumuli as the tombs of their earliest leaders.[1345]

The Bak families had thus been two or three years on the way since their departure from their original settlements in West Asia, but one year only from the west of Karashar. The probable date of their arrival was 2282 B.C.

Notes—

1330) *Shan Hai King*, kiv. ii. f. 18-4.

1331) *Yung* 5984 instead of 4422, Bas. Mount *Mit* reminds us of Mount Mirdjai, all of jade at 230 *li* of Yarkand. Cf. *Description de la Chine Occidentale*, trad. Gueluy; Muséon, Juin, 1885, p. 312. The same mount is called *Miritan*, in the *Si yu wen kian tu*, k. 2, f. 15 *v*. It was at proximity of Pu-tchou-shan or Badakshan.

1332) *Suprà* note 1292.

1333) This legendary statement of the existence of jade there, which existence was unknown of the later Chinese is most remarkable, as nephrite-jade has indeed been found in the Nan Shan by European travellers. Cf. P. Martin *C. R. Ac. Sc.*, Paris, 1891, cxii, 1153, H. Fischer, M. Anthr. Ges. 1879, 50; A. B. Meyer, *Neue Beitrage zur Kenntniss des Nephrit und Jadeit*, Berlin, 1891, p. 12. Cf. also *Marco Polo* on the river of Peih, edit. Yule, i. 198.

1334) *Lieh-tze*, kiv. ii., where it is made the occasion of an alleged dream. Cf. also the remarks of Hwai-nan-tze on the subject. T. P. Y. L., 79, 4 *v*.

1335) *Shan Hai King.* T. P., 178, 8. On the *Yao Min*, cf. *Shan Hai King*, 7, 8; 16, 2 v.

1336) *Sui yng tu:* T. P., 872, 12. *Tsih sien luh:* Kin ting ku kin t'u shu tsih tcheng.

1337) *Shan Hai King*, xviii. 1 r.

1338) The own legend of *Lei tsu*, says only that she was a girl of the West Ridges, which is correct from China. T. de L., *The Silk Goddess of China and her Legend*, par. 46.

1339) Tchwang-tze, *Nan hwa tcheng king*, xii. 4. The *Shan Hai King*, xi. 3, says that it flows into the *Nan hai* (a lake) east of the *Yen hwo*, or Fire Mountains, therefore near the *Tien Shan* range.

1340) *Shan Hai King*, xi. 8; xvi. 4 v. All this will be explained more fully in my *History of Chinese Civilisation*. The most important identification are those of the *Joh shui*, or Weak Water, with the river of Kantchou, eastern affluent of the Etsinai; Red Water, with the *Hung shui* and *Tolai* river; Black Water, with the Bulunghir.

1341) The route *tao* upon which Hwang-ti enquired there has been understood by the Néo-Taoists as referring to their own *tao*, and Kwang-tchen-tze, the old man in question, has been supposed by them to have taught their doctrines to Hwang-ti. The mountain was called *Kung-tung*. It has been identified with one of the hills of the Nan shan range, south of Suh tchou, and a monument has been built there in ancient times. Cf. the *Tchu Shui King*, in T. P. Y. L., 44, 3.

1342) For the ancient Chinese the *Kuen-lun* embraces the Altyn tag range and the mountains south of it, all westwards; the *Tchung shan* included the *Nan shan*, *Ala shan*, and *Yu shan* ranges, extending from the Kuenlun to the north of China. The point of junction appears to be south of Suhtchou.

1343) *Shan Hai King*, ii. 14-15. *Pao Kiang*, or *Tsu Kiang*, is the name given in the legend, as that of the principal of the followers of Hwang-ti who had lost their life. About the *Tchung shan*, cf. *suprà* § 351 and note 1333.

1344) Szema Tsien, *She Ki*, i. 4 v. *Shan Hai King*, vii. 3; xvi. 3 v. *Ti Wang She Ki*, &c. The legend says that this state, *i.e.*, that settlement, lasted 800 years, *i.e.*, until the country was occupied by the Tchou-ites. The name of *Hien yuen*, which we have already met, and which means *Kom-the-long-robed* (*sup.* 348), explains the saying hitherto unclear of olden times, that it was sufficient that Hwang-ti, Yao, and Shun should wear their long robes for everything to be in order in the empire (cf. *Yh King*, Hi-tse, ii. 16).

1345 *Suh Han shu*, Kiun Kwoh tchi: T. P., 165, 1 r. Szema Tcheng, *Wu Ti pên ki*. Hwang P'u-mi. *Hou Wei Fêng tu ki:* T. P, 44, 3. Tchu Kung Yang, *Lih tai ling ts'in pei k'ao*. Grosier, *De la Chine*, i. 162.

From South-West Kansuh to South Shansi.

(Circà 2282-2275 B.C.)

354. Yu-nai Hwang-ti, as principal leader of the emigrants, was the first, with a portion of his followers, who penetrated south as far as the present Kung-tchang fu. From there he was enabled without delay to advance eastward along the north side of the valley of the Wei river as far as the *Loh* which flows into the Hwang-ho,[1346] near the mouth of the Wei itself. Arrived there in the fiftieth year of his reign,[1347] he was greeted by the appearance of phœnixes, the bird of good omen, and he offered a sacrifice. There also cupules, or cup-marks, graven on the cliff by former inhabitants, were then discovered and being looked upon as a divine script, have become the *Loh shu* of the legend.[1348] Several years, probably seven, were then spent by Hwang-ti in establishing in his new country his final settlements, government and imported civilisation.[1349]

355. Another portion of the Bak Sings, perhaps the bulk of them, had remained behind and settled along the Nan shan range on the south-east, from the present Kan-tchou fu to the north of Kung-tchang fu. They were under the command of Tsing-yang, titled Shao-hao, elder son of Hwang-ti by his first wife.[1350] During his government of some thirty years there, in the name of his father, gold was discovered at *Ku-wu* (Liang-tchou) and at Kang (Kin tchen or gold city, of Lan-tchou). Several native tribes submitted,[1352] and pitchers in agate were brought from *Tan Kii* (Turfan).[1353] Shao Hao was venerated in after times (*i.e.*, 669 B.C.) as the White Ti (Regent of the White West), who had ruled by the virtue of gold.[1354]

(Circà 2275-2255 B.C.)

356. Two native populations of unusual aspect, reported themselves to Hwang-ti, in his 59th year. Their names *Kwan-hiung* and *Tchang-ku*, which have been taken in their proper sense of " Pearced-breasts " and " Long Legs," by the mythological ethnology of the *Shan Hai Hing*[1355] refer to peculiarities less momentous than that; such for instance as tatooing and the use of tooth picks[1356] in the one case, and a real appearance of long legs in the other.[1357] These tribes were probably in Honan. There was also a tradition that some southern

tribes had presented a white deer and some aromatic liquor. But these legendary statements are beyond our possibility of investigation.

357. It was in these years that took place the unsuccessful and fabled expedition of Hwang-ti to the north of Shansi and in Tchihli. Marching northwards in the east of Shensi, beyond the present Sui-teh department where he had a regular settlement, the chief of the Bak Sings crossed the Hwang-ho, probably by the north ford[1358] (between Fu-kuh of Shensi and Pao-teh of Shansi), and proceeded east in north Tchihli, where he founded a city.[1359] Then he is reputed to have gone to the sea-shore, where he caught some kweis, or sea-oxen, from whose skins he made drums.[1360] From there he advanced south to the site of the later Yung-tcheng (present Sin-'an hien in Pao-ting fu of C. Tchihli) where he organised the calendar;[1361] hence he came further south as far as Ta Kwei in Kiü-tze (later Kiü-tchou, present Shun teh fu, S. Tchih-li), where numerous spirits and demons were worshipped.[1362] But he could not advance any further, nor remain there, as he was attacked by some Tchi-yü or Tchi-vus enemies[1363] as far back as his new city. A version of the legend says that with the help of the goddess of Drought, *Pat*, whom he invoked for that purpose, he could withdraw with his followers. He returned by Mount Shao-hien, next to the ford of the Ho, and near there he saw *Ya-yühs*, dragons (sort of alligators), which were caught for him by an officer named Ni-fuh; he brought them back to his settlements of Mount Shu shuk, near the present Sui-teh.[1364]

358. So much of mythology has grown over the events that it is most difficult to discriminate the substratum of truth in the circumstance. *Tchi-vu* the common appelation of the first enemies of the Bak Sings on their north, as we have seen previously, was used again in this instance as also later on at the time of Tchuan-hiüh; and the assumption that it was the personal name of a single individual has thrown a good deal of confusion into these legends which consequently have not been clearly distinguished one from the other as they ought to have been. *Tchoh-lu* did not exist in ancient Chinese geography;[1365] it has been repeated from one legendary account to another, and it is only during the HAN dynasty when geographical localisations for ancient stories were sought for in China proper, that the name was erroneously supposed to have existed in the present Tchihli in high antiquity, simply

because a concatenation of legendary traditions pointed out to a temporary sojourn of Hwang-ti in that region. When the historical legend of this new encounter of Hwangti with Tchi-vus was restored and developed by the compilers, they supposed most conveniently but most erroneously that there was only one such encounter, and they have arranged the story accordingly; furthermore they appear to have worked, having in their mind, a Persian legend which we quote in another page (add. 153).

359. In the 77th year of Hwang-ti's reign, or 2255, his second son, Tchang-y, was sent on the Joh river of north-west Szetchuen to establish a colony. This is the first intimation of the natural route famous in later ages and followed to the present day which connects Kun-tchang fu to Lin-tao, present Min-tchou, to Si ku tcheng, Sungpan ting and the north west of Szetchuen (note 919). He married there a native princess named Tchang-Pu (of Shan race), who bore him Kao-yang, the future Tchuan-hiuh. The local tradition wants him to have gone as far south as Kwan-hien, west of Tcheng-tu. But he proved incapable in his government, which means that he was driven back by the natives, and little more is heard of him in history.

NOTES—

1846) This river was the *Loh tchuen* of the modern maps, and not the *Loh ho*, of later historical importance, which flows into the Hwang ho near Honan fu.

1847) *Tchuh shu ki nien*, I., i. 3. The fiftieth year is the date commonly accepted, but some editions give the fifty-seventh year. The latter figure would make the whole length, or 100 years of the reign of Hwang-ti, with the forty-three years alluded to by Lieh-tze, kiv. ii. (T. P., 79, 4 *r*.) There was a tradition that after a period of fifteen years of difficulties in his government, Hwang-ti had ruled in peace twenty-eight years more. The seven years after the sacrifice should thus have been spent in organisation.

1848) *Yh King*, Hi tse, i. 73. *Shui King*, T. P., 62, 5. On these cup-marks, cf. my *Beginnings of writing*, sections 83, 227.

1849) We shall resume the most important items of that civilisation, sections 383-389 below. An important geographical statement in in the legendary accounts on the subject is that Hwang-ti commanded his officer Ling-lun to get bamboos from the country lying in the west of Ta Hia, and arrange the system of modulated sounds. Cf. *Lu she Tchun tsiu*, of the third century B.C. The *Ta Hia* of that time was the present Ho tchou in Lan tchou fu of south-west Kansuh. The text of Liu she says: on the north of the Kuen-lun, or of *Yüan yu* (cl. 85 + 375-5075 Bas). Cf. T. P., 656, 6 v.; 963, 8. Cf. however § 298 and note 1193 *suprà* on the possibility of another *Ta Hia*.

1350) Shao Hao was son of Hwang-ti by the first in date of his four wives, Niu-tsieh of the Fang-lei family. Cf. Pan ku, *Tsien Han Shu*, Ku kin piao. *Ti wang she ki*. T. P., 79, 8 and 135, 7 v. Szema Ts'ien, *She Ki*, i. 5, has mistaken the first wife in rank for the first wife in date, and thus made Shao Hao the son of Lei-tsu, which the sequence of events does not permit.

1351) *Kiu tchou yao ki*. *Han tchi*. T. P., 165, 2 ; 50, 8. Gold is obtained still at present from the sand of most of the streams and rivers of Shensi and Kansuh, especially near Lan-tchou. Cf. A. Williamson, *Journeys in North China*, i. 170 ; and W. W. Rockhill, *The Land of the Lamas*, 46.

1352) A curious legend has crept in with reference to Shao Hao and to native tribes of Pongs, which unhappily I have recorded, *suprà* p. 46. See the rectification, *add.* 216.

1353) *Shih y ki:* T. P., 808, 3.

1354) *She Ki*, v. 5 ; xiv. 14, 19 v; xxviii. 3, 8 v. Also *suprà* section 153, note 538, and *add.* 538.

1355) *Tchuh shu ki nien*, I., i. . *Shan Hai King*, vi. 3 ; vii. 4.

1356) Cf. T. de L , *The Negrito Pygmies of Ancient China*, 15, 16. The use of tooth-picks among the natives of Indo-China when reported by early travellers has given rise to a fable of the same kind. A legend in the *Kwa-ti-tu* explained the denomination of the Pierced-breasts by the circumstance that two of the ancestors had once committed suicide in piercing themselves with swords. Cf. T.P., 790, 2 v.

1357) Cf. for instance Dr. Thorel, in *Voyage d'Exploration en Indo-Chine*, ii. 317, on such a peculiarity among the Mois, Penongs, and Khas of Indo-China. Mr. A. H. Savage Lindor, *Alone with the Hairy Ainu*, 1893, p. 300-4, shows by Anthropological measurements the great length of the arms of Ainu race.

1358) There is another ford more south with a route from Tai-yuen, but it can be used only by travellers on foot. Mount Shao-hien spoken of in the recit shows that it was by the north ford that the expedition crossed the river.

1359) The name of *Tchoh-lu* (in memory of the similar name in the West ?) has been commonly mentioned as that of this town since the HAN period when geographical localisations within the Chinese dominion have been sought for all the traditions of antiquity. If it has been done so after a genuine tradition, we must confess our complete ignorance about it. Several traditions pointed out to a temporary appearance of Hwang-ti in that part of the land, but this is all. The name in question was given only during the HAN dynasty to a locality in Shan Kiü kiun, near present Pao-'an of Tchih-li, north-west of Peking.

1360) Near Liu-po shan on the shores of the Tung-hai or Eastern Ocean. *Shan Hai King*, xiv. 5 *v*. Hwang P'u mi : T. P., 899; i, 582, 4.

1361) *Shi pên* : T. P., 16, 7 *v*. The geographical name has been taken as that of an officer of Hwang-ti from that circumstance. There is about the first making of a calendar by Hwang-ti an interesting tradition which shows the foreign origin of Hwang-ti's knowledge, in Szema Tsien, i. 4 and, xxviii. 48. He says that Hwang-ti had acquired (by conquest or otherwise is not said, but the word *kwoh*, 9860 Bas. suggests the first), a precious tripod, and that he observed the sun, *yng jeh*, and arranged accordingly the lists, or written tablets (*t'ui ts'eh*) that were in or on that tripod. The latter circumstance is suggested by a spurious legend, kiv. 28, fol. 82, when the 19-year cycle is attributed to Hwang-ti, but where the circumstance above referred to as : *Hwang-ti teh pao ting shen ts'eh*, *i.e.*, that Hwang-ti got—the precious tripod and the mysterious tablets, or the mysterious tablets of the precious tripod. In western antiquity written texts on vegetable material were usually kept in pots or jars.

1362) Ping, Duke of Tsin, 557-531 B C. ; She Kang ; Han Feitze : T. P., 79, 6. *Tchwang tze*, kiv. 24, T. P., 79, 5. This was the country of *Kiu* and *Li*, of which we shall hear again under the government of Shao Hao and the reign of Tchuan-hiuh. What sort of defeat this historical legend covers may be easily inferred from the result.

1363) On that meaning of *Tchi-vu*, cf. *suprà*, note 1316, and below.

1364) Cf. *She Ki*, i 3. *Tchuh shu ki nien*, i. 1. *Shan Hai King*, 3, 5 ; 10 : 3 ; 11 : 1, 2, 4 ; 12 : 1 ; 17 : 3, 4. *Ti Wang She Ki :* T. P., 79, 1, 2. *Yuen ho Kiun hieu tu :* T. P., 164, 10. The dragons, *yah-yü*, had dragon's heads and serpent's bodies ; mewling like children, they devoured the men they caught. Some lived near the Weak Water, as well as on the banks of the Ho. During Yao's reign, they were once so numerous that it was necessary to send archers to kill them. Cf. T. P. Y. L., 908, 4.

1365) The *Han shu*, Ti li tchi, said that a Tchoh-lu hien had existed in high antiquity (near present Pao-'an, north-west of Peking), in the Tchoh Kiun, but other commentators have remarked that the statement was erroneous. Cf. comm. *She Ki*, i. 3.

1366) *She Ki*, i. 5. *Tchuh shu ki nien*, I., i 5. *Shuh Ki* : T. P., 44, 4, 5 ; 166, 8.

(*Circâ* 2250 B.C.)

360. The failures of Hwang-ti in the north and of Tchang-y in the south in their attempts at opening new lands, had left the Bak families limited chiefly to the west of the Hwang Ho. They had

certainly multiplied during their thirty years of occupation, and it became imperatively to advance eastwards and find new grounds for a portion of them. It was Shao Hao who was the leader of the migration, and his ox-waggons advanced forward through and between the native centres and states on the south of the Yellow river until he found lands suitable for a final settlement.

Passing north of the native state of *Yu Hu* (Honan W.), they advanced at first as far east as the banks of the *Ti Kiang* (near Lu shan, C. W. of Honan). Thence continuing eastwards, they past south of the *Yu Sin* (west of Kai-fêng fu) of the *Yu Kwei* (Kai fêng fu), and through the country of the *Tchu Siang*, with whom Shao Hao made a treaty of alliance which permitted him to go further east; then leaving the *Shuh Ki* (east of Kwei-teh) on the right, and the *Tsao Jungs* (Tsao tchou fu) on their left, they arrived to the hills of West Shantung, near which they founded *Kiung sang*, the capital city of Shao Hao (modern Kiuh-fou, in Yen tchou).[1367]

Shao Hao remained there some thirty-seven years, and gradually strengthened his colony, without however aggrandizing his territory, as he was hemmed in all round by native states which he could not conquer.

(Circà 2235-2232 B.C.)

361. Hwang-ti, then a very old man, made three sorts of copper vases at Head-hill, *Shou Shan*, near Mount King (in Shang Loh, south-east Shensi), where he had found the metal.[1368] This was not long before his death,[1369] which occurred after a reign of one hundred years. He was buried on a Mount Kiao in the north-east of Si-'an fu.[1370] After the death of his master, Tso-tch'ih, one of his officers, carved a wooden image of the deceased and covered it with his garments, cap, and staff, that it should be venerated by all the officers and people.[1371]

(Circà 2225-2213 B.C.)

362. Shao-Hao being too far away in the east, with defective intercommunications with the west, to exert any effective authority on the Bak families of Shensi, Tchuan Hiith, grandson of Hwang-ti, was elected chief in Kung-tchang, and ruled there for twelve years.[1372]

Intercourse continued with the *Tan Kiü* country, or Turfan, and water pitchers in agate were imported again.[1373]

(*Circâ* 2213 B.C.)

363. Shao-Hao had died eighty-four years old, after having governed portions of the Bak families for many years, and without having ever been able to cross over to the left side of the Hwang-ho because of the enmity of the native *Li* tribes. He was buried at Kiuh fu (West Shantung), where a stone pyramid, unique in China, is still shown as his tomb.[1374]

Tchuan-Hiüh, his successor, removed from Kung-tchang to the east, and established his central quarters at *Puh* (present Puh-tchou north of Tsao-tchou), somewhat more east than those of his predecessor. He was then enabled to cross the Ho, then running north-east, and to extend the Chinese dominion to the north side of the river. He crushed the *Kiu* and the *Li* who had opposed Shao-Hao, and he is praised for having then upheld the religious principles of his ancestors. He conquered a part of Shansi as far north as Tai-lu, later Tai-yuen, and south-west of this region the native states of *Tao*, or Potters, and of *Tang*.

Tchwan-hiüh was an energetic ruler who did much to enlarge the Chinese dominion in the east, and to secure the communications with the western province. About 2180 he subdued the native state of *Yü Sin* (west of Kai-fêng fu) for that purpose, and *c.* 2147 he smashed the *Shuh Ki*, who had moved north and attempted to interfere with the works of damming the river which were going on since the reign of his predecessor because of local floods.

(*Circâ* 2147 B.C.)

364. Ti Kuh Kao Sin,[1379] great grandson of Hwangti, and heir associate since twelve years, at Poh, modern Kwei-tch fu, succeeded to Tchwan-hiüh. He married four wives from states on the borders of his dominion to strengthen his power, and he conquered several minor native princedoms. He employed a Tchung-li (anciently *Tungli=* Tengri,=h e a v e n in Tartar languages, therefore a foreigner), to describe the zodiacal stars and explain their time to the people.

His son, Ti-Tchih, made heir associate in 2112, was disallowed nine years later, and Yao, another son of his by a native wife of West Shantung, was appointed in his stead.

In 2085 he died and was buried near his predecessor.

(*Circâ* 2085 B.C.)

365. Ti Yao (heir associate since eighteen years) on his accession to the throne, established his capital at Ping-yang, in south west Shansi, and organised his government. He does not seem to have had any other title than Prince of T'ao and T'ang. In 2042 B.C. occurred a great overflow of the Yellow River, which flooded a large track of land, principally the lands of the *Li-min*, corresponding to the present Tchang-teh fu, and the surrounding region (*i.e.*, part of the country of the *Li* conquered by Tchuen-hiüh). Twenty three years of engineering work (ten under the superintendence of the great Yü) were spent before the course of the river was regulated again.

In 2033, more by the force of circumstances than otherwise, Yao made alliance with Shun, a prince of the native state of Yü, yet independent, in south-west Shansi. He gave him his two daughters in marriage, and at the expense of his own son and heir, associated him to the supreme authority. This permitted the submission of several native states, and the final establishment of the Chinese dominion on the two banks of the Yellow River as far east as the west of present Shantung province.

During his reign, intercourse continued with Karashar, and Hou-y, the Chief Archer, could get in 2076 from there some of the famous fir-balsam of asafœtida of the Si Wang Mu.

366. We have thus followed the gradual advance of the Baks and their final settlement from the north-western borders of China to the centre of Shansi. And we have just seen the transmission of the supreme authority over the civilised Bak Sings of YAO to SHUN, which is an event of great importance in the history of the country. We can understand at present without difficulty how the joint control of the two rulers has come to be looked upon in the traditions as the real beginning of Chinese history. YAO, notwithstanding the native blood of his mother, was a genuine descendant and representative of the chieftains that had led the Bak tribes in the Flowery Land. SHUN on the contrary, was an indigenous prince, belonging to a family of native rulers in possession of a part of the country long before the arrival of the civilisers from the west. Their association closes the period of foundation of the Chinese dominion.

Tradition has preserved the names of only the most important of the leaders of the Bak Sings at a time, and even these most important were contemporary for a certain extent. Shao-Hao was contemporary of Hwang-ti and of Tchwan-Hiüh. Ti Kuh was for twelve years contemporary of the latter, and he saw himself for eighteen years the rising authority of Yao. We have seen that the rulers of the Bak Sings in China were neither the ragged chieftains of straggling tribes, nor the glorious autocrats of a great empire, that they have been supposed to be. They were simply the chiefs of some intelligent tribes, as much civilised as their proximity to the old centres of civilisation in Anterior Asia had permitted them to be, and with as much knowledge of that western civilsation as they were able to preserve in distant lands and different surroundings.

NOTES—

1367) Szema Tsien, i. 5. *Ta Tai Li. Ti Wang she ki.* T.P.Y.L., 79, 8. *Shan Hai King*, 14, 1. All the names of native states here are found in subsequent history when they were subdued, viz., *Yu sin* before 2175; the *Yu Kwei* in 2145, she *Shuh ki* in 2147, the *Tsao Jungs* and *Yu Hu* in 2018. The treaty with the *Tchu siang* is specially mentioned in the traditions. All the evidence shall be found in my large history.

1368) Szema Tsien, *She Ki*, xxviii. 33; xii. 8 *r*. *Tsien Han Shu:* T. P., 813, 1 *r*. *Sang fu hwang tu*, iii. 8 *r*. *Shan Hai King* and T. P. Y. L., 49, 1-2.

1369) Liu shu, *Wai Ki*.

1370) *Tchuh shu ki nien*, I., i. . Szema Tsien, i. 5 *r*. Hwang Pu-mi: T. P., 79, 1-2. *Lih tai ling ts'in pei k'ao*, ii. 5 *r*. Another localisation in the same region, more north, was preferred during the Han dynasty, near *Sui-teh*, but was given up soon afterwards.

1371) *Tchuh shu ki nien*, I., i., note 8. *Poh wuh tchi*. T.P.Y.L., 79, 7.

1372) *Tchuh shu ki nien*, I., iii. Hwang Pu-mi, l.c.

1373) *Shih y ki* : T. P., 808, 3.

1374) Szema Tsien, i. 5. *Ti Wang She Ki:* T. P., 79, 8. Tchu Kung-yang, *Li tai ling ts'in pei k'ao*, iii., 1. A. Williamson, *Journeys in North China*, i., 234. How far the present monument represents faithfully the original one remains to be seen.

1375) *Tchuh shu ki nien*, 1., iii.

1376) It must be remembered that the Hwang-ho was then running north-easterly where at present flows the Tchang river; cf. J. Legge, *Chin. Class.*, iii. 185.

1377) The names of these tribes appear variously written *Kiü*, 619 Bas., which has appeared in the account of Hwang-ti, *Kiü*, 51 Bas., and *Li*, 13125 Bas.; the two latter have thus been wrongly supposed to mean the nine Li; they were a population of husbandmen extensively addicted to Shamanism or spirit worship, between Lu-'an fu of south-east Shansi to Shun-tch fu of south-west Tchih-li. All sorts of erroneous theories have been built up on these simple facts because the geographical location had been overlooked. Traditions wanted the *Kiu* and *Li* to have been ruled by a Tchi-yu who used to take metal for his weapons and mails at the Lu shan (near present Tsi-ning, West Shantung). Cf. *Kwoh yu*, Tsu ii; *Kung-'an Kwoh*: Legge, *Chin. Class.*, iii. 590. *Kwan-tze*: T. P., 810, 5 r. Playfair, *Cities and Towns*, 2322, 4128, 4555; 4587, 655. The *Tchung mu ki*, by Hwang Kien, of the Tang period or before, says that a great tumulus, seventy feet in height, was looked upon as the tomb of Tchi-yu at Kwan-hiang town, Shou tchang hien, Tung ping kiun, West Shantung. Sacrifices were offered to Tchi-yu in the tenth month. Cf. T. P., 875, 10. On such tumuli, cf. *Tso tchuen*, VII., xii. 3. There were in the vicinity several tumuli of Tchi-yus. Cf. comm. on *She Ki*, i, 3. The worship of Tchi-yu has continued to the present day. A red vapour in the sky like a falling scarf, says Hwang Kien, or a sort of comet, says Szema Tsien, was called *Tchi yu ki*, or Tchi-yu's banner. Cf. T. P., 875, 10.

1378) *Tchuh shu ki nien*, I., iii. 5. *Shan Hai King* xviii. 5-6.

1379) The sources of the present and following sections are the *Tchuh shu ki nien*, Hwang P'u mi; *Ti Wang She ki*, Szema Ts'ien: *She Ki* and the *Shu King*.

CHAPTER XI.

ADDITIONS AND EMENDATIONS OF PRECEDING CHAPTERS.

Chapter III.

367. The suggestion, page 5, that some of the Bak families migrating to the Flowery Land had branched off and passed northwards in the region of the Yenisséi must remain a moot-point. The Chinese characters found near Abakansk, are cyclical signs in the *tchuen* style which may have been engraved there at any time in antiquity. Most of the Siberian inscriptions belong to the Pseudo-Runic style of comparatively modern times, viz., from the sixth to the ninth century, which has nothing in common with the Chinese script. We have explained the matter in our *Beginnings of Writing*, sections 32, 235, 237-242.

Chapter IV.

368. *Elements of Culture received by the Civilisation of China from Babylonia and Elam. Sciences and Arts.* The discovery which I made during the printing of the present work, that traders of the Erythœan Sea frequented the coast of Shantung after 680 B.C. and imported into the Middle Kingdom some more Babylonian notions, has led me to reconsider carefully the provisory list pages 9-27; further reconsiderations resulting from fresh investigations have also touched them; the result is that we must cease to claim an importation by Hwang-ti and his Bak families of the following items: twelve Babylonian months, astronomical instruments, 19-years cycle, colours of the planets, *yn* and *yang*, which were all introduced subsequently. On the other hand numerous additions which have to be made have been duly entered in the chronological lists.

ADDITIONS AND EMENDATIONS.

24) On the ancient Chinese calculations of the year cf. two papers written by Dr. Fr. Kuhnert: *Der Chinesische Kalender*, nach Yao's Grundlagen und die wahrscheinlichste allmähliche Entwicklung und Verwollkomnung desselben : in *T"oung pao*, Avril, 1891, vol. ii· p. 49-80 ; und *Heisst bei den Chinesen jeder einzelne solar term* auch tsiet k'i und ist ihr unsichtbarer Wandelstern k'i thatsächlich unser sonnen cyclus von 28 julianischen Jahren : Z.D.M.G., 1890, vol. 44, f. 256-266. On the four divisions of the day, cf. *Tso tchuen*, ann. 541; *Chin. Class.* v. 580 ; and on the six modes of dividing time, *ibid.*, ann. 535 and p. 619. On the 24 *tsieh* in high antiquity, cf. the enquiry made by Yang Tsiuen, *Wu li lun*, of our era.

25) On the seventh day, cf. *Yh King*, kwa 24 ; also G. Schlegel, *Uranographie Chinoise*, p. 645.

25) The *Tso tchuen*, Duke Tchao, year vii. 1 (*i.e.*, 535 B.C.) tells us that "as Heaven has its ten suns, men have their ten classes." Dr. J. Legge, *Chin. Class.*, v. 616, has translated : " the day has its ten divisions of time," which would be against the statement of our text about the 12 double-hours. But this translation is incorrect, and the statement must be understood in other ways. *Tien yu shih jih* may mean that heaven has its ten days, alluding to the denary cycle applied to the supputation of days, which was a fact as we know by the *Shu King* at the time of the great Yü. This view is that of several commentators. Or it may be an allusion to the famous phenomenon of parhelions, or mock-suns, which is said to have occurred in the last year (*i.e.*, c. 1737 B.C.) of Yn-Kiah, otherwise *Kiu*, the thirteenth ruler of the HIA dynasty, when ten suns appeared in the sky (*Tchuh shu ki nien*, III., xiii. 8). A similar phenomenon was also attributed to the time of Yao. The ten suns affair is spoken of by Tchwang-tze, Hwai-nan-tze, Kiü-yuen, the Kwei-tsang's commentary, &c. On this event and a phenomenon of the same kind in Java, cf. G. Schlegel, *Problèmes Géographiques* I.; T'oung Pao, Mai, 1892, p. 115-6. On the other hand the most probable meaning is that which is explained in the *Tchou-li*, xxiv. 30-31 ; tr. Biot, ii. 84, by the ten *hwei*, or light's influences, those which affect the sunlight in the sky. With reference to the above ten suns, let us remember that the Pythagoricians, such as Philolaüs, c. 450-375 B.C., believed in ten celestial bodies (sun, earth, planets, &c.) circulating in the sky around the central fire. Cf. J. Lieblein, *Les Anciens Égyptiens Connaissaient-ils le Mouvement de la Terre ?* (Congr. Provinc. Oriental, St. Étienne, 1880), p. 137. A Hindu symbol represents four suns on the trunk and branches of a tree. Cf. Creuzer-Guignaut, *Symbolique*, iv., pl. 2, fig. 16, and Cte Goblet d'Alviella, *Les Arbres Paradisiaques*, Bruxelles, 1890, p. 81.

33) We may enumerate also : hundred, which was for them a standard number (sections 321-329) as among the Semitic Assyrians (Cf. A. H. Sayce, Hibb. Lect. p. 366). Avoidance of regular figures as ominous. Cf. J. Oppert, *Soc. Philologique*, 1880, i. 55. A special bird of good omen, the *fung*, or phœnix (cf. the Egyptian *bennu*).

36) On the eight wands of fate, cf. Lenormant, *Chaldæan Magic*, pp. 287-8.

39) The list of the ancient twenty-four lunar stations of Chaldea is given in C. I. W. A., v. 46; Fritz Hommel, *Die Astronomie der alten Chaldäer*, III., 1892, Sonderabdr. 4, 18.

41) We cannot give more than a few names in this note to show that the earliest civilisers of China were acquainted with Babylonian names of stars: Aldebaran, *pidnu* Bab., *pit* Chin., yoke or net; Great Bear, a chariot, Bab. Ch.; Draco, an enclosure, Bab. Chin.; Orion, military chief, Bab. Chin.; Pleiades, *mul* Bab., *mao* Chin.; Polestar, star of God, Bab. Chin.; Regulus, Royal Star, Bab. Chin.; Sirius, Bow-star and Dog-star, Bab. Chin.; Spica, *Ku* Bab., *Kio* Chin.; &c. Cf. the Bibliography Note 1262 and G. Schlegel, *Uranographie Chinoise*.

42) Dr. John Chalmers, *The Chinese Ch'ih Measure*, 1885, has remarked that once corrected of clerical errors which have crept into the text, the figures given by Szema Tsien of the twelve notes, correspond to those of the chromatic scale; the matter being however theoretical as far as the bamboo tubes are concerned, because it is only applicable to strings.—Szema Tsien starts from the mystical measure of eighty-one units for his longest tube, as this number was then supposed to be full of special virtue, and had also been applied to the Calendar. Lu-Pu-wei, in the third century, had only said that thirty-nine was the difference between the longest and the shortest. Cf. T. P., 16, 1. Also the twelve strings of the harp at Tello: Perrot-Chipiez, *Art Antique*, ii. fig. 291.

44) Herewith a list revised to date of the old forms of the Chinese cycle of ten *Kan* with the Akkadian numerals: (1) Akk. *ge=Kah* Ch. (2) Akk. *gash=êt* Ch. (3) Akk. *bish=binh* Ch. (4) Akk. *shin=dinh* Ch. (5) Akk. *bar=bau* Ch. (6) Akk. *'ash=ket* Ch. (7) Akk. *gim=kam* Ch. (8) Akk. *ussa* (?)=*sên* Ch. (9) Akk. *ilim=nham* Ch. (10) Akk. *gu=kwi*. For the Akkadian cf. especially F. Hommel, *Dei Sumero-Akkadische Sprache*, and others, but there is no certainty about several of the names beyond five. The days were first reckoned by decades (*Shu King*, I. 8; III., iii. 1), and these ten numerals of Akkadian-like source were first used for denominating the days as shown by the *Shu King*, *Yh tsih*. The cycle of twelve derived from the names of the zodiac of similar source were, curiously enough, not used for months denominations, but for a years' cycle, and appears in connection with the cycle of ten to make the names of the sexagenary cycle applied to the days in the *Shu King*, IV., iv. 1, and in the *Tchuh shu ki nien*, iii. 4, *i.e.*, in 1667 and 1904 B.C. It appears also under Hwang-ti in the latter work.

45) The only cycle of twelve which must be mentioned here, since the full names of the months belong to the seventh century (cf. § 105, note 890), is the zodiac which I have explained in *The Zodiac and Cycles of Babylonia and their Chinese derivations*: Academy

Oct. 11, 1890. Herewith the list with some additions: I. Bab. Offspring, TE=TU, mod. *tze*, child, Chin. II. Bab. *Twins*, MASH-MASH=*tcheu*, manacles, Chin. III. Bab. A crab?, namgaru=JEM, *yn*, earthenware, Chin. IV. Bab. Water, son, ME=Mo, *mao*, springing, Chin. V. Bab. Growth? SHERU=TCHAN, *tch'en*, pregnant, Chin. VI. Bab. Empty? ZAB=SZE, exhausted, Chin. VII. Bab. A sting, GIR=GU, *wu*, a club? Chin. VIII. Bab. Leafy top of a tree, PA=VE, *wei*, upper sprout of a tree, Chin. IX. Bab. Sea-goat? SAHU = TZAN, *shen*, stretched, Chin. X. Bab. Overflowing, GU=HIU, *yu*, a vase full, Chin. XI. Bab. Threshold, ZIB=SUH, guard, Chin. XII. Bab. Dog, *kalbu*, KU=HAI, a quadruped, Chin. In some cases the respective meanings could be improved by subsequent researches. For the meanings in Babylonian, cf. the works of Epping, Jansen, Brunnow, Sayce, and Chossat; in Chinese the *Shwoh wan* and *Kwang-hi tze tien*. In the above comparative list the numbers are those of the Chinese; the Babylonian would be XII., I., II., III., &c., the twelfth of the latter corresponding to *Taurus*, and the first to *Aries*. This shows that the borrowing by the Bak Sings, or some intermediary, took place before the Babylonian revision of the Calendar (Note 1209). The date of this revision has not been ascertained, but Astronomy says that it cannot have taken place before 2540, and traditions in Greek authors point out to the twenty-third century. The oldest astronomical observations sent by Kallisthenes from Babylon to Aristotle in B.C. 331 reached back to B.C. 2234 (Aristotle), or 2243 (Berosos, in Pliny). Ktêsias (ap. Georg. Synk.) made the reign of Bêlos, "who first reigned over the Assyrians," and of whom Pliny remarks, "Inventor hic fuit sideralis scientiæ," last for fifty-five years from B.C. 2286 to 2231. It ought therefore to be under his reign that the revision of the calendar was made. Khammurabi who ruled fifty-five years about that time ought to be the sovereign in question, but Assyriologists disagree about his exact date.

47) An instance of the cycle of 19 occurs in the *Tso-tchuen*, V, v. 1, *i.e.*, 655 B.C. *Chin. Class.*, v. 144. *Khang-hi tze tien*, s.v. *tchang*, 117, 6, f. 102 r. Also J. B. Biot, *Astronomie Indienne et Chinoise*, p. 47. It must be enumerated therefore among the astronomical notions introduced by the Erythræan Sea traders at Lang-ga and Tsih-moh. But it was not often utilised, and we see it again mentioned in 112 B.C. Cf. Szema Tsien, *She Ki*, kiv. 28, fol. 32, mixed in a legend of Hwang-ti.

50) Prof. J. Oppert has communicated to the Academie des Inscriptions et Belles Lettres, 20 Sept., 1889, some proof of the decimal notation in cuneiform texts.

52) The Chinese notion was that the sky was a vault (*kai*) revolving (*hwan*), and that the earth was square (*fang*) under it. While in Chaldea the sky was a vault revolving and the earth like an overturned boat (which does not mean round nor circular). Cf. *Dio-*

dorus Siculus, ii. 31. Fritz Hommel, *Der Babylonische Ursprung der Altgyptischen Kultur*, Munchen, 1892, p. 8. P. Jensen, *Die Kosmologie der Babylonier*, 1890, p. 10, 11, 160, &c.

52) The Cosmic Egg appears also in China but in later times. Several writers of the first centuries of our era describe the sky as the shell of an egg whose yellow in the centre is the earth. Cf. T. P., 2 : 4 *c.*, 8-9.

54) The third series of Akkadian words found in China are those which have entered through intermediary and later channels. On this question and the relation of the Chinese and Sumero-Akkadian languages, cf. pp. 106-108 of my work, *The Oldest Book of the Chinese*, vol. i., 1892. In my lecture on the *Early History of the Chinese Civilisation*, 1880, p. 19-21, I gave a list of fifty words identical in the two languages, but I was afraid of going on because of the pit-falls of monosyllabic comparisons, especially with a neo-monosyllabism like that of the Chinese. The two languages belong to the same original stock, but their grammar has diverged in course of time by external influences of a different character. Cf. T. de L., *Accadian and Sumerian in comparative Philology*: B. & O. R., Nov., 1886, *The Languages of China before the Chinese*, 1887, §§ 8-10, and 20-26; and *The Oldest Book of the Chinese*, 1892, p. 106-108. Dr. J. Edkins published an *Accadian and Chinese* vocabulary in 1887, China Review, xv. 295-8; but the relationship of the two vocabularies has been established finally but by the Rev. C. J. Ball's *The New Accadian*, 1889-90, and *Accadian Affinities*, pp. 677-728, of Trans. Ninth Congress Orient, 1892-93. On the neo-monosyllabism of Chinese (a happy term of Mr. Ball, p. 712), cf. T. de L., *Early History*, 1881, p. 19; *Beginnings of Writing*, 1885, §§ 49-55; *The Languages*, 1887, pp. 119, 137-9; *Tibet, Philology*, Encyclopædia Britannica, 1888; *Le Non-Monosyllabisme du Chinois Antique*, 1889; and the concurring works of Prof. R. K. Douglas, *China*, 1882, p. 346, and various articles, Herbert Baynes, *Die Indo-Chinesische Philologie*, Zeits. f. Volkerpsychol. 1888, xviii. p. 284, on my lectures at University College; Alfred Maury, *Journal des Savants*, Sept., Oct., 1889; Dr. R. de la Grasserie, *Des Recherches Récentes de la Linguistique relatives aux langues de l'Extreme Orient*, 1891; C. de Harlez, *Existe-t-il des langues purement monosyllabiques ?* 1893.

61) And also, stamping occasionally the bricks (cf. Perrot, *Art Antique Chaldée*, ii. 117, and F. Hirth, *Anc. Chin. Porcel*, 27); doors on sockets (cf. Perrot, *ibid.*, 254, those of Telloh, and W. Gill, *Golden Sand*, i. 99); orienting buildings by the sun shade (*Shi King, ibid.*); washing the war weapons in prisoners' blood (Pinches, *Guide Nimroud*, p. 38; *Tso-tchuen*, V. xxxviii. 2, and X., vi. 6; *Mencius*, I., 1, vii. 4); cutting the left ear of slain on battlefield (cf. *Shi King*, III., i., ode 3; *Tso-tchuen*, V., xxix. 14 and VI., ii. 1); &c.

62) On works made to embank the rivers, vid. under Tchuen hiüh, the statements of the *Tso-tchuen*, Duke Tchao, year I., 1. Under Yao, vid. the *Tchuh shu ki nien*, Yao, years 19th, 61st, 75th. For further comparison with Chaldean works, cf. the interesting mono-

graph, *Les Travaux hydrauliques en Babylonie*, by P. A. J. Delattre, Bruxelles, 1188. There is no late Chinese invention in the art of sinking wells as at the time of Hwang-ti they knew it (cf. *Kih tchung Tchou shu*). And under the reign of Shun, sinking wells was in the administration of *Peh yk*, one of his nine ministers (cf. *Shu pêu*). The Chinese mode of sinking a well, as described in Huc, *L'Empire Chinois*, 3, I., 316, is similar to that used in the ancient west, notably that in Egypt. Cf. Ch. Lenormant, *Acad. des Inscr.*, 12 Nov., 1852; Ed. Fournier, *Le Vieux Neuf*, ii. 78. It is entirely different from the pot-wells and *pucka*-wells (or brick wells) of India, on which cf. Ed. Balfour, *Cyclopædia of India*, iii. 1064. The well was looked upon in ancient China as the necessary centre and market place of every eight tribes or families, settled in as many square plots of land around it, as shown by the form of the written symbol *tsing* (70 Bas.) used for it. On the ancient process of piercing, cf. Wang-tze nien, *Shih y Ki:* T. P. Y. L., 189, 1 and 8. Also W. Gill, *The River of Golden Sand*, i. 298-9. One of the secondary chieftains of the Bak Sings, at the time of their immigration was called Chief of the Potter's Wheel. Cf. *Shan Hai King*, ii. 14; xvi. 3; xviii. 5 *v.* The oldest written symbol for it in Min Tsi Kih, *Luh shu tung*, ii. 21 *v.*, and other similar works looks like a lost-sight of pictograph. It is *kiün*, 1568 Bas. Cf. also *Shan Hai King*, xvi. 1-2.

63) We must add also the ox as driving beast; the horse and the ass as pack animals (cf. the two oldest symbols for *ma*, horse, figuring one with long ears and no mane, the other with no ears and a long mane; also the sign *lok*, 12518 Bas., made of a horse and a bag); the sheep, the dog, and the fowl of Media.

65) The importance attached to the observation of the stars, and the building up of *Tai-s*, or towers, may be deduced from the celebrity of the observatory of King Wen, called the Marvellous Tower, *Ling Tai*, *Shi King*, III., 1., VIII. It seems from Mencius' remarks on the subject (I. i., II. 3), that the entire population of the tribe had united in its construction. Cf. Edouard Biot, *Recherches sur les mœurs anciennes des Chinois, d'après le Chi-King*, Journal Asiatique Nov., Dec., 1848; J Legge, *Chinese Classics*, vol. ii., p. 4; .vol. iv., pp. 162, introduction, and 456. On the Ziggurats and the Chinese Tai, cf. A. H. Sayce, *Relig. Babylon*, 96; P. Jensen, *Kosmologie*, 255; Paléologue, *Art Chinois*, 100-4. History reports the building of Tais at the beginning of the HIA dynasty.

66) Dr. J. Edkins has an interesting note on *Seals* in *China Review*, 1888, xvi. 372-4. The Babylonian use of personal seals existed also in Egypt, where cylinder seals often met with in early times disappeared almost entirely by the eighteenth dynasty. Cf. Flinders Petrie, *Ten years digging in Egypt*, 1892, p. 145. Babylonian seals have been found near the Pamir on the oldest trade route to China.

67) Wells Williams, *Syll. Dict.*, p. 454, says that the *Lip-kuh* were followers carrying screens over a general in his chariot, such as is seen in Assyrian sculptures. "In the warfare of the early times of

China chariots were much used. The ordinary war chariots for the troops contained only three men—an archer on the left, a soldier armed with javelins and pike or spear on the right, and the charioteer in the centre. This continued down to the Tchou dynasty. The pictures of those chariots are not unlike those reproduced on Assyrian monuments." Legge, *Chin. Class.* iii., p. 154, n. Les Egyptiens ne mettaient que deux hommes sur leurs chars, mais les peuples voisins en mettaient souvent trois. Cf. *Congrès Oriental St. Etienne*, 457. We must notice also here the simple (tik) and the double (*kwan*) flute, the bell, two drums, a sort of reed organ, imported by the Bak Sings. Cf. *Shu King*, II., iv., 9; *She pên: Shan Hai King*, xviii. 5; *Ti Wang She Ki;* T. P., 580: 1, 5-6. The three-holed flute (*yoh*) was introduced by the Tchou: cf. T. P., 580, 6: *Shi King*. The *mu-nao*, or sistrum, was introduced in the fifth century. Cf. *Tchwang-tze: Tchou-li*, 29, 15; T. P., 39, 5.; cf. also G. von den Gheyn, *Die Speeltingen te Babylon*, pp. 81-90; Dietsche Warande, 1888; F. Vigoureux, *La Musique Babylonienne*: O. C., iv. 475-493; A. Buckland, *Primitive Instruments of Music*, p. 249 sq. Anthropological Studies, 1891. Cf. also T. de L., *On the ancient Bronze Drums of China, Indo-China, and the Archipelago*, April, 1894.

68) The emblematic figures on the robes of the first Chinese sovereigns (on which see J. Edkins, *China's Place*, p. 14), remind us of the emblems figured on the Babylonian bas-reliefs of kings, on their dress and round their neck.

69) And also Rafts of inflated skins (cf. P. Piassetsky, *Voyage en Mongolie et en Chine*, 392), as on the Assyro-Babylonian monuments. The *Tung Kwan Han Ki*, of the second century A.D., speaks of coracles in use in the west as far south as Fông-tchu'an in Ta li fu, of W. Yunnan, T. P., 769, 1. The *Sui shu* says that the *Kia-laug y* used to make coracles. The *Shih tao tchi* says the same thing of the inhabitants of *Yueh-sin Kiun*. The first inhabited near Man tchou in the north-west of Szetchuen, on an affluent of the Yang-tze Kiang. The second on the borders of that great river in South Szetchuen. Cf. T. P., 166, 8; 788, 6; 165, 3; 769, 1. W. W. Rockhill, in the eastern part of Tibet, has seen numerous skin coracles, on the Dré tch'u, or upper Yang-tze Kiang; cf. *The Land of the Lamas*, 1891, pp. 197, 198, 199 (plate), 200 and 228; cf. our section 229. On round coracles among the Aleutian Islanders and in North Europe in the middle ages, cf. David McRitchie, *The Finn Men of Britain*, i.: The Archæological Review, 1889, iv., 13-14.

369. *Writing and Literature.* There is nothing to modify in this section, as further facts have confirmed the statements therein.

ADDITIONS AND EMENDATIONS.

72) A large amount of evidence of the derivation of the oldest Chinese characters from those of Babylonia and Elam in their

transitory forms between the ages of Gudea and of Khammurabi will be found also in the following works: T. de L., *From Ancient Chaldea and Elam to Early China*, par. 14-32 : B. & O. R., v., Feb., 1891, where I have shown some survivals of the cuneiform shape of characters in China; *Catalogue of Chinese Coins*, 189z, intr. 33-4 ; C. J. Ball, *The New Accadian*, 1889-90; *Ideograms common to Accadian and Chinese*, 1890-91; *The Accadian affinities of the Chinese*, 1893.

76) The above note and text were published in the B. & O. R., of March, 1889. In the *China Review*, at the end of the following year, 1891, xix. 56-7, Dr. J. Edkins, in *Cuneiform Writing in China*, said : " For myself, after some consideration, I have come to the conclusion that what early Chinese writers mean by tadpole is cuneiform writing." Cf. also the same scholar, *The Ancient Tadpole Writing was Cuneiform* : *ibid.*, xix. 255. Some more information on the preservation of the ancient Chinese texts and characters are given, pp. 102-5 of my book *The Oldest Book of the Chinese*, 1892. Hü shen, when compiling the *Shwoh Wan* in A.D. 89, has preserved 441 *Ku-wen* characters that differed from his adopted rules of formation. The scholar who deserves the most under that respect was Lü-shen, of Jen in Shantung, whò flourished about 265 A.D., and published in his *Tze-lin*, or grove of characters, all the characters still visible on the lacquered tablets of antiquity yet preserved in the Royal Library of Loh Yang, and destroyed not long afterwards in the fourth Bibliothecal catastrophe, 311 A.D. (cf. Ma Tuan-lin, *Wen hien tung k'ao*, kiv. 189; T. Watters, *Essays on the Chinese Language*, 1889, p. 40). The art of block-printing has been invented earlier than is commonly supposed. The *Shuh tchi* of the fifth century, a description of Szetchuen, gives the name of Hiangliang, styled *Kiu-to*, who being eighty years old, first printed books, about 330 A.D., at Tcheng-tu, which was then the capital of the Non-Chinese State of Tcheng. Before 420 A.D. it was established at Nan-King, and before 558 at Loh-yang, where printing halls were organised with eighty hands in memory of the old age of the inventor (cf. *Shuh tchi; Hon Tchou shu* : T. P., 618, 4, 4 *r*.) In 593 the first Imperial decree mentioning printing was issued ; it is this date which has been published by Stan. Julien in 1847.

88) Prof. De Harlez has published since then *Le Yih King*, texte primitif, rétabli, traduit et commenté, 4to, 155 pp., Bruxelles, 1889 ; *Le Yi-King, sa nature et son interprétation* : J. A., Jan., Feb., 1891, pp. 164-170 ; *Le Yi-King au Tchun-tsiu et au Tso-tchuen*: *ibid.*, 1893, 1, pp. 198 f. ; Review of Philastre's translation ; *T'oung-pao*, March, 1894, pp. 93-98 ; *The True Nature and Interpretation of the Yi-King* : Asiastic Quarterly Review, April, 1894. The learned author has endeavoured to establish his theory as applying to the earliest period of the work ; but this theory is met at the outset by the facts, that he has made no preliminary criticism of the text, that this text is avowedly altered from what it was, and that the little that we know of these alterations are against his view

for the primitive period of many chapters. It will be only when we are enabled to study the *Ku-wen* text of the *Yh*, that we shall see if the various meanings of each heading of the chapters had remained in most cases as simple lists, or if they had already been worked out into sentences.

89) Cf. also the decisive confirmation of sections 146-148 of my work, *The Oldest Book of the Chinese and its authors*, vol. i. History and Method, 1892. It has been most favourably reviewed, *The London and China Telegraph*, May, 1893, *Manchester Guardian*, March 24, 1894, &c. Several suggestions and interpretations, pp. xiii. and xv. of the introduction are only provisory, and will have to be tested by a study of the Ku-wen text, when available, before being finally accepted.

91) The late date of some of the parts of the Shan Hai King may be appreciated by some internal evidence like the following: Kai Ming, the name of the kings of Shuh after 450 B.C. is mentioned xi., f. 3. The state of Ts'u is spoken of as Tṣ Tsu, xiii. 2, a peculiarity of circà 350 to 250 B.C., when the two big states of Ts'in and Ts'u of the Chinese agglomeration were fighting for the Empire. It shows moreover that the author of chapter xiii., and probably of the chapters vi. to xiii., was belonging to the state of *Ts'u*. We can surmise that parts of the survey made in that state in 548 B.C. (cf. § 211) has thus found its way into that part. As explained, p. 19 *supra*, the *Shan Hai King* was made of five different works, written in different times, containing in some cases some valuable geographical knowledge of difficult elucidation. Prof. L. de Rosny has completed his translation in two vols., 1892. Prof. G. Schlegel, in his *Problemes Géographiques* has shown in several instances the high value of the geographical information therein. Prof. Ch. de Harlez in the *T'oung-pao* of May, 1894, pp. 114-122, has written against the *Shan Hai King* a plea which calls for another plea in favour of this very valuable composite work. On the other hand there are reasons to believe that the *Shui King* which was incorporated in the thirteenth book of the *Shan Hai King* by Kwoh-poh in the third century A.D., is the original work of Sang K'in who wrote it at the beginning of the Christian era. The separate work under the same title and same author's name, which exists at present with a commentary by Li Tao-yuen of the fifth century, is said, according to A. Wylie's *Notes on Chinese Literature*, p. 43, to be the production of some unknown hand during the time of the Three Kingdoms, 220-277 A.D. It certainly exhibits a more accurate knowledge on some rivers of the south-west than the first work.

370. *Institutions and Religion* (p. 19). The use of the divine prefix may have been an afterthought, and the identification proposed for the six *Tsung* is not confirmed as far as the names in question are concerned. On the other hand further confirmation has come forward of a quasi-monotheism in Anterior Asia.

ADDITIONS AND EMENDATIONS.

96) Like that of Hwang-ti in the legendary account reported, § 845, which we have understood as referring to the period of his reign preceding his migration eastward, since several only of the same appear later on distinctly in China, the first government described in the *Shu-King* comprehended ten chief officers or ministers:— (1) A Prime Minister, titled *Peh-kwei*, or General Regulator; (2) a *Se-yoh*, litt., Four Mountains, a sort of adviser consulted by the sovereign; (3) an Officer of Agriculture; (4) of Instruction; (5) of Crime; (6) of Works; (7) of Forests; (8) of Worship—of the spirits of heaven, of earth, and of men; (9) of Music; (10) of Advice (II., i. 2, 17-25). An interesting comparison could be made between the legendary administration of Hwang-ti and the latter which has all the historical character which the *Shu King* can impart. With the twelve pastors they made a total of twenty-two great officers of state.

97) The appellative of Midddle Kingdom appears in the *Shu King*, Yü Kung, I, ii. 15. On the Black Heads, cf. my monograph, *The Black Heads of Babylonia and Ancient China*: B. & O. R., v. 233-246. The word *Li*, 13125 Bas., in *Li-min*, which has been understood in that sense since remote times has had several acceptations, or at least perhaps it has come to represent three different words or acceptations. At the first it appears (*Shu-King*, I., 2, II., 18; *Kwoh-yu*, Ts'u 2, &c., cf. *suprà* note 1377) as that of agricultural populations on the left bank of the Hwang-ho, which opposed Shao-Hao, were subdued by Tchuen-hiüh, and were reduced to starvation by the great overflow of the Yellow River under the reign of Yao; secondly, the able, black-haired ones, as shown in the pre-cited monograph; thirdly, many, numerous, the people at large, in later instances.

100) Add an important social status for the wife and for the mother, and probably some peculiarities in the right of ownership. On these points cf. amongst others G. Bertin, *Akkadian Precepts for the conduct of man in his private life*, 1884; V. et E. Revillout, *Sur le droit de la Chaldée au XXIIIe et au Ve siècles avant notre ère*: pp. 273-530 of *Les Obligations en Droit Égyptien*, 1886; Bouinais et Paulus *Le Culte des morts dans le Céleste Empire*, pp. 199-237; Chr. Gardner, *Chinese Laws and Customs*, 1883, &c. Miss Edith J. Simcox, in an important work on *Primitive Civilisations, being first chapters in the history of ownership*, which will appear when the present pages are printed, has given a large share to China; and she has kindly informed me that she has found only recognised in Chinese law the antichretic mortgage which the Revillouts have discovered in ancient Egypt and Chaldea. As the Chinese laws are reputed to have so little altered since remote times, that it is with reference to them that it has been said : " We survey a living past and converse with fossile men," it is not uninteresting to remark that one of the oldest Chinese inscriptions in existence, that of the *San she p'an*, is a deed of property which as far as I am

aware has not yet been deciphered and translated. We must add also *Notions of Eschatology*. Cf. on the double soul of the Assyro-Babylonians, J. Halevy, *L'Immortalité de l'Ame chez les Sémites:* Rev. Archeol, xliv., 1882, p. 44. Jeremias, *Die Babylonisch-Assyrichen Vorstellungen vom Leben nach dem Tode*, 1887. Among the Egyptians the *ka* and the *baï* or *khu*; G. Maspero, *Histoire des Ames dans l'Egypte Ancienne:* Rev. Scientif. 9 Mars, 1879. Among the Chinese, the *hwun*, or spiritual soul, or *k'i*, breath the of *shen*, of spirit's nature; and the *p'eh*, animal soul of the *kwei*, of ghost's nature; cf. *Tso tchuen*, X., vii. 4; *Li Ki*, xxi. 2, 1; ii. 2, 3, 13; *Kia yu*, xvii; and C. de Harlez, *Le Huan et le Pe, les deux Esprits de l'homme:* Muséon, 1893, Nov., 375-381. In later times the Platonician notion of the triplicity of the soul appears to have been imported into China, as it was adopted by the Neo-Taoists; cf. also on the subject the interesting work *Le Culte des Morts dans le Céleste Empire et l'Annam comparé au culte des Ancêtres dans l'Antiquité Occidentale*, by Col. Bouinais et A. Paulus, 1893.

102) Mr. Theo. G. Pinches, at the Victoria Institute, April 16, 1894, read an important paper on *The Religious Ideas of the Babylonians*, in which he has shown that there existed among them a quasi monotheism, because most of the deities were usually identified with one supreme god.

103) The statement that the names of the S i x T s' u n g s referred to in the *Shun tien* of the Shu-King, have been preserved in the literature of the Han period, and were similar to those of the six minor gods of Susiana, was premature and must be cancelled. We do not decidedly know the names of the six Ts'ungs. They may or they may not have been the six minor gods in question, one cannot tell. They may have been the six predecessors of Shun, viz.: Hwang-ti, Shao-Hao, Tchwan-hiüh, Ti Kuh, Ti Tchih, and Yao, but there are some difficulties in these names because Ti Tchih had been only heir associate and Yao was still alive. Perhaps that some other names were on the list, to begin with that of Shen-nung. The Chinese themselves have never been able to agree on the matter, and curiously enough the commentators of the Han period have suggested astronomical or meteorological explanations which, as far as we know do not find the slightest support in collateral evidence. Cf. also *Ancestral Worship in the Shu King*, by M. H. Blodgel: J. Peking Orient. Soc., 1892, iii. 123-156.

371. *Historical Traditions and Legends.* (p. 21). The ten *Ki*, the thirteen heavenly and eleven terrestial kings with their mythical chronology have decidedly no right to be enumerated there as they belong to the introductions of the fifth century; they appeared late in literature, and always with the nine human kings, making thirty-three fabulous beings spoken of in section 193. The legendary fishmen, carriers of

writing, and the calendar tree, on reconsideration, appear also to belong to the same later date.

ADDITIONS AND EMENDATIONS.

120) Mr. Robert Brown, Jun., in a later article on *The Ten Patriarchs of Berosus* (The Academy, June 15, 1893, p. 56), has given reasons which make the names of "the ten kings appear to be impersonations of natural phenomena, afterwards adapted to an astronomical cycle."

126) Cf. Note 719 and *add*. In a special paper on *The Flood Legend and its remains in Ancient China* (B. & O. R., lv., 15-24, 49-56, 79-88, 102-111), I have pointed out several traces in Chinese literature of the western story of the deluge, and I have shown that the well known legend of Nükwa, known in fragments of the Shang literature, is based upon some incidents, as in the Story of the Flood, in the Nemrod Epos of the Chaldean poet. A peculiarity of the Chinese account that Nükwa repaired the rent of heaven with stones of five colours has been found also in the Chaldean account, where the "great goddess raises an arch of precious stones," or raises up the great intaglios made by Anu. Cf. also T. de L., *On the Ancient History of Glass and Coal and the Legend of Nü-kwa's coloured stones in China* (T'oung Pao, 1891); and *The Oldest Book of the Chinese*, i., 1892, xvi. 113-114, on the same legend in the *Yh King*, and our note 719. For the demonstration about the Chaldean account, cf. P. Jensen, *Die Kosmologie der Babylonier*, pp. 380, 381 and 439-440. A peculiarity which I take to show that the legend was an adaptation by the Bak Sings themselves is the connection established therein with the Pu-tchou-shan, Badsakshan or Badakshan, a country through which their traders in jade used to travel.

127) Cf. also W. St. Chad Boscawen, *The Elamite Origin of Chinese Civilisation*: B. & O. R, Sept., 1893, p. 17, and *Beginnings of Chaldean Civilisation*: B. & O. R., Oct., 1893, pp. 29-30.

131) Cf. also T. de L., *The Calendar Plant of China, The Cosmic Tree, and the Date Palm of Babylonia*, 22 pp., 1890, and *Chaldean and Egyptian Trees on Chinese Sculptures of 147 A.D.*: 1883, B. & O. R., vi., 283-7, and erratum vii. 96. The "Fabulous Fishmen" and the "Tree of Life as a Calendar Tree," were most probably introduced only in 500 B.C. by the traders of the Erythroean Sea in Shantung.

372. In the fifth chapter (p. 25) the entry concerning the six *ts'ung*, as pointed out out already, must remain an open question. Further evidence of the Elamite character of a large part of the civilisation imported by the Hwang-ti-ites has appeared in chapter X. sections 343-348. Mr. W. St. Chad Boscawen in favour of the same view has written *The Elamite Origin of Chinese Civilisation*, Sept., 1893.

373 ADDITIONS AND EMENDATIONS of Chapter VI. pp. 29-83.

150) The Bamboo Annals register the first arrival of tribes reckoned among the ancestors of the Tchou as follows:—" The Jung, barbarians of *Ki-Tchung*, came to make their submission in the sixth year of Kwei of Hia." The country of the *Ki-Tchung*, 2284 or 10639-10728 Bas., is spoken of in the *Shan Hai King*, iv. 6, and viii. 3, as situated beyond the shifting sands in the north. They introduced with them hemp in south-west Kansuh. Cf. my paper *On Hemp from Central Asia to Ancient China*, 1700 B.C.: B. & O. R., vi. 247-253, and vii. 96.

151) The people of Kwarism, Khorasmia, east of the Caspian, dated from the beginning of their colonisation of their country, 980 years before Alexander. They distributed the twenty-eight lunar mansions over the twelve signs of the zodiac, for which they also had special names in their language. Cf. Al Biruni, *The Chronology of Ancient Nations*, tr Sachau, pp. 40, 226. On the importance of the Khorasmian dominion and civilisation of that remote time, cf. the suggestive remarks of Sir Henry Rawlinson, *Central Asia:* Quarterly Review, Oct., 1866 : *England and Russia in the East:* 1875, p. 461-502 ; and *Comments on some recent Pehlvi decipherments*, by Ed. Thomas, 1872, p. 18 ; *Did Cyrus introduce writing into India?* by T. de L. : B. & O. R., Feb., 1887, p. 61 ; cf. also *Hecataeus*, frag. 178 ; *Herodotus*, iii. 93 ; Arrian, iv. 15, 4.

153) The oldest references to the notions of *yn* and *yang*, the two principles of nature, obscurity and light, female and male, &c., appeared also with the Tchou people. For instance *Shu King*. V. iv. 1, and xx. 5; *Shi King*, III. ii. Ode 6; *Yh King*, appendice *Twan*, k. 11, attributed to Wen Wang, but not in the text of the book. It cannot be denied that views and ideas which afterwards have been preserved in the *Zend-Avesta* were current in the west of Anterior Asia at very ancient dates. Some of them were already current when the Bak Sings left the Dakthyari hills ; others have come to China through the Tchou (Aryanised Kirghizes) and their relations with the west. Further investigations in that field of research would certainly be rewarded by fresh disclosures of the same kind. For instance the *Pat*, female demon of drought, spoken of in the ode *yun-han* of the *Shi King*, III. iii. 4. 6, at the occasion of the drought of 802 B.C., is found also in the combination of legends heaped under the name of Hwang-ti in the introductory note of the *Tchuh shu ki nien*, older than 296 B.C., and in the last book of the *Shan Hai King*, xvii. 4 (added before A.D. 57 by Liu-hin from older documents ; cf. *suprà* note 91). The latter documents make Hwang-ti seek the help of this *Tien-Nü*, or Celestial woman called *Pat*, against *Tchi-yu* who had hidden himself behind mists and rains to escape attack. Now this is clearly an allusion to the struggle of *Apaosha* (cf. *Pat*) the demon of drought, against *Tishtrya* (cf. Tchi-yu), the producer of rain, in the Avesta ; cf. J. Darmesteter, *Le Zend-avesta*, vol. ii., p. 241-422, on these two mythical beings.

157) Boulders of a beautiful dark green nephrite have been found in the valleys of the Batougol Mountains, west of Irkutsk, by Mr. Alibert. Jadeeite is now found at Shunning and Yun-fu of Western Yunnan, and at Teng-yueh, further south on the frontier.

159) Cf. also *On the source of the Jade used for ancient implements in Europe and America*, by F. W. Rudler, of the Anthropological Institute, 1891, a short and clear resumé, with useful references, and L. Conradt, *Die Nephritgruben von Schachidula und die schleifereien von Chotan:* Z. f. Ethnolog., 1893, xxiii. 692. Dr. Arzuni, *Nephrit von Schachidula, ibid.,* xxiv., 10-38. A. Martens, *Undersuchung des nephrits von Schachidula, ibid.* xxiv. H. Haberlandt, *Ueber nephrit und Jadit Gegenstaende aus Central Asien*, Wien, 1891. On a mine of jadeite at Roquedas, on the sea shore of Morbihan, cf. E. Cartailhac, *La France Préhistorique*, 1889, p. 267. Also Kristian Bahnson, *On objects of nephrite and Jade in Europe*, 1889: Mém. Soc. Antiq. du Nord. The most important work on the subject is the *Neue Beitrage zur Kenntniss des Nephrit and Jadeit*, Berlin, 1891, by Dr. A. B. Meyer of Dresden, and his former paper *Die Nephitfrage kein ethnologisches Problem*, Berlin, 1883.

161) Cf. R. Virchow, *Eine Sammlung Assyrischer Steinearteefarkte*, namentlich solcher aus Nephrit: z. f. Ethol. 1887, xix, 456-61, 724. *Nephrit-Ring from Erbil:* ibid., 1892, xxiii. 81.

162) The jade question has made great progress since the last few years. Dr. Arzuni, of Berlin, and other scholars have shown that the microscopic structure of nephrite and jadeite differs according to localities. The nephrite implements of Switzerland have thus been proved not to be Asiatic, while on the contrary the nephrite implements of Assyrio-Babylonia belong to the Turkestan mines. Therefore most part of the speculative views quoted in the first part of this note is now baseless, as the polytropic origin of the jades has become evident. An exception however is made for the white jadeeite, which had been found in Turkestan, and of which implements have been discovered in the oldest ruins of Hissarlik. Cf. *Schliemann's Excavations*, by C. Schuchhardt, London, 1891, p. 38.

164) The *Shan Hai King*, vii. 2, speaks mythologically of the *Nü Tsi* and of the *Nü Ts'ih* (*Nü*=woman) states in the north-east of Tibet. On the two kingdoms ruled by queens in the north-west and east of Tibet; cf. the *Peh she* and the *T'ang shu's* notices translated in S. W. Bushell, *The Early History of Tibet*, n. 42: J. R. S. A., xii., Oct., 1880, and Woodville Rockhill, *The Land of Lamas*, pp. 389-41, from the *Sui shu*, kiv. 83, and from the *T'ang shu*, kiv. 122.

171) Abdallah Beidavi, who died in 1292, cannot have been the author of the *Tárikh-i-Khata*, or History of China, which is dated 1317. The work was in reality written by *Benaketi*. Cf. E. Quatremère, *Histoire des Mongols*, pref. 4, 85, 99; E. Bretschneider, *Mediæval Researches*, i. 196, n. 532. Although mentioned by

Firdusi, b. A.D. 940, in his famous poem, the *Shah nameh*, the marriage of a Chinese Imperial Princess by Djemshid is not spoken of in Mirkhond's *History of the early kings of Persia*, fifteenth century, cf. trsl. David Shea, p. 99-122.

172) Subsequent researches have convinced me that the Ring Money had come earlier to the cognisance of the Tchou, who included them in their financial enactments of 1091 B.C. Cf. my *Chinese Coins*, early period, p. x. They had learned it with the other notions of civilisation from Baktria and Khorasmia, which had come to them. The system had been introduced in Anterior Asia by the Egyptian conquest of the eighteenth dynasty.

177) The book called *Kwan-tze*, name of the able minister of Ts'i, who lived in the seventh century, contains a great deal about his deeds and sayings but was compiled much later, perhaps about 400 B.C. (cf. B. & O. R., May, 1893, p. 264). It contains also much later matter, such as sayings of Tze-hin, who died about 406 B.C. (cf. T. P., 928, 6). It ought not to be used without caution as evidence of the seventh century. The late Prof. Georg. von der Gabelentz has given *L'Œuvre du philosophe Kuan-tsi;* specimen du texte, traduction et notes : *Le Lotus*, v. 81-103.

184) To the names given in the text must be added those of *Kamalanka* (i.e., Pegu or old Hansawadi, and the delta of the Irawadi); also Langkawi near Kedah, *Ling-ga* island, south of the Malacca Peninsula, *Ling-ka-poh-pah-to* island, opposite the Lin-yh or North Cochinchina; cf. S. Beal: *Buddhist Records of the Western World*, 1884, vol. ii , p. 200. W. P. Groeneveldt : *Notes on the Malay Archipelago and Malacca, compiled from Chinese sources*, Batavia, 1876, pp. 79, 10. Prof. Leon de Rosny, *Les Peuples Orientaux connus des Anciens Chinois*, 1881, p. 64, edit. ii. 1886, pp. 208, 252, places *Lang-va-siu* at the south point of Cochinchina. These various stations were not contemporary, and some of these names have been transformed by local folk etymology.

185) She Hwang-ti built there the Lang-ya t'ai, an edifice of several stories. It was in the modern district of Tchu tch'ong, on the south of the Shantung peninsula; cf. W. F. Mayers, *Chinese R..M.*, i. 335 ; cf. our section 225.

189) It is not exact at present to state with the authorities quoted here that the Chinese had no knowledge of the Sunda Islands before the sixth century. As shown in several parts of the present work, sailors' yarns about these islands were heard of 400 B.C.; they became less fabulous about our era ; but in the third century some extensive and accurate notions were obtained and published, notably by K'ang-tai and Tchu yng. Unhappily fragments only remain of their works.

190) The country of *Shou-mi* is mentioned in the *Shan Hai King*, xvi. 5, among the unknown countries outside the border lands at the time.

195) This was in the third year of Tchou Tcheng Wang, 1101 B.C. The NÊRE in question is written *Ni-li*, 4926-11932 Bas., while the Nala of Asoka is written 4926-5673 Bas. Cf. *Shih y ki*, kiv. 2, fol. 6 ; *Lih tai ki sze nien piao*, kiv. 6, fol. 9 ; Stan. Julien, *Simple Exposé*, 1842, p. 204-9. Stan. Julien, like myself, judging from the mountainous lands travelled through by the envoys of Nêlê had looked for their native country beyond the south-west borders of China. It is there that the roads over high ridges are often in the clouds and fogs, that rivers run through caves, and that the traveller passing under downfalls of water hears their noise over him, as described by modern travellers (Giles, Colquhoun, Baber, &c.), and in the account of their journey by the envoys from Nêlê. Dr. G. Schlegel has kindly communicated to me (6 May, 1894) a first proof of his *Problèmes Géographiques XIII. Ni-li-kuo* from which it appears that the *Shih-y-ki* in the fifth kiv. mentions a mission of a Nêlê country in 193 B.C. from beyond *Fusang* (=Sakhalin). Dr. S. identifies it with the country of the Tchuktchis, and his identification appears probable. But the name of this Nêlê is written like that of 1100 B.C., and the Chinese compilers, for that reason, have concluded that the first mission had come from the same country as the second. The evidence appears not to be sufficient under that respect, as the *Kiu shui* crossed by the old mission was a name of the Lang-tsan Kiang.

196) In the fifth year of the King Hien, the thirty-second ruler of the Tchöu dynasty, *i.e.*, 364 B.C., it rained *pih* stones in Tch'ing, which place corresponds to the district of Kiang-ling, department of King-tchou, in the south of the province of Hupeh. Cf. *Tchuh shu ki nien*, Tchen Hien XXXII, 5. It seems to be a poetical reference to an arrival of jade stones brought in by some trading parties.

196) It is said that the discovery of green jade in Burma was accidentally made by a Yunnanese trader in the 13th century ; cf. *Proc. of Chief Comm., Burma*, Aug., 1888, Rangoon, and Dr. Noetling's *Report on Jade in Upper Burma*, 1892. On the amber trade, cf. note 998.

216) When I wrote that Shao-Hao had remained in the west, I ought to have added that it was only for a time. The fact is that Shao-Hao governed the west, c. 2282-2250 B.C., until he removed to the east, and established a colony on the south-west of Shantung, in the interest of his father, Hwang-ti, until his death, *circa* 2213. But being far from the centre of the Bak families (Kung tchang fu of south-west Kansuh), he did not succeed to his father (2282) and *Tchuen Hiüh* in 2225 was elected sovereign there.

As to the statement that *Pong*, or Phœnix, tribes brought books to Shao-Hao, I have not been able to find a tithe of probability in favour of such a construction put erroneously upon a statement which bears another complexion. The story of the *Tso tchuen* is a systematized account under one system of explanation of various facts which differed originally. A legendary account wanted phœnixes, as birds of good omen, to have appeared during Shao-

Hao's government, and to have suggested to him to distinguish henceforth his various officers by feathers of birds (to their caps!) arranged according to their duties and the seasons which concerned them. The full account of the pre-cited chronicle does not leave any doubt on the subject. But the ambiguous terms of one or two sentences when separated from the context (a most dangerous process in Chinese) have been the cause of the misconception, thus: " there appeared phœnixes and he recorded by birds," hence the legend of phœnixes or Pongs bringing in some records or books. As a fact the Bak Sings had heard of this custom before their migration from Anterior Asia, where it was practised to a certain extent. Cf. for instance the Assyro.-Babylonian *pihâtu*, a swallow, prefect, governor (Brunn. List, 2099), and other cases.

249) On the Dahae, who are said to be an Elamite tribe (cf. Sayce, on Herodotus, *l.c.*) See also Fr. Lenormant, *Lettres Assyriologiques*, i. 61 ; F. Vigouroux, *La Bible*, iv. 260.

270) The suggested restoration of *Ts'u* into *Tseru*, and therefore as a possible antecedent of the name of *Ser* in the west, rests on the reading of the character as a phonetic compound made Ts*uh*, cl 157, and LAM=RAM, mod. *liu*, 4136, Bas, over it for the final. But the name *Seres* is better explained as I have done in, note 985.

275) The conquest of *Shuh* by the Ts'inites took place according to the *She Ki*, Tchang-y-tchuen, kiv. 70, fol. 4 v., in the ninth year of TS'IN Hwui wang, *i.e.*, 329 B.C., or according to the same work, *Luh kwoh nien piao*, in the twenty-second year of the same king, *i.e.*, 316 B.C. It suggests two successive attacks.

281) Kang-tai is the officer of the Wu-kingdom, who was sent in a mission to *Funam* (=Phnom=Cambodja), after 226 A.D. to report upon the southern countries. *Peh-lu* is written 188-3027 Bas., in the *Shan Hai King*, and 953-8690 Bas., in his work. It might perhaps be identified with Perak. As India used to be provided with tin from the west as stated in the *Periplus*, and not the reverse, it is interesting to note this earliest date known of the trade of Malayan tin.

310) Let us remark the confirmation given by that name, and that of *Tsin* in the Burmese chronicles (note 290 and text) to our reading of the ancient name of the Tsu-ite kingdom of *Tsen* in Yunnan.

331) Further investigations have shown me that while the general results of Richtofen's and Yule's work on the subject are correct, their identification of Kattigava with Hanoi was premature. Cf. note 1036.

335) The date 1777 B.C. for the first approach of the Chinese to the sea is that of the Bamboo Books. 1801 is that of the rectified chronology.

336) The black stone object representing a wig and hair and hair-dress is in black steatite, and it bears a dedication by Dungi to a deity, whose name Mr. T. G. Pinches tells me is partly obliterated and cannot be deciphered. My lamented friend Consul E. Colborne

Baber called my attention on the explanation afforded by pl. 215 in Perrot-Chipiez, *O.C* II, p. 481, to the Chinese town gates, and he had promised to contribute an article on the subject in the B. & O. R., but his departure for Burmah-China prevented the fulfilment of his promise.

337) At Khotan the native population was most probably that of the Issedons whose name was subsequently altered into the Sanskrit *Kustana* to fit a local myth. We hear of them in the poetry of Alkman of Sparte, 671-681 B C., fragm. 94, in Aristeas, of Prokonnesus, 600 B.C., IV., 3, in Hecatæus of Miletus, fragm. 160, and in subsequent classical writers, but in a very vague manner. Cfr. E. H. Bunbury, *History of ancient Geography*, vol. i. pp. 102, 141, 190, ii. 598, and McCrindle, *Ancient India of Ptolemy*, p. 295. On the extension of the Chaldeo-Elamite civilisation towards the east, cf. *Cuneiform Inscriptions near the Pamir*: B. & O. R., vi. 168.

340) We are afraid to have unduly minimised here the probability of some foreign missions, probably caravans from the west arrived during the reign of SHANG Tai Mou. Further justice is meted to them in section 392 below. The dates pp. 75-76 are those of the Bamboo Annals.

342) On Wu-hien as a foreigner, cf. section 309 and notes 965, 1238, and add. 1238.

344) The Bamboo Annals record that in the sixth year of K'i of Hia (*c*. 1941 B.C.), *Peh-yh*, who had been Chief Forester under Shun, and had helped the great Yü in his works (*Shu King*, II. i. 22, and ii. 4, 6, 21), died, and that a sacrifice was appointed to him.

345) On the tabued words, cf. Hilderic Friend, *Euphemism and Tabu in China*: Folklore Record, 1881, iv., 71-91. R. K. Douglas, *On Tabu-ed Characters*: Chinese Manual, 1889, 372-6. F. Garnier, *Voyage d'Exploration en Chine*, ii. 171. Liu-hie, *Sin lun*, kiv. 6, f. 31 of 500-550 A.D. T. P. Y. L., 562, 8-9. T. de L., *Catalogue of Chinese Coins*, xxxvi.

346) *Tchou*, name of the famous dynasty, is written by the Tibetans *Tchigur*, according to Sarat Chandra Das, *Sacred Literature, &c.*, *of Ancient China*, translation of Dub-thah Selkyi Mélón. Dr. J. Edkins has suggested that it was TOK in olden times, in his *Introduction to the study of Chinese Characters*, p. 87; while Mr. Kingsmill has preferred *Djow* in his paper on Myths. The Archaic dialects do not help because they are too late (*tchou, tchĕu*), and a comparison of the *Djüs*, hord, of the Kirghises-kaïsaks would not be justified. The old word did contain a final *k* or *ku*, as shown by the preservation of a guttural final in phonetic derivates, as Dr. Edkins has pointed out. On the other hand the composition of the character ought to be decisive in the matter. It is made of DJONG (mod. *vung*, use), and of KU (mod. *kou*, mouth), suggesting DJO-KU for the ancient sound of the name. We might compare it to DJAGATAI or the like. The explanation of *Kilik* by Kirk, Kirkhizes,

is perhaps not quite safe, because it may be as well explained by *Kutlug*, lucky, happy, a title among the Turks-Tartares. Cf. also *La Nationalité du peuple de Tcheou*, by C. de Harlez : J. A., 1892, xx. 335 f.

347) In the time of Muh Wang, the Jungs and the Tehs having ceased to pay tribute, the monarch invaded the *K'üen Jung* in the west and captured five of their kings; obtaining also four white deer and four white wolves. The monarch then removed Yung to T'ai yuen (at present the capital of the Shensi provinces). *Hou Han Shu*, kiv. 117, tr. Wylie.

356) According to Mr. Thomas Ferguson, *Chinese chronology and cycles*, p. 220, the origin of the Duodenary cycle (of animals) may be traced to a systematic connection with the twenty-eight *siüh*, and its Chinese historical origin can thus be only synchronical with the appearance in China of the twenty-eight *siüh*. Prof. G. Schlegel, *Uranographie Chinoise*, p. 963, has collected evidence showing that it was known during the Tchou dynasty; the earliest instance cited is said to belong to the reign of Tchou Süan Wang (*Shi King*, II. iii. 6).

357) *On the Nakshatras.* They seem to have been mapped out on the heavens as groups of stars, not far from the ecliptic, readily recognizable, and by the position of the moon and planets could be readily indicated (James Burgess, J.R.A.S., Oct., 1893, p. 753). Alb. Weber, *Hist. Ind. Lit.*, p. 30, says that they are enumerated singly in the *Taittirya-Samhita*, and the order in which they occur is one which must necessarily have been established somewhere between 1472 and 536 B.C. Cf. *suprà* note 1222 for a probability of the twelfth century.

They do not appear in Babylonia earlier than on astronomical tablets of the Greek period, namely on calendaric tablets of 122 and 100 B.C. Cf. their names in P. J. Epping, *Astronomisches aus Babylon*, pp. 117-133 : Ergänzungshefte zu den "Stimmen aus Maria-Laach." 44; Freiburg, 1889. Dr. P. Jensen, *Die Kosmologie des Babylonier*, Strassburg, 1890, has nothing important on the subject. The Babylonian names in twenty-one cases out of twenty-eight are purely descriptive; for instance : II, *mahru sha rishu ku*, i.e., W e s t-o f-t h e-h e a d-o f-k u, or β Aries ; III, *Arku sha rishu ku*, i.e., E a s t-o f-t h e-h e a d-o f-k u, or Aries ; XXI, *Mûru sha shûtu*, i.e., S o u t h-o f-Nûru, or *a* Libra; &c., and these descriptions show that the knowledge of these twenty-eight lunar mansions were a foreign importation, which the Babylonians grafted on their own previous knowledge of ecliptical constellations. Prof. W. Whitney, in his studies on the Nakshatras published in the *Journ. Am. Orient. Soc.* in 1866, has come to the conclusion that, considering the concordances existing among the three systems" of the Hindoos, Chinese, and Arabians, it can enter into the mind of no man to doubt that all have a common origin, and are but different forms of one and the same system." These concordances coupled with the foreign character and late appearance of the lunar mansions in Babylonia and the ancient existence of such a system with the old Khorasmian astronomers, points to the latter's country as the focus from where it spread to China and through the channel of the Persian dominion, to India, Babylonia, and Arabia afterwards. Comparative lists of the lunar mansions are given in various works. The most recent are: James Burgess, *Notes on Hindu Astronomy :* J. R. A. S., 1890, p, 756; J. Norman Lockyer, *Early Asterisms*, iii., Nature, 28 Dec., 1898; T. W. Kingsmill, *A comparative table of the ancient lunar Asterisms :* J. Ch. Br. R. A. S., 1891-2, xxvi. p. 44-79.

363) We may mention also as evidence of relations with the west of the Pamir range the following circumstances: Under the reign of Tcheng-wang, according to the *Tchou shu*, if not already under Wen Wang, according to the *Shwoh wan*, the *Küan Yung*, also called *K'üan-fêng*, of the west presented a beautiful horse, the body white, mane red, and eyes like gold, named *Kih-liang* or *Kih Kwang* (cf. *Tchou shu : Shwoh wan ; Shan Hai King*, xii. 1 v.). It became the fashion at court in China to dye the manes and tails of horses red. Cf. *Shu King*, V. xxiii. 1, edit. Legge, p. 562; *Tso tchuen*, XI. Ting Kung, x. 12, edit. Legge, p. 778. The practice was a direct importation from Khorasan and Persia. ·Cf. also Edw. Balfour, *Cycl. of India*, p. 37.

---

874. *Chapter VII. Part I. and II. pp. 85-129.*

369) *First prison in China.* About 1803 B.C., the eighth ruler of Hia dynasty is reported in the annals of the Bamboo Books to have made a circular enclosure *for a prison.* The words in italics are additions of the commentators, as the original text says only that he *tso kwan t'u*, made a circular enclosed ground. The matter by itself would have little significance, were it not the fact that prisons are or were unknown to the Altaic races, and Vambery testifies that amongst the Turkomans the prisoners who are not put to death or do not become slaves are attached simply by a chain to the ground. Mr. F. Geo. Mohl, in a recent review of some works of the late Prof. August Ahlgvist, of Helsingfors, has remarked that in Vogul and Ostiak the terms for 'jail' are simply translations of a Russian appellative (*Mém, Soc. Ling.*, 1892, vii. 481). The notion of making a prison was therefore another foreign importation into the Flowery Land. The remote date of the event is interesting to note.

372) On imbrication of bronze and iron welded together, and of damaskeening in Assyria, cf. Dr. Percy's note in Layard's *Discoveries*, p. 670; Perrot-Chipiez, Hist. Art Ant., ii. 721-2; in Egypt, cf. A. H. Sayce, *Herodotus*, p. 257; Wilkinson, *Ancient Egyptians*, ed. Birch, ii. 257-8, Perrot-Chipiez, *O.C.*, i. 889; at Hissarlik and Mikenæ, cf. *Schliemann's Excavations*, by Dr. C. Schuchhardt, pp. 230, 264, 297, &c.

384) It is exact to say that the state of *Yueh* does not appear in the

Tchuntsiu before 587, but the *Tso-tchuen* mentions it first in 601. Therefore it may have been included in 584 with that of Wu in the astronomical distribution.

391) Herewith the comparative List of names (of the months) in Babylonian, and (of a cycle of twelve) in Chinese: Bab. NISAN= *Nuy-han*; Bab. Propitious bull=generous cattle. Bab. SIVANNU= *Tihfannoh* in ancient and tchihfanjoh, in modern Chinese. Bab. TAMUZ=*Tam-ot*, tan-oh. Bab. AB=*Hephap*, hich-hiah. Bab. KINSUKUSH = *Kentuk*, yen-mou. Bab. DULKU—*Tsayah*, tsoh-oh. Bab. ARAK-SHAMMAH=*Loktomany*, Ta-mang-Loh Bab. GANGANNNA *gangan*, ta-yuen-hien. Bab. TEBIT=*Tibtu*, tchihsiu. Bab. SHEBAT =*Shepti-koh*, sheh-t'i-koh. Bab. SEKINTAR=*Ta kwan tun*, kwan-tun. The Chinese list was dislocated, and its order different. It looks like a corrupted transcription.

The Babylonian names and colours of the planets which appear to have been imported into China with the names of the months, &c., by the west traders with Shantung, have also been preserved in astrological works in a curious state of dislocation:

1. Bab. *Kairanu*   Saturn   Black
   Chin. *Hih kwan ki*   Mercur   ,,
2. Bab. *Pitsu*   Venus   White
   Chin. *Pih tchao kiu*   ,,   ,,
3. Bab. *Nwuau*   Jupiter   Brown red
   Chin. *She tchu niu*   Saturn   Yellow
4. Bab. *Dawinu*   Mercure   Blue
   Chin. *Lingweinjang*   Jupiter   Green
5. Bab. *Nibatanu*   Mars   Red
   Chin. *Tsihpiaonu*   ,,   ,,

392) The names of the 10th, 11th, and 12th of the Chinese list of the 12 *ts'e* are fuller than given here and read respectively *shun shou, shun ho, shun wi*, i.e., head, fire, tail of the bird quail, or eagle (Eitel), corresponding to the celestial quadrant of the Red Bird, or *Tchu-nio*, the Summer One. There are no other names concurring with the three other quadrants, viz., *Tsang Lung*, or Azure Dragon for spring, *Hiuen Wu*, or Black Warrior for winter, and *Peh hu*, or White Tiger for autumn, corresponding to east, north, and west. The four animals of the quadrants therefore were only partly known at that time. It is what we should expect from their western origin. In the time of Nebukadnezzar, as far as they are described, in the vision of *Ezekiel*, their inception was probably achieved although each of the four beings therein shared the particularities of a man, lion, eagle, and cherub. This astronomical character is shown by the eyes (i.e., stars?) that covered their bodies (i. 18, x. 12) by their wheels (revolutions), and by the "likeness of a firmament" above them (i. 22). In the *Apocalypse* they appear distinctly. I do not know of any evidence showing that the Chinese had become acquainted with these four denominations before the HAN period. They were not known by the compilers of the *Er-ya*, nor by Kü-yuen (end of the 4th cent. B.C.) who in his *Li Sao*, where he had plenty of occasions to mention them, speaks only of the *Hien*

tchi, which name occurs in the *Tien kwan shu* book of the *She Ki* as that of the quadrant afterwards called the *Peh-hu*, White Tiger. Lü Pu-wei, who died in 237 B.C., did not know them, and the *Li ki*, is also silent. Szema Tsien in the precited *Tien kwan shu* appears to have been the first who mentions them with the exception referred to. And they appear all four in the *Wen yao kau* of the first century B.C. The commentators of the *She ki* have not been able to quote any older authority. No historical inference can be drawn from the fact that the first of the Chinese lists corresponds to the fourth of the Babylonian, since they were used only for astrological purposes and fixed in China according to prejudices foreign to any scientific object, and only in the seventh century B.C. Tso-kiu-ming, of the fifth century, in his own remarks (*Tso tchuen*, I. v. 7), speaks of the *Lung hien*—appearance of the dragon—season, with other names for the three other seasons, so that the case suggests only a partial knowledge.

396) Similar sacrifices were made in Szetchuen. When Tchao Wang of Ts'in (after 305 B.C.) invaded the Shuh country, and that Li-ping was prefect there, it had been customary to give every year to the Spirit of the River, two young girls for wives. Cf. *Tong suh tung*: T. P., 882, 4.

The practice extended northwards along the sea coasts. An annual offering of a maiden to the sea existed about 200 B.C. amongst some populations north-east of Corea. Cf. D., Hervey St. Denys, *Ethnographie de Matouanlin*, i. 327. J. Klaproth, *Aperçu Général des Trois Royaumes*, 149. Cf. also: *Some vestiges of Girl Sacrifices*: J. Anthrop. Inst., May, 1882.

414) The woodwork of Chosroes Palace in the ruins of Ctesiphon has been found by Dr. Sprenger to have made of teak wood. J.A., Mai-Juin, 1863, p. 309.

416) Under Usurtasen III. of the twelfth dynasty, an expedition was made against the country of Houâ (near Punt, between the Nile and the Red Sea, about Dongolah, Berber, or Khartum), but this was made by the Nile, not by sea. Cf. G. Maspero, *Revue Critique*, 15 May, 1892, reviewing *Bubastis* (1887-89) of Edouard Naville, 1891. Cf. also on Egyptian Journeys, Chabas et Goodwin, *Voyage d'un Egyptien au XIV. Siècle Av. n.è.*, 1868; W. Golonischeff, *Sur un ancien conte Egyptien*, of 2000 B.C. Verh. Orient. Congr., Berlin, 1881, II. iii. 100-120.

423) The Chinese transfer of the name of the *Saew* under the Han dynasty way S a k, 1673 Bas., now read *Sai* in Pekinese, *Seh* in central Mandarine, *Sak* in Cantonese, and erroneously transcribed *Sae* or *Sse*, *Tze* in historical works by Europeans. Mr. T. G. Pinches, in the *American Journal of Archæology*, 1893, has described a Babylonian tablet, dated 539 B.C., showing the figure of an Indian humped ox, referred to in the inscription on the other side of it.

441) Our section 117 was printed in July, 1892, of *The Babylonian Record*. The P. A. J. Delattre, *Une flotte de Sennacherib sur le Golfe Persique*, p. 18, article which appeared in the same month and

year in the *Revue des Questions Historiques*, has come to the same conclusion about the Phœnician influence of that fleet on the sea trade.

444) I had spoken of the *Muh t'iên tze tchuen* there on its former reputation, which the publication of Dr. J. Eitel has caused to reconsider. The geographical identifications which I have been able to make in the sections 284-296, show on the contrary that it is a most valuable relic of antiquity which has escaped the transcription of the Han commentators, and contains many characters which had ceased to be understood in later ages.

455) In the descriptions of the Fairy Islands, the words " trees of pure white coral" are a mis-translation. The text says that the trees were like pure white silk and that their stems were of pearl, *Shun-kao tchu kan*. Coral was not yet known, white pearls just first imported had the interest of novelty.

474) Le détroit séparante Java de l'Ile de Babli a été formé en 1204 à suite d'éruptions volcaniques. Cf. Henri Courtais, *Le Volcan de la Malaisie*, Sumatra-Java : Bull. Soc. Geogr., Toulouse, 1888, p. 521-529 ; Bull. Soc. Acad. Indo-Chin., 3, 527.

477) It seems however that the statement of the *Shan Hai King* on bamboos large enough to make boats growing on the Wei hills is not entirely improbable for that time. Marco Polo in Tchekiang speaks of the largest and longest canes that are in all Manzi (South China), " four palms in girth and fifteen paces in length." Cf. Yule edit. 2, vol. ii. 208. In Sze tchuen, according to Richtofen's *Letters*, bamboos are very large. Cf. E. Bretschneider, *Botan. Sinic.*, ii. 565. Tung-Fang So, *Shin y King*, reported that in the vastness of the southern regions some *p'ei* bamboos of an enormous size (fabulous dimension given) were used to make ships. T. P., 963, 6. Ktêsias mentioned the fact that in India small boats were made of one bamboo, which could hold not more than three men. Cf. Pliny, *Hist. Nat.*, xvii. 3 ; *Ancient India as described by Ktêsias the Knidian*, by J. W. McCrindle, 1882, p. 71. At Yung-tchang, says the *Kwan-tchi* of the fourth century, there are bamboos three feet round. Cf. T. P. Y. L., 963. 5 v. Dr. J. Edkins, *Bamboos in North China*: Ch. Rev., has collected evidence of the former existence of Bambu in Shantung, Honan, and South Shensi. The climate seems to have been warmer than at present.—The earliest European boats were nothing more than tree trunks hollowed out. Cf. O. Schrader, *Prehistoric Antiquities of the Aryan Peoples*, p. 278.

479) Hwai nan tze gives the word for boat in the Yueh and Shuh regions in the following statement: The bow of the *Wu-hao*, in the south-west borders, and the cross bow of the *Ki-tze* (valleys of West Hunan), cannot shoot without string ; the *K'ung*, small boats, of *Yueh*, and the *t'ing*, long narrow boats of *Shuh*, cannot float without water. T. P., 848, 6.

482) The *Heh-tchi*, or country of the black teeth, i.e., where they

chew betel, or lacquered their teeth, was beginning with Si-tu, the present Hue of Annam (cf. *Nan tchou y wuh tchi:* T. P. Y. L., 790, 9r.), and the *Lo,* or naked people country, with the Malacca peninsula and any of the Sunda Islands.

482) In the wars of the states of Ts'u and of Wu, sixth century B.C., the latter used boats to attack the former. In 525, according to the chronicle of Tso-Kiu, the king's vessel, called the 'Ultra Sovereign,' *Yü hwang,* the vessel of our former kings, said an officer Wu, was temporarily seized by the troops of Ts'u, and retaken with great slaughter by the Wu soldiers. It was then the habit of dragging the boats to shore, and there it was taken. The men of Ts'u digged a ditch all around it, and along the channel between it and the river, piled lighted charcoal. Notwithstanding this the Wu troops could carry away the royal ship, which must have been small indeed.

495) The water wheel innovated by Ma Kiun in 227-237 A.D. at Loh-Yang, *and which children were turning.* Fat or *Fan-kiü* (13308, cl. 159 Bas.), or flying cart. Cf. Fu-tze. T.P., 752, 7. The phonetic *fan* or *fat* used in the compound character is that for foreign. Liu-Tsih, of the Ming dynasty, in his commentaries on Kwan-tze, says however that it was the same thing as the *yt-hui,* 5136-4937 Bas., which goes against the stream ; *Khang hi tze tien,* s.v. In Sing and the Pendjab, the Persian bucket wheels in use there are called *pe-cottah.* Cf. Ed. Balfour, *Cyclop. of India,* ii. 377, 380, and iii. 1064.

498) In Delhi and Bundelkand, this water-raising implement is called d a h, d u-g l a, d u l i a (cf. Ed. Balfour, *Cyclop of India,* ii. 880), which remind singularly the Babylonian words, and show from where India has derived it.

504) Also: Fried. Wilh. Noack, *Laótsee, Taotek-king,* aus dun Chinesischen, Berlin, 1888, 61 pp.

506) According to the description of Shuh, or Sze-tchuen, *Shuh-tchi,* the ancient chiefs of the country used to wear their ears long stretched. Cf. T. P., 366, 2 *r.* and section 215.

513) The history of Khotan (*Pien Y tien,* kiv. 55, which Remusat has translated), says that five *lis* from there was the *Pima* temple where Lao-tze, after having made the barbarians convert to his views became (a) Buddha (p. 20). Pao-poh tze=Ko-hung, of the fourth century, and the *Wei-lioh* of about 300 A.D., speak of the journey of Lao-tze to the west.

517) Cf. also the chapter lxi. of the *Tao teh King* where another allusion is made to the Animal Mother (*p'in*). Dr. J. Edkins has given a short article on the *Foreign Origin of Taoism,* in China Review, 1891, xix. 397-399, where he claims Babylonian and Hindu ideas in the Taoism.

538) The latter statement must be restricted to the identification of the Five Tis with historical personages ; as the Five Regents of space which appear to have been worshipped long before the Han

dynasty, were explained by Confucius, according to tradition, as the genii of the five elements. Cf. on this point, C. de Harlez, *Les Religions de la Chine*, Leipzig, 1891. p. 121, 138, 139 : *Kung-tze kia yu*, v. 3; trad. Harlez : B. & O. R., vii. 1894.

546) Mr. A. Reville, in *Revue des Religions*, 1893, has come again to the subject in reviewing Dr. de Harlez's work on *La Religion Chinoise, Aperçu historique et critique*, Leipzig, 1891, 8vo. 271 pp., but he has only been able to show that a proper acquaintance with the Chinese original texts is absolutely required for a study of this sort. Cf. the rejoinder of Prof. de Harlez in the *Muséon* of Juin, 1893.

548) On widow burning recognised in India 600 B.C., and a translation of the Sutras of Asvalâ Yana ; cf. Max Muller, *Anthropological Religion*, 1892, p. 241 sq.

553) A woman was buried alive *(siün)* at the burial of Tcnou Ling Wang in 545 B.C. Cf. T. P. Y. L., 50, 7 r.

The *siün* practice of burying alive persons with a deceased sovereign seems to have been followed at Emperors' funerals much later than is here stated. The *Kwoh she lioh*, quoted by Palladius, N. C. B. R. A. S., x. 13, mentions the abolition of the practice in Japan in A.D. 646, and reproaches China with continuing it. But as stated in *China Review*, xviii. 261, there must be some mistake of date there. In our note 568, we have cited from the *Ko-ji-ki*, the suppression of the practice about A.D. 200. At his death in 1464, Ki-tchen, the MING Emperor Yng Tsung, left instructions that no concubines should be *siün*, i.e., buried alive. Cf. *Li Tai Ti Wang nien piao*. In the geography of the Sung dynasty it is reported that among the *Fu-yü*, in north of Corea, the practice of the princes was to slay several hundred people to be interred with a deceased ruler, *China Review*, xix. 287.

Burying alive is a Persian custom, says Herodotus, vii. 114, who quotes several instances of such mode of human sacrifices, not at funeral, but for propitiating or thankoffering to Earth Gods. He quotes also an instance of the Magi sacrificing white horses to make streams favourable, *ibid*. 113. On burying queens, servants and slaves with a departed king among the Scythians; cf. Herodotus, iv. 71-2. They were however strangled before.

650) On sacrifices of horses under the Ts'IN last princes and the Ts'IN dynasty, cf. Szema Tsien, *She Ki*, kiv. 28, fol. 16. On the altars of the four Tis, on which cf. note 588 *supra*, four foals were sacrificed, also a wooden image of a dragon-curved-tie-beamed chariot, *Lang lwan kiü*, 13287-4588-10840 Bas., with four horses. In 103 B.C. the living pony for sacrifices was replaced by a wooden image, save for the sacrifice of the fifth month. Cf. *She Ki*, kiv. 28, fol. 44 r.

569) In confirmation of my opinion that the human sacrifice made in the nineteenth year of Duke Hi., i.e., 641 B.C., in Honan was a result of foreign influence from West Asia, I have just seen in a valuable paper, *On star naming among the ancient Chinese*, by Dr. J.

Edkins, *China Review*, xvi. 389, that *Tu yü refers it to the practice of the Persian religion*. He was a famous commentator of the classics who lived in A.D. 222-284, according to Mayers, *Ch. R M.*, 684. On the same subject, cf. also J. Edkins, *Persian Sacrifices in China:* China Review, 1891, xix. 55-6, and F. Lenormant, *Chaldean Magic*, p. 531. In 532 the *Tso tchuen*, X. x. 3, says: " Ping-tze, of Lu, invaded *Kiü* and took Kang. In presenting his captives, he for the first time sacrificed a human victim at the altar of *Poh*." The fact was not approved. *Kiü* was narrowly connected with the foreign colonists of the Gulf of Kiao-tchou.

586) Prof. Ch. de Harlez has written an elaborate paper on *Le Style de Kong-fou-tze, Kong-tze-a-t-il interpolé le Shu King et composé le Tchun-tsiu:* in the T'oung Pao, Juillet, 1893, p. 248-297. He shows that none of the peculiarities of the style of Confucius appears in the first, second, third, and beginning of the fifth book of the *Shu King*, and he concludes therefrom that the Book of History has not been interpolated by the Sage of Lu. And with regard to the *Tchun-tsiu*, Dr. De H., wants to show that references are made by the Sage to another *Tchun-tsiu*, which would have been lost, but the suggestion seems difficult to accept, considering the care of his disciples for all he had taught them.

592) Prof. De Harlez has called my attention to the fact that in the words "he retained and *developed*," the last is an overstretched translation of Prof. J. Legge, of the character *Kiü*, 8705 Bas., which means "to extol" and not develop." Confucius therefore may not have altered the *Shu King*, save by substitutions of characters in transcribing it. But nothing shows that he has not suppressed parts of it still existing in his time. Fragments which have been preserved suggest that he did so. Furthermore it is rather suggestive in favour of this view that several of the very parts which are missing are exactly those where we should have expected views and circumstances contrary to his philosophy. Cf. the list of the original hundred books of the *Shu King* in the preface attributed to him. He apparently only transcribed the parts which he approved. Twan Yuh-Tsai in his work *Ku-wen Shang shu siuen y*, in the last century has collected a large amount of information on the subject.

602) Ti Tchih was only heir associate and did not rule, cf. § 364.

614) The adverse circumstances of the Chinese state or states, according to the period, hardly permitted any serious study of their ancient traditions. During the Hia and Shang dynasties their dominion was from time to time at so low an ebb, and in so constant a state of warfare, either internal or with the border tribes, that it did not allow science and literature to flourish. During the short period of power of the Tchou dynasty the chief object was to enhance their glory. Then came the period of Wonderism, Taoism, Neo-Taoism, and Confucianism which we have described. On the other hand we are aware that many ancient books have disappeared.

627) Lieh-tze speaks of Siang-tze of Tchao who ruled in 549-426

B.C. Cf. T.P., 869, 8. Hu-tze as a name for the teacher of Lieh-tze is rather suggestive. Although written with a character seldom used, *Hu* is homonymous of *Hu* the West Asiatics, and suggests that in Hu-tze we should see a makeshift for Hu-tze, the bearded foreigner, inasmuch as the bulk of notions, ideas, and legends in Lieh-tze's teaching is originary from the Erythræan Sea through the Erythræan traders and colonists in Shantung.

650) We know that at *Tsih Moh* there was a special calendar, *Tsien Han Shu*: T. P., 16, 9 *r*., and that in later times, i.e., before our fifth century, while making excavations there, one found in an ancient funeral mound, a golden bull. Cf. Liu Kiang Shu, *Y Yuan*: T. P., 811, 3 *r*. Can this have been an idol of the Erythræan Sea-traders and colonists? It looks like it.

651) The custom of cold food was suppressed only in the fifth century by Wei Wu Ti ; cf. Mayers, *Ch. R. M.*, 253. Another custom, that of the Easter Eggs, ornamented and coloured, boiled and given away, was probably introduced at the same time. *The oldest author on the subject* is Tze-Hia of the fifth century B.C., who is quoted in the book on *Kwan-tze*, cf. T. P., 928, 6. Dr. G. Schlegel, *Chinesische Bräuche und spiele in Europa*, 1869, p. 5, and *Easter Eggs in China*: N. and O., Hong Kong, 1868, p. 21-22, was the first to call attention to the custom. Cf. also J. J. M. de Groot, *Les Fêtes à Emoui*, i. 220-9.

665) Dr. J. Edkins, in *Worship of the Gods of Fire*, a note from the China Review, which he has kindly sent me, has attributed this worship to a Persian influence.

671) Among the Avestic notions introduced at that time we may also mention the figure of a four yellow-eyed animal dispelling bad spirits at funerals. Cf. *Zend-Avesta*, *Vendidad*, Fargard, viii. 41 : ed. Darmesteter, ii. 123, and *Tchou-li*, xxxi. 28, ed. Biot, ii. 225. Prof. C. de Harlez, *The Four-eyed Dogs of the Avesta*, 1886: B. & O. R., i. 36-8, 64, thinks that the Avestic notion was derived from Western Tartary. On the later development of the above superstition in China, cf. J. J. M. de Groot, *The Religious System of China*, 1892, i. 161-2. It may have been introduced earlier, i.e. by the Tcnou themselves, but the evidence is too late to prove it.

684) The *Yang sui* was spoken of by Tchwang-tze of the fourth century ; cf. T. P. Y. L., iii. 4 *r*.

688) A fire-syringe from the extreme south-east of the Malay peninsula has been sent over here ; cf. F. W. Rudler, in J. A. I., 1893. Cf. par. 229 for a knowledge of pyrite in 220 B.C. It would seem that it was long known amongst the Tartars. For instance, the Toba Tartars relate that fire was invented by Ulgan's three daughters striking iron against a stone. Cf. W. Radloff, *Proben der Volkslit. den Turk. Siberiens*, i. 286, *Folklore Journal*, Sept., 1892, iii. 318. A Mongol hymn is addressed to Mother Ut, Queen of Fire, whose father is hard steel and mother is Silex ; cf. Goblet d'Alviella, *Histoire Religieuse du Feu*, 1887, p. 81.

691) Cf. also C. de Harlez, *Un Philosophe Poète du IXe Siècle*, *Tchwang-tze*: Muséon, 1892, xi. 5-16, 116-128.

697) We ought to have recorded here in the text that in the fifth century Yakut rubies from Badakshan, pearls from the Persian Gulf, mother-of-pearl from the Erythraean Sea were among the staple articles imported at the emporium of Shantung; cf. par. 199, 203, notes 750, 767, 772. Mother-of-pearl was used to adorn the tomb of Duke *Yu* of Tsin, who died in 419 B.C.; cf. *Si King tsa ki:* T. P., 808, 7 r.

707) Pan Ku, in the *Tsien Han Shu*, Kiao Ki tchi, has given the same statement as Szema Ts'ien, about the Eight Gods, from India.

715) Cf. also J. Darmesteter, *Le Zend-Avesta*, 1892, i. 18-14. The list of thirty-three Ratus was given in one of the Nasks, the *Pajag*, according to the *Dinkárt*, viii. 7, 17; *Pahlavi Texts*, by E. W. West, iv. 1892, p. 18. The oldest references to these fabulous thirty-three beings in Chinese literature occurs in the *Tchou shu*. The Heavenly and Terrestial Kings of p. 23 *supra* do not seem to have been introduced before that time, probably with the ten *Ki*.

719) The story of *Nü-Kwa* is given in the Lieh-tze as a quotation from Hia-Koh of the Shang dynasty; cf. T. P., ii. 2.

722) The knowledge of some narcotics seems to have been also introduced by the same channel. For instance, *aconitum* was known first in the fourth century, and in that part of China under the name of *Otu*, modern *Wu-tou*, crow's head, from the Skr. *Ativisha*, Telug. *Ati-*vassa : cf. *Tchun-tsiu hou yu* and other works in T. P. Y. L., 990, 1-2 : cf. note 1012, on a later introduction.

729) Wang-tze-nien, *Shih y luh*, of the fourth century, has preserved a most curious tradition about the men of Muk-tu, Magadha, the country of Sila, as reported by him. His description answers exactly to the figure of a Hindu deity, such as Siva or Mahadêva, as figured in Moor's *Hindu Pantheon*, pp. 24, 45, 82, 104.

731) Magnifying glasses were made in Assyro.-Babylonia as early as the seventh century, and probably long before ; cf. Perrot-Chipiez, *Histoire de l'Art*, vol. ii. p. 718. In Greece, cf. E. Egger, *Mém. hist. anc.* 136, 415.

732) We must add here that some chrysolite from Kutcha=*Si Wang-Mu* was presented to King Tchao of *Yen*=Tchih li, in 311 B.C., by the north route; cf. Wang-tze-nien, *Shih-y-ki*: T. P., 178, 1-2 ; M. Gueluy, *Description de la Chine Occidentale* : Muséon, Juin, 1885, p. 303 ; the fame of this kind of stone came to the ears of Mandeville ; cf. *Globe*, 8 Août, 1826 ; V. Fournel, O.C., ii. 156.

734) On the name Hu, the word Hu means properly d e w l a p, that which hangs under the chin of a wolf, *Shi King* I. xv. od. 7 ; of a bull, *Shwoh wen:* or of objects (*Shih Ming*) like hooked spears, *Tchou li*, &c. Hence its application to old people, because of their hanging chin and neck, and by contempt to foreign bearded races.

741) *Tch'u* of HIA, c. 1855-1838 B.C., successor of Shao Kang, is reported to have introduced buff-coats in China, through his relations with the Tung-hu *Kiueh-Kung*, of North Shansi; cf. *Mih-tze* ; *Shi-pên*. T. P., 355; 1, 6 r. *Tchen lin wu ku fu:* T. P., 856, 3 r. *Tso tchuen*, V. xxviii. 8; X. xv. 6; XI. iv. 4. Yuen Yuen, *Tsih ku tchai tchung ting y ki kwan tchih*, 1804, i. 4. According to the legendary account in our p. 319, some sort of mail-coats were known in the west at the time of Hwang-ti.

748) The *Tchou-pi* says that the sun shines at a distance of 81 myriads of *li*, T. P., iv. 2. The number *eight* there is ominous, and suggest that the statement has come from the same source as that of Eratosthenes' (B.C. 276-196) calculation giving the distance of the sun as over *eight* hundred thousand stadia, 804,000,000. The source was probably Chaldean.

762) The genuine Asbestos is not yet known from the Dutch Eastern Archipelago. On Timor, near Atapupo, occurs however the so-called serpentine asbestos which externally often is much alike to the true asbestos, but differs chemically (note of Dr. A. B. Meyer, of Dresden). The external resemblance was quite sufficient for the assimilation made in the reports. As Timor stands last of the Sunda islands just south of the Banda Sea and Moluccas, we may understand that the sea traders were then passing there, and thus reached the native countries of the nutmeg and clove.

785) Yng-Shao, of the second century, says that the *Hwang-tchi* were in the south beyond Jeh-Nan=Nhit-nam ; and the *Si yü tchuan* connects them with the Tiao-tchi near the Western Ocean; cf. *Khang-hi tze tien*, cl. 65. Tiao-tchi were near the Persian Gulf. A garbled quotation given without source says that from the *Kan tu lu* state you go by ship about two months to the Hwang-tchi state, where the customs are much like those of the Tchu-yai (Hai-nan); cf. note 1037. I suspect this *Kan-tu-lu* to be the same as *Kan-to-li*, modern Palembang, of Sumatra, on which, cf. Groenevell, *Malay Archipelago*, p. 60, and L de Rosny, *Peuples Orientaux*, p. 285-6.

796) This informal entry of arrivals from the South in 591, indicates most probably the introduction of several things from India, mentioned § 209.

805) Cf. also H. Giles, *Chinese Dictionary*, s. v. Tou, Nos. 11427 and 11429.

811) We may add also the jaggery, or sugar of palm, par. 252, peacocks, note 1025, before 300 B.C.

The game of *Siang-ki*, which is much like our chess, was introduced about that time, as shown by its first mention in the elegies of Ts'u ; cf. *Ts'u-tze*, tchao hwun. Meng Tch'ang Kiun of Ts'i, who died in 279 B.C., was an adept at the game (Liu-hiang, *Shwoh yuen*). On subsequent instances, cf. H. F. W. Holt, *Notes on the Chinese game of the Chess*, J. R. A. S., 1885. See also Karl Himly, *Anmerkungen in Beziehung auf das Schach- und andere Brettspiele:* Z. f. D. M. G., 1887, xli. 461-484. The *Wei ki*, a sort of game of draughts, well known at the time of Confucius, had been attributed by the *Poh wuh tchi* to the age of Yao and Shun, but Ho Fah-tcheng a century later, in the *Tsin tchung hing shu* remarked that the attribution was inexact, as the game of *Wei ki* had not been introduced before the reign of Shou-Sin, the last ruler of the Shang-yn dynasty, cf. T. P., 753, 1-5.

825) Dr. P. Piassetsky, travelling from Han-tchung fu to ‎‏'‎Lan-tchou fu passed by another route. viz.: by *Mien* hien, *Lioh-yang* hien, *Hwei* hien and *Ts'in* tchou; from there two roads branch off; one, the shortest, is available only for horses and pack animals; the other, which was taken by the Russian expedition, and is a carriage road, passes through *Fuh-kiang* hien, *Kung-tchang* fu and *Ti T"ao* tchou to *Lan* tchou fu; cf. his *Voyage à travers la Mongolie et la Chine*, 1883, pp. 340-379.

876. *Chapter VII. (continued), Part III., pp.* 203-263.

ADDITIONS AND EMENDATIONS.

866) The two characters *tchou* and *tan* are much like one another, whence the confusion. *Tan* is cinnabar. It was used for painting purposes by the Romans, as shown by H. Davy, in *Annales de Chimie*, 1815, clvi, 72, &c.

867) *No silk in ancient N. W. China.* This is shown by the report of Li-sze to the future First Emperor in 236 B.C. The inquiry carried on in T. de L., *The Silk Goddess and her Legend*, 1891, par. 14, had led me to the same conclusion. The report of 86-73 B.C., mentioned in F. Hirth, *Roman Orient*, p. 226, mentions silk only in the *Yen, Yu,* and *Ho* districts, i.e., Shantung, Honan, and Shansi S. Not Kansuh as mistaken there.

875) Cf. also De Guignes, *Histoire des Huns*, ii. 19-20. A. Wylie, *History of the Hiung-noo*, 405-6.

879) P. Gaubil in his *Traité de la Chronologie Chinoise*, p. 65, remarks that " Li-sze and the Emperor She Hwang-ti were infatuated with the principles of the Taoist sect, and it is therefore probable that a strict search was not made for the books of that sect.

884) Cf. also the Japanese history *Koh shi ryak*, in H. F. Balfour, *Leaves from my Chinese Scrap Book*, pp. 24-27; *Le Lotus*, viii. 52. Some interesting details are given in another chapter of Szema Ts'ien, *She Ki*, 118, 11 r., which made this expedition a real attempt at colonising; 3000 people, goods, cereals, &c., and experienced operatives were sent.

914) It seems that we may recognise an interesting synchronism of the mission sent to India by Ming-ti in search of Buddhist infor mation, 64-5 A.D., in a tradition reported by the pilgrims Hiuen-F'ang and Hwei-lun. Under the reign of Kanishka, about twenty men having come from *East China*, or *Sze tchuen*, to pay homage, he assigned to them three convents as residences during their

sojourn according to the three seasons. In Kapisa the convent was
called *Sha-lo-kia* (which Beal understood as *Sérika*). Their winter
residence was called *Tchinapati*, near the Sutledj. They introduced
the p e a c h and the p e a r, hitherto unknown in India, and which
were called from them *Tchinâni* and *Tchinâradja putra*. The
peach has preserved that name to the present day; cf. S. Beal,
Records of Western Countries, i. 57, 174; *Life of Hiuen Ts'ang*, xxvi.
54; and Alex. Cunningham, *Arch. Surv. of India*, xiv. 54. The
p e a c h of China had been transplanted in Persia in the fourth
century, *suprà* p. 47. The p e a r is originary of anterior Asia, not of
China. The Chinese mission consisted of Ts'ai-yu, Ts'in King, of
the rank of Po-sze, Wang Tsun, and others, altogether eighteen
men; cf. Beal, *Buddhist Literature*, 3.

923) In the valley of the Ak-Baital river, near the Rang-Kul in the
Pamirs, Lord Dunmore saw immense beds of sulphur on the slopes
of the mountains; cf. his narrative, *The Pamirs*, 1893, ii. 179.

926) Stone-coal, Greek, *Lithanthrax:* Chinese, *Shih-t'an*, was then
also known for the first time in China. Theophrastes, 371-286 B.C.,
says that in his time, the founders and smiths of Greece made a
great use of *fossil coal* from Liguria and Elide, which they called
stone-coal. Hwai-nan-tze, who was acquainted with all the Greek
notions then reaching China, was the first Chinese writer who
spoke of coal; cf. T. de L., *On the ancient history of Glass and Coal
in China:* T'oung-pao, Sept., 1891.

The death of Hwai-nan-tze took place in 122 B.C. according to
his biography in Szema Ts'ien, *She Ki*, kiv. 118, fol. 7-18, and the
political circumstances which have led to his suicide. The date
of 122 B.C. is given rightly by Mayers, *Ch. R. M.*, 412. It is stated
also in the *Lih-tai Ti Wang nien piao* in that year. Dr. De Harlez,
Textes Taoistes, 1891, p. 171-2, thinks that he must have lived later,
but the Chinese authorities are most precise on the subject.

934) We may mention also amongst other things; the Calippus period
of seventy-six years, called *pu*, and attributed to Li-fang (a visibly
crippled and approximative transfert of the name of the Greek
astronomer; cf. P. Gaubil, *Traité de l'Astronomie Chinoise:* Souciet,
1732, iii. 21; Th. Ferguson, *Chinese Chronology*, p. 229. It was
employed by Szema Ts'ien for his calendar of 104 B.C. I do not
know the passage of the text of Hwai-nan-tze on the circulating
movement of the earth in the heavens alluded to by P. Cibot and
L'Abbé Grosier. But I may quote the following: "The sky is
like the awning of a carriage where the earth is the carriage and
the seasons the horses." T. P., 17, 5. Dr. J. Edkins has a note on
The Earth a Sphere: China Review, 119-20. In Lu she *Tchun-tsiu*,
a century before Hwai-nan-tze, I find a similar idea expressed as
follows: The sky is the wheel of the earth—chariot; in winter it has
gone to the extreme end and then it comes back;" cf. T. P., 2, 3 r.
During the reign of HAN Wu-Ti, one Loh Hia-hung, in 104 B.C.,
made a figure of the heavens after the *Kai-t'ien*, or vault of heaven
method; the sky was fixed, divided into seasons, and the earth was

revolving in the centre. The degrees had been marked by Sien-yü Wan jen; cf. T. P., 2, 10 r.

968) J. T. Reinaud, *Relations de l' Empire Romain avec l' Asie Orientale*, pp. 181, 186, 189-194, quoting *Florus*, iv. 12, and *Horat.* iii. 29, iv. 15, has shown that travellers from the country of the Sêres, after four years' journey, visited the Roman Emperor Augustus at Samos with an Indian Embassy in 20 B.C.

975) The ostrich eggs were an imported article of trade and industry, notably among the Egyptians and Phœnicians, who used to decorate them with paintings and carvings; cf. Perrot-Chipiez, *Hist. Art Antique*, iii. 855-61. The circumstance is interesting, as it has had most probably an influence on ancient Chinese art. Some of them were sent to China in several instances; the dates of 115 B.C , 101 A.D., &c. (cf. § 245), are mentioned in history.

980) The *Pan-ku yü ti Tchao shu*, or Records of Pan-ku and his brother Tchao, report that an officer of Tou, the commander in chief in Turkestan, A.D. 87, conveyed 700 pieces of cloth of various colours, and some *su-hoh* perfume sent by the *Yueh-ti*, i c., storax made in Syria; cf. T. P., 982, 1 r. On the *su-hoh*, cf. F. Hirth, *China and the Roman Orient*, pp. 263-6. E. Bretschneider, *Ancient Chinese and Arabs*, p. 20. H. F. Hance, *Notes and Queries*, iii. 81. Dan. Hanbury, *On Storax*: Pharm. Journ., 1857, xvi.

985) About Ngansi tchou of north-west Kansuh, the *Description de la Chine Occidentale*, tr. M. Gueluy, Muséon, Mars, 1885, p. 148, says: Ou suppose que là se trouvait l'ancien royaume de *Choul*; les renseignements positifs manquent, mais il y a là une rivière du nom de *choul*.

994) Another sort of precious spice had been sent by the same king in 98 B.C.; cf. Tung Fang So, *Shih tchou Ki*: T. P., 8, 5.

998) Amber was an article of exchange produced by the *Lendjabalous* Islands, according to the Arab travellers of the ninth century; cf. Reinaud, *Relation*, pp. 8, 16-7; also Maçoudi, I. pp. 338-9.

1000) The saltpetre, *siao shih*, and sulphate of copper, *shik tam*, are also mentioned by the *Fan tze ki jan* as imported through the Lung tao; T. P., 988, 2, 4. *Siao*, the Chinese term for saltpetre, is a trade word derived from Persian and Hindu *shora*: its first importation from from India was by the *Yh tchou* route about 100 B.C. Cf. *Pen tsao King*, ibid. The *Yh-tchou* was first established about 108 B.C. Saltpetre is extracted from an immense cave near Kung tia pin, north-east of the lake of Ta-ly fu, according to F. Garnier, *Exploration en Indo-Chine*, i. 521.

1006) According to the *Shih tao tchi* topography of the ten provinces (*tao*) into which China was divided in the seventh century, by Liang Tai yen of c. 800 A D., the country of *Ngou-loh*, or at least the eastern part of it, extended to P'an tchou, i.e., the present Kao-tchou fu in Kuangtung west; cf. T. P., 172, 9; and Playfair, *O.C.*, 4980. The description of the two provinces of *Nan-hai* and *Siang*-

kiun of Tchao-t'o show that they extended much beyond those first established by Jen Hiao spoken of in our note 1005.

1024) In the Kilian Mountains of North-west Tibet, the Earl of Dunmore, *The Pamirs*, 1893, i. 236, saw " a peacock-blue head, a magpie body, and the brightest of bright red tails. The birds are very numerous on the plains of Western Tibet, although we saw but two all the time we were riding through that country."

1076 In A.D. 84, the Chinese government commissioned Tcheng-hung, then commanding in *Kiao tchu*, on his own report, to establish officially the route by Ling-ling, present Yung-tchou, and *Kuei-yang*, also in Hu-nan, for the facility of the trade from that county ; De Mailla, iii. 384. This was the route by the Tchi-ling pass and Y-tchang, south of it, on the head waters of an affluent of the north river of Kuang-tung ; cf. G. James Morrison, *Journey in the Interior of China :* Proc. R. G. S., 1889, p. 152. *Tung-yeh*, present Fuhtchou, then the port for intercourse by the trading ships of Nhitnam, with the Chinese authorities, was said to be too far away.

1123) The nutmeg, Chin. *nah-tou-kou, ju-tou-kou* (cf. *jadikai* Tamil, *jadikaia* Telugu) does not appear, at least under that name, in Chinese literature before the *Nan fang ts'ao muh tchuang* of 300 A.D. Cf. T. P., 971, 6 *v*. The name often appears curtailed in *tou-kou* ; according to the *Wu-ti-ki*, in the years 220-227 A.D., the WEI of Loh-yang sent to Nanking to get some of these nuts. The *C. R. Acad. Scienc.*, xxxiv. 775, state that nutmegs have been found in the shells of late Egyptian mummies. Should the statement be true we could not be surprised since the traders in clove must have known them.

1128) Cf. also *Les Juifs et les Chinois*, by M. Cordonnier : Soc. de Geogr. Oran., 1892, xii. 52, 123- 9.

1137) Herewith an earlier instance of pleasure boats manned by ladies of the palace. In the year 656 B.C. we read that " the Marquis of Ts'i and Ki of Ts'ai, one of the ladies, were in a boat on a lake in the park, when she made it rock. The Marquis was afraid, changed colour, and forbade her ; but she persisted ; cf. *Tso tchuen*, V. iii. 7.

377. *Chapter VIII. Excursus.* pp. 264-290.

ADDITIONS AND EMENDATIONS.

1168) It was probably at that time also and not later that *Muh Wang* was offered by envoys from the country of *Kiü-su*, modern Wakhan), some objects in amber, according to a tradition which I have overlooked. On that country, cf. note 1187.

1184) In perusing the legends concerning Si Wang-mu in mythological books I find also the name of Kam-mu, modern *Kin-mu*, Golden Mother, for the same being. This is an unexpected confirmation of the name given in our text.

1187) We have overlooked here an important instance of distant intercourse with the west. The *Tchuh shu ki nien*, sixteenth year of Yao, reports that some Kiü-sou people came to China. In the *Yü-kung* the same name occurs again as importing carpets and furs, with the *Kuen-lun* and the *Sih-tchi* in a statement intended to include the most distant lands then known in the west. The *Kiü-sou* or *Kiü-su*, 5078-2550 or 3522 or 8176 Bas., was also called *Fu-kiü-su*, and later *P'o-han*, 11572-4850 Bas., modern Wa-khan, — in the Pamirs; the *Sui shu*: T. P., 793, 8 v., says that it was situated 500 *li* west of the Tsung-ling's entrance and 1000 *li* from *Su-leh*=Kashgar. The identification is therefore clear. Communications with the same country are mentioned under the reign of Tchou Muh-wang and in 571 B C. In Kiü-su and *Fu-kiü-su* we can recognize the name of Waksh, the river of Wakhan, of which the Greeks have made Oxus, and the Turks *Aksu*, as has been suggested.

1223) Cf. also J. Edkins, *On Chinese names for Boats and Boat Gear with remarks on the Chinese use of the Mariner's Compass:* J. N. Ch. Br. R. A. S., Shanghai, 1877, xi. 123-142.

1234) A common saying in China is that the first armillary sphere was made by Tsien-yoh of the Liu-Sung dynasty, 420-477 B.C. Cf. J. H. Stewart-Lockhart, *Manual of Chinese Quotations*, p. 293. Cf. add. 984, p. 368.

1238) In the name of *Fuh Muh*, the *Muh* is the same that appeared afterwards as a name of the district established 59 B.C. in exactly the same spot by the newly-established Governor-Generalship at *Wu-ley;* cf. note 965.

§ 378. *Chapter IX. Meeting of Objections.* pp. 291-315.

1254) Even supposing that some decisive evidence should be found in favour of a genuine antiquity of some parts of the Chinese astronomy, this would not affect the western origin of the Chinese civilisation, since Dr. G. Schlegel contends that the names of his asterisms refer only to the stone age.

1259) A shooting star is held among the Karens to be "a youth going to meet a maiden-star;" cf. Dr. Mason, *Notes on the Astronomy of the Karens:* J. A. S. B.; A. R. McMahon, *The Karens of the Golden Chersonèse*, 1876, p. 283. This looks like a parallel explanation of the Chinese myth of the Cowherd and Weaving Damsel, inasmuch as the Karengs are originary from China.

1262) According to De Mailla, *O. C.*, viii. 648, Chinese astronomy was rectified fifty times between Hwang-ti and the Sung dynasty, and fourteen times during the 250 years following.

§ 379. Chapter X. Essay of Reconstruction. pp. 316-337.

1313) It may be that some foundation in fact exists historically for the vague traditions that the Bak Sings or their ancestors had been submitted for three centuries to the successors of Sargon=Shennung before the accession of Hu Nak Kunte, and that seventy reigns or generations had elapsed between Shennung himself and the latter. Three hundred years before 2332 beginning of Hwang-ti, make the twenty-seventh century, which befits the age of Dungi, under whose reign the Bak Sings claim to have learned the art of writing. Assyriologists esteem that Dungi must have lived before 2500 B.C., and some give 2800 as his possible date. Now, as the second point, seventy reigns at an average of twenty years a reign would make 1400 years, 3750 before Hwang-ti. The date of Naramsin, son and contemporary for a time of his father Sargon is given by Nabonidus as 3750 B.C. The coincidence in the two cases it rather suggestive.

CHAPTER XII.

CHRONOLOGICAL SKETCH OF THE PRE-CHINESE AND IMPORTED
CIVILISATIONS OF CHINA IN ANTIQUITY.

I.—*Native Civilisation of the Pre-Chinese*.

380. Before proceeding to the arrivals in China let us first enumerate briefly what the civilisers found in their adopted country. The civilisation of the Pre-Chinese populations, when the Chinese Baks arrived into the land, and for long afterwards in the parts of the country which remained independent and outside their influence, was heterogeneous. Several distinct races, originary from the north and from the south, were occupying the basin of the Yang-tze kiang and that of the Hwang-ho. They had already come near one another, with their respective idioyncracies and acquisitions from their native lands, but they had not intermingled, and the country was sparsely populated. Notwithstanding the remote times we are referring to, i.e., some 4000 years ago, the racial distinctions of later ages seem to have been as clearly marked as they long remained afterwards. No leading state, nor any great power had arisen among them. As they appear to us, they seem to have been in that stage of everlasting immanence of the undeveloped and low civilised communities which change only when an outside influence arouses them to competition and progress.

381. The information on the subject is poor and scanty; only a few peculiarities have been stated, or may be inferred from the statements at our disposal, but they are sufficient to show how different was that heterogeneous civilisation from that imported into the country by the Chinese Bak Sings.

The dwellings of the native tribes consisted either of caves dug out in the loess country,[1380] especially in Shensi, or of houses on piles (in north Kiangsu and Anhwui, &c.),[1381] or of various sorts of sheds, or of large houses for a whole community (in the Centre, &c.) As vegetable food they used to eat Italian millet, *setaria ital.*, soy beans, rice, jujubes, radishes, peaches, apricots, plums, oranges, &c., and as intoxicating beverage some spirit made from rice.[1382]

They made fire by the ploughing or by the sawing process; their weapons and tools were either in scorched wood or in stone, some having the peculiar shape commonly called shouldered celts; they had bows of the plain type and arrows in wood or in bamboo, with or without stone-heads. Some of them knew copper, and others, chiefly in Szetchuen, knew iron and natural steel. Spinning and weaving grass and silk, dyeing with indigo and several other plants, lacquer, hand-made pottery, &c.,[1383] were among their rude industrial accomplishments.

Some knew the five tones of music, and others had special taste for clinkstones, numerous in the country.[1384] The Tchu-siang tribes had a five-chord harpsichord.[1385] Their trade was made by barter, and also with cauries, which they employed for ornaments.[1386] Tattooing was practised by many tribes for the same purpose. They had no written characters, but they had some embryo-writings, such as cup-marks on rocks and cliffs, knotched sticks and knotted cords.[1387] They were addicted to Shamanism, and generally worshipped spirits of rivers, mountains, and of everything in nature.[1388] Some were star-gazing, and had connected the yearly recurrence of stars in certain positions with their occupations, principally for sowing and harvest times, which for some plantations occurred twice in each year, and therefore caused a frequent confusion in later symbolism; the four and three stars of the Great Bear, called also the Seven Directors, appear to have been for them an object of peculiar attention under that respect.[1389]

Their marriage rules were various, as shown in after times: some were polygamous,[1390] others had gynecocratic institutions, and many had no family names. For the funerals they used to dispose of their dead either by putting them in the bush on the soil, or on piles or trees.[1391] Others, *especially in the east, placed them in egg-like urns, of earthenware, which urns in their turn were put severally in larger ones.*[1392]

382. Much more could be added about the customs and habits of the native tribes, should we have sought information from sources of later date, but we have been careful to avoid this convenient means, as some of the other peculiarities may have arisen in course of time through outside influences of variour sorts. We think it better not to encroach any further than we are afraid to have already done on late illustrations of the brief and limited suggestions of the primitive period. Nothing at all was known for a long time of the populations inhabiting the south of the Yang-tze Kiang, and therefore it is sufficient to say that they were not better than those north of the great river.

NOTES—

1380) *Shi King*, III. i. and modern travellers.

1381) Cf. the *Tsao* or Nest-dwellers as a soubriquet of a population of Anhwai. *Shu King*, iv. 2, 1; *Tchuh shu ki nien*, Hia, xvii; and modern descriptions Chinese and European. Also *Kai shan tu* by Sun Kia : T. P., 78, 2 *v.*

1382) As shown by the story of Y-Tek in the *Tchen Kwoh tsih* and the *Shi Pen :* T. P., 848, 1. Also in Mayers, *Ch. R. M.*, 230 and 682. Y-Teh had made some of this spirit by order of a wife of Shun. Shao Kang (*c.* 1875 B.C.) is reputed to have first made some spirit beverage from a variety of the *setaria italica*.

1383) Cf. the *Tao*, or potters' country in C. Shansi, conquered by Tchuan Hiüh after *c.* 2213 B.C., and the *Yao*, also potters, further south.

1384 Cf. *Shu King*, II. i. 23, 24, and iv. f. 10. Kuei, name of the appointed director of music by Shun, was the chief of a native tribe; we find it in 634 B.C. settled in the present Kwei-tchou fu similarly written in the extreme north-east of Sze-tchuen ; cf. *Tso tchuen Tchun tsiu*, Hi kung xxvi. 6 ; and Playfair, *Cities and Towns*, n. 3888.

1385) Luh she, *Tchun tsin :* T. P., 576, 3-5.

1386) *Shu King*, Yü Kung ; cf. T. de L., *The Silk Goddess of China and her Legend*, § 9. *Yh King*, Kwa 61, in *The Oldest Book of the Chinese*, 1892, vol. i., p. xviii.

1387) There is considerable evidence on this subject collected in my *Beginnings of Writing in C. Asia*, which it would be too long to reproduce here. That they had no written characters is shown by the complete absence of anything like a hieroglyphic inscription in China, and by the fact that all the natural products of the country had to be written by the newcomers with compound characters of their own script, while it would have been easier with a system open to any addition like their own to adopt any pictorial symbols previously in existence for the objects in question.

1388) For instance the *Kiu* and *Li* on the left banks of the Hwang-ho in North Honan were strongly addicted to spirits worship. They were conquered by Tchuan-hiüh after c. 2213 B.C. And also among the Miao-tze.

1389) Cf. *supra* § 309 and note 1284.

1390) Yao, a Chinese, sent his two daughters in marriage to Shun, a Non-Chinese ; cf. *Shu King*, Yao tien, 12. And on the subject, cf. J. Kohler, *Rechtsvergleichende Zkizzen :* z. f. vergl. Rechtweis. viii., 1888, p. 80, and Edw. Westermarck, *The History of Human Marriage*, 1891, pp. 20, 396.

1391) The first fashion (practised in Hupeh) is mentioned in the *Yh King*, Hi tze, it. 22 ; the second comes also from Chinese descriptions of native customs, such as in the *Mao Man hoh tchi*, iv., 8.

1392) "In the time of Shun, of Yü, they used earthenware coffins," *Li Ki*, T'an Kung, I. i. 12. These urns were called *op-ü* (Chin. oh-yü). On a find of such ancient urns in A.D. 506 in South- Kiangsu, cf. *She-hi :* T. P., 780, 2 *v.*

II.—*Imported Civilisation by the Chinese Bak Sings.*

383. The imported civilisation of the Baks, came into contact under the reign of Yao and Shun, with that of the indigenous which belonged to a low standard. We have already described briefly the last, and we must now examine the other in its complexity.

The following lists compared with those given in Chapters IV. and V., with corrections in the following and especially in the eleventh chapters, differ from them thus far that they contain only, to the best of our knowledge, a series (much more complete) of the elements of western civilisation imported into China by the emigrants of *circa* 2282 B.C., i.e., the Baks under the general leadership of Hu Nak Kunte or Yu Nai Hwang-ti, and that it leaves to be entered under their respective dates in the present chronological sketch the items of the same and other sources that were introduced in later times.

384. Comparative research into the Chinese traditions, checked by our knowledge, however incomplete it may be for the present, of the Chaldeo-Elamite culture, shows that among the many elements of western civilisation which the Bak Sings have imported with them from Anterior Asia, we may enumerate with great chance of historical accuracy all these items; they correspond to the very stage of development and progress which had been reached in western Asia a little after the middle of the third millenium B.C., neither before,

afterwards, or elsewhere. A few of the entries cannot be identified with Chaldeo-Elamite antecedents, although clearly imported from Anterior Asia; the civilisation of Babylonia and Elam was certainly paramount there, but it had not extended beyond its original centre over new lands and peoples without giving rise to local divergencies. Borrowed culture is seldom servile, and it requires and undergoes almost always a certain amount of transformation and adaptation to its new environment. Moreover every race has its own peculiarities and idiosyncracies, and we are well aware that the Bak Sings were no exception to the rule.

385. With all reservation necessitated by the obscurity of a subject so remote in times, and the frequent one-sidedness and lateness of the literary information from which the inferences and evidence can be drawn, it seems to me, in the present stage of my inquiry after many years labour, that we can ascribe to the Bak Sings themselves: A fair complexion, blue eyes, no black hair, and no high cheek bones, artificial tapering of the head; the ancestral worship;[1393] veneration of the sky-heaven, whose acknowledged son was their leader, T'ien-tze; building in pisé;[1394] clay-vaults for tombs;[1395] scorching the tortoise-shell for divination instead of the central Asiatic usual omoplatoscopy;[1396] a special taste for jade; important traditions concerning their relations with Chaldeo-Elamites and other princes of western Asia;[1397] that Tsang-kieh (old T'an-kih=Dungi)[1398] was their first initiator in the art of writing, and that their leader did get some precious vases with inscribed tablets; an adaptation of the Chaldean version of the deluge to the mountainous region of Puh-tchou-shan (=Badsakshan, modern Badakshan, through which they used to travel);[1399] the name of Hu Nak Khunte for their leader,[1400] and other things.

NOTES—

1393) The Ancestral Worship appears in the first chapters of the *Shu King*. Shun was appointed in the temple of *Wen-tsu*, or accomplished ancestor, II. i. 4. *Yü* was also appointed in the temple of *Shin Tsung*, or honoured spirits, II. ii. 19. Shun was worshipped in the *Wen-Tsu* temple, II. i. 14, and once coming back from a tour of inspection, went to the temple of *Y'tsu*, or cultivated ancestor, where he offered a single bullock, II. i. 8.

1394) Cf. W. Simpson, Tr. S. B. A., 1888, ix. 2; *Shi King*, III. i. Ode 3; *Tso tchuen*, VII. xi. 2.

1395) Still practised to the present day in the Pamirs.
1396) On the Omoplatoscopy, Mr. Woodville Rockhill has collected some data in *The Land of the Lamas*.
1397) I have utilised them in the *Reconstruction*, Chapter X.
1398) Dungi is the Chaldean King renowned for his numerous inscriptions, for whom Gudea conquered Anzan and Elam. Szema Ts'ien, *She Ki*, i. 4, xxviii. 32, 43, has preserved the tradition that Hwang-ti obtained some valuable vases with written tablets. The Chinese text as usual is rather vague in its construction, but we may understand it as meaning that the written tablets were inside the vases, as was customary in Chaldea, Egypt, Greece, and Rome.
1399) On Badakshan, cf. notes 1288, 1290, 1329.
1400) Derived like that of Kudur Nakhunte, his contemporary, from that of Nakhunte, chief of the gods of Susiana; cf. T. de L., *The Onomastic similarity of Nai-Hwang-ti of China and Nakhunte of Susiana*, 1890, and the Elamite inscription of Undas Arman where Nakhunte is called *Sulla Annap*, caput deorum.

386. When they arrived in the Flowery Land, the Chinese Bak Sings, besides their own achievements which we have just enumerated, were altogether acquainted through their relations with Chaldea and Elam, with the following elements of western civilisation which they introduced with them:—

The sky as a vault and round, the earth like a square raft underneath; the sun, male, and the moon, female; the five planets and some of their attributions; the solar year and the twelve lunar months, with an occasional intercalary month to adjust it roughly; year divisions into twenty-four parts and into periods of five and ten days; the division of the day in four parts and into fixed hours; a certain use of a period of seven days; four seasons in the year, the winter solstice as beginning of the calendar; and the vernal equinox for the year;

The four points of space with their symbols denoting a peculiar shifting, and their special colours; many names of stars and constellations, twenty-four stellar points; the sky as a figure of the earth surface; probably the five elements;

Standard measures of length and weight, such as the half cubit and the mina; balance scales; the gnomon but probably not the clepsydra;

The zodiac with the name of its twelve objects, used as a cycle of twelve for years, and as part of a cycle of sixty; the use of cycles, of ten, derived from the Akkadian numerals, of twelve, of sixty as a divisible unit, of seventy-two, &c.; the decimal notation and local value of the figures; the musical chromatic scale of twelve, &c.; but they had no 19-years cycle nor astronomical instruments;

Notions of hidden properties and harmonies of numbers, superstitions concerning certain lucky and unlucky days, belief in the repetition of events after certain periods, special practises of divination such as oneiromancy, belomancy, the eight wands of fate, avoidance of regular figures, hundred as a standard number.

387. They had learned from the same sources:—Building in claybrick instead of stone; stamping occasionally the bricks; doors on sockets; pillars for houses and great importance given to the roof; orienting buildings by the sun shade; special disposition of town-gates; erection of lofty terraces for astronomical purposes, and of large square altars; brick vaults for tombs; coracles, or skin-boats and rafts on inflated skins;

Making canals; embanking rivers; sinking wells; boiling the brine; works of irrigation for agricultural pursuits; extensive husbandry;

And they brought with them the wheat and the barley, the small garlic, the vine, the common millet, &c.

The composite bow, the archer's thimble, the sword, the potter's wheel, the mortar, the smith's bellows, the West-Asiastic plough, the plumb-line, the wedge, the balance-scales, manacles, ox-waggons, light and heavy with spoked wheels, one curved pole and yoke for animals abreast; bells hanging from the animal; a canopy over light chariots;

The use of gold, silver, copper, lead, and tin (but not of iron nor bronze), and the arts of casting them into vases, bells, war weapons, and other implements; cinnabar;

Long dresses; peculiar head-dress; special emblems on their rulers' robes and royal staff with auspicious bird on top, and state umbrellas, fans, walking staffs, rings, personal seals; shoes and sandals; stools, bedsteads, and mats;

Customs of mulcts instead of corporal punishment, tattooing for ignominy; cutting the left ear of slain on battlefield; besmearing the war weapons with the blood of prisoners;

Notions of eschatology (double soul); the nose as beginning of a human being; 120 years natural length of life; importance of personal names and their inscription for preservation by after generations;

As domesticated animals they had the ox as driving beast, the horse and perhaps also the ass as pack animals, the dog, the sheep, the fowl of Media, &c.

Some peculiarities of art designs; the single and the double flute; the drum, in earthenware and leather, and the tambourine; sort of reed organ and the bell; &c., &c.

388. They were acquainted also from Elam and Chaldea with the imperial system of government, the Four Regions, a title of Chief of the Four Mountains, the Susian duodenary division of states, the title of Pastor for their twelve leaders of these states, the appellatives of Middle Kingdom for their country, and of Black-headed people for their population; a prime minister, state astronomers, and several other special officers; change of name when ascending the throne; the leader as first husbandman of the state;

Bestowing a cup (*tsiok*), as a distinction like that of the cup-bearer (rab-sag); the right side a place of honour; titles of officers by birds' names; the worship of a personal God, called *Shang-ti*, several demigods and spirits; an important social status for the chief wife and for the mother, and probably some peculiarities in the right of ownership;

The art of writing the Babylonian characters in columns, strokes thick and thin, semi-ideographic semi-phonetic, such as they were written between the times of Gudea and Khammurabi; systems of syllabaries, phonetic and ideographic; and most probably some written texts; the custom of writing inscriptions inside of vases, across statues, &c.; a few traditions and legends concerning Sargon=Shennung, some ancient kings and systematic periods of history, a Babylonian cosmogony, and other legends, &c.

389. As previously stated, the ancient existence in China, after the arrival of Hwang-ti and his followers, of these 160 items of civilisation traceable to antecedents in Western Asia, is vouchsafed by statements in the history, traditions, and legends. Some of them are still in existence, others have disappeared in course of time, either by neglect or by better substitutions. But we know that (subject to further

research and revision, which may invalidate a few of them, and make some additions), they formed with subsequent introductions from the outside, and the natural evolution and progress of the Chinese themselves, the basis of their civilisation.

III.—*Chronological List of Western Relations with China and their Importations from* 2300 B.C. *to* 220 A.D.

§ 390.—*From Hwang-ti to the* HIA *dynasty.* c. 2282-1954 B.C.

c. 2282 B.C.

Arrival of Hwang-ti from the west in the fiftieth year of his reign, first leader of the civilised Bak Sings, on the Banks of the Loh, where he sacrificed. List of civilisation (sections 383-388).

c. 2260 B.C.

Pitchers of agate were brought to Shao-Hao from *Tan-kiu* (Turfan).

c. 2225 B.C.

Intercourse with Turfan during the first years of Tchuan-Hiüh.

c. 2147 B.C.

A Tartar named Tungli (=Tengri, heaven), was astronomer of Ti Kuh Kao-sin.

c. 2076 B.C.

Intercourse with West Karashar (country of the Western Wang-mu). Some fir-balsam was procured from there by Hou-y, who made the journey.

c. 2061 B.C.

In Yao's 16th year arrival from *Kiu-su* (later *P'o-kan*=Wa-khan).

c. 1996 B.C.

Intercourse with West Karashar. The West Wang-mu sent jade rings and archers' thimbles to Shun. Wan-ming, the great Yü is said to have gone there in his youth.

§ 391.—*From the* HIA *to the* TCHOU, *c.* 1954-1110 B.C.

c. 1954 B.C.

Reign of the Great Yü. Issue of the Brief Calendar of Hia (on fourteen astronomical statements, ten which can be verified have been found exact for the twentieth century).

c. 1950 B.C.

Introduction of yoked or car horses by Hitchung and Kikwang.

c. 1904 B.C.

On the 12th of May, 1904, solar eclipse at Tchin-sin (astronomically verified by G. Schlegel and F. Kuhnert).

c. 1903 B.C.

Arrival by the Kukunor, of the Kun-wus, clever craftsmen, acquainted with metallurgy (selection of ores), pottery, and roof tiling, astronomy, &c.

c. 1803 B.C.

First prison made in China. A western notion.

c. 1775 B.C.

Arrangement made with foreigners, east and west.

c. 1741 B.C.

Fresh arrival of Kun-wus who settled in Wei (north-east Honan). Kitan their chief introduced the art of bronze (= *tung*, i.e. mixed metal), probably alum, &c.

c. 1734 B.C.

Kung-kia in his third year became acquainted with iron (= *tieh*, i.e., barbarian metal,) from the natives Unsuccessful trial of iron swords.

c. 1800-1700 B.C.

According to the *Yü kung*, relations existed with the country of Kiu-su (=Aksu river, later called *P'o-han*=Wakan) from where carpets were imported. Jade (from Khotan-Yarkand) was also a staple article of importation by the north-west.

c. 1712 B.C.

Arrival of Ki-tchung tribes from beyond the Flowing Sands, reckoned among the ancestors of the Tchou because of their settlement in south-west Kansuh, and introduction of hemp.

c. 1690 B.C.

Arrival of Lao shih shing, from or by Karashar, at the court of Kieh Kuei, last ruler of the Hia dynasty.

§ 392.—*The* SHANG YN *Dynasty*, 1686-1111 B.C.

c. 1686 B.C.

Foundation of the SHANG, i.e. Merchants' Dynasty, of Shang-kiu, or Merchants' Hill (Kwei-teh fu, Honan). Intercourse with the west continued.

c. 1558 B.C.

Mokan (=Wu-Hien), a foreigner who had come from Karashar, officer of SHANG Tai Mou, made the first catalogue of stars, arranged prayers to the hills and rivers, and introduced the use of the divinatory plant *shi* (ptarmica sibirica).

c. 1538 B.C.

In Tai Mou's twenty-sixth year arrivals from a western state near Karashar. Wang-Mêng was sent there with presents, and also to the West Wang-mus to get some of their famous balsam.

c. 1394 B.C.

SHANG Yang-kiah made an unsuccessful expedition as far as Turfan.

c. 1331 B.C.

Under YN Wu-ting, arrivals of missions from six foreign states, using several interpreters. Some from the west were probably among them. Introduction of the yeast.

c. 1325 B.C.

Immigration of the TCHOU at K'i, in south-west Shensi. They appear to have been red-haired Kirghizes aryanised to a certain extent.

c. 1255 B.G.

Tsu Kia of the YN dynasty, in his twelfth year, made an expedition outside the western frontiers.

c. 1190 B.C.

Horses (of Khorasan) are said to have been brought to the chief of the TCHOU, Wen Wang; they had red manes, white bodies, and eyes like gold.

c. 1170 B.C.

Arrivals from the west to the seat of the TCHOU.

c. 1136 B.C.

Lunar eclipse of January the 29th, twenty-six years before the foundation of the TCHOU dynasty (astronomically verified by S. M. Russell).

c. 1180 B.C.

Importation of Jade from Turkestan, and probably of the game of draughts.

§ 393.—*The West* TCHOU *Dynasty*, 1110-770 B.C.

c. 1110 B.C.

Overthrow of the SHANG-YN dynasty and conquest of the country by the TCHOU, with the help of native tribes. They introduced with them ring-money, clepsydra, polarity of magnet, names of stars, the twenty-eight lunar mansions, duodenary cycle of animals, worship of heaven and earth, notion of the Yn and Yang (perhaps still crude), use of the flagrant *tch'ang* "bringing down the spirits," dog sacrifice, dyeing red the manes of horses; eunuchs and slavery, castration as a punishment; three-holed flute, and other things, all notions most originary from Bactria and Khorasmia.

c. 1105 B.C.

Tchou Wu Wang opens routes for intercommunications with all the foreigners. Importation of mastiffs from West Tibet.

c. 1099 B.C.

Arrivals from the west; presentation of clever embroiderer women from *Yen-ki* (Karashar), of peacocks from *Ku-tze* (Kutcha), asbestos cloth from Badakshan.

c. 1097 B.C.

Arrivals of missions from the south-west: *Shou-mi* with Indian monkeys; *Nélé* with calendars and astronomy; *Yueh shang* with elephants and pheasants.

1092 B.C.

Arrivals from Kashgar with moral laws.

1079 B.C.

Several arrivals from distant countries.

1017 B.C.

In the twenty-fourth year of Tchou Tchao Wang, arrivals from the south-west by *Tu* and *Siu*.

c. 990 B.C.

Some tribes from the west brought to Muh-wang some asbestos from Badakshan.

c. 986 B.C.

Journey of Tchou Muh Wang, to Turfan, Karashar, the Yulduz plateau and further west, perhaps as far as Kashgar. He brought back with him several clever artificers, the arts of inlaying metal and of making paste-gems, &c., some jade from Khotan-Yarkand, amber through Wakhan, &c., Marionnettes, and other things.

c. 984 B.C.

A prince of the Si Wang-mus came to visit Muh Wang, and brings some white jade objects.

c. 881 B.C.

First settlement of Semi-Chinese of Ts'u on the south of the Yang-tze Kiang.

860 B.C.

The usual route by the north-west being stopped by unruly tribes since the days of Muh Wang, the jade traffic, on a smaller scale, was carried by a route more south, reaching China by the north-east corner of Tibet, the present Sung-pan ting route.

c. 800 B.C.

Foundation of Tagaung in Burma by Hindu colonists arrived through the land route.

§ 394.—*The Eastern* Tchou *Dynasty*, 770-481. B.C.

770-678, &c., B.C.

Practices of burying alive at funerals were then introduced by the Western Tartars in the State Ts'in (Shensi and Kansuh) as well as several barbarian sorts of worship.

About 680-642 B.C.

Within twenty years of the introduction by Sennakherib of the Phœnician navy in the Persian Gulf, traders from the Indian Ocean (Erythrœan Sea) arrived in the Gulf of Kiao-tchou (South Shantung), where perhaps their ships were first carried by chance of sea voyage like the one carrying Fa-hian to Canton, who arrived at the same spot in 400 A.D.) They established there colonies named Lang-ya (Lanka ?) and Tsih-moh (Saphar ?), and issued soon afterwards in the latter place the first inscribed coinage of China. The joint-issues of coins show that these marts, for two centuries, established trade relations with cities in N. W. Shantung, S. C. Shansi, E. and S. E. Shensi, and C. Honan, and therefore that alone would suggest that the influence of these foreign merchants must have been extensive.

They came on ships having birds' or animals' figure with two big eyes on the bow, and two sculls at the stern, which have remained in the Chinese navy of later times. They introduced into the country besides the coinage standards of weight and measure (mina of Karkhemish and Babylonian empan); quince fruits of Media; notions of Sorcery and astrology, mythological imaginery, the twelve *tze*, or zodiacal signs (adapted from corrupted Babylon names of the months), for astrological purposes, and the 19-year cycle, from Assyria; the Phœnician custom of putting in tombs figures of horses and carriages in earthenware, and other things.

641-600 B.C.

During the following years, the items and notions introduced by the foreign sea-traders coming to Shantung were different from those of the first forty years, and came evidently from the border lands of India and Persia. In 631 their leader had a Sanskrit name, *Gotra*. Herewith a summary list: human sacrifices near river; exposure of victims for droughts; cold food at vernal equinox, and exchange of painted eggs; tempering iron; worship of the fire god of the earth; sesamum (under its Indo-Persian name); mercury; etc.

626 B.C.

You-yu, a barbarian of the west, became adviser of Muh Kung of Ts'IN.

600-575 B.C.

Opening of relations between India and the Non-Chinese west of Szetchuen. Arrival and settlement in the caves near the Min river of Brahmanist colonists, long-eared, eating Soma, and living like Anachorets. Arrival in 591, in T'SU, through the same route of travellers from the south (India). Introduction there of the use of stamped ingots of useless shape for currency, horse-shoe shape of tombs and Wei-kan pillars (both symbolising the natural worship; the shaduff; and other things.

571 B.C.

Arrival in TCHOU of travellers from *Kiü-su* (=Wakhan) who presented camels with rich saddles.

565-525 B.C.

A further change occurred then with the Erythrœan Sea traders frequenting Shantung. They introduced fire worship, dualist worship and the five Avestic fires; some superstitious practices such as the figure of a four yellow-eyed animal dispeller of spirits at funerals; writing on skins; and other things. This was due to the fact that Persian influence became paramount at that time. Cyrus conquered Babylon in 539.

§ 395.—*Period of the Contending States*, 481-221 B.C.

500-450 B.C.

The influence exercised in China by the Erythrœan traders became again Babylonian with a strong Indian tinge in some cases, and its activity was rather important. The Persians had obviously given a new life to the outside relations of the old Babylonians. The following items were then introduced into Shantung and neighbouring provinces: Astronomical and mathematical notions (*Tchou pi*), counting rods, cementation of metal (*c.* 500), a sort of catapult (*c.* 475), concave metallic mirrors (*c.* 450), the Semitic names of the twelve Babylonian months, ten other names of the same nature, ten *Ki* as historical periods, mythical chronology of Babylon, thirty-three kings heavenly, terrestial, and human ; fabulous notions of fishmen carriers of civilisation, tree-of-life and calendar tree, hippocentaurs, semi-animal beings ; Egyptian phylacteria ; and other things.

475 B.C.

T'u-yü, a prince of Indian origin, founder of the Kingdom of Snun, was then ruling at Tcheng-tu, in Szetchuen.

473 B.C.

Foundation by the King of *Yueh* of an emporium at *Kwei-ki*, near the Hang-tchou bay, which the Erythrœan traders began to frequent. In 472 their ships carried soldiers of Yueh to Lang-ya.

c. 470 B.C.

Foundation of a second Hindu colony in Burma, said to have been made by a band of Kshatriyas from Gangetic India, on the east bank of the Irawaddy.

c. 450 B.C.

Foundation of a colony in Ukkalamandala, near Rangoon, by Taphussa and Bhallika, two Hindu merchants, not Buddhists, from Orissa.

425-375 B.C.

The trade from the Erythrœan Sea to the eastern coasts of China (Shantung, Tcheh-kiang) was then entirely changed. It seems to have passed chiefly into the hands of Indian mariners who did not, as their predecessors, navigate through the Malacca Straits, and came by the south of Sumatra and Java. They imported mother-of-pearl of the Indian Ocean, large pearls of the Persian Gulf, yakut stones of Badakshan ; narcotics such as aconitum ; the *mu-nao* or sistrum ; fabulous accounts of the storm bird, avatar of Kurma (tortoise), the Sumeru, Rishis and their drug of immortality (*soma*), Indian cosmogony ; worship of the eight Hindu *Vasus ;* fabulous accounts of five islands of the blessed and their reduction to three, as stations of their sea voyage ; process of casting coins, &c., in clusters ; mercury ; and other things.

c. 890 B.C.

Since the middle of the previous century the Kings of Ts'ɪɴ (Shensi) were extending their sway westwards. About 390 B.C., the Ts'inites were going west in Outer Kansuh as far as Kwa-tchou (present An-si), to communicate with western traders, without any help of their government.

634 B.C.

Importation of jade from Yunnan-Burma into Hupeh through the south-western route.

330 B.C.

Foundation in Yunnan by an army from Ts'ʊ of the Kingdom of Tsᴇɴ, whose name in later times became for the southern traders, that of Cʜɪɴᴀ.

c. 327 B.C.

Foundation of *Mon* (=exchange) as an emporium for foreign trade, near the present Ningpo.

325-310 B.C.

Tung-yeh, present Fuhtchou, of Fuhkien, became then an emporium for foreign sea-trade, and the imports there, at *Mon*, and at *Kwei-ki*, consisted of rhinoceros horns, ivory, carved vases, lamps with asbestos wicks, yakut rubies, western rope, peacocks, ear-haired rhinoceros, sugar of palm ; perfect dancers ; notion of a three-legged bird in the sun ; the chess-game ; &c. Transhipments were made from there to the ports in the north.

305 B.C.

Arrival of the Hindu Sila at Yen (Tchihli) from Magadha, by Tung-yeh (probably) or by the south-west route, after five years journey. He brought with him some magnifying glasses.(?) The inhabitants of Magadha he described as the Hindu statues of gods.

311 B.C.

Relations were then existing between Karashar-Kutcha (=*Si Wang-mu*) and the Kingdom of *Yen*=Tchihli, by the north route. Importation there of chrysolites of Kutcha.

c. 280 B.C.

Military expedition of the King of Tsᴇɴ (Yunnan) towards Old Pagan on the Irrawaddy, in Burma, which facilitated commercial intercourse with the Hindu merchants of Pegu. Arrival afterwards in south-west Hunan of bearded merchants with valuable spices, *ugai-nap*, or mint palm, and *mi-sung*, a narcotic from the western ocean.

237 B.C.

Jade from Turkestan was then imported in the north-west. The fame of Alexander-the-Great and his deeds had reached the state of Ts'in, then rising to the empire.

§. 396.—*The Chinese Empire*.

221 B.C.

Foundation of the Chinese Empire by She Hwang-ti who seems to have endeavoured to imitate Alexander-the-Great in several respects.

220 B.C.

Arrival at Lin-tao, on the borders of Kansuh south-west, and Tibet, through Szetchuen, of Hindus, or western men, professing Hinduic views. They introduced the use of pyrites.

220-217 B.C.

First arrivals of Buddhist missionaries, Tzekao, Tcheng Pehkiao, Tsili Fang, &c., who were unsuccessful in their religious propaganda.

201 B.C.

The Erythræan Sea traders had given up Kwei-ki as an emporium because it had fallen into the hands of the Chinese, and had made for a time *Tung-yeh*, which was still independent, their chief station. They imported there big pearls from the Persian Gulf (transhipped to Kwei-ki, which was a market for them), and for the first time some sugar-of-cane from India. Wu-tchu, the King of *Min-Yueh*, could send as a present to the Chinese Emperor, HAN Kao-tsu two *huk* measures of the foreign dainty.

195 B.C.

The same sea-traders in view of commerce with the new Semi-Chinese Empire of Nan-Yueh (204-111 B.C.) frequented then *Hoppu*, or Estuary of Meeting (near the present Pakhoi, south-west Kwang-tung), in connection with the market place of Hêng-shan inland. They had imported there jasmine from Persia, and sambac from south India, peacocks, &c. They became known as *Hwang-tchi*, or yellow fingers, from their habit of dying their fingers with *henna*, and their home was *Hormuzia*, near the Persian Gulf.

179-150 B.C.

The Hormuzian sea-traders shifted again their landing place, on the conquest in 179 by the Nan-Yueh Emperor of the country westward, including Tung-king. They selected a convenient spot (near present Ha-tinh, south of Nghê-an province), on the outskirts of his dominion, where the colony of *Kattigara* was founded. They established also pearl fisheries at *Tchu-yai*, or coast of pearls, in the Isle of Hainan.

164 B.C.

The jade traffic of Turkestan was then continuing as shown by a jade cup procured in that year by the Chinese Emperor HAN Wen.

145 B.C.

Greek ideas and notions penetrated then into China by the west trade route inland, such as Alchemy with the use of orpiment and cinnabar for transmutation into gold, &c.

140 B.C.

First arrival in South China, probably at Hoppu, of Tats'in=Tarshish merchants, with a large quantity of red corals from the Mediterranean, via Reckem, Ailana, and the Red Sea. Tchao-t'o, the Emperor of Nan-yueh, sent 462 branches to the Chinese Emperor HAN Wu, who ornamented with them the Tsih-tsao pond of the Shang-lin park of the capital Tchang-'an, inaugurated in 188 B.C. The sea route was then passing south of Sumatra-Java and the Sunda Islands near Timor; serpentine asbestos found in the latter was the occasion of several fables.

139 B.C.

Sea-going ships were then built for the first time in China, in imitation of those of the Erythrœans, by the Semi-Chinese State of Min-yueh (Fuh Kien).

139-126 B.C.

First mission of the Chinese government to the West for political motives. Tchang-kien, the envoy, went as far as the Oxus and Baktria, where he saw goods from Szetchuen imported there through India.

133 B.C.

Importation by the west trade route inland of brimstone from Tsiü-mi (800 li of Karakhodjo), alum shale from Kutcha, and a large metallic mirror which required rubbing with felt and powder of black tin to be kept shiny (of Greek make), and jade.

130 B.C.

In Shuh-Szetchuen importation from Burma of cocoa nuts and bananas.

127 B.C.

Importation in Nan-yuch of the *henna* plant from India, and of Nard from north-west Sumatra, by Tats'in=Tarshish merchants.

126 B.C.

On the return of Tchang-kien, the Chinese Emperor HAN Wu adopted his report proposing a conquest of Bactria by way of India. Some ten missions were sent during the following years to find the routes, but they were stopped in Yunnan and in south-west Szetchuen.

126-122 B.C.

Introduction by the west route inland of further Greek notions, such as astronomical speculations, circulation of the earth, the 76-year cycle, knowledge of stone-coal, burning lenses, &c.

119-116 B.C.

Second mission of Tchang-kien to the Wu-suns in Ili. He opened by himself and his assistants intercourse with some ten states of central Asia. After his return the state mint was reorganised like those of Athens and Rome.

115 B.C.

Alum-shale from Kutcha, amber objects from Kabulistan, ostrich eggs of Mesopotamia (probably decorated with pictures as was usual), and jugglers from Reken, sent by the Parthians, were then brought into China. A regular intercourse was then established between west Turkestan and China.

Lucern, vine again, cucumber, and safflower with their Greek names, walnut tree with its Aryan name, common bean, parsley, great garlic, hemp and sesamum again, pomegranate of Parthia, were then introduced into the Flowery Land and carefully transplanted at first in a park of the capital.

113-108 B.C.

Several missions were sent by the Chinese Emperor without success to the Greek State of Yuan=Yaon, Ferghana, with goods and presents, to get from the king some of his Nisæan horses (of classical fame) blood perspiring.

111 B.C.

Conquest of the dominion of *Nan-yuch* by the Chinese. Unsuccessful transplantation in the *Fuli* gardens at Tchang-'an of native plants from the new provinces, and besides several already named, of some which had been introduced by the foreign trade, such as sweet flag of south India, Indian shot, *Quisqualis Indica*, &c.

110 B.C.

The Chinese conquest having included *Kattigara*, which they called *Nhitnam* (Jihnan) the Hormuzian sea-traders removed once more their chief landing place; they established it further south, on the west of Cape Cambodia, east side of the Gulf of Siam, in Tcham, the *Zabai* of Ptolemy. They came from there to Kattigara and Hoppu, bringing pearls of the Persian Gulf, coloured glass of Kabulistan, precious stones and strange objects such as a big pearl, perfectly spherical, &c. The Chinese Emperor HAN Wu being desirous of getting some more coloured glass was obliged to send a ship for that purpose to their Emporium.

108 B.C.

Merchants from Tats'in-Tarshish arrived at Hoppu with red corals for the market of Hêng-shan, and with a *hwa-ti-niu*, or flower-hoofed bull, which they presented to court. They taught a process for dyeing black with the leaves of the *mu-lan*—magnolia.

102-100 B.C.

After several abortive attempts, frustrated by the Hiung-nus, a Chinese army reached and conquered the Greek State of *Yuan*=Yaon, Ferghana. A new king was enthroned, and ten Nisæan horses were brought back in triumph. The results of this expedition were important, as they gave to the Chinese empire a prominent position which was acknowledged in western and eastern Turkestan.

100 B.C.

Trade with India by the Szetchuen route was active. Sugar of cane, aconitum, and saltpetre from India were then imported at Wu-tu (near present Kiai-tchou, south-west Kansuh). In 78 B.C. a small mirror in an amber case was imported from Kabulistan through India by the same route to HAN Suan-ti.

98-87 B.C.

Trade continued uninterrupted with Turkestan, &c. Alum-shale, saltpetre, sulphate of copper, *mung*-dogs from the Kuen-lun are recorded importations. In 87, the King of the Yuch-ti sent to the Chinese Emperor some precious spice of Socotra. Another sort of spice had been sent by him in 98 B.C.

73 B.C.

Ships from India and from Tats'in-Tarshish arrived at Kattigara, the Chinese port. Some twenty years later ships of Oman arrived with the founder of Cambodia at Zabai. Kalingas in Java, 75 B.C.

59 B.C.

Establishment of a General-Governorship of the *Si-yü* or Western Regions, at Wu-luy, near Karashar, by the Chinese, with jurisdiction over thirty-six states of east and west Turkestan.

51 B.C.

Si-kiun, a Chinese princess, who in 105 B.C. had been sent in marriage to the King of Wusuns in Ili, came back introducing into her native country the *p'i-pa* or Persian *tamburah*.

50 B.C.

Chinese authority was powerful enough in central Asia to instate Hermæus, a Greek prince, on the throne of Kabulistan. But this authority lasted only a few years there.

20 B.C.

Travellers from the country of Sêres (a name meaning yellow and oriental, given to the Chinese by their western neighbours), after four years journey, reached Samos with an Indian embassy to the Roman Emperor Augustus.

12 B.C.

Some cotton paper, *haktai*, had been brought from India to Loh-yang.

11 B.C.

Arrival of travellers from the Wusuns (Ili), *Kang kiu* (Samarcand), and *Pan-tu*—Parthia.

2 B.C.

Y-tsun-kou brought Buddhist books to China. At that time fifty states of the Si-yü were receiving investiture from China, and 876 princes and officers there were holding Chinese seals of office.

1-37 A.D.

New instances of intercourse with the south. In A.D. 1 arrival of a mission from Yueh-shang (south Indo-China). In A.D. 2, Hwang-tchi, or Hormuzian, ships arrived at Kattigara and Hoppu. In 37, arrival of another mission from Cochinchina.

10-75 A.D.

In 10-16 A.D. revolt of the states of the Si-yü (with the exception of Yarkand until 41 A.D.) against the Chinese government. Interruption of regular intercourse for 65 years.

41 A.D.

Rachias envoy of Ceylon to Rome, said that his father used to trade beyond the Himalayas with the red-haired Sêres. Since 108 B.C. the red-haired Kunmings were subjects of the Chinese in south-west Szetchuen, where the trade route was passing.

47-85 A.D.

First practical use of the monsoons in 47 A.D. by Hippalus, of Alexandria, who sailed direct from the Red Sea to Muziris on the Indian coast. The *Periplus*, about 85 A.D., shows that the Greek merchantmen did not go beyond Nelkynda of south India.

67 A.D.

Return of a Chinese mission sent to India. Official introduction of Buddhism into China. Adoption of seven musical notes as in India.

69 A.D.

The 'Ai-Lao advancing north-west, cut the route through the Kunmings, and submit to China. Foundation amidst them of the great mart of *Yung-tchang* (present Tali fu) for foreign trade. The imports then consisted of copper, iron, lead, tin, gold, silver, bright pearls, amber, crystal, vitreous ware, kassia-grubs, oyster pearls, peacocks, kingfishers, rhinoceroses, elephants, apes, and tapirs; all products from Shan-Burma, Malacca, Ceylon, India, Kabulistan, but nothing from the Red Sea.

c. 72 A.D.

Arrival of the first Jewish colony in south-west China.

84-89 A.D.

Mission from Cambodia arrived in 84 to the Chinese court. In 89 Hindu traders arrived at Kattigara and Hoppu.

87-106 A.D.

From 73 to 98, the Chinese gradually re-established their authority and prestige in central Asia. The General Pan-tchao in 97 went as far as Antiochia Margiana, and sent Kan-yng who travelled as far as the Persian Gulf. In 87 a Parthian mission arrived with lions, *fu-pao*, 700 pieces of cloth of various colours, and some *su-hoh* perfume (Storax made in Syria), sent by the Yueh-ti King. In 101 another Parthian mission, sent by Pacorus II., brought lions and ostrich eggs. In 106 a last mission from Parthia arrived. All the Si-yü revolted then against the Chinese. The preceding years were those when the agents of Maës Titianus were trading with China probably through the Parthian Missions.

97-131 A.D.

Missions from the Shan States in 97, 120, 124. The second mission presented jugglers from Tats'in, with which country relations had began by the south-west. The Greek Alexander from whom were derived the information in Marinus of Tyre had then travelled on board ship as far as Pegu.

119-150 A.D.

Attempts at re-opening communications with the Si-yu and reconquest as far as Karashar in 126. In 134 a mission came from Kashgar. In 147, 148 Buddhist missionaries arrived from Parthia.

159 A.D.

Hindu merchantmen arrived at Canton via Kattigara. The King of Saurashtra Mandala (Guzerat) was then sending ships to Mahacina, Cina, and Bhota. First importation of cloves (chicken tongues) of the Moluccas in China. For two hundred years afterwards the landing place of the Indian and Omanite ships was chiefly Funam-Cambodia, from where the goods were transhipped for the Chinese ports.

166 A.D.

Arrival of Roman merchants, of whom An-tun (Marcus Aurelius Antoninus) was the Emperor, at Kattigara and Canton to open intercourse. The Parthian war had interrupted the communication inland which, however, was restored in the years 172-187 as shown by fresh arrivals of Buddhist missionaries from Parthia and Samarkand. Later arrivals of Roman traders were reported at Canton in 226, 284, &c.

* * *

397. The relations of the west with China since the second century which became more frequent, are beyond the scope of the present work. We have had occasion to mention a few of them in the course of our enquiries and they may be referred to in the alphabetical index.

398. Arrived at the end of these laborious pages, we think it necessary to mention once more an important principle in all comparisons of civilisations. It is that borrowings of elements of culture, except in material cases, having required necessarily a certain amount of mental activity from the borrowers, cannot be blind copies and

servile imitations, specially when carried to distant lands and different surroundings, and not kept up by a continued intercourse with the mother country. We have not included as borrowings many strong suggestions whose western character was often quite clear, which would have lengthened sensibly several of the lists we have established, and we have counted only as units such comprehensive elements of civilisation as writing and astronomy.

399. The conclusion of the present work is that some 370 items of civilisation have been introduced in China from Anterior Asia and also W. India during the twenty-five centuries covered by the investigations it contains or summarizes. About 2282 B.C. some 175 of these were imported by the Bak Sings themselves, including more than 160 derived from the Chaldeo-Elamite civilisation, such as it was at that time neither before nor afterwards. During the Hia and Shang dynasties only twenty-five appear to have been introduced from western and central Asia. The Tchou themselves introduced about twenty-five, mostly Baktrian and Khorasmian. The traders of the Erythræan Sea, who began to arrive on the Chinese coasts in the seventh century, introduced sixty-six items, of Assyrian 12, Indo-Persian 7, Mazdean 4, Indo-Assyrian 14, Indian 16, and mixed 18, sources successively, and in homogeneous groups, while 6 came direct inland from India, all before the Empire. During the four centuries of the Ts'in and Han dynasties about 70 ″ ..s were introduced, viz.: 10 Greek, 24 from Parthia, 22 from India and Burma, and 16 by the traders of the Indian Ocean. All these elements of western culture, with a limited contribution of the Pre-Chinese, form with the own adaptation, progress, and evolution of China, the real bases of the Chinese civilisation.

§ 400.—*Comparative Chronology.*

Egypt 5500 B.C. Chaldea 4500 B.C. China 2300. Egœan, Mikænian, Pseudo-Hittite, Assyrian, 2000 B.C.

CHINA.	Rectified.	Bamboo Annals.	Common.
Hwang-ti	c. 2332-2232	2388	2698
Shao-Hao	c. 2282-2213	(not)	2598
Tchwan-hiuh	c. 2226	2288	2514
Ti-Kuh	c. 2147	2208	2436
Ti-Tchih	,,	,,	2366

China.	Rectified.	Bamboo Annals.	Common.
Ti Yao	c. 2085-2076	2146	2357
Ti Shun	2004	2043	2255
Hia Dynasty	1954-1687	1990-1594	2205-1767
Solar eclipse	**1904**	1948	2155
Shang Dynasty	1686-1111	1558-1051	1766-1123
Tai Mou	1568	1475	1637
Wu Ting	1336	1274	1324
(3rd year of Wu Wang)	**1120**	1061	1132
Tchou dyn. 1st year	1110	1050	1122
Tcheng Wang	1103	1044	1115
Muh Wang	1001	962	1001
Li Wang, 12th year	841	841	841
W. Tchou dynasty	770	770	770
Contending States	461	461	461
Foundation of Empire	221	221	221

ALPHABETICAL INDEX.

ABBREVIATIONS.

Ch. = *China, Chinese.*   Isl. = *Islands.*   Mt. = *Mountain.*   Nat. = *Natives.*

R. = *River.*   S. = *See.*   S.V. = *Sub verbo.*   St. = *State.*   Tr. = *Tribes.*

W. = *Wang or King.*   A star indicates a *rectification.*

Abakansk 338
Abhirâja 56, 59, 60, 117
Abiria 100
Abricot 47, 49, 198, 374
Abyss, female 127
Acclimatation, 230, 246, 391
Agôkarama 57
Aconitum 236, 365, 387, 392
Acrology 186
Addumu 103
Advance, S.W. 249, 250
Aeng pass 251
Aepyornis 170
Agate 267; pitchers of, 328
  333, 381
Agathou daimonos nêsos 111
Ag-daimon 113
Aghic 272
Agriculture 11, 379, s. Husbandry
Aham metal 99
Ahaziah 244
Ahura mazda 95
Ailana 390
Ai-Lao 41, 252, 253, 394
Ak-Bozat 289
Akhæmenians 157
Akhaz 278
Akkadian 293; and Ch. 342;
  numerals 340; orientation
  11, 29; words 10, 13, pass.
Aksu, Oxus 371
Akurgal 307
Alaka-Khotan 74
A-lan-na 311
A-la shan 327
Aleutian 344
Allas strait, 111, 181
Alchemy, Greek, 214.217,390
Alchemists 214
Alectromancy 218
Alexander 240, 244, 395

Alexander the great, 38, 158,
  203,-5,-6,-14,-43, 389; wall
  of 209
Alexandria 268, 271
Alligators 208, 329 *
Allophylians 317
Allusions, valuable 316
Aloes paper 245,-6
Altars, square, 11, 379
Altering texts 140, 143
Altin kazuk 289
Alum, 230,-2, 382, 390,-1,-2
A-man 58
Amber, 39, 41, 230, 231, *232
  369,-7, 314, objects 391,
  case 392, 394
Amesha gpentas 81, 83
Anachorets 196, 200, 386
Anaximander 278
Ancestral worship 74, 79,
  139, 160, 162, 377
Ancient documents, 127, 141,
  143,-7-8, 151-2, 175, 288
Andamon isl. 111
Angular Bow 194
Animal: cycle 356, 383;
  ethnics (318) 323; mother
  126, 361; quadrants 298,
  358
Animals, domesticated 380;
  pack-312
Anku-Angha 58
Annam, coast 68, 240; history 44, 45, s. Tung king
Annius Plocamus 251
Anro-Mainyus 95
An-shi-Kao 248
An-shih-lu 230
Ansih-Andhra 58
Ansik 224, s. Parthia
Antimony 85
Antiochia Margiana 222, 394

Antun = Antoninus 245, 395
Anu and Anah 10
An yang 156
An yang wang 236
Anzan 378, 26
Apaosha 350
Apes 99, 252, 394
Apocalypse's Animals 358
Apsu 127
Arabian sea 89,96, 102; traders 111, 211; in India
  97, 107; Bengal* 119; 277
Araktu 109
Archaian white races 80
Archaic Ch. 17 s. Ku-wen
Archeology, Ch. impeded
  368
Archer's thimble 195, 264,
  379, 381
Archery 176
Archiver of Tchou 127
Arcus 194
Areca catechu 246 252
Arghamak 224
Argyrê 251
Aristolochia 252   [379
Arithmetical notation 13,
Arkan-jolduz 289
Armillary sphere 289, 371
Armlet-mana 97, 101; in
  India 101
Aromata of Socotra 230, 231;
  coast 96
Arrakan 102
Arrows 179, 195, 374
Arsaces 214, 222, s. Parthia
Art designs 380; B. & Ch.
  72; 391
Artificers, clever, 382, 384
Aryan Influence 30, 73;
  ,, Words 31
Asafœtida 265, 270

400   ALPHABETICAL INDEX.

Asbestos 35, 77, 182, 187, 309, 318; a bark 188; cloth 384; hair 188; jokes 187; legends 259; wicks 180, 388; in Ch. 187, 188, Sunda Islands 188, *366, 390
Ass 343, 380; and Horse 343
Assurbanipal 101
Assyria and India 97
Assyro-Babylonia 30, 71, 73; Art in Siberia 14; Bronzes 88 :, Words 13
Astrognosie 291-8-9
Astrological Books 206
Astrology 89-92, 385
Astronomy 8, 74, 76,(77, 80) 82, 93, 297, 383-4, 387; Unscientific 294-5; Foreign 179, 287, 295, 382; Greek 217, 282, 391; Instruments of 10, *338, 368, 379; Native 286, 294, 374; Public Officers 20, 380; South 108, 158, 159, 190, 290, 296-7; Tartar 289; Towers for 379, 343, 11; Verifications of 6, 8, 39, 88, 179,* 277, 297, 381; Work on 287-8, 290; Observations 341
Augustus 393
Autocracy 203
Avatars 173, 387
Avestic infl. 82, 173, 157, 364 387; five fires 164, 166
Azure Dragon 358

Bàa-n-pe 283
Baba kul 273
Babylon 102, 157, 230; civ. in Ch. 70; and India 96, 97, 101; Cosmogony 127, 175; Fire-drill 168; Fire-mirrors 168; Imagery 91; Months, 12 Signs 94, *338, Names 358; Navy 102, 105; Sea-trade 91; Ships 105; Zodiac 90, 341; India, influences, 386
Bab-salimeti 103, 105
Bactria 82, 315, 321; Chin. Coins 226, 309; Conquest projected 250-1, 254, 391; India-China 50; to Jade Mines 321
Bactro-Pali 198
Badakshan 73, 77, 80, 180, 377, 384; Route 75, 225, 308
Bagaratch kul 267
Bagdad 26

Bagistan 26, 305
Bagla 262
Bahrein isl. 96, 103
Bahr Yukhre 169
Bak, etym., 303, compounds, 307 : ethnic 22, 26, 302
Bak-Fêng 304
Bakh, Baku 305
Bakhdi 26, 305, 307
Bakhtan 26
Bakhthyari 26, 305, 317, 350
Bak kwan 304
Bak Li 304
Bak mes nagi 26
Baks, Bak Sings, 14, 20, 27, 104, 141, 161, 195, 264, 302-7, 310, 318, 372; Advance 316; Beginn. 320; Chiefs of 320, 305, 319, 336; Civilised 336, 377; Date 341; Migration 71, 288, 291, 321; Multiply 332-3; Trade in Jade, 32, 309; Physical Type 318, 377
Bak wang 304
Balance Scales 378-9
Bali 110, 113; Strait of, 360
Balsams, 99, 270. s. Fir balsam
Baltic Amber 231
Bamboo 104, 266; Bark 14; boats 114,* 360; Staves 198, 200; Tubes 340
Banana 246, 390
Banca 108, 255
Banda 259
Bangka 108, 111
Banners 204
Bantam 108, 111
Bantings 260
Barbarous Customs 131-3, 385
Barbarikon 51, 53
Barkul 311
Barley 379
Barter 251, 374
Barugaza 51
Basiati 100
Battle ships 115
Bean, common, 227, 391
Bear, Great,(374) –
Bearded Merchants, 250, 389; Races 365; s. Hu
Bedstead 379
Beginn. of day 79; of year 79
Behistun 157, 305
Beidawy 35,* 351 •
Bell 210b, 380. Hanging 379; of Peking 167

Bellows 379
Belomancy 379
Bêlos 341
Benaketi 351
Bengal, Bay of, 111,* 119
Bennu 339
Berosus 37, 96
Bhiennaka, 56, 60
Bhota 247, 395
Bibliotecal   Catastrophes 345
Bingani-Sariris 297
Bintang 180, 186
Birds, enormous 170; footprints 14, 318; fronting 72; head-ships 385; officers 353, 380; path 289 : stations 271
Bit-yakin 102
Black hair, no., 85, 87, 318, 377
Black heads 20, 96, 97, 98, 380
Black, obelisk 97, 182; people 109; river 266-9; teeth 38, 115, 360; warrior 358; water, 325-7 3·5ϒ
Blessed, Isles of 387; S.- Fairy isl.
Block printing 345
Blood, besmearing 342, 379; drank 313 : perspiring 219, 224, 391
Bloodshed, wholesale 207
Blue eyes 85, 318
Boats, char. 15; inv. 114; 179, 360; Chaldean 105; Indian 260
Bogdo-Ola 269
Bogh 305
Bolor 308
Bonze 207b
Book of Hwang-ti 126, 127
Boots, leather 176
Borrowings, adapted 396; first 380; x, xi
Botany, historical 230
Boussole 31; s. Compass
Bows, composite 194, 379; native 360; plain 374; star 298, 340; symbol 194, various 194-5
Bower, MS. 313
Brahmans, ascets 108, 197, 200, 210, 386; influence 107, 118, 122, 128, 197
Branches, twelve 341
Bricks, building 11, 13, 379; stamped 342; vaults 379
Brimstone 213, 215-6, 390
Brine, boiling the 379
Brinjal 269, 270

ALPHABETICAL INDEX. 401

Bronze 86, 88, 379, 382; art 286; ingots 118; and iron 357; statues 211, 214; weapons 214
Broussonetia papyrifera 251
Buddhagosha 104
Buddhism, early 211; introd. 210, 212, 389, 394
Buddhists 249, 389, 394; books 209b, 211b, 393; first 207b, 389, images 207b, 210b
Bucket-wheels 361
Buff coats 184, 366
Bull: Flower-hoofed, 392, 242; Golden 364
Bulunghir 266-9
Buried Cities 309, 310
Burma: 117; Amber 39, 41, *232; Jadeite 40, 41, 388; Nagas 89; Sources, 56, 117-8; to Szetchuen 64, 65; Tsenites in 56, 388
Burning: the Books 36-7, 205-6; Lenses 219, 391
Burying alive 132-3, 138, 210, &c., s. Siun

Cakes, Sugar, 237
Calendar 92, 288, 384; Babylon reform 230, 279, 281, 288, 341; Hia 6, 143, 381; Hwang-ti 329, 331; Tchuen Hiûh 81; Tree 24, *387; Tsih-Moh 364; Vedic 281-2; Yueh shang 46
Canals 11, 379
Canarium 246
Canopy 379
Canton 241, 245, 247, 248, 395
Capitals, s. Kung-shan, Kung-sang, Puh, Poh, Ping-yang
Carchemish 36. s. Karkemish
Cardinal points shifted 11, 288, 299, 321, 378
Carmania 232
Carpets 371
Cassia 193, 194; grubs 234, 288, 394
Casting: Coins 388; Metal 379
Castration 384
Catapult 194, 387
Catalogue of Lit. 151, 210; of 3tars, s. v.
Cauries 235, 374; Metallic 118
Cavalry 176

Cave-dwellings, 196, 197, 278, 374
Celts, Shouldered 374
Cementation 165, 167, 387
Central Kingdom 151
Ceylon 36, 37; to Ch. 107, 251; Egypt 98; Rome 251
Chaldean: Astron. 302, 341; Boats 105
Chaldeo-Elamite civil.in Ch. 376-8
Chance Sources 181-2
Changes of Name 380; in Sea-trade 81, 156-8, 239-241, 259, 387-392
Chantabon 262
Chaotic Creatures 171, 387
Characters changed 140, 184
Chariots 179. 379
Charles the Fifth 187
Chau: kung 163; ma 163
Chersonese trade 260
Chess 366, 388
Chichiklik pass 309, 312
Chicken tongues, s. cloves
Chiefs early, 336
Ch'ih measure 340
Childish ditties 92
China's: name 39, 63, 64, 66, 67, 68, 193, 207; Antiquity 142; Astronomy 371; Boating 112, 115; calendar 389; chronology 6; historians patriotic 317; isolated 20; histories 71; linguistic 293, 342; literature intricate 298, wrecked 206; natives 114, 373-4; navy 106, 240; outside relations 315, 381-396; pearls 242; poor states 314, 339; religion 135, 362, pass.; writing 15, 345: to Ceylon 261: Herat 268, 311, Hira 261, India 61, Pegu 56
Chinese, character 147; in Kansuh 328, Shensi 328, Honan 333, Shantung 333, Shansi 335; in Central Asia 221, 392, 394; v. Hiungnus 219, 220
Chorasmians, s. Khorasmians
Choul, Shul, 369
Chronology 6; rectified 88, 143, 179, 192, 354, 381; table 397
Chrysolite 365, 388
Cina 248, 395
Cinnabar 214, 367, 379, 390

Cinnamon 191, 193, 194, 246
Circulation, Earth, 368; ix
Civilisation borrowed 71, 378; native 373-5; imported 381-396; how divided 396; ix
Claws of birds 14, 318
Clay images 136, 138; vaults 377
Clepsydra 10, 78, 281-2, 378, 383; Egypt 279, 281; India 280
Climate, warmer 360
Clinkstones 374
Cloth: coloured 369, 394; striped 291; woollen 200 s. Asbestos
Cloud-thunder orn 72
Cloves 181, 252, 253, 257, 259, 366, 395
Cluster casting 179, 388
Coal burning 272; stone 368, 391
Coasting navigation 261
Cocoa-nuts 251, 390
Coffins in earthenware 374, 376
Coinage 89, 214, 385; shapes useful, useless 118
Cold food 160, 386
Collyrium 99
Colours symbolical 10; horses 211; planets *338, 358; of space 135, 208b, 211
Compass, mariners 31, 45, 261, 283-5
Complexion fair 377
Composite Bow 194-5
Concave mirrors 165, 387
Conversation 168
Cone fruit figure 72
Conflict, schools 138, 147
Confucius 74, 118, 119, 125, 140-1, 180, 166; character 139; editor 143, 363; historian 139; and Laotze 139, 142
Confucianism 138, 142, 147; Books burnt 206, 209
Conquests, projects of 203, 207, 249, 253, 315, 391
Contending states 70, 145, 386
Convex sky 10, 378
Cook, First, 161
Copper 85, 87, 252, 333, 374, 379, 394; and tin 85; vases 333; sulphate of 369, 392
Coptos 96, 98 [379
Coracles 11, 114, 208b, 344,

Corals; Red 235, 243, 390, 392; fishery 237; white 109, *360
Corea 114, 119, 362
Cos, cloth of 200
Cosmic egg 342
- Cosmogony: female 126, 208b; male and female 127; Bab. 380; Ind. 387 174
Cosmography 288
Counting rods 387
Cow, mythical 126, 129
Cowherd and Sp. D. 301, 371, cf. 289
Cross-bow 192, 194-5, 360
Cross-legged 114
Crow, Sun, 193
Crystal 252, 394, 247, 182
Cubebs 180
Cubit, half, 378
Cucumber 220, 227, 391
Cuneiform, 14, 318, 380; in C. Asia 312, 321, 322; latest 231
Cup, bearer 380; bestowing 380
Cupmarks, cupules 328, 374
Cupid's bow 194
Curios, trade, 179, 182, 204, 246
Cycles, 10; of ten 10, 379, twelve 379; 78, 93; nineteen 288; sixty 379, 10, 78; seventy-two 379; seventy-six 368, 391
Cylinder seals 343
Cyprus 102, 105, 187
Cyrus 102, 157; and India 198

< Dahae, Daoi, 53, 354
Dakshina 122
Damaskeening 357
Dams 11, 334, 341, 379
Dancers 388; Girls 180; see Jugglers
Darchiendo 50
Darius 157
Days by five, seven, ten 340, 378
Daza rāja 56
Dead on bush, piles, trees, 374
Decimal Notation, 101, 341, 379
Deluge 97, 100, 173, 324, 349, 377
Demavend 219
Demi-gods 172, 280

Democrites 217
Demon Classifier 323
Denary Cycle 10, 339, 379
Deneb 299
Derivation of writing 345, 14, 15, 17
Dermata Sérica 51
Desarēnē 251
Destruction of Relatives 132
Difficulties of Journey 308-314
Diglat 22
Dintih-Babylon, 22, 23, 25, 313
Diodotus 214
Disorder, General, 145, 146
Distant regions 76
Divination 10, 92, 377, 379
Divine: prefix 20, *346; Self-ruler 151
Djemshid 85 --)
Djurtchen 138, 198
Documents suppressed 363
Dogs: 380; Keepers 81; Mung 392; Mastiffs 47, 48, 49, 197, 384; Sacrifice, 79, 132, 384; Star 298, 348
Domesticated Animals 11, 176, 343, 380, 381, 386
Double-banked boats 260; Crops 298; Eyed-ships 106, 178, 385; hours, 9, 339
Draconis Pole Star, 289 /
Draco 302
Dragon: Season 359; five 175
Draughts 367, 383
Dravidian words 89, 100
Drawings of statues 210b
Dress Emblems 11, 379, 344
Driving Animals 343
Drought: Goddess of, 329, 350; Superst. 90, 386
Drums 204, 208, 329, 380
Dry Sea, Han hai, 314
Dualist worship 90, 386
Dulati 120
Dumang 23, 318
Dungi 5, 14, 15, 24, 26, 32, 318. 372, 377, 378
Duodenary Cycle 10, 340-1, 378; Animals 356; Months 358
Dyavaprithivyau 81
Dye of Magnolia 242, 244, 392

Ea 105
Eagle wood 247
Eannada 307, 324

Ear; Elongated 121, 124, 361, 386; haired rh. 388, 182; left cut off 342, 379
Earth flat 341, 378; circulation 216, 368
Earthen: carriages 136, 137, 385; coffins 374, 376; drums 380
Earthquake 261
East Barbar 134, 144
Easter Eggs 386
Ebony wood 247
Eclipses, 39, 88, 297, 382, 383
Egg: cosmic 343; easter 386; tombs 374
Egypt 3, 15, 80, 97, 106, 157, 183; Animal worship 171; and Ceylon 168; and India 99, 100, 169; influence 86, 37, 76, 169, 352; journeys 359; phylacteria 169, 170, 171, 387
Eight: Hindu Vasus 156, 171-2, 387: hundred years of Hien-yuen 327: wands 10, 340, 379
Eighteen small states 210
Eizion-gaber 102, 243
Elam, Nam 25, 26, 102, 105, 157, 318, 320
Elephants 252, 384, 394; Ch. 184-186; India 100; tails fired 167, 186
Elixir of immortality 107, 108 s. Immortality
Embanking rivers 11, 35, 334, 379, 342
Emblems on robes 11, 344, 379
Embroiderers 204, 384
Empan 385
Emperor 151, 336; two great 203
Empire 76, 203, 389
Emporia successive, s. Tsihmoh, Kuei-Ki, Mou, Tungyeh, Hoppu, Kattigara, Zabai
Eratosthenes 367
Erh-fu, s. Ni-fu 329
Erh-sze, s. Ni-sze
Eridu 96
Erythrœan sea traders: 96, 106, 198, 169, 181, 233, 298, 338, 385, 387; changes 81, 156-8, 239, 241, 259, 387, 392; navy 106, 178, 262, 387
Esag-gil 231
Eschatology 348, 380
Estrangement of Ch. st. 138

Etymology Ch. 295
Eunuchs 384
Euphrates 102, 105
Europe 114, 344
Exposing for drought 90, 386
Eyes: blue 87, 377, 318; two on ships 106, 178, 385
Ezekiel's animals 358

Fabulous figures 169
Fahien, Fahian 87, 45, 313, 385
Fairy islands 107, 108, 109, 111, 113, 114, 158, 173, 178, 218, *360, 387
False: gems 268, 271; hieroglyphs 185
Family names 374. s. Sings
Fang-hu 107, 108, 109, 113; Fangtchang 108, 110, 113, *180, 181; Lwan-wei 110
Fang-kiu-Pêng-lai 110
Fan-li 182, 191
Fans 379
Fan-tsiuen 318, 323
Feathers; hill 187; mud 232; shed 267; wild birds 76
Female; abyss 126, 128
Fên-tien 128, 147
Ferghana: conquered 220-1; route 308
Feudal princes 75
Figures local value 379
Fines 379
Finger nail flower 190, 246
Fir-balsam 265, 270, 381, 383
Fire: Avestic sorts 164, 166; central 339; director 161, 162; drill 11, 166, 167; female 160: flint 166, *208b, 210b, 364, 389; friction 11, 13, 168; goddess 160; gyration 11 168; invented 364; isl. 269, 262; of literature 140; mirrors 165, 166, 167, 364; Mt. 215, 272; ploughing 168, 374; processes 168; renewal 160; sawing 168, 374; syringe 168, 364; Vedic 166; worship 90, 94, 386
Fish-hawk's head 106
Fishmen 24, 97, 169, *349, 387
Fish oil 180
Five: fires 164, 166, 386; days 9, 378; dragons 175;

elements 79, 81-3, 174, 214, 362, 378; fairy isl. supr; notes 374; planets 288, 358, 378; regents 361; Tis 361
Flint 166, 168, *208b, 210b, 364, 389
Floods 21, 173, 334, 335, 347
Flower boats 262, 370
Flowery-land 4, 71, pass. 310
Flowing sands 213, 382, pass.
Flutes: single, double 344, 380; three-holed 384
Flying-bridge 58
Fords 329, 331
Foreigners: adviser, 215, 207, 386: aversion 204; Lin-tao 207b, 208b; avoid 239; lore 141; ships 259; useful 204; welcomed 134, 138, 204, 382, 384 388
Fortunate isl s. Fairy isl.
Fossile men 347
Four: cardinal points, s.v.; div. day 339, 378; eyed animal 364, 386; mountains 19, 20, 347, 380; seasons 9, 378
432 years 23
Fowl 380
Fox, nine tails, 75
Fright, Elixir for 231; figure, 72
Friction. s. Fire
Fu, mirror 165, 167
Fuh 132
Fuh-hi 22, 109, 149, 169
Fu-li-garden 246, 391
Fuh-muh 289, 371
Funam - Phnom - Cambodia 188, 240, 247, 261, 354 395; ships 115-6, 260
Funerals, nat. 374
Fung-ho. 235
Fung-hou 324; Fung-hu 324
Fung-kü 319, 324
Fu-pa 394, 222
Furnace, worship, 160, 162 217
Furs, precious 51, 198, 371
Fusang. 353
Fu-tcha 262
Fu-tze 236
Fu-yh 209b
Fu-yu 362

Gablan, Gobharana 213
Gandalarit, Gandhara 56, 60

Garlic: great 230, 391, small 379
Garuda, 169, 179
Gate: of gates 209; of heaven 301; Town 375, 379
Gâthas 157
Genii, isl. 173, s. Fairy isl.
Geometry 183
Ghari 280
Girls: dancing 180; nice 204; sacrifice 90, 359
Glass 268, 271; sent for 261; coloured 182, 216, 247, 392
Glutton figure 71
Gnomon 10, 150, 277, 378, Bab. 279; pierced 78, 277
God: chief 320; darkness 90; drought 329; fate 162; fire 90, 94; hearth 162, 386; local 151; north 173; personal 380; roads 211; and spirits 91; star 300
Gog and Magog 205
Golanagara 57
Gold 85, 88, 204, 252, 328, 331, 379, 394; Ants 271; horse 223; ox 364; statue 208b, 209b, 220; mother 370
Gotra 89, 386
Grass: cloth 374; dogs 137; pampas 267, 271
Graving knife 15
Grease, valuable 180
Great men, sacrificed to 355, 79
Great wall 205, 209
Greco-Bactrians 214, 224: Lycians 82; Romans 244
Grecque scroll 72
Greek: Alchemy, 214, 217, 390; Astronomy 282; Astrology 89-92, 385; civilisation 217; influence 216, 230-1, 390-1; merchantmen 394; state conquered 392, 224; words 220, 224-5; Lesser state 225;
Green-paint 204
Gryphon 169
Gtsub 13
Gudea, 14, 15, 26, 32, 96, 345, 378
Guild-Merchants 156
Gulel 195
Gurra 127
Gynecocracy 374, 32, 351
Gyration, fire by, 168

Hagar 103
Hainan isl. 110, 115, 240, 241; pearls 241;
Hair: animal 188; dress 72, 354, 379; pins 204
Haktai 250, 393
Hami 314
Han: dialect 243, dyn. 60, 62, 92, 108, 206, pass; Huanti 253; Wenti 390; Wuti 53, 112, 113, 203, 207b, 219, 230, 231, 235, 250, pass, Yuanti 225
Han-hai 314
Han state 146, 152
Handswipe, s Shaduf
Hanoi, not Kattigara 61, *242
Hantchung 212, 215, 367
Harpagornis 170
Harpsichord 374
Hatshopsitu 97, 99
Hatti 102
Head: dress 82; tapered 307, 318, 324, 377
Hearth, gods of, 163
Heaven: cult of 20, 139, 377; and earth 79, 126, 128, 165, 378, 384; fire 166; Lord of 172; Son of 377
Heavenly kings 23, *348, 365
Heft-iklim 309
Heh: r. 266-9; tchi 115, 360
Helike 289
Hemodii mts. 251
Hemp 350, 382, 391
Hêng-shan 240-1, 242, 389, 392
Henna 182, 235, 238, 246, 389, 391
Herat 268, 311
Hermæus 221, 223, 225, 393
Hermit caves 196, 197, 386
Hero-worship 79, 355
Hi-Ho, 286
Hia: 69, 150, 223, 381; calendar 3, 47, 48, 381 ;═ Ketchi 307; in Ki 74, 140 ;═Sha 321
Hia: hou ki 151; Ti Mang 94; Ti Sieh 94
Hiafei 261, 284
Hia-fu-tchi 160
Hiaiki rhin. 179, 183
Hia-koh 276, 365
Hiang-liang 345
Hiao Wenti 218
Hien: r. 313; tchi 358-9; tu 222, 226, 311
Hien-yuen 318, 326, 327; chiefs 322

Hieroglyphs 19, 292, 375
High-cheek bones 377
Hills and rivers worsh. 287, 374, 383
Hindus: colonies of 56, 57, 91, 108, 117, Burma 121, 250, 387, Java 259; Szet chuen 52, 54, *196, 363, 387; cosmography 173; cosmogony 173-4; gods figures 169, 170, 173, 365, 388; influence 91, 157, 158, 173, 187, 208b, 389; sea-traders 158; names in Indo-China 158
Hindu Kush 110; Hien-tu shan 311
Hints 292
Hippalus 243, 394
Hippocentaurs 169, 387
Hippostratus 224
Hippuri 251
Hiram 102, 243
Hissarlik 351
Historical: periods 380; works 317
Hittites 4, 15
Hiuen :—Ming 90, 95, 160; pu 266 ;-tchi 266 ;-Tsang 267-313 ;-Wu 358
Hiungnus 50, 60, 61, 190, 249, 254, 392; incursions 218-9; language 190, 223; not a race 223 —
Hiu-tu 211
Hoh kwan-tze 149, 289
Hoh-liü, Ho-lü, 133, 165
Hoh:-she 216; tchi 325 ;-tchung 237
Hô-kiu-ping 208b
Ho-ku 301
Ho-ling 113, 262
Honey, stone, 234
Hooked spear 192
Ho P'eh 90, 94, 268
Ho-pei-tsien 118
Hoppu 241, 246, 389, 390, 392, 393, 394
Horary vase 280-1
Hormuzia trad. 182, 240, 241, 235, 387, 389, 390, 392, 393
Horns 180, 204, 234, 244, 388
Horse 204, 207, 208, 222, 343, 357, 380, 383; harnessing 11, *381; Manes dyed 357, 383-4; blood perspiring 219, 224, 391; Nisaean ibid -riding 176; sacrifice 137, 362
Horse-shoe tomb 119, 191, 386

Ho-tih 114
Ho-tsung 268, v. Ho peh
Hou 150 :-Y 265, 335
Hours, double 9, 339: fixed 378; variable 230, 282
House 162, 374, 379 ;-cricket 163
Hu, bearded barbar. 176, 207, 234, 249, 275, 314, 365, 389
Hwa ;-kwa 114 ;-Miao 125 ;-sü 325 ;-ti niu 242, 392
Hwai-wan-tze 284, pass.; death 368
Hwan: kung 151; tchou 110; yuen 148
Hwang 151; ho 80, 224, 336; Lao 148, 149, 151, 209b; p'u mi 2, 6, 151, 317, 324; shu 266; tche or Hormuzians 181, 182, 189, 282, 235, 240, 246, 366, 389, 393
Hwangti, pass. ; arrival 381; death 333; migration 321; officers 347; in Tchuh 141; unsuccess 329; years 330
Hwei: r. 179; influencing light 389; luh, Hwuy-luh, 90, 95, 160, 162
Huk 236
Hukit 219
Huliang 113, v. Holing, Java
Huma 230, v. Sesamum
Human: figures 133, 137, 138; fire 166; rings 348; sacrifices 132, 134, 138, 359, 362-3
Hu Nak-Khunte 27, 319, 320-1, 372, 377, v. Huangti
Hundred: families, inexact, 24, 209, 306; standard 339, 379
Hung: li 319; In 266, 269; shui 325
Huns 215
Hunts, royal, 184, 268
Huo, or Hwo: Kuan 166, *208b; lin :—Huliang═Holing═Java 181; shan 215; tchou 269, 276; tsi 268
Hupeh 231
Husbandman 380, 379
Hu-shen 208
Hu-sheng 284
Hu: suan 229; sui 227; tcheng 192; tou 227; tze 149, 364
Hwun, Hwan 348

Hydraulic works 342-3
Hydropyrum latifolium 217, v. Soma
Hypobarus 232

Iaon, yuan, 221
Ideographical reform 86
Identities 292
Id-lal 120
I-hi-wei 123, 125
Ikshvākus 236
Ilu 266
Image, wooden, 333, 362
Imagery 89, 91, 114, 169, 385
Imbrication 357
Immanence of uncivilised 373
Immortals 109, 114
Immortality, drug of, 107, 108, 197, 206, 214, 217, 233, 270, 387; shrub of, 114, 237
Imperial government 19, 380
Importations of the Baks 141, 377, 378-380; by Shuh 191, 198; General 381-96
Increase of writing 87, 375, 184, 185
India and: Arabia 97: Ass.-Bab. 97, 101; Indo-China and Ch. 67; Judæa 99; Shuh-Szetchuen 64, 65, *196, 197, 369, 386, 392; Ts'u 117, 118, 170, 386
Indian: Archip. 114; Coinage 119; Cosmogony 387; Influence 104; literature 174; monkeys 38, 78, 97, 100; ocean trade 89, 91, 107, 108, 158, 166; paper 251, 393; plants 247, 391; rhinoceros 179, 183; ships 247, 248, 260; shot 247, 391; synchron. 367; trade 51, 66, 107; east coast, 56, 78, 102, 103, 108, 109, v Orissa; Tuyü 387, v. Anachorets, Buddhists
Indo-China, route 158
Indo-Erythræan influence 387; Persian 386, traders 233, 234, 240, 258
Indonesia 111
Indigo 87, 374
Inlaying metal 86, 384
Inscription of Yü 192; inscriptions 380
Intercalary month 9, 11, 79, 288, 378

Intercourse, west 131, 391
Invention for Adoption 279
Irano-Indian influence 73
Irawady, colonies 56, 387
Iran 85, 201, 252, 371, 379, 382, 394; south-north 283; ware 198
Irrigation 11, 379
Ish-ban 324
Iskandar 205, 208
Isolation of Ch. 29, 308, 310 314
Issedons 355
Ivory 99, 184, 204, 245, 388

Jade 41, 204, 31, 34, 40; chisel 34; cup 390; microscope on 351, *312; mines 309, 312-3, 325, in Burma *353, Nan-shan 325, 326, Turkestan 389, pass.; objects in Ass. Bab. 32, 34, 309, 312, Hissarlik 351, India, 42; polytropic *351; rings 264, 265; taste for 377; traffic 30, 46, 207, 382-3-4, 390, routes 309, 385; white and dark 313, 318, 325, 384
Jadeite 33, 39, 40, 41; Burma 388; pik 41; Yunnan 41; white 351
Jaggery 366
Jahve 122
Jail 357
Jangars 260
Japan, ancient 138; colonized 210, 367; no navy 119
Jasmine, Jessamine 182, 234, 389
Jasper 33
Java 37, 45, 108, 113, 181, 189, 247, 259, 261, 280, 398; J-Bali 360
Jch-kwei 277
Jch-nan, jihnan 68
Jehoshaphat 243
Jen, tribes 61, 66
Jen-Hiao 287, 370
Jen-Kia-Man 66
Jeti-Karakchi 289
Jewel of Tch'en 135
Jews 166, 168, 253, 256, 257, 370, 394
Joan of Arc, Tungkinese 261
Joh shui 327, 330
Joshua's feat 218
Jugglers 391, 394
Juh r. 266-7

Jujube 47, 198, 374
Julian year 339
Jungs 30, 31, 75, 76, 91; Tartar 207; Teks 80, 284
Junk 26); largest 26
Junk-Ceylon 256
Jupiter cycle 78, 93
Ju-tou-kou 370
Jyotisha 282

Ka, Bai, Khu, 318
Kabulistan 221, 393, 311
Kachab 300
Kachins 168
Kai-lo-shen 215
Kai-mings 52, *196, 199, 346
Kai-t'ien 179, 308; yang 156
Kalang 189
Kalas 280
Kalingas 113, 114, 181, 247; java 113, 393; navy 257
Kalmucks-Torguths 311
Kam-mu 273, 274, 325, 370
Kan: ten 340; kung 287, 298 lan, ran 246, 255; to-li, tu-lu 366; tsiang 105; tsiao 246; yng 223, 394; yü 246
Kandar pass. 309, 312
Kang, c. 328; mt. 134; kiu 219, 222, 309, 393, tai 261
Kanishka 367
Kansuh S.W. to S. Shansi 328
Kao, 118, 120; duk 68; hou 187 kiu 223; Pen jung 315, she 207b; Sin Ti Kuh 76, 140, 141, 143, 161, 162, 334, 336, 381; Tsu of Han 161, 235, 389; YangTchuan hiüh s.v. 76, 141, 143,
Kap, Gafi, Kafu 99.
Kapilanagara 59; Kapila-vastu 56
Kapisa 368
Karashar 212, 265, 267-8, 272, 298, 325, 335, 381, 382-3-4-8, 393, 395
Karens, Karengs 59, 371, 254
Karkemish 36, 105
Kasan 216.
Kashgar 308, 384, 395
Kashtu 321, 324
Kasiap Matang 213
Kassi 321; Kassite 323
Kassia, v. Caasia
Kattigara 68, *240-2, 244, 247, 261, 390, 392-395
Kauthala, Oudh 59
K'eh 280
Kentu, India 50, 53, 122

Ke-p'in 311, 221, 393, 280
Kerwankush 289
Kesho 67. 68, *242
Khaidin Kua 267
Khaidu gol 267
Khamil 314
Khammurabi 101, 320, 341, 345
Khas 331
Khest wood 99
Khorasan 383, x
Khornsmians 12, 30, 31, 38, 73, 77, 78, 350, 357, 384
Khorsabad 105
Khotan 74, 75, 77, 195, 312, 361
Khrysê 51
Khshathra-Vairya 74
Ki.-ten 23, *348, 387; hundred 78
K'i 348
Kia, Sing 307
Kiah of Yn 339
Kiaï 92
Kia-lang-y 314
Kiang r. 199; liang 173; Taikung 171-2; Ts'en 67
Kiangs tr. 61, 66, 73, 219, 249
Kiao mt. 333; tchi 67, 261, 370
Kiao-tchou, gulf, 89, 103, 157, 158, 178, 240, 385
Kiao-tung 215, 218
Kieh, spear 192; Kao 119; Kuei 275, 382; shih 149, 174, 207b
Kien, drum 208; tchang 113; tchang 52; wei 60, 62, 254
Ki-fu 58; Ku luh 317; lian 370; lien 190; lik of Tchou 80, *355; lü 266
Kiln-huts 278
Kimbun-Lusar 311
Kin Tartars 138; Mu 370; lin 255; sui 166; pei 326
King st. 190; lu 211; ti of Han 182, 214; tsing 230, 231; of Ts'i 262; tcheng 328
Kings, mythical, 22, 377, 380
Kingfishers 204, 208, 234, 252, 394
Kirghizes 30, 304, 355, 77. v. Ki-lik
Ki-she, penality 209; shit 256
Kitan 382
Kitchen god 160, 161, 162, 163, 287

Kitchung 350, 382
Kit-hu 281
Ki-tze 17, 192, 195, 360
Ki-wei 160, 161
Kiü, st. 89, 196; extol 363; shu 195; sou or su, Wakhan 321, 370, 371, 381, 382, 386; Sze-Kao-tchang 215, 308
Kiu: and Li 332, 334, 337, 376; lung 67; to 345: tse-Kutcha 86: yuen 252
Kiuch Kung 366
Kiuen-jungs err. for Kuen-jungs
Kiüh-ti 204, 208
Kiuh-lao 270
Kiuns 36
K'iun-yüh 266,-9
Kiung 198, 254; sang 333; Tsoh 60; yuk 48
Kiüt 195
Kun-wu, Kungu, 86, 286, 310, 382
Ki-yng 277
Knotted cords 374
Ko-hung 299
Kök-bozat 289
Kokhab 299
Kokonor 86, err. Kukunor
Kolandiophanta 260
Kom - the - long - robed 318, 323, 327, 379
Ko-ngai 167
Kophen 221, 230, 311, 393
Ko-tou, Koh-tou 15, 16, 20, 192
Ko-tchung 234, 237, 252
Kotymbæ 260
Kou: chen 300; K'i 270; tche daria 269; tsien 262, 178
Krakatao 113
Kü, shui 353
Ku, tr. 326; wu 328
K'u 266; K'i 270 Kwa 270; shan 266-9
Kua or Kwa, lu 314; tchou 216, 388
Kuan or Kwan 161; Fêng 357; hiung 328; shu 214; y wu 89; tze 33, 37, 45, *352, pass.
Kuang or Kwang; si 110; tchen tze 327; tchu 41, 256; yuen 267
Kuarism, Kwarism, v. Khorasmians
Kudang 38
Kudremale 255
Kudur Nakhunte 6, 24, 26, 320, 321, 375

Kuei or Kwei 216, 277, 348, 375; Ki 115, 178, 182, 183, 230, 234, 263, 387, 388, 389; Kuh tze 284; lin 55, 58, 193, 236; shan 220, 224; shin 242; tsang 147, 151, 175; yang 370; yu kiü 323
Kuen-jungs 35, 89, 187; removed 356, 357
Kuen-lun, Kün-lun 4, 32, 173, 246, 252, 256, 327, 371
Kufas 114, v. Coracles
Kukunor 86, 187, 313
Kumongs 66
Ku Nak Khunte, v. Hu Nak Khunte
Kün-kuei 192
Kun-mi, Kun-mo, Kun-mings 61, 62, 66, 115, 223, 249; fair haired 250, 252, 273, 275, 394
Kung: kia 319, 382; ku 114; kung 161; Ngan kwoh 140; shan 326; sun 318; Szeyu 179; tchang fu= shan 326, 328, 330, 367; tia pin 369; tsiok 237, v. peacock, tung 327; wu 262
Kurla 325
Kurma avatâra, 107, 109
Kushites 80, 96, 98, 102
Kustana 355, v. Khotan
Kutcha, Kutze 222, 216, 267, 365, 384, 388
Kutche 324
Kut-lu 89
Kutthi 26
Kuvera, 74, 174
Ku-wen 15, 17, 27, 345, 346; spell. 185, 186, 199, 226, 300, 303, 354, 355
Kü-yao 275
Kwun 170

Lack of criticism 317
Lacquer 374; lacquered tablets 345
Ladies boats 262, 370
Lagash 307
Lamps, abestos 180, 388
Lan: tai 213; tchou 367; tsang kiang 252
Lang-ya, lang-ga 36, 89, 90, 93, 107, 134, 137, 147, 148, 152, 155, 156, 158, 160, 166, 240, 385; Tai 352
Lanka 86, 103, 106, 107; to Lang-ga 36, 352; Barusæ 112

Lao-shan 109; shih shing, shing shing 275, 382
Lao-tze 91, 95, 125, 139; journey 122, 211, at Khotan 361; no love 126, 127; origin 120-2, 124, 192, 197
Lapislazuli,187, 309, 312, 318
Law, in Egypt, Chald., Chin., 347
Lead, 252, 379, 394
League, Su-Ts'in, 177
Leather drums 329, 380
Lei-tsu 325, 331
Lendjabalous 36, 369, v. Nicobar
Lenses, burning 391, 216
Leopard skins 99
Li 121, 123, 124, 335, 337; tr. 334; coracles 215; of Kiang 196; v. Kiu and Li
Li: fang 208b, 209b, 368; Kwang-li 220; Laotan 120; min 305, 335, three meanings 347; ni 55; pei 252; shu 204; sze 149, 204, 207; tchao Kiun 214; tchi 246
Liang 198; Hwei of 170; hi 187; north 271
Library: state 125, 127, 210, 317, 345
Lieh-tze, Lieh-yu kou 91, 107, 126, 149, 152, 168, 170, 173, 180, 189, 364, pass. v. Hu-tze
Life of 120 years 11, 24, 380
Light of Asia 210
Likien 58, 222, 224
Limurykè 51
Lin: erh 211; hu 176; tao 207b, 210b, 213, 214, 215, 330, 389
Ling: drum 208; ling 370; lun 330; shan 269; wang 287
Lions 222, 237, 394
Lists of civilisation 9-27; corrected 376
Literary mosaic 55
Liu: 301; Kiu-tze 246; li 256; po shan 332; sha 310; shang 115; shu 317; tcheng 222; yng of Ts'u 209b
Lo 115
Loadstone 45, v. compass
Lob and Kank 310
Localisations, late 329
Lofty terraces 11, 343, 379, v. Tai

Loh, r. 320, 328, 330; shu 328; tchi 266; yang 125, 78, 150
Lolo writing 45, 198, 201
Lombok 110, 113
Long: armed 269; dresses 318, 323, 327, 379; eared 121, 124, 361, 386; legs 328, 331
Lopnor 224, 267, 313
Lou 300; iron 85; fan 172; lan 219, 254; tchuen 260-2
Love, no in Lao-tze 125, 127
Lo-yueh 236
Lü; shan 253; shen 345
Lu 90, 94, 146, 156, 160; 'an sheng 231; sheng 207b
Luan-ta 207b, 214; wei 110
Lucern 219, 220, 229, 391
Lucky, 10, 379
Lufen 58
Luhkia 233-4
Luk, jadeite 41
Lumbini 211
Lun-tai 225
Lunar mansions 28, 30, 78, 81, 340, 350, 356, 378, 383
Lung: hien 359; kia 305; pak 107, 109, 111; tsiuen 207; yen 246
Lycium 270
Lydian coins 118, 191, 193, 217
Madratæ 260
Maes Titianus 222, 240, 243, 395
Magadha, Muktu 174, 176, 365
Magi 82; Magical tricks 174, 175
Magnet 283, 284, 383
Magnetic iron 45, 269
Magnifying glasses 176, 182, 268, 365, 388
Magnolia 242, 244, 392
Mahacina 247, 395
Maiden drowned v. girl's sacrifice
Magpies, "Celestial" 301; cf. 289, 371
Mailcoats 319, 366
Makiun 45, 284
Malabar coast 99, 260
Malabathrum 66
Malacca: peninsula 37, 291; straits 111, 113, 255, 259, 261; avoided 181, 387
Malei 56
Mallai 234
Malûth 278, 279
Man tr. 196

Mana, Mina 10, 36, 101, 104, 378, 385
Manacles 379
Manazils 78; v. lunar mansions
Mandshu Tartars 136
Manes dyed 357, 383-4
Mang tr. 61
Mango 238
Ma-ngu isl. 253, 256, 262, v. Moluccos
Man-tze caves 197
Mao, Pleïades 300-1, 340; yü 200
Marcius Philippus 278
Marco-Polo 169
Marduk 22
Margarita 189
Mariba 102
Marinus Tyrius 222, 242, 395
Marionnettes 384
Marine terms 105
Market of the valley 213
Marriage laws 374; Muh Wang's daughter 35, 268, 271, 352
Marvels, taste for 208b
Mass of gems 266, 267, 272
Mastiffs, Tibet 47, 48, 49, 197, 384
Masula boats 260
Mats 379
Mathematics 179, 189, 387
Matsya-Avatara 109
Maurya script 198
Me, bleating 190
Meandre 72
Measures, standard 89, 378, 385
Medicine books 152, 206
Media 82, 90, 93; trade 159, 380, 385
Mediterranean 390, v. red corals
Megas 220
Meh-ti, Mih-tze 149,152,180
Mōngs, Muongs 186
Mèngtien 205
Mèngtze, Mencius 6, 149
Merchants' hill 382
Mercury 386, 388; and Mica 218, v. Cinnabar
Merkhet 281
Merv, amber of 231
Meshed, tin of 26, 309, 311
Meslem 90
Metallic cauries 118
Metallurgy 11, 85-6, 165, 167, 379, 382, 386
Meton 10
Miao-tze 125

ALPHABETICAL INDEX.

Microscope on jade 312, 351
Middle Kingdom 20, 22, 315, 319, 380
Midian coast 96
Midnight: day 73
Mien, r. 196
Migrations 310-1, 321
Mih-hiang 246
Milfoil 92
Military Art 164, 166
Milky-way 289, 299
Millet, Ital 374, Comm. 379
Min, r. 40, 179, 196, 199; caves 197, 208b, 386; shan 184; tchou 215, 330; yueh 115, 179, 209b, 233, 234, 260, 380, 300
Minæans 100
Mincopies 113
Ming—ho-tchi 261, 285; ki 134, 136; ti of Han 209b, of Wei 284; yueh,-guet 180, 189, 204, 246, 255
Ministeries, six ideal 151; ten, 319, 347
Minnagara 100
Mint, state 217, 391
Mintpalm 250, 389
Minutiæ, historical 251
Mirdjai, Miritan, Mit, mt. 31, 325-6
Mirrors, 251, 268, 392; concave 165; metallic 213, 216, 390; sun 167; moon 168
Missions foreign 38-44, 51, pass.
Missions to Central Asia 50, 62, 200, *219, *253, 219-222, 230, 390-1; to India 61, 249, 391
Missouri Kurds 97
Mi-sung 250, 389
Mock objects, 134, 136, 137, 385; Suns 218, 379
Mogan 290
Mogaung 40, 42
Moh-ya 165, 207
Mois 381
Mo-li 234
Moluccas 253, 256, 259, 366, 395
Momien 39, 41
Momordica charantia 269
Monetary Unions 385, 89, 155
Money, metallic 36, v. coins, ring-money
Mongol sacrifice, 80
Monkeys 38, 78, 97, 99, 100, 182, 384
Monosyllabism 293-4

Monotheism 346, 348
Monsoons 214, 394
Months names 9; Akka, Bab. 94, 385; Sem. Bab. 9, 93, 358, 385
Moon female 168, 378
Moral laws, foreign, 381
Mortar 379
Mortgage, antichretic 317
Mosaic, literary 55
Mother of Pearl 98, 365, 387
Mother, status 380; Universe 126, 128; writing 14, 305, 380
Mou 179, 183, 388; y 195; yuen 266, 273
Mountains, opened 319: reverer 323
Muh Kung of Ts'in 207, 215, 386
Muh-Kua 93, v. Quince, Papaya
Muh T'ien tze tchuen 189, 265, 313, *360
Muhuratas 280
Muh Wang 32, 77, 80, 119, 131, 173,* 175, 265-71, 310, 313-4, 384
Mu-Koh, 262; Ian 242, 392; nao 344, 387; pang 67
Mal 300
Mulcts 379
Music, Duodenary scale 10, 330, 340; seven 394; on stones 374
Muslin pearled 257
Mutsri 97
Muziris 99, 394
Mythical chronology 387, 23; Kings 22, 29, 323
Myths 89, 91, 141, 168, 170, 188, pass.
Mythography 163

Nabonidus 320; Nabonassar 87
Nacreous mussels 180, 188
Naga race 35
Nagar 59
Nagit 102
Nai Hwangti 26, 269 v Hwang-ti
Naked men 38
Nakhunte 4, 26, 320, 378
Nakshatras 355 v. Lunar Mansions
Nala 40
Nam-Elam 26
Names, personal 74, 79, 380
Nana 320
Nancowry isl. v. Nicobar

Nan-hai 235, 236, 369; ho 301; shan 308, 313; tou 299
Nan-yueh, Empire. 58, 62, 186, 209b, 233, 234, 235, 240, 249, 250, 260, 389, 390, 391
Nar 37, 229
Naramsin 372
Narcotic 250, 365, 387, 389
Nard 235, 391
Narru Marratu 102
Nasks 206, 365
Native tr. 75; civilisation, 373-5
Navel of Heaven 172
Navigation 91, 92, 261, 181, 113
Navy, Ch., 112, 260, 262, 390; foreign 103, 113, 115, 178, 181, 259-263
Nayee 282
Nearchos 108, 157, 158, 189, 190
Nebuchadnezzar 98
Negrito-Pygmies 111, 244
Negroes 80
Neko II. 106
Nèlè, Nèrè, Nili, 39, 40, 255, 353, 384
Nelkynda 394
Nèma serikon 51, 53
Neo-Monosyllabism 293, 342
Neo-Taoism 145, 147, 151, 176, 206, pars.
Nephelium longam 246
Nephrite Jade, 73, 77, 213, 351
Nest dwellers 375
Ngai-lao, v. Ai-lao
Ngai-Nap 250, 389
Ngan-Ki Sheng 207b, 218
Ngao mastifis, 197; shin 162
Ngou-lo 233, 236, 369; ye 165
Nhitnam. Jehnan, 240, 241, 392, pass.
Nicobar isl. 36, 108, 110-115, 233, 369
Ni-fu Erh-fu, 329
Nimrod 98
19-year period 10, 288, 332, *338, *311, 379, 385
Nineveh 102
Ning 5, v. 333
Ninus 38
Nippur 297
Ni-sze, Erh-sze, 220
Nisœan horses 219, 224, 391, 392; general 220
Niu 301

ALPHABETICAL INDEX. 409

Nomes 36
Nomi-no-Sukune 137
Non-Chinese st. 209b; Confucianists 142; first printing 345
Noon, day, 78
Noras 39, 42
North-god 173; influence 176; Pole 299; Route 249
Nose, beginning, 306, 380
Notched sticks 374
Novelties, liked, 180
Nu, crossbow, 195
Numerical properties 10, 82, 83, 379; names 304
Nü-kwa 169, 175, 349, 365
Nü Tsi 351; Tsih 351; or Niü-tsieh 331
Nutmeg 181, 253, 366, 370

O 114
Oannès 97
Observations, gnomon 78
Official intercourse 227
Oh-pak 94
Old: and new ideas 147-8; texts 17; traditions 147;
Oman 190; amber 223; ships 247, 393, 395
Omoplatoscopy 377
Oneiromancy 379
Onesicritos 108, 158, 190
On-Khilien 149
Onomancy 92
Opening with W. 223
Ophir 39, 97, 99, 100
Orange 247, 374
Ordo 212
Ores, special 88, 382
Organ, Reed 380
Orientation 162, 277; of buildings 342, 379
Origin, W. 292; to Jade Mines 317
Orissa 56, 117, 251; to Burma 387
Orkham 322
Orpiment 214, 217, 390
Ostanes 214
Ostrich eggs, painted, 99, 225, 369, 391, 394
Ownership 347, 380
Ox: driving 380; waggons 333, 379
Oxus, 110, 371; Aksu 371
O-yk-shan-li 268
Oyster pearls 252, 394

Pa region, treaty 54; tchung 52

Pack-animals 312, 343
Pacorus 222, 230, 394
Pagan, old 56; new 59
Pah shen 171, 172; sien 172
Painting 208, 367
Paktyeia 157
Palmistry 92
Pamir, routes 308, 312, 321
Pan, bow 195; Keng 170; Ku 317; tchao 221, 222, 394; tu 222, 393; tchu 256
Papaya 93
Paper, Indian 250; rags 251; silk-refuse 251; cotton 393; implements 136
Parhelion 218, 339
Parrots 252
Parsindu 104
Parsley 229, 391
Past, living 347
Parthians 214, 222, 214, 391, 394
Paste-gems 268, 384
Pastors 20, 380
Pat 329, 350
Patamar boats 260
Patna, route 50, 51, 197. 62
Patriotic histories 317
Peach 47, 198, 368, 374
Peacocks 90, 234, 237, 252, 366, 370, 384, 388, 389, 394
Pear 368
Pearls trade 180-182, 189; Ceylon 189, 237, 252, 255-6, 324; Hainan 189, 240, 390; Persian Gulf 180, 189, 234, 255, 365, 387, 389, 392; Muslin 256; pierced 241; spherical 247, 392
Pegu 91, 102, 106, 113, 117; Shensi to 55, 64; yoma 56
Peh, or Poh 348; ho 301; hu 358; Ku 55; lu 55, 255, 354; ma 209b; shan 216, 272, 308; yh 355; yng 114; yüh 269; yung 52, *196
P'ei 125
Pellet bow 194, 195
Pencil 204
Pendant pearls 204
P'êng 168
Pêng-lai 38, 107, 108, 109, 110, 111; v. Tang-kiu, yun-shuh; zi-la-vie 59
Penongs 331
Perak 255
Periods 69, 70; disorder 145; numerical 10, 378

Persia 35, 38; and India 158; v. Indo-Persian; and Muhwang 35, 268, 271, 352
Persian 230; five elements 81-2; gulf 96, 101, 157-8, 394; seal 207; legends 330, 350; words, pass.
Personal names, v. Names
Pheasants 384
Phylacteria 169, 170, 171, 387
Philippines isl. 111
Phœnician navy 96, 102, 106, 109, 157, 243, 360
Phœnixes 328, 339, 353
Piao 277; p'iao 41
Pictorial characters 86, 185, 292
Pidjan 267
Pien-ho 204; piao 317; tsiao 218
Pierced breasts 328, 331; gnomon 78, 277
Pih 234; Pihwuy 79
Pih, Pik, Jadeite 41, 353
Pihâtu 354
Piled houses 374
Pilgrims 367
Pima temple 361
Pine's fingers 270; fat 270
Pinlang 246, 252
P'ipa 222, 393
Pippilika 271
Pisciculture 182
Pisé: building 377
Pi-Ts'ao, 162, 287
Pi-yh 196
Planets: colours and names 10, 288,* 338, 358
Pleiades 10, 78, 289, 300-2, 340.
Plough, W. Asiatic 379
Plowing, fire 168, 374
Plumb-line 379
Po r. 308; P'o tr. 61; dji 235
Poh 334; yao 268
Points of space, v. Cardinal points; colours 10, 135, 208b, 379
Poisoned: four emperors 214, 217
Polarity 283, 383
Pole, curved 379; star 10, 289, 292, 299
Poli 108, 110
Pomegranate 227, 231
P'ong tribe 46, 48, 331, *353, 354
Pool of Heaven 168
Pooped junks 260

Population removed 210b, 263, 356, pass.
Potters 334, 375; wheel 343, 379
Pot-wells 343
Pottery 374, 382
Prahus 260
Pre-Chinese 168, 209b, 291; astronomy 286, 289, 295, 371; civilisation 371-3
Prime Minister 319, 347, 380
Princess Imperial 105—51 B.C., 222
Printing, first 345
Prison 382, 357
Profit on trade 244
Prognostication 78, 92
Prome, earthquake 261
Pseudo-Runic 338
Ptarmica Sibirica 383
Ptolemies 243
Pu : coins 156; lai 95; lo-ki 223; shao 207, 220, 224; tchang hai 224
Pucka: wells 343
Puh 334; Hai 107, 109, 207b; Szemin 114, 233; Tchou Shan 234, 349. 377, v. Badak-han ; T'ing-hu-yu 114
Punt 99
Puppets in graves 132
Py 301
Pygmies 115
Pyramid, stone 331
Pyrites 156,* 208b, 210b, 364, 389
Pyrolatry 90, 157, 159, 160, 386

Quadrants, Animals, 358, 298
Queendoms 35, 273, 351
Quelpaert 110, 115, 210
Quinces 91, 93, 159, 180, 182, 385
Quisqualis Indica 247, 391

Rachias 251, 394
Radishes 374
Rafts 344, 379
Ragha 82
Rain of stones 353
Rama bridge 58
Ramesses 111. 106
Ramuth 236
Rarities 179, 182, 204, 246
Rastaban 299
Rats, gnawing, 271 ; s. yellow R., sand R.

Ratus 365
Recluses, *Sien*, 196, 208b, 210b
Reconstruction 316
Red berries 270; Bird 358 ; corals 235, 243, 390, 392 ; green 208 ; hair 49, 250, 251 ; manes 357, 388-4 ; River 64, 266, 268, 325; sandal 252; water 327
Red Sea trad. 96, 102, 106, 157, 235, 249, 390, 394
Redeemed punishments 379
Reform of writing 86
Regents of Space 131, 135
Regularity avoided 339, 379
Rekem, Ailana, 243, 245, 390
Relatives destroyed 132
Religion Ch. 135, 362
Rent in heavens 175, 349
Repetition of events 10, 379
Reskem Daria 313
Res-mehit-ba 283
Revolving sky 341
Rhinoceros 246, 252, 394 ; ear-haired, India, 182; Assyria 182; in Ch. 183-4 ; hides 184 ; symbol 184; s. horns
Rice 374
Richis, *Sien*, 197, 387, 107, 109
Rig Veda 173, 174
Right hand side 20, 380
Rimaku 22
Ring money 35, 78, *119, 352, 383
Rings Jade 32, 379, 381
River : boating 115 ; god 90; sacrifice 90, 381, 386
Roads, god, 215
Rock crystal, s. Crystal
Rofia palm 170
Roman Empire: name 242, 244; trad. in Ch. 244, 395; Ceylon 251 ; Sères in 393
Roof : tiling 382; importance 379
Rope : foreign 192, 388 ; asbestos 187
Routes, Trade : difficult 65, 308 ; long-lived 53 ; southwest 249-253 ; Jade traffic 309 ; by : Badakshan 225, 308 ; Burma to Szetchuen 64 ; Ceylon to Ch. 251 ; Ferghana 308 ; Hantchung to Lan-tchou 367; Herat to Ch. 268, 311 ; India, Indo-China 67 ; India to Szetchuen,

64, 65 : Kashgar 308 : Khotan 50 ; Kiang 61, 66, 219, 249; Kungtchang to Szetchuen 330 ; Ling ling 370 ; Lin tao 213, 214, 215, 219 ; Min-tchou, Sung-pan-ting 215 ; Nan Shan 308 : Ningyuen 40 ; North 249 ; Pamir 308, 312, 321 : Patna 50, 51, 197 : Peh-shan 249, 308 ; Shan Burma 253 ; Shensi-Pegu 55, 64 : Shuh 60, 61 ; Sining to Min-tchou 215 : Sung-pan-ting 218, 384 ; Tatsien lu 50 ; Ta-yao 40, 255 : Tai-yuen 331 ; Tchengtu 40 ; Tung-King to Szetchuen 64, 65 : Tsih-shih 66 ; Ts'in-Shuh 199 ; Tsung-ling 308 ; Yarkund 308 ; Yemtsai 309; Yung-tchang 56
Routinism 139
Royal boat 361
Royalty weak 69, 70
Rubies 309, 318, 365
Rude mercantile writing 199
Rukh 169

Saba, Sheba, Queen of 35, 264
Sabæans 240; colonies 97, 99, 102, 103
Sabæo-Phœnicians 157
Sabbath 12, 378
Saccœ, Sak 100, 359
Sacrifice first, 320, 328, v. Girls, Human, Horses
Sada 251
Saddles 386
Sadin, not Sindu 104
Safar, Zabai 92
Safflower 220, 229, 391
Sailors' yarns 107, 114, 168, 170
Sakwala Cosmogony 174
Salamander 188
Salar, Turks, 311
Salmanazzar 182
Salomon 39, 99, 102, 234, 243
Salt 318
Saltpetre 369, 392
Sambac 182, 234, 389
San-fûn 128, 140, 113 ; shep'an 347: shou 75
Sand rats 270-1
Sandalwood 99, 252
Sandals 379
Sanf 240, 242

Sangani 297
Sangara; 260
Sangir 262
Sapta-sindu 97
Sapy straits 181, v. 366
Sargon-Shennung 26, 318, 320, 372, 380
Sari 23
Saribas-Dayaks 168
Sankara 234
Sarmatia 216
Sassanides 82
Saurashtra Mandala 247, 395
Savul 168
Sawing fire 168
Scientific expedition 261-2
Screens 343
Sculls, double 385
Scythian bow 194
Se or Sze, tr 61, 359 ; Ming 162 ; Tche 325 ; yep or yip 213 ; yoh 347, v. Four Mountains
Sea, arrival 69, *354, 329 ; going vessels 102, 105, 259, 260, 390 ; hunters of Tats'in 245 ; oxen 329 ; traders, 37, 96, 107 ; change 91, 156-8, 239-41, 366, 387-92
Seal, character 88, v. Tchuen ; seals personal 11, 343, 379 ; ribbons 221, 393
Seasons, four, 9. 378
Seed-pearls 180
Sekiz-jolduz 289
Self-growth 292, intr.
Semi-animals 387
Semi-ideographic 15, 87, 380
Semitic works 10, 90, 317, v. months
Sennacherib, fleet 101, 102, 105, 359, 385
Sera, Serica, Seres, 51, 222, 224, 226, 227, 251 ; yellow, east, 226-7, 393; red haired. v. Kunmi ; at Samos 369, 393 ; and Sinæ 255
Sesamum 180, 182, 229, 231, 386, 391
Sesatai 166
Sesostris 76, 183
Setaria 374-5
Seven days 9, 12, 38, 378 ; directors, 374 ; kings 146 ; month 7th day 302 ; musical notes 394
76 year cycle 368, 391
Sexagenary cycle 10, 78, 378
Sha-Hia 321 ; Kiu 221, 308
Shaduff 118, 119-20, 191, 386
Shah Rukh 313

Shalmanazar II. 97
Shamanism 147, 374
Shamans, Sramans 210, 207b, 208, 209b
Shan, not Tan, st. 59, 252-3, 395 ; jugglers 59 ; Burmese rante 253
Shan-hai King 19, 189, 192, 346 ; Hu 235 ; Kiang 246 ; Kin Kiun 332
Shang dyn., Shang-yn 5, 30, 69, 140, 143, 150, 170, 183, 190, 382 ; Ritual 149, 208 ; in Sung 74, 140, 143
Shang-kiu 382 ; Kiun 205 ; Lin Park 230, 390 ; Tai Mon s.v. ; Wu-ting s.v.
Shang-ti 20, 21, 139, 380
Shantung : foreign traders 36, 78, 89, 91, 96, 103, 107, 156-7-8, 168, 170, 173, 365, 383-6-7
Shao-Hao 46, 95, 141, 143, 316, 328, 331-6, 347,* 353, 360, 381
Shao-hien 329, 331, ong. 214
Sheb 281
Shebat 94, 358
Sheep 380
Sheh-ti-K'oh 93
She Huang-ti 132-3, 152, 172, 203, 205, 207b, 208b, 236, 389 ; Neo Taoist 149, 204, 206
She Ki, pass., deficient 317
Shell-cups 252
She-lo, Sila 174, 175, 207b, 365, 388 ; Yh 287
Shen 318 ; Shen 308; Tsè 214 ; Tsing 237 ; Tu 174 ; Yu 254
Shensi-Pegu route 55, 64
Sheng-tu 114
Shennaar-Singar 27
Shennung-Sargon, v. Sargon
Shennung-hwang-tchih 319
Sheshonk 194
Shi 383
Shifting of capital, s.v. ; cardinal points, s.v. ; emporia, v. changes
Shih-hu 261, 284 ; Liu Hwang 215 ; Shen 287, 298 ; Tan 368, 369
Shin-Tsung 377 ; Tuh 60, 61 ; Yoh 197
Shindu cloth 119
Shining at night 179
Ships : battle 115 ; red, 180 ; Funam 115, 116 ; Indian 260, v. Sea-going vessels, Navy

Shiraz 189
Shoes 379, v. boots
Shooting stars : myths 302, 371, cf. 289
Shora 369
Shou of Shang 184 ; Mi 38, 41, 97, 117, 255, 352, 384 ; Shan 333 ; Sin 367
Shouldered Celts 374
Shu 95 ; Drum 208 ; Ban 299 ; Sha 275 ; Shan 318 ; Shuk 329
Shu King 5, 139, 140, 363, pass.
Shuh history 51, 52, 120,* 196, 237, 387 ; conquered 54, 354; articles 50, 65, 219 ; traders 46, 48, 50, 55, 61, 77, 117,* 197, 198, 207, v. Routes
Shuh-Han. dyn 67 ; Yao 276 ; Ki 333-6
Shwe-Dagon 56
Shui Kia 45 ; King 346
Shun of Yü, a native 5, 141, 143, 144, 195, 265, 287, 335 ; in Tchen 141
Shun-ho, Shou, Wi, 358 ; Wei 223 ; Yü Kwan 149
Shwoh-wen 208, pass.
Si : rhin. 184 ; Fan 299 ; Hu 269 ; Kiun 293 ; Shi 262 ; Wang Mu, s.v.
Si Yü 229 ; gov. gen. 221-2, 225, 393-5
Siang 185 ; Ki 366 ; Kiun 186, 236, 370 ; Wang of Ts'u 179
Siao-Shih 369 ; Tchuen 88, 205 ; Yuan 225
Siberia, Ass. Bab. 14 ; inscriptions 338
Sidonians 102
Sieh 5, 30
Sien 173, 196 ; jen tchang 270 ; Pi 176 ; Shing 107 ; tch'uei 161
Sih-Schi 371
Sila, v. She-lo
Silence, western 314
Silk : cloth 200, 204, 374 ; districts 367 ; stuff 200 ; trade 244 ; worms 196, 200
Silky amianthus 187
Silver 85, 87, 204, 252, 318, 379, 384 ; mines 199, 255
Simen Pao 90, 94
Simple char. 198
Simurgh 169
Sin-Yuen-Ping 218
Sindhn, not Sindu, 101 : cloth 104, 200-1

Sing, name, 24, 303, 306 ; Kia 307 ; Ki 92 ; Su hai 223
Singhalese traders with Ch. 251
Sinim, not Chinese, 68
Sining 215, v. Routes
Sirius 298, 340
Sirpurra 307-8
Sistrum 344, 387
Siu-fuh 115, 210, 221, 367 ; Hi 95
Siuen of Tchou 184 ; of Ts'í 174
Siuh 93, v. lunar Mansions
Siün, sacrifice, 132-138, 362
Siun-ki 289
Six, div. of time, 339 ; periods 69 ; states 145, 148 ; stores 81 ; Tsung 20, 26, 81, 348, 349
Sixty, cycle, 10, 78, 378
Skin, boats, 11, 114, v. coracles ; writing 169, 171, 386 ; of iguana 204, 208
Skull, deformed, 307, 318, 324, 377
Sky, figure of earth, 378 ; a vault 10, 341, 378 ; earth, water, gods, 173 : Heaven, cult., 20, 377
Skylax 157-159
Slavery 384
Small ; 18 States 218
Sockets of doors 379
Socotra 230, 231, 392 ; cf. Mi-sung
Sofala 99
Sogdiana, Ch., 314
Solanum Melangenum 269
Solar, distance, 366 ; year 9, 378
Soma, Tze-mai, 107, 109, 110, 173, 210, 386-7
Somali coast 96
Son of Heaven 151, 377
Sona and Utara 57
Soothsayer 207b
Sorcery 89, 92, 385
Soul, double, 348, 380 ; triple 348
South, Açôka, char., 198 ; Arabia 80 ; Burma 59
South pointing boat 261, 285 ; chariot 45, 283-6
South regions and Ts'u 234 ; west trade 119
Soy beans 374
So-yep, Sui-yep, 215
Spica 302, 340
Spices, precious, 369, 392
Spinning 374 ; damsel 301-2 ; v. cowherd

Spirits worship, 139, 208b, 280, 329, 374 ; of furnace 161 ; awe of 292 ; bringing down the 386 ; dispeller of 386
Spirituous beverage 374, 375
Spoked wheels 379
Sramans, first, 174, 234
Staffs 333 ; royal 379 ; walking 379
Stamping : bricks 342, 379 ; coins 104, 118, 156, 385 ; ingots 191, 386
Standard measures and weights 10, s.v.
Starry animals, v. quadrants ; beast 129
Stars, Bab., Ch., 298, 300, 302, 340, 383 ; catalogued 286, 287 ; gazing 374 ; Tartar 289 ; star - points 24, 10, 12, 24, 378 ; also v Lunar Mansions, Astronomy
State diviner 92 ; seal 204, 207
Stations at Sea 388, 235 ; v. Fairy isl.
Statues 211, 214, 220, 333, 362
Steel, natural, 374 ; and silex, v. Fire
Stems, ten, 340
Stitched boats 260
Stone : age 24, 295, 371, 374 ; bird 131 ; classics 17 ; coloured 349 ; coal 368, 391 ; heads 374 ; oxen 190 ; sculptures 36, 38, 44 ; tower, 51, 222, 312 ; wicks 187 ; wig 354
Stools 379
Storax 369, 394
Storm bird 158-9, 170, 387
Straits, v. Malacca, Sunda, Bali, Allas
Striped cloth 201
Su-lioh 359, 394 ; Jen 138 ; Lih 308 ; tchou 158 ; Ts'in 149, 176, 207
Suh-kiü 262 ; Shin 31 : Teh 311
Sugar 182 ; drug 234, 236 ; cane 236 ; of cane 233, 234, 389, 392 ; of palm 233, 366, 388
Sui dyn. 215 ; tr. 61 ; fire 166 ; Ho 204 ; Jen 162 ; Min 138
Sulla Annap 378
Sulphur 213, 215-6, 368, v. Brimstone

Sulphurous gas 272
Sumatra 238, 255 ; N. 110 ; N.W. 235 ; S.E. 108 ; Java 38, 113, 297
Sumbawa 113, 181
Sumbul 235
Sumero-Akkadian 22, 96, 98, v. Akkaian
Sumeru 173, 387
Sun, bird 193, 217, 388 ; male 378 ; mirror 168 ; stopped 218 ; mock v. Parhelion
Sun-K'ing 149, 204, 207 ; Kwang 218 ; Shuh ngao 118 ; Wu 164-6
Sunda isl. 188, 236, *352, 366 ; straits 111, 113, 181, 261
Sundering of the earth 175
Sundial 277-9
Sung 90, 92, 94, 133-4, 140, 146, 166-9 ; kia 305 ; panting 215, 219, 229, 300, 385 ; Wu ki 149, 207b, 218 ; yung 310
Sunrise, day 99
Suppressed texts 363
Surnames, first 303
Survey, v. Yü kung ; of Ts'u 192
Susa, Susiana, civil, 21, 22, 26, 83, 318, v. Elam
Susu, se 182
Sutra in 42 sect., 209b, 213
Suttism 132-3, 135, 362
Suvanna Bhumi 57
Suy r. 134
Swallow, prefect 354
Swan-pan 13
Sweet-flag 236, 246, 391 ; tree 233
Swords 165, 167, 204, 379 ; iron 207, 382 ; famous 207
Syllabaries 16, 129, 380
Symbolism stretched 295-6
Syria 102, 104
Sze, rhinoc 179, 184 ; lo 58
Szema-Kuang 317 ; Siang ju 230, 247, 250, 254 ; Tsien 211, 317, pass. ; pin 58, tao 58 ; Tchou 86 ; Tchuen, v. Shuh, and Routes ; yoh, v. Four Mountains

Ta-Hia 50 219, 275-6, 330 ; Hung 319, 323-4 ; jen 114 ; Kwei 329 ; shik 211 ; tchuen 8S
Ta-ts'in 55-58, 122, 222, 235 ; muddle 55, 58, 276 ; sea-hunters 245 ; Tarshish 182,

ALPHABETICAL INDEX. 413

187, 243-4, 390, 392, 395;
traders 240, 242, 252
Ta-Ts'u 345; yao 255; yb
113; yuan-laon 219, 220,
221, 309
Taas 99
Tablets, city of 196; and
tripod 332, 378
Tabu-ing names 30, 74, 79,
216, 355
Tadpole char 20, 345
Tad-svad-kama 123
Tagaung 56, 59, 117, 216, 385
Tagh Dumkash valley 312
Tai, towers 11, 343, 379
Tai Shans 190
Tai Kung Wang of Ts'i 171,
172, 183; Ho 156, 172
Tai-lu, Tai-yuen 334
Tai-mou of Shang 73, 74, 76,
265, 275, 286, 355, 382
Tai-ngo 204; yu 107, 109;
yuen 331 route
Takla-Makan 310
Tall men 314
Tamburah 222, 393
Tambourine 380
Tamdin 22
Tamerlan, tombstone 313
Tan 367; v. Cinnabar; erh
115, 124 ! fu 278; kiu 328,
333, 381; tchi 33; tchou
110
T'an 195
Tang 334; Mei 287; Sien
319; Tien 324; t'u 138
Tao 334, 375; the 122, 125;
of Huangti 327; and Tang
335
Tao-sze-ism 95, 145, 147,
217 cradleland
Tao-sze-ists 91, 169, 173
Tao-teh-king 91, 120-1-2-3-4
Tao-t'iet 71
Taoism 95, 138, 147
Taoists 148-9, preservers
141; Books 367
Taphussa, Bhallika 56, 387
Tapi 79
Tapirs 252, 394
Taprobane 58, 251
Tarshish navy 99, 243, 245
Tartar influence 131-2-3, 207,
215, 284-5, 385
Tarym r. 4, 267, 309
Tash kurgan 312
Tatsienlu, Route 50, 197
Tattooing 328, 374, 379
Tchai-ling 220
Tchaispaish, Teispés 157
Tcham 240, 392
Tchampa 242

Tchang, flagrant 384; Heng
284
Tchang-Kien 50, 62, 200;
two journeys 219; dates
253; Assistants 219-22,
230; report 249; in Tsen
250; 390, 391
Tchang-ku 328; kung 269;
lo 231; pu 246, 8, 330; y
46, 52, 149, 325, 330,
332
Tch'ang Hwang 91, 95;
hung 287; tch 189
Tchan-tan 252
Tchao 146, 149, 179, 287,
304; After 261, 284;
Hwang-hou 250; Siang
Wang 203; t'o 62, 233-4-
5-6-7, 241, 390; Wang
384; of Tchou 184: of
Yen 174, 180, 365; Yun
325
Tche-pu, Java 189; tsiang
233
Tchehkiang 107
Tcheh-kwan 196; Muh 92
Tch'eh-fu 266-9
Tch'en 145; t'oh 287
Tcheng st. 90, 92-3, 146, 149,
152, 162, 167, 170; hiuen
93; hung 370; Mao 208;
peh kias 149, 207b
Tcheng or Tching; Tang
169, 170; tu 54, 196, v.
Shuh, routes; Wang 81,
38, 43, 51, 169, 186, 208,
255, 352, 357
Tchi-gur 355; Kia-hua 190,
235, 246, v. Hunna
Tchi-yu, or vu 318, 319, 323-
4, 329, 330-7, 350; anc.
Tchi-vu 328; yu-ki 337
Tchih r. 266; Wu 266
Tchinani 368
Tchinapati 368
Tchoh-lu 329, 331-2
Tchou 30, 91, 95, 115, 120,
141, 151, 183, 283, 350, 382;
East 70, 89, 177, 385;
West 69, 383; origin 77,
310, 355, 383, v. Shang
199; late weakuess 146,
190
Tchou Kung 31, 43, 146, 151,
278, 283; Siuen, Wang 86;
y Wang 46
Tchou, boat 262; Kwan
145; Li 146, 150, 175;
Ling 95; Mi 38; pei or-pi
179, 278, 366, 387; shu
38; sin 33
Tchu, of Hia 366; hi 162;

ju 115; Ko liang 63; nio
358; po 240-1, 255; she
196; Siang 333-8, 374;
tchung 183, 234; Wen of
134; yai 115, 124, 240, 366,
390; yng 261; Fahlan
215.6
Tchuang or Tchwang, of
Ts'u 118, 184, 190; Lao
148; tchou, or tze 91, 95,
118. 133, 136, 149, 153,
168, 170, pass.
Tchuen, boat 252; style 88,
198, 205, 338
Tchuen, or Tchuan, or
Tchwan-hiüh 95, 140, 141,
143, 148, 190, 192, 269, 286,
288, 316, 329, 330-4, 336,
347. 353, 381; calendar 81
Tchun-tsiu 139, 143, 363
Tchuh, priests 141; lu 319;
lin 266; yung 161-2
Tchuktchis 393
Tchung-erh 121; Kia 305;
Li 161, 286, 289, 334;
Tyng-li 381; shan 266,
268-9, 325-7; shang 149,
211
Teak wood 96 98, 101, 359
Teeth lacquered 361; v.
Black teeth
Teh-Hien 317
Teks, Red 161, 161, 162;
White 326
Temir Kazuks 289
Tempering iron 79, 81, *86,
90, 167, 386
Ten: celestial bodies 339;
days 378; Hwei 339; Ki
23, *348, 387; Ministers
319, 347; months 24, 319;
names, cycle, 90, 387;
Patriarchs 340; suns 339
Terrestrial kings 33, 348, 365
Thatun, Sadun, 57
Thaumaturgists 218
Thein-ni 67; cf. Thinai
Thimble, Archer's, 195, 264,
379, 381
Thinai 51, 68
33 demi-gods 173-5, 348, 365;
kings 365, 387; Ratus 365
36 st., Turkestan, 393
3 fairy isl. 206, s.v.; legged
bird 193, 217, 388
300 winters 322; years 322
376 officials 376
Thuc 236
Ti, divine, 190; tr. 61; white
328; Kiang 76, 333; Kuh-
kao-sin 334, 336, 381, 396;
Ti Tchih 143, 334, 396

Tiao-tchi, or Ti, 55, 58, 227, 366
Tiawat. Tiamat, 127
Tibet 13, 114, 344; bricks 13; fire 13; mastiffs 197
Tieh, tiet, 85, 382, v Iron; mt. 266, 269
Tien, dyn. of Ts'i, 159, 171; Ho 156; Ping T'ien-tze 149; Tsen 67; Yueh 56, 62, 66
T'ien, heavens, 20-1; Huang Ta Ti 300; Tchang 159; Tchu. err. for Tsen-tu, 172, 247-8; T'o 54; Tze 150, 319, 377; Ts'in 299 Ts'ing 270
Tigers 184
Tiglath-Pileser 100, 278
Tigris 102, 319
Timor 366, 390
Tin 85, 86, 255, 354, 379, 394; Meshed 318, 322; Peh-lu 55, s.v.; powder 213, 222, 390; Yüt for Tsen-yut 66
Tinning mirrors 216
Tishtrya 350
Tithes. Ch. rulers, 150
T'o 208
Toad, red, 163
Tokhari 53
Tombs, horseshoe 119, 191 386; vaults 379; v. Deads
Toothpicks 328, 331
Torguths 311
Tortoise, Avatar 173; mt. 274; shell 92, 244; scorched 377
T'ou 236; Tou-hien 215
Towers, Astron. 11, 343, 379
Town-gates 355, 379
Tong-ti-jen 115 or Tung-ti-jen
Tong-King or Tung-King v. Nhitnam, Nan-yueh, Kattigara
Trade; profit 244; routes 30, s.v., N. E. 321, S.W. 48, 394, Turkestan 320; unnoticed 314
Traditions and legends 377, 380
Transformation 208b, 214
Transmogrified Notions 33
Transmutation 89, 214, 390
Transplantation 230, 246, 391
Transhipments 388
Trappage 260
Travellers on Pamir 312

Travelling Merchants 314, cf. Shuh, &c.
Tree of Life 24, 387, *349
Trien 236
Trigonometry 183
Triple Walled 314
Tripod and Tablets 332, 378
Trisula 197
Trung-trac 260
Tsab Mandas 317, 319
Tsai 138, 145-6; Ki 317; Kia 305
Tsampenago 56
Tsan 300-1; Tsung 196
Tsang-hieh or Kieh, Dungi 5, 7, 24, 27, 318, 377
Tsang-ko 65: lung 358; wu 208
Ts'ao 145; Jungs 333, 336; ling 134, 137; nu 266; shin 161, 163
Ts'e, not Tz'e 12, 94, 358, 385
Tsen, st. 39, 52, 61-3, 191, 209b, 233, 388; routes 63, 191; stops 250; China's names 63, 91, 354; exp. in Burma 56, 60, 63, 191, 250, 388; not T'ien 67; Yueh 56, 61, 62
Tsen-pho 63; Tang Kiang 62; tchen 67
Tseng 134
Ts'i, st. 146, 148-9, 155, 156, 159, 172, 214, 218; Hiai book 170; Siuen, W. 108, 170; Wei, W. 108, 110
Tsiang Kiu-ju 160-1
Tsie-lan 58
Tsich 24, 339
Tsien, r. 196, 199; Li 204, 207; shan 196; Sing Tze 246
Tsih-Moh 36, 89, 92, 106, 107, 109, 118, 134, 137, 147, 156, 158; ruined 178, 206, 364, 385
Tsih-shih 66; Tsao 390
Tsin 188; former 187; W. 261; Hou 284; Wen 160
Ts'in, st. 51, 55, 57, 60, 77, 92, 95, 115, 131, 133, 145, 146, 162; Empire 203; Than-Tan, 51, 55, 57, 244, 246; not China 63, 64, 66, 67, 68, 193, 207; books saved 205; and Han 210; Hiao Kung 149; Hwei, or Hwuy Wang, 52 Muh Kung 133, s.v.; SheHwangti, s.v.; and Shuh 199, 354; westwards 207, 213, 388

Tsing-ling 52, 54; Muh 252; Yang 328
Tsiü-Kiü 268, 271; Ni 213, 215
Tso-Kiu Ming 148, pass.; Tch'ih 333
Tsoh, Tsok 60, 61, 254
Tsou-hien 149, 173, 174, 180, 207, 207b
Tsu, Kia, 383; Tchou 114
Ts'u, st. 51, 115, (117)(118) 120, 134, (138) 146, 149, 156, 167, 207, 208; hist. 190, 191, 287; Tchwang, W. 118; Wei, W. 52, 55, survey 171, 192, 346; Taic Shan 193; Tseru 51, 354; and India 170; Peh-yung 197; Shuh 54, 354; south 191; Ts'in 179, 190; Wu 186, 361; Yuch 178, 191
Tsü Kwot 230
Tsuan, Charat 198; Mu 235; Shin 161-2
Tsung: six 20, 26, 81, 316,* 348: Ling 308
Tu, and Siu 384; kun 216
T'u: kwei 277; Sui 236; Yü 52, 54, 196, 363, 387
Tuh-kiüh 225
Tul-Barsip 102
Tumuli, old 326, 337
T'un-liu 210b
Tung, valley 312, 382 v. bronze; hai 179, 209b, 233; hu 176, 366: kien kang muh 75, 76, 317; kien wai ki 317; king 44; ngou 233, 260-2, 299; yao 92; ye, yeh 115, 179, 234, 370, 388-9; yueh 233, 260: yun 186
Turfan, Tan-kiü 267, 333, 383-4
Turiva 231
Turkestan 220, 250, pass.
Turkoman horse 220, 224
Turquoises 318
Tusks 180, v, ivory
Tusser silk 105, intr.
Twelve, hours 279; leaders 20; months 9, Bab. 10, 12, *93, *338, 385; notes 340, 379; states 92, 380; Ts'e or Tz'e 94, 358, 385; years 10; zodiac 92-3-4, 340-1, 350, 378
24 year-parts or tsieh 9, 339, 378; stellar points 340, 378
Two fairy isl. 109, 111, 181; sosses 24, 380
Tyr, Tyrians 102, 243

ALPHABETICAL INDEX. 415

Tze: kang 133; kao 207b, 210b; kwei 196; mai, or wei 107, 109, 173, 220; shen 91; tch'an 152; Tch'ang 91, 95: wei 287; yang 170
Tzen, or Tsen, tu, not Tientchu 246-7

Uan-na-sha 311
Ubua 105
Udumi 100
Ugro-Altaic 317
Ukkalamandala 56, 387
Uknu 34
Ulai 105
Ulgan 364
Umbrellas, state, 379
Unas, pyramid, 283
Uncivilised immanence 373
Undas Arman 378
Unlucky: days 10, 379; words 10
Unsuccess of Huangti 329
Urba'u 22
Urn burial 374
Urnina 307
Ursa-major 286, 289, 374; minor 300
Ur-sze for Ni-sze 227
Uruk 22
Usurtasen III., 359
Ut 364

Vadjra 197
Vases 379; Carved 180, 388; Copper 333
Vasus, Eight 156, 171-2, 387
Veda 166
Veined Stone 188
Vermilion 204
Vernal Equinox, year 79, 378
Vertical Writing 15, 380
Victims 137
Vine 223, 230, 379, 391
Vitreous Ware 252, 394
Vrihashpati 93, 94

Wakhan, Kiü-su, 308, 324, 371, 381-2, 384
Waksh, Oxus 371
Walnut tree 225, 229, 391
Wan 204; Min 304; Sing 304
Wang 150; Müng 70, 265, 383
Wang-Mu, Si, 32, 35, *264, 266-7, 272-4, 325, 335, 365, 381-4, 386

Wang-shen 216; Sun Mwan 6; Tcheng 203-4; ti 196
War, chariots 11, 344; for horses 220
Washing the Weapons 342, 379
Water; male 160; basins 197; sweep 361, v shaduff; wheel 45, 120, 361
Weak water 268, 327, 332
Weaving 374
Wedge 379
Wei, st. 90, 94, 146-9, 162, 179, 190, 287; Hwei W. 149; and Tsin 301; of Ts'i 173
Wei, Northern 45, 187, 218
Wei-Kan 119, 191-3, 386; Ki 366; tien 196; yen 171
Weights and Measures 10, 93, 378, 385
Welding 375
Wells 343, 379
Wen, of Tsin 161; Shan 66; Tsu 377; tze 149, 152; Wang 30, 190
West, char. for 5; trafic 309
Western Civilisation 396
Wheat 11, 379
White, Ti 323, v. Five Tis; Tiger 358; victims 80
Wild silk 198, 200
Wind, char. 15; S.W. demon 72; sacrifices 138
Winter, solstice 378; year 79
Woman status 347, 380
Wonderful 88, 91, 138, 147, 166
Wood, boats 114; figures 134; scorched 374
Woollen cloth 200-1
Worships, new, 131-5
Writing, Ch.; Origin 14, 15, 18, 292, 380 v. Ku-wen; Reform 86, 204, 185; and India 198: v. Hieroglyphs
Writing; Embryo 374; Djurtchen 198; on Skins 169; Lols 198; Shui Kia 198; Tsuan 198
Wriggling Char. 192
Written Tablets 332, 377; Texts 382; v. tripod
Wu, st. 92, 145, 155, 158, 162, 165, pass.
Wu-hao 360; heng 82; Hien of Mokan 74, 76, 286, 289, 298, 355, 371, 382; hwan 176; Ki 191; Kiang of Yueh 178, ley or luy 221, 225, 393; ling of Tchao 176

Wu-suns 15, 218, 222, 224, 230-1, 250, 254, 391, 393; tchu 236, 389; tien 128, 140; Ting 78, 383; tou 365; tu 213-4, 234; Wang 115, 146, 149, 190, 384; y 268

Y tr. 75; Mou 195; Tsu 377; Tsun Kou 211, 222, 393; Yn 275-6
Ya, Tchou, 40, 61
Yah 314; Yü, or Ya-yüh, 329, 332
Yak 100
Yakut 179, 182, 365, 387-8
Yang: barrier 308; r. 266; Kiah 383; kwuh 273; mirror 167, 364; Tze Kiang, crossed, 193, 384; mouths 158, 178, 190; Tchu 149, 152; Yh 156
Yao, or Ti-yao, 141, 143, 144, 237, 334-5; Ki-Tchou 141; and Shun 6, 114, 140-1, 169, 335
Yao 252, v. Ta-Yao; hills 326; potters 375; Jen 530; Min 325; Shui Kia 198; Tchi 266
Yaon, Ferghana, 391
Yarkand, route, 308, 393; Daria 309, 313
Yavnai 105
Yazatas 83
Ye-Kwang 179, 180, 204; Lang 62, 193; Si-Ming 234
Year, divisions 9, 378; great 11; name 13; solar 378; ten months 24, 319; vernal equinox 79; winter solstice 79
Yeast 383
Yeh 90, 94, 261, 285
Yellow r. 5; fingered 181-2, 246, 389, v. Hwang-Tchi; rats 188, 266-7
Yemen 99
Yem-Tsai 309, 311, 224
Yen, of Tsin, 92; mt. 266; nat. 184; st. 146, 148, 174, 176, 180, 207b, 218, 388; Tchao W. 108, 149; Hwo-Shan 272, 327; Ki, Karashar, 212, 222, 309, 384; Ling 191, Tou 115; Tze-Shan 269
Yenissei 5, 383
Yh-King 16, 30, 147, 151, 345; Shou 106; Tchou 41, 63, 115, 369

Yn dyn. 115, v. Shang-Yn
Yn and Yang 10, 125. 148. 165, 174. *338, 350, 384
Yn-han 266; Kao 287; T'ang 170
Yng-ling 156; Lung 319; Tchou 107-9
Yoke 379; of heavens 300; of horses 381
Youi 119
You-yü 207, 211, 386
Yü the Great 32, 169, inscript. 192, 195; st. 335; — Hjung 190; Hwang 361; Kiang 109, 173; Kung 6, 33, 180, 186, 190, 192; Lo 58; Men 308, 310; She 33; Siang 186; Tchang 115; Wei 52, 196; Y 110, 196
Yu-Hu 333, 336; Kiu-li 225; Kwei 333, 336; Nai Hwang, ti 27, 88, 127, 150, 319, 328

v. Hwangti; Shan 327; Sin 333-4, 336; Siüh 246; Yü 207
Yuan-Yaon 221, 392; Kiü 208b
Yueh, st. 92, 107, 155-6, 158, 165, 178-9, 218, 262,* 357, 360, 387; mariners 112, 115, 260, 262; and Wu 182
Yueh-pan, Sol-pan 215-16; Shang 31, 43-4, 46, 384, 393; Wang 193; Sui, or Hi 61, 344; Ti 50, 60, 218, 223, 250, 269, 275-6, 369, 392-394
Yuen-Kiao 107, 109, 114; Kiu 236; Ling 140
Yüh-heng 289
Yulduz, plateau 273, 276, 284
Yun-lei-wen 72; Shuh 110

Yunnan 56; Jade 34; Jadeite 41; Pegu 389
Yung 137, 208b; tr. 199; Kiu, Greek 225; Shing 266; Tchang 39, 253, 394; Tcheng 329
Yüs 304

Zab r. 319
Zabai 240, 242, 246, 392, 393
Zafar 100, 109
Zejan-jolduz 289
Zend-Avesta 164, 166, 323, 350, 365
Ziggurats 343
Zikura 129
Zikuv 127, 129
Zodiac 92, 93, 94, 340-1, 350
Zodiacal names 378, 385; stars 286, 334
Zoroastrism 157

List of Important Errata.

Page.	Line.	Read.
10	23	ten Akkadian or cognate
11	3	the notion that
13	21	Wylie, *Notes* 86.
„	28	diverged 3) those which have entered China through intermediary and later channels.
14	1	63) Wheat . . .
„	13	*Trans-Kaukasische*
15	6	called *Ko-ton*
16	12	*the Yh-King*
17	7	which have
20	4	country (yü kung, I, ii, 15)
„	27	that *Shun* venerated
21	5	p. 486) and
21	23	*Shangti* and *T'ien*
24	11	in 2285 B.C.
26	8	that Kutchi or the like
„	25	in 2285 B.C.
27	22	n. 103.—Vigoureux, *La Bible*, iv, 463
30	17	however reckoned as
33	8	tchou and Liang-tchou
34	4	Yung-tchang
„	18	Bk. II, fol. 19
„	28	Jade of Turkestan
36	12	having entered China in the
„	39	discovered, which, though
40	20	of Switzerland
45	9	Wei dynasty, cf. T. P. 752, 7. The
47	23	indegenous in China, and
48	3	SHANG-YN dynasty
„	n.218	*Shuh wang pen-Ki*
50	20	sent in *159* B.C.
„	24	Bactria in *128* B.C.
„	34	Tchang Kien
52	6	circâ *475* B.C.
55	24-5	*Li-ni*—parted ears
57	n.275	afterwards, by Fah-hien
60	last	returned in *126* B.C.
69	21	1777 or better *1801* B.C.
70	2	from *Shensi* to Tchihli
„	5	capital eastwards
73	28	B.C. 1466 or better 1554 B.C.
„	29	B.C. 1269 or better 1331 B.C.
74	3	a blank, and not
75	4	about *243* B.C.
„	31	1845 or 1848 B.C.
„	42	1710 or 1775 B.C.
„	44	1596 or 1724 B.C.
„	47	1584 or 1712 B.C.
„	48	1575 or 1686 B.C.

Page.	Line.	Read.
76	4	1557 or 1668 B.C.
„	5	1466 or 1554 B.C.
„	13	1450 or 1537 B.C.
„	16	1414 or 1503 B.C.
78	10	Chinese, does not seem to
„	11	about 1091, not 1032 B.C.
83	2	*origines et leur*
85	13	B.C. 2282, arrival
89	38	ideas of transformation but not of alchemy
86	1	a branch
90	24	time of drought
92	36	have a song
93	28	in China by
94	13	in 655 (5, v, 9)
100	n.420 l.4	note 422. Mr. Houghton
„	„ 5	the Hanuman of
„	n.424 3	of Manu and the Fish
101	n.425 6	pp. 125-6, and
109	l.1	(ought to be at the foot of the page)
109	n.453 l.2	*Sapphur* metropolis
„	n.456 „	*Pêng-lai*
110	n.467 l.8	(Bas. 2375-7896)
„	„ 11	or Barbarians in the South-East
114	n.477 l.9	*Shan Hai King*, 18, 5
119	n.490 l.5	the *Wei kan*
120	l.6	third century
121	l.22	Abhiraja
131	title	FOURTH PERIOD: 770-481 B.C.
„	l.15	in the west, in 986 B.C
133	18	Daughter, an undescribed
138		(paragraph) 155 (not 147)
140	8	he retained and *extolled*
143	n.589 l.3	p. 32 and 212
143	n.599 l.2	of the Shang-Yn
„	n.602 l.3	Kao-yang Tchuen hiuh
145	title	481-221 B.C.
151	l.1	she Hwang-ti
158	l.35	since the previous
160	30	the teeth of the standing sacrificial
161, 162, 163		have been misnumbered 155, 156, 157
166	n.668, l.2	Kiv. 869, f. 5 c. and Kiv. 321, f. 1
170	n.692, l.7	13239-10157 Bas.
187	n.761, l,9	Reinaud
188	n.762, l.6	Sunda islands except Timor
189	n.772	Emerson Tennant
193	n.796, l.11	The Kassia forest
204	l.23	and gold and tin

LIST OF IMPORTANT ERRATA.

Page. Line. Read.
208, l. 6   HAN Wen-ti
209, l. 7, c 350 A.D.
210 n. 888, l. 2   Tchang-sha
  „   „   l. 3   Kiu Kiang
  „   „   l. 6   Liao-tung
210· following pages numbered 207b,
           208b, 209b, 210b, 211
222   20   marriage in 105 B.C.
  „   21   came back bringing home
246 l. 3   *Fu-li* gardens
  „ l. 18 and *Kan tsiao*
282 n. 1219, l. 1   Shway yio
284 l. 32   Shih-hu, third king
312, n. 1291, l. 12   Badakshan
319 l. 6   (paragraph) 345
325 l. 25   of the *Tchao Yun*
328 l. 22   and at Kang (Kiu-tcheng
             or
  „   l. 30   Pierced breasts
337 n. 1379   *Ti Wang She Ki*

Page. Line. Read.
341 add. 47, l. 4   p. 331 it must
344 a. 69, l. 7   *Yueh-sui kiun*
  „   „   l. 10   788, 6 ; 65, 3 ; 769, 1
349, a. 126, l. 6   incidents, like those in
353, a. 195, last   the Lan-tsang Kiang
354, a. 331, l. 3   of Kattigara with
356, a. 347, l. 4   removed the Jungs to
357, a. 363, l. 4   the *Küen Jungs*
359, a. 396, l. 4.   Cf. *Fung suh*.
359, a. 414, l. 2   by   Dr.   Spranger,
             made of
360, a. 474, l. 1   séparant...Ile de Bàli
362, a. 560   (not 650)
371, a. 1259, l. 6   from China, cf. p. 289
374, l. 23   cliffs, notched sticks
375, l. 5   of various sorts
376, n. 1391, l. 3   *Miao Man hoh tchi*
381, § 391   *to the* SHANG, c. 1954-1686
             B.C.
386, l. 7   fire god of the hearth

www.ingramcontent.com/pod-product-compliance
Lightning Source LLC
Chambersburg PA
CBHW051726300426
44115CB00007B/482